Mara Wantuch-Thole

**Cultural Property in Cross-Border Litigation**

# Schriften zum Kulturgüterschutz / Cultural Property Studies

Herausgegeben von /
Edited by
Professor Dr. Wilfried Fiedler, Saarbrücken
Professor Dr. Dr. h.c. Erik Jayme, Heidelberg
Professor Dr. Kurt Siehr, Hamburg

Mara Wantuch-Thole

# Cultural Property in Cross-Border Litigation

Turning Rights into Claims

DE GRUYTER

ISBN 978-3-11-035543-7
e-ISBN (PDF) 978-3-11-035577-2
e-ISBN (EPUB) 978-3-11-038660-8

**Library of Congress Cataloging-in-Publication Data**
A CIP catalog record for this book has been applied for at the Library of Congress.

**Bibliographic information published by the Deutsche Nationalbibliothek**
The Deutsche Nationalbibliothek lists this publication in the Deutsche Nationalbibliografie; detailed bibliographic data are available on the Internet at http://dnb.dnb.de.


Printing and binding: CPI books GmbH, Leck
♾ Printed on acid-free paper
Printed in Germany

www.degruyter.com

# Acknowledgments

I would like to express my sincere gratitude to my supervisor Norman Palmer, who sparked my passion for cultural heritage law. He very patiently guided my work on this thesis and led me both through the good and rough patches. His enthusiasm and knowledge of the subject accompanied me for most of the time. I also thank Prof. John Phillips from King's College London for teaching me a great deal about academic writing and structuring, as well as Prof. Stefan Grundmann from Humboldt University Berlin for taking me on the course, although I took him by surprise, and for his fast and thorough examination of my thesis. I am also very much indebted to Prof. Eric Jayme, who's seminar in Art Law I already attended in my very early years at Heidelberg University and who persuaded me to go to London in the first place. Of course, I am indebted to Prof. Kurt Siehr for being the secret "Doktorvater" of most PhD students writing a thesis in cultural property. His infamous doctoral seminar was academically a great support as well as a breeding ground for long lasting friendships.

I have to thank my husband Jan Eike for his constant support, for diligently editing this work, for tolerating my absent-mindedness and furious mood swings during the time when this book was written, and for looking after our children when I could not be there.

In no particular order, many thanks also go to Ruth Redmond-Cooper, for her guidance at the Institute of Art and Law and for always being kind, to Matthias Weller for his clever comments, to Friederike Brühl for being a good friend and colleague on our course at FU Berlin, which constantly helped staying in touch with the subject, to Breva Capitaine for retouching the illustrations, to Andrzej Jakubowski, who always listened, to Robert Peters and my colleague Anna Distelkamp for their comments on the title to this work, to Robert Kugler for reliable knowledge on Mexican and German cultural property law, to Tony Doubleday from the British Museum, to Jeremy Scott, to Sophie Vigneron from Kent University for her help on French law. I am also greatful to my friends Lisa and Anne Tlach, for keeping me from desintegrating, to Jacek Sternal, to Jan Konetzki, to Katja Lubina for being a great PhD flat mate in London, to Carola Thielecke and Dorothea Kathmann, who gave me the opportunity to work for the Prussian Cultural Property Foundation, to Sarah Cakebread and Anne Vins-Niethammer for our genious time in London and Budapest and to Shoshana Berman, my "oldest" friend – thank you for showing me around Cesarea.

I dedicate this book to my son Benjamin, who supported me through the last two chapters of the thesis although he was only small like a pea, and to my daughter Emma – she attended my defence without knowing. Thank you, the two of you, for making me laugh, when sometimes there was nothing to laugh about. Of course, without my parents, the work on this book would never have been possible.

Mara Wantuch-Thole
Berlin, 24. July 2014

# Preface

The legal discipline of cultural property law is a fairly young one compared to the main areas of law practiced throughout the legal community. Owing to the growing awareness of the value and meaning of art and cultural heritage for humankind, however, it is becoming a fast evolving subject with a constant flow of new legislation being enacted both nationally and internationally. The monetary value of art and archaeological artefacts has experienced an exponential growth in the past three decades and so has the illegal market in such objects. The recent conflicts in the Middle East have curbed the illicit trafficking in archaeological objects from the region, where plunderers are said to control archaeological sites and the export of cultural heritage.

Once however, art or cultural property has found its way onto the black market, claims for its return to the original owner have proven to fail, notwithstanding the vast body of domestic and international laws. Litigation is often complex, both in terms of procedure and substance. It involves a mix of domestic civil and criminal law, European Human Rights and EU law, Private International Law as well as Public International Law. Successful litigation, however, would increase the awareness of illegal dealings with such goods. Returns of movable antiquities to its source countries could help diminish the destruction of archaeological context caused by looting, if they succeed in serving as a deterrent to prospective purchasers and thereby providing a disincentive to looters and illicit traffickers. In support of this contention, this book upholds the view that the return of illegally excavated and exported cultural objects is an imperative based on legal argument.

The research consists of two parts. The first part comparatively delineates different means of acquiring or retaining rights in cultural objects. They may be property rights, interests that equal property or interests that do not count as property, but serve as a mechanism to protect movable cultural heritage. The second part of the thesis will be devoted to investigating and delineating ways to enforce interests in cultural objects and to turn such interests into claims.

The thesis that served as a breeding ground for this book has been admitted as a PhD research project at King's College London in 2007. The upgrade defense took place in 2009. The project was further accepted as a doctoral thesis at Humboldt University Berlin in 2010 and jointly supervised by Prof. Norman Palmer and Prof. Stefan Grundmann. The defense took place at Humboldt University in 2013. The main manuscript has been completed with the defense of the doctoral thesis, however, several amendments had to be undertaken until its actual publication. This includes amongst others EU Regulation 1332/2013 concerning restrictive measures in view of the situation in Syria, which was enacted as a result of the exponentially increasing illegal trafficking with Syrian cultural heritage following the intensification of political upheaval in the Middle East as well as recent case law on the enforcement and justiciability of claims involving cultural objects.

Berlin, 10th October 2014

# Contents

# List of Abbreviations

| | |
|---|---|
| AAL | Art, Antiquity & Law (Institute of Art and Law) |
| ABl. EG | Amtsblatt der Europaeischen Gemeinschaft, jetzt Union |
| Abs. | Absatz (German: paragraph) |
| A.F.L. Rev. | Air Force Law Review |
| Am. J. Archaeol. | American Journal of Archaeology |
| American J. Int'L Law | American Journal of International Law |
| Am. J. Int'l L. & Pol. | American Journal of International Law and Politics |
| Antiquity | The Antiquity Journal |
| Annu. Rev. Anthropol. | Annual Review of Anthropology |
| Asian Pac. L. Pol. J | Asian Pacific Law & Policy Journal |
| ARCHAEOLOGY | Archaeology Magazine |
| Ariz. J. Int'l & Ccmp. L. | Arizona Journal of International and Comparative Law |
| Art. | Article |
| Arts. | Articles |
| Aboriginal History | Aboriginal History Journal |
| Athena Review | Athena Review: Journal of Archaeology, History and Exploration |
| AöR | Anstalt und Archiv des öffentliches Rechts |
| Bd. | Band (Series) |
| BGB | Bürgerliches Gesetzbuch (German Civil Code) |
| BGBl. | Bundesgesetzblatt (German Official Journal) |
| BGH | Bundesgerichtshof (German Supreme Court) |
| Brit. Y.B. Int'L L. (BYIL) | British Year Book of International Law |
| Brooklyn Journal of Int. L. | Brooklyn Journal of International Law |
| BT-Drucks. | Bundestag Drucksache (Parliamentary Debate, Germany) |
| Boston U. L. Rev. | Boston University Law Review |
| CA | Court of Appeal |
| Calif. L. Rev. | California Law Review |
| Cardozo J. of Int'l & Comp. L. | Cardozo Journal of International & Comparative Law |
| CASE W. RES. J. INT'L L. | Case Western Reserve Journal of International Law |
| cert. denied | certiorari denied (Appeal denied by U.S. Supreme Court) |
| Ch. | Chapter |
| Chi. J. Int'l L. | Chicago Journal of International Law |
| C.L.J. | Cambridge Law Journal |
| Colum. L. Rev. | Columbia Law Review |
| Colum. J. L. & Arts | Columbia Journal of Law and Arts |
| Colum. J. Transnat'l L. | Columbia Journal of Transnational Law |
| Conn J. Int'L L. | Connecticut Journal of International Law |
| Cornell Int'l L.J. | Cornell International Law Journal |
| Cp. | Compare |
| DePaul-LCA J. Art & Ent. L. | DePaul University Journal of Art and Entertainment Law |
| Der Tagesspiegel | Daily German Newspaper |

| | |
|---|---|
| DöV | Die öffentliche Verwaltung (Journal) |
| Duke L.J. | Duke Law School Law Journal |
| e.g. | exempli gratia ("for example") |
| ed | editor |
| eds | editors |
| Emory Int'l L. Rev. | Emory International Law Review |
| E. J. Comp. L | Electronical Journal of Comparative Law |
| Environs Envt'l L. Pol'y J. | Environs Environmental Law and Policy Journal |
| Envt'l L.Rev. | Environmental Law Review |
| EWHC | High Court of England and Wales (UK) |
| EWCA | England and Wales Court of Appeal (UK) |
| et seq. | and the following (pages or items in a list) |
| F. 2d | Federal Reporter (US) |
| F. Supp. | Federal Supplement (US) |
| Fordham L. Rev | Fordham University Law Review |
| Germ. YB Int'l L. | German Yearbook of International Law |
| Harv. Int'l L.J. | Harvard International Law Journal |
| Harv. L. Rev. | Harvard Law Review |
| Hastings L.J. | Hastings Law Journal |
| Hous. J. INT'L L. | Houston Journal of International Law |
| ibid | footnote or reference that was cited in the preceding footnote |
| ICLQ | The International and Comparative Law Quarterly |
| ICRC | International Committee of the Red Cross |
| i.e. | id est ("that is") |
| IFAR Journal | International Foundation of Art Research Journal |
| IJCP | International Journal of Cultural Property |
| ILM | International Legal Materials |
| IPrax | Praxis des Internationalen Privat- und Verfahrensrechts |
| ITAP | Report of the Ministerial Advisory Panel on Illicit Trade 2000 |
| J. Inst. Just. Int'l Stud. | Journal of the Institute for Justice and International Studies |
| JuS | Juristische Schulung |
| K.L.J. | King's Law Journal |
| KUR | Kunst und Recht Journal |
| LQR | Law Quarterly Review |
| Loy. L.A. Int'l & Comp. L.J. | Loyola Los Angeles International and Comparative Law Journal |
| LJ | Lord Justice |
| Lloyd's Rep. | Lloyd's Law Reports |
| LMCLQ | Lloyd's Maritime and Commercial Law Quarterly |
| Melb. U. L. Rev. | Melbourne University Law Review |
| Melb. J. Int'l L. | Melbourne Journal of International Law |
| Mich. L. Rev. | Michigan Law Review |
| New Eng. Int'l & Comp. L. Ann. | New England International and Comparative Law Annual |
| NJW | Neue juristische Wochenschrift |
| Notre Dame L. R. | Notre Dame Law Review |

| | |
|---|---|
| N.Y. City Ct. | New York City Court |
| N.Y.S. 2d | New York Supplement |
| N.Y. Sup. Ct. | New York Supreme Court |
| N.Y.U. L. Rev. | New York University Law Review |
| N.Y U. J. of Int'l L. and Pol. | New York University Journal of International Law and Politics |
| NWVBl. | Nordrhein-WestfälischeVerwaltungsblätter (Journal) |
| OJLS | Oxford Journal of Legal Studies |
| OGEL | Open General Export License (UK) |
| OIELs | Open Individual Export Licenses (UK) |
| para. | Paragraph |
| PIL | Private International Law |
| Public Archaeology | Public Archaeology Journal |
| QC | Queen's Council (UK Barrister title) |
| RDU | Revue de droit uniforme |
| Rev.crit.dr.int. pr. | Revue critique de droit international privé |
| RSDIE | Revue suisse de droit international et européen |
| sec. | Section |
| SPA | Spoliation Advisory Panel (UK) |
| Stan. L. Rev. | Stanford University Law Review |
| Suffolk Transnat'l L.J. | Suffolk Transnational Law Journal |
| Syr. J. of Int'l Law and Com. | Syracuse Journal of International Law and Commerce |
| SZIER | Schweizerische Zeitschrift für internationales und europäisches Recht |
| t. | tom (polish: volume) |
| Tex. L. Rev. | Texas Law Review |
| Tex. Int'l L. J. | Texas International Law Journal |
| Tit. | Title |
| Tul. J. Int'l & Comp L. | Tulane Journal of International and Comparative Law |
| Tul. L. Rev. | Tulane Law Review |
| Transnat'l L. & Contemp. Probs. | Transnational Law and Contemporary Problems |
| U.C.C. | Uniform Commercial Code of the United States |
| UCLA L. Rev. | University of California Law Review |
| Uniform L. Rev. | Uniform Law Review |
| UNESCO | United Nations Educational, Scientific and Cultural Organisation |
| UNIDROIT | International Institute for the Unification of Private Law |
| Vand. J. Transnat'l L. | Vanderbilt Journal of Transnational Law |
| Vand. L. Rev. | Vanderbilt Law Review |
| Vill. Sports & Ent. L. J. | Villanova Sports and Entertainment Law Journal |
| Virginia L. Rev. | Virginia Law Review |
| Willamette L. Rev. | Willamette Law Review |
| Yale L.J. | Yale Law Journal |
| YPIL | Yearbook of Private International Law |
| YIHL | Yearbook of International Humanitarian Law |

# Chapter 1.
# Introduction

## § 1. The Illicit Trade in Cultural Objects – A Scope of the Problem

### I. General Remarks

National and international trade of art and cultural property has significantly increased in the past three decades.[1] On the one hand the market allows individuals and institutions to study, possess, display, and preserve art and a cultural interchange is encouraged from a cultural and educational perspective. On the other hand, it is the trade that causes theft destruction and looting of cultural objects and sites all over the world. Nowadays, art and antiquities crime is considered to be one of the most remunerative businesses on the black market.[2] It includes the theft of famous works of art from private individuals or museums, the illicit excavations and sale of archaeological artefacts, the illegal export of cultural items by its owner or non-owner without the necessary authority,[3] or the unauthorised reproduction of an artist's work.[4] In the case of illicit archaeological excavations, the depredation of significant cultural objects is particularly severe, as it involves the removal of unrecorded objects and the irreversible obliteration of the historical context.[5]

---

1 See e.g. Seventh Report of the Ministerial Advisory Panel on Illicit Trade in Cultural Objects 2000, Department of Culture Media and Sport (ed.), Annex A of the Report, providing for statistics and evaluating data concerning the scale of the illicit trade in the UK and various other countries [hereinafter: Report ITAP].

2 See e.g. www.Interpol.int/Public/WorkofArt/woafaq.asp. However, Interpol stated that there exist no figures which would enable to claim that trafficking in cultural property is one of the most common form of illicit trafficking, although this is frequently mentioned at international conferences or the media. In fact, they claim, it is very difficult to gain an exact idea of how many items of cultural property are stolen through the world and it is unlikely that there will ever be an accurate statistics', see Interpol, Stolen Works of Art, frequently asked questions, at www.Interpol.int/Public/WorkofArt/woafaq.asp. Cp. also FBI Law Enforcement Bulletin, March 2012.

3 Cp. Report ITAP 2000, Annex A.

4 Geerally on the unauthorised reproduction of art, see e.g. Simon Stokes, Art and Copyright (2003); Carolyn Olsburgh, Authenticity in the Art Market: A Comparative Study of Swiss, French and English Contract Law (2005), including French and Swiss law.

5 For the meaning of the notion 'historical context' see this Chapter, at § 4 III.

In Afghanistan, for example, more than 55.000 art objects that were looted from all over the country since the 1980s are missing.[6] In Britain, when in 1984, a site in Wanborough was systematically looted by metal detector users, following the initial discovery of the so called Wanborough Hoard, 1.041 coins in all were recovered but it is believed that the total find may have consisted of at least 9.000 coins.[7] In Germany, the famous sky disc of Nebra had nearly disappeared on the black market, after being illegally excavated by looters in 1999.[8] Iraq was particularly affected during the two Gulf Wars. Following the outbreak of the war in April 2003, the National Museum in Baghdad was ransacked. The official U.S. investigation reported that at least 13.515 objects had been stolen from the museum,[9] of which by June 2004 approximately 4.000 had been recovered while the larger part did or will appear on the black market in the near future. Archaeological sites all over the country are being systematically plundered. The systematic looting of archaeological sights all over Syria has only just started with the beginning of the Syrian crisis. In the ancient city of Dura-Europos, which is known as the "Pompeii of the Syrian desert" an estimated 80 % of the site has been plundered by illegal excavation.[10] The provenance papers for such objects are being forged by the looters and in that way the artefacts infiltrate the international market.[11]

Nowadays, there are probably more collectors of art and antiquities than ever before. The volume of antiquities on the market, however, cannot legitimately equal the demand.[12] The sources to legally obtain cultural objects are limited and fixed: the volume of antiquities entering the international art market is very restricted by local legislation, trying to keep heritage within the source

6 See 'Treasure troves and lack of supervision turn Afghanistan into looter's paradise', International Herald Tribune, February 2, 2007, quoting archaeologist Prof. Zemayalai Tarzi; A.W. Feroozi/Z.Tarzi, The impact of war upon Afghanistan's cultural heritage (2004), at www.archaeo logical.org/.

7 Neil Brodie/Jenny Doole/ Peter Watson, Stealing History-The Illicit Trade in Cultural Material (2000), at 22.

8 The disc has been seized by the police during a simulated transaction in 2002. On the whole affair see e.g. Die Welt, Himmelscheibe von Nebra, 14.04.2011; available at http://www.welt.de/wissenschaft/article13174437/html.

9 See M. Bogdanos, Iraq Museum investigation: 22 Apr–8 Sep 2003, at www.defenselink.mil/news/Sep2003/d20030922fr.pdf

10 Javier Pes/Emily Sharpe, Vol XXIII, NO. 255 The Art Newspaper, March 2014.

11 The Italian archaeologist Paolo Matthiae, who has worked in Syria for many years warned collectors "to be very careful about artefacts of Mesopotamian origin", Vol XXIII, NO. 255 The Art Newspaper, March 2014.

12 Cp. J.D. Murphy, Plunder and Preservation: Cultural Property Law and Practice in the People's Republic of China (1995).

countries' borders. States ban the export of certain types of cultural property or pass laws declaring artefacts, discovered or undiscovered, to be the property of their government. Artefacts immediately have to be reported after their discovery. The purpose of theses statutes is to reduce illicit trade in antiquities through the fear of sanctions. Although there are no statistics as to how successful these laws are at curbing the incentive for finders of newly discovered antiquities to turn to the black market, the vibrant black market for cultural property is evidence that many finders do not consider the legislation much of a deterrent.[13] Finders receive no or hardly any finder's fee. From an economic perspective, it is understandable that the finder of cultural property is reluctant to report the find and rather turns to the black market as, in many cases, artefacts have a greater monetary value outside their country of origin.[14] Companion studies of exhibition and sales catalogues have shown that upwards of 70 % of archaeological objects that come onto the market or that are contained in recently assembled collections are without any indication of provenance.[15] The clear implication is that they have only recently entered circulation and are probably stolen, looted, or fake.

On top of the issue sketched above, the enforcement of national antiquities laws is poor. Art rich source nations do not have enough resources to afford for the protection of their cultural heritage. As a result, professional traffickers are able to outmaneuver the relatively weak enforcement agencies.[16] But also in the art importing countries, the weaknesses in law enforcement work are considerable. In the United Kingdom, inter agency rivalry between police forces and customs constantly hinders the effectiveness of joint operations. For example,

---

**13** See e.g. Jane Warring, Underground Debates: The Fundamental Differences of Opinion that Thwart UNESCO's Progress in Fighting the Illicit Trade in Cultural Property, 19 Emory Int'l L. Rev. (2005) 227, at 229; Thomas O'Connor, Intelligence-Led Policing and Transnational Justice, J. Just. Int'l Stud. (2006) 233, at 233; Peter Wedel, Protecting Newly Discovered Antiquities: Thinking outside the "Fee Simple Box", 76 Fordham L. Rev (2007) 1015, at 1042.

**14** See the case of an Italian antiquities trafficker who was caught offering Hellenistic marble statues of Marsyas and Apollo for $850,000. The statues were originally purchased from a Turkish farmer for $7,000, cp. Lisa Borodkin, The Economics of Antiquities Looting and a Proposed Legal Alternative, 95 Colum. L. Rev. (1995) 378.

**15** Cp. Christopher Chippindale/David Gill, Material Consequences of Contemporary Classical Collecting, 104 Am. J. Archaeol. (2000) 463; Ricardo Elia, Analysis of the Looting, Selling and Collecting of Ampulian Red-Figure Vases: A Quantitative Approach in: N. Brodie/J. Doole/C. Renfrew (eds.), Trade in Illicit Antiquities: The Destruction of the World's Archaeological Heritage (2001) 145; Elizabeth E. Gilgan, Looting and the Market for Maya Objects: A Belizean Perspective, in: N. Brodie/J. Doole/C. Renfrew, Trade in Illicit Antiquities (2001) 73.

**16** Cp. Lisa Borodkin, The Economics of Antiquities Looting, 95 Colum. L. Rev (1995) 378, at 384.

there are 50 separate police forces, five regional crime fighting priorities and agencies[17] Moreover, in a lecture given at the Institute of Advanced Legal Studies in 2006, Simon Mackenzie identified another problem which he referred to as the **"national self-interest":** the primary aim of the art importing countries' enforcement agencies lies understandably in local protection and safety rather than in helping foreign countries, to combat the looting of antiquities.[18]

Another reason for the illegal trade in cultural objects is rooted within the traditions of the art market. It is steeped in secrecy and what passes for "gentleman informality", provides ideal opportunities for introducing illegally acquired antiquities into the legal art market. Traditional methods of art dealing help to obscure the origins of rare artefacts. The numerous levels of the antiquities trade – looters, smugglers, intermediaries, auctioneers, dealers, purchasers – insulate each participant from knowledge of incriminating evidence and reduce the sense of guilt associated with each transaction. The art auction system can operate to obscure the origins of objects, while establishing sale records that can simulate provenance. According to the English law of agency, an auction house entertains a fiduciary relationship to its vendors/consignors,[19] while buyers need not identify themselves, nor even be present at the sale, in order to make a purchase.[20] The majority of cultural property transactions do not involve an exchange of information on title history.[21]

Three major theories are being maintained on how to take measures with the illegal trade in cultural objects. They reflect the tension between the desire to conserve the cultural heritage of source states and the desire to encourage free trade in antiquities and the acquisition of historically valuable artefacts by collectors and museums.[22]

---

**17** Cp. Charles Hill, Recovering stolen art: practical recovery issues and the law of the law enforcement agencies, in: Norman Palmer (ed.), The Recovery of Stolen Art (1998) 171, at 181.

**18** For a detailed account of this lecture see Katja Lubina, The Dealing in Cultural Objects (Offences) Act 2003 put through its paces, Issue 199, The Art Loss Review (2007) 25.

**19** For a detailed analysis on the fiduciary relationship see Bowstead/Reynolds on Agency (19th ed. 2010) articles 45–50.

**20** Most auction houses will take written bids or allow purchasers to bid by telephone. In fact, fine art auctions can provide an ideal method for laundering the proceeds of another illicit activities, such as drug trafficking. The buyer can buy art in cash, then use it as a collateral. Later on the money can be recouped with a receipt, see Anthony J. Del Piano, The Fine Art of Forgery, Theft and Fraud: Corruption in the World of Art and Antiquities, 8 Crim. Just. (1993–1994), at 16, quoting Richard Ellis, former detective of the Art and Antiquities Squad, Scotland Yard.

**21** See also Brian W. Harvey/Frank Meisel, Auctions Law and Practice (2nd ed. 1995), at 246.

**22** For an account of the debate see e.g. Susan Kean McIntosh, The Good Collector: Fabulous Beast or Endangered Species? 1 Public Archaeology (2000) 73; John Henry Merryman, A Licit

The first theory argues that source nations shall prevent and control illegal excavation by implementing more or less retentive laws which try to disable the uncontrolled outflow of antiquities to market countries by practically closing off the market.[23] This view is popular with source nations and archaeologists, and dominated by the idea that "collectors are the real looters".[24]

The second major approach is to create a licit and free market that will compete with the black market.[25] This, let us name it 'free market-approach', suggests that retention and repatriation do not protect cultural objects, but rather serve to form a vigorous black market.[26] By denying the opportunity for a licit market, ownership and export embargo-laws drive the trade underground, assur-

---

Trade, IJCP (1995) 13, reprinted in: Kate Fitz Gibbons (ed.), Who Owns the Past – Cultural Policy, Cultural Property and the Law (2005); Michele A. Miller, Looting and the Antiquities Market, 4 Athena Review, No 2, editorial notes.

**23** See e.g. Ihsan Ali/Robin Coningham, Recording and Preserving Gandhara's Cultural Heritage, 3 Culture Without Context (1998) 10; J. Blake, Export Embargoes and the International Antiquities Market – The Turkish Experience, 2 AAL (1999), 233; Colin Renfrew, in: N. Brodie/J. Doole/C. Renfrew (eds.) Trade in Illicit Antiquities (2001); Katherin Walker Tubb, Antiquities Trade or Betrayed- Legal, Ethical and Conservation Issues (1995).

**24** See Colin Renfrew, Collectors are the Real Looters, 46 Archaeology (1993) 16.

**25** See for example, Paul Bator, An Essay on the International Trade in Art, 34 Stan. L. Rev. (1982) 275, at 317 (the article was later published as a monograph, Paul Bator, The International Trade in Art (1983)); John Henry Merryman, A Licit Trade in Cultural Objects, 4 IJCP (1995) 13; Steven Vincent, The Good Collector, Debates between Susan Keach McIntosh and Colin Renfrew, in 1 Public Archaeology (2000) 73, at 80; A.K. Bordkey, The Failure of the Nationalisation of Cultural Patrimonies, in: M Briat/J.A. Freedberg (eds) Legal Aspects of International Trade in Art (1996) 135; P. Marks, The Ethics of Dealing (1998); George Ortiz, The Cross Border Movement of Art in 3 Art, Antiquity and Law (1998) 53–60; Dalia N. Osman, Occupiers' Title to Cultural Property: Nineteenth-Century Removal of Egyptian Artefacts, 37 Colum. J. Transnat'l L. (1999) 969 (advocating for a repeal of the prevailing source country retention model and adoption of a managed market model).

**26** See J. H. Merryman, A Licit Trade (1995) 13, suggesting a more "liberal" form of the 'free market approach', based on a model of a rationalised market. Merryman argues that cultural property should be made available for the free trade if it is either movable and bears a significant relation to the national culture, such as Hitler's water colors which Italy refused to allow to leave its national territory, or, for redundant archaeological objects, meaning surplus archaeological objects that are being held in source nation's storages and that are of known provenance. On the other hand, trade with stolen objects or objects that are too fragile or too dependent on context for their significance to allow removal· such as parts of buildings and monuments, should be considered illicit. The same would be true for objects orphaned by removal from their historical record without adequate documentation, or objects whose removal causes significant damage to the objects themselves, or equally, objects that are immovable for cultural reasons, such as the Liberty Bell for the Americans or, the Crown of St. Stephen important to the Hungarians.

ing the existence of an active and profitable black market in art.[27] Ownership vesting laws deny opportunities for licit export and dictate that the trade will be inevitably clandestine, unregulated, untaxed and undocumented.[28] According to the proponents of this approach, the only way to protect cultural objects is to create a regulated, licit international trade. This view is being supported by the international art and antiquities trade. It emphasizes humanity's common interest in its past and employs terms such as "the cultural heritage of all mankind."[29] Supporters of the antiquities trade note that many source countries, such as Egypt or Greece, maintain warehouses and storerooms filled with thousands of uncatalogued artefacts, many of which are "rotting away" without being seen by the public and that, via the art market, these objects could be seen and appreciated by people throughout the world.

The third approach, let us name it the 'demand-reduction-approach', is based on an economic analysis of the market for antiquities and tries to eliminate, or more realistically, to reduce the demand for illicitly obtained cultural objects by placing liability for the purchase of stolen antiquities on buyers.[30] By reducing the demand for a good through creating deterrence to the purchasers in market countries, the supply of the goods in question is being decreased in the source countries.[31] Consequently, where demand remains at high levels in economically rich nations, not much can be gained solemnly by enacting legislation in source countries.[32]

Each of these three approaches has its core of unquestioned validity. In their application to concrete problems the three images sometimes conflict and sometimes reinforce each other. The first step to create a globally working cultural

---

**27** Cp. Paul Bator, An Essay on the International Trade in Art, 34 Stan. L. Rev. (1982) 275, at 317.
**28** Cp Merryman, A Licit Trade, at 18; A.K. Bordkey, The Failure of the Nationalisation of Cultural Patrimonies, at 138.
**29** The quoted words are taken from the Preamble of the 1954 Hague Convention on Protection of Cultural Property in the Event of Armed Conflict, May 14, 1954, 249 U.N.T.S.215.
**30** See e.g. Jonathan S. Moore, Enforcing Foreign Ownership Claims in the Antiquities Market, 97 Yale L.J. (1987–1988) 466, at 480; Simon McKenzie, Going, Going, Gone: Regulating the Illicit Market in Antiquities (2005); S. Mckenzie, Dealing in Cultural Objects – A new criminal law for the UK, 71 Amicus Curiae (2007) 8; Christine Alder, The Illicit Traffic in Asian Antiquities, Paper presented at the Australian Registrars Committee Conference, 9 October 2001; Patty Gerstenblith, Schultz and Barakat: Universal Recognition of National Ownership of 14 AAL (2009) 21; P. Gerstenblith, The Public Interest in the Restitution of Cultural Objects, 16 Conn J. Int'L L. (2000–2001) 197.
**31** P. Gerstenblith, Schultz and Barakat, at 22.
**32** Cp also Katja Lubina, The Dealing in Cultural Objects (Offences) Act 2003 put through its paces, Issue 199 The Art Loss Review (2007) 25.

property regime however, is to accept that that the problem with illicit cultural property is complex and there is no simple one dimensional solution to the illegal trade with movable antiquities.

## II. Cross-Border Recovery of Misappropriated Cultural Property

In an attempt to revert the wrongs of the development sketched above, litigation related to cultural property by both states and individuals have grown significantly. Such litigation is often complex in terms of procedure and substance. It can involve a mix of domestic civil and criminal law, European Human Rights and EU law, private international law as well as public international law.

With regards to the recovery of misappropriated heritage items by individuals, inconsistent policies and differences in domestic legislation in many art collecting nations such as the different attitude of nations to the good faith acquisition of stolen goods, or the limitation periods for claims play a part in contributing to the poor recovery rate of art and antiquities. While in some states the good faith acquisition of stolen goods is impossible, in others stolen items can be acquired if the buyer can prove that he was bona fide.

State claims on the other hand are largely based on the individual state's specific legislation aimed at inhibiting the illicit trafficking in antiquities. Such legislation may be composed of offences of public laws (e. g. illegal export) or offences of laws vesting ownership in the specific state. Whereas courts of all countries are in theory open to actions for the recovery of property stolen from individuals, the main obstacle for states to recover misappropriated heritage items is the principle of territoriality, a legal institute largely admitted in international comparative law, under which a state cannot use its respective public law as the basis of an action it brings abroad when its claim amounts to an exercise of a sovereign right on foreign territory.[33] As a result of this principle sovereign claims for the recovery of cultural heritage were on many occasions rendered non-justiciable, in the sence that they could not be enforced.[34]

---

**33** See e. g. H Battifold-P. Lagarde, Private International Law (7th ed., Vol. 1, Paris 1982) at 248; P. Mayer, Private International Law (Paris 1987) at 199. For a recent analysis see, Cedric Ryngaert, Jurisdiction in International Law (2008) Chapter 3, 41 et seq.

**34** Therefore, D. McClean/K. Beevers err when they thinkthat "the conflict of laws is mainly concerned with the interest of private persons and not with the interest of states". They continue that it " has to be dounted whether governments are really interested in having their law applied (...), cp. Morris, Conflict of Laws (6th ed.) 2005, at 537.

The international community enacted several international treaties aimed to promote the protection of cultural property some of which may facilitate claims for the return of unlawfully removed antiquities to their countries of origin. The Hague Convention 1954, for example, provides amongst others for the return of artefacts removed during the times of war. The 1970 UNESCO Convention deals with the recovery of illegally exported and stolen heritage items in the times of peace. The 1995 UNIDROIT Convention is aimed at harmonising national private laws as well as the mutual recognition of export legislation. The European community enacted EEC Regulation No. 3911/92 and EC Directive 93/7/EEC. The most recent initiative was the draft of a Model Law convened jointly by UNESCO and UNIDROIT, the objective of which is to assist states of origin in reforming their domestic law in order to facilitate the recognition and enforcement of the state's property rights in cultural items. We will see however in Chapter 4 that the effect of international public law instruments is still limited. The recovery of items that are not subject to international legislation is governed by the national law of the forum, and automatically questions of justiciability arise.

## 1. The Principle of Justiciability

The principle of justiciability is a chameleon. It is a doctrine of private international law infiltrated with considerations of public international law.[35] It can encompass elements of jurisdiction, standing, mootness, ripeness, admissibility of evidence and even the appropriateness of remedies,[36] but at the same time it can also encompass elements of democracy and of the separation of powers.[37]

If a claim is declared to be non-justiciable, it means that it cannot be enforced. In specific, the principle of justiciability requires the court to withdraw from adjudication of a claim on the grounds that the substance of the claim is such that the court is not competent to decide.[38] As opposed to a procedural bar to the claim, as would be the case with the principle of state immunity,

35 On the intersection of private and public international law in regard to justiciability, see Dominic McGoldrick, The Boundaries of Justiciability, 58 ICLQ (2010) 981. Similarly, Christian von Bar/Peter Mankowski, Internationales Privatrecht Band I (2nd ed. 2003) 235 et seq.

36 Richard H. Fallon, Justiciability and Remedies—And Their Connections to Substantive Rights, 92 Virginia L. Rev. (2006) 633; J.S. Harbison, Private Enforcement of Public Values in US Courts: Justiciability Barriers in Environmental Law, 4 Environmental L. Rev. (2001) 264.

37 Jeff A. King, Institutional Approaches to Judicial Restraint, 28 OJLS (2008) 409.

38 Wilfried Bolewski, Diplomacy and International Law in Globalized Relations (2007), at 99; Anthony Aust, Handbook of International Law (2010), at 146; A. Scott, The Non-Justiciability of Foreign Sovereign Claims, LMCLQ (2007) 296.

non-justiciability is a substantive bar to adjudication.[39] A claim is thus non-justiciable if the substance of the claim is of such nature that the court may not decide about it. This substantive bar can be of legal, political or policy nature of the right, interest, decisions or questions at issue.[40]

The principle of justiciability is being invoked in relation to claims involving foreign affaires or claims involving the public law of a foreign state. Justiciability or non-justiciability of claims involving foreign affairs is a consequence of the territoriality doctrine.[41] The Permanent Court of International Justice once contended that the first and foremost restriction imposed by international law upon a state is that, it may not exercise its sovereignty in any form on the territory of another state.[42] For decades, the principle of territoriality is or was an almost "universal principle".[43]

In most countries justiciability is determined as a matter of jurisdiction.[44] A court does not have jurisdiction to entertain an action that is non-justiciable.[45]

---

**39** D. McGoldrick, The Boundaries of Justiciability, at 984.

**40** See J.A. King, The Pervasiveness of Polycentricity, Public Law (2008) 101.

**41** Cp. e.g Jan Kroppholler, Internationales Privatrecht (6th ed. 2006) at §22 II 2; Ivo Schwander, Einführung in das internationale Privatrecht Bd 1 (3rd ed. 2000), at 73.

**42** Cp. the case of the S.S Lotus (Series A), No 10, 18, 19.

**43** Cp. Dicey/Morris/Collins, Rule 3 (1) para 5R-019; Williams and Humbert Ltd v W&H Trademarks (Jersey) Ltd. [1986] A.C 368, 428, per Lord Templemen, Derby & Co Ltd v Weldon (No 6) [1990] 1 W.L.R 1139 (CA) at 1154 per Staughton J.

**44** In England, the doctrine of justiciability was established in Buttes Gas & Oil Co v Hammer (No.3), [1982] A.C. 888, a case concerning the dispute between two American Oil firms competing for the right to exploit a discovery of oil in the Arabian Gulf. See also Kuwait Airways Corporation v Iraq Airways Corporation [2002] 2 AC 883; Mbasogo v Logo Ltd and Others [2005] EWHC 2034, (2005) 102(39) LSG 32. For German law, see Christian von Bar/Peter Mankowski, Internationales Privatrecht (2nd ed. 2003), at 235 et seq; Rudolph Heiz, Das fremde öffentliche Recht im internationalen Kollisionsrecht (1959) 50 – 54; Gerhard Kegel/Klaus Schurig, Intrnationales Privatrecht (9th ed 2004), at 1092 with further reference. For US law see e. g. R.W. Galloway, Basic Justiciability Analysis, 30 Santa Clara Law Review (1990) 911; Dapo Akande, The Act of State Doctrine in the United States, The Act of State Doctrine, in: P. Cane/J. Conaghan The New Oxford Companion to Law (2008) 932. For a comparative account of Australian and UK law on justiciability cp. Sim Cameron, Non-Justiciability in Australian Private International Law: A Lack of "Judicial Restraint"? 10 Melb. J. Int'l L. (2009) 102.

**45** The Prinicple of justiciability was central in the English cases, cp. the English cases Mbasogo v Logo Ltd and Others [2005] EWHC 2034; (2005) 102(39) LSG 32; The Campaign for Nuclear Disarmament (CND) v The Prime Minister of the United Kingdom and Others [2002] EWHC 2777, where CND sought an advisory declaration as to the true meaning of Security Council Resolution 1441 (in respect of disarmament) particularly as to whether it authorised States to take military action in the event of non-compliance by Iraq with its terms. The court held that it had 'no ju-

However, in the language used by courts and commentators, it is often unclear whether the principle of justiciability is distinct from that of jurisdiction and often the term is used ambiguously by courts and commentators.[46] Sometimes the terms jurisdiction and justiciability appear to be used interchangeably.[47] It has been suggested that justiciability should be formulated as a distinct rule of admissibility of the claim which stands aside the determination of jurisdiction.[48] However, this question is only of theoretical relevance as it does not change the substance of the rule itself. Hence, for the purpose of this research, an issue may thus be considered to be justiciable in a particular forum if it is capable of being decided in that legal forum and it is considered appropriate to do so on legal, political or on policy grounds.

According to the procedures of international private law, justiciability is determined as a preliminary issue. If a matter is considered to be non-justiciable, the court dismisses the issue without full consideration of the substantive case.[49] The effects of the non-determination of a particular issue maybe threefold: First, the court may consider that the whole case cannot be determined at all because the central issues are non-justiciable as a matter of principle.[50] Secondly, it may be that only certain issues in the case are non-justiciable. This is the situation where the court considers that it cannot make determinations of the legal validity of the acts of sovereigns within their own jurisdiction. As a consequence, the court treats such acts and laws as valid and the courts decision is then made on that basis. The third situation is where courts will not allow themselves to be used to assist the enforcement of particular acts or laws of foreign states outside of their own jurisdiction. In the UK, this third option is enshrined in Rule 3 of the Conflict of Law classic "Dicey, Morris and Collins", which states that:

---

risdiction' to declare the true interpretation of the Resolution which had not been incorporated into English domestic law.

**46** Cp. CND v The Prime Minister of the United Kingdom and Others [2002] EWHC 2777, where Mr Justice Maurice Kay observed that in the course of proceedings, there was some debate over whether any obstacle in the way of CND's application is properly categorised as one of jurisdiction, justiciability or discretion", at 50.

**47** C.A. Whomersley, Foreign States and British Courts 125 LQR (2009) 227, at 234; D. Goldrick, at 983.

**48** Thus it has been said that non-justiciability, 'is or leads to a form of immunity ratione materiae', cp. Kuwait Airways Corporation v Iraq Airways Corporation [2002] 2 AC 883 (CA), at para 319.

**49** For example in Buttes Gas & Oil Co v Hammer (No.3), [1982] A.C. 888, per Lord Wilberforce, stating that the non-justiciability principle is, "not one of discretion, but inherent in the very nature of the judicial process",. per Lord Wilberforce.,at 932.

**50** As in e.g. the English case Aksionairnoye Obschestvo A. M. Luther v James Sagor & Co [1921] 3 KB 532 (effect was given to Russian laws vesting property in the Russian State).

> "English courts have no jurisdiction to entertain an action for the enforcement either directly or indirectly, of a penal, revenue or other public law of a foreign State."

It is this third option which countries of origin struggle with when claiming for the return of cultural objects. Statutes which grant property rights in antiquities to sovereigns are public laws. Their primary purpose is not to regulate the relations of individuals inter se, which is the essence of private law, but rather to exert public control over cultural objects. The main value of such laws seems to be that they give the state an interest which it can enforce. However, according to the above stated principle, that states do not enforce the penal, revenue and public laws of another state, it would seem to follow that claims for the recovery of misappropriated antiquities may be rendered non-justiciable in foreign courts.

### 2. Misappropriated Cultural Objects in Litigation

Claims to cultural objects based on foreign cultural property legislation has been the central issue of two cases, the legal divergence of which gave the idea to this thesis: the famous case *Attorney General of New Zealand v. Ortiz and Sotheby's*[51] and *Government of the Islamic Republic of Iran v. The Barakat Galleries Limited.*[52] While in *Ortiz*, the state was unable to recover its cultural heritage on the basis of its cultural heritage statute, in *Barakat*, the government of Iran was capable to rely on its legislation protecting cultural property to be the ground of a claim for some heritage items. Both cases will be discussed in detail throughout the thesis but shall be briefly summarised in order to illuminate the research task:

#### a. Attorney General of New Zealand v. Ortiz

*Attorney General of New Zealand v. Ortiz and Sotheby's*[53] concerned five carved wooden panels which at one time were the end wall of a Maori pataka, or raised store house, hidden during the displacements of the 1800s.[54] Both the outsides and the insides of pātaka were often decorated with elaborate carvings. They

51 [1982] 1 Q.B. 349, [1982] 3 WLR (Q.B. and C.A.) 432, [1984] AC 1, [1984] 2 WLR 809.
52 [2007] EWHC 705 (QB); [2007] EWCA Civ 1374; [2008] 1 All ER 1177; QB 22 [2009].
53 [1982] 1 Q.B. 349, [1984] AC 1; [1984] 2 WLR 809; For comment see P.J. O'Keefe, Export and Import Controls on Movement of the Cultural Heritage: Problems on the National Level, 10 Syracuse J. Int'l L. & Com. (1983) 352, at 354.
54 Hannah Fleming, Push for funds to restore ancient epa (2012) available at http://www.stuff.co.nz/taranaki-daily-news/news/6936469/Push-for-funds-to-restore-ancient-epa Accessed on 5 July 2014.

were found in a swamp by a Maori tribesman in Tanarakt, New Zealand in the 1960ies and exported from New Zealand by the dealer and art trafficker Lance Entwistle and taken to New York.[55] In the thought, Entwistle was the rightful owner, the items were bought by the famous Swiss art collector George Ortiz, who brought them to London. In 1978, the items were about to be sold at an auction at Sotheby Parke Bernet & Co., London, when it turned out that no export permit had been issued for the carvings to leave New Zealand, as required by the then extant New Zealand legislation, the Historic Articles Act 1962.

The New Zealand Government sought an interim injunction to prevent the sale and to secure the return of the panels to New Zealand. Ortiz sought trial on two preliminary issues: 1) whether the New Zealand Government had become the owner and was thus entitled to possession of the artefacts and 2) whether New Zealand legislation was enforceable in England. In the first instance, Staughton J. found that under the New Zealand Historic Article Act 1962, such articles if exported without a licence were automatically forfeited to the Crown, making it the owner of the artefacts despite the fact that the New Zealand government had never obtained physical possession of the items and further, that this legislation was enforceable in England. Conversely, the Court of Appeal held that forfeiture did not take place automatically but only upon the seizure by the Crown. For that reason the title to the panels did not vest in the New Zealand government unless they had obtained physical possession of them while still on New Zealand territory. Furthermore the Court of Appeal found that the Historic Article Act 1962 was classified as both a public and a penal law and was held to be unenforceable in England. Lord Denning, contended that a successful recovery of the carvings would constitute the enforcement of the New Zealand Cultural Historical Articles Act 1962 and this would amount to an extra territorial effect of a public law, which would be a direct infringement of the territorial theory of sovereignty[56]. The House of Lords, to which the case was further appealed, also ruled in favour of George Ortiz and, as a result, the panels remained in his possession until his death in 2014, when the panels where returned to the Te Papa National Museum. Allegedly, Ortiz ruled in his will that he wished the

---

**55** Christopher Finlayson, "Motunui Panels Returned to New Zealand" National Party Press Release 4 July. Available at: https://www.national.org.nz/news/news/media-releases/detail/2014/07/04/motunui-panels-returned-to-new-zealand2014.

**56** See on this e. g. Adam Rushworth, Assertion of Ownership by a Foreign State over Cultural Objects Removed from its Jurisdiction, 3 LMCLQ (2007) 123; C.J.S. Knight, Of Coups and Compensation Claims: Mbasago Reassessed, 19 (1) K.L.J. (2008) 176; Petty Gerstenblith, Schultz and Barakat, Universal Recognition of National Ownership of 14 AAL (2009) 21.

panels to retrun to New Zealand. [57] This landmark case laid the foundations for the view that property rights in heritage items arising from foreign export legislation were incapable of being enforced in foreign courts, rendering most national laws dealing with the illegal export of cultural goods ineffective.

**b. Government of Iran v. Barakat Galleries Ltd.**

The *Barakat-case*[58] concerned a claim for the return of artefacts allegedly originating from Iran and bought by the London-based Barakat Galleries.[59] The subject of the claim were 18 antique jars, bowls and cups dating from before 2000 B. C. which in all likelihood had been excavated in the Jiroft region of Iran and then exported illegally. The two preliminary issues of the case were whether Iran could show that it obtained title to the antiquities it claimed under Iranian law, and if Iran could show it obtained title, whether that title would be recognised and enforced in English courts to the extent that it would satisfy a revindication claim.

In the court of first instance Gray J. followed the reasoning of the *Ortiz-decision* answering both questions to the negative:[60] He first held that the Iranian provisions could not be construed as vesting title to the antiquities in the Iranian state. Moreover, he arrived at the conclusion that even if he had held Iran to be the owner of the antiquities in question, this title could not be enforced in English courts as Iran never obtained possession of the artefacts before they left Iranian territory and, as a consequence, their recovery would amount to an act jure imperii and thus an exercise of a sovereign right.[61] Thus, his ruling went even further than *New Zealand v Ortiz* in that all property rights based on a nation's cultural property statute were incapable of being enforced in England. Although he mentioned that the Iranian provisions granted Iran an immediate right of possession to the antiquities he did not find it worthwhile considering whether this property right was justiciable in England.

The Court of Appeal[62] overruled the decision of the first instance court holding that Iran had obtained both ownership and an immediate right of possession

---

**57** Reportedy, the New Zealand Government paid 4.5 $ million NZD for the panels return and legal fees, cp. Finlayson.

**58** Government of Iran v Barakat Galleries Ltd. [2007] EWHC 705 (QB); [2007] EWHCA Civ 1374; [2008] 1 All ER 1177; QB 22 [2009].

**59** [2007] EWHC 705 (QB).

**60** [2007] EWHC 705 (QB), at 98–99.

**61** In the following: CA.

**62** [2007] EWCA Civ 1374; [2008] 1 All ER 1177

in the antiquities in question and that both rights, if once acquired within the territory of a state, would be recognised in England, despite the government's lack of possession.[63] The CA considered the case to be different from *Att Gen of New Zealand v Ortiz*, owing to the fact that Iran's immediate right of possession would be acquired while the property was within Iran's jurisdiction. According to the CA, a property right of this kind would not be questioned in an English court despite Iran not having acquired possession. Although the court found that the provisions relied on by Iran where indeed 'public' as they "seek to enforce a governmental interest",[64] the claim put forward by Iran was construed as a claim in property and not a prerogative claim, as in Ortiz, where the foreign state had gained no title to the historic article before the object left its territory. Accordingly, the CA held Gray J.'s ruling to be contrary to the doctrine of vested rights and English case law.

In consequence, the CA found that although Iran based its claim on a public law, this claim was one to assert rights of ownership, rather than to enforce export legislation and was therefore to be regarded a patrimonial claim. Under the reservation that the foreign law was non-confiscatory, as opposed to confiscatory, there was no principle reason not to recognise the state's title despite the lack of possession.[65] The claim was one of recognition and not one of enforcement. On the other hand, the court held that in case a state acquired ownership through confiscation, then the state has to reduce the property to possession while the property is still located within the state.

Importantly, the CA stressed in its ruling that in fact there is no decision, which binds the court to hold that there is a rule generally preventing the enforcement of all foreign public laws. Rather the court found that the rule is one of public policy and where a claim for the recovery of antiquities which form part of its national heritage is concerned, there are positive reasons of policy why such a claim should be enforced. The court stressed the importance of countering the trade in cultural heritage and referred to the UNESCO and UNIDROIT Convention to underline this view. As a consequence, Iran's claim was held to be justiciable in England.

---

**63** [2007] EWCA Civ. 1374, at 118 and 125. The court resorted to the definition of public law proposed in the Spycatcher-case, see Att-Gen (UK) v Heinemann Publishers Australia Pty Ltd. (1988) 165 CLR 30.

**64** [2007] EWCA Civ 1374, at 149.

**65** Cp. Patty Gerstenblith, Schultz and Barakat, at 46, stating that the CA's approach in Barakat recognises the fundamental problem with "undocumented" antiquities – that is antiquities that are looted directly from the ground and are therefore unknown and unrecorded before their theft.

Contrary to the court of first instances decision, the CA in *Barakat* succeeded to distinguish between the recognition of a foreign nation's ownership right and the enforcement of a foreign nation's laws in UK courts. This new development acknowledges the problem of illegally excavated antiquities where the state regularly cannot have obtained possession of them before they leave the territory of its country of origin.[66] Although the decision still awaits the determination of whether the artefacts were discovered in Iran and whether they were removed from Iran after the enactment of the laws in question, the preliminary trial marked a giant step towards the protection of illegally excavated cultural property in front of English courts, and will be critically discussed throughout the thesis.

## § 2. Objectives of the Book and Research Task

This thesis will argue in favour of the 'demand-reduction-approach'. It holds the view that aside from criminal and administrative legislation, successful returns of illicitly obtained heritage items to their countries of origin may be used as an additional route to reduce the demand for illicitly obtained cultural property. Successful litigation to recover cultural objects would equally increase the awareness of illegal dealings with such goods. Returns of movable antiquities to its source countries would help diminish the destruction of archaeological context caused by looting, if they succeed in serving as a deterrent to prospective

**66** In the United States, individuals have found that objects which at times cost millions of dollars have been seized and returned to their rightful owner, or have been returned as a result of negotiation prompted by legal proceedings. See for example the Lydian hoard-case, Republic of Turkey v Metropolitan Museum of Art, 762 F. Supp.44 (S.D.N.Y. 1990); the Elmali Hoard-case, Republic of Turkey v OKS Partners, No CIV. A 89–3061-WJS, 1994 U.S. Dist. LEXIS 17032 (D. Mass June 8, 1994), also United States v McClain, 545 F.2d 988, 100 (5th Cir. Tex., 1977); United States v Schultz, 333 F.3d 393 (2nd Cir.2003), cert. denied, 72 U.S.L.W. 3446 (U.S. Jan.12 2004) (No 03–592); the Phiale-case, US v An Antique Platter of Gold, 991 F. Supp. 222 (S.D.N.Y. 1997). For a detailed analysis of the American case law see e.g. Lawrence M. Kaye, The Future of the Past: Recovering Cultural Property, Cardozo J. of Int'l & Comp. L. (1996) 23; L. Kaye, Cultural Property Disputes in Foreign Courts, in: E.Schneider/R.Schneider (eds.), Cultural Property Protection, Deutsch Türkische Rechtsstudien Band 4 (2005) 43; L. Kaye & Carla T. Main, The Saga of the Lydian Hoard, Antiquities Trade or Betrayed (1995). The notion of deterrence here includes not only the threat of the imposition of the criminal law, but in addition civil sanctions such as seizure by customs officials or loss of the material as a result of a suit seeking recovery of stolen objects.

purchasers and thereby providing a disincentive to looters before the objects are taken from the ground.[67]

In support of this contention, it is necessary to prove that aside the enactment and implementation of international treaties, the return of illegally excavated and exported cultural objects is an imperative based on legal argument. The maintenance of the principle of state sovereignty should not hinder the vindication of sovereign rights in cultural heritage. Therefore, the overall aim of this thesis is to investigate the development of justiciability of sovereign claims to misappropriated cultural property, and ideally, to prove that there exists a rule of law which renders such claims to be justiciable. In the alternative case that no such rule can be revealed, the thesis will make a recommendation on the quality of the property interest which may best ensure to render such claims justiciable in foreign courts.

In order to meet this goal the research will have to take the following direction: The first task will be to identify "rights" or "interest" in cultural objects which are capable of being enforced in foreign courts and, second, to elaborate means to turn such rights into claims fit for litigation. The main concern will be on rights adhering to states on the ground of public and administrative law, while the second concern will be on rights adhering to states arising from civil law. The term "rights" is being used in this context as a single term detached from its usual counterparts intentionally as not all models analysed in this study necessarily constitute a property, proprietary or possessory right in the understanding of either civil or common law. The research results can be of use for states who want to improve or draft legislation concerning cultural property in order to grant their heritage a better protection from illicit trafficking with antiquities. The second task will be to investigate how these "rights" practically work if presented in a foreign forum.

For this purpose it is necessary to:

- Examine and compare legislative models that have been adopted at the national level to ensure the protection of movable cultural property and to extract rights granting an interest in these special objects that are capable of being made the subject of a revindication claim

67 The 1970 UNESCO Convention works with the term "cultural heritage", which is defined in Art. 4, and "cultural property".

Furthermore it is necessary to:
- Examine international treaties in relation to the revindication of such rights and their effect on the justiciability of claims based on those rights
- To analyse the law on justiciability of claims in relation to cultural property in selected market states

The legislative programs of various nations for the protection of cultural property are characterised by a great number of differences reflecting the variety of opinions and national policies which prevailed when each system for protection was created. It is impossible to provide an exhaustive study concerning the protection of cultural property of all jurisdictions. However, in order to give a systematic overview, the author decided to present the different national legislative schemes by grouping legal systems into singular models of protection. In order to present and analyse each legislative model, specific jurisdictions were chosen which are representative of the model's distinct character. The study could also have been conducted on a region-by-region basis. This approach was rejected because legislation aimed at protecting cultural property can, but does not necessary show similarities depending on the geographical region. In fact, legislation can vary immensely, although the countries that enacted it can be counted to one geographical area. Furthermore, the aim of the study was to introduce the different legal tools of which a statute could consist of in detail, in order to be able to determine which models are more favourable than others to either source or market states.

## § 3. Terminology and Delimitation

### I. Movable Cultural Property

There is no recognised definition of what constitutes a cultural object, nor has any general definition of cultural property been agreed upon in the course of both the 1970 UNESCO Convention[68] and the 1995 UNIDROIT Convention[69], the main international conventions governing the protection of cultural goods. Only general guiding principles could be settled upon, and it was eventually

68 Convention on the Means of Prohibiting and Preventing the Illicit Import, Export and Transfer of Ownership of Cultural Property, Nov. 17, 1970, 823 U.N.T.S. 231 [hereinafter UNESCO Convention].

69 1995 UNIDROIT Convention on Stolen or Illegally Exported Cultural Objects, June 24, 1995, 34 I.L.M. (1995) 1330; reprinted in 5 IJCP (1996) 155 [hereinafter: UNIDROIT Convention].

left to the individual states to define cultural property pursuant to their own methods. Thus, most states have their own definition of what constitutes cultural property or what constitutes an archaeological artefact. It falls beyond the purpose of this work to address the controversy relating to the definition of cultural property or cultural heritage.[70] The same is true for the definition of what is to be considered an antiquity. Hence, for the purpose of this research, cultural property is considered to be paintings, sculptures, carpentry, coins, and objects belonging to more recent historical periods, but may include even ceremonies, songs, language, and other forms of cultural expression. Antiquities will be objects that have been made or modified by humans, and date to earlier periods of human history or are of considerable age, often obtained through archaeology or by chance.[71]

Movable as well as immovable cultural property each of its own entails a vast regulatory system of protection.[72] Movables require different legal treatment from immovables owing to their portability and the legal consequences thereof. The protection of immovable cultural property on the other hand pursues different goals. Immovables in the first place have to be protected from deterioration and destruction by vandalism or building measures, while movables additionally have to be protected from theft, looting, illegal excavation and illegal export. Movables can travel from one jurisdiction to another. They can be acquired in good faith, through adverse possession or forfeiture. It is movable cultural heritage that is subject to recovery cases on the ground of national cultural property laws. The comparative analysis of legal systems undertaken in this study is thus confined to movable cultural property and cultural property which has been made movable.

**70** Similarly, Patrick J O'Keefe, Trade in Antiquities – Reducing Destruction and Theft (1997), at 12. For attempts of a definition see however for example J. Blake, On The Definition of Cultural Heritage, 1 ICLQ (2000) 49, at 60 and references; Kerstin Odendahl, Kulturgüterschutz (2005), at 386 et seq; K. Lubina, Contested Cultural Property (2009), at 39 et seq.

**71** Underwater cultural heritage is not directly addressed in this thesis. However, many laws which vest ownership of antiquities in the state cover antiquities that were found in the sea bed.

**72** As antiquities form only a fraction of the cultural object and all laws analysed in this paper have a general application to cultural property, the analysis will also entail objects, which do not qualify as 'antiquities', but which do fall within the general definition of 'cultural property'.

## II. Antiquities

Although the findings of this research generally apply to all cultural objects, this thesis is especially relevant to antiquities. Owing to their status as 'mixed goods',[73] antiquities hold an exceptional position within the cultural property total: they have a physical component (the object itself) and an intangible component (the archaeological or historical context). Each time, an antiquity is discovered and removed from a site without first being studied and categorised by professional archaeologists, the historical context *in situ* is destroyed. Most ancient art on the market has no record of either provenance or provenience. For a long time, this total lack of documentation has traditionally been seen as sufficient evidence that such objects belong to no one, or to anyone. If, however, questions of ownership in antiquities become more clear, this might make illicit trade in them less fruitful. Apart from losing valuable information gathered from the context of the archaeological site, archaeological artefacts are more susceptible to damage than objects that are already in a museum or private collection. Treasure hunters have been known to destroy and to break up artefacts, behead statutes, destroy human remains, melt down ancient coins, chisel reliefs from tombs, as well as to amputate portions of fixed monuments. Cultural policy ought to insure future generations continue to be able to view, possess or study antiquities.

Movable antiquities can be divided into two categories: (1) newly discovered antiquities that have not (yet) been reported to the state, and (2) previously discovered antiquities that the state knows about but which are still in the ground and at risk of being stolen. Protection of the latter is primarily a question of countries providing adequate resources to deter criminal activity. Protection of the former, the newly discovered antiquity, is more difficult in that the source countries do not know of the antiquity unless and until the finder reports his or her find to the proper authorities.[74]

---

**73** The term provenience is used in this thesis to indicate the modern history of an archaeological object back to its find spot in the ground. The term provenance refers to the history of the ownership of an object, but in the case of an archaeological object this history will necessarily be complete back to the moment at which it was removed from the ground, cp. Patty Gerstenblith, The Public Interest, footnote 7. Defining provenance as including both, origin and the history of subsequent transaction of an object, see Patrick O'Keefe, Provenance and Trade in Cultural Heritage, Brit. Colum. L Rev. (1995) 259 (Special Issue).

**74** Explaining the meaning of context in detail, Clemency Coggins, United States Cultural Property Legislation, 7 IJCP (2005) 94; Lyndel Prott, The International Movement of Cultural Objects, 12 IJCP (2005) 225; Petty Gerstenblith, Controlling the International Market in Antiquities: Reduc-

The first concern of this study is with antiquities taken from the ground in contravention with national regulations, or from their place as an integral part of, or attachment to an ancient structure.[75] The second concern is with objects taken illicitly from the possession of individuals, institutions (such as museums or churches) or other resting places which do not harbour any archaeological interest in their link with the object itself.[76] The term "illicit" includes trade in cultural objects that has been conducted in violation of legal regulation, national or international.[77] In cultural property law, the first category of cultural objects that had been taken from the ground is generally being referred to as "looted", while the term "stolen" sometimes includes both the first ('looted') and the second category. Some of the second category of objects stolen from individuals or institutions may of course have been looted prior to becoming part of those collections. In order to avoid this confusing terminology and differentiation, all situations of theft, looting and equally illegal export of cultural objects are being referred to as "misappropriated".

## III. Archaeological and Historical Context

Although it is a notion used by archaeologists and anthropologists, for purposes of the present research task, it is important to inform the reader about the meaning of 'context'.[78] The manner in which artefacts are recovered from the ground only became important after the development of archaeology as a science, with examples of stratigraphic excavations and recordings dating back as early as the seventeenth century. Stratigraphic excavation requires that each layer be removed in reverse chronological order and that the remains be recovered separately by each stratum, with all the remains of the same period in association with each other.[79] In this way, the archaeologist can determine the spatial and

ing the Harm, Preserving the Past, 8 Chi. J. Int'l L. (2007) 169; Derek Fincham, The Fundamental Importance of Archaeological Context, in: Noah Charney (ed.), Art and Crime (2009) 1.

**75** The following differentiation was suggested by Simon MacKenzie in Going, Going, Gone: (2005), at 3.

**76** See P.J. O'Keefe/ L.V. Prott, Law and the Cultural Heritage, Vol. 3 Movement (1989), at 147.

**77** See Peter Wedel, Protecting Newly Discovered Antiquities, at 1016.

**78** See E.g. W.J. Mayer-Oakes, A Stratigraphic Excavation at El Risco, Mexico, 103 Proceedings of the American Philosophical Society (1959) 332; L.R. Lyman/M. J. O'Brien, Americanist Stratigraphic Excavation and the Measurement of Culture Change, 6 Journal of Archaeological Method and Theory (1999) 55; David L. Browman/Douglas R. Givens, Stratigraphic Excavation: The First "New Archaeology", 98 American Anthropologist (1996) 80.

**79** P. Gerstenblith, Controlling the International Market, at 170.

chronological relationship of all the remains, and many aspects of past life can be reconstructed including economics, trade, health, diet, religious ritual and function, burial methods, family structure, political organisation, technology, and literature.[80] The archaeological heritage consists of this fragile and non-renewable physical evidence of humankind's origins and behaviour. Carefully preserved artefacts in their original location can furnish the data upon which the reconstruction of our past depends. This historical record that can be constructed through scientific evaluation of the object *in situ*, the archaeologists call 'context'. Finds are often dated according to the 'context' in which they have been excavated. Older artefacts in a younger archaeological context can be used as proof of the persistence of certain traditions and rites.[81] Thus, the most important indirect quality of archaeological objects as compared to other kinds of cultural objects is the context in which they are discovered. With some exaggeration, from a scientific perspective the context of discovery of archaeological objects is more important than the objects themselves.[82]

### IV. Source Nations and Market Nations

This book will discuss regulations concerning the protection of cultural property in source nations and market nations. Most of the case law concerning cultural property involves claims by source nations against consuming market nations rather than vice versa. This is due to the fact that in source nations, the supply of desirable cultural property exceeds the internal demand.[83] Nations like Mexico, Egypt, Greece, Italy and India are examples. They are being considered rich in cultural artefacts. In market nations, the demand exceeds the supply. France, Germany, Japan, the Scandinavian nations, Switzerland and the United States are examples. When, as is often (but not always) the case, the source nation is relatively poor and the market nation wealthy, an unrestricted market will

**80** Clemency Coggins, United States Cultural Property Legislation (2005), at 98.
**81** Ricardo J. Elia, Looting, Collecting, and the Destruction of Archaeological Resources, 6 Nonrenewable Resources (1997) 85, at 93 (discussing the destruction of an artefact's original archeological context as the most serious consequence of looting); L. Borodkin, The Economics of Antiquities Looting, at 382.
**82** J.H. Merryman, Two Ways of Thinking about Cultural Property, 80 Amer. J. of Int'l. L. (1986), 831; E. Willis Lindsay, The Recovery of Cultural Artefacts: The Legacy of our Archaeological Heritage, 22 Case W. Res. J. Int'L (1990) 165, at 167 (debating relations between art-rich and art-poor nations).
**83** Cp. J. H. Merryman, Two Ways of Thinking about Cultural Property, at 833.

encourage the export of cultural property from source to market nations.[84] Many countries, however, can be both source states and market states. Australia, for example, is the source of Aboriginal remains and artefacts, and also runs a small market in international antiquities. China, maintains one of the largest art markets in the world while at the same time being rich in artefacts which flow outwards from China into both wealthy Asian countries as well as the traditional market centres of London and New York.[85] The United Kingdom, is one of the worlds leading art market countries but on the other hand is rich in a wide variety of antiquities, including many from the former Roman Empire. The U.S. can show a respectable excavation history of native American graves. An analysis of the international art market however proves that the U.S. and the UK are the biggest consumer states.[86]

## § 4. The Structure of the Book

This thesis consists of two parts. The first part comparatively delineates different means of acquiring or retaining rights in cultural objects. They may be property rights, interests that equal property or interests that do not count as property, but serve as a mechanism to protect movable cultural heritage. The second part of the thesis will be devoted to elaborating ways to turn interests in cultural objects which derive from national cultural property legislation into recovery claims. The main focus will be on finding methods which apply to such interests in a foreign forum.

Chapter one provides a general introduction to the book. After presenting a background on the scale of the illicit trade in antiquities and explaining the reasons why the law in this area needs to be reviewed, it outlines the main objec-

84 For information on the Chinese art market see Kathleen Anderson, The Illicit Traffic in Asian Antiquities (2001); Michael Dutra, Protecting Cultural Relics in the People's Republic of China, 5 Asian-Pacific L. & Pol'y J. (2004) 62.

85 Cp. Simon McKenzie, Going, Going, Gone (2005) at 8.

86 For instance, the protection of immovable structures is regulated in laws concerning the environment, building, space, planning, and structural development. International instruments protecting immovables and natural structures are The UNESCO Convention for the protection of the World Cultural and Natural Heritage 1972, and the Venice Charter 1964 on Architectural Conservation. Note, that the Common Law does not use the distinction between movable and immovable in its legislation. Objects that are associated with an immovable fall into a special legal category called "fixtures", while movable objects are called "chattels". In England, immovable cultural objects are amongst others protected by The Ancient Monuments and Archaeological Areas Act 1979 (as amended by the National Heritage Act 1983).

tives of the study as well as the methodology that will be followed to assess them. It also outlines the scope and limitations of the thesis and considers terminological and definitional issues.

Chapter two focuses on sovereign rights to movable cultural objects. It will draw a systematic overview of the current legal techniques. It presents the different ways in which countries impose control on fortuitously discovered heritage objects. It will discuss the acquisition of ownership to such objects and methods of retaining cultural heritage within the public domain according to public law. Firstly, it outlines the specific mechanisms of supervising the export of heritage items. Further it presents how different jurisdictions protect heritage items through a right of pre-emption.

Chapter three will comparatively analyse under which circumstances a state acquires title to discovered objects, which do fall foul of the special cultural property regime, on the grounds of the law of finds. In a first part, it examines the acquisition of title in common law jurisdictions, focusing on English law. In a second part, it discusses finder's law as it is practiced in civilian jurisdiction.

Chapter four evaluates the relevant international statutes in relation to the recovery of movable antiquities. It will analyse whether the current regime in force provides means for the enforcement of interests to public or private cultural objects on which claims to such objects are founded.

Chapter five will elaborate upon the application of foreign cultural property laws within the framework of private international law. It will discuss which law should govern the rights and obligations of the disputants once a looted, stolen or illegally exported artefact surfaces.

Chapter six deals with the justiciability of foreign law in national courts. It analyses, how rights derived from public cultural property statutes are applied in foreign courts in international litigation. The chapter focuses on the law in England, the USA, Germany, and Switzerland, as being the main market states for cultural goods.

# Part I: **Rights to Cultural Objects**

The first part of this book focuses on the various types of "rights" a state may have or may obtain in cultural objects, in particular movable antiquities. The very general term "right" is an intentional choice as opposed to the more differentiated term "property right", as, first, it would go beyond the scope of this work to determine the bounderies of what constitutes a "property right" and what does not. This would, however, be a necessary step if choosing that specific term. Second, the term "right" encompasses equally other interests in cultural objects, such as rights of immediate possession, pre-emption rights or de-accession provisions of public institutions which do not constitute a property right in the traditional sence of some legal systems and as such would fall foul of the analysis. However, it was thought necessary to include the whole palette of "rights" in order to draw a complete picture of legal problems that cross-border litigation involving cultural objects may entail.[87] Depending on the quality of the right a state (or an individual) may have in a missappropriated cultural object, the item in question may or may not be successfully recovered.

Consequently, Part I of this analysis consists of two chapters, of which the first will scrutinise the quality of the right or interest which states may obtain in cultural objects and equally rights that a sovereign may already hold in such objects. In order to delineate the findings of the analysis of many national legal systems aimed at the protection of cultural property, different mechanisms of controlling the rights to cultural objects have been identified and are being presented in this chapter. The second chapter is devoted to rights that states may hold in newly discovered antiquities, in the event they are not covered by a special cultural property regime, as outlined in the previous chapter. For this reason, the study examines the allocation of title to finds according to the civil law of finds. The extrapolation in Chapter three equally adheres to private individuals who furtuitoudly discover treasure.

---

87 The research excludes intellectual property rights.

# Chapter 2.
# Sovereign Rights to Movable Cultural Objects

## § 1. Introduction

Initially, movable antiquities were governed by the ordinary civil law of finders.[88] During the nineteenth century, source countries began to reconsider the law-of-finders-approach to newly discovered antiquities. This philosophical change coincided with the advent of "cultural property".[89] Mexico for example, made some attempts to nationalise its cultural objects as early as 1897 but did not fully establish ownership until 1972. Greece claimed state ownership to all antiquities and maritime finds in 1932 and Egypt in 1983. So far, no unified system of state ownership of antiquities exists. In 1956, the UNESCO International Principles Applicable to Archaeological Excavations recommended that "each member should in particular define the legal status of the archaeological sub-soil and, where state ownership of the sub-soil is recognised, specifically mentioning the fact in its legislation.[90]

Today, states protect their antiquities through various legal mechanisms granting them sovereign rights of which some may constitute property rights and some may not. Which sovereign right constitutes at the same time a property right has an enormous impact on its recognition and enforcement in foreign courts as, so far, only property rights may be recognised in the international arena. Property rights in that sense may be (1) direct ownership, (2) confiscatory ownership, or (3) an immediate right of possession based on a duty to deliver the item to the state.[91] The purpose of this chapter is to determine which sovereign rights aimed at the protection of cultural property at the same time constitutes a property right that may be capable of being recognised or enforced in a foreign court. In order to conduct this analysis different legal mechanisms have been ex-

---

**88** Cp. Patty Gerstenblith, Controlling the International Market in Antiquities: Reducing the Harm, Preserv ing the Past, 8 Chi. J. Int'l L. (2007) 169, at 174; Peter Wendel, Protecting Newly Discovered Antiquities, at 1022.

**89** Peter Wendel, supra, at 1025. On the "advent of cultural property" see also John Alan Cohan, An Examination of Archaeological Ethics and the Repatriation Movement Respecting Cultural Property (Part One), 27 Envt'l L. Pol'y J. (2004) 1, at 7; John Henry Merryman, The Public Interest in Cultural Property, 77 Cal. L. Rev. (1989) 339, at 341.

**90** UNESCO Recommendation on International Principles Applicable to Archaeological Excavations 1956, Art. 5.

**91** Of course direct ownership and confiscatory ownership may also constitute an immediate right of possession.

trapolated from various national cultural property statutes that provide the government with a sovereign right. Paragraph two of this chapter deals with mechanisms of acquiring antiquities for the state which are not yet in its possession or ownership, whereas paragraph three looks into mechanisms which attempt to retain objects for the state which are already a part of the public domain.

## § 2. Mechanisms of Acquiring Rights to Cultural Objects

In order to analyse legal frameworks aimed at acquiring property rights to cultural heritage as to the quality of its proprietary title, following major control mechanisms have been identified: explicit ownership declarations, laws granting an immediate right of possession, export legislation and pre-emption rights.

### I. Property Rights on the Ground of Ownership Declarations

#### 1. Umbrella Statutes

The strongest possible protection is being achieved by so called 'blanket' or 'umbrella' laws.[92] They provide for state ownership of all cultural objects, whether they have been excavated, are still buried or whether they are in private or public hands.[93] The main purpose of blanket legislation vesting the state with what is called *ipso iure* ownership[94] is to protect national cultural heritage by not allowing precious objects to remain ownerless until the state acts to acquire them.[95] A country enacting such vesting legislation remains the owner of artefacts within its territory, on the understanding that the item in question must have been in the territory at the time of enactment, until it expressly states that it revokes its ownership.

---

92 Generally, laws which vest the ownership of antiquities in the state may also be called vesting laws, patrimony laws or found in the ground laws.

93 Cp. Kurt Siehrt, Reforms and Developments in the Member States of the European Union, in E. Schneider/ R. Schneider (eds.) Cultural Property Protection, Deutsch-Türkische Rechtsstudien Band 4 (2005) 77.

94 Ownership "ipso jure" means that the object becomes property of the state as soon as it is discovered, without seizure, without any kind of appropriation by government officials or without first having to purport an administrative act or court order, cp. e. g. Kurt Siehr, Reforms and Developments, at 78.

95 Cp. Sibel Özel, The Basel Decisions: Recognition of the Blanket Legislation Vesting State Ownership over the Cultural Property Found within the Country of Origin, 9 IJCP (2000) 325.

Such vesting legislation can vary in terms of the definition of the protected objects or the time period of objects covered by the protection of the law. Some countries provide for a total embargo on all objects belonging to the cultural heritage of the country. One of these countries is *Egypt.*[96] In 1983, it enacted one of the most restrictive patrimony laws which declares all antiquities discovered after the enactment of the statute to be the property of the Egyptian state.[97] The law provides for all antiquities privately owned prior to 1983 to be registered and recorded, and makes private ownership or possession of antiquities found after 1983 illegal. Art. 6 reads as follows:

> "All antiquities are considered to be public property – except for charitable and religious endowments. It is impermissible to own, possess or dispose of antiquities except pursuant to the conditions set forth in this law and its implementing regulations."

An antiquity is defined to be "every building or object that is a product of the Egyptian civilisation or any further civilisation."[98] It is also a product of art, science or religion on Egyptian soil from the pre-historic era up to 100 years before present time. An antiquity also covers any item with a historical, archaeological or artistic value that has contributed to the Egyptian civilisation or was created in Egypt for any other civilisation. It also covers anything produced in Egypt or bearing any relation to Egypt's history. All human remains are considered as antiquities.[99]

The Egyptian umbrella law does not only prohibit the unearthing of artefacts but even the sole possession of antiquities, with the exception of these whose ownership or possession was already established in 1983, before the law was enacted.[100] Egyptian government officials testified that there is no legal way for a private individual to retain possession of an antiquity discovered after

---

**96** But see also for example the legislation in Afghanistan, where Art 8 of Law on the Protection of Historical and Cultural Properties 2004 provides that all historical and cultural properties, movable or immovable, in Afghanistan, discovered or hidden in the earth, are the property of the State by virtue of this law. Thus any kind of transfer of such property without permission is considered as theft.

**97** Law No 117 on the Protection of Antiquities (1983). In the following, all legal acts cited without the exact source, from where they were obtained, can be downloaded at the UNESCO cultural property database at http://www.unesco.org/culture/natlaws/index.php?&lng=en. For the Egyptian Act, see also United States v Schultz, 333 F. 3d 393 (2d Cir. 2003), where Law 117 was analysed by the U.S. Court of Appeal.

**98** Art. 1 Law No 117.

**99** Art. 1 Law No 117.

**100** Art. 8 Law No 117.

1983, and that all such antiquities are seized by the government.[101] The Egyptian parliament recently agreed to amend Law No 117 which shall now also prohibit all antiquities trading and cancel the 10 per cent of unearthed goods previously granted to the foreign excavation missions who discovered them.[102]

*Mexico*'s Patrimony law is also considered to be one of the strictest protective regimes.[103] Objects covered by the act however, are divided into three categories of heritage items. According to the most recent Mexican protection act[104], cultural property protected by the act is: archaeological monuments, which consist of real estate and movable property that are products of cultures preceding the establishment of the Hispanic culture on national territory, as well as human, flora and fauna remains related to those cultures,[105] artistic monuments,[106] and historic monuments.[107] According to Art. 27 of the Mexican Federal Act such artefacts are the property of the state even if they are still buried or underwater.[108] However, private ownership of antiquities, as opposed to the regime in Egypt, is permitted in limited cases, namely only in relation to archaeological movable her-

**101** Parliament agreed on Article 8 forbidding trade in antiquities but allowing possession of antiquities for some individuals, on condition that they did use them for benefit, and did no damage or neglect them, cp. Christine Irsheid, The Protection of Cultural Property in the Arab World.

**102** For information on the new law see http://weekly.ahram.org.eg/2010/984/eg3.htm. The new law also doubles the previous penalties. Anyone who steals, hides, or collects authentic artefacts, or owns them without permission, will be imprisoned for 10 years and fined from LE 50,000 to LE 250,000 instead of three years' hard labour and a smaller fine. According to the new law, stealing or helping to rob a part of a genuine piece or any deliberate intent to disfigure it will land a sentence of 15 years and a fine of from LE 50,000 to LE 100,000.

**103** Generally on Mexican cultural property law, Jorge Sanchez Cordero, The Protection of Cultural Heritage – in: T.Kono/S.Wrbka (eds.), The Impact of Uniform Laws on the Protection of Cultural Heritage and the Preservation of Cultural Heritage in the 21st Century (2010) Mexican Report, 495–560.

**104** Federal Law on Archaeological, Artistic and Historic Monuments and Zones 1972 (Ley federal sobre monumentos y zonas archeologicas, artisticas e historicas, most recent amendment published in the official Gazette of the Federation on 13.01.1986).

**105** Art. 28 of the 1972 Act.

**106** Art. 33 of the 1972 Act: Artistic Monuments are real estate and movable properties that have relevant aesthetic value. The works of living artists that have the characteristics of movable goods may no be declared artistic monuments.

**107** Art. 35 of the 1972 Act: Historic monuments are those linked to the nation's history, from the establishment of Hispanic culture in Mexico, under the terms of the respective declaration or as determined by the Law.

**108** They are also inalienable and imprescriptible, Art 27 of the 1972 Act. In any case, discovered or found archaeological objects have to be reported to the INAH within 24 hours, leading to state ownership.

itage privately owned prior to 1972. However, their use and holding was confined to national territory.[109]

The same is true for *Italy*, which permits private ownership of both immovable and movable cultural property, although the main proprietor of cultural heritage is the state.[110] The status of privately owned goods as cultural property is not presumed *per se* as is the case with objects belonging to the state. Their status must first be recognised via an administrative procedure called 'declaration of the cultural interest' contemplated by Art. 13 Code of Cultural Property and Landscape 2004. As a consequence, privately owned objects are considered cultural property and made subject of the measures of protection reserved to cultural heritage pursuant to the relevant legislation only after their cultural significance has been specifically declared through an ad hoc procedure of designation.[111] At the end of the procedure, the Declaration of Cultural Interest is issued irrespective of the consent of the private proprietor of the object concerned who may only bring administrative recourse against the Declaration according to Art. 16 of the Heritage Code. Once a 'cultural interest' has been recognised by the procedure, the ownership of the item in question is limited and constrained to the extent necessary to ensure preservation and public fruition of the relevant heritage.[112] There is no acquisition of property rights by private persons on the basis of original title. Thus, Article 91 of the 2004 Code establishes that all objects found in the ground or in sea beds are considered property of the state, and they become part of the national domain or of the not-disposable heritage.[113] The idea of state ownership of newly discovered antiquities was introduced into Italian law in 1939 and is an exception to Italian treasure law which generally awards the treasure to the owner of the locality where it was found.[114] Before 1939, Art. 714 of the Italian Civil code of 1865 declared that all

**109** Cp. J.S. Cordero, Mexican Report, at 527.

**110** Section 1 Code of Cultural Properties and Landscapes 2004 (Codice dei beni culturali e del paesaggio, D. Lgs. 22 January 2004, No 42, Gazz. Uff. 24 Feb 2004, No 45, Supplement). The Code is the final result of a long evolution in the Italian legislation concerning the protection and management of cultural heritage. It superseded Law No 1089, 1 June 1939, which was in force for over 60 years. For a detailed account of the new Italian legislation see Federico Lenzerini, Italian Report, in: T.Kono/S.Wrbka (eds.), The Impact of Uniform Laws on the Protection of Cultural Heritage and the Preservation of Cultural Heritage in the 21st Century (2010) 439.

**111** Cp. F. Lenzerini, Italian Report, ibid, at 447.

**112** Cp. F. Lenzerini, Italian Report, ibid, at 448.

**113** For the concept of public domain, see this Chapter at § 3 I at seq.

**114** Compare also Chapter 3 on private rights to antiquities. Artcile 932 of the Italian Civil code states that "Treasure is any movable thing of value, hidden, or buried, of which no one can prove he is the owner".

excavations belonged to the owner of the land and were not considered treasure.[115] Article 91 additionally declared that all things found during licenced archaeological excavations are state property.

Other countries have chosen to employ a wider definition of protected objects as it only affects objects which were found underground but not on the surface of the soil. One example is the new Macedonian Law on the Protection of Cultural Heritage 2004 which states in its Article 10 (3) that "cultural heritage and goods which are commonly presumed as cultural heritage which shall be found under ground or underwater, regardless of whether or not it was excavated, shall be treated as state property".[116]

### 2. Conditional Ownership Declarations

Some countries provide for an *ex lege* state ownership of specific archaeological objects but allow for the private acquisition of ownership or private possession of some categories of movable antiquities, the cultural importance of which first has to be determined by a special cultural committee. The state thus acquires ownership of an antiquity based on the condition that it belongs to a certain category of protected objects.

*Greece*, for example, maintains a system of protection which contrasts between three major categories of movables that are treated entirely different concerning their acquisition. The main distinction adopted by the fairly recent Greek Act on the Protection of Antiquities and Cultural Heritage 2002[117] is that between monuments dating from the very remote past until the year 1830 (ancient monuments) and those dating after this year (modern monuments). In addition, the ancient monuments are further divided into those from before 1453 and those between 1453 and 1830, the year of 1453 being the end of the Byzantine Empire, and 1830 marking the creation of the modern Greek state.[118]

**115** Cp. Fabrizio Lemme, Il "Korous" ritrovato: riflessioni e meditazioni, Il giornale dell'arte, Mar. 1990, reprinted in: Tra Arte Dirtto (2d ed. 1996) 63, at 64.

**116** Law on Protection of Cultural Heritage (Official Gazette of the Republic of Macedonia, No. 20/2004).

**117** Act No 3028/2002. The act replaced Act 5351 (1932) which remained in force for 70 years, and was, from time to time, modified and completed by other rules, especially by Act No. 1469 of 1950, see M. Anastassopoulos, The new Act on the protection of antiquities and cultural heritage in general – Survey of the Act No 3028/2002, 6 Environment and the Law (2002) 685.

**118** Similarly, the Art 12 of the Norwegian Cultural Heritage Act 1978 provides for state ownership of heritage items up to the year 1537, as well as for coins from before 1650 and Sami objects which are more than 100 years old. Other objects become the property of the finder. In Venezuela the State owns archaeological property dating from before the conquest. According to the UK

All ancient monuments[119] dating from before 1453 are considered to be the property of the state *ex lege*, meaning without needing the intervention of the Cultural Ministry.[120] They are rendered *res extra commercium.*[121] However, property rights to religious objects dating from before 1453 and previously belonging to the church or to other ecclesiastical or religious bodies are conditionally recognised if they are not the result of an excavation.[122]

The same regime applies to ancient monuments dating from 1453 until 1830 that have been discovered during an excavation or any other archaeological research,[123] and that have been detached from an immovable structure, or which constitute a religious icon or ritual object.[124] Whoever finds or discovers such a monument must declare it without undue delay, to the nearest archaeological, police or port authority.[125] However, monuments dating up to 1453 and belonging to the state may be subject to private possession if the government grants a permit for possession.[126] An object may even be released for the free use of the finder if the finder has declared it accordingly and if it is of very small scientific or commercial value.[127]

As far as concerns artefacts which have not been discovered during an excavation and which have not been detached from an immovable and are not religious icons or ritual objects, but dated between 1453 and 1830, they may also be

Treasure Act 1996, the state owns objects other than coins that are at least 300 years old and have a minimum precious metal content of 10 % and all groups of coins from the same find at least 300 years old, cp. sections 1, 2 and 3 of the Treasure Act 1996.

**119** The concept of 'monument' does not coincide with the concept of 'cultural object' mentioned in Art. 1 par. 2 of Act no 3028, cp. Y. Karymbali-Tsiptsiou, Monuments and their Possession (2004) at 21–47. Art 1 par 2 states that "the cultural heritage of the country consists of cultural objects located in Greece" and in Art 2 (a) that "cultural objects" mean's "the testimony of the existence of individual and collective human activity".

**120** Art. 21 (1) reads "Movable ancient monuments dating up to 1453 belong to the state in terms of ownership and possession. They are imprescriptible and extra commercium according to 966 of the Civil Code".

**121** On the concept of *res extra commercium* see this chapter § 3 I.

**122** If they originate from an excavation they belong to the state, Art. 21 para. 2, combined with Art. 33 para. 3.

**123** Art. 21 (1) (b).

**124** Art. 21 (3).

**125** Art. 24 (1). The declaration shall include the exact location where the antiquity has been found, the manner in which it came to the possession of the discoverer and also personal data of the previous holder, if the antiquity has not been fortuitously discovered.

**126** Art. 23 (1).

**127** Art. 23 (5). The decision is made by the Minister of Culture, following an opinion of the Council.

subject to private ownership and possession. According to article 20 (1) they are qualified as monuments owing to their social, technical, folkloric, ethnological, artistic, architectural, industrial or general historic or scientific importance. They are not protected *ex lege* but by virtue of a decision of an administrative act.[128] The crucial element of their protection is not their age but their cultural importance.[129] They may be owned by private individuals and transferred under the terms and conditions of the act.[130] The same applies to "modern monuments", the third category of movables protected under the act. All modern items, in order to be protected, must first be characterised as monuments by virtue of a decision of the Minister of Culture and published in the Government Gazette.[131]

Monuments which do not automatically belong to the state *ex lege*, are being protected through a reporting duty and pre-emptive rights of the government. Any person who acquires ownership or possession of a monument of this kind shall submit a declaration on the circumstances in which it came to his possession and the personal data on of the previous holder without undue delay to the authorities.[132] In the event that possession of the antiquity passes to the state, reward shall be paid to the person which made the declaration.[133] Consequently this means that the government is not automatically the owner of such monuments but is only entitled to a right of possession to such objects in order to determine its cultural importance. The wording of Art. 24 II stating that "any person who acquires ownership of a monument dating after 1453" makes clear that the finder or the buyer becomes the owner of such items in the first place.

### 3. Mixed Law of Finders and State Ownership Approach

Today, many market nations and countries which are poor in antiquities follow a moderate law of finders approach, where the finder generally becomes the owner of found objects unless the objects belongs to a certain category of protected objects. In the latter case, the heritage item explicitly becomes the property of the state upon its discovery.

---

**128** Art. 20 (2), the decision of the Minister is issued after the report of the Authority and opinion of the competent council.

**129** Spyridon Vrellis, Protection of Antiquities and Cultural Heritage in Greece, in: E. Schneider/ R. Schneider (eds.), Cultural Property Protection (2005) 97, at 109.

**130** The conditions are stated in article 28 of Act no 3028.

**131** Art. 20 (2)-(3), see further A. Papapetropoulos, The Decision of the Council of State, 7 Environment and the Law (2003) 693.

**132** Art. 24 (3) Law 3028.

**133** Art. 24 (3) Law 3028.

### a. The UK Treasure Act 1996 – A Market Nation's Protection Scheme

In England and Wales, for the last 700 years title to objects discovered in the ground was governed by two complementary sets of rules: the private law of finders and the royal prerogative of treasure trove.[134] Generally, finds were governed by the ordinary law of finders unless they fell under the ancient law of treasure trove[135] which provided that certain objects belonged outright to the Crown. To qualify as treasure trove, an object had to fulfil three tests: (1) it had to be composed substantially of gold or silver,[136] (2) it had to have been deposited in the ground by someone who intended to return and retrieve it later,[137] and (3) its present owner had to be unknown. In order to vest ownership in the Crown, all three criteria had to be fulfilled. The second test caused insurmountable problems, as it was often impossible to determine the state of mind with which a person came to leave an object in the ground many centuries ago.[138] The law did not include the protection of important historical objects as its original purpose was the prospect of increasing revenue.[139] According to Carman, "it was a form of taxation of secret wealth long after the death of the taxee"[140]. The 'gold or silver'- test automatically excluded from Crown ownership objects made wholly or substantially of baser metals, objects not made of metal at all, and objects which contained and were found along with treasure trove. For example, in

134 On the law of treasure trove see e. g. George Hill, Treasure Trove in Law and Practice (1936); John Carman, Valuing Ancient Things – Archaeology and Law (1996); Neil Cookson, Archaeological Heritage Law (2000), at 229 et seq; and especially N. E. Palmer, Bailment (3rd ed. 2009), at 26 – 062 et seq.

135 Treasure trove derives from the old French treasure trove, found treasure.

136 A.-G. of the Duchy of Lancaster v. G. E. Overton (Farms) Ltd [1980] 3 All E.R. 503 (Dillon J.), affirmed [1982] 1 All E.R. 524 (C.A.); see also N. Palmer (1981) 44 Mod. L.R. 178. According to Lord Denning it should be 50 per cent or more gold or silver before it could be described as a gold or silver object": [1982] 1 All E.R. 524, at 530.

137 A.-G. v. Trustees of the British Museum [1903] 2 Ch. 598,; A.-G. of the Duchy of Lancaster v. G. E. Overton (Farms) Ltd [1980] 3 All E.R. 503, at 508 per Dillon J., affirmed without reference to this point [1982] 1 All E.R. 524 (C.A.); Webb v. Ireland and A.-G. [1988] I.R. 353, 373; See also Hill, Treasure Trove Law and Practice (1936).

138 Cp. N. E. Palmer, Bailment, at 26 – 063.

139 It was not until the mid-nineteenth century that this law began to be used fro the purpose of state acquisition of antiquities. By that time, the historical worth of objects became more important than their worth as valuable metals. As such, an incentive was needed to ensure uninformed finders did not melt down their discoveries for their precious metal content. In 1886 the government instituted a rewards scheme where finds claimed as treasure trove were offered to museums and finders were paid a reward. Of course, this was a period of extreme prosperity in much of the United Kingdom, cp. Hill (1936), at 239.

140 Cp. John Carman, Valuing Ancient Things – Archaeology and Law (1996), at 49.

*Attorney General of the Duchy Lancaster v G.E Overton Ltd*,[141] the court refused to classify a hoard of almost 8000 third century Roman coins as treasure trove because its silver content ranged from less than 1 % to approximately 18 % . As a result, the coins have been awarded to the landowner.

The definition of treasure trove received significant criticism in that they were too restrictive and could result in the division of a single archaeological find between the Crown and either the landowner or the finder.[142] The definition excluded many valuable finds and meant that historically important and valuable objects that fell outside the scope of common law treasure trove were not subject to crown ownership. Hence, the existing legal framework was not valuing the historical and archaeological value of finds. The 'intention to return' test excluded from Crown ownership anything deliberately abandoned or inadvertently lost, rather than deliberately deposited, so that objects like a mediaeval gold brooch in *Waverley Borough Council v Fletcher*[143] was not considered treasure trove.[144]

After several attempts to reform the law of treasure trove a new act, The Treasure Act 1996, is now in force. The Treasure Act removes much of the deficiency of the old treasure trove by abolishing the need for inquiry into the mental state of the loser, abandoner or depositor.[145] The place of find is generally irrelevant: the object can be above or below land, or concealed in part of a building. The law covers England, Wales, and Northern Ireland. The old definition has been replaced with a new objective formulation, supplemented by the Treasure (Designation) Order 2002.[146] The following objects are now considered treasure:

---

**141** A.-G. of the Duchy of Lancaster v. G. E. Overton (Farms) Ltd [1980] 3 All E.R. 503; [1982] 1 All E.R. 524 (CA)

**142** See Norman Palmer, Treasure Trove and Title to Discovered Antiquities, 2 IJCP (1993) 275, at 278–281 (arguing that such a division diminished the historical value of the collection as a whole).

**143** [1996] Q.B. 334 (CA).

**144** N. E. Palmer, Bailment, at 26–063.

**145** Cp. James Carleton, Protecting the National Heritage: Implications of the British Treasure Act 1996, 6 IJCP (1997) 343; but also Clive Cheesman, Religious Offerings and the Intention to Recover in the Law of Treasure Trove, 1 AAL (1996) 27.

**146** The act can be obtained via: http://www.opsi.gov.uk/si/si2002/draft/20022470.htm. The Treasure (Designation) Order 2002 extends the definition of "treasure" in section 1 of the Treasure Act 1996 ("the Act") by designating under section 2(1) of the Act two classes of prehistoric base-metal assemblages as being of outstanding historical, archaeological or cultural importance. This definition will safeguard finds such as the Bronze Age metal smith's hoard found near Salisbury and looted in the 1980 s, which would otherwise go out of the public domain unrecorded, cp. N. E. Palmer, Bailment, at 26–077.

- Objects other than coins that are at least 300 years old and have a minimum precious metal content of 10 %
- All groups of coins from the same find at least 300 years old[147]
- Objects found in association with other treasure objects
- Groups of prehistoric base-metal objects from the same find

Finders are required to report treasure to the coroner within 14 days of the discovery, or within 14 days after realising that the find may be treasure. If the object is deemed to be a treasure, the finder is entitled to a reward based on the market price of the object. Under section 8 (3) of the Treasure Act, if individuals fail to report a find, they may be imprisoned for up to three months, fined, or both. In proceedings against a finder for an offence under this section, it is a defence for the finder to show that he had, and has continued to have, a reasonable excuse for failing to notify the coroner.[148]

After the notification, the Crown is expressly empowered to designate, by order, "any class of object which it considers to be of outstanding historical, archaeological or cultural importance," or, "to disclaim treasure which vests in it under the Act"[149]. If the Crown does disclaim, the effect is retrospective: the disclaimed treasure is deemed not to have vested in the Crown under the Act and can (without prejudice to the interests and rights of others) be delivered to any person.[150] Finds that are not deemed to be a treasure are subject to the regular law of finds.[151] The person to whom title is awarded under private law is free to deal with the object virtually as he wishes.

The new section 8 A of the Treasure Act 1996[152] additionally imposes a duty to notify upon acquirers of treasure.[153] It applies to persons who "acquire property in an object, believing or having reasonable grounds to believe both that the object is treasure and that the appropriate statutory notification in respect of it has not been given. Such individuals must now, within a strictly defined peri-

**147** Single coins found on their own are not treasure and groups of coins lost one by one over a period of time will not normally be treasure, see www.ni-environment.gov.uk/treasureact.pdf
**148** Sect. 8 (4).
**149** Sect. 6 (3).
**150** Sections 6 (4) (a) and 6 (4) (b).
**151** The acquisition of title according to the private law of finders is dealt with in Chapter 3.
**152** The section has been added to the principal Act by section 30 of the Coroners and Justice Act 2009. For a detailed account of the new provisions see especially Norman Palmer, Acquiring Property in Treasure and the Duty to Notify: The Coroners and Justice Act 2009 and the New Criminal Offence, 15 AAL (2010) 125.
**153** Compare the broader approach of the Dealing in Cultural Objects and (Offences) Act 2003 which applies to persons who "deal in" a relevant object.

od[154], notify the Coroner for Treasure. Their failure to notify the Coroner for Treasure before the end of that period may constitute a criminal offence and may result in a penalty on summary conviction of either imprisonment for a term not exceeding 51 weeks, or a fine, or both, if firstly, that notification in respect of the object has not in fact been given under section 8 (1) or section 8 A (1), and secondly if there has been no investigation in relation to the object.[155]

The new section 8 C of the Treasure Act places the prosecution of both offences, the failure to notify a find and the failure to notify of an acquisition, under a limitation period. Proceedings for such an offence may be brought six months from the date on which evidence sufficient to institute a suit became known to the prosecutor.[156]

What the law maker has not considered is the fact that the acquisition of property under section 8 A (1) may collide with the possessory title of the landowner, from whose land the object was excavated without consent.[157] If the person who has excavated property never acquires property due to the landowner's overriding title, the statutory period for the giving of notice would never begin to run. A preferable approach might have been to impose the duty to notify on any person who "deals" in treasure in the sense acknowledged by the Dealing in Cultural Objects (Offences) Act 2003, or indeed on any person who comes into possession of treasure, knowing or having reasonable grounds to believe that it is treasure.[158]

The new provisions of the Treasure Act do not come into force until April 2012.[159] According to Art 11 of the Treasure Act 1996, the Act itself is to be complemented by a code of practice, which must in particular set out the principles

---

**154** Either within fourteen days beginning with the day after the day on which the person acquires property of the object, or, within fourteen days of the day on which the person first believes or has reason to believe that the object is treasure, and that notification in respect of that object has not been given under section 8 (1) or under section 8 A (1).

**155** In this section "investigation" means an investigation under section 26 of the Coroners and Justice Act 2009 by which the Coroner for Treasure may conduct an investigation concerning an object in respect of which notification has not been given under section 8(1) of the Treasure Act 1996 whenever the Coroner has reason to suspect that the object is treasure, cp. N. Palmer, The Coroners and Justice Act, note 14. By section 25 (3) of the Coroners and Justice Act 2009, the Coroner for Treasure may also conduct an investigation concerning an object if he or she has reason to suspect that the object is treasure trove. No investigation is to be conducted, however, where the Crown disclaims the find.

**156** Cp. N. Palmer, The Coroners and Justice Act, at 131.

**157** For the title of the landowner according to the common law of finders see Chapter 3.

**158** Cp. also N. Palmer, The Coroners and Justice Act, at 134.

**159** Cp. N. Palmer, The Coroners and Justice Act, at 129.

and practice to be followed by the secretary of state when considering to whom treasure should be offered, when making determination in relation to the reward and where the Crown's title to treasure is disclaimed.[160] It also complements the new law in making account for the various procedures for reporting finds and notifying occupiers of land, the valuation of treasure for reward, or the process by which objects are offered to and accepted by museums. It also contains useful advice about the care and safekeeping of finds.

### b. Germany: The "Schatzregal"

In *Germany*, the title to finds is governed by § 984 of the German Civil Code (Bürgerliches Gesetzbuch – BGB), unless they fall under special provisions concerning movable cultural property. According to Art. 73 EGBGB[161] the German Federal Counties are entitled to implement the so-called "Schatzregal", that is, state ownership of movables having a cultural or scientific value.[162] The "Schatzregal" stems from 1224 A.D. and hence also constitutes one of the oldest cultural property protection regimes providing for state ownership of treasure.[163]

So far, 13 of the 16 German federal counties have enacted laws which vest title to cultural objects in the state. For example, the county Baden-Württemberg claims "all cultural objects that are lost or which have been hidden so long that the owner cannot be established, if they have been discovered during an official excavation or in an designated area of archaeological interest or, if they are of outstanding scientific value."[164] The provisions in Saarland and Niedersachsen (Lower Saxony) only encompass objects which have been found during an official excavation or in a designated area, virtually excluding all chance finds

**160** Art. 11 sec (a) Treasure Act 1996.

**161** Preliminary Provisions of the German Civil Code.

**162** This is an optional provision, meaning the counties are not bound to enact state ownership of antiquities into their lex-specialis codes. For a detailed account on the "Schatzregal" see e.g. E-R. Hönes, Das Schtazregal, DöV 1992, 425; N. Bernsdorff/A.Kleine-Tebbe, Kulturgutschutz in Deutschland (1996); Ralf Fischer zu Cramburg, Das Schatzregal (2001); K. Odendahl, Kulturgüterschutz (2005), at 439.

**163** For the historical development of the German "Schatzregal" see e.g E-R. Hönes, Das Schatzregal, DöV 1992, 425, at 427; Ralf Fischer zu Cramburg, Das Schatzregal (2001), at 47 et seq.

**164** Art. 23 Denkmalschutzgesetz Baden-Würtemberg. Similar provisions can be found in Berlin: Art. 3 sect. 2 DSchG; Brandenburg: Art. 20 DSchG; Bremen: Art. 19 sect. 1 DSchG; Hamburg: Art. 18 sect. 3 DSchG; Mecklenburg-Pomerania: Art. 13 DSchG; Lower Saxony: Art. 18 DSchG; Rhineland-Palantinate: Art. 19a; Saarland: Art. 23 sect. 1 DSchG; Saxony: Art. 23 sect. 1 DSchG; Saxony-Anhalt: Art. 12 sect. 1 DSchG; Schleswig-Holstein: Art. 21 sect. 1 DSchG; Thuringia: Art. 17 DSchG.

which have been found outside of such a designated area of archaeological interest.[165] Objects which are covered by these acts become state property *ipso iure*, which is as soon as they are discovered. No special act of designation is necessary.

Conversely, Bayern (Bavaria), Hessen, and Nordrhein-Westfalen (North Rhine-Westphalia) have abstained from enacting the "Schatzregal". They leave the acquisition of treasure to the ordinary law of finds according to § 984 German Civil Code.[166] However, they provide for a reporting duty and where relevant for a right of expropriation.[167] This mechanism constitutes a relatively weak system of protection, as the objects falling into the protection frame of the "Schatzregal" only cover a small amount of valuable objects.[168]

#### 4. Dual Regime between Finders Law and Cultural Property Law

Many countries do not follow a complementary mechanism between finder's law and treasure trove, as in the case of Britain or Germany, but rather a dual regime between civil law and newly enacted statutes deemed to protect heritage items. Both finders' law and cultural property legislation equally vest title to treasure in the state. Before cultural property protection was an issue, many countries already provided special provisions for the state or crown ownership of treasure in their civil codes. In order to follow the development of the law, many countries have enacted special provision on heritage protection which simply adopted the

165 Art. 23 I Saarland DSchG; Art. 18 Lower Saxony DSchG.

166 For the German law of finders see Chapter 3 § 2.

167 Baden-Württemberg: Art. 25 sect. 2 DSchG; Bavaria: Art. 18 sect. 2 DSchG; Berlin: Art. 17 sect. 1 DSchG; Brandenburg: Art. 29 DSchG; Bremen: Art. 20 sect. 2 DSchG; Hamburg: Art. 20 Nr. 1 DSchG; Hessen: Art. 25 sect. 1 Nr. 2; Mecklenburg-Pomerania: Art. 21 sect. 1 lit. b DSchG; Lower Saxony: Art. 30 sect. 2 DSchG; Rhineland-Palantinate: Art. 30 sect. 1 Nr. 1; Saarland: Art. 25 sect. 1 Nr. 2 DSchG; Saxony: Art. 27 sect. 1 lit. a DSchG; Saxony-Anhalt: Art. 19 sect. 1 Nr. 2 DSchG; Schleswig-Holstein: Art. 26 sect. 1 DSchG; Thuringia: Art. 27 sect. 1 Nr. 2 DSchG.

168 A similar approach has been adopted by Slovenia, where according to Art 53 (1) Slovenian Law of Property Act 2001, treasure generally belongs in equal parts to the finder and to the owner of the movable or immovable on which it was found. However, Slovenia employed a broader definition of treasure which includes "things of substantial value that have been hidden for so long that it is no longer possible to ascertain its owner", Art. 53 (2). State ownership is vested in heritage items which, according to Art 2 of the Slovenian Heritage Protection Act 1999, are deemed to be items and groups of items of historical, artistic, anthropological, art-historical, archaeological, ethnological and natural-scientific value which are testimony to historical developments in Slovenia. Art. 58 of the Heritage Act stipulates that "an item assumed to be a heritage item which is found on the surface of the earth, underneath the surface of the earth or in underwater shall be the property of the state."

provisions already provided by civil law. Consequently, both civil law and cultural heritage law provide for state ownership *ipso iure*, from the time the objects has been discovered. This mechanism is predominant in the new Eastern European states, where after the fall of Communism, modern laws were drafted in order to improve the outdated system of cultural heritage protection and in order to be inline with European Legislation.

In *Poland*, for example, according to Art. 189 of the Polish Civil Code, "an object of material, scientific or artistic value which has been found in such circumstances that the owner of it is unknown belongs to the state. The finder has to inform the proper authority and is entitled to a reward". In 2003, Poland has enacted a new statute dedicated to the protection of the national heritage.[169] The act distinguishes between relics and archaeological artefacts, both movable and immovable.[170] A movable relic is an object of historical, artistic or scientific value, irrespective of whether it has been listed in the national register.[171] As examples, the act specifically mentions pieces of fine arts and craftwork, coins, medals, orders and stamps, technological products, library materials, musical instruments, ethnographical objects, as well as memorabilia eternising historical events. Conversely, archaeological artefacts are subsoil and superincumbent objects, as well as objects found under the surface of the water, which constitute remnants of human existence.[172] The act does not specifically ascertain a time frame or date for the determination of an antiquity.[173] According to Art. 35 (1) of the Polish Cultural Heritage Act 2003 "archaeological objects which have been discovered by chance or excavated as the result of an archaeological research are the property of the state." Art. 33 (1) states that chance finds which may constitute an archaeological artefact have to be left untouched in the place of its discovery and after the findspot of the artefact has been indicated, the responsible authority has to be notified immediately. Art. 34 provides for a reward, if the reporting duty in Art. 33 has been complied with. It can be assumed that archaeological artefacts are objects of material, scientific, or artistic

---

**169** Act on the protection of monuments and the guardianship of monuments (enacted 23 July, 2003, published in: Polish Journal of Laws No 162, Item 1568).

**170** The previous Act on the Protection of Cultural Heritage dating from 1962 used the general term "cultural property". The definition was constructed in this wide sense in order to cover all heritage items in Poland, see Monika Drela, The Ownership of Relics (in Polish: Własność zabytków, 2006), at 46.

**171** Articles 3 (1) – 3 (4) Polish Act 2003. See also Monika Drela, The Ownership Of Relics, at 48.

**172** Art 3 (4) Polish Act of 2003. See also Zbigniew Kobyliński, The Protection of Archaeolgical Artefacts in Europe (in Polish: Ochrona dziedzictwa archaeologicznego w Europie, 1998), at 261.

**173** But see for example Norway, where archaeological artefacts are objects dating from before 1573 A.D., cp. Art. 12 Norwegian Act 1978.

value in the sense of Art. 189 of the Polish Civil Code. Art. 33 – 35 of the Polish Act 2003 thus repeat the provision in the civil code, additionally specifying a reporting duty. As a result, both provisions are simultaneously applicable to chance finds, as opposed to a confluence of norms resulting in the exclusive application of the more special provision.[174]

A similar system can be found in *Estonia*. There, the general rule is that treasure belongs to the person on whose property it was found.[175] Under the Law of Property Act 2001, treasure is defined to be "money or valuables such as gems, pearls or precious metals buried in the ground or hidden in any other manner whose owner cannot be ascertained".[176] State ownership is only vested in treasure with special value, being defined in Art. 105 (1) of the Law of Property Act as "a thing with historical, scientific, artistic or other cultural value". The provision in the Civil Code is repeated in Estonia's Heritage Conservation Act[177], which states in Art. 30 (2) that "finds of cultural value belong to the state". According to Art. 30 (1) "a finding of cultural value is a movable find in the ground or on the surface of the ground, inside a construction, under water or in the sediment of a body of water, which is either a natural feature or has historical, archaeological, scientific, artistic or other cultural value and which has no owner". According to Art. 32 (1) a finder of a thing specified in subsection 30 (1) of this Act is required to preserve the place of the finding in an unaltered condition and to notify the National Heritage Board and the rural municipality or city government promptly of the finding. Paragraph (2) states that a found thing shall be left in the place it is found until it is delivered to the National Heritage Board. The object may be removed from the place it is found only if its preservation is endangered. It can be argued that Estonia's provisions constitute blanket protection for all antiquities as the categorisation of finds covered by the state ownership rule is so general as to exclude only finds of minor archaeological or cultural significance.

In *Croatia*, the protection and preservation of movable tangible cultural heritage under Croatian law is basically regulated by one of the most comprehensive

---

**174** M. Drela, Ownership of Relics, at 199. See however, J. S. Piątkowski The system of private law (in Polish: System Prawa Cywilnego, 1977), at 372 (arguing that the treasure trove provisions in the old Polish cultural property act are lex specialis to the Civil Code and exclusively applicable).

**175** 103 (2) Estonian Law of Property Act 2001, available at: http://www.lexadin.nl/wlg/legis/nofr/oeur/lxweest.htm.

**176** 103 (1) Estonian Law of Property Act 2001.

**177** Cultural Heritage Conservation Act 2002.

national legal statutes in the field of cultural heritage[178], the 1999 Croatian Cultural Heritage Act.[179] Article 8 of the CHA defines the term movable tangible cultural heritage by giving various examples of respective objects ranging *inter alia* from museum collections to church objects, from archaeological finds to pieces of art. Article 19 of the Act states that objects presumed to have the capacity of a cultural object and which are located or found under ground, in the sea or water are the property of the Republic of Croatia.[180] Objects that are found are governed according to the regulations on the finding of treasure.[181] However, the same provision is reflected in the Croatian Ownership Act[182] with regard to treasure trove. Found treasure must be handed over to the Republic of Croatia which becomes the owner of such an object right from the moment of discovery, but in return has to pay an award up to 10 % of the market value to the finder as well as to the owner of the land where the object is found. The finder and the land owner can however – subject to a state option – become co-owners instead of the Croatian Republic.

### 5. Reporting Duties and Rewards

In order to work, most of the vesting statutes consequently have to be complemented by reporting duties and fines, as wells as pecuniary rewards for the reporting of discovered artefacts. If no pecuniary incentive is provided, the finder will be tempted to sell the antiquity on the black market with the result that the

**178** For a detailed account of the new Croatian regime, see Toshiyuki Kono/Stefan Wrbka, General Report, in: T. Kono/S.Wrbka (eds.), The Impact of Uniform Laws (2010) at 129 et seq.
**179** Protection and Preservation of the Cultural Heritage Act, Official Gazette (OG), 69/99, 151/03, 157/03. For the basic text see http//www.nn.hr/clanci/sluzebno/1999/1284.html. The CHA replaced the Protection of Cultural Monuments Act 1965 and the very basic Act on Cultural Monuments 1971. There are a substantive number of bylaws, to enforce the new CHA, such as the Ordinance of the Register of the Cultural Heritage of the Republic of Croatia (OG 21/86 and 4/08), or the ordinance on Conditions for Obtaining the Permission to Export of Cultural Heritage from the Republic of Croatia (OG 141/06), the Ordinance on Archaeological Research (OG 30/05) or the ordinance on Determining that Cultural Goods that are Considered National Treasure of the EU Member States (OG 38/04).
**180** Art. 19 para. 1 of the Croatian Act on the Protection and Preservation of Cultural Objects 1999.
**181** Art. 19 para. 2 of the Croatian Act 1999.
**182** Law on Ownership and other Real Property Rights (adopted 1996, English translation available with the Commercial Law Reform Project Croatia).

object itself and the precious information on context is lost for good.[183] There are several variations to this approach, but each basically requires the country to compensate the finder in exchange for the state taking possession and ownership of the newly discovered antiquity.

In common with many market nations, *England* possesses a very liberal system of rewards, combined with a duty of notification upon the finder. Whereas, under common law, a finder is under no obligation to report a find, Section 8 of the Treasure Act 1996 provides that anyone who does not report a find within 14 days of its discovery or within 14 days from the date that person believes (or has reason to believe) that the object is treasure shall be guilty of an offence and could be liable upon conviction to three months imprisonment and/or a fine of up to £ 5,000. Any find declared to be treasure that a museum wishes to acquire must be valued by the Treasure Valuation Committee, which consists of independent experts.[184] The total reward must not exceed the treasure's market value, Art. 10 (4) The details of allocating rewards is set out in the Code of Practice, accompanying the 1996 Act.[185] For example, if the finder does not remove the whole of a find from the ground but allows archaeologists to excavate the remainder of the find, the original finder will normally be eligible for a reward for the whole find. Rewards will not normally be payable when the find is made by an archaeologist. Where the finder has committed an offence in relation to a find, or has trespassed, or has not followed best practice as set out in the Code of Practice, he may expect no reward at all or a reduced reward. Landowners and occupiers will be eligible for rewards in such cases. The Code of Practice states that the finder should receive a reward within one year of having delivered

**183** See Peter Wendel, Protecting Newly Discovered Antiquities, at 1115 (discussing the return to the traditional law of finders as as an alternative means of protecting newly discovered artefacts).

**184** The Committee will commission a valuation from one or more experts drawn from the antiquities market. The finder, together with the museum that wishes to acquire the find and any other interested party, will have an opportunity to comment on the valuation and to send in a separate valuation of your own, before the Committee makes its recommendation. The Committee shall also take account of the archaeological and historical significance of the effect of illegal or improper behaviour involved in the specific circumstances or a particular case. In such cases the interested parties will have the opportunity to submit evidence to the Committee. If the finder is dissatisfied with the decision, he can appeal to the Secretary of State for Culture, Media and Sport. For a detailed account on the work of the treasure valuation Committee see articles by Trevor Austin, member of the Treasure Valuation Committee, in "The Searcher" and "Treasure Hunting" magazines, e.g. July 2004, August 2004 October 2004, March 2005, information found on www.ncmd.co.uk/tvc.htm

**185** Cp. above.

the find, although this may take longer in the case of very large finds or those that present special difficulties. If no museum wants to acquire the find it should be disclaimed within six months or within three months if it is a single object.

Additionally, rewards are to be paid to any person who gave notice under the new section 8 A in respect of the treasure.[186] The normal expectation is that the acquirer's reward will reflect an appropriate proportion of the overall value, pitched according to the particular circumstances, including the merits of the acquirer's conduct. Where the identity of the owner of the find spot is known, the acquirer and that owner will normally each receive a half-share of the full value of the object.[187]

In comparison, only a handful of source countries offer the finder a reward in exchange for reporting the find. *Italy* offers a percentage which in no event can exceed twenty-five percent of the value of the found antiquity, but the government determines the fee.[188] If there is a disagreement over the value of the fee, a three person commission is established.[189] The problem is that the reward is usually either a fixed sum that is substantially less than the market value (or the black market value) of the antiquity or a percentage of the fair market value as determined by the government.[190] Thus, despite the provisions on rewards, the black market in Italy is very strong since the government greatly limited the legal trade in antiquities through the provisions such as nationalisation of all archaeological finds and through export control found in the 2004 Act.[191]

The current practice of finders favouring the black market over offers of rewards from the source country supports the conclusion that finder's fees would have to be significantly increased to create the necessary incentive for finders to come forward with a newly discovered antiquity.[192] The ultimate reward would be to require the state to either purchase the find at full market value, or to

---

**186** See section 30 (2) of the Coroners and Justice Act 2009, which adds a new sub-section 10 (5) (d) to the Treasure Act 1996.

**187** Cp. N. Palmer, The Coroners and Justice Act, at 134.

**188** Code of Cultural Property and Landscape 2004, articles 92 and 93.

**189** Code of Cultural Property and Landscape 2004, art. 93 (3).

**190** In some countries, after reporting the find, the state may even take the land where the object was found, without compensation, because of its archeological significance, cp. Dalia N. Osman, Occupiers' Title to Cultural Property, at 993.

**191** Cp. Stephanie Doyal, Implementing the UNIDROIT Convention into Domestic Law: The Case of Italy, 39 Colum. J. Transnat'l L. 657 (2001), at note 88; George Ortiz, The Collectors and the Regulation of the Art Market, in: La Libre Circulation des Collections d'objects d'art (1993) 147, at 153–155.

**192** See P. Wendel, Protecting Newly Discovered Antiquities, at 1049; S. Doyle, Implementing the UNIDROIT Convention, at 677.

pay an *ex gratia* rewards amounting to the full market value of the object, as is the approach adopted by England. However, England is a country that is relatively rich in revenues. The English approach is applied in a few hundred cases a year so it costs relatively little. On the other hand, most source countries are antiquities-rich but revenue-poor. They will not have the resources to purchase all found antiquities it wished to retain. The full compensation-approach, from a practical perspective, is politically and economically unacceptable to source countries such as Egypt or Greece. The result is that most of the newly discovered antiquities end up on the legal international market for antiquities and as such, are ultimately being transferred to museums or collectors in market countries. So far, the problem could not be solved to every party's satisfaction.[193]

### 6. The Quality of the Proprietary Title

Some of the aforementioned statutes explicitly or under a certain condition vest title to the protected object in the state, but in order to be read, understood and applied in the international arena, they have to be drafted very diligently.[194] Any ambiguity in the language of the statute may prevent the return of an object which was illicitly excavated and exported from the territory of the state of origin.

Source countries have experienced the consequences of ambiguity in their statutes several fold:

#### a. The Elmali Hoard-Case

In the American case regarding the *Elmali hoard*[195], where the Republic of Turkey sued a business-man from Boston for a precious hoard of ancient Greek and Lycian coins, the state ownership to the treasure became a main issue of the trial.[196] The collection of over 2000 silver 5th-century BC Greek coins were illic-

193 But see P. Wendel, ibid, at 1052, suggesting a possessory estate and future interest approach. A possessory right to excavated antiquities could in his view be awarded to both the finder and the source country: The finder could be awarded a term of years, and the country could be awarded the future interest in fee simple absolute.

194 Cp. K. Siehr, Reforms and Developments in the Member States of the European Union, in: Schneider E./Schneider R (eds.) Cultural Property Protection, Deutsch-Türkische Rechtsstudien Band 4, (2005) 77, at 78.

195 Republic of Turkey v OKS Partners, No. Civ.A.89 – 3061-WJS, 1994 U.S. Dist. Lexis 17032 (D. Mass. June 8, 1994).

196 For an account and comments on the case see Lawrence M Kaye, Cultural Property Disputes in Foreign Courts, in Schneider/Schneider (eds.) Cultural Property Protection (2005) 43, at 49;

itly excavated at Elmali (near Antalya) in 1984 and illegally exported to Germany and later shipped to the US.[197] The defendants questioned whether Turkey had a sufficient proprietary interest in the *Elmali hoard* to give it a standing to sue in this case. They argued that Turkey's 1983 Law on the Protection of Cultural and Natural Assets[198] had changed the meaning of the phrase 'state ownership' of antiquities, used in the 1906 and 1973 versions of the law, to a lesser property interest of 'having the property of state ownership'. The defendants argued that the 1983 law should be read not as an ownership law, but rather, as an export control law.[199]

The Turkish 1983 Act states in its Art. 5 that "movable and fixed cultural and natural assets that are known to be present or may occur in the future in the fixed assets of the state, public organisations and agencies, and the fixed assets possessed by real and corporal persons subject to the provisions of private law and that require to be protected, qualify as state property." Art. 5 of the 1983 law is complemented by Article 697 of the Turkish Civil Code, which reads as follows: "Rare natural objects which nobody owns and which are of rare significant, scientific value and antiquities are the property of the treasury."[200]

Experts for Turkey testified that the change in wording in the 1983 Act did not signify any change in meaning. Turkish commentators and academics mutually agree that both provisions provide for state ownership *ipso iure* of newly found antiquities, the moment they are discovered, and no further act of acquisition is required.[201] The court accepted that Turkey had an unconditional right of possession from the moment of the discovery of the antiquities. On this basis, it ruled that Turkey did have a sufficient proprietary interest in the hoard through

---

Howard N. Spiegler/Lawrence M. Kaye, American Litigation to Recover Cultural Property, in: N. Brodie/ J. Doole/ C. Renfrew (eds.) Trade in Illicit Antiquities (2001) 121; Jason McElroy, War against the Illegal Antiquities Trade: Rules of Engagement for Source Nations, 27 Hastings Comm. & Ent. L.J. (2004–2005) 547, at 557; Janet Blake, Illicit Antiquities and International Litigation- The Turkish Experience, Antiquity (1998) 824.

**197** Janet Blake, The Turkish Experience, at 829.

**198** Law on Antiquities No 2863 (enacted 21.7.1983). Some parts of the law were amended in 1987 via law No. 3386.

**199** Republic of Turkey v OKS Partners, No. CIV.A.89–3061-WJS, 1994 U.S. Dist. LEXIS 17032 (D. Mass. June 8, 1994).

**200** The 'treasury' is the cultural property department of the Turkish Government (note of the author).

**201** See e.g. Ergun Zsunay, Protection of Cultural Heritage in Turkish Private Law, 6 IJCP (1997) 278; Sibel Özel, The Protection of Cultural Properties in Turkey, in Cultural Property Protection, 23–41; S. Özel, The Basel Decisions: Recognition of Blanket Legislation Vesting State Ownership over Cultural Property Found within the Country of Origin, 9 IJCP (2000) 315.

its absolute right of immediate possession to maintain all the claims contained in its complaint.[202] Although Turkey was able to recover the coins at the end, the question whether Turkey had ownership over the coins was resolved to Turkey's favour only after the Court directed depositions of legal experts on both sides and held a four day trial to hear their testimony on the meaning of the language of the Turkish law. [203] If the court had accepted that the Turkish law was to be understood as an export law, it would have meant that the United States would not have enforced this export prohibition and the coins would not have been returned. As a result of the case, a recent translation issued by the Directorate General for Cultural Heritage and Museum of Turkey, changed the wording of Art 5 of the 1983 Act into "are the possession of the state". Unfortunately, the statute does still not use the term "property", why the amendment of the Turkish Statute might not prevent further problems in interpreting the statute's meaning.

**b. Turkish Republic v The City of Basel**

The second provision vesting all newly discovered antiquities in the Turkish state, Art. 697 of the Turkish Civil Code (hereinafter: TCC), has been analysed by the Swiss courts in several instances in the case Turkish Republic v The City of Basel.[204] This case concerned the recovery of five gravestones that were found in Turkey and were on display at the Antiquities Museum in the city of Basel.[205] The issue was whether the Swiss courts would apply Turkish law on antiquities. As the TCC is based on the Swiss Civil Code, the court analysed Art. 724 Swiss Civil Code (hereinafter: SCC), which is the Turkish counterpart. The court concluded that according to Art. 724 SCC, ownership of a newly discovered object does not pass to the Swiss cantons ipso iure but rather the canton has a right to acquire the object, meaning that it has an immediate right of possession which it may or may not choose to exercise.[206] Thus, the law conferred quasi-ownership but not state ownership. In the view of the court, the Turkish state failed to ex-

**202** Cp. Janet Blake, The Turkish Experience, at 829.
**203** Republic of Turkey v OKS partners, No. CIV.A.89 – 3061-WJS, 1994 U.S. Dist.lexis 17032 (D. Mass. June 8, 1994).
**204** Turkish Republic v the Canton of the City of Basel and Prof. Ludwig, decision delivered by the court on August 16, 1993.
**205** A detailed analysis of this case is provided by Sibel Özel, The Basel Decisions, Recognition of Blanket Legislation Vesting State Ownership over Cultural Property Found within the Country of Origin, 9 IJCP (2000) 315, at 325 – 340.
**206** See Turkish Republic v The Canton of the City of Basel and Dr. Professor Ludwig; Peter Liver, Das Eigentum, in Schweizerisches Privatrecht, Band V, Sachenrecht, Basel und Stuttgart (1977) at 366 – 367.

ercise an act of acquisition and, therefore, waived its ownership rights by inactivity. The court of appeal adopted this approach, as well.[207] According to the Swiss Court of Appeal, it was necessary that the Turkish state clearly informed private persons involved (the finders and the owners of the land), whether it was asserting or waiving its right of ownership or acquisition. Otherwise, ownership of the object would constitute *bona vacantia* for decades, which would be irreconcilable with the nature of ownership.[208] The Federal Court, affirming this decision, stated that "negligence with regard to such notice was equal to the return of the objects to the private finder".[209] The case shows again that the terms used in cultural property legislation vesting antiquities in the state have to be drafted carefully in order to be construed as creating an explicit ownership right.

#### c. Government of Peru v Johnson

A disappointing experience has been made by Peru in the American case *Peru v Johnson*.[210] The case concerned some eighty-nine allegedly stolen pre-Columbian gold, ceramic and fabric objects in the defendant Johnson's collection.[211] After a thorough examinination of Peru's antiquities laws, the Distrcit Court of California rejected Peru's own analysis of the laws which Peru claimed vested ownership in the state of some plundered pre-Columbian artefacts it sought to recover. The court in *Peru v Johnson* concluded that none of the provisions provided for ownership of antiquities in the national government with sufficient clarity to make them comprehensible by and binding on American citizens.[212] While the laws of Peru asserted the interest of the government in preserving its cultural heritage and prohibiting the export of artefacts, this assertion was not equivalent

**207** Court of Appeal decision, 18 August 1995.
**208** Cp. Sibel Özel, The Basel Decisions, at 334.
**209** Federal Court Decision, 22 May 1996.
**210** Peru v Johnson, 720 F. Supp. 810 (C.D. Cal.1989), aff'd by unpublished order, 933 F.2d 1013 (9th Cir. 1991).
**211** For a detailed analysis of the case see e.g. J.H. Merryman/ A. Elsen/S. Urice (eds.), Law, Ethics and the Visual Arts (2007) at 223; J.H. Merryamn, Limits on Sate Recovery o Stolen Artefacts: Peru v Johnson, 1 IJCP (1992) 169; Lawrence M. Kaye, Cultural Property Disputes in Foreign Courts, in Cultural Property Protection (2005) 43, at 51 et seq.; Judith Church, Evolving U.S. Case Law on Cultural Property Disputes, 2 IJCP (1993) 47, at 54 et seq.
**212** Peru v Johnson, ibid, at 812. The appellate court affirmed the rejection of Peru's claim on an entirely different ground – the identity of the objects. The lower court also held that Peru has failed to prove that the objects at issue had come from a site in Peru.

to a declaration of national ownership.[213] For example, Heritage Law No. 6634 of June 13, 1929 which pronounced historical monuments and unregistered artefacts to be property of the state, did not preclude possession of artefacts by private parties and their subsequent transfer. Law No. 24047 of January 5, 1985 and the language of the Supreme Decree of February 27, 1985, which proclaimed pre-Hispanic artistic objects belonging to the nation's cultural wealth were untouchable, and their removal from the country was categorically forbidden, were considered by the trial court to be too vague to be a declaration of state ownership. Equally, Statute of June 22, 1985, which was not referred to by number could not be construed as vesting state ownership in excavated antiquities. This statute provided specifically that all archaeological sites belong to the state[214], but the law did not appear to pronounce objects which have not been found at an archaeological site to be state property. This leaves a potentially large class of objects within the domain of private ownership.[215] The court, reading the Supreme Decree and Statute together determined that any artefacts privately excavated between January 5 and June 22, 1985 would constitute private property.[216] Additionally to the fact that the provisions did not vest ownership in the government with sufficient clarity, the court also found that Peru had made no real effort to enforce those laws, which was one more reason the judge believed it would be inappropriate to allow Peru to rely on its law in a U.S. court.[217]

As for today, Peru has enacted a new cultural heritage statute, Law No. 28296 of 1st June 2006[218] , which specifically proclaims that undiscovered cultural property, movable or immovable, belongs exclusively to the state.[219] However, private property of already discovered movable cultural arefacts is allowed and ownership thereof can be transferred free under any title as long as it is transferred within the borders of the Peruvian territory.[220]

---

**213** Peru v Johnson, ibid, at 814. See also Judith Church, Foreign National Ownership Statutes in U.S. Courts, 30 Colum. J. Transnat'l L. (1993) at 193.

**214** Peru v Johnson, at 814.

**215** See L. V. Prott/P.J. O'Keefe, Law and the Cultural Heritage- Vol 1 Discovery and Excavation (1984), at 191.

**216** Peru v Johnson, at 814–815.

**217** Peru v Johnson, at 814.

**218** General Law of the Cultural Heritage of the Nation 2006, Law N° 28296 published on July 22, 2004 – Pages N° 272925 to 272932 – edition N.L.N: 8797 – Lima, December 04, 2007 (Regelemento de la Ley General del Patrimonio Cultural de la Nacion). The new Act is being complemented by the Executive Order No 011–2006 –ED.

**219** Art. 5 Law No 28296.

**220** Art. 7 (1) – (4) and Art. 9 (1) Law No 28296.

### d. United States v McClain

An exegesis of the Mexican heritage laws was undertaken in the *McClain-cases.*[221] The two related decisions by the Fifth Circuit Court of Appeal, involved U.S. defendants who excavated pre-Columbian artefacts in Mexico and exported them without licence or permit into the United States. Mexico claimed ownership of the items by virtue of several umbrella statutes: Art. 1 of the Law on Archaeological Monuments, May 11, 1897 made "archaeological monuments, the property of the nation."[222] While this law appeared to vest ownership of such monuments in the government, private individuals were allowed to possess pre-Columbian artefacts. However, the class of artefacts at issue in *McClain* were covered by Article 6 of the 1897 law which provided only for a prohibition on export.[223] There was nothing in this language that could lead the court to a determination that the artefacts were owned by the state. In 1930 Mexico enacted a broader statute.[224] The 1930 law covered objects of "artistic, archaeological or historical value, whether movable or immovable." An object was, declared to be a monument if it came under the auspices of the Secretariat of Public Education or was declared to be a monument by the Department of Artistic, Archaeological and Historic Monuments. Monuments were to be protected, but could be privately owned and alienated subject only to a right of first refusal in the government. This law was also determined not to amount to a declaration of ownership.[225] A third law, with still broader impact, was enacted in 1934.[226] The definition of monuments was expanded to include "all vestiges of the aboriginal civilization dating from before the completion of the Conquest." All immovable archaeological monuments were declared to belong to the nation including "objects which are found [in or on] immovable archaeological monuments." The

---

**221** United States v McClain, 545 F.2d 988 (5th Cir. 1977), rehearing denied, 551 F.2d 52 (5th Cir. 1977) [hereinafter: McClain I]; United States v McClain, 593 F2d 658 (5th Cir. 1979), cert. denied, 444 U.S. 918 (1979) [hereinafter: McClain II].

**222** Diario Oficial de 11 de mayo de 1897, in: XIV Annuario de Legislation y Jurisprudencie (1897), (discussed in United States v. McClain I, 545 F.2d, 998).

**223** Article 6 provides: Mexican antiquities, codices, idols, amulets and other objects or movable things that the Federal Executive deems interesting for the study of the civilisation and history of the aboriginal and ancient settlers of America and especially of Mexico, cannot be exported without legal authorisation.

**224** Law on the Protection and Conservation of Monuments and Natural Beauty of January 31, 1930, in: 58 Diario Oficial 7, 31 de enero de 1930 (discussed in McClain I 545 F.2d, 998).

**225** McClain I, 545 F.2d, 988 (5th Cir 1977).

**226** Law for the Protection and Preservation of Archaeological and Historic Monuments, Typical Towns and Places of Scenic Beauty of January 19, 1934 82 in: Diario Oficial 152, 19 de enero de 1934 (discussed in McClain I, 545 F.2d, 998 (5th Cir. 1977)).

1934 law continued to recognise private ownership of archaeological monuments. Privately owned objects had to be registered and all transfers were to be recorded.[227] The court concluded that artefacts found in or on immovable monuments were a subset of all pre-Columbian artefacts. If an object was not within the subclass it was not owned by Mexico. The final law considered by the court was the Federal Law on Archaeological, Artistic and Historic Monuments and Zones of May 6, 1972.[228] For the first time this law declared unequivocally that "archaeological monuments, movables and immovables, are the inalienable and inprescriptable property of the Nation."[229] Article 28 defined archaeological monuments as "movable and immovable objects, products of the cultures prior to the establishment of the Spanish culture in the National Territory." The 1972 law "extended national ownership of the cultural patrimony to private collections and forbade absolutely the export of pre-Columbian items." The 1972 law still protected private ownership rights to the extent these had been previously created by registration under the 1934 and 1970 laws. Thus, there was a dual ownership system with the same types of objects owned by the state through legislation, or by private persons through registration. The Court of Appeal held that a national ownership declaration could not be enforced in the Uited States unless the relevant ownership declaration is clear enough for U.S. citizens to understand.[230] After the examination of all relevant statutes, the Court found the Mexican ownership laws "too vague to be a predicate for criminal liability," the court reversed the substantive count against the defendants but allowed a conspiracy conviction to stand.[231]Although this was a case under criminal law, the courts reasoning in respect of the quality of Mexico's propriety title reflects the necessity of a very precise and diligent statute drafting.

**227** Article 9 required the 'Register of Private Archaeological Property' to maintain a record of movable artefacts and Article 10 required any transfers to be recorded.

**228** 312 Diario Oficial 16, 6 de mayo de 1972.

**229** Article 27, Federal Law on Archaeological, Artistic and Historic Monuments and Zones of May 6, 1972.

**230** McClain II, 593 F.2d 658 (5th Cir. 1979) at 670.

**231** McClain II, 593 F.2d 658, (5$^{th}$ Cir. 1979), at 670 – 672. For a thorough analysis of the McClain decisions cp. Chapter 6, § 4 I – The U.S. approach on the justiciability of claims to cultural objects.

## II. Property Rights on the Grounds of an Immediate Right of Possession

When there is no express declaration of state ownership or when the cultural property statute's wording cannot be construed as conferring clear title, it can become very difficult to determine a right which may amount to full property. Some countries do not provide for express ownership declarations of all newly discovered finds, but, intentionally or unintentionally, rather sustain a system where the state is granted an immediate right of possession to fortuitously discovered treasure. Although some statutes do not mention the phrase ownership or property, or for some other reason clear ownership cannot be established[232], the previously mentioned reporting and delivery duties may for example create an immediate right of possession in the state. In *United States v McClain*[233], the legal expert presented by the Mexican government testified that, regardless of the exact wording or specific provisions of the laws, the Mexican government had intended to own pre-Columbian artefacts from as early as the Cultural Property Act dating from 1897. He maintained that the combination of the default ownership provisions and the Mexican Constitution was a sufficient declaration of ownership.[234] Similarly, in the *Elmali Hoard-case*, the court ruled that Turkey did have a sufficient proprietary interest in the hoard through its absolute right of immediate possession to maintain their claim.[235]

This reasoning has recently been affirmed in *Government of Iran v Barakat Galleries*[236], where the Court of Appeal held that an immediate right of possession may be interpreted as a real ownership right. The court based its conclusion on the grounds that it is not the label that foreign law gives to the legal relationship, but its substance.[237] The case concerned the illegal export of certain Iranian antiquities allegedly excavated in the Iranian Jiroft-region, the facts of which have already been summarised in the introduction to this research. Although rich in antiquities, Iran is one of those countries that did not implement an express vesting of title to antiquities in their law.[238] Conversely, different acts contain several ambivalent provisions as to the rights and obligations of finders of

**232** Cp. this chapter § 2 I 6, above.
**233** For an account of the case see this chapter § 2 I 6 d.
**234** McClain II, 593 F.2d 658 (5$^{th}$ Cir. 1979), at 667.
**235** Cp. this chapter, § 2 I 6 a.
**236** [2007] EWHC 705 (QB); [2007] EWCA Civ 1374; [2008] 1 All ER 1177; QB 22 [2009].
**237** [2007] EWCA Civ 1374, at 49. For the question whether an immediate right of possession is sufficient to be the basis for a recovery claim in a foreign court, see Part II, Chapter 6 § 2 II 3 a.
**238** Note that Iran has been populated by various cultures including the Medes, Bactrians, Parthians, Saasanids, Scythians, Sarmatians, Assyrians, Greeks, Romans and Persians.

antiquities. According to Art. 10 of the National Heritage Protection Act 1930,[239] half of the property or an equitable price as considered by qualified experts shall be transferred to the finder. It is implicit that if the latter option is adopted the state becomes the owner of the property in question. The section further gives the state the option "to appropriate or transfer the other half of the finder without recompense". This gives the state the option of becoming the owner of the other half. However, Art. 5 of the 1930 Act permits private ownership of Antiquities by individuals. Art. 9 of the Act requires the owner to inform the government before a movable property is sold. The same duty is imposed on anyone who finds movable property. There is a reference in Art. 9 to a government right of pre-emption and in Art. 10 to payment by the government of an equitable price to a chance finder.

According to section 2 of the Iranian Legal Bill 1979[240], the finder of antiquities is required to hand them over "as soon as possible". Once the antiquities are handed over, they become the property of Iran. If they are not handed over, but are transferred by the finder to another party, the third party will get no title and the antiquities will be subject to seizure. Where antiquities are discovered in the course of illegal excavation, they will be subject to seizure, whether they remain in the possession of the finder or are transferred to a third party.[241] Seizure can only take place upon conviction of an offender in a criminal court for undertaking unlawful excavations or digging, or where by virtue of paragraph 4, discovered objects are offered for sale or purchase. In summary, there is a lack of clarity in these provisions about precisely how and when the state becomes the owner of its share of antiquities that are discovered in lawful excavation. Irrespective of whether it also has become the owner, however, the Iranian government has an immediate right of possession to each antiquity fortuitously discovered on its territory.[242]

Sir Sydney Kentridge QC submitted on behalf of the government of Iran that the *cumulative effect* of the relevant Iranian provisions was to vest ownership of newly discovered antiquities in the state.[243] In order to prove this contention for its validit, the CA scrutinised the relevant provosions by a reverse process of elimination: who was the owner of newly discovered antiquities, if it was not

**239** National Heritage Protection Act (enacted 3 Nov. 1930), discussed and reprinted in Iran v Barakat Galleries Ltd. [2007] EWHC 705 (QB).

**240** Legal Bill Regarding Prevention of Unauthorised Excavations and Diggings (enacted 17th May 1979), discussed and reprinted in Iran v Barakat Galleries.

**241** Section 1, 1979 Legal Bill.

**242** Cp. also Iran v Barakat [2007] EWCA Civ. 1374, at 84.

**243** [2007] EWCA Civ. 1374, at 53.

Iran? Under the 1979 Legal Bill, the Court was unable to identify anyone other than Iran as the owner of antiquities that are discovered.[244] Lord Phillips of Worth Matravers held that the finder of antiquities is not entitled to keep possession of them nor to transfer title to anyone else. His only right is to receive a reward for handing them over to the relevant authority.[245] The finder thus has no ownership right in the antiquities that he finds. His Lordship went on that given the conclusion that the finder does not own the antiquities he excavated there are only two possibilities to allocate property rights: Either finds are *bona vacantia*, to which Iran had an immediate right of possession and which would become Iran's property once Iran obtained possession of them or they belonged to Iran from, at least, the moment they were found.[246] He considered the first option to be artificial. The CA thus held that Iran was to be the owner of both fortuitously and illegally excavated heritage items.[247] As opposed to the High Court which held that the Iranian provisions cannot be construed as conferring title *ipso iure* to newly discovered antiquities in the state,[248] the Court of Appeal took the view that all relevant Iranian provisions viewed in a coherent context are to vest ownership of antiquities in the Iranian state. It further concluded that the general purpose of the Legal Bill 1979 was to prevent the pillaging of antiquities which took place immediately after the revolution of 1979 and the draftsmen of the Bill must have started from the premise that antiquities were owned by Iran. The Court's approach finding that Iran was the owner of the antiquities in question although the Iranian legislation at no single point mentioned the words 'property' or 'ownership' in the direct context of Iran's right to them proves the Court's willingness to endorce foreign national claims for the recovery of cultural property.

Generally, it can be said that all states providing for reporting requirements, duties of delivery and criminal penalties instead of express ownership declarations have a right of immediate possession to discovered antiquities. Thus, for example, in the case of the German Federal states that have opted for the "Schatzregal" or in cases of objects which are not covered by the "Schatzregal" the federal counties have implemented a duty to deliver the object to the relevant

---

**244** [2007] EWCA Civ. 1374, at 80.
**245** [2007] EWCA Civ. 1374, at 64.
**246** [2007] EWCA Civ. 1374, at 80.
**247** [2007] EWCA Civ. 1374, at 80.
**248** [2007] EWHC 705 (QB), at 45 per Justice Gray.

authority.[249] In those Federal Counties, which do not provide for state ownership, title to treasure vests in the landowner and finder according to the ancient roman law of Hadrian[250], however, the objects must be delivered to the authorities, followed by the payment of a reward. But even in the light of the *Barakat-decision*, such provisions would most probably not be viewed as conferring a real ownership right in favour of the German government, as they do not imply ownership in favor of the government, as was the case in *Barakat*.

### III. Property Rights on the Ground of Export Legislation

Much of the artistic patrimony in both market and source countries is in state ownership. There is, however, also a significant amount of cultural property in private hands and it is these items that are subject to state intervention in an attempt to retain them within national boundaries. Likewise, illegally excavated antiquities may become subject to the acquisition of the state on the grounds of export legislation if a state does not provide for automatic state ownership *ipso iure*, in case artefacts are fortuitously discovered.[251] Some of these laws grant property rights in the form of confiscatory ownership or an immediate right of possession whereas some may purport to confiscate but they entail only criminal or pecuniary sanctions without granting any property right or possessory title to the state.

#### 1. The Ambit of Export Legislation

##### a. No Export Controls

Only very few states have no export control over cultural objects. For example, in the *United States*, the export of cultural property is not restricted.[252] If, however,

**249** E.g. Art. 24 I Hessen DSchG, Art. 17 North Rhine Westphalia DSchG. Bavaria is the sole federal state not having a reporting or delivery duty, cp. Kerstin Odendahl, Kulturgüterschutz, at 442.

**250** On the ancient law of Hadrian, see Chapter 3 at § 3 IV 1.

**251** For example Latvia, Act on the Protection of Cultural Monuments 1993 (as amendment 2005), which operates only as an export prohibition, cp. section 4 of the Act, and a pre-emption right, section 8 of the Act. According to Art 952 of the Latvian Civil Code, treasure discovered on one own's land or ownerless land belongs to the finder.

**252** L.D. DuBoff, Art Law in a Nutshell, (2nd ed. 1993), at 16; J.H. Merryman, American Law and the International Trade in Art", in Pierre Lalive (ed.) International Sales of Works of Art (1985), at 425; Generally on US cultural property export law see K. D. Vitale, The War on Antiquities, 84

an object is obtained in violation of another law, such as the Archaeological Resources Protection Act 1979 (hereinafter: ARPA)[253] or the Native American Graves Protection and Repatriation Act 1990 (hereinafter: NAGPRA)[254], then its export is also prohibited.[255] The ARPA criminalises the excavation, removal, damage, alteration, or defacement of archaeological resources without permission.[256] Moreover, it prohibits anyone from selling, exchanging, transporting, or dealing in any way in archaeological resources excavated or removed from public or Indian lands in violation of ARPA[257] or from trafficking in those archaeological resources contrary to federal, state, or local law.

Similarly, many *Swiss* cantons do not provide for special prohibitions on the export of cultural goods.[258] According to the narrow interpretation of the Cultural Property Law of the *Canton Tessin*[259], the export of some of the collection of the Thyssen–Bornemisza from the city of Castagnola to Madrid was possible.[260] Owing to a lack of export prohibitions in the state of *Lichtenstein*, in 1967, the Duke of Lichtenstein was able to sell Leonardo Da Vinci's portrait of Ginevra dei benci to the National Gallery in Washington.[261]

---

Notre Dame L. Rev. (2009) 1835; P. Gerstenblith, Art, Cultural Heritage and the Law – Cases and Materials (2nd ed 2008), at 635 et seq.

**253** 16 U.S.C. §§ 470. For details on the Act cp. P. Gerstenblith, Art, Cultural Heritage and the Law (2009), at 782 et seq.

**254** 25 U.S.C. §§ 3001–13. See the collection of articles and and legislative reports collected in a symposium issued devoted to the enactment of the NAGPRA, Symposium, The Native American Graves Repatriation and protection Act of 1990, and Stated-Related Legislation, 24 Ariz. St. L.J. (1992) 1.

**255** P. Gerstenblith, Art, Cultural Heritage and the Law, at 635.

**256** Id § 470 ee (a). Archaeological resources are defines as "any material remains of past human life or activities of archaeological interest" that are at least one hundred years old, 16 U.S.C. §§ 470aa-470bb (1).

**257** Id § 470ee (b).

**258** K. Siehr, International Art Trade and the Law (1993), at 162; B. Knapp, La protection des biens culturels, in Rapports suisses présentés au XIII Congrès international de droit compare (1990), at 227 at seq. and 241 et seq.

**259** Tessin, Art. 15 de legge del 15 aprile 1946.

**260** Keine Ausfuhrbehinderung für Thyssens Bilder-Nachlese im Tessiner Kantonspalast: Neue Zürucher Zeitung, 23.04.1988, 33.

**261** Kurt Siehr, Nationaler und Internationaler Kulturgüterschutz. Eingriffsnormen und der internationale Kunsthandel, in: B. Pfister/M.R. Will (eds.) Festschrift fur Werner Lorenz (1991) 526, at 531.

### b. Export Embargos

Most source countries on the other hand enacted total export embargos of virtually every piece of cultural property without distinguishing between classified or registered items and unclassified and unregistered ones or between national treasure and pieces of looted art. *Italy*'s export control, for example, is one of the strictest in Europe. According to Art. 65 of the recently enacted Code of Cultural Property and Landscape 2004, the export of protected cultural property within the sense of Art. 10 of the Code is forbidden. Anyone wishing to export any of the objects subject to Art. 10 must have a licence. Export may be prohibited completely, if it would constitute damage to the heritage of the nation. According to Art. 10, cultural property consists of immovable and movable things belonging to the state, the regions, other territorial government bodies, as well as any other public body and institution, and to private non-profit associations, which possess artistic, historical, archaeological or ethno- anthropological interest. As well as almost any antique object, whether artistic or not.[262]

### c. Classified National Heritage

Some states on the other hand prohibit only the export of classified or designated items, or likewise, items which are registered in a national inventory. *France* for example opted for a division into various categories of importance: (1) national treasures are subject to strict export prohibitions making exceptions only for special temporary exports under the control of the Ministry of Culture; (2) other movable cultural properties are subject to various licences with different systems for exports to EU Member States and non-EU Member States; and (3) movable cultural objects, which due to their minor value may be exported freely.[263]

In order to grant specific protection to objects from private collections against their export, the *Netherlands* employ a sophisticated list system.[264] Currently, there are 240 single objects and 23 collections designated under the Dutch Cultural Heritage Act 1986 and listed in the specific inventory to be maintained by the Minister.[265]

---

**262** Compare Art. 10 (2) (a) – (j) Code of Cultural Property and Landscapes 2004.

**263** See Marie Cornu, French Report, in: T. Kono/S.Wrbka, The Impact of Uniform Laws, 337, at section 2.2.4.4.2.1.

**264** For an account see K. Lubina, Dutch Report, in: T. Kono/S.Wrbka, The Impact of Uniform Laws, 563; K. Lubina, Contested Cultural Property, § 2 I 1 at 235.

**265** Art. 3c Dutch Cultural Heritage Preservation Act 1984.

A precondition for designation of an object is that it is deemed both irreplaceable and indispensable for Dutch cultural heritage.[266] Hence, not every object of cultural-historical value is included on the list of protected objects. Instead, only if there are no similar objects present in the Netherlands[267] (the criterion of irreplaceability) and if the object fulfills one of the following functions stipulating indispensability will it be protected under the Act: a symbolic function, a "linking function" or a "reference function".[268]An object has a symbolic function if it serves as memory of historically important persons or events. Examples are the "Portrait of Jan Six" by Rembrandt and the decorated furniture in the castle of Amerongen, which was a present by Willem III. The other two (alternative) criteria for judging indispensability are overlapping: a "linking function" is explained as the "functioning of an object or collection as an essential element in a development that is of great importance for the exercise of scholarly work, including the science of culture."[269]An object is considered to have a "reference function" if it "served as starting point for the development for other scientific or artistic objects."[270] In case an object fulfills the criterion of irreplaceability, and one of the three criteria stipulating its indispensability, it can be designated as a protected object under the CHP Act and will hence fall under the Dutch export regime.[271] According to Lubina, working with a set and known number of objects has the advantage of allowing for greater legal security and visibility, while the disadvantage consists in lesser flexibility and and an increased need to evaluate cultural objects prior to an envisaged export. [272]

A similar system can be found in *Germany*. Germany uses a list system, where heritage items are subject to an export prohibition if they are recorded in a "registry of valuable cultural property".[273] So far, however, the registry only contains approximetly 2700 objects. It is only since 2007, that objects which are in public hand can be registered in the inventory.[274] This also includes archived documents. The registry is subjects to a complicated beaurocratic pro-

**266** Art. 2.
**267** Art. 2 (2).
**268** Art. 2 (3).
**269** Art. 2 (3) (b).
**270** Art. 2 (3) (c).
**271** Art. 1.
**272** K. Lubina, Contested Cultural Property, at 235.
**273** Verzeichnis wertvollen Kulturgutes Cp. the German statute (Gesetz zum Schutz deutschen Kulturgutes gegen Abwanderung vom 10. August 1955 in der Fassung vom 8. Juli 1999 (Kulturgutschutzgesetz – KultgSchG).The registry is accessible at http://www.kulturgutschutz-deutschland.de/DE/3_Datenbank/3_datenbank_node.html.
**274** 18 II KulturgSchG.

cedure. According to the "Recommendation of the Conference of Cultural Affairs for the Register of Cultural Property of National Importance"[275], objects may be registered in the inventory if they have been created by an artist of national importance, or, if they are considered to be of outstanding importance for German history and culture. All cultural objects which are not registered are virtually unprotected. There is no obligation for private collectors to register an item and thus, the German government every now and then ends up buying back its cultural heritage on the international market, in the case a collector decides to sell an item abroad.[276]

*Australia* uses a dual control list system for regulating the export of cultural property.[277] Under the 1986 Protection of Movable Cultural Heritage Act, a permit is required to export any item on the National Cultural Heritage Control List/Prohibited Export List. A key criterion used in establishing the content of the list is "significance to Australia" which means the object must be of Australian origin, have substantial Australian content, or been used in Australia together with additional significant associations".[278] The control list is divided in two classes A and B. The former cannot be exported from Australia unless they have been imported temporarily and a certificate of exemption for their re-export has been granted. As currently defined, Class A objects are indigenous, sacred and secret ritual objects, carved tree bark and log coffins used as burial objects, rock art and human remains.[279] All other controlled objects fall within class B and can be exported only with permit or certificate.[280] Permits can be denied if the object is deemed important enough. Any protected object exported without a permit or the appropriate certificate is forfeited and an offence is committed by the person responsible.[281]

**275** In German, available at http://www.kmk.org/fileadmin/veroeffentlichungen_beschluesse/2010/2010_04_29-Verzeichnis-Kulturgut-Archive.pdf

**276** The German system is currently being revised, cp. Report of the Federal Government on the Protection of German Cultural Heritage April 2013, available in English at http://www.bundesregierung.de/Content/Infomaterial/BPA/BKM/2013-08-12-bericht-kulturgutschutz-englisch.html

**277** For an indepth account of the Australian export system see Patrick J. O'Keefe, Commentary on the UNESCO Convention (2nd ed. 2007, at 100 – 102.

**278** P. J. O'Keefe, Commenatry, at 100.

**279** P. J. O'Keefe, Commentary, at 101

**280** This accords with Art. 6 of the UNESCO 1970 Convention.

**281** 1986 Protection of Movable Cultural Heritage Act, section 9.

## 2. Confiscatory Laws

Many cultural property export laws are of a confiscatory nature. Confiscatory laws are laws, which are penal or financial in nature, and the private owner affected by them is not entitled to compensation.[282] As opposed to confiscation, expropriation or compulsory acquisition is the taking or use of property by public authority with adequate compensation.[283] Insofar as the confiscation affects cultural property situated within the territory of the confiscating state, its effect may be the transfer of title to the confiscating state, even if the confiscated object did not belong to a national of that state.[284] The government then obtains ownership. In other circumstances, it can be difficult to construe a property right vesting in the state, in the event export laws are violated.

### a. Confiscatory Ownership *ex lege*

In some laws, confiscation of a relic in favour of the state occurs automatically as an act of law on commission of the illegal export. Automatic forfeiture[285] thereby creates a real ownership right *ex lege* without first having to obtain an administrative decision or court order, provided the object is within state territory. The benefit of this mechanism is two fold: First, the state emphasises that contrary to the all consuming umbrella states it does not proclaim all artefacts to be the property of the state, but only in the case of an illegal export. Second, in case the cultural heritage of a specific nation is effectively endangered the state can retain the object by becoming the owner without the need of any additional administrative decisions.[286] However, if the wording of the statute is unclear or if the time and place of forfeiture is not sufficiently indicated, this mechanism may create problems with regard to the justiciability of such provisions.

#### (1) Automatic Forfeiture

Whether the statute requires an additional administrative act or and act of seizure or whether it vests the ownership automatically depends on the precision of the statute's wording.

---

**282** Cp. Cheshire/North/Fawcett, Private International Law (14th ed. 2008), at 132.

**283** Cp. George A. van Hecke, Confiscation, Expropriation and the Conflict of Laws, 4 ILQ (1951) 335, at 345–346.

**284** Cheshire/ North/Fawcette, Private International Law, at 132.

**285** According to the Oxford English Dictionary the definition of "forfeit" is: "to lose, lose the right to; to render oneself liable to be deprived of (something).

**286** Cp. A. Müller-Katzenburg, Internationale Standards (1996), at 84.

The importance of this fact became apparent in *Attorney-General of New Zealand v Ortiz*[287], where *New Zealand* tried to recover some precious Maori artefacts which had been illegally exported and offered for sale at Sotheby's London by the Swiss art dealer Ortiz. The case has already been briefly introduced in Chapter 1 of this book. New Zealand footed its claim on sect. 12 (2) of the Historic Articles Act 1962 which stated that a historical article knowingly exported or attempted to be exported in breach of this act "*shall be forfeited to her Majesty*" by operation of law and that such transfer takes effect when the article is seized. While in the first instance Staughton J found that the wording of the statute provided for automatic ownership of the state, on the grounds that the purpose of the Historic Articles Act 1962 was to secure the enjoyment of historic articles for the people of New Zealand and this purpose was plainly advanced if articles exported unlawfully automatically became the property of the Crown,[288] the Court of Appeal and the House of Lords both rejected this interpretation and found that "shall be forfeited" meant that an act of seizure was prerequisite to becoming owner.[289] As a result, the Maori artefacts were not held to be the property of the state, as seizure had not taken place.

When, in 1983, Francisco de Goya's 'Marquesa de Santa Cruz' was illegally exported to England, it was *Spain* who had to encounter that its Cultural Property Act in force did not provide for a possibility to recover art objects of national importance.[290] Consequently, in 1985, the Spanish government enacted Art. 29 (1) of the Ley del Patrimonia Historico Espanol, which states that "any movable property belonging to the Spanish Historical Heritage that is exported without the authorisation required under Art. 5 of this Law belongs to the State." It is inalienable and cannot lapse. The state thus automatically becomes the owner of the illegally exported object.[291] Art. 29 continues to say that the state administration shall carry out any actions leading to total recovery of illegally-exported property.

**287** Att-Gen. of New Zealand v Ortiz [1982] 1 Q.B. 349; [1984] 1 A.C. 1. Cp. Part II, Chapter 6.

**288** [1982] 1 Q.B. 349, at 362.

**289** [1984] 1 A.C. 1, at 49.

**290** See Kingdom of Spain v. Christie's [1986] 1 W.L.R. 1120 (Ch.D.). For a detailed account of the case see e. g. K. Siehr, International Art Trade and the Law, at 198; A. Müller-Katzenburg (1999), at 82.

**291** However no provision in the law elucidates at what time exactly the artefact is vested in the state.

Similarly, the *Australian* Protection of Movable Cultural Heritage Act 1986 is clear in stating in section 9 that an object protected under the act is forfeited if it is exported other than in accordance with a permit or certificate.[292]

**(2) Moment of Forfeiture**

The second issue at concern is that automatic forfeiture m ust take place on the territory of the state in order not to violate the principle of territoriality.[293] According to the principle of the *lex situs*-rule,[294] an ownership right may only be recognised in a foreign court if the property right has been vested in the state before it crossed the borders of the territory of the state in question.

In New Zealand, the Historic Articles Act 1962 has been replaced with the Antiquities Act 1975,[295] which was not applicable in *Ortiz*, but even the defendants were convinced that contrary to the older Historic Articles Act 1962, the Antiquities Act 1975 "undoubtedly" provides for automatic forfeiture.[296] However, it obviously went unnoticed that by referring to sect. 69 of the Customs Act 1966, the Antiquities Act 1975, determined the time of export, but neither the provisions on forfeiture (sections 269–274) of the Customs Act, nor the two New Zealand Cultural Property Acts themselves made clear that forfeiture takes place at the time of the illegal export, meaning on the state's territory.[297]

---

**292** Similar mechanisms to be found in *Greece*: Art. 69 (1) provides that the confiscation of cultural objects which are subject of illegal export or attempted export is imposed compulsory; *Kuwait*: Princely Decree No 11 of 1960, Art. 41, 43; *Lebanon*: Art. 97 and 107 Arrêté No. 166 LR du 7 Novembre 1933 portant règlement sur les Antiqués; *Mauretania*: export of classified heritage items is prohibited, art 4 Loi No 71 160 (31.7. 1972). In case of an attempted export, the object will be forfeited and seized, Art. 4(1); *Marocco*: Art. 55 Law No 19–50 (15.6.2006), modifying Law 22–80 (25 Dec 1980) providing for the confiscation upon illegal export; *Sweden*: Art 17 Chapter 5 Swedish Heritage Act No 950 of 30.6.1988, referring to Smuggling Penalties Act 2000, according to which illegally exported objects become the property of the state.

**293** Another question is whether the state has to obtain factual possession of the object through seizure in order not to violate the principle of territoriality, see further on this Part II, Chapter 6, § 3 II 2.

**294** For a more detailed delineation of the lex situs rule see Chapter 6 at § 3 II 1.

**295** Antiquities Act 1975, Reprinted Statutes of New Zealand, Vol. 26 (1979), at 31–46.

**296** See Paul Baker, Q.C. and Nicholas Patten for Ortiz, [1984] 1 A.C. 1, at 39.

**297** Sec 69 of the Customs Act 1966 reads: "For the purpose of this Act the time of exportation of goods shall be deemed to be the time at which the exporting ship leaves the limits of her last port of call in New Zealand, or at which the exporting aircraft departs from the last customs airport at which it landed immediately before proceeding to a country outside New Zealand."

Conversely, the most recent New Zealand Protected Objects Act, which was enacted in 2006,[298] refers the New Zealand Customs and Excise Act 1996, which on the other hand exactly determines the moment and place of forfeiture in respect of an attempted illegal export. Section 225 (2) of the Customs and Excise Act deems objects to have been exported as soon as they are placed in or on any craft for exportation.

Equally, the Australian Movable Cultural Property Act of 1986 explicitly determines the moment at which forfeiture takes place. In section 9 (4) it states that an object shall be taken to be exported at the time when (a) "the object has been placed on board of a ship or aircraft in Australia with the intention that it be taken out of Australia by that ship or aircraft and the departure of the ship or aircraft has commenced" or (b) "the object has been delivered as a postal article into the control of the Australian Postal Commission at a particular place in Australia with the intention that it be sent out of Australia by post and the movement of that article from that place has commenced." The export is thus executed with the charging of the transporting vessel or with the disposal of the article in question at the post office.[299]

Another example is *Afghanistan*, where the export of historical and cultural property is prohibited except for temporary international exhibitions, for scientific research, for restoration of the property or in exchange for historical and cultural property conserved in foreign museums, upon the approval of the Council of Ministers.[300] Article 77 provides, that a person, who contrary to Article 66, exports or takes historical and/or cultural property out of the country, faces, in addition to seizure of the property, imprisonment from six months, up to ten years. Article 67 makes clear that "historical and cultural property is considered to be exported when the process by which it is to be removed from Afghanistan has commenced", even though it has not left the territory of Afghanistan.

Thus, this minimal differentiation in a cultural property statute may be decisive whether a statute vests confiscatory ownership within its sovereignty or whether the provision constitutes a mere export prohibition.

**298** Protected Objects Act 1975 No 41, available at http://www.legislation.govt.nz/act/public/1975/0041/latest/DLM432116.html. On the new Act see Piers Davies and Paul Myburgh, The Protected Objects Act in New Zealand: Too Little, Too Late, 15 IJCP (2008) 321.

**299** Cp. K. Siehr, Nationaler und Internationaler Kulturgüterschutz, in: FS Werner Lorenz (1991) 526, at 529.

**300** Art. 64 of Heritage Law 2004.

#### b. Confiscatory Ownership based upon an Administrative Act

Legislation that requires an additional administrative act upon which the state may become the owner of illegally exported heritage items may possibly violate the principle of territoriality, as clearly neither ownership nor an immediate right of possession will have been vested in the state at a time where the object was present on the territory of a claimant state. Provisions of this kind only constitute "pure" export prohibitions. This would be the case e. g. in *Germany*, where Art. 16 (3) of the "Gesetz zum Schutz deutschen Kulturgutes gegen Abwanderung of 1955" states that cultural property subject to illegal export "may be confiscated on behalf of the federal county where it has been registered in the inventory." Once the object has left the borders of Germany, the government will have no possibility to recover the artefact as seizure would take place outside of German territory.

Similarly ineffective legislation can be found in *Italy* where Art. 174 of the Code of Cultural Heritage and Landscapes 2004 provides that confiscation may take place in accordance with custom provisions[301], in *France*[302], as well as in *Fiji*, where "objects of archaeological interest may be confiscated and disposed of as the Ministry may direct", if a permit to export is not provided.[303]

### 3. Export Laws Granting a Right of First Refusal

Some jurisdictions opted for an export system where the attempt to export an art object may lead to a pre-emption right, or an obligation of the state to acquire the object. It has to be noted that this system concerns only privately owned cultural objects which are intended to be sold abroad by their owners in order to achive a higher price. For this scenario, several jurisdictions, which may be characterised as liberal, provide for a compulsory purchase offer upon the denial of a licence. In such states, the prohibition to export a certain piece of art is com-

**301** See Tommaso Alibrandi/Piergiorgio Fierri, I beni culturali e ambientali (1985) at 682.

**302** Art. L. 111 2–4 of the French Cultural Heritage Code (Code du Patrimonie 2004, established by Order 2004–178 and entered into force on 20 February 2004) in combination with Executive Order 93–124, Décret n°93–124 du 29 janvier 1993 relatif aux biens culturels soumis à certaines restrictions de circulation, JO 30 janvier 1993, p. 1600 as modified by Décret n°2001–894 du 26 septembre 2001 modifiant le décret n° 93–124 du 29 janvier 1993 relatif aux biens culturels soumis à certaines restrictions de circulation, JO 29 septembre 2001, p. 15393. Generally, on French law see this Chapter, available online at: http://www.legifrance.gouv.fr. Formerly, Art. 4 Loi du 23 juin 1941 relative à l'exportation des oeuvres d'art, JO 19 juin 1941.

**303** Art. 19 (4) Preservation of Objects of Archaeological Interest Act 1940. On cultural heritage protection in Fiji see Erike J. Techera, Safeguarding Cultural Heritage: Law and Policy in Fiji, 12 J. Cultural Heritage (2011) 329.

bined with an offer to purchase the object. Some of these laws prohibit only the export of certain objects which are designated in an national inventory[304] while other jurisdictions deny the export after an evaluation process qualifies the object to be of national importance.[305] Conversely, retentive systems, where export is generally prohibited, provide for an optional purchase offer on behalf of the state which it may or may not exercise and which cannot be refused. This mechanism more resembles a compulsory acquisition rather than a right of pre-emption. Some of the laws granting a right of first refusal are confiscatory while others only entail criminal sanctions.

### a. Compulsory Purchase Offer

Jurisdictions which opted for a compulsory purchase offer have in common that the owner may deny the government's purchase offer if it does not match the free market value.[306] During a deferral period, if no offer is made to purchase the object at or above the fair market price, an export licence is normally granted. If an offer is made and accepted by the owner, the licence application will lapse. If an owner does not accept an offer at or above the market price, an export licence will normally be refused. The compulsory purchase offer thus serves as a quasi-compensation for the refusal of the export licence. As a consequence, however, this 'buy out' – system does not grant a right of immediate possession that may be enforced in a foreign court, unless the state has obtained ownership and possession through purchasing the object.

#### (1) The Waverley System

As the centre of international art trade in Europe, the United Kingdom opted to employ this liberal and flexible system defining the range of items subject to regulation as narrowly as possible. The current system is based on the Export Control Act 2002 and, for antiquities, the Export of Objects of Cultural Interest (Control) Order 2003. As a general rule under the Export Order 2003, all objects of cultural importance, which were manufactured or produced more than 50

---

304 For example in the Netherlands, Art. 3c Cultural Heritage Protection Act 1984 – for details see also K. Lubina, Contested Cultural Property, at 235 et seq.

305 For example in England, where the evaluation process is based on the "Waverley Criteria"; Denmark, sec. 3 para 2 Law Nr 404 (1987); Norway, sec. 5 Regulations on the export and import of cultural objects 2007; Canada, arts. 10 and 11 Cultural Property Export and Import Act 1985.

306 C. Maurice/R. Turnor, The Export Licencing Rules in the United Kingdom and the Waverley Criteria, 1 IJCP (1992) 273.

years before the date of the export may only be exported under the authority of a licence granted by the Secretary of State.[307] Any license application is evaluated by an Expert Adviser, who may refer the matter to the Reviewing Committee of the Export of Art and Object of Cultural Interest.[308] In case an object qualifies under certain criteria, export may be delayed to give domestic institutions an opportunity to purchase the object. If an export permit has been denied, "the owner must be assured of an offer to purchase at a fair price".[309]

Until 1939, the UK had no controls on the export of cultural property.[310] The outbreak of the Second World War however, made it necessary to impose controls on the export of goods in order to preserve national resources. As part of the legislation to deal with the wartime, the Emergency Parliament enacted the Import, Export and Customs Powers (Defence) Act 1939, which was later replaced by the Export Control Act 2002.[311] The 1939 Act was not drafted with a view to addressing the problems of the loss of Britain's national heritage but rather with the intention to prevent the export of all types of goods, such as military equipment and weapons and other exports which might prejudice national security.[312]In 1949, a number of works of art were refused export because they were national treasures. [313] The debate surrounding these developments led to the appointment of the Waverley Committee, chaired by Lord Waverley, to advise the government on the best way to control the export of art and antiquities. The committee suggested that the existing export licencing framework should be used to prevent the loss of national treasures.[314] It rejected other means of control such as a tax on art exports, or the provision of public funds to enable these objects to be purchased. [315] One of the main concerns was ensuring that any sys-

---

**307** Sec. 2, Export of Objects of Cultural Interest Oder 2003.
**308** [hereinafter: The Reviewing Committee].
**309** See Report of the Waverley Committee on the Export of Works of Art (HMSO, 1952) (hereinafter: The Waverley Report). Exempt from the requirement to obtain an export licence are postage stamps and other articles of philatelic interest, as well as personal papers and goods exported by their maker or his or her spouse, widow or widower, Schedule 1, Art. 1 Export Order (2003).
**310** Cp. M. Polonsky/ J-F. Canat, The British and French System of Control of the Export of Works of Art, 45 Int. & Comp L.Q. (1996) 557.
**311** The Act was adopted after the so-called Scott inquiry, which had identified a number of limitations in the 1939 Act, including the lack of parliamentary scrutiny of secondary legislation made under the Act and the absence of any indication of the purposes for which export controls may be imposed, see Sir Richard Scott's Report on the Inquiry into the Export of Defence Equipment and Dual-Use Goods to Iraq and Related Prosecutions in February 1996.
**312** See C. Maurice/ R. Turnor, Export Licencing Rules, at 274–275.
**313** Cp. M. Polonsky/ J-F. Canat, British and French System of Control, at 561.
**314** C. Maurice/ R. Turnor, Export Licencing Rules, at 275.
**315** Waverley Report, 121–24, 110–13, 114–17, 118–20.

tem would not punish owners by artificially reducing prices.[316] Accordingly, the Waverley Committee recommended to introduce purchase offers at a fair market price in case an export permit should be denied.[317]

The committee identified three test questions, which needed to be applied in order to determine whether an object ought to be prevented:

1. Is the Object so closely associated with our history and national life that its departure would be a misfortune?
2. Is the Object of outstanding aesthetic importance?
3. Is the Object of outstanding significance for the study of some particular branch of art, learning or history?

Since the "Waverley Criteria" have been introduced in 1952, their wording has been unchanged. Their interpretation, however, has been broadened to some extent:[318]

The first criterion, asking whether an object is so closely connected with the history of the UK and national life that its departure would be a misfortune, refers to national treasures whose export would constitute a loss for the country for the object's outstanding artistic, historical, or archaeological value. Under the original interpretation, this criterion referred to objects of truly national relevance only. Under the revised interpretation, however, also items that are of major importance for local history, items that have been part of collections which are of great historical significance, or objects which are associated with significant historical events, people or places can qualify under the first Waverley criterion.[319]

The second criterion, investigating whether an object is of outstanding aesthetic importance, is a subjective one. The assessment whether an object is of outstanding aesthetic importance is judged on a case by case basis even where it concerns work by great artists. It is not the case that any work by a

---

**316** M. Polonsky/ J-F. Canat, British and French System of Control, at 562.

**317** Cp. The Report of the Committee on the Export of Works of Art (HMSO 1952). But see also the Danish System, where a refusal to issue an export licence leads to the state's obligation to purchase the object at market price, though without having any right of first refusal on this account, Section 11 (1) of the Danish Cultural Assets Act.

**318** See 2003 Quinquennial Review of the Reviewing Committee of the Export of Works of Art of Cultural Interest, published 8. December 2003 and accepted by the DCMS in 2004 [hereinafter: Quinquennial Review].

**319** Examples of the first criterion under the broadened interpretation are: the deposit from the'royal' ship burial from Sutton Hoo, the Middleham Jewel or decorations awarded to Sir William Carnegie in connection with the battle of Trafalgar, see Quinquennial Review, at 44.

great artist is outstanding in the sense of the second Waverley criterion. Instead, the assessment includes also the condition as well as the quality of the work in question, as well as the extent of damages and restorations, leading to even works of great artist being rejected if this criterion is not fulfilled.[320]

The third Waverley criterion, looking at an object's significance for the study of some particular branch of art, learning or history, assesses whether the object is outstanding in significance either on its own account or in connection with a person, place, event, archive, collection or assemblage.[321] Under the revised interpretation of the Waverley criteria "learning" in relation to culture covers a wide number of disciplines, such as art history, archaeology, ethnography, anthropology, paleontology, science, engineering, architecture or literature.[322]

The Criteria are being alternative. Hence, if the Export Adviser comes to the conclusion that at least one of the criteria is met, the application is referred to the Reviewing Committee.

The Reviewing Committee decides whether to recommend to the Minister that an export licence should be granted, or whether to defer the application to allow for an offer to purchase the item at or above the fair market value as recommended by the Reviewing Committee.[323] The usual deferral period is between two and six months; however, a period for up to twelve months may be used for exceptional items.[324] Where the State or its public institutions do not succeed in raising the necessary funds by the end of the deferral period, an export licence will be granted despite the fact that the object is considered a national treasure.

The liberal UK system effectively precludes the motivation to sell many works on the black market. However, in a period of growth on the art market, it may become increasingly difficult to raise the requisite funds.[325] For this rea-

---

**320** See Quinquennial Review, at 44.

**321** K. Lubina, Contested Cultural Property, at 268.

**322** The Reviewing Committee stressed that this list is illustrative and not comprehensive, Quinquennial Review, at 44.

**323** C. Maurice/ R. Turnor, Export Licencing Rules, at 286; C. McAndrew/J. O'Hogan, Export Restrictions, Tax Incentives and the National Patrimony, 2000 Trinity Economic Papers, at 3. On the fair market value see M. Polnsky/ J-F Canat, British and French System of Control, at 567.

**324** D. Finchham, Why U.S. Federal Criminal Penalties for Dealing in Illicit Cultural Property are Ineffective, and a Pragmatic Alternative, 25 Cardozo Arts & Entertainment L. J. (2007) 597, at 636.

**325** This issue has been addressed in recent years with the setting up of the Department of National Heritage in 1992, which funds the National Heritage Memorial Fund. The Fund provides money directy to museums and galleries to purchase art worls of artistic and historic interest on the condition that they also raise part of the funding themselves or from public or private sources. The National Lottery Fund has also been established which gives 20 per cent of its

son, in 1991, the Reviewing Committee recommended that purchase offers may also be submitted by private individuals.[326] The decision was induced by the license application for the export of Antonio Canova's neo-classical marble statute, *The Three Graces*, originally housed in the especially designed Temple of the Graces at Woburn Abbey.[327] The Trustees of the Bedford Estate sold the sculpture to a private company, the Fine Art Investment, which later, in March 1989, entered into an agreement with the Californian John Paul Getty Museum to to sell the statue for £7.6 million.[328] The decision to grant the export licence was repeatedly defered as the Reviewing Committee believed that the sculpture indeed met all three Waiverley Criteria and should remain British Heritage.[329] As not enough money could be raised by a public body in order to meet the asking price for the sculpture, the Secretary of State for National Heritage, Nicholas Ridley, decided that from that moment purchases by private individuals shall also be taken into account. Indeed, a private buyer came forward, however, the Fine Art Investment refused to accept the offer. When September 1993, the Getty Museum submitted another purchase offer and Fine art Investment yet again applied for a new export licence, the Reviewing Committee recommended a deferral of the licence for an unprecedented 18 months in order to allow for funds from the National Lottery via the National Heritage Memorial Fund. Owing to a number of large donations, the Victoria and Albert Museum and the National Museum of Scotland were able to purchase the sculpture jointly. Initiated by the Getty Trust, the National Heritage Secretary's decision to defer the

net marginal revenue to the National Heritage Memorial Fund for distribution to national heritage concerns. For details see www.hlf.org.uk.

**326** Report on the Reviewing Committee for 1990/1991. See also C. Maurice/R. Turnor, The Export Licensing Rules, at 288. Before March 1990, it was implicit that any offer to purchase an item, where a licence to export had been deferred, would come from a public institution. The theme of the Waverley Report in relation to finance was that the British tax payer should be paying, cp. C. Maurice/ R. Turnor, The Export Licencing Rules, at 291.

**327** The History of the Three Graces and he principal events concerning the attempts by the Getty Museum to purchase at are described in the Reports of the reviewing Committee for 1988–1989, at 834, para. 27 and case 23; for 1989–90 at 1225 para. 53–57 and for 1993–1994 at 2710 para. 3–7 as wall as and case 11. Further details can be found in the unreported judgments of Laws Journal (13 Sept 1994) and the Court of Appeal (27 Oct 1994), which dismissed the application for judicial review of the decision in August 1994; For an account of the case see Nicholas Bamforth, Protecting the National Heritage? Judicial Review and the Three Graces, 1 AAL (1996) 147; Sara E. Bush, The Protection of British Heritage: Woburn Abbey and The Three GracesIJCP (1996) 269.

**328** M. Polonsky/J-F. Canat, British and French System of Control, at 569; D. Finchham, U.S. Criminal Panalties, at 638.

**329** Cp. N. Bamforth, Protecting the National Heritage, at 148.

export was later subject to judicial review by the Divisional Court and the Court of Appeal.[330] The Getty Trust submitted that the deferral decision was against their legitimate expectation which they enjoyed a sa result of assurances made by the previous Secretary of State that no further deferral will be allowed.[331] Furthermore the Trust believed that the decision was *Wednesbury* unreasonable,[332] as well as in violation with Art. 87 EC Treaty (ex Art. 92 Treaty of Rome) which forbis state aid that distorts competition between Member countries. However, the court found Getty's arguments to be of little merit and the case was dismissed.[333]

The new system which allowes private owners to buy national heritage in order to prevent it from leaving the country was viewed critically.[334] Some proclaimed that it may distort the market by deterring buyers from bidding at auction, in the expectation that a decision on the licence application would be deferred if an overseas buyer eas successful and they could make an offer at that stage, or deterring overseas buyers, who would resent the uncertainties connected with applying for a license.[335] Indeed, controveries such as that involving *The Three Graces* raise the question what respeonsibilties private collectors owe to the community in respct of art in their ownership. Indeed, sometimes it might be preferable to "loose" a heritage item to a foreign national museum such as the Getty Trust where it will be available for study and display and not to retain it in Britain where it will be in possession and control by a private owner who may prove to be uncooperative.

In the event of breach of the English provisions on export control, Section 7 of the new 2003 Control Order refers to the Customs and Excise Management Act 1979. There, section 69 paragraphs (2) and (3) of the Customs and Excise Manage-

---

**330** R. v. Secretary of State for National Heritage, ex parte John Paul Getty Trust, 13 September 1994, unreported, Divisional Court (Laws J); 27 October 1994, unreported, Court of Appeal (Neill and Hoffmann L.J.J., Henry L.J). Cp. also N. Bamforth, Protecting the National Heritage, at 148.
**331** In the UK, the law of legitimate expectation is a still emerging concept of public law, see e.g. PP. Craig, Legitemate Expectation: A Conceptual Analysis, 108 L.Q.R. (1992) 79. R Bhatt Murphy and others v Independent Assessor; R (Niazi and others) v Secretary of State for the Home Department [2008] EWCA Civ 755.
**332** This legal concept is standard of unreasonableness used in assessing an application for judicial review of a public authority's decision and was enunciated in Associated Picture Houses v. Wednesbury Corporation [1948] 1 K.B. 223, at 228–30 per Lord Green M.R.
**333** Cp. Transcript of Court of Appeal decision (LEXIS), where Neill L.J. described the Getty"s submission, as "hopeless", at 18. See also N. Bamforth, Protecting the National Heritage, at 150.
**334** For the different points of criticisim see Cp. C. Maurice/R. Turner, The Export Licencing Rules, at 291.
**335** Report of the Reviewing Committee for 1989–1990, paragraphs 11 to 31.

ment Act 1979 provide that any person knowingly concerned in the exportation of any goods with a view to evading any prohibition or restriction with respect to those goods commits an offence. On conviction on indictment in the Crown Court the penalty is a fine of an unlimited amount or imprisonment for not more than seven years or both.[336] Additionally, section 3 (1) and section 139 of the old Customs and Excise Management Act 1939 provide that, if any goods are exported in contravention of regulations affecting the export of goods, those goods shall be forfeited to the state. This provision renders the British Export Control System a public "confiscatory" law in the sense previously discussed in III 2 of this Chapter, which means that goods which have been exported in contravention with those rules may be deemed non-justiciable in foreign courts.[337].

A similar system as in the UK has been employed in *Canada* via the Cultural Property Export and Import Act of 1985. In Canada, an omission to apply for a licence also entails the confiscation of the object in question.[338]

### (2) The Dutch System

The Netherlands also operate a sophisticated system but do not provide for criteria to judge which objects ought to be denied export and which ought not to be. This decision already has been made in order to decide whether an object should be registered in the national inventory.[339] Compared with the UK system under which all objects above a certain threshold have to be judged by the Waverley criteria in order to obtain a permit, the Dutch system is rather inflexible and not apt to quickly react to potential exports of not yet registered but nevertheless relevant objects for Dutch cultural heritage. For this reason, an emergency procedure has been introduced.[340] As opposed to Britain, the Netherlands do not provide for a possibility to forfeit the illegally exported object on behalf of the state. A failure to comply with the current export regime only entails criminal sanctions.

According to the Dutch Cultural Heritage Act of 1984, any transfer in property or relocation of a registered object, even if within the Netherlands, is prohib-

---

**336** Consultation of the DCMS on a Draft Order to be made under the Export Control Act 2002, see: http://www.culture.gov.uk/images/consultations/Export_Controls_Draft_conspaper.pdf

**337** This depends of the question whether the court interprets the term "public law" in the way the English courts recently did in Government of Iran v Barakat, cp. in detail Part II, Chapter 6, at § 3 I 3.

**338** Art. 9 (1) Cultural Property Export and Import Act 1985.

**339** Cp. this Chapter, at § 2 III 1 c.

**340** Dutch Cultural Heritage Preservation Act 1984, Art. 3 a.

ited without prior notice to the inspector appointed by the Minister to oversee compliance with the Act.[341] In cases of cultural objects to be exported abroad for sale and other (e. g. exhibition) purposes, the Minister of Culture can grant permission. State Inspectorate and Minister have four weeks to react upon an owner's notice. The Minister can extend the period for another eight weeks. Upon lapse of the four (and if applicable eight) week period, the owner is notified by the State Inspectorate, respectively the Minister as to whether or not the object is protected by the Cultural Heritage Preservation Act 1984 (CHP 1984). In case of an affirmative reaction by the State Inspectorate /Minister, the owner is free to carry out the notified action for a period of a year. In case the Minister denies the export on behalf of a sale abroad, the denial holds at the same time the State's offer to purchase the object.[342] In case the State and the owner cannot agree upon a price of sale, the District Court of The Hague has jurisdiction to determine the price.[343]

One case in which the District Court of The Hague was called upon to determine the sales price concerned a painting by Cézanne.[344] 'Paysage près d'Aix avec la tour César' had been designated as protected object under the Dutch Cultural Heritage Act in 1985. In 1995, the owner of the painting informed the Minister about his intention to sell the painting abroad. The export was denied on the ground of the painting's importance for the Dutch Cultural Heritage. The State made an offer to acquire the painting for 6.5 million Dutch Guilders. The owner rejected the price that did not reflect full market value. When it became evident that the parties could not agree upon a price, they turned to the District Court in The Hague. The Court sought expert opinions on the value of the painting and set the price at 15 million Dutch Guilders, more than twice the amount initially offered by the State.[345] As a consequence, the Cézanne was the first painting designated as cultural heritage that could not be acquired by the State. However, before the painting was taken abroad for sale, a private individual acquired the painting and gave it in loan to the Museum Boijmans Van Beuningen in Rotterdam where it still remains as of today. Had the owner of the Cézanne, or any other owner of an object protected under the CHP Act violated the Act, e. g. by relocating or even selling the protected object without notifying the

**341** Dutch Cultural Heritage Preservation Act 1984, art. 7.

**342** Dutch Cultural Heritage Preservation Act 1984, art. 7, art. 10 and art. 12.

**343** Dutch Cultural Heritage Preservation Act 1984, art. 12.

**344** For a deailed account of the case, see K. Lubina, Dutch Report, in: T. Kono/S.Wrbka, The Impat of Uniform Laws (2010) 563, at 601.

**345** District Court of The Hague, 14 January 1998, Prg. (1998) at 395. Excerpts from the case are published in: P.S. Sjouke, Wet tot behoud van cultuurbezit (2007), at 86.

State Inspectorate or Minister, he or she can expect to be prosecuted under Criminal Law. Violations of the Cultural Property Act qualify as an economic crime.[346]

### b. Optional Purchase Offer

The previously described system has to be distinguished from the system in more retentive jurisdictions where export generally requires a licence and the state has a right, not the obligation, to acquire the antiquity whether it denies or permits the export, as is the case in *Saudi Arabia*. According to Art. 46 Law No 2435[347] the export of antiquities shall be subject to a special licence which shall be granted by the Department of Antiquities. The Department has the authority to refuse to allow the exportation, if it finds that this would impoverish the country's archaeological or artistic heritage. After studying the antiquities for which an application for export has been submitted, the Department of Antiquities has the right to allow or disallow exportation, or to buy such antiquities as it desires at the price quoted in the application for export.

In *Spain*, the application for an export licence indirectly contains the owner's irrevocable sale offer to the benefit of the state.[348] The value of the object contemplated in the export application at the same time constitutes the price for which the government can acquire the object.[349] In case the state refuses to grant the export certificate, it has the option to accept the offer within 6 months and pay within a year. It is important to note that the denial of the export licence does not constitute the acceptance of the offer. After the expiry of the preemption right deadline the owner may sell the object on the free market within Spanish territory.

---

**346** Art. 1(2) of the Wet op de Economische Delicten (WED, 22 juni 1950) WET van 22 juni 1950. The santion can range between a maximum of six years in prison and a fine in the fifth category if the violations has been deliberately, to custody for a maximum o f a year and a fine of the forth category (Art. 6).

**347** Law No. 2435 concerning the Regulations of the Export of Antiquities, 18 August 1972.

**348** Art. 35 Spanish Decree 1985. See the very helpfull account in Matthias Plutschow, Vorkaufsrechte im internationalen Kulturgüterschutz (2002), at marginal note 68.

**349** Art. 33, Spanish Decree 1985. Similar provisions can be found in *Italy*, where the ministry has the right to purchase the object at the declared value within 90 days of presenting the object for permission to export, Art. 39 Law 2004; *Iran*: Art. 18 of the National Heritage Protection Act 1930 (reprinted in Iran v Barakat, [2007] EWHC 705 (QB); [2007] EWHCA Civ 1374; [2008] 1 All ER 1177; QB 22 [2009]); *Lebanon*, Art. 104 (1) Law no. 166 on the Regulation of Antiquities (1933); *Luxemburg*: Art. 9 (2) Law 1966 concerning cultural property. For details see generally M. Plutschow, Vorkaufsrechte (2002).

*Mauritania*, operates an especially strict regime.[350] According to Art. 4 of the Heritage Law No 72 160, the export of designated heritage items is prohibited and any item attempted to be exported illegally will be forfeited and seized. The export of an object which is not designed, because the identity of the person in possession of them was unknown, but the object is indeed of particular significance for the Mauritanian culture, requires a license.[351] In this event, the State has a preemptive right to purchase the object regardless of whether an export license has been de facto granted or refused.[352] Even after a license has been issued the State has a right to buy the object, provided that it pays a fair price determined by a mutual agreement or by expert opinion.[353]

In *Venezuela*, the export licence will not be granted unless the exporter has offered the object for sale to the government.[354] The export of objects without having it first offered the object in question to the state for purchase and without obtaining licence is a criminal offence.[355]

Whether these optional purchase offer-provisions grant the state an ownership right in form of an immediate right of possession depends on the proprietary nature of options and pre-emption rights and will be discussed in paragraph IV 3 of this chapter.

### 4. Export Laws not granting Property Rights

Some systems do not provide for a possibility to confiscate heritage items upon illegal export and as a consequence they neither grant any kind of confiscatory ownership nor an immediate right of possession. They entail only criminal sanctions and pecuniary penalties or a right to claim damages for the loss of the object for the national heritage but do not grant any property right in the object.

The Dutch-System, for example, prohibits the export of classified items but does not provide for the forfeiture or confiscation of an object that has been exported in violation of the export prohibition or in attempted export of a classified

350 For a detailed account of Mauritanian cultural heritage law see Christine Irsheid, The Protection of Cultural Property in the Arab World, 6 IJCP (1997) 11, at 28 et seq.

351 Art. 4 (2) Law No 72 160.

352 Christine Irsheid, The Protection of Cultural Property in the Arab World, 6 IJCP (1997) 11, at 28.

353 Art. 4 (1) Mauretanian Law No 72 160.

354 Ley de proteccion y defensa del patrimonio cultural 1994 (enacted 5 Aug 1993).

355 Art. 41 of Law 1994.

item. Violations of the Dutch Cultural Heritage Act however qualify as an economic crime.[356]

Similarly, *Denmark*, that also employed a right-of-first-refusal mechanism does not provide for an option to confiscate the object upon violation of the export prohibition. The Danish Cultural Heritage provisions are mainly based on three codes, Act No. 332 of June 1986 on the Protection of Cultural Assets, Act No. 331 on the Protection of Cultural Recourses, as well as Executive Order No. 404 of 11 June 1987 on the Protection of Cultural Assets.[357] According to Art. 1 of Order No. 404 (1987)[358] and Articles 3 and 4 of Act No. 332 (1986), the export of cultural goods covered by those acts is prohibited and subject to a licence.[359] On refusal of an export licence the Cultural Assets Commission must make a compulsory purchase offer to the owner of the object, Art. 3 (4) Executive Order 404. [360]Art. 13 of Act No. 332 only provides that the non-compliance with the export provisions shall be punishable by a fine. The Danish Criminal Code stipulates that fines are subject to the discretionary authority of the court and administration. [361] Compared to other jurisdictions, the sanctions for the violation of export provisions is relatively low, if not non-existent.

*Norway* has a peculiar handling of the non-compliance with its export laws. Norwegian Cultural Heritage Protection is based on the Cultural Heritage Act

**356** Article 1(2) of the Wet op de Economische Delicten (WED, 22 juni 1950) WET van 22 juni 1950. The sanction can range between a maximum of six years in prison and a fine in the fifth category if the violations has been deliberately, to custody for a maximum o f a year and a fine of the forth category (Article 6).

**357** See especially Frank Kohls, Kulturgüterschutz – Die Wirkung von Verstössen gegen Ausfuhrverbote und Möglichkeiten der Rückführung illegal verbrachter Kulturgüter, Eine vergleichende Untersuchung mit den rechten Dänemarks, Norwegens und Schwedens (2001).

**358** Executive Order No. 404 of 11 June 1987 entered into force on 1st January 1987.

**359** The Act covers: (1) cultural asset from the time before 1660, (2) cultural assets which have the value of DKK 100.000 or more and are older than 100 years, (3) photographs which have the value of DKK 30.000 or more as well as (4) other assets after a specific decision by the Miniter of Cultural Affairs in pursuance with sec 2(4) of the Act. Such a decision can only be made when the Cultural Assets Commission makes a proposal hereof, and when special circumstances speak in favur hereof, Art 1 Executive Order No. 404.

**360** An application for an export licence will normally be processed within one month. If on special grounds the processing of any application cannot be completed within this period, the Commission shall notify the applicant hereof, as well as of the time at which the decision is expected to be available, Art. 7 (1). In the event that a decision is not available three months at the latest from receipt of the application by the Commission, the latter shall issue a statement to the effect that the export licence may be considered as granted in pursuance of section 6 (2) of the Act, Art. 7 (2).

**361** Art. 6 preliminary provisions of the Danish Criminal Code (1930).

No. 50 of 1978[362] and the complementary Executive Order of 1979.[363] In case, an object has been exported without first obtaining an export licence and awaiting the result of the evaluation process, the State can claim damages for the loss of the object.[364] It also provides for fines and imprisonment up to 6 months in severe cases, Art. 23 of Law No. 50 (1978), but not for the possibility to forfeit or confiscate the item upon its export.

Surprisingly, the new export regime in *France* has not introduced stricter export rules. With the adoption of the new Cultural Heritage Code (CHC) in 2004, the newly introduced export regime was incorporated in Book I of the Code, but the older Act No. 92–1477 of 31/12/1992[365] and Executive Order No. 93–124[366] are still in force. According to Art. 111–4 of the Code du Patrimonie 2004, cultural objects that qualify as national treasures may not be exported.[367] While the wording of Art. L. 111–4 CHC suggests that the licence that is required for export "may" be refused for national treasures,[368] there exists general agreement in the literature that the provision is badly drafted and that, in accordance with its legal history, must be understood as prohibiting the granting of an export licence to national treasures rather than only providing the possibility for

**362** 9 June 1978 entered into force 15 February 1979.

**363** 15 February 1979.

**364** Art. 27, Law No 50. See also Frank Kohls, Kulturgüterschutz, at 79.

**365** Loi n° 92–1477 du 31 décembre 1992 relative aux produits soumis à certaines restrictions de circulation et à la complémentarité entre les services de police, de gendarmerie et de douane, disposition relatives aux biens culturels, JO 5 janvier 1993, p. 198.

**366** Décret de 29.1.1993 relatif aux biens culturels soumis à certaines restrictions, JO 30 janvier 1993, p. 1600. The executive order was revised by two further executive orders: Décret no 95–24 du 9 janvier 1995 modifiant le décret no 93–124 du 29 janvier 1993 relatif aux biens culturels soumis à certaines restrictions de circulation, JO 11 janvier 1995 and Décret n°2001–894 du 26 septembre 2001, JO 29 septembre 2001, p. 15393.

**367** Julia El-Bitar, Der deutsche und der französische Kulturgüterschutz nach der Umsetzung der Kulturrückgaberichtlinie (2006), at 30 and 34.

**368** "Le certificat ne peut être refusé qu'aux biens culturels présentant le caractère de trésor national. Aucune indenité n'est due du fait du refus de délivrance du certificat. Il est accordé aux biens culturels licitement importés dans le territoire douanier depuis moins de cinquante ans. S'il existe des présomptionsgraves et concordantes d'importation illicite, l'autorité administrative peut exiger la preuve de la licéité de l'importation du bien et, en l'absence de preuve, refuser la délivrance du certificat. Le refus de délivrance du certificat ne peut intervenir qu'après avis motivé d'une commission composée à parité de représentants de l'État et de personnalités qualifiées et présidée par un membre du Conseil d'Etat. Un décret en Conseil d'État fixe les modalités de désignation de ses membres et les conditions de publication de ses avis".

doing so.[369] In case an object has been illegally exported, French Law does not provide for the possibility to confiscate it.[370]

### 5. Export Restriction and EU Law

Within the European Union, the question has been raised whether export restrictions among European Union nations violate the EU's Treaty of Rome principle of free movement of goods. In 1993, the European Union issued Directive 93/7/EEC of March 15, 1993 (hereinafter: the Directive),[371] on the return of cultural objects unlawfully removed from the territory of a member state, as well as Council Regulation No 3911/1992 on the export of cultural goods,[372] in order to deal with cultural property questions arising from the establishment of the European Single Market. The Directive controls the movement of cultural objects within the Community, while the Regulation inhibits the export of such articles from the Community. Their effect is to provide unconditional Community enforcement of the export controls of each of the member nations. The authority for the Directive and Regulation derives from Article 36 of the Treaty on the functioning of the European Union (ex Art. 34 Treaty of Rome), which authorises national limitations on the principle of free movement in order to protect "national treasures." However, Member States give no guidance on when cultural objects meet the definition of "national treasure". Hence, Art. 36 and the term "national treasure"

---

**369** Cp. K. Lubina, Contested Cultural Property, at 286; J.F. Poli, La Protection de biens culturelles meubles (1996) at 78; Marc Weber, Unveräußerliches Kulturgut im nationalen und internationalen Rechtsverkehr (2002), at 295.

**370** Articles 4–15 of the LOI n° 92–1477 du 31 décembre 1992 relative aux produits soumis à certaines restrictions de circulation et à la complémentarité entre les services de police, de gendarmerie et de douane.

**371** Council Directive 93/7, 1993 O.J. (L 74) 74–79, amended by Council Directive 2001/38, 2001 O. J. (L 187) 43–44. The statutory instrument which implements the Directive in the UK came into force in 2nd March 1994, The Return of Cultural Objects regulations 1994, SI No. 501 of 1994. For the German implementation see Richtlinie 93/7/EWG des Rates vom 15. März 1993 über die Rückgabe von unrechtmäßig aus dem Hoheitsgebiet eines Mitgliedstaates verbrachten Kulturgütern, ABl. EG Nr. L 74 vom 27. März 1993, pages 74–79, and Gesetz zum Schutz deutschen Kulturgutes gegen Abwanderung, 06.08.1955, as amended on 8. Juli 1999 (BGBl. I 1999, S. 1754), and on 18.5. 2007 (BGBl. I 2007, S. 761–762).

**372** Council Regulation (EEC) No 3911/92 of 9 December 1992 on the export of cultural goods, OJ No L 395, 31.12.1992, p. 1, as amended by information of 27 March 1993, OJ No L 74, 27.3.1993, p. 80.

have been accorded divergent interpretations resulting in two conflicting trends[373]:

Countries largly exporting cultural objects, such as Italy, Spain or France, who aim to enforce tight restrictions through broad definitions support an extensive interpretation of the term. On the opposite, importing countries rather advocate for a restrictive interpretation in order to be able to obtain the cultural wealth of other countries.[374]

In addition, the former Treaty of Rome was written in several authentic language versions and the different translations of "national treasure" have different meanings. Professor Manlio Frigo argues that the extensive application of "national treasure" by France, Spain, Italy and Portugal can in part be attributed to the problem of translating various concepts into different legal languages.[375] While, according to the Italian (as well as the Spanish and Portuguese) text of Art. 36 of the Treaty on the Functioning of the European Union, the provisions of Article 34 and 35 (ex Art. 28 and Art. 29 EC-Treaty) shall not preclude prohibitions or restriction on imports, exports or goods in transit justified on grounds of the protection of the 'patrimonio artistico, historico o arqueologico nazionale', other authentic texts (notably the English and French texts) refer to the protection of 'national treasure of artistic, historic or archaeological value and to "tresor nationaux ayant une valeur artistique, historique ou archaeoligique'.[376] In other words, it is clear that "national heritage" and "national treasures" evoke two different concepts. Consequently, the Italian, Spanish and Portuguese texts appear prima facie to give the national authorities a broader discretionary power in deciding on the categories of goods to be included in the national protective legislation, and more specifically on the limitations of their movement.[377]

---

**373** At this time, there are no decisions by the European Court of Justice on the meaning of this term.

**374** Andrea Biondi, The Merchant, the Thief and the Citizen: Circulation of Works of Art within the European Union, Common Market Law Review, Vol. 34 (1997) 1173 (opining that the correct interpretation of term "national treasures" should not refer to the generality of all art or cultural goods, but to a specific category that forms an indissoluble link with the cultural heritage of a particular nation); Barbara T. Hoffman, European Union Legislation Pertaining to Cultural Goods, in: Barbara T. Hoffmann (ed.) Art and Cultural Heritage (2006) 191, at 192.

**375** Manlio Frigo, Cultural Property v. Cultural Heritage: A "Battle of Concepts" in International Law?, Vol. 86 International Committee of the Red Cross (2004) 367, at 369.

**376** The German text of Art. 30 EU-Treaty refers to 'Kulturgut von künstlerischem oder archäologischem Wert'.

**377** Cp. B. T. Hoffmann, European Union Legislation Pertaining to Cultural Goods, in: B.T. Hoffmann (ed.) Art and Cultural Heritage (2006) at 193.

The World Trade Organization (WTO) in Article XX of the General Agreement of Tariffs and Trade (GATT),[378] and the North American Free Trade Agreement (NAFTA) which refers to GATT, likewise exempt "national treasures" from the prohibition on controls that restrict the movement of goods. However, no international court or tribunal has yet defined the term "national treasure".[379] It has been thought that the Council of the European Union would treat the term "national treasures" as a restrictive one, applicable to only a small group of a nation's important objects, however, so far all of the objects included in the broad categories of cultural property whose export is controlled by the national laws of such nations as Greece, Italy and Spain qualify as "national treasures" within the meaning of Article 36, EU-Treaty.[380]

In the *Walter-case*,[381] the French Court de Cassation endorsed the extensive interpretation of the term "national treasure". In this case, the great grandson of a prominent Parisian art dealer, Jacques Walter, whose family has donated some 144 master paintings to French museums, intened to sell a Van Gogh's *Jardin à Auvers* to a foreign buyer, but the French Minister of Culture refused to issue an export licence on the grounds of the French law of 31 December 1913.[382] Instead, the painting was listed as a "national treasure" with the consequence that it would not leave the country if sold. The French state chose not to exercise its right of pre-emption under the 1941 law, as abviously that would have meant to pay for the paitning.

Owing to the classification as a national treasure and the subsequent prohibition to export it, the Van Gogh was auctioned in France for an amount three times less than its expected international art market value. For this reason, in 1992, Walter sued the French state for asking for compensation in the amount

**378** 33 I.L.M. 1125–1154.

**379** The Court will of course be called on only to deal with that term in applying the EC-Directive, which deals with intra-Union trade. Article 36 of the Treaty does not apply to trade with nations outside the Union, cp. Fraijcois Rigaux, Libre circulation des biens culturels et protection des tresors nationaux, 2 European Review of Private Law 95 (1994); Daphne Voudouri, Circulation et protection des biens culturels dans 1'Europe sans frontières, Rev. de Droit Public (1994) 479, at 483 et seq.

**380** J.H. Merryman, Cultural Property, International Trade, and Human Rights, Occasional Papers in Intellectual Property from B. N. Cordozo Law School University No 9 (2001); J.H. Merryman, A Licit Trade, 4 IJCP (1995) 13, at 15.

**381** Agent Judiciaire du Tresor v Walter Cass. Civ. Ire, 20 February 1996, Bulletin de la Cour. For a detailed account of the case see: Timothy P. Ramier, Agent Judiciaire du Tresor v Walter: fait du Prince and a King's Ransom, 6 IJCP (1997) 337; Merryman/Elsen/Urice (eds.), Law, Ethics and the Visual Arts (2006), at 135.

**382** Loi du décembre 1913 sur les monuments historiques, JO 1 janvier 1914, p. 129

of 250 million French Francs for calssifying the painting as a "national treasure" under the 1913 law.[383]

The Court of Appeal in Paris held that the Van Gogh indeed was to be classified as a national treasure. It based its finding on the painting's importance to the national patrimony in France and its position in the history of art it was to be classified as a national treasure and therefore the Frech state had to pay indemnity under the 1913 law.[384]

In the *Walter-case*, the connection between a Van Gogh and the French culture has been obvious, however, in other case where France prevented the export of works of art, the interpretation of the term national treasure has been by far stretched, for instance when the export permit for some Chinese jars was denied, or equally where the permit for a Turkish scene painted by Swiss-French artist Jean-Etienne Liotard was concerned.[385]

The European Court of Justice (ECJ) has the ultimate authority to decide whether a Member State is following the law and to draw the line between national treasures and cultural objects. It may invalidate the government's restriction on export and hold the Member State to have violated its free trade treaty obligations. So far, no decisions by the ECJ on the meaning of this term exist as potential disputing litigants have chosen to avoid the ECJ. However ultimately, an official clarification from the ECJ would settle the matter and solidify the guidelines.

## IV. Property Interests on the Ground of Pre-Emption Rights

Pre-emption rights do not only serve as a mechanism to prevent export and to retain cultural property within state borders. They may serve as a vehicle to acquire fortuitous finds or as a mechanism for the integration of antiquities that are being legally sold on the free market from private owners into national collections.

---

**383** Article 16 of the 1913 law stated that: "Classification gives rise to the payment of an indemnity representing the resulting injury to the owner by the application of the servitude resulting from classification (....)."

**384** Agent Judiciaire du Tresor v. Walter (06/07/94), Cour d'Appel de Paris, Ire Ch. A., D. S. Jur. 1995, at 254.

**385** Cp. J.M. Cheng, The Problem of National Treasure in International Law, 12 Oregon Rev. Int'L L (2010) 141, at 168.

### 1. Pre-Emption Rights as a Mechanism to Acquire Fortuitous Finds

If archaeological treasures are not *ipso facto* state property, some jurisdictions provide that the state may exercise a right to acquire them from the private owner. Such a right can be exercised only so long as the object is located within the territory of the state exercising this right. This type of pre-emption right is indeed not a real pre-emptive mechanism as it is vested in the state by the operation of law and not by an act of disposal by the owner of the property.

In *France*, for example, the state does not become the owner of excavated objects automatically, but "may in the sole interest of public collections, claim the ownership of the resources excavated or fortuitously discovered with compensation paid to the owner of the object".[386] The ownership of excavated finds is basically decided by the general Civil Law rules, leading to a shared ownership between the finder an the landowner.[387] The item belongs to the owner of the land.[388] The finder can claim half of the value of the antiquity that he found, the other half belongs to the owner of the land.[389] According to section L 531–14 of the Cultural Heritage Code, the finder and the owner must declare the find to the mayor of the town. The mayor will then inform the government representative. The find should be delivered to the relevant authority upon request for a period of five years maximum.[390] If the antiquity is of interest for the state, it can buy it by compulsory purchase for an amount agreed with the owner and the finder. If there is a disagreement, an independent appraiser will value the find.[391]

A coinciding but more protective regime can be found in *Sweden*. There, according to Chapter 2 of the Swedish Heritage Conservation Act[392], ancient finds that have no owner when found and that are discovered in or near ancient monuments and remains and are connected with them accrue to the state.[393] Ancient finds that are found in other circumstances and are presumably at least one hundred years old accrue to the finder.[394] He is, however, duty bound to invite

**386** Section L. 531–1 Code du Patrimonie 2004. Cp. also M. Cornu, French Report, in T. Kono/S. Wrbka, The Impact of Uniform Laws, 337 at sect. 2.2.1.2.2.1.

**387** Ibid, section 2.2.3.3.2.4.

**388** Section 552 of the French Civil Code, absolute right of ownership of land and things below and above it.

**389** Section 716 of the French Civil code

**390** Section L. 531–16 Code du Patrimonie 2004.

**391** M. Cornu, French report, in: T. Kono/S.Wrbka (eds.), The Impact of Uniform Laws (2010) 337, at section 2.2.3.3.2.3.

**392** Heritage Conservation Act 1988:950 (last amendment 2002).

**393** Chapter 2, Art. 4 and Art. 3 (1) of the 1988 Act.

**394** Chapter 2, Art. 4 and Art. 3 (2) of the 1988 Act.

the state to acquire it in return for payment if (1) the find contains objects partly or wholly of gold, silver, copper, bronze or any other copper alloy, or if (2) the find consists of two or more objects, which were presumably deposited together.[395] Other countries providing for means of acquiring fortuitously found antiquities via a right of pre-emption include, *Belize,*[396] *Botswana,*[397] *Finland,*[398] *Luxemburg*[399] and *Senegal.*[400]

After the purchase has been exercised the state obtains full ownership. For the purpose of cross border claims, such a mechanism of acquisition is unfruitful, as the state does not obtain legal title *unless it* excercised its right of pre-emption. In case an object illegally leaves the country, the state will be unable to recover it because indeed it never became the owner of the object.

### 2. Pre-Emption Rights as Means of Acquiring Property from Private Collectors

In case, an antiquity is sold on the free market, many jurisdictions stipulate that the state has a pre-emption right to acquire the object. Usually, this kind of pre-emption right will serve as a mechanism to retain valuable heritage items within the borders of a state's territory or equally as a means of making cultural heritage that so far has been kept in private collections available to the public by including it into public collections and museums. Several different pre-emption models to acquire private property could be identified while analysing specific legal systems of cultural property protection. Some of them are more effective in its compatibility to retain national cultural heritage within state borders than others.

#### a. Option to Purchase

The clearest and strongest right that can be granted to a party is an option to purchase. The option grantee is given the right, but not the obligation, to

---

**395** Ancient finds discovered on or beneath the seabed beyond the limits of national jurisdiction and salvaged by a Swedish vessel or taken to Sweden, also accrue to the state. A shipwreck discovered on or beneath the seabed beyond the limits of national jurisdiction and salvaged by a Swedish vessel or taken to Sweden, accrues to the state if at least one hundred years have presumably elapsed since the ship was wrecked.

**396** Sect. 14 of the Ancient Monuments and Antiquities Ordinance 1971.

**397** Art. 11 Monuments and Relics Act 1970.

**398** Art. 16 and 17 Antiquities Law 1963.

**399** Article 10 (2) of the Luxemburg Act of on the conservation and protection of sites and national monuments (18 July 1983).

**400** Articles 14, 19 and 21 Loi No 71–12 du janvier 1971.

lease, buy or otherwise control a specified asset in the future.[401] According to Black's Law Dictionary, an "option to purchase" can be defined as "a contract by which an owner of an object enters an agreement with another allowing the latter to buy the property at a specified price within a specified time, or within a reasonable time in the future, but without imposing an obligation to purchase upon the person to whom it is given".[402] The grant of the option imposes no obligation on the purchaser,[403] but merely confers on him a contractual right to call for the relevant disposition provided that he has satisfied any conditions to which the option was made subject. Control over the exercise of the option lies wholly in the hands of the purchaser. To be enforceable, the option should set forth exactly what asset is subject to the option, the price and terms on which the optionee can exercise the option, the date or dates on or between which the option is exercisable, and the corresponding dates for closing or delivery of the optioned asset.[404]

Many legal systems provide for a mechanism of cultural property protection or acquisition that is akin to an exclusive option to purchase granted by contract. For example, some states operate a system where the owner or seller of a heritage item is bound to notify the state of his intention to sell the item in question. It is then the government who makes a sales offer to the seller while he is constrained to accept the offer made by the state. This mechanism can be found for example in *Israel.*[405] There, Art. 25 of Antiquities Law 5738 of 1978 stipulates that the government may request the object to be sold or transferred to the state to a price it finds appropriate. In case the seller is not satisfied with the consideration offered by the state, he may turn to the court for it to be decided. Aside from the ordinary right of first refusal where the state is being notified about an intended sale and where it might decide to buy the item instead of the potential contracting party, the state may also request an item to be sold if it regards it to be of

---

**401** Cp. e.g. Kevin Gray/ Susan Francis Gray, Elements of Land Law (2005), at 774; Roger Sexton/Barbara Bogusz, Complete Land Law: Texts, Cases and Materials (2009), at sect. 1.3.10; Marc P. Thomson, Modern Land Law (4th ed 2009), at 78; John Stevens/Robert Pearce/Nicola Jackson, Land Law, ($4^{th}$ ed 2008), at 18–007.

**402** Brian A. Garner (ed.), Black's Law Dictionary (8th ed. 2004), at 118. The definition indeed concerns options to buy real property.

**403** See for example Spiro v Glencrown Properties [1991] Ch 537, at 543 per Hoffmann J.

**404** K. Gray/S.F. Gray, at 772; Phillip H Kenny, What is a Right of Pre-Emption? Conveyancer and Property Lawyer (2001), 295, at 296; Quentin Smyte, Pre-Empting the Problem, 109 Property Law Journal (2003) 10; see also Black' Law Dictionary, at 1127–1228.

**405** Articles 19, 25 and 26, Antiquities Law 5738 of 1978 (passed by the Knesset on 31. January 1978, published in Sefer Ha-Chukkim No. 885 5738, $10^{th}$ February 1978, at 76; the Bill and Explanatory Note were published in Hatza-ot Chok No. 1250 of 5736, at 314 et seq.

national value.[406] In case the antiquity is an integral part of a group the state may only request that the item is being sold in respect of the group as a whole.[407] In the event that the state and the possessor of the antiquity cannot reach an agreement regarding the price of the heritage item, the matter shall be decided by the court.[408] An interesting feature of this model is the presumption of the sellers knowledge about the item's quality as an antiquity. Art. 20 of Law 1978 provides that the plea of a dealer who presumably did not know that an artefact he was about to sell was an antiquity in terms of Law 1978 should not be heard. A similar system can be found in *Uruguay.*[409]

Another model of property protection is the obligation of the owner or seller to submit a sale offer to the state. [410] Legal systems which provide for a rule that requires to declare the intention to sell a heritage item which at the same time must contain the exact price and conditions of the sale contract are equally similar to an exclusive option to purchase. It can be assumed that a declaration of the intention to sell a heritage item can account for a concrete sales offer if it contains the exact price and other conditions of sale.[411] The owner is thus constrained to offer the item to the state before he concludes a sales contract with the potential third buyer. Specific for this system is also the fact that the state is compelled to acquire the object in question at the same conditions as are outlined in the declaration of sale. This system can be found for example in *Spain.* There, Art. 38 of Law Nr 16/1985 stipulates that any person trying to sell property declared of cultural interest or included in the General Inventory shall notify the state and declare the price and conditions proposed for the sale.[412] Auction houses must give notification in advance of public auctions in which it is planned to sell any property forming part of the Spanish Historical Heritage. Within the period of two months subsequent to the notification referred to in the above section, the state administration may use its right of pre-emption to purchase the property for any public corporation, entering the obligation to pay the agreed price or, where appropriate, the auction price within a period not exceeding two financial years, unless an agreement is reached with the inter-

**406** Ibid, Art. 19 (b).
**407** Ibid, Art. 19 (d).
**408** Ibid, Art. 19 (c).
**409** Art. 16 Law Nr. 14.040 of 20 October 1971.
**410** See also M. Plutschow, Vorkaufsrechte, at 201.
**411** M. Plutschow, Vorkaufsrechte, at 201.
**412** Art. 38 Law 16/1985 dated 25 June, on the Spanish Historical Heritage (Patrimonio Historrico Regulatión, Official State Bulletin of 29 June 1985) and Art 41 Law Nr 111/1986 (Real Decreto 10 enero 1986, num. 11/86 (Presidencia).

ested party on other payment terms.[413] In the event, the intention to sell is not correctly notified, the state administration may, in the same terms as those for the right of pre-emption, exercise its right of redemption within a period of six months after the date on which it receives reliable information on the sale.[414]This model is a strong mechanism of protection as it allows the state to enter the agreement in lieu of the potential buyer. The contract is thus concluded and binding the moment the government notifies the seller of its intention to exercise the pre-emption right. In the event that the state does not accept the owner's offer, the owner is free to divest of the property.[415]A similar system can be found in *Greece,*[416] *Brazil*[417] or *South Korea.*[418]

### b. Right of First Refusal

Unlike an option, a "right of first refusal"[419] does not entitle the holder of the right to force the other party to sell the asset.[420] An option gives the holder the power to compel the owner to sell the property regardless of the owner's desire to do so. In contrast, a right of first refusal does not give the holder the power to compel the owner to sell but merely requires the owner, if and when he or she decides to sell, to offer the property first to the holder. Obviously, a right of first refusal is much weaker from the standpoint of the holder than an

**413** Art. 38 (2) Law 16/1985.

**414** Art. 38 (3) Law 16/1985.

**415** See for example in Greece, Art. 28 Act No. 3028/2002; Lebanon, Arrêté No. 166 LR. 7 November 1933.

**416** Art. 28 Act No. 3028/2002 on the Protection of Antiquities and Cultural Heritage.

**417** Art. 22 Decree No. 25 of 30 Nov 1937 (Decreto-Lei No. 25, de 30.11.1937, Organiza a proteção do patrimônio histórico e artistico nacional).

**418** Art. 26 (1) and 27 Law No. 3644 of 31 Dec 1982, no official translation was available, but see Pai Hyung, Nationalism and preserving Korea's buried past: the Office of Cultural Properties and archaeological heritage management in South Korea, Antiquity (1999), available via www.highbeam.com

**419** In common law, so far as there is any distinction between "pre-emption right" and "right of first refusal", a "right of first refusal" describes a preferential right to refuse an offer of sale at the price at which the grantor is willing to sell, whereas a "right of pre-emption" commonly denotes a preferential right to refuse to purchase at a fixed price, see Kevin Grey/S.F. Grey, Elements of Land Law, at 774; cp. also Birchahm & Co Nominees (2) Ltd. v Worrell Holdings Ltd (2001) 82 P & CR 427 at 31 per Chadwick LJ. For the purpose of this study, however, it has been thought useful to employ the term "pre-emption right" as the more general term as opposed to the notion of "right of first refusal".

**420** Phillip H Kenny, What is a Right of Pre-Emption? Conveyancer and Property Lawyer (2001) 295, at 296; Quentin Smyte, Pre-Empting the Problem, at 11.

option: it does not set the price for the asset in advance, and it allows the owner of the asset to decide whether and when to sell or lease. The grantee of a right of first refusal is clearly not entitled to compel any transfer. The decision whether to sell at all lies within the discretion of the grantor of the right.[421]

Such a system of pre-emption can be found in *Italy*, where the owner may enter into an agreement of sale with a third party but is later constrained to notify the state about the deed's exact conditions.[422] Every time an antiquity is to be sold, the seller or the buyer are bound to inform the ministry within 30 days from the conclusion of the contract. The state then either accepts the original contract or it disagrees and exercises its right of pre-emption. According to Art. 60 (1) Code of the Cultural and Landscape Heritage 2004, it is then entitled to purchase the object by pre-emption at the price established in the deed of transfer.[423] But it is not bound by the clauses of the contract of sale.[424] In the case in which the Ministry exercises its right of pre-emption, the buyer is entitled to rescind the agreement with the seller.[425] The state has to notify the seller and the buyer about its intention to exercise the right of preemption within sixty days of receipt of the contract.[426] Upon notification, ownership to the object automatically passes to the state. While the time limit of sixty days is pending, the effects of the deed of transfer between the seller and the third party are suspended until the exercise of pre-emption occurs and the seller is forbidden to carry out delivery of the heritage item.[427] When the seller does not wish to accept the assessment established between him and the state, the monetary value of the object is being determined by a third party, designated by agreement between the seller and the state exercising pre-emption. Although the Italian system is characterised as a preemption right, the fact, that the seller can enter an agreement with a potential buyer before the state exercises that right, makes it seem more like a mechanism of expropriation. By entering the agreement, the buyer becomes the new owner with the consequence that any subsequent involvement of the state should be treated as a quasi-expropriation

**421** A right of first refusal operates thus as a "negative covenant on the part of the vendor not to part with his interest in the object until the first opportunity to purchase is accorded to the covenantee", see Canadian Long Island Petroleums Ltd v Irving Industries Ltd. (1975) 50 DLR (3d) 265 at 279, as well as, Dear v Reeves [2002] Ch 1, 43.

**422** Section II Code of the Cultural and Landscape Heritage 2004, Articles 60 and 61.

**423** Art. 60 (1).

**424** Art. 61 (5).

**425** Art. 61 (6).

**426** Art. 61 (1).

**427** Art. 61 (4).

### c. Right of First Negotiation

The weakest system of protection may be called "right of first negotiation".[428] It merely obliges the owner of a good to undergo exclusive good faith negotiations with the rights holder before negotiating with other parties.[429] It provides, that the owner must notify the holder of such a right that the owner intends to sell or lease his or her property. The parties then have a specified period of time in which to negotiate, on an exclusive basis, a mutually acceptable deal. A right of first negotiation does not give the holder of the right any assurance that the parties will reach final agreement on the price and terms for the transaction.[430] If the exclusive negotiation period lapses without an agreement on price and terms, the owner generally is free to sell or lease the property to a third party free and clear of the rights of the holder of the first-negotiation right.

Many cultural property codes stipulate that the owner concerned by the pre-emption right has to give the government an opportunity to make an offer for the antiquity, but he is not obliged to either make a sale offer to the state or to accept an offer made by the State, as in the previous examples. This mechanism for example exists in *Poland*. What is interesting about the Polish system is that it is not the state, which is entitled to exercise a right of pre-emption, but the museum entities themselves.[431] According to the Museum Act 1996, museums are public bodies (fiscal institutes), but they are not necessarily state-owned. Art. 20 of the Act provides that registered museums shall be entitled to a pre-emptive right to purchase artworks from entities whose activity is based on offering artwork items for sale within 14 days of the date on which the museum declares the intention to buy the objects. [432] The wording of the statute suggests that the right of pre-emption is only activated when a sale offer already exists. The museum becomes an alternative contracting partner and can obtain ownership of the object in question by accepting the seller's offer according to Art. 15 Polish Civil Code

**428** Indeed, the notion stems from real estate law, but it has been thought usefull to adopt the term for the purpose of this research. See e.g. Paul S. Rutter/ Duane M. Montgomery, Options, Rights of First Refusal, Rights of First Negontiation and Rights of First Offer-A Guide Through the Maze, California Real Estate Journal (1999) 1.

**429** Cp. P. Rutter/ D. Montgomery, at 3.

**430** Cp. P. Rutter/D. Montgomery, at 3.

**431** In Poland, museums are governed by the Museum Act of 21.11.1996 (ustawa o muzeach, Dz. U. z 1997 r Nr. 5 poz. 24 ze zm.) and the Act on the Organisation and Adminstration of Cultural Activities 2001 (ustawa o organizowaniu i prowadzeniu działalności kulturalnej, tekst jedn. Dz. U. z 2001 r. Nr 13, poz. 123 ze zm.). The current 2001 Museum Act partly contains of provisions stemming from the old Act on the protection of Cultural Property and Museums 1962 enacted by the polish socialistic regime.

**432** Art. 20 (1) Museum Act 1996.

(PCC). In case, no sales offer previously existed, the pre-emption right is not activated. The museum thus cannot force the seller to submit an offer. In this context, a useful tool in Polish law is Art. 543 Polish Civil Code which stipulates that exhibiting a priced heritage item accounts for a sales offer.[433] The entity submitting the sales offer to the museum does not necessarily have to be the owner of the heritage item, but an intermediary or a commissioner. The seller of the object however must be a person whose commercial activity is based on offering artwork for sale, which considerably narrows down the scope of the pre-emption right. The museum has to notify the seller about its interest in the object within 14 days and accordingly is entitled to acquire the item for the price contained in the sales offer. By declaring its interest in the object the museum can practically inhibit the possibility of third parties to accept the sellers offer. In case the object is offered at a public auction, Art. 20 (2) provides that the museum is entitled to buy the item at the bid out price. Art. 20 only provides that the museum has the right to become the exclusive contracting partner but the seller is not obliged to conclude the agreement with the specific museum. The Act does not provide for any rules for the situation that the seller delivers the object to a third party contrary to the museums pre-emptive right. Polish academics however contend that the sale of a heritage item in violation of the museum's exclusive right to acquire the object by selling it to a third party renders the latter contract null and void, according to the general principles of Polish civil law.[434] In the event, the museum does not show any interest in the object within 14 days, the seller is free to divest of the object as he wishes. In consequence, this model is a very weak mechanism to acquire cultural property in order for it to be included in public collections.

Conversely, in *Argentina*, the owner is not obliged to sell the object to the state. If however, he refuses to do so, the state is entitled to expropriate the owner, if the object is of exceptional value to the heritage.[435]

---

**433** By comparison, advertisements and price tags are considered to be an "invitatio ad offerendum" – an invitation to the potential buyer to make an offer, Art. 71 PCC.

**434** Art. 54 Polish Civil Code. See also S. Grzybowski, Prawo Ciwilne, (Warsaw 1986), at 269; Z. Radwanski, System Prawa Cywilnego, t. I, at 522 and System Prawa Prywatnego, t. II, Prawo Cywilne – Czesc Ogolna, (Warsaw 2002), at 224.

**435** Art. 19, 21 Decreto No. 81.005 de 1941 (Dicta el reglamento de la Comision Nacional de Museos y de Monumentos y Lugares Históricos (Boletin Oficial 28/2/1941).

### 3. The Proprietary Nature of Options and Pre-Emption Rights

If the state has a statutory pre-emption right and has exercised it, it achieves title to the heritage item subject to the possibility that the owner or possessor did not have title himself. If then the object is being removed from the state's territory, the state has a proprietary interest in the heritage item and thus a claim to recover the item. As a pre-emption right is only a contingent right of ultimate possession, in the sense that it is entirely dependent on a future contingency which is uncertain -the grantor may never decide to sell the property- it is very questionable whether the pre-emption right grants the sovereign a property interest in the event the object is being sold and exported contrary to the state's right of pre-emption and before it could exercise that right and gain possession of the item in question.[436] The answer to this question may depend on whether the pre-emption mechanism the state operates grants the state an option, a right of first refusal or a right of first negotiation.

In *England*, for example, it is widely believed that an exclusive option to purchase granted by contract gives the option holder an equitable interest in the object, particularly if the object had been performed by a decree of specific performance.[437] Even before it is exercised the option confers upon the grantee a so-called "equitable interest"[438] in the item in question.[439] The full interest in the object passes to the purchaser on the exercise of the option followed by completion of the transaction.[440]

---

**436** The state does not have a right of immediate possession, as pre-emption rights are only contingent rights of ultimate possession.

**437** See London South Western Railway Co v Gomm (1822) 20 Ch D 562, at 581 per Jessel MR; Armstrong & Holmes Ltd v Holmes [1993] 1 WLR 1482, at 1488; Spiro v Glencrown Properties Ltd [1991] Ch. 537 at 544, per Hoffmann J.

**438** An *equitable interest* is an interest in property originally recognised by the English Court of Chancery, as distinct from legal interests recognised in the common-law courts. It arose in cases when it was against the principles of equity for a person to enforce a legal right, cp. Introduction to English law, William Geldart/David Yardley (11th ed. 1995). Today, in common law, an equitable interest is an "interest held by virtue of an equitable title (a title that indicates a beneficial interest in property and that gives the holder the right to acquire formal legal title) or claimed on equitable grounds, ", cp. Black's Law Dictionary (2nd Pocket ed. 2001), at 361. One example for an equitable interest is the institute of trust, whereby one person (the trustee) holds property, for the benefit of another person (the beneficiary). Here, the trustee holds a legal interest and the beneficiary holds an equitable interest, cp. for example, D. Hayton/ C. Mitchell, The Law of Trusts and Equitable Remedies (12th ed. 2005), at para. 1–01 to 1–04;

**439** See for example Stephens v Gulf Oil Canada Ltd (1976) 65 DLR (3d) 193, at 215; London & Blenheim Estates Ltd. v Ladbroke Retail Parks [1992] 1 WLR 1278, at 1282.

**440** See London and South Western Railway Co v Gomm (1882) 20 Ch. D. 562 at 581, per Jessel MR.

Conversely, there has been an extensive debate in recent years, concerning the proprietary status of rights of first refusal,[441] which according to Kenny, have the "odd floating position between a contractual right and a proprietary right".[442] The grantor of a right of first refusal is under no positive obligation to sell. He is only under a negative obligation to refrain from selling the property without first giving the grantee the opportunity to purchase it in preference to any other buyer. The grantee is free to accept or reject the offer as he chooses. Until the grantor decides to sell there is only a possibility or hope that the grantee might have an interest. For many years, it was also believed that this mere possibility or hope is insufficient to amount to either a thing in action or a future or contingent interest and that accordingly, a right of first refusal confers insufficient property in the object in order to qualify its recipient as an owner of an equitable entitlement capable of protection. In *Pritchard v Briggs*[443], an English case concerning the question whether the right of first refusal could be registered as a land charge, it was stressed that this right does not of itself create an equitable interest since it amounts merely to a positive obligation to make an offer to sell to the landlord before the leasehold interest is disposed of to anyone else.[444] This analysis is probably correct in reflection for the highly contingent nature of the unfructified right of first refusal, but was later reversed in a different case

**441** For an overview see e.g. Marc Pawlowski, Rights of Pre-Emption, Lord & Tenant Law Review (2004) 39; Phillip H Kenny, What is a right of pre-emption? Conveyancer and Property Lawyer (2001) 295; Quentin Smyte, Pre-Empting the Problem, 109 Property Law Journal (2003) 10. Concerning Land Law, much of the controversy surrounding the right of pre-emption has now been removed, with prospective force, by the Land Registration Act 2002, see LRA 2002, section 115(1)–(2).

**442** H. Kenny, What is a right of pre-emption, at 296.

**443** [1980] 1 Ch. 338 at 418, per Templeman LJ and 423b, per Stephenson LJ.

**444** To this extent, a right of pre-emption is distinguishable from an option to purchase. For American law see e.g. Stuart Kingston v. Robinson, 596 A.2d 1378, 1383–1384 (Del. 1991) ("Although the rule is most often applied in the construction of testamentary devices, it applies equally to rights of first refusal, also known as preemptive rights, to acquire interests in land. Despite the view of some courts that preemptive rights are merely contract rights and not direct interests in property, a vast majority of courts and commentators view such rights as equitable claims sufficient to support an action for specific performance if the property owner attempts to sell to someone other than the owner of the right of first refusal. Because the holder of the right of first refusal acquires merely an equitable interest, it remains inchoate until the owner decides to sell thus triggering the right of first refusal"), or, Lake of the Woods Assoc. v. McHugh, 380 S.E.2d 872, 874 (Va. 1989) (rejecting a request to treat first-refusal provision as procedural right that could be saved by application of "wait and see" doctrine). But for a different view see Murphy Exploration & Prod. Co. v. Sun Operating Ltd. Pshp., 747 So. 2d 260, 265 (Miss. 1999).

called *Deer v Reeves*.[445] The issue in this case was whether a right of first refusal belonging to a bankrupt was property which vested as part of the bankruptcy estate at the commencement of the bankruptcy pursuant to section 283 and section 436 of the Insolvency Act 1986. As opposed to *Pritchard v Briggs*, the English Court of Appeal in *Deer v Reeves* held that a right of first refusal was sufficiently proprietary to vest property in a trustee in bankruptcy, at least for the purposes of the 1986 Insolvency Act. The CA stated that the right had a distinguishing feature of a right of property in that it was assignable and that, although it might be difficult to put a value on a right of first refusal since the grantor might never decide to sell the property, it was not necessary for a right to have any present or immediate value for it to be "property" within section 436 in the 1986 Act.[446] Furthermore, the CA found that a right of first refusal was indeed a "thing in action" since there existed a negative obligation not to sell the property to anyone without first making an offer to the grantee which would not exist but for the deed of pre-emption and, in the event of a decision by the grantor to sell the property, the obligation was enforceable by legal action by the grantee or his assignee for an injunction to restrain sale of the property to another person until the grantor had first made an offer to the grantee and the grantee had failed or refused to take it up.[447] Finally, the CA held that a right of first refusal could properly be described as an "interest" which was "future ... contingent ... [and] incidental to, property" within the meaning of section 436 of the Insolvency Act and consequently a right of first refusal was therefore "property". [448]

Despite of the interesting development in *Deer v Reeves*, for the purpose of international cultural property law, it must be assumed that a right of first refusal is too uncertain a right in order to be awarded the stability of a property right for it to be enforceable in a foreign court before it has actually been exercised by the state. But considering the interpretation of the proprietary interest of the Iranian provisions in the *Barakat*-case[449] and the recent developments in Cultural Property Law, a pre-emption right may be treated as a contingent interest in property for the purpose of enforcement under the patrimonial interest, if it does provide for a specific degree of certainty.

The proprietary nature of a pre-emption right could also depend on its legal consequence provided within the statutory framework. If the pre-emption provisions give rise to a confiscation right or even an automatic forfeiture, they may be

**445** [2001] EWCA Civ 277.
**446** Deer v Reeves, ibid, at para. 10, per May LJ
**447** Deer v Reeves, ibid, at 41.
**448** Deer v Reeves, ibid, at 42.
**449** [2007] EWHC 705 (QB); [2008] 1 All ER 1177; QB 22 [2009].

considered proprietary for the purpose of enforcement of cultural property rights. In most jurisdictions, transactions which violate a state's pre-emption right will be proclaimed null and void, but they do not give rise to the confiscation of the object nor do they vest ownership of the object in the state upon its violation. Some countries however do provide for a confiscation right on behalf of the state in case the object is sold without having notified the government.[450] In some countries, the violation of a pre-emption right even entails the automatic forfeiture to the state, as is the case e.g. in *Bangladesh.*[451]

### 4. Pre-Emption Rights and the ECHR

Pre-emption rights were put to the test as to whether they are compatible with the European Convention of Human Rights in *Beyeler v Italy.*[452] There, the European Court of Human Rights examined to what extent a state may rely on a right of pre-emption and which measures it may take to control the sale of art by means of pre-emption rights. The main question was whether the pre-emption right excercised by the Italian government did violate the right of peaceful enjoyment of possession as codified in Art 1 of the Protokol No. 1 of the European Convention of Human Rights.[453]

The case involved a painting by Vincent Van Gogh, "Portrait of a young Peasant", which Beyeler bought in 1977 for 600 million lire (300.000 Euros) through an intermediary without disclosing his identity to the vendor. The Italian Cultural Property Statute which was in force until 2004, Law No. 1089 of 1939, required that any transaction transferring full or partial title or possession of a work of

**450** For example, *Brasil*, Art. 22 Decree No. 25 of Nov 1937; *Burkina Faso*, Art. 30 of Law No. 85–049 of 29 Aug 1985 (Ordonnance No 85–049 portant protection du Patrimonie culturel (1985); *Lybia*, Art. 56 lit a) and d) of Antiquities Law No. 40 1968; *Maroc*, Articles 53 and 55 Dahir No. 1–80–341 or Law 22–80 du 25 Dec 1980, and, in *Bahrain*, Art. 25 lit a) of the Bahrain Antiquities Ordinance 1970.

**451** Art. 9 (4) Antiquities Act 1968 (An Act to Consolidate and Amend the Law Relating to the Preservation and Protection of Antiquities, 12 Dec. 1986, Act No. 14 of 1968.

**452** Beyeler v Italy (Application No 33202/96) [2000] ECHR 1; (2001) 33 EHRR 52; (2003) 36 EHRR 5; [2002] ECHR 466, available at http://www.echr.coe.int/ECHR/EN/hudoc. For comments on the case, see Barbara T. Hoffmann, European Union Legislation Pertaining to Cultural Goods in: B.T. Hoffmann (ed.) Art and Cultural Heritage (2006) 191, at 193; Beate Rudolph, Beyerler v Italy, Am J. Int'l L, Vol. 94 No. 4 (Oct. 2000), pp. 736–740; Jan Sikuta/Eva Hubalkova, European Court of Human Rights, Case-Law of the Grand Chamber 1998–2006 (The Hague 2007) at 104; Marc André Renold, A Landmark Decision in Art Law by the European Court of Human Rights: Beyeler v Italy, 5 AAL (2000) 73.

**453** Note that the case has been decided under the old Italian Cultural Property Law Nr 89/1939, available at http://www.echr.coe.int/eng/Judgments.htm

art had to be declared to the Ministry of Cultural heritage.[454] Consequently, the declaration of sale, which the vendor filed with the Italian ministry of Cultural Heritage in accordance with the requirements of Law No. 1089 did not mention Beyeler's name.[455]

The Italian government learned that Beyeler was the real purchaser of the painting in 1983, when Beyeler informed the Ministry that he intende to sell the painting to the Peggy Guggenheim Collection in Venice. He offered the painting to the state for $ 11 Million. The painting was ordered to be placed in temporary custody. Owing to the fact that Beyeler did not disclose his name in 1977, the Ministry claimed that the ownership of the paitning was uncertain. In 1988, it finally decided to exercise its right of pre-emption according to section 31 of Law 1089 however at the 1977 sale price of about 300.000 Euros.[456] The Italian Ministry declared that by failing to inform the Ministry of the 1977 sale, Beyeler violated Law No. 1089 and his title to the painting was void. The work of art was thus sold directly to Beyelers intermediary. As a result, the Ministry retained its right of pre-emption indefinitely under section 31 of the old 1939 law, and as a consequence exercised its right of pre-emption in relation to the sale of 1977 to the small price of 300.000 Euros instead of $ 11 million Euros.

Beyeler unsuccessfully challenged this decision through all Italian instances. In front of the Corte Constituzionale, he claimed that section 31 of Law 1939 was unconstitutional. But the court found against him on the premise that the special nature of cultural objects justified their being treated differently from other property.[457] It also underlined the punitive character of section 61 of the 1939 law, which confers an indefinite character of a right of pre-emption.

Before the European Court of Human Rights, Beyeler alleged that the facts of the case constituted a violation of the protection of property guaranteed by Art. 1 of Protocol No. 1 of the European Convention of Human Rights. Art. 1 provides that:

---

**454** § 30 of the former Italian Law No. 1089.

**455** The Van Gogh had to be declared as it had been registered as a work of special artistic interest in 1954 and was thus covered by the 1939 law.

**456** Sections 31(1) and 32(1) of the old Law No. 1089 of 1939 provided that the Ministry may exercise a right of pre-emption over the work within two months from the date of the declaration referred to above, at the agreed price as set out in the deed of transfer if the transfer is for value (section 31(1): "*Nel caso di alienazione a titolo oneroso, il Ministro per l'educazione nazionale ha facoltà di acquistare la cosa al medesimo prezzo stabilito nell'atto di alienazione*"; section 32(1): "*Il diritto di prelazione deve essere esercitato nel termine di mesi due dalla data della denuncia*").

**457** For the judgment of the Corte constituzionale, June 14 1995, No. 269, see Foro It.1996, I. 807, 809–11.

> Every natural or legal person is entitled to the peaceful enjoyment of his possession. No one shall be deprived of his possession except in the public interest and subject to the conditions provided by law by the general principle of International law.
> The proceeding provisions shall not, however, in any way impair the right of a State to enforce such laws as it deems necessary to control the use of property in accordance with the general interest or to secure the payment of taxes or other contributions or penalties.[458]

Beyeler's primary claim was for restitution of the painting. In addition, he claimed compensation for the damage sustained as a result of the length of time for which he had been deprived of the treasure and the consequent loss of use of the amount he would have received had it been possible to perform the contract signed with the Guggenheim Foundation in 1988.[459] The court in *Beyeler* held that the exercise of the Italian right of pre-emption was an interference with Beyeler's right to the peaceful enjoyment of his possession but the nature of the violation did not allow for the restitution of the property. Instead, Beyeler would be compensated for the loss sustained as a result of being paid a considerably lower price for the Van Gogh than he was entitled to.

As Italy did not recognise Beyeler's title to the painting, due to the violation of Law No. 1089, the first question to be answered by the court was whether Beyeler had a property interest that was protected under Art. 1 of the Protocol. The court observed that the term possession has an autonomous meaning under the ECHR which is independent of national laws.[460] The court pointed to several indications proving that Italy had recognised Beyeler's proprietary interest in the Van Gogh. For example, the Ministry had twice informed him of its interest in acquiring the painting. Moreover, it had granted him permission to move the work to Venice. Additionally, Beyeler had been allowed to inspect the painting and was given the right to access it while it was in temporary custody. The court considered it irrelevant that the proprietary interest was revocable under certain circumstances through the exercise of the state's pre-emption right. It concluded that the Van Gogh was Beyeler's "possession" in the sense of Art. 1. The exercise of the right of pre-emption thus constituted an interference with that right.

After finding that the Van Gogh was Beyeler's possession under Art. 1 of the Protocol, the court then went on to consider whether the exercise of Italy's pre-emption right struck a "fair balance" between the "demands of the general inter-

---

**458** Protocol to the Convention on the protection of Human Rights and Fundamental Freedoms, Mar. 20 (1952 Art.1, 213 UNTS 262.

**459** His total claim amounted to more than 14.000.000 Euros.

**460** It referred to the case Gasus Dosier-und Födertechnik v Netherlands, 306-BEur.Ct.H.R. (ser. A) 46, at 53 (1995).

est of community" and the "requirement of the protection of the individual's fundamental rights".[461] In determining this proportionality the ECHR weighed Beyeler's dishonest behaviour in deliberately withholding his identity in order to prevent the right of pre-emption against the Ministries conduct in having waited for five years to act after learning that Beyeler had been the end purchaser in the 1977 sale. The court concluded that the Italian authorities had derived an unjust enrichment, as the delayed exercise of pre-emption regarding the 1977 sale had permitted the state to make a "good deal" and acquire the valuable treasure at a price considerably below its market value, and that such an unjust enrichment was incompatible with the requirement of a "fair balance" within the meaning of Art. 1 of the Protocol. Italy's conduct thus violated Art. 1 of No. 1 of the ECHR.[462] The court decided that Beyeler should be compensated for the loss sustained as a result of being paid a lower price, without any adjustment and that Beyeler should be compensated for the legal costs he had incurred between 1984 and 1988 in determining his ownership in regard to the painting.[463] The court's reasoning implies that the measures taken might have conformed to the Convention if Italy had exercised the pre-emptive right to obtain the painting earlier. It pointed out that the right of pre-emption was not unlawful as such. The court furthermore recognised that a state enjoys a wide margin of appreciation when determining the general interest". The reference to the UNESCO Convention in this context – an unexpectedly positive aspect of the judgment- indicates that the court will consider international law in determining the limits of a state's discretion in exercising a pre-emption right.

### 5. Pre-Emption or Expropriation

Instead of a pre-emption right, some countries choose to retain valuable cultural objects which are sold on the market or which are about to be exported by expropriating the object on behalf of the state. However, the difference between a pre-emption right and an expropriation is difficult to determine. In both cases, the owner of an antiquity is restricted in the peaceful enjoyment of his

461 Beyeler v Italy (Appl No. 33202/96) [2002] ECHR 466, at 107.

462 Beyeler v Italy (Appl. No. 33202/96) [2002] ECHR 466, at 117. There was no need to give a separate ruling on the question whether Beyeler had suffered discriminatory treatment contrary to Artcile 14 of the ECHR and no separate issue arose under Article 18 ECHR.

463 According to Article 41 of the Convention, the Court "shall afford just satisfaction to the injured party, if it finds that there has been a violation of the Convention or the protocols hereto, and it the internal law of the High Contracting Party concerned allows only partial reparation to be made". Cp also Beyeler v Italy (Appl. No. 33202/96) [2002] ECHR 466, at 130.

possession, as he is unable to freely dispose of his property as he pleases. Under the term 'freely disposing of his property', it is understood that the owner cannot choose his contract partner and sometimes has to deliver to different conditions than initially intended.

Characteristic for an expropriation right is the power of the government to divest of or dispossess an owner of his property through the exertion of a sovereign right and upon the payment of an adequate compensation.[464] On the other hand, where an owner becomes the subject of a pre-emption right, the state is entitled by statute to conclude a private agreement or contract.

An indicator for a pre-emption right may be the fact that the state has to meet the conditions of the contract or sales agreement between the owner and the hypothetical buyer of an antiquity as is the case in *Brasil*[465], *Burkina Faso*[466] *Morocco*[467] or in the *Netherlands*[468] or in *Spain*[469], *Tunisia*,[470], or similarly, a relatively flexible price determination.

Some states, for example, stipulate that the price for the heritage item has to be negotiated between the state and the owner of the object. In case, mutual consent cannot be achieved, the price may be set by an independent export committee or even the court as is the truth for *Chile*[471], *Mauretania*,[472] and *the Netherlands*.

Where the pre-emption right correlates with an export prohibition, in most cases, the price to be paid by the government will match the value of the object that has been the subject of the export licence or the market value of the object. In *Canada*[473], *Denmark*[474] or *Turkey*[475], the price will be determined by an expert committee.

---

**464** M. Plutschow, Vorkaufsrechte, at 37.

**465** Art. 22, Decreto-lei No. 25, de 30.11 1937, Organiza a protecao do patrimonio historico e artistico national

**466** Art. 19, Ordonnance No. 85–049 portant protection du Patrimonie culturel (1985).

**467** Art. 41 Dahir No. 1–80–341, 25 December 1980.

**468** Paragraph 11, of the Dutch Cultural Heritage Preservation Act 1984.

**469** Art. 38 of Spanish Cultural Property Law of 1985 and Art. 1521 Spanish Civil Code.

**470** Law No. 94–35 (24 Feb. 1994) Code concerning the protection of the Archaeolgical, Historical and Artistic Heritage ( Journal Officiel No. 17 du ler mars 1994, 355).

**471** Law No. 17288 of January 1970 (no engl. Translation available. The text can be found in UNESCO (ed), The Protection of Movable Cultural Property, Paris 1984, at 86).

**472** Law No. 72 160 of 31 July 1972 relative à la sauvegarde et à la mise en valeur du Patrimonie national, préhistorique et archéologique .

**473** Art. 29 Cultural Property Export and Import Act 1985 (Consolidated Statutes of Canada, Chapter C-51).

**474** Art. 11 Act on the Protection of Cultural Assets in Denmark No. 404 (1987).

**475** Art. 30 Law No. 2863 (21.07.1983, Resmî Gazete Nr. 18113).

The question whether a pre-emption right at the same time constitutes an expropriation also has been subject of dispute in *Beyeler v Italy*[476].

Beyeler unsuccessfully challenged the Italian exertion of its pre-emption right before the administrative tribunal. The Consiglio di stato affirmed this judgment on appeal, holding that in the case of a defective declaration the state was entitled to exercise its right of pre-emption at any time and that the limitation period would have started to run only when a properly executed declaration was made. On further appeal, the Corte di Cassazione confirmed this reasoning but noted that the exercise of the right of pre-emption amounted to an expropriation. It expressed doubt about the constitutionality of the treatment of Beyeler since, in contract to that in a "ordinary" expropriation, his compensation did not reflect the actual value of the object at the time the pre-emption right was exercised.

The European Court of Human Rights however did not consider it necessary to examine the case under the second sentence of Article 1 (1), which is the rule expressly concerning expropriations. Because of the complex legal situation, the Court instead decided to examine the case under the general principle set forth in the first sentence of Article 1 (1), which guarantees the peaceful enjoyment of possession. By failing to analyse the case under the provisions of Protocol No. 1 on expropriation the Court reduced his judgment to a mere balancing of interest. This approach clearly deprived Beyeler of the special protection Art. 1, namely the entitlement to compensation in accordance with the "general principles of international law".

Although this difference was at the end not decisive in the case, the court set a precedent: the requirement that the amount of compensation due shall be balanced against other factors, opens the door to finding no fault with the expropriation of a foreign national's property even if no "prompt and adequate compensation will be paid, contrary to the rules of general international law".

## § 3. Mechanisms to Retain Ownership of Cultural Objects in the Public Domain

Some cultural property laws and statutory restrictions may convey the impression of a very liberal attitude towards a free circulation of heritage items, as

**476** Cp. above, Beyeler v Italy (Application No 33202/96) [2000] ECHR 1, (2001) 33 EHRR 52; (2003) 36 EHRR 5, [2002] ECHR 466.

does for example the *UK* system, or equally *Denmark*[477] or *the Netherlands.*[478] However, many jurisdictions employ mechanisms to retain cultural heritage which is already in their possession or ownership. They may be provisions prohibiting any legal transfer of title without the authorisation of public authorities or provisions on the de-accessioning of objects from museums which are state owned, with the consequence that their treasures can only be sold or divested of by governmental permission. Such provisions on restricting the trade in cultural property and antiquities do not create property rights upon their violation. Thus in the present situation most countries will not recognised foreign statutes on inalienability and therefore objects that have been obtained by violation of these laws may be validly sold outside their countries of origin and acquired in good faith.

## I. Objects Res Extra Commercium

Aside from fortuitously discovered cultural objects which are being declared to be state property through vesting legislation, many other items are in the property of the state, whether in museum collections, archives or national libraries. Sometime those objects subscribe to a special regime of protection. In several countries heritage items in public property may be subject to certain exception within the rules of private commerce. They are inalienable, imprescriptible and cannot be seized. They are objects *res extra commercium.*

'Inalienability' means that an object cannot be sold or otherwise be transferred by any legal transaction.[479] Any transfer of an inalienable object is void.[480] 'Imprescriptibility' refers to the owner's right of revindication. If an object qualifies as imprescriptible, its owner can at all times seek revindication of the object. Consequently, legal title to an object from the collection cannot be acquired by a good faith purchaser by means of legal transaction nor as a result of adverse possession.[481] On top of that, the action to revindication is not subject to any extinc-

**477** For an account of cultural property legislation in Denmark see Ditlev Tamm/Anne Ostrup, Danish Report, in: T.Kono/S.Wrbka, The Impact of Uniform Laws (2010) 297.

**478** For an account of Dutch cultural property legislation see K. Lubina, Dutch Report, in: T. Kono/S.Wrbka, The Impact of Uniform Laws (2010) 563.

**479** K. Siehr, Reforms and Developments, at 80; Amalie Weidner, Kulturgüter als res extra commercium (2001), at 10.

**480** K. Lubina, Contested Cultural Property, at 278.

**481** Julia El-Bitar, Der Schutz von Kulturgut als Res Extra Commercium in Frankreich (2006), at 182–183.

tive limitation period.[482] The owner of an object can at all times recover the object. Therewith, imprescriptibility prevents involuntary loss of title, even against a purchaser in good faith.[483] Furthermore cultural objects belonging to *res extra commercium* or the acquisition through adverse possession is excluded.

In *Italy*, for example, Art. 823 (1) of the Italian Civil Code reads: Property that forms part of the public domain (*domanio publico*) is inalienable and cannot be the object of rights in favour of third persons, except in the way and within the limits established by the laws concerning it.[484] The same is provided for by Art. 53 of the recently enacted Code of Cultural Property and Landscapes for cultural property that belongs to the state, the regions and other territorial public authorities and that compose the *state cultural domain.*[485]

Similarly in *Switzerland*, the Cultural Property Transfer Act 2003 amended Article 724 of the Swiss Civil Code which now states that "antiquities of scientific value may not be sold without the permission of the competent cantonal authorities, neither can they be acquired by adverse possession nor acquired by good faith. The claim to return the object is not subject to a statute of limitation."

Mexico's Federal Act of Archaeological, Artistic and Historic Monuments 1972 declares movables and immovable within Mexico to be the "inalienable and imprescriptible property of the nation".[486]

Such provisions on inalienable cultural objects prevent any legal transfer of title in the country of origin without any official authorisation by public authorities.

---

**482** M. Cornu, French Report, in T. Kono/S. Wrbka, The Impact of Uniform Laws (2009) 337, at 341; K. Lubina, Contested Cultural Property, at 277.

**483** Guido Carducci, La Restitution Internationale des Biens Culturels et des Objets d'Art (1997) at 64.

**484** Goods that form part of the domanio publico are defined by Art 822 Italian Civil Code. However, goods that are part of the domanio publico have to be distinguished from goods that are patrimonio indisponibile, that means, goods that are considered as patrimony of the State, and although not included within the concept of domanio publico, also cannot be used for purposes different from the public one to which they are devoted, except according to the modalities established by the specific laws dealing with them, see F. Lenzerini, Italian report, in T.Kono/S. Wrbka, The Impact of Uniform Laws, at 445.

**485** The concept of *state cultural domain* is more limited that the concept of public domain as it only includes those goods which are part of the state domain and at the same time qualify as cultural property pursuant to the Italian Cultural Heritage Code 2004. According to Lenzerini, the relationship between the two concepts corresponds to that existing between two concentric circles, in which the '*state cultural domain*' is the smaller one, which is embraced by the larger one, the 'State domain', see F. Lenzerini, ibid, at 445.

**486** Art. 27, Mexican Law of 1972, but see also Spain, Art. 44 Ley del Patrimonio Historico 1985.

An elaborate system of *res extra commercium* protection can be found in *France*. There, case law and academia has developed the doctrine on the *domaine public*.[487] The doctrine constitutes a specific regime of protection under French law for public property, which is not limited to objects of cultural relevance.[488] It differs between two categories of state property (domaine de l'Etat): the *domaine public* and the *domaine privé*. The legal consequence of an object belonging to the *domaine public* has been codified in Art. L.52 of the Code du Domaine de L'Etat: "property belonging to the domaine public is inalienable and imprescriptible." This provision is an exception to Art. 2279 of the French Civil Code, providing that possession of movable property gives title, and the registration provision allows the owner of a classified object to bring an action to recover possession at any time and against anyone, even a *bona fide* purchaser.

For a long time the doctrine has been based on customary law and the criteria that determine as to whether an object falls in the *domaine public* have been developed in case law[489]and academia from the nineteenth-century onwards.[490] With regard to public collections of cultural objects, however, which serve the public cause of preserving and exhibiting cultural objects on behalf of the public, their belonging to the domaine public is generally accepted.[491] However, not all cultural objects in State ownership fall in the *domaine public*: those objects, which do not strictly serve the public cause, e.g. cultural objects decorating or antique objects furnishing the buildings of the public authorities, fall in the *domaine privé*.[492]

---

**487** Especially Victor Proudhon, Traité du domaine public ou de la distinction des biens considérés principalement parrapport au domaine public (1833). The treaty is considered the birth hour of the domaine public doctrine.

**488** K. Lubina, Contested Cultural Property, at 271; M. Weber, Unveräusserliches Kulturgut, at 64; A. Weidner, Kulturgüter als res extra commercium, at 47.

**489** On the development of the domaine public in case law see e.g, B. Hervé, A quoi sert le domaine public mobilier, L'exemple des biens culturels, 1993 AJDA, 675; M. Weber, Unveräusserliches Kulturgut, at 69–75.

**490** J. Chatelain/F. Chatelain, Oeuvres d'art et objets de collection en droit français (1990) at 18.

**491** F. Chatelain, Rapport national sur le sujet 1. Liberté des musées de procéder à des transactions d'objets d'art, in: Briat, M./Freedberg, J., A. (eds.), International Sales of Works of Art: International Art Trade and Law (1991) 109, at 111; M. Cornu, Le droit culturel des biens – L'intérêt culturel juridiquement protégé, (1996) 476–477; Cour de Cassation, decision of 2.04.1963, at 486: "Les biens des etablissements public sont partie du domain public des lors que (...) leur conservation et presentatin au public sont l'objets meme du service public", J. Chatelain/F. Chatelain, (1990), at 18.

**492** J. El-Bitar, Der deutsche und der französische Kulturgüterschutz (2006), at 180.

In 2006, with the introduction of the General Code Regarding the Property of Public Entities[493] (hereinafter: "GCRPP"), certain aspects of the notion of the *domaine public* have been codified for cultural property. Art. L. 2112–1 GCRPP confirms the status of several (collections of) movable cultural objects as belonging to the *domaine public* by stating that they are "part of the movable public domain of the public entity owning property with a public interest from the perspective of history, art, archaeology, science or technology". Furthermore in 2004, the new French Cultural Heritage Law[494], introduced special provisions concerning the "Musée de France" collections.[495] According to Art. L. 441–1 of the Code du Patrimonie, the label "Musée de France" can be granted to national museums, as well as to museums belonging to other legal entities under public law or legal entities under private law with a charitable cause. Different from the *domaine public* outlined above which consists only of objects in public ownership (not including objects in the domaine privé), the label "Musée de France" can also be granted to entities under private law with charitable cause. A number of museums have automatically been designated as "Musée de France" by Art. L. 442–2 Code du Patrimonie. According to this provision, the national museums, classified museums (musées classés), as well as state museums whose status has been determined by executive order, qualify as "Musée de France" as of 5 January 2002. Other museums have to follow the designation procedure as outlined by Art. L. 422–1 Code du Patrimonie: as first step, the legal entity owning the collections has to make a formal application. The requirements that must be fulfilled are more stringent for collections owned by legal entities under private law with charitable cause in order to compensate for the lesser influence on the collection management by public authorities. The subsequent step consists of hearing the High Council (Haut Conseil) of the French Museums.[496] The hearing of the High Council is mandatory. The ultimate decision power lies with the Minister of Culture.

**493** Code général de la propriété des personnes publiques. The Code was established by Ordonnance 2006–460 (21 April 2006).

**494** Code du Patrimoine 2004. Available online at: http://www.legifrance.gouv.fr.

**495** The protection corresponds with the protection reviosly granted by Law No. 2002–05 relating to French Museum, Loi n°2002–5 du 4 janvier 2002 relative aux musées de France, JO 5 janvier 2002, page 305. The Law relating to French Museums was adopted to replace an earlier order whose application to museums of fine arts was considered too limited: Ordonnance n°45–1546 du 13 juillet 1945 modifiée portant organisation provisoire des musées des Beaux-Arts. Cp. Julia El-Bitar, Der deutsche und der französische Kultugüterschutz nach der Umsetzung der Kulturgüterrückgaberichtlinie (2006) at 43.

**496** Art. L. 430–1 Code du Patrimoine outlines the general composition of the High Council.

According to the first sentence of Art. L. 451–5 Code du Patrimonie "objects constituting collections of the Museums of France, and belonging to a legal personality under public law, are in the domaine public and are hence inalienable (...)".[497] The provision contributes to legal security by clearly stating that objects from the collections of publicly owned Musées de France cannot be sold or otherwise transferred by any legal transaction. It does not, however, change or extend the protection that had already been granted to the objects under the notion of the domaine public.[498]

Furthermore, Art. L. 451–3 of the Code du Patrimonie makes clear that collections of the Musées de France are imprescriptible. Together, the traits of inalienability and imprescriptibility render an object that belongs to the *domaine public* (res) extra commercium.[499] It is only after its de-classification from the domaine public that an object is no longer inalienable and imprescriptible and can be legally transferred.[500]

According to Art. L. 2311–1 CGPPP and Art. 451–10 Code du Patrimonie, objects in the domain public and especially the collections of the Musées de France are "insaissable", which means they cannot be seized or be subject to any levy of execution.[501] This prevents that private creditors seize heritage items in order to satisfy their pecuniary claims or in the belief of being the rightful owner of the item in question.

## II. Movable Cultural Objects dedicated for Public Use

### 1. The "öffentliche Dienstbarkeit"

Most countries decided not to adopt the theory of *domaine public* and objects which belong to the state or its administrative entities succumb to the ordinary rules of commerce, however, certain cultural objects, in private or public hands, may be dedicated for public use and subject to a specific regime of protection.[502] In *Germany*, for example, there is no express regulation which may declare cul-

**497** Art. L. 3111–1 GCPPP confirms the general rule with regard to objects in the domaine public, i.e that these objects are "inalienable and imprescriptible".

**498** Art. 2112–1 (sub 8) also certifies museums owned by public persons to belong to the domaine public.

**499** A. Weidner, Kulturgüter als res extra commercium, at 9.

**500** C. Debbasch, Droit administrative des biens (1994), at 101.

**501** J. El-Bitar, Der deutsche und der französische Kultugüterschutz nach der Umsetzung der Kulturrückgaberichtlinie, at 183.

**502** In this sence, such a legal regieme may be called "extra commerciality in a narrow sence", cp. Michael Anton, Zivilrecht-Guter Glaube im Internationalen Kunsthandel (2010), at 272.

tural property of importance as goods *res extra commercium*. Instead, property in public ownership, due to its special appropriation and public purpose,[503] may be charged with a kind of public servitude, that is a real property right and assigned to its legal successor in case the object is being sold or otherwise divested.[504] Such is the nature of the German doctrine of the *öffentlich-rechtliche Dienstbarkeit*, which constitutes an unwritten rule of German administrative law and for the purpose of this study is regarded to be a right *ipso iure*.[505]

Art objects, museum and library collections, as well as archives in publicly accessible facilities are counted among public property which may be charged with the "*öffentlich-rechtliche Dienstbarkeit*". The consequence of the "*Dienstbarkeit*" would be the owner's liability to acquiesce to any use of the object within the limit of its specific public purpose. This does not necessary mean that property charged with a "*Dienstbarkeit*" is exempt from private commerce. In contrary, such object can be sold, bought or encumbered, however under the premise that the chattel is charged with a real right, which grants the public body an immediate right of possession.[506] Good faith acquisition of the object without the servitude or the acquisition by adverse possession, however, is precluded.[507]

---

**503** In German, a so-called "Widmung", cp. e.g. P. Axer, Widmung als Schlüsselbegriff des Rechts der öffentichen Sachen: Zur Identität des Rechst der öffentlichen Sachen als Rechtsgebiet (1994), at 49 and 98 et seq.; Hans-Jürgen Papier, in: Enrichsen/Ehlers, Allgemeines Verwaltungsrecht – Recht der öffentlichen Sachen (13th ed. 2005), at 782–791; Oliver Lepsius, Besitz und Sachherrschaft im öffentlichen Recht (2002), at 143 et seq.

**504** A. Müller-Katzenburg, Internationale Standarts, at 76.

**505** A. Müller-Katzenburg, Internationale Standarts, at 76; K. Siehr, International Art Trade and the Law, at 66. Compare also the similar Italian concept of "patrimonio indisponibile", Marc Weber, Unveräusserliches Kulturgut, at 134 et seq.

**506** A. Müller-Katzenburg, Internationale Standarts, at 76; M. Anton, Guter Glaube im Internationalen Kunsthandel, at 278.

**507** This legal doctrine is called the "doctrine of modified private ownership", which is based on a dualistic concept of property. The object in question may be in private ownership but succumbs to a public servitude, cp. H-J. Papier, in: Enrichsen/Ehlers, Allgemeines Verwaltungsrecht – Recht der öffentlichen Sachen, at 782–791; P. Axer, Widmung als Schlüsselbegriff, at 49. Conversly, at the beginning of the last century, German public law championed the doctrine of "public ownership", which was developed according to the principle of the French domaine public. This doctrine followed the view that objects which succumbed to public possession where to the free disposal of public bodies and the rules of private law where not applicable to such objects, cp. Otto Mayer, Der gegenwärtige Stand der Frage des öffentlichen Eigentums, AöR 21 (1907) 499, at 502; Casjen Peters, Die Ersitzbarkeit von Gegenständen öffentlich–rechtlichen Eigentums in besonderer Beziehung auf Stücke aus Archiven des Staates oder anderer öffentlich-rechtlicher Körperschaften in Preussen, in VerwArch 24 (1916) 167, at 170.

The doctrine has been tested in the infamous *Hamburg Stadtsiegel-case,*[508] which was fought before both, the civil and administrative courts. The case concerned the recovery of an antique seal belonging to the City of Hamburg that had been stolen from the archives of the city during the war, and later sold by auction to a bona fide purchaser. The seal had been used for sealing documents as early as 1306 and was kept in the city archives from 1820 onwards. The City of Hamburg turned to both, the civil and administrative court, to recover the seal from its possessor:

In front of the civil courts, the city requested the return of the seal on the grounds that the dedication of the seal by the public authorities for public use never ceased to exist and consequently, an acquisition in good faith according to §§ 935, 936 German Civil Code (BGB), or an acquisition based on adverse possession according to § 947 German Civil Code, was precluded.[509] The court of first instance in Cologne rejected this proposition on the grounds that the principle of good faith acquisition in German law "beyond any doubt overrides the *öffentliche Dienstbarkeit.* [510] The German Federal Supreme Court (BGH) followed the first instance Courts' reasoning. It rejected the idea of *res extra commercium* in German law in holding that objects may be charged with a public servitude due to its special appropriation and public purpose, but this does not exempt them from private commerce, and good faith acquisition of such objects as well as adverse possession is possible.[511]

Hamburg then turned to the administrative courts for the return of the seal.[512] The central question of the case was the city's civil suit for recovery based on the ground that the seal was an object dedicated for a public purpose. The city claimed that due to this public purpose it holds a public claim in conversion which is recognised in German customary law. The trial court gave judgment for the City of Hamburg. It stated that according to the "doctrin of modified private ownership",[513] which allows for the private ownership of objects in public

---

**508** For a detailed accunt of the case, cp. Michael Anton, Guter Glaube in Internationalen Kunsthandel, at 276–286; Gerrit Manssen, Der Hamburger Stadtsiegelfall, JuS (1992) 745; P. Axer, Das Hamburger Stadtsiegel – ein Problem des Rechts der öffentlichen Sachen, NWVBl. (1992) 354; Anette Hipp, Schutz von Kulturgütern in Deutschland (2000), at 355 et seq.

**509** The German Civil Code permits for the good faith acquisition of stolen goods at public auction, see Sec. 935 German Civil Code.

**510** LG Köln 25 Feb. 1988 [8 O 473/87]; OLG Köln 2 Nov 1988 2 U 52/88.

**511** BGH 9. Zivilsenat, Judgment of 5 October 1988 2 U 52/88. Az: IX ZR 265/88; MDR 1990, 238; JA (1990) 128; JuS (1990) 441.

**512** Adminstrative Court (VG) Köln NJW (1991) 2584; Appelate Court (OVG) Münster NJW (1993) 2635; Federal Administrative Court (BVerwG) NJW (1994) 144.

**513** Cp. above, note 507.

possession, objects which are dedicated for public use may be acquired by private individuals only subject to the condition that they are charged with a real right. Based on this principle, German customary law grants the public body a claim in conversion based on its immediate right of possession stemming from the *öffentliche Dienstbarkeit.*[514]

On appeal, the decision was reversed by the superior administrative court on the ground that no statutory rule existed which would allow for a dedication of the seal for public use. As the court pointed out, such a dedication cannot be substituted by custom or case law.[515] Dogmatically, this result is correct according to German law. Because Germany allows for private ownership of cultural property, a claim in conversion by a public entity against a private owner which is not based on codified legal authority, constitutes a gross infringement of Art. 1 of the European Convention of Human Rights 1998 (ECHR), which provides that every natural or legal person is entitled to the peaceful enjoyment of his possessions. According to Art. 20 II of the German Constitution[516], such an interference with the private owner's property right deriving from the ECHR requires a direct authorisation of the German parliament.[517] Hence, a revindication claim can only be successful, if the dedication of the property as a *öffentlich-rechtliche Dienstbarkeit* is based on legal authorisation deriving from public law. Additionally, even if it does derive from public law, the statute must be compliant with the European Convention of Human Rights. Ergo, a heritage item charged with the *Dienstbarkeit* that is based on direct legal authorisation by a public statute can be subject to an immediate right of possession of the German state, within the limits of its dedication. As opposed to *France*, where the extra commerciality of cultural property has found a codified legal authorisation in the Code du Patrimonie 2004, so far, no such authorisation exists in German cultural property law. The enactment of a provision which would allow for a dedication of cultural property for public use failed due to difficulties in solving who has the leg-

**514** In German, a so-called "öffentlich-rechtlicher Herausgabeanspruch".

**515** Federal Administrative Court (BVerwG) NJW (1994) 144.

**516** Grundgesetz – German Constitution.

**517** Anette Hipp, Schutz von Kulturgütern, at 364; J. El-Bitar, Der Schutz von Kulturgut als res extra commercium in Frankreich: Ein Vorbild für Deutschland? In: Im Labyrinth des Rechst? Wege zum Kulturgütershcutz, Koordinierungsstelle für Kulturgutverluste (ed.) (2007) 173, at 188; Reinhard Mussgnug, Museums- und Archivgut als res extra commercium? in: Dolzer R./ Jayme E./Mussgnug R. (eds.) Rechtsfragen des internationalen Kulturgüterschutzes (1994) 199, at 200. See also Art 1 II of the ECHR which states that "no one shall be deprived of its possessions except in the public interest and subject to the conditions provided for by law (..)."

islative competence to formulate this provision.[518] Given that the German legislator would enact a provision allowing for the dedication of cultural property for public use, theoretically, public bodies may be granted a claim in conversion for cultural objects on the grounds of the *öffentlichen Dienstbarkeit.*

### 2. The "dominio eminente"

The notion of the German "*öffentliche Dienstbarkeit*" can be compared to the Ecuadorian "*dominio eminente del estado*".[519]

According to the Law of Ecuador archaeological objects form part of the "patrimnio cultural de la nación".[520] This does not mean that these objects are public property. They may be private property charged with the limitation of a "*dominio fiscal o eminente*".[521]

Although private parties may own pieces of "*patrimonio cultural de la nación*" they cannot make a transfer without permission of the Cultural Institute of Ecuador.[522] The State always keeps an immediate right of possession to recover the chattel in order to display it on its territory. The imposition with a *dominio eminente* never expires and precludes the good faith acquisition of the object free of the real right.[523]

In *Casa della Cultura Ecuadoriana v Danusso.*[524], the *dominio eminente* has already been the subject of a claim in front of the Italian *Tribunale di Torino.* The claim concerned the recovery of some Ecuadorian antiquities that were sold in Ecuador in breach of the "*dominio eminente*". At that time, the language of the Ecuadorian law fell short of claiming ownership of all antiquities and was

518 Cp. J. El-Bitar, Der Schutz von Kulturgut als res extra commercium in Frankreich, at 191; R. Mussgnug, Museums- und Archivgut als "res extra commercium"?, at 201 et seq.

519 K. Siehr, International Art Trade, at 83.

520 Art. 58 of the Constitution of Ecuador of 1967.

521 Art. 623 of the Civil Code of Ecuador. See also Nicolás Granja Galindo, Fundamentos de derecho administrativo (Quito 1984) at 388 and 468.

522 Note however that Ecuador also provides for state ownership of all artefacts. Art. 7 of Law Nr 3501/1979 proclaims that property included in the catalogue also provided by Art. 7 to be the property belonging to the cultural heritage of the state. However private ownership of antiquities so far is still permitted as it is stated in Art. 11 of the law: "The declaration which confers the status of property belonging to the Cultural Heritage of the Nation as stipulated in Art. 7 of this Act, shall not deprive its owner of the exercise of ownership right over this property, within the limit laid down by the present Act."

523 Leonardo Rivas Cadena, Derecho Civil, Bd I (Quito 1974), 140.

524 Tribunale di Torino 25 march 1082, 18 Rivista di dritto internazionale privato e processuale, at 625 (1982). An extensive discussion of the case scan be found in Manlio Frigo, La protezione dei beni culturali nel dritto internazionale (1986), at 315 et seq.

interpreted by the Italian Court to create the "dominio eminente". The court concluded that he defendant could not acquire legal title from the sellers and the Ecuadorian government had a valid claim for the recovery of the chattels. It gave judgment for the Ecuadorian government. The original owner remains the owner of the artefact but the Republic of Ecuador can make use of the artefacts as *dominio cultural de la nación.*[525]

## III. Restrictions on Disposal

### 1. De-accession Provisions

Although they are not charged with the status o being *res extra commercium*, in some jurisdictions, national museum collections are subject to restrictions on the deaccession[526] of cultural objects. For example in the UK, restrictions on disposal of cultural property in the ownership of public bodies arise from museum governing statutes, or equally from the Law of Trust and the Law of Charity.[527]

#### a. Arising from Trust

The institute of "trust" is unique to the Common Law System and is a creation of equity consisting of a relationship based on fiduciary confidence between the trustee and the beneficiary.[528] Created by legal instrument, a trust vests legal title to the property in the trustee who is bound to administer the property for the benefit of the beneficiary who has equitable or beneficial property in accord-

---

**525** Cp. K. Siehr, International Art Trade, at 83.

**526** The notion "de-accession" refers to the procedure to remove an object from a public collection. It has been mainly used in the United State as referring to the "removal of an entry from the accessions register of a museum, library, etc., usually in order to sell the item concerned. For a long time, the word 'de-accession' did not appear in any dictionary, but it has now found a place in the Concise Oxford English Dictionary (The Oxford English Dictionary, 11th ed. 2009). There the meaning given is: "officially remove (an item) from a museum or art gallery in order to sell it". As for today, it has been adopted as a general term by the museum sector, for example, in the ITAP Report, 2000, at para. 166). The definition presupposes that the object in question was once accessioned and that it was formally accepted and recorded as an object worthy of collection status. See. also Marie C. Malaro, A legal Primer on Managing Museum Collections (2nd ed. 1998), at 217; A. Calhoun, De-accessioning: Why not? (1985), at 14–15.

**527** On the US Law on "de-accession", see Derek Fincham, Deaccession of Art and the Public Trust, Electronic copy available at: http://ssrn.com/abstract=1470211; on Australian legislation see Norman Palmer, Museums and the Holocaust, at 164.

**528** D. Hayton/C. Mitchell, Commentary and Cases on the Law of Trusts (13th ed 2010), para. 1–01 to 1–05; J.E. Penner, The Law of Trusts (5th ed. 2006), at para. 2.1.

ance with the terms of the trust and usually without personal benefit to the trustee.[529]

Most of the UK national museums and galleries have been established by trust, whereby the museum trustees hold the collections in trust for the public as the beneficiary. Generally, a trust can be enforceable at law only if there is certainty about the identity of the beneficiary of the trust. Charity law provides an exception to this rule. As the law developed, a set of public interest purposes for which a trust could be said to exist have emerged as a matter of charity law, even though an individual cannot be identified as a beneficiary, and the Attorney General became the guardian of the so called beneficial interest in a charitable trust. The consequence of this system is that national museums and galleries must conform to certain requirements of charity law.[530]

Broadly speaking, in England and Wales public institutions operate with limited powers of disposal, with the consequence that a disposal without possessing the power to do so constitutes a breach of trust or duty with the potential to expose the trustees to personal liability for any loss to the institution.[531] As a result, any national museum which is a charity cannot dispose of its charitable assets other than in the interest pursuant to its own charitable trust.[532] If no authority, express or implied for the disposal can be found in the constitution of the charity, then external authority for the disposition can be sought from the Charity Commission, the Courts or the Parliament.

### b. Arising from Museum Governing Statutes

As statutory corporations, national museums created by statute will have only whatever power of disposal is given to them expressly by statute in relation to their own collections.[533] The regimes are not consistent and some institutions

**529** L. Prott/P.J. O'Keefe, Movement (1989), at 403.

**530** Report ITAP 2000, at para. 138.

**531** Cp Edward Manisty/Julian Smith, The Deaccessioning of Objects from Public Institutions: Legal and Related Considerations, Vol. XV, Issue 1, AAL (2010) 1, at 18.

**532** Constraints under the law of trusts or penalties under the law of contract can exist, neither of which need necessarily to have been reduced to writing in order to be effective

**533** On the other hand non-statutory museums which in general do not include local authority museums or galleries are either governed by a trust deed (or with those trusts set out in a Charity Commission Scheme), by Articles of Association (in the case of a charitable company), or, by more esoteric forms of constitution (eg Royal Charter). Whether or not such a charity has the power to deaccession will be governed first by its constitution, which might or might not provide an express power, cp E. Manisty/ J. Smith, ibid, at 21.

clearly have greater latitude than others.[534] For instance, the British Museum, which is governed by the British Museum Act 1963, provides for "the duty of the Trustees of the British Museum to keep the objects comprised in the collections of the Museum within the authorised repositories of the Museum (...)".[535] Temporary removals of objects from the collection are allowed only for administrative reasons or the management of the collection, or in the form of loans for public exhibitions (whether in the United Kingdom or elsewhere).[536] Section 3 (4) of the British Museum Act complements the positive duty of the Trustees to keep the objects from the collection within the authorised repositories of the museum with the explicit prohibition of disposing of any objects vested in them otherwise than in accordance with section 5 and 9 of that Act, or section 6 of the Museums and Galleries Act 1992. Under section 5 (1), the British Museum may only dispose of items vested in the Trustees if:

a. the object is a duplicate of another object, or
b. the object appears to the Trustees to have been made not earlier than the year 1850, and substantially consists of printed matter of which a copy made by photography or a process akin to photography is held by the Trustees, or
c. in the opinion of the Trustees the object is unfit to be retained in the collections of the Museum and can be disposed of without detriment to the interests of students..."

Similar conditions apply to the Natural History Museum, the British Library[537], the Victoria and Albert Museum, the Science Museum, the Armouries and the Royal Botanic Gardens[538] and to the Tate Gallery.[539] The National Portrait Gallery misses the option to dispose of an object that is considered "unfit to be retained". The Trustees of the National Portrait Gallery have, however, been granted a *sui-generis* disposal power, which mirrors the mission of the museum as National Portrait Gallery: in cases where the identification of the sitter of a portrait

534 For example, the Act for Settling and Preserving Sir John Soane's Museum, Library and Works of Art, in Lincoln's Inn Fields, dating as early as 1833, not only prohibited the disposal of any item in the collection but also required its trustees to retain Soane's house (No. 13, Lincoln's Inn Fields) in the form in which it was left on his death, cp. E. Manisty/J. Smith, The Deaccessioning of Objects from Public Institutions, at 80.

535 Sec. 3(1) British Museum Act 1963.

536 Sec. 3(1) and sec. 4 of the British Museum Act 1963.

537 British Library Act 1972, sec. 3(5).

538 National Heritage Act 1983 sections 6(3) (b), 14(3)(b), 20(3)(b).

539 Museums and Galleries Act 1992, sections 4(4)(b).

has been discredited, the Board of Trustees may dispose of the portrait by whatever means.[540]

### 2. Exceptions to the Rule

### a. Through Act of Parliament

For the time being the general principle remains that statutory restrictions on disposal can be waived only by an act of parliament.[541]

This stringent concept has been questioned in *AG v Trustees of the British Museum*[542], a claim concerning some four drawings from the collection of the British Museum which were looted in the Nazi era. In response to a return request advanced by the Commission of looted Art in Europe, the Museum asked the Attorney General whether it would be able to return the paintings to the heirs of the late Dr. Feldmann on moral grounds. Arthur Feldmann, a Jewish lawyer in the Czech town of Brno, bought the disputed drawings at an auction in Switzerland in 1934. The Nazis invaded Czechoslovakia on March 15, 1939, and the Gestapo had occupied Dr. Feldmann's home and evicted the family. In many countries, the Nazis sent scouts to search for valuable art collections before invading, and the quickness with which Feldmann's house was occupied has led researchers to believe that the Nazis knew about his large art collection. Feldmann was tortured and killed in a nearby fortress, and his wife ended up in Auschwitz, where she died.[543]

The British Museum wanted the Attorney General to authorise the Museum's Trustees to meet a moral claim that arises from the Holocaust without the need for amending the British Museum Act (1963) by an Act of Parliament. The Museum argued that section 27 of the Charities Act 1993 would enable the Attorney General and the British Museum to take account of these matters in considering a claim for the return of works looted during the Holocaust period.[544] Section 27 of the Charities Act 1993 provides that

> "*.....the commissioners may by order exercise the same power as is exercisable by the Attorney General to authorise the trustees of a charity to make any application of property of the char-*

540 Museum and Galleries Act 1992 s 44.

541 "An Act of Parliament can always be amended in general or specific terms by another Act of Parliament", cp. E. Manisty/J. Smith, The Deaccessioning of Objects from Public Institutions, at 21.

542 Attorney-General v Trustees of the British Museum [2005] EWHC 1089.

543 For further details see Nathaniel Popper, British Museum in Moral Quandary Over Stolen Art, NY Forward, 10.06.2005.

544 Attorney General v. Trustees of the British Museum (2005) EWHC 1089.

> *ity, or to waive to any extent, on behalf of the charity, its entitlement to receive any property, in a case where the charity trustees have no power to do so, but in all the circumstances regard themselves as being under a moral obligation to do so."*

The court stated that, unless the heirs of Dr. Feldmann could establish title to the drawings in other proceedings with the consequence that they will never have been "part of the collections of the museum", sect. 3 (4) British Museum Act will preclude a disposition by the trustees in the family's favour. Morrit J rejected the possibility of an implied exception to sect. 3 (4), on the ground that "the very existence of exceptions in sect. 3 (4) negatives the recognition of further but implied exceptions". A further point is that the enactment of the Museums and Galleries Act 1992 provided a parliamentary opportunity to insert a further exception but the parliament decided not to do so.[545] It was held that only statutory authority would justify a departure from statutory obligations imposed on trustees. Consequently, the Feldmann-drawings could not return to their rightful owners. After the judgment, the case was referred to the Spoliation Advisory Panel, an independent body established in February 2000 to facilitate claims concerning the 1933–1945 period, which resolved the case by recommending financial compensation to the descendants.[546]

As a result of the case, and due to various recommendations by the Spoliation Advisory Panel to amend the British Museum and the British Library Act[547], the Parliament has enacted the Holocaust (Return of Cultural Objects) Bill 2009. The Act gives the trustees of national institutions in Britain the necessary statutory power to de-accession any artefacts or cultural objects currently held in their collections which were stolen by or on behalf of the Nazi regime between 1935 and 1945.[548] The law provides that this power can only be exercised where the return is recommended by an advisory body established by the Secretary of State[549] and where the Secretary of State accepts that body's recommendation.

A similar provision which provides an exception to the statutory disposal restrictions is section 47 of the Human Tissue Act 2004, which confers a power

**545** Fact is that parliament was not aware of the holocaust problematic at the time of drafting the 1992 Act. Restitution and repatriation claims started to appear in the middle of the 90's, which initiated the Washington conference on Holocaust Era Assets in 1998.

**546** See Report of the Spoliation Advisory Panel on the Feldmann Drawings at www.culture.gov.uk/what_we_do/cultural_property/3296.aspx.

**547** See for example, the Benevento Missal-case, 2005 Report of the Spoliation Advisory Panel available at www.culture.gov.uk/what_we_do/cultural_property/3296.aspx.

**548** For a detailed analysis of the Act cp. Norman Palmer, Responding to Conscience -The Holocaust Return of Cultural Objects Act 2009, 15 AAL (2010) 87.

**549** That is the Spoliation Advisory Panel.

upon national museums to de-accession human remains, "if it appears to them appropriate to do so for any reason whether or not it relates to their other functions." The power applies only to human remains which are reasonably believed to be of a person who died less than 1,000 years before this section comes into force.

### b. Through Voluntary Surrender of Title

It seems that restricted national museums have no choice but to refuse any demand for the return of artefacts. However, it is possible that in proceedings regarding the return of an object, the claimant may establish title to it with the consequence that it will never have been 'part of the collection of the museum'.[550]

If the object has not clearly and conclusively become part of the permanent collection of the institution, then on its leaving the collection, whether by way of sale or otherwise, *prima facie* legal and ethical implications associated with deaccession will not be an issue.[551]

A *bona fide* compromise of the issues in the claim may therefore involve a recognition that the object in question is not subject to the prohibition of deaccession contained in sec. 3(4). If a claimant could raise serious doubt as to the museum's title to the object, achieving a *bona fide* compromise, the object could be relinquished to the claimant without offending the statutory provisions.[552] This possibility was considered in the *Feldmann-judgment*[553], where the court made clear that the power to compromise is "not an unexpressed exception to sec. 3(4) but the consequence of its limited application to objects, which never became part of their collections." Thus, a *bona fide* compromise is not a 'disposal' in the sense of the statute.[554] Notwithstanding, the trustees still might decide the object to be 'comprised in the collection'[555] and so within the ambit of the

---

**550** E.g. section 3 (4) British Museum Act 1963.

**551** Cp also E. Manisty/ J. Smith, The Deaccessioning of Objects from Public Institutions, at 2.

**552** Sir A. Morritt in the BM Judgment: "...the compromise of a claim by the heirs of Dr. Feldmann to be entitled to the drawings does not involve any breach of sec. 3(4)."

**553** See above.

**554** A bona fide compromise is as binding as a decision of the court, see Binder v Alachouzos [1972] 2 QB 151.

**555** Sec. 3(4) British Museum Act 1963, which is the provision prohibiting disposal other than by statutory exemption, applies to objects that are vested in the trustees as a 'part of the collection'. On this point the act is unclear.

act. [556] In addition, a possibility to compromise would not apply where the museum derives its title from a *bona fide* purchase while the item was situated in a country which recognises such an acquisition as conferring title. It follows that the restitution of objects other than from the Holocaust period is not impossible. On the contrary, museums seem to be allowed to divest themselves of items where, in respond to a claim, the museum believes reasonably and in good faith and having taken counsel's advice that the claimant had a good arguable case and a realistic prospect of success.

Equally, the object may never have been part of the collection, if it was a loan instead of a gift or bequest,[557] or where although the object is owned by the institution it has not been 'accessioned' into the permanent collection.

## § 4. Conclusion for Chapter 2

This chapter scrtinised existing national legal frameworks concerned with the protection of cultural heritage for interests granted to their sovereigns in relation to antiquities and their quality as "property". For the purpose of this analysis these interest were divided into two broad categories, namely legal mechanisms that aimed at acquiring property rights to antiquities which were not yet in the ownership or possession of the state, and legal mechanisms that were meant to retain cultural items already held by the state within the public domain. The analysis of the first category revealed that while all national legal frameworks grant their sovereign certain rights to heritage items upon their discovery or export, there exist a great variety of forms and techniques employed to empower the state with property rights to cultural heritage. Such included property interest based on declarations of ownership, interests based solely on rights of immediate possession, and property interests arising out of export declarations and rights of pre-emption.

With regard to declarations of ownership, the analysis exposed that umbrella legislation which is often employed by source states, grants the sovereign the strongest possible property right as long as the heritage item remains within the

556 See Norman Palmer, Repatriation and Deaccessioning of Cultural Property: Reflections on the Resolution of Art Disputes, in: Current Legal Problems (2001) 475, at 506.

557 See for example the dispute relating to the ownership of objects placed by the first Lord Beaverbrook with the New Brunswick Provincial Art Gallery ('The Beaverbrook Art Gallery') at Fredericton, New Brunswick, Canada. For an account of the case see Ina Jahn, Loan versus Gifts, Determining the Donor's Intention, Lord Beaverbrook v. The Beaverbrook Art Gallery, 12 AAL (2007) 81.

territory of the state. Some umbrella statutes even prohibit the private possession of artefacts. In the event a heritage item has left the state's territory illegally, umbrella laws have often proven not to be a useful tool for their recovery for the reason that the legislative text not always has been drafted diligently and courts decided to interpret ownership declarations concerning cultural heritage narrowly. Recent case law however suggests that foreign courts started to view ownership declarations more in favour of the claimant state. The analysis exposed that even rights of immediate possession may amount to a real ownership right if its cumulative effect can be viewed as conferring title. In the light of *Government of Iran v Barakat*, a state may be able to prove that regardless of the exact wording of the statute specific provisions such as reporting and delivery duties amount to conferring title if the overall aim of the state's law was for the sovereign to own tainted artefacts.

Conversely, many market states preferred to adopt a system where title to finds is governed by the law of finders, unless they fall under the special provisions concerning movable cultural property. They too create explicit title in the state, however, within a narrower frame than most source countries have opted for. As a consequence, the acquisition of antiquities by public individuals is possible for a specific category of finds. Many of the new Eastern European Member States on the other hand show to have adopted a dual regime where both, the civil law of finders and cultural heritage legislation, to the same extent vest title to all newly discovered heritage items in the state. Private ownership of heritage items is only permitted for items that have already been owned before the enactment of the special legislation.

In relation to property rights granted on the basis of export laws, the analysis concluded that some states acquire property in antiquities in the form of confiscatory ownership upon the illegal export of a heritage item, if the confiscation occurs automatically as an act of law. In order for such legislation to grant a proper ownership right the wording of the statute has to be clear in relation to the time and place of forfeiture. Conversely, legislation that requires an additional administrative act upon which the state may acquire confiscatory ownership of illegally exported heritage items will violate the principle of territoriality. The same is true for export laws which grant a right of first refusal and are confiscatory upon its violation. States where the illegal export of heritage items entails solely criminal or pecuniary sanctions do not grant any property rights to their sovereign upon their violation.

Concerning the quality of property interests granted by a right of pre-emption, the extrapolation allows to conclude that a state achieves title only if it has a statutory pre-emption right which it exercised. In the event it did not, the author adopted the view that pre-emption rights do not confer title upon their violation as their nature brings with it that they entirely dependent on a future contingency which is uncertain. If, however, the pre-emption right provides for a specific degree of certainty, it may be treated as a contingent interest in property for the purpose of enforcement under the patrimonial interest. The same is true if the pre-emption right gives rise for an automatic forfeiture in favour of the state. In relation to pre-emption rights and their compatibility with human rights, this chapter revealed that pre-emption rights do not interfere with the ECHR as such but the exercise of such rights have to struck a "fair balance" between the "demands of the general interest of community" and the "requirement of the protection of the individual's fundamental rights". So far, the violation of the ECHR was never made the basis of a restitution claim.

The analysis of the second category dealing with mechanisms to retain cultural property in the public domain discussed national regimes which provide for provisions that render cultural objects to be inalienable and subject to exceptions within the rules of private commerce as well as regimes which restrict the disposal of objects from public collection.

This is especially the case in the *UK*, in *Italy* and in *France*. All three regimes are characterised by a general ban on the disposal of objects from their collections. The ban on the disposal of objects from UK public collections originates from restraints on the museums' rights to disposition, whereas the ban on the disposal of objects from French and Italian public collections results from *res extra commercium* legislation. Although such rules provide the state with an interest, in the sense that they prevent an involuntary loss of the state's title, they do not create property rights upon their violation and are thus not capable of being enforced in a foreign court in that event.

This may be different with the German "*öffentliche Dienstbarkeit*" where the art object can only be divested under the premise that the chattel is charged with a real right for the object to be used only within the limits of a specific public purpose. A heritage item charged with the "*Dienstbarkeit*" that is based on direct legal authorisation by a public statute can be subject to an immediate right of possession of the German state within the limits of its dedication, and may become subject of a vindication claim in the event of its violation.

The same is true for the Ecuadorian "*dominio eminente*", a real right *ipso jure*, similar to the "*öffentliche Dientbarkeit*" which precludes the good faith acquisition of the object free of this right. The state thus always has an immediate right of possession to recover the chattel in order to display it on its territory. So far, the "*dominio eminente*" has been the only right subject to a successful recovery claim in a foreign court.

# Chapter 3. Title to Cultural Objects under the Private Law of Finds

## § 1. Introduction

The previous chapter has elaborated different ways in which states can obtain or keep an interest in cultural property on the grounds of cultural property legislation. Many countries passed legislation declaring certain types of heritage items to become the property of the state. However, if a finder discovers an object which falls foul of these *lex specialis* provisions in that it is not encomepasse by the definition of the statute of what constitutes protected cultural property, the title to the found object is being determined by the private law of finds. In fact, some civilian jurisdictions chose not to adopt state ownership at all and preferred to continue protecting movable antiquities solely through finder's law. In these circumstances, the sovereign in whose jurisdiction a precious object is found may acquire title to it only under two conditions: Either, the object has been found on land which belongs to the public authority. In this case, the sovereign will become owner of the object if the private law of finds allocates title to the object to the land owner. In case, the object was found on private land, the sovereign will only acquire title to the object, if the title holder to the find, may it be the finder or the landowner, transfers the object to the sovereign, for example in return for a reward, or because criminal law or public law provisions oblige the finder to do so.

In order to provide for an integrated approach on the acquisition of title to antiquities by sovereigns, it will be thus imperative to elaborate how title to fortuitously discovered antiquities is allocated under the private law of finds. It would be a Sisyphean task to discuss all possible regimes regarding the allocation of title to found chattels under private law. Consequently, the author decided to conduct an analysis of the common law regime and a few selected civil law jurisdictions. Hence, in a first part, the chapter examines the acquisition of title in common law jurisdictions, focusing on English law. The extrapolation can be equally applied to determine title to antiquities to an individual finder. In a second part, it discusses finder's law as it is practiced in civilian jurisdictions. Finally, it considers whether finder's law forms a feasible mechanism to protect antiquities from illegal removal and to counter illicit trade.

## § 2. The Common Law of Finders

The common law of finders attempts to navigate its way through the collision of two notions of English law: One is the common belief that "finders are keepers", the other is the legal rule that an owner or lawful possessor of land owns all that is in or attached to it.[558] The title to the find has to be identified as between the finder of the object and the possessor or the rightful occupier of the land. The rights of both seem to depend upon the fact *where* the chattel was discovered.

Generally, lost objects can fall into three classes: those which become part of the soil, those which are within the soil but do not form part of it and retain their identity as a chattel, and those which are merely on the soil.[559] English law chose to allocate title to finds according to this threefold distinction. Objects which became part of the soil cease to be chattels on integration with the land and thereby become the property of the landowner.[560] Chattels which have been found on the surface of the land can be kept by the person in priority of possession of the item.[561] The owner of the premises will regularly be in priority of possession if he succeeded in manifesting an intention to control chattels which have been lost.[562] As regards objects which were discovered underneath the land but did

**558** General literature on English Finder's law, see Norman Palmer, Bad Apples and Blighted Windfalls: Finding, Bailment and the Fruits of Crime, in: F. Meisel and P.J. Cook (eds) Property and Protection: Essays in Honour of Brian Harvey (2000) 1; N. Palmer, Quality and Duration of the Finder's Title: Free-Standing of Free-For-All? 3 AAL (1998), 223; N. Palmer, Title to Antiquarian Finds: Perpetuating the Inpenetrable, (1996) AAL, 157; Palmer on Bailment (3rd ed. 2009), Chapter 26; Robin Hickey, Curbin the Enthusiasm of Finders, in: Elizabeth Cook (ed), Modern Studies in Property Law Volume 4 (2007) 97; David C. Hoath, Some Conveyancing Implications of "finding" Disputes, Conveyancer and Property Lawyer (1990) 348; R.H. Helmholz, Equitable Division and the Law of Finders, 52 Fordham L. Rev. (1983–1984) 313. On Australian Law see Joyce Tooher, Jubilant Jamie and the Elephant Egg: Acquisition of Title by Finding, 6 Australian Property Law Journal (1998) 117.

**559** See Norman Palmer, Quality and Duration of the Finder's Title, at 228. See for the somewhat similar three-fold classification recognised in cases concerning fixtures e.g. Elitestone Ltd v Morris [1997] 2 All E.R 513, HL (where a house intended to form part of the realty was assigned to be an attachment that merges into the land and become part of it although it rested on the land solely by virtue of its own weight); Melluish Inspector of Taxes v BMI (No 3) Ltd [1995] 4 All E.R 453 (concerning the lease of machinery to local government authorities, who owned the freehold where the machinery was installed. It was held to be "fixtures, although it could be removed at the end of the lease). But cp. Simmons v Midford, [1969] 2 All E R 1269; [1969] 2 Ch 415, where it was held that an underground drain had not become part of the land owing to the intention of the parties in the particlar agreement relating to it.

**560** Elwes v Brigg Gas Co (1886) 33 Ch D 562 at 567, 568, [1886–90] All ER Rep 559, at 561–562.

**561** Parker v British Airways Board [1982] 1 Q.B 1004, at 1019.

**562** Parker, at 1019.

not become part of the soil, English law rejects the requirement of manifest intention in relation to chattels subsoil, on the grounds that an object subsoil is to be treated as an integral part of the realty as against all but the true owner.[563]

The law is not clear as regards chattels which the finder obtained by committing trespass. It leans towards the suggestion that a trespassing finder is disentitled in favour of the occupier or owner of the land, especially when concerning heritage items.[564]

If the finder discovers a chattel in the course of employment the law will regularly award the title to the employer.[565] The difficulty lies here in determining whether the act of finding is related to the servant's employment or whether the finding merely occurs wholly incidentally.

Parallel with the development of the law, the following paragraph will discuss the law of finds as regards chattels discovered on the surface of the land, following by an analysis of the law regarding items found below the ground. It continues with presenting the situation when chattels where found by a trespasser and by an employee. It will also illustrate the general obligations a finder has to fulfil.

## I. Superincumbent Finds

### 1. Priority of Possession

On a general basis, the right to discovered objects is based upon the priority of possession: If the owner does not claim his property, the party first in possession is said to have title against anyone except the true owner.[566] This rule has been set out in the case *Armory v Delamirie*[567], where the plaintiff being a chimney sweeper's boy found a jewel and carried it to Delamirie's shop (who was a goldsmith) to inquire what it was. He handed it over to an apprentice to ask for a val-

---

**563** Parker, at 1010; Waverley Borough Council v. Fletcher [1996] QB 334 (CA) at 345.

**564** Cp. Webb v Ireland and the Attorney General [1988], I.R 353, at 379 – 380, Waverley Borough Council v Fletcher [1996] QB 334, at 344.

**565** Parker v British Airways Board [1982] 1 Q.B 1004, at 1017.

**566** The Winkfield [1902], at 42, a case concerning the ownership quality and the possessory title; Armory v. Delamirie (1722) 1 Stra. 505; 93 E.R. 664; Bridges v. Hawkesworth (1851) 15 Jur. 1079, 21 L.J.Q.B. 75; Kowal v. Ellis (1977) 76 D.L.R. (3d) 546, at 548; Pierce v Bemis, The Lusitania [1986] 1 Lloyd's Rep. 132 at 141 – 142; Parker v. British Airways Board [1982] Q.B. 1004, at 1019 per Eveleigh L.J. at 1009, Donaldson L.J. also accepted the general validity of the proposition stated by Pratt C.J. in Armory v. Delamirie, observing that otherwise: "lost property would be subject to a free-for-all, in which the physically weakest would go to the wall".

**567** (1722) 1 Stra. 505.

uation. When the apprentice suggested some paltry sum, the boy requested back the jewel, but only the empty socket was returned. The chimney sweeper brought an action in trover[568] against Delamirie. Pratt C.J. gave the judgement of the Court: "the finder of a jewel, though he does not by such finding acquire an absolute property or ownership, yet he has such a property as will enable him to keep it against all but the rightful owner, and consequently may maintain trover."[569] Similarly, in *Bridges v Hawkesworth*[570], it was held that the finder of bank notes dropped by someone unknown accidentally on the floor of a shop had a better title to them than the shop owner, who did not know about them until the finder drew his attention to them.

The modern authority for the rule as set out in *Armory* was *Parker v British Airways Board*[571], in which the plaintiff, Mr. Parker, found a gold bracelet lying on the floor while he was waiting as a passenger in the executive lounge at Terminal One of Heathrow Airport. He handed the bracelet in, provided his name and address and requested that the item be returned to him should the true owner not be found. British Airways subsequently sold the chattel, causing Mr Parker to initiate an action for damages in the county court. Donaldson L.J. held that Mr Parker was entitled to the gold bracelet as against the airline company.

A similar conclusion was reached in the Canadian case *Kowal v Ellis*[572], where a finder happened upon a pump which was lying unattached on somebody's land. The landowner subducted the pump from the finder and the finder sued for its recovery. The Monitoba Court of Appeal held that the finder was entitled to possession of the pump.

Although the law of finders in the common law jurisdiction is founded on priority of possession, it does not lend much support to the colloquial "finder's keepers, losers weepers"- maxim. Unless he has not abandoned the object,[573] or

---

**568** Trover is the ancient legal remedy in common law for the wrongful appropriation of the plaintiff's personal property, see e.g. in Isaac v Clark (1614) 2, 306; Wilbraham v Snow (1670) 1 Modern Reports 30; Gordon v Harper(1796) 7 T.R. 9. For more information on Trover see also Edward H. Warren, Trover and Conversion: An Essay (1936); C.H.S. Fifoot, History and Sources of the Common Law, Trover and Conversion, (London 1948) 102 et seq.

**569** (1722) 1 Stra, 505, at 507.

**570** Bridges v Hawkesworth, (1851) 21 L.J.Q.B. 75.

**571** Parker v British Airways Board [1982] 1 Q.B 1004.

**572** Kowal v Ellis (1977) 76 DLR (3d) 546.

**573** A chattel is not of course abandoned merely because its owner has lost it, cp., e.g. Moffatt and Another v. Kazana [1968] 3 All E.R. 271, at 274. Indeed, in the case of valuable items, there appears to be a presumption against abandonment, cp. e.g. R. v. Peters (1843) 1 Car. & K. 245, at 247. However, it is still not clear whether English law recognises the general concept of "divest-

lost his title due to the operation of the Limitation Act 1980[574], in common law the owner can recover the lost item from the finder or occupier of the land upon which the chattel was found.

Furthermore, a claim to the object could also be made by a previous owner of the relevant land or building.[575] In the context of the sale of goods in *Merry v Green*[576], where money was discovered in a secret compartment of a bureau which had been sold at auction: the court was prepared to assume that even after the sale the seller retained a right to the money which was good against all but the "true owner" thereof, and that no right to possession of the money passed to the buyer even though the seller had been unaware of the hidden money. The decision has been criticised[577] and should be regarded as confined to the old law of larceny. If, however, the *Merry v Green*-principle does represent the law as between vendor and purchaser of land, the current occupier at the time of the find would, at least in theory, be exposed to the undesirable risk of an indefinite chain of claims from previous owner-occupiers or their personal representatives; the *locus standi* of such a claimant will indeed be better documented than is likely to be the case where chattels have changed hands, and there could be no question of time running against him under the Limitation Act 1980 until the item is actually discovered.[578] The issue was also argued in *Moffat and Another v. Kazana*[579], where the predecessor in title died before the hearing. However, the case was decided on the basis that the predecessor in title had been the "true owner" of the banknotes, and had intentionally secreted them; thus it was not necessary to consider whether he could have qualified as a "prior possessor" of the banknotes if he had been at all times unaware of their presence during the period of his ownership of the dwelling.

---

ing abandonment", see on this A. H. Hudson, Is Divesting Abandonment Possible in Common Law? 100 LQR (1984) 110, Note however, the recent case Robot Arena Ltd. v Waterfield and Others [2010] EWHC 115 (QB), concerning the sitution that a landlord wishes to dispose of goods that a former tenant left behind. The landlord may become liable to the tenant for damages unless he proves an intention on the part of the tenant that he abandonded the goods. The court found that the landlord will not be liable if he did not know of the identity of the former tenant.

**574** See Limitation Act 1980 sections 3 and 4.

**575** Cp. David C. Hoath, Some Conveyancing Implications of "Finding" Disputes, Conveyancer and Property Lawyer (1990) 348.

**576** (1841) 7 M. & W. 623; For further details on the case see A. Samuels, Comment, 116 National law Journal (1966) 1009.

**577** See, e.g. the anonym note in (1964) 80 LQR, at 151–152.

**578** See Limitation Act 1980, sec. 2.

**579** [1968] 3 All E.R. 271; see also case note in (1969) 85 LQR, 460.

## 2. The Manifest Intention-Test

Where a "lost" article is found in a place more or less under private control, the question whether the colloquial finders keepers – maxim prevails over the rights of the owner or occupier of the premises upon which the chattel was found can sometimes be difficult to ascertain. The problem involves the inquiry as to who had possession of such an article while in the state of being "lost", the last possessor or the one in control of the place.[580] The landowner can only sustain his claim on the basis that he had rights in relation to the object immediately *before* the finder discovered it and that these rights are superior to the finder.

In the *Parker* – case, Donaldson L.J. held that the right of the occupier to exercise control over his land is not in itself enough to obtain possessory title over a disputed chattel. An occupier must have "manifested an intention to exercise control over the building and the things which may be upon it", in which the "manifestation of intention may be express or implied from the circumstances."[581] In all other circumstances the finder would obtain possessory title and accrue the right to maintain the object against all but the true owner.[582]

The theory underlying the rule in *Parker* has been established in *South Staffordshire Water Co v Sharman*[583], where the defendant was employed by the occupier of land to remove mud from the bottom of a pond. He found two gold rings embedded in the mud. The daimant occupier was held to be entitled to the rings. Lord Russel of Killowen, C.J. relied on a passage in Pollock and Wright - Possession in the Common Law - stating that "the possession of land carries with it in general, by our law, possession of everything which is attached to or under that land, and, in the absence of a better title elsewhere, the right to possess it also." Lord Russell further agreed with Pollock and Wright that "it makes no difference" that the possessor is not aware of the thing's existence.

According to Lord Russel of Killowen, "the general principle seems to be that where a person has possession of a house or land, with a manifest intention to exercise control over it and the things which may *be upon or in it*, then, if something is found on that land, whether by an employee of the owner or by a strang-

**580** Anonym comment, Possession of Lost Goods, in Columbia Law Rev, Vol. 20, No. 7, (Nov., 1920), at 780–787.

**581** Parker v British Airways, at 1018; Kowal v Ellis (1977) 76 D.L.R. (3d) 546. Followed by the Supreme Court of New Zealand in Tamworth Industries Ltd. v Attorney General [1991] 3 NZLR 616 at 621–624; but see also approved but distinguished in Waverley Borough Council v Fletcher [1996] Q.B. 334.

**582** Hannah v. Peel [1945] K.B. 509, at 520.

**583** [1896] 2 Q.B. 44.

er, the presumption is that the possession of that thing is in the owner of the *locus in quo*."

The decision in *Parker* and *Sharman* is in contradiction with *Bridges v. Hawkesworth*[584], where the notes where found in a shop and the finder was entitled to keep them. There, Patteson J. expressed the view that it should make no legal difference where they were found and that the principle in *Armory* should prevail.[585] However, *Bridges* could be explained by reliance upon the fact that the notes were found in what may be described as the public part of the shop. The tenor of the judgment suggested that no prior possession could have existed without the defendant's knowledge of the presence of the goods. Partly, perhaps of this reason, *Bridges v Hawkesworth* was criticised in some quarters to be a misconceived judgment.[586]

In *Parker*, Donaldson L.J. endorsed Lord Russell of Killowen's statement of the general principle in *Sharman*, provided that the occupier's intention to exercise control over anything, which might be on the premises, was manifested.[587] The manifestation of intention may be express or implied from the circumstances including, in particular, the circumstance that the occupier manifestly accepts or is obliged by law to accept liability for chattels lost upon his "premises".

The types of precaution necessary to establish the occupier's possession will naturally vary according to the circumstances of the land and the character of the entrances. In *Bailment*, Palmer suggests that the most effective measure is likely to be some form of publicised announcement to visitors which stipulates that their permission to enter the land is subject to the condition that all articles situated on it are deemed, in the absence of the real owner, to be in the occupier's possession and control and must, if found, be surrendered to him.[588]

---

**584** 21 L.J.Q.B. 75, per Patteson J.
**585** 21 L.J.Q.B. 75, Patteson J., at 77–78.
**586** Its correctness was doubted by Hart J. (dissenting) in Byrne v. Hoare [1965] Qd R. 135, at 168–169; see also the observations of Wells J. in Minigall v. McCammon [1970] S.A.S.R. 82 at 93. But cp. On the other hand South Staffordhire Water Co. v. Sharman [1896] 2 Q.B. 44 at 47; McFadyen v. Wineti (1908) 11 G.L.R. 345; Hannah v. Peel [1945] 1 K.B. 509, at 515–517; Byrne v. Hoare [1965] Qd R. 135, at 139 per Stable J. (cf. at 146 per Gibbs J.; Minigall v. McCammon [1970] S.A.S.R. 82, at 88 and Kowal v. Ellis (1977) 76 D.L.R. (3d) 546, where Bridges v. Hawkesworth was approved, albeit not infrequently on grounds that it was a highly special case.
**587** Parker v British Airways, at 1014.
**588** Cp. N. Palmer, Bailment (2009), at 26–047, citing the British Rail's "Conditions of Carriage of Passengers and their Luggage", which formerly provided, inter alia, that "all articles found in or upon any of the British Railways Board's premises or trains shall, as between the finder and the board, be deemed to be in the possession of the latter and must be given immediately into the custody of its staff", (September 1984), Condition 22(1).

Eveleigh L.J. has observed in *Parker*, the firmer the control which the occupier exerts over his premises, "the less will be the need to demonstrate independently the *animus possidendi*" over chattels lying thereon.[589] Since, in *Parker* there was no evidence that British Airways showed an intention to control all things which might be upon or in the premises where the bracelet was found (such as by regular searches) Mr Parker had the better right arising from his possession of the bracelet.

In contrast to *Parker*, the necessary manifestation of intention will invariably exist where the premises are a private residence.[590] There, it is held to be a rebuttable presumption that the householder intends to exercise control over everything within the domestic premise.[591] A recent authority for this presumption is the Australian decision *Flack v Chairman, National Crime Authority and Another*[592]. In this case, the police found a briefcase containing Australian $ 433,000 while searching the home of Mrs Flack in connection with a drug crime. The briefcase had been concealed at the back of the cupboard and Mrs Flack denied all knowledge of the money. The search had been conducted under a warrant and the subsequent removal of the briefcase and its contents by the police was lawful, but no charges were brought and the police eventually conceded that there was no "current operational necessity" for the money to be retained. They refused to return the money and Mrs Flack sued on the strength of an alleged pre-existing possessory title, derived from the presence of the money in her home. Hill J. (upheld by the full Federal Court) held that she had the prior and superior possession and that this gave her an enduring right to the find once the right of the police to retain it for purposes of investigation and prosecution had come to an end. In upholding Mrs Flack's possession, Hill J. accepted that the *Parker* principle of "manifest intention" applies to above-ground finds in Australia.[593]

---

**589** Parker v British Airways Board, at 1020 per Everleigh L.J.; Webb v Ireland and the A.-G. [1888] I.R. 353, esp. at 378–379, per Finlay J.

**590** Flack v Chairperson, National Crime Authority and Another (1997) 150 A.L.R (Fed. Ct., Australia, Hill J.) 501.

**591** Flack v Chairperson, at 514–515 per Timberlin J. See also Foster J's judgment, who refers to a "very strong" but rebuttable presumption of fact and expressly denies a presumption of law, ibid., at 506

**592** (1997) 150 A.L.R. 153 (Fed. Ct., Australia, Hill J.).

**593** (1997) 150 A.L.R. 153, at 159–163.

## II. Subsoil Finds

The law is reasonably clear in respect of lost chattels that are attached to realty when they are found. The rationale of this rule is that the chattel is to be treated as an integral part of the realty against all but the true owner.

Authority for this view is to be found in *Elwes v Briggs Gas Co.*[594] in which land had been demised to a gas company for ninety-nine years with a reservation to the lessor of all mines and minerals. A pre-historic boat embedded in the soil was discovered by the lessees when they were digging to make a gasholder. Relying on the passage in *Pollock and Wright* set above[595], Chitty J. held that the boat, whether regarded as a mineral or as part of the soil in which it was embedded when discovered, belonged to the landowner.[596]

This brings us to the situation, where the found thing was embedded in the soil but did not form part of it and remained a chattel. In *Elwes*, Chitty J. set out that in the alternative view of the pre-historic boat still being a chattel, it clearly belonged to the owner of the land, "even if he was not aware of its existence".[597] In the *Sharman*-case, this principle has been affirmed in that a person who has possession of house or land, the presumption is that the possession of a thing found is in the owner of the *locus in quo,* as long as he had "a manifest intention to exercise control over it and the things which may *be upon or in it*".[598] *Sharman* thus seems to be extending the test in *Elwes* as the notion "upon or in it" used by the chief justice are wider than "attached to or under".

A later judicial authority for Lord Russell's test has been *City of London Corporation v Appleyard*[599], concerning a dispute about the entitlement to banknotes found in a wall safe on a building site. McNair J accepted Lord Russell Killowen's statement of the general principle provided that the landowner's intention to take control over things in or on the ground was manifest. However, he rejected the contention that the mere right of an occupier to exercise control over his land creates sufficient rights in lost property as that would mean to overrule the decision in *Bridges v Hawkesworth.*

---

**594** (1886) 33 Ch D 561–562 and at 567–568, per Chitty J.

**595** See Sir Frederick Pollock and Samuel Wright, Essay on Possession in the Common Law (Oxford 1888).

**596** Elwes v Briggs Gas Co., 33 Ch. D. 562; City of London Corporation v Appleyard (1963) 1 W.L. R. 982.

**597** Ibid, at 564.

**598** See F. Pollock/S. Wright, Essay on Possession, at 41.

**599** (1963) 1 W.L.R. 982.

In the recent decision *Waverley Borough Council v Fletcher*[600], the question of who has the better right to lost chattels found subsoil and which degree of control was required by the landowner was again debated. There, Auld L.J. rejected the requirement of manifest intention in relation to things subsoil, stating that un object subsoil is to be treated as an integral part of the realty as against all but the true owner because in detaching the object the finder would become a trespasser. In this case, Mr Fletcher, a metal-detectorist, who, in the course of pursuing his hobby in a local park, found a medieval gold brooch that he subsequently claimed for himself.[601]

In his judgement Auld L.J. did not see the necessity to apply the manifest intention test to things subsoil and relied on the test set out in *Elwes*. He stated that he can see no basis for not applying the general rule that an owner or lawful possessor of land has a better title to an object found in or attached to his land.[602] He cited Finlay J in *Webb v Ireland*[603] stating that "the decision of Chitty J. in *Elwes* was a very persuasive precedent".

Auld L.J. was "satisfied that that the true legal position is that there must be distinguished, with regard to the question of control, things which are on land and things attached to it"[604]. In Auld L.J.'s view, practically, the extent to which an absence of control may deprive the owner against the finder is probably limited to cases such as *Hanna v Peel*[605], where the owner of a house has never entered into possession of it though the title has devolved upon him. Auld L.J. precised the manifest intention test set out in *Parker* accordingly that:[606]

(1) Where an article is found in or attached to land, as between the owner or lawful possessor of the land and the finder of the article, the owner or lawful possessor has the better title and
(2) where an article is found unattached on land, as between the two, the owner or lawful possessor has the better title only if he exercised such manifest control over the land as to indicate an intention to control the land and anything that might be found on it.

One might be forgiven a suspicion that *Waverley* was fashioned to make room for the controversial decision in *Bridges v Hawkesworth*. In the Queensland Supreme

**600** (1995) 3 W.L.R. 772, (1996) QB 334
**601** Waverley Borough Council v Fletcher [1995] 4 All E.R. 756 C.A; (1996) QB 334
**602** Ibid, at 350.
**603** [1988] I.R.353.
**604** Ibid, at 344.
**605** (1945) K.B. 509.
**606** Ibid, at 345 per Auld J.

Court decision *Byrne v Hoare*, Hart J. even favoured the opposite view in that an occupier intends to exclude things under the surface and that intention might even extend to superincumbent finds.[607] Hart J. thought that *Bridges v Hawkesworth* was wrongly decided and should not be followed. Indeed, it seems artificial why it should make a legal difference if a find is on the surface or just underneath and the physical position of a find should have an influence on the degree of control the owner or occupier of the land has to manifest. Admittedly, it is quite a minor factor to be able to determine who has the better possessory claim to a property. Some support to this allegation has been given in the first instance of *Waverley*. There, Judge Fawcus expressed the view that "the general rule that an owner of land owns everything that is in it up to the centre of the earth, would be applicable to things that are naturally there, as for example minerals. But why in the case of lost or abandoned chattels there should be any difference as to who has the better possessory claim dependent merely upon whether the chattel is above or below the ground, I wholly fail to understand." If an intention to exert exclusive control over superincumbent chattels is the true criterion of the occupier's possession, it might be argued that such a criterion should equally apply to burried goods.[608]

### III. The Trespassing Finder

In common law, possession gained by trespass may be ineffective against the occupier on whose land the trespass occurred, although the occupier had no possession of the object itself.[609] The contention has been made that a finder who discovers goods as a result of trespass should not be entitled to keep the object, as it would enable him to profit from his own wrong.[610]

A case commenting upon this theory is *Byrne v Hoare*[611], where a police constable found a gold ingot near the approach road of a drive-in cinema, on land occupied by the cinema company. In the dissenting judgment of the Queensland Supreme Court, Hart J. concluded that the trespassing finder should get "*no rights*" as against the person in possession of the land and further that the tres-

---

**607** See Byrne v Hoare [1965] Qd.R. 135, at 174.
**608** Cp. N. Palmer, Bailment (2009), at 26–038.
**609** Parker v British Airways Board [1982] 1 Q.B 1004, at 1009, 1010, 1017; Webb v Ireland and the Attorney General [1988], I.R 353, at 379–380, Waverley Borough Council v Fletcher [1995] 4 All E.R 756, at 766–767.
**610** See e.g. Webb v Ireland (1987) I.R 353, at 29; Parker v British Airways Board, at 1009.
**611** [1965] Qd R. 135.

passing finder should get merely "*bare possession.*"[612] By bare possession, he means "the possession of a person with no other title to or interest in the property other than his possession, there being another known person with a better right to immediate possession than the finder."[613] Hart J. further followed that "the right of any finder must depend on the extent to which the person in possession of the land has consented to his acquiring them."[614] The essence of this is that to get anything more than bare possession, a finder must obtain the consent to remove lost items by the possessor of the land. In the *Byrne-case*, the constable failed to obtain an agreement or permission from the land owners that he should get possession of the ingot, but Hart J.'s judgment has been overruled and the constable was granted the recovery of the find from the Crown on other grounds.

In *Parker v British Airways*[615], Donaldson L.J. also expressed the view that public policy forbade the trespassing finder to acquire any rights to the find, in order "to avoid a possessory free for all". In the case of trespass, he identified the occupier of the land as the obvious candidate to the title of the object, the true owner being unknown.[616]

This proposition is acceptable when the dispute lies between the occupier and the trespasser. In cases however, where the trespassing finder seeks to defend his possession against a third party, the proposition that he acquires "no rights" or "bare possession" appears contrary to the principles that possession counts as title (as established in *Armory v Delamirie.*) Under the doctrine of the *Winkfield*, a possessor of goods who is wrongfully dispossessed by another can recover their full value in an action for conversion, that includes also the thief, from whom a chattel was taken by a third party.[617] To the contrary, granting no rights to the trespassing finder would produce the free-for-all situation, in that anyone can take the article from the trespassing finder. It must be noted that in the end, in Donaldson L.J.'s summary of the finder's legal position in *Parker*, he states that "the finder of a chattel acquires *very limited rights* over it if he takes it into control...in the course of trespassing."[618]

**612** Ibid at 161.
**613** Ibid, at 161.
**614** Ibid, at 174.
**615** Parker v British Airways Board [1982] 1 Q.B., 1004.
**616** Parker, [1982] Q.B. 1004, at 1009; see also Webb v Ireland and the A.-G. [1988] I.R. 353, at 379–380 per Finlay C.J.
**617** The doctrine goes back to the case *The Winkfield* [1902], cp. N. Palmer, Treasure Trove and Title to Discovered Antiquities, in: Palmer and McKendrick (eds.), Interests in Goods (1993), at 287. On the law of conversion note also Chapter 6 § 3 II 2.
**618** [1982] Q.B. 1004, at 1017.

The principle that trespass disentitles a finder of his discovery may however be stronger established when it comes to chattels obtained through digging and removing them from the ground. In *Webb v Ireland and the Attorney General*[619], a case tried at the Irish Surpreme Court, Finlay C.J. concluded that although the plaintiffs entered the premises of the landowner with an implied permission, the act of digging was an act of trespass "*ab initio*". The case concerned a father and a son, who discovered a silver chalice with a metal detector on land near Derrynaflan Tipperary, which was jointly owned by some Mr O'Brien and some Mr O' Leary. The Webbs delivered these articles into the care of the National Museum of Ireland "for the present and pending determination of the legal ownership". While still in possession of the antiquities, the museum approached the owners of the land and agreed to acquire the entire interest in what became known as the *Derrynaflan Hoard* which led to the Webbs bringing an action for recovery of the items.

Finlay C.J. held that "in the course of trespassing, an occupier of land has rights superior to those of a finder over chattels in or attached to that land and that the finder of a chattel acquires *very limited rights* over it if he takes it into his care and control...". He further stated that "the fact that these plaintiffs are finders by an act of trespass would disentitle them to any rights in the objects found, certainly as between them and the owners of the land.[620] According to Finlay C.J. this principle is based on the common good that the "ownership and right of possession of land shall be protected from an unlawful invasion of it."[621] One cannot however ignore, that in the first instance the learned judge ruled in favour for the Webbs and held, that the fact that the Webbs obtained the hoard by an act of trespass did not affect their title and right to the return of the hoard.

The decision in *Webb* was again reaffirmed in *Waverley v Borough Council*[622], where Auld L.J. concluded that Mr Fletcher's metal detecting, digging and removal of a gold brooch did not accrue to a recreational activity and was thus an act of trespass. In his view, Mr Fletcher had no right to dig or remove the brooch without an explicit licence from the council to excavate.[623] In his decision Auld L.J. also referred to the *Elwes-case*, where Chitty J. said that a "licence to dig does not amount to a licence to take away".

---

**619** Webb v. Ireland [1987] IESC, 2; [1988] I.R. 353.

**620** [1987] IESC, at 33, per Blayney J.

**621** See Webb v Ireland [1988] I.R. 353, at 379. Similarly, Waverley BC v Fletcher [1995] 4 All E.R. 756, C. A; [1996] Q.B 334, at 348.

**622** Waverley Borough Council v Fletcher [1995] 4 All E.R. 756 C.A; [1996] Q.B. 334.

**623** [1996] Q.B, 334 at 350.

It follows that regarding chattels found in or attached to the ground, the right of any finder depends on the extent to which the person in possession of the land has consented to the finder acquiring them. The trespassing finder has, by virtue of his possession alone, a better right to the chattel than anyone who subsequently divests him of the goods, but he will not have a better right than the owner or rightful possessor of the land.

As finds on the ground are concerned, the law in the words of Finlay J. "leans towards the disentitlement of the trespassing finder" however owing to the lack of judicial authority in this field no secure contention can be made. In *Bailment*, Palmer even argues against the disentitlement of the finder and believes it "preferable to conclude that the mere trespass *per se* should not divest the finder of the primacy of title, as the occupier will always have his remedy for trespass."[624] Dogmatically, this reasoning must be the only correct solution, as in accordance with the general principle under English law, possession counts as title, and so far this principle has been found fundamental to English law.[625] The occupier will be able to sue for damages on the grounds of trespass and likely will receive a sum to represent the loss of his opportunity to find the chattel for himself.

## IV. The Employee versus his Master

In Common law there is a general rule that an employee who obtains goods as a result of his employment holds for his employer and does not acquire independent possession.[626] Donaldson L.J. in *Parker*[627] contended that:

> Unless otherwise agreed, any servant or agent who finds a chattel in the course of employment or agency and not wholly incidentally or collaterally thereto and who takes it into his care and control does so on behalf of his employer or principal who acquires a finder's rights to the exclusion of those of the actual finder.

---

**624** See N. Palmer, Bailment, at 26–055.

**625** Parker v British Airways, at 1019 per Eveleigh L.J., where he stated that "against all but the true owner a person in possession has the right to possess."

**626** This could be one of the explanations proffered for the result in Sharman, in which a man employed to clean a pool of water was held not entitled to the rings he found embedded in the mud at the pool's bottom, as against the locus owner who had hired him. The case however, was decided on different grounds, cp. South Staffordshire Water v Sharman [1896] 2 Q.B 44.

**627** [1982] Q.B. 1004, at 1017.

The difficulty lies here in determining whether the act of finding is related to the servant's employment or whether the finding merely occurs wholly incidentally. Clearly, the principle will apply when the discovery occurs on the employer's premises. There it can be assumed that the master was in possession of the goods when the finding occurred. Thus a shop assistant who picked up a jewel from the shop floor was held to have reduced it into her employer's possession.[628] In an 1848 U.S. Oregon-case, it was held that a chambermaid was not entitled to the $ 800 she discovered while cleaning a hotel room. The court said: The decisive feature of the present case is the fact that the plaintiff was an employee or servant of the owner of the premises and she was simply performing the duties of her employment.[629]

The situation is more complex in cases of off-premise findings, as was the case in *Byrne v Hoare*[630], where a policeman found a gold ingot in the approach of a drive-in cinema. The court held in this case that the fact that the finder of the ingot was a policeman on his duty merely afforded the opportunity which led to the finding and could not be considered to have happened in the course of employment.

Following the test adopted by the Queensland Court in *Byrne*, as a general rule, the servant will not acquire possession of goods lost on his masters premises, goods found while conducting a search for his master and goods concealed within real or personal property upon which the servant is working or with which he is dealing in the course of his employment. The necessary degree of proximity between the employment and the discovery has to be determined by the facts of the particular case.

## V. Finder Obligations

There are very few direct authorities in common law that unequivocally discuss the obligations a finder owes to the true owner. The vast majority of litigated finding disputes are cases between finders and non-owing possessors, to which the obligations of a finder to a loser are not immediately relevant.[631] Moreover, in most of the reported finding disputes which are discussed above, finders

**628** White v Alton Lewis Ltd (1975) 49 D.L.R. (3d) 189. See also McDowell v Ulster Bank Ltd. (1899) 33 Ir.L.T.J. 223 (the possession gained by a porter sweeping out a bank and finding lost notes on the floor was "the possession of the bank itself").

**629** Jackson v Steinberg, 186 Or. 129, 136, 200 P.2d 376, 378 (1848).

**630** [1965] Qd R. 135.

**631** Cp. Robin Hickey, Curbing the Enthusiasm of Finders, at 104.

have behaved reasonably or honest and have not needed their conduct curtailed by positive obligations. In *Waverley*[632], M. Fletcher reported his find to the coroner in the belief that it might be treasure. In *Hannah v Peel*[633], a soldier on duty reported his find to a commanding officer as soon as he believed the brooch to be of value. In *Parker*, Donaldson L.J. thought that the claimant finder "acted as one would have hoped and expected him to act".[634]

In the absence of any direct authorities, English courts have tended to rely on the idea that a finder is a bailee to the loser to justify the supposition that he owes obligations.[635] However, in the 2nd edition of *Bailment,* Norman Palmer describes the equation of bailee and finder as "partial and imperfect" and concludes that finding represents one of the "more questionable forms of bailment."[636] Firstly, there is no contract or agreement between the loser and finder.[637] Secondly, bailment seems to be unworkable in the cases of finding as bailment stems from the time when bailments occurred only by way of delivery[638] and there is no delivering or handing over to the finder. Modern authorities however preferred to define bailment as depending only on the voluntary assumption of possession, and not on the literal transfer of possession from bailor to bailee.[639]

In *Parker,* Donaldson L.J. remarked *obiter* that an occupier who demonstrates the intention to exercise control over articles lost on his land so as to acquire a possession superior to that of a finder will owe three correlative obligations:[640] First, he must take reasonable steps to ensure that chattels lost upon his premises are found. Secondly, he must take reasonable steps to acquaint the true owner of the finding of any such chattel, whether it is found by the occupier himself or by a third party. Thirdly, he must take reasonable care of any such chattel,

**632** [1996] Q.B. 334.
**633** [1945] K.B. 509.
**634** Parker v British Airways, at 1017.
**635** Newman v Bourne & Hollinsworth Ltd (1915) 31 T.L.R. 209; Helson v McKenzies (Cuba St) Ltd [1950] N.Z.L.R. 878, Grafstein v Holme and Freeman (1958) 12 D.L.R. (2d) 727, at 738–739, Kowal v Ellis (1977) 76 D.L.R. (3d) 546, at 547.
**636** Palmer, Bailment (2nd ed 1991) at 1418. In the 3rd edition of Bailment, Palmer states that "finding represents one of the more ambiguous forms of bailment" and admits that "the equation between findings and ordinary bailment is harder to sustain", cp. at 26–001.
**637** R. Hickey, Curbing the Enthusiasm of Finders, at 108.
**638** The word bailee derives from the French word bailer, meaning to deliver or hand over.
**639** For example, Morris v CW Martin & Sons Ltd [1966] 1 QB 716 (CA); Gilchrist Watt and Sanderson Pty Ltd v York Products Pty Ltd [1970 3 All ER 825 (PC).
**640** Parker v British Airways, at 1018.

at least until the owner has had a reasonable opportunity to claim it.[641] As regards the first obligation, in many cases this requirement will already coincide with the relevant manifestation of intention to control which in most circumstances will be expressed in a way that the occupier will have a special lost and found diary or his employees will be advised to report any lost items.

There seems little doubt that the loser can sue if the finder fails to fulfill the obligations identified in *Parker*. After all, the loser has the immediate right of possession and this will be enough to sue in negligence, conversion or breach of bailment under English law. More difficult is the question whether the finder's breach of this obligations will affect the nature of the finder's own possessory title, in a way it does in the civilian jurisdictions.[642] So far as concerns a finder who is not an occupier or owner, his title is subordinate to that of the loser in any event and it makes no difference to the finder's title. But where the finder is indeed an occupier or landowner and the object was buried on his land and the finder would normally get possessory title, it could be argued that the finder's breach of the *Parker* obligations puts him in a similar position to a trespasser with only a diminished possessory title.

## VI. Concluding Remarks to the Common Law of Finders

It can be concluded that the position of the finder concerning the acquisition of title to found objects is unpredictable and contains many unsolved questions.[643] Distinctions are being drawn between finds on the ground and finds that are attached or merely loose in the ground. It seems artificial to make a legal difference if a find is on the surface or just underneath. The physical position of a find should not have an influence on the degree of control the owner or occupier of the land has to manifest. It only adds to the plethora of legal uncertainly that the common law of finds brings about, for example, the allocation of title to a trespassing finder who acquires "very limited rights" or "bare possession". Terms of this kind are unlegal and should not be employed to delineate the strength of a proprietary interest under civi law. As regards the protection of heritage items, cases such as *Waverley* today would fall under the Treasure Act, which means that title to the bracelet would vest in the crown and the finder

641 Parker v British Airways, at 1017

642 See this Chapter § 3 I.

643 In 1971, the Law Reform Committee reported that it was by no means clear who had the better claim to lost property when the protagonists were the finder and the occupier of the premises where the property was found.

has a duty to report it. If however, an item does fall foul of the special cultural property regieme, the mere factor that a thing was found on land that does belong to a public authority does not render the object property of the sovereign. Despite the attempt in the *Parker* – case by Donaldson L.J. to set out "the general principles or rules of law" applicable to finding disputes, neither the case itself nor the other "finding" cases provide any clear guidance as to the entitlement of the previous landowner or the current landlord to the object which has been found. Those leading decisions are so uncertain in their rationale that it is difficult to fit new fact situations into established patterns. The same seems to be valid for the trespassing finder and the owner of the land where an object was found.

Regarding the position of the employee versus his master, the situation of the finder has to be determined by the necessary degree of proximity between the employment and the discovery. This again is being decided on a case-to-case basis.

When applied to movable antiquities, the result is that a finder can keep the artefact against the sovereign if (1) it is not treasure as set out in sect. 1 of the Treasure Act 1996, (2) if it has not been found subsoil and did not become part of the land where the item was found and (3) in the case the thing was discovered on the surface of the land, if the public owner of the land where the item was discovered did not manifest an intention to control it. Possibly, the finder may be disentitled if he (4) obtained the chattel by trespass, or (5) if he discovered it in the course of employment. Under common law, the finder has no duty to report the find or to deliver the find to the autorities, if it does not fall under the Treasure Act. This leaves the return of antiquarian finds to the discretion of the finder.

## § 3. The Civilian Law of Finders

The statutory civilian law of finders differs from common law generally in the way lost objects are being acquired. As opposed to common law, the title to the find depends on the finder's fulfillment of specific obligations. After complying with those duties, the finder can keep the object even against the true owner. The situation is also different between the master and his employee. Civilian law seems to favour the finder as to the employer. As regards the acquisition of treasure, civilian private law has developed a special mechanism, solving the conflict between the finder and the owner of the land. It allocates the title to the discovered treasure by dividing it equally between finder and landowner. Such allocated ownership can then serve as a ground for determining compensation or rewards according to special statutes protecting cultural property. The opinion as to the situation of the trespassing finder, however, seems to be equally divided as in the common law of finders.

## I. The Acquisition of Title in General

In most civil law countries, the finder of a lost object becomes the owner therof after notifying the relevant authorities and subject to the expiry of a specific notification period in which the real owner has the possibility to collect the object. As opposed to common law, where the true owner (or even the predecessor in title) can still recover the lost object, in civilian jurisdictions the former owner's title is being extinguished after the expiry of the notification period providing the finder with a 'good title'.[644] Until the notification period is expired, the finder has the immediate right of possession or, in jurisdictions where he has to deliver the found item to the municipality, a kind of expectant right.

This notification period varies between 6 months and three years. Such provision can be found for example in *Poland*[645], *Slovenia*[646], *Estonia*[647] or *Germany*[648].

In *Hungary*, if a thing has no owner, anybody may acquire ownership by taking possession thereof.[649] In the case, where an owner presumably exists, the finder acquires ownership, if he has done everything prescribed by law in order to return the thing to its owner, and the owner has not come forward to take possession of the thing within one year of the day on which it was found.[650]

In *Albania*, the finder of a lost object acquires ownership thereof after he has handed it over to the relevant administrative unit, which will keep the object for three years. After the expiry of that period this object or the sale price of it will be transferred in ownership to the person who has found it, who will pay the expenses of keeping it.[651] *Estonia* provides for a special provision regarding objects which are expensive or difficult in safekeeping, during the notification period.

**644** See for example Hans Joseph Wieling, Property Law, Vol. I: Chattels, Possession and the Rights to Movables (1990).
**645** 1 year, Articles 183–187 Polish Civil Code.
**646** 1 year, Art. 52 Slovenian Law of Property Act.
**647** 1 year, Art. 100 Estonian Law of Property Act 2001
**648** § 965 German Civil Code (BGB)
**649** Sect. 127 Hungarian Civil Code.
**650** Sect. 129 Hungarian Civil Code.
**651** Articles 184 and 186 Albanian Civil Code.

After public notification, a finder has the right to sell the thing by public auction if safe-keeping of the thing is excessively expensive, if the thing is highly perishable or if a public establishment or the police have kept the thing for six months.[652]

There are countries where the finder has no duties to fulfil, however, his possessory title is subject to a limitation period. In *France*, for example, possession of a lost thing counts as title against everyone but the true owner. After three years, the owner simply loses the right to recover the item.

However, in a few former communist states, all found objects become state property, regardless of their material or historic value. The acquisition of title to lost items simply does not exist. In *Bulgaria*, the person who has found a lost object must immediately turn it over to the relevant Municipal Property Office.[653] In case the real owner does not come forward to collect it within one year, the finder is only entitled to a reward, which amounts up to ten percent of the value of the object. The reward however may be reduced by the court, taking into consideration the property status of the person who has lost the property or when the full amount of the reward is excessively high.

A similar provision can be found in the *Czech Republic*, where after a certain lapse of time, found objects ipso jure pass into the ownership of the state.[654] After the object was handed over to the authorities by the finder, the owner has got one year to collect the thing in question. In case he does not, the object becomes the property of the State, instead of the finder's property.[655] The finder is only entitled to be reimbursed for his cost as well as to a reward, which amounts up to 10 % of the value of the object.

## II. Master versus Servant

As opposed to common law, civil law courts generally seem to favour the finder to the employer or owner of the premises where the item was found.

Although many civil law countries adopted the principle that the servant holds possession for the master, this principle only applies in cases where the employee has been explicitly advised to safeguard eventually found things by

652 Art. 99 Estonian Law of Property Act 2001.
653 Sect. 88 Bulgarian Civil Code.
654 Sect. 135 Czech Civil Code.
655 Sect. 135 (1) Czech Civil Code.

contract.[656] In German law, employees generally acquire possession of found items even if they have been found on the premises of the employer when the find did not occur in the course of employment. Thus, for example a factory worker would be entitled to keep the wallet of a customer found on the parking lot belonging to the factory.[657] To determine the proximity between the employment and the discovery, civil law courts only refer to the servant's contract of employment, which has to be interpreted according to the facts of the specific case.

In the German *Cinema-case*, an usher found a brilliant ring worth 2500 former Deutsche Mark (DM) and claimed title to it as against the owner of the cinema.[658] According to her employment contract, the cinema has to be inspected for lost objects after the last screening and all found objects are to be returned to the cinema management. The *Bundesgerichtshof* (BGH) held in this case, that the usher was not the finder of the object according to § 965 BGB, as she was only the employer's agent. Upon the finding of the ring, her employer immediately acquired possession to it according to § 855 BGB, and was thus held by the court to be the finder of the ring. Similarly, a waiter working for the German railway was not entitled to keep found items he discovered in the restaurant carriage of the train.[659]

The question was also discussed in relation to found valuables, where it was held that the test similarly applies to treasure finds. In the *Lübeck hoard*-case[660] a dredge operator who has happened upon gold and silver coins during some demolition works in the Hansetown of Lübeck, Germany, was held to be entitled to keep them as against both the landowner and the employer. The gold was found on land belonging to the county Schleswig-Holstein. The contract between the county and the independent contractor whom the county had hired to conduct the demolition works contained a provision which provided for the county's right to retain built-in-parts, chattels of historical value or parts which had the quality to be reused in later construction works. The dredge operator was an employee of the independent contractor. He happened upon the coins during construction works for a building and immediately informed his employer who then in turn informed the respective Institute for Prehistory and Early History. All three, the dredge operator, the independent contractor, and the county claimed

---

**656** Cp. the Lübeck hoard-case, BGH Z 103, 101 (1988), below. But cp. also e. g. the Austrian Civil Code, art. 401, where this principle was codified.
**657** J v. Staudinger, Commentary to the BGB (Kommentar zum Bürgerlichen Gesetzbuch, 2005), § 965, at 11.
**658** BGHZ 8,130 (1952).
**659** LG Frankfurt NJW 1956, 573, at 574.
**660** BGHZ 103, 101 (1988).

title to the treasure. In this case, the court pointed out that "in awarding the finder with the title to the finder's share, § 984 BGB wants to reward the person whose agency contributed to the treasure being returned into circulation."[661] The court held that the dredge operator's discovery was merely the occasion of the discovery or merely afforded the opportunity for it. The court denied the county's and the contractor's claim because the dredge operator had not explicitly been advised to deliver occasional finds to his employer.

A similar case was decided in the *Netherlands*, where during construction works, not qualifying as licenced archaeological excavation, an employee of the company found a helmet dating from Roman times and subsequently sold it for 6000 Guilders.[662] The City of Woerden tried to recover the helmet, arguing that the employee did not have the right to dispose of the helmet without the city's consent. According to the city, the employee could not have acquired property of the helmet. The reasoning of the city would have been correct had the helmet been found during licenced archaeological excavations: according to Art. 50 of the Monuments and Building Act 1988 which deals with the protection of immovable property[663], ownership of objects found during archaeological excavations is granted either to the municipality in whose territory the object was found or the province. However, the Dutch Monuments and Historic Buildings Act did not apply in this case and title was allocated according to the Dutch implementation of the equitable division principle.[664] The employee was granted half of the find. As a consequence, the employee did have the right to dispose of his share ownership with respect to the helmet. Given that no action of recovery exists against a co-proprietor, the City of Woerden could not recover the helmet from the person who acquired half of the property from the employee.

In *Austria*, this favourable treatment of the employee has even been codified in Art. 401 of the Austrian Civil Code, stating that workmen, who discover treasure, are entitled to a third of its value, regardless whether the find was made in the course of employment, subject to the exception of workmen hired for the purpose of archaeological excavations.

**661** RG (Supreme Court of the *German Reich*) [1896] 12, 14, RG Z 70, 308, at 311.

**662** District Court Utrecht 5 February 2003, NJ 2003, 211, AF4007.

**663** Monumentenwet 1988. In 2008 the Monuments Act was amendeed by the Act on the Managment and Care of Archaeological Monuments to ensure the implementation of the Valetta Convention 1992, see Katja Lubina, Dutch Report, in T. Kono/S.Wrbka, Uniform Laws, at 564.

**664** Art. 5:13 Dutch Cultural Heritage Code.

### III. Finder versus Occupier

In order to elaborate the relationship between finder and landowner/occupier in civil law, a few mechanisms of civil property law have to be briefly illustrated.

There are different types of possession in civilian property law. To take German law as an example, differentiates between direct possession, which is the factual power over an object (§§ 854 I and 872 I BGB) and indirect possession. Indirect possession under § 868 I BGB is created through the establishment of a contractual or non-contractual relationship allowing indirect possession (*Besitzmittlungsverhältnis).* The main requirement characterising a relationship of indirect possession between the direct possessor (*unmittelbarer Besitzer*) and the indirect possessor (*Besitzmittler*) is the indirect possessor's right to claim for the return of the object. This legal construction can be equated to the common law of bailment, where the bailee would have direct possession and the bailor indirect possession. In most civil law countries, possession can be either for oneself or for another. In German law, § 855 BGB concerning the possessor's agent, states that a person is not a possessor if he exercises the factual power over an object for another in someone else's household, business or a similar relationship.

The finding of a lost object is to be classified as a case of agency. As we have seen above, the person who finds a thing has to fulfil certain duties towards the loser of the property in order to gain title. A possessor's agent cannot become possessor of found objects. In these cases, possession is immediately established for the person he is the agent of, as in the forth mentioned *Cinema* – case, where an usher found a brilliant ring and claimed title to it as against the owner of the cinema.[665] The *Bundesgerichtshof* held in this case, that the usher was not the finder of the object.

In cases, where the finder has no contractual relationship to the owner/occupier of the premises, the conflict between finder and owner/occupier of the land or the premises where the object was found is solved through a 'manifest intention' – test, similarly as it is the case under common law. It is generally assumed that the owner or occupier of the premises has the intention to control and possess all objects that can be found upon or in it. This intention, however, has to be manifested. In the *Supermarket* – case[666], the court held the manifest intention-test is sufficed when supermarket employees were advised to return all found objects to the store manager, where they were registered in the lost prop-

**665** BGHZ 8, 130 (1952).
**666** BGHZ 101, 186 (1987).

erty register. In the case, a customer discovered a 500,– former Deutsche Mark[667] note under a shelf and claimed to title it upon the expiry of the notification period and after he had notified the store management. The court awarded title to the money to the supermarket company.

As a result, under German law, chattels on these premises do not count as lost and consequently cannot be found by a random finder but only by the occupier/owner himself, where a manifest intention of the owner/occupier could be identified. The finder again does become the possessor's agent.

In *Swedish* law, the collision between finder's and landowner's rights has been abolished. There, landowners have no title to finds discovered on their land. The landowner will prevail only insofar as a "find" is a fixture or a fitting to real property and not a movable.[668]

## IV. Fortuitously Discovered Treasure

Many civil law countries incorporate special provisions concerned with the fortuitous discovery of treasure in its civil codes. The main concern was to solve the finder/ landowner conflict, which turned out to be the clear downside of the common law of finders. The so-called *Hadrianic Partition* or the principle of *equitable division* derives from ancient Roman law and contains one of the oldest known dispositions on treasure trove. According to the Justinian Institutes, the Emperor Hadrian allowed the finder of treasure trove to keep all trove found on his own land or found accidentally on sacred or religious land. If anyone fortuitously found treasure on another man's land, the Emperor allowed half of it to the owner of the soil.[669] Consistently with this, he decided that treasure found on his private domain was half to go to the finder and half to the Emperor. If found in a place which is public or belongs to the fiscus, half goes to the city or the fiscus, half to the finder. Treasure is defined as "movables hidden long ago by unknown owners".[670]

---

**667** Deutsche Mark (former German currency).

**668** Thomas Adlercreutz, Property Rights and Protection of Cultural Heritage in Sweden, 7 IJCP (1998) 410.

**669** Fritz Schultz, Classical Roman Law (1951), at 362; R.W Lee, Elements of Roman Law (1956), at § 211 et seq.

**670** R.W. Lee, Elements of Roman Law, at § 185.

### 1. The Allocation of Title based on Equitable Division

Today, the majority of civil law nations adopted the *Hadrianic Partition* or a variation thereof and split treasure trove in equal shares between the owner of the property and the finder.[671] In most codes, *treasure* is similarly defined as "chattels which have been hidden for such a long time that the owner cannot be ascertained."[672]

In some countries, such as *Italy, Malta, Slovenia or Austria*, the equitable division principle is still valid law, however it is subject to a reservation in cases of objects of special historic, archaeological, paleontological or artistic value. Then cultural property law provisions come into place which vest title in the state.

One of the few countries which still solely relies on the ancient principle is *Latvia.*[673] Sections 952 and 953 of the Latvian Civil Code state that ownership of concealed property discovered on one's own land or on ownerless land accrues to the finder,[674] whereby those who accidentally find concealed property on the land of another person shall acquire half thereof and the other half accrues to the owner of the land. Sect. 953 specifically prohibits searching for concealed property on land of another person and sanctions the trespasser with the lack of acquisition of title.

According to the Cultural Heritage Code, the finder has to notify the state inspection within 10 days and finds have to be delivered to the heritage office, where a decision is taken of the inclusion of such objects in the list of state protected cultural monuments.[675] If a find is being included into the list, the state has then a right to inspect, preserve, and if necessary expropriate the object and in the case of a sale, it has the right of first refusal[676]

As opposed to *Latvia*, some of the new Eastern European Member States preferred to abolish the *Hadrianic Partition* altogether in favour of new cultural property statutes which have been incorporated into the civil codes after the

**671** See also R.H. Helmholz, Equitable Division and the Law of Finders, at 314.

**672** Art. 716 French CC, whereby here only objects count as treasure, which have been discovered by chance; also Malta: Sec 563. (1) CC, Moldavia, art. 327 CC, Germany § 984 BGB (in lands without "Schatzregal" e.g. Hessen, Bayern, Nordrhein-Westfalen) Netherlands, Art. 5:13 (1) CC, Turkmenistan, Art. 215 CC, Italy Art 932 CC; Slovenia, Art. 53 CC, Belgium, art 716 CC; Latvia, sec. 953 CC, Austria Art. 399 CC; but equally in the USA, the Louisiana, La. Civ Code art 3420.

**673** Similarly Belgium, which only provides for a reporting requirement, see Johann van Heesch, Belgian Laws Regarding Coin Finds, 43 CIN, Compte Rendu (1996) 34.

**674** Concealed property means all valuable property buried in the earth, immured or in any other way concealed, whose owner due to the length of time elapsed is no longer able to be known, see sec. 953 Latvian Civil Code.

**675** Sect. 17 Latvian law on Protection of Cultural Monuments 1995 (amended 2005).

**676** Sections 10, 11 13, Monuments Act.

legal reform. In *Poland*, formerly title to treasures was shared between the finder and owner of the land where the treasure had been discovered,[677] whereas today, the chattel becomes the ownership of the state, if it is of material or scientific or artistic value and the finder has to deliver the object to the relevant authorities.[678]

*Hungary* previously had a preemption right to all finds of cultural significance, the compensation being divided between the finder and the owner of the land, whereas after the law reform the ownership of all archaeological objects found on or beneath the soil, in the water beds or elsewhere vests in the state.[679] The same is valid for objects having historical, monumental or museum value, which were hidden by unknown persons or the ownership of which have been forgotten.[680]

In countries who opted not to adopt state ownership of fortuitously discovered artefacts but prefer a right of pre-emption or compulsory acquisition, the equitable division principle provides for an allocation of title and is complemented through provisions in special codes designed to protect heritage items, which contain reporting or delivery obligations and rules of conduct in the case a heritage item is found.

On the ground of title being allocated through division, the finder and the occupier of land are entitled to a reward or compensation. For example, in the county of *Nordrhein-Westfalen, Germany*, § 16 of the Cultural Heritage Code prohibits any further activities on the site after the discovery of an archaeological artefact. The find has to be reported and is not allowed to be removed until three days after the heritage office was informed of its whereabouts. The heritage office is entitled to excavate and to evaluate the site, as well as to keep the found items in its possession for a period of six months. § 18 I CHC rules that the heritage item has to be delivered to the heritage office upon the payment of compensation. The person who is losing the ownership to a found treasure by expropriation is then entitled to a compensation of the full market value of the chattel.[681] According to *equitable division*, the finder and landowner acquire title to the dis-

---

**677** Edward Muszalski, Civil Codes Binding in Central Poland (in Polish, Kodeksy cywilne obowiązujące na Ziemiach centralnych Polski, Warsaw 1936), at 669.

**678** Art. 189 Polish Civil Code.

**679** Section 172 (a) Hungarian Civil Code and sect. 8 of Act LXIV of 2001; cp. on this David Papp, paper presented at a conference organised by the Institute fo Art and Law, Hungary Pecs, Hungary, 12–13 July 2007, available over www.ial.co.uk

**680** Sect. 132(3) Hungarian Civil Code.

**681** See § 17 DSchG, § 18 Abs. 3 DSchG and § 34 Abs. 3 Satz 2 DSchG Nordrhein-Westfalen.

covered object, and based on that are entitled to compensation against each other.

Similarly, in *France*, according to Art. 716 French Civil Code a treasure belongs to the person who finds it on his own land, but if the treasure is found on the land of another, one half belongs to the discoverer and the other half to the land-owner. The finder and the owner must declare the find to the mayor of the town.[682] The mayor will then inform the government representative. The find should be delivered to the relevant authority upon request for a period of five years maximum.[683] If the antiquity is of interest for the state, it can buy it by compulsory purchase for an amount agreed with the owner and the finder. If there is a disagreement, an independent appraiser will value the find. If the state decides not to exercise its pre-emption right, the find can be kept by the finder and owner.

### 2. The Conflict between Civil and Public law

Problems can arise when *equitable division* collides with prohibitions contained in the cultural heritage statutes, which constitute public law instruments. Where a finder fortuitously discovers an archaeological artefact and complies with all requirements inflicted upon him by the Cultural Heritage Code obliging him to immediately suspend any activity in order to enable professional excavation, the question arises as to who is the "finder" of the successive finds made in the course of further excavations conducted by professionals. Such a situation arose in a German case concerning the discovery of some ancient roman tombs.

In this case, ancient Roman tombs were discovered during construction works in the German town of Düsseldorf.[684] The tomb was intact and included precious grave goods. The grave was found by the builder-owner and according to § 15 I of the Cultural Property Code of the county Nordrhein-Westfalen, immediately reported to the regional Historic Buildings and Monuments Office. The office made use of its right to excavate the site and eight other tombs including grave goods were found. The Historic Buildings office contended that it was the discoverer of the eight remaining tombs and thus the builder-owner's claim for the finder's share of the whole treasure had been declined by the cultural ministry.

---

**682** Sect. L 531–14 Code du Patrimoine.
**683** Sect. L. 531–16 Code du Patrimoine.
**684** OLG Duesseldorf (1993), at 106–107.

The result of the case largely depended on whether the discovered treasure is held to be a whole single entity or whether each individual piece has to be regarded as a separate chattel capable of being acquired.[685] If the treasure was regarded as one single entity although successive finds might still be buried in the ground, certainly the first discoverer will be entitled to the finder's share of the whole entity. If however, the treasure is held to be consisting of many singular pieces, then theoretically a subsequent finder could be entitled to the finders share to those pieces by unearthing them. In the *Lübeck – hoard* case, concerning the discovery of a hoard of precious gold and silver coins, the German Supreme Court held that the first discoverer should be entitled to the whole hoard without even considering the forth mentioned questions.[686]

In the *Roman tomb* – case, the appellate court concluded that the discovery of a fragment of the treasure suffices to claim the finder's share for the whole treasure, provided that the whole treasure was excavated right upon the discovery by authorised members of the Historic Monuments Office. The court held that "the first discoverer should be awarded as only through his discovery any further excavations were rendered possible. Another outcome would contravene the law whose purpose is only the protection and preservation of German heritage and not the expropriation of owners without providing for compensation."

The facts of the *Roman tomb* – case accentuate the problems that can arise from the application of the *equitable division* principle when applied together with the provisions contained in the cultural heritage codes. But the result in the *Roman tomb* – case seems to be one with which future courts would generally endeavour to conform.

As a general rule, the first finder will therefore acquire title to half of the finds subsequently discovered, if (1) the subsequent finds were excavated in close spatiotemporal proximity to the first find, (2) if the finder abstained from further excavations owing to a statutory prohibition, and (3) if it can be assumed that he would have discovered the subsequent treasure if it was not for the statutory prohibition. That will regularly not be the case if the excavation of it required special archaeological knowledge or specialist archaeological equipment or tools.

**685** For a thorough discussion of this question see Heinrich Dörner, Zivilrechtliche Probleme der Bodendenkmalpflege (1992), at 29 and 57.
**686** BGHZ 103, 101 (1988).

### 3. Treasure Acquired through Trespass

There is virtually no case law and no codified law in mainland Europe on the question whether a finder who violates statutory prohibitions concerned with the protection of heritage items still acquires title to them as a consequence of applying finder's law. Certainly, he will be subject to criminal sanctions and fines.

As between a trespassing finder and the landowner, many civil law countries provide codified provisions concerning the acquisition of title. Thus in *Austria*, sect. 400 of the Austrian Civil Code provides that a person who commits trespass on another's land or who otherwise wrongfully interferes with another's property and by virtue of this wrong discovers a treasure, the title to this treasure vest in the owner of the property, or in the case an owner does not exist, it vests in the state. The same provision can be found in *Latvia*, where the civil code prohibits searching for treasure on another's land and the title to such found treasure should belong to the owner of the land where the chattel was found.[687]

In countries where the prohibition of trespass has not been codified in the civil code, the scholarly opinions are divided as to whether a person who violates provisions which are designed to protect cultural property can still acquire valid title to them. Some hold that the finder's rights are not being affected by trespass, as the purpose of cultural heritage protection laws is only to prohibit illegal excavation but not to allocate property rights. Thus, the trespassing finder acquires title to the discovered object even if he becomes subject to charges and penalties according to the Cultural Heritage Code.[688] If the treasure was discovered in a country which provides for state ownership of antiquities, the result is simple: the state becomes the owner of the antiquity ipso iure.

The finder's rights as against a third party however are much clearer than under the Common Law, where the trespassing finder acquires "bare possession" or "no title at all." Under civil law, the trespassing finder acquires possessory title.[689]

## V. Concluding Remarks to the Civilian Law of Finds

As opposed to common law, it could be observed that the civilian law of finds is more generous to the finder. Firstly, the finder gets good title after the expiry of a

---

**687** Sect. 953 Latvian Civil Code.

**688** See J. v. Staudinger, Book 3: Property Law (Sachenrecht), at § 984; H. Dörner, Zivilrechtliche Probleme, at 65.

**689** Cp. J.v. Staudinger, ibid, §§ 858, 1007.

certain notification period even against the true owner. As regards the finder/landowner conflict in respect of treasure, the finder is entitled to half of the find. The old roman concept of *equitable division* provides a reasonable way to resolve competing claims between the finder and landowner that are apt to be about equally strong. The rule avoids the fine and artificial distinction that common law has created between things in or attached to land and superincumbent chattels as well as chattels that have been naturally in the ground and chattels that have been lost or abandoned.

However, *equitable division* was not meant to protect heritage items but to settle questions of ownership to precious objects found in the ground. For this reason the draftsmen of the civil codes in civilian jurisdictions did not necessary troubled themselves for clear definitions of what constitutes treasure for the purpose of the the equitable division rule. In the codes analysed above, nothing is said about quantity or the value of the find. In *France*, the additional requirement is that treasure has to be discovered by chance, meaning that theoretically metal detectorist searching methodically for antiquities would not fall under this rule and ownership automatically passes to the landowner.

A further downside proves to be that finders lie about where they have found the hoard, and always claim that it was on their own land.[690] In some civil law countries there is no reporting requirement to the owner of the land, but the finder becomes subject to criminal charges for trespassing or fraudulent conversion if he fails to inform the owner of the discovery.

## § 4. Excursion: Finders Law as a Means of Protecting Antiquities

This paragraph discusses the general suitability of the common and civilian law of finds as a mechanism to protect movable antiquities. It elaborates upon the question which legal regieme gives a finder more incentive to report the find of a precious item instead of turning to the black market. The last part of this paragraph presents the Portable Antiquities Scheme, an alternative method introduced by the English government to secure data derived from archaeological finds which are not covered by the English Treasure Act 1996.

690 As for Belgium, see Johann van Heesch, Belgian Laws Regarding Coin Finds, 43 CIN, Compte Rendu (1996) 82.

## I. The Need for an Incentive to Return Archaeological Finds into Circulation

The goal of antiquities protection is to safe the tangible and intangible value contained in heritage items. Ultimately, this means that artefacts should be left *in situ* where they where discovered in order to enable professional archaeologists to excavate the find. At least however, the aim is to record and safe the data derived from archaeological objects and to preserve their tangible value for future generations. Finder's law should thus be constructed as to make sure that the finder at least returns the find into circulation. However, the finder will go public with the find only if he can be certain that he can keep the find or, alternatively, receive compensation, a reward, or other recognition. Although in most cases keeping the find would entail prosecution under criminal law, sanctions have proven to be a small deterrent.[691]

Moreover, going public with the find gives the finder free publicity, thereby establishing some record of the antiquity's provenance and helping to create a market for the antiquity.[692] An antiquity's provenance constitutes added value. Where it was found and how it was found contribute to the archeological and historical value of the antiquity. In addition, the better the condition of the antiquity, the more money it commands on the market.[693]

Under common law, the position of the finder concerning the title to fortuitously discovered antiquities has proven to be uncertain, if not unpredictable. The law leans towards awarding the title to the owner of the land on which the item was found, leaving the finder with nothing if he goes public with the find. Hence, from a law and economics perspective, a finder has no incentive to go public with found property.[694] The legal uncertainty concerning the finder's title to fortuitously discovered antiquities can rather lead to finders concealing their find and turning towards the black market.

In civil law jurisdictions, if the finder goes public with the find, and the true owner does not claim the item within a reasonable period of time, typically the finder is awarded title to the found property. On the other hand, if a finder does not come forward with his or her find, he or she does not gain title to the item,

---

**691** See e.g. David Loewenthal, Why Sanctions Seldom Work: Reflections on Cultural Property Internationalism, 12 IJCP (2005) 393.

**692** See Lindsay E. Willis, Looting in Ancient Mesopotamia: A Legislation Scheme for the Protection of Iraq's Cultural Heritage, 34 Ga. J. Int'l & Comp. L. (2005) 221, at 224 (describing Iraqi law granting the first right of publicity to the finder subject to detailed accounts of excavation and any publications about the antiquity).

**693** See Lisa Borodkin, The Economics of Antiquities Looting, at 387.

**694** Cp. also Peter T. Wendel, Protecting Newly Discovered Antiquities, at 1015 et seq.

and he or she may be subject to civil and/or criminal penalties. Regarding archaeological finds, the discovery is awarded to the finder if found on his own land. If found on another's land, the finder is awarded half of its value.

The civilian "finders" approach to newly discovered antiquities creates a strong incentive for a finder to go public with the find, and as part of that process, providing at least some information concerning the antiquity's provenance. As opposed to common law, the finder who finds an antiquity on another's land can be sure that he will be awarded a share of the value of the find. Hence, a development of the common law towards this approach would be constructive both for the legal certainty concerning ordinary finds and for the protection of movable antiquities.

The benefits of the civilian concept of *equitable division* for the common law have already been recognised by common law academics in the past. The first source suggesting the division of the find between the finder and the owner of the premises was a comment published in *Fordham Law Review* in 1939.[695] The comment reviewed the categories that the law has developed to resolve finder's cases, setting out the relevant English and American authorities. It pointed out the difficulties attendant upon these categories and advocated a rule that would divide found property between the person who discovers it and the possessor of the *locus in quo*.[696] The comment argued that a finder who is being deprived of his share of the find is being encouraged to dishonesty and therefore the law fails its primary goal – the protection of the owner. In the case of archaeological finds, it fails to protect the information encoded in the object and returning the heritage item back to circulation. As a practical matter, a solution was needed that encouraged honesty of the part of all concerned. Hence the comment proposed that the owner of the premises and the finder should share in the goods equitably.

The lead was picked up by R.H. Helmholz, in an article published in *Fordham Law Review* in 1984.[697] In this paper, Helmholz concluded that despite the absence of explicit judicial recognition, the evolving American case law does provide authority in some situations for the application of *equitable division* between the finder and the owner of the *locus quo*.[698] Helmholz argued that the existing case law is moving closer to the concept of equitable division under the principles of joint finding. He advocated that claims which are evenly balanced

**695** Anonymous Comment, Lost, Mislaid and Abandoned Property, Curbing the Enthusiasm of Finders, 8 Fordham L. Rev. (1938) 222.

**696** Curbing the Enthusiasm of Finders, ibid, at 237.

**697** Cp. R.H. Helmholz, Equitable Division and the Law of Finders, at 314.

**698** R.H. Helmholz, Equitable Division, at 317.

and where *equitable division* is possible, the fairest course would be to divide the property.[699]

Under this principle, it is enough that when several persons participate in a finding, they are joint finders with equal rights in the property found.

This result was reached in the American case *Keron v Cashman*[700], an 1896 New Jersey case, in which one of five boys walking along a railway track came upon an old sock tied on both ends. He threw it at one of his companions and they tossed it back and forth. At length, it broke and money fell out. The boy who had first picked it up claimed it all, but the New Jersey Court of Chancery held that the finding had not occurred until the sock burst and divided the money equally among all boys. What made the sharing of the money the correct result, according to this case, was the equivalent status of the finders. They were walking together until they had treated the sock as common possession. More recent cases however, go beyond these requirements. It is now clear, that common possession before discovery of the real value of the item is not necessary for joint finding to occur. It is enough that if several persons participate in a finding, they are joint finders. This was the result in *Edmonds v Ronella*, an American case where two boys picked up a manila envelope in a grocery store parking lot.[701] Uncertain about what to do with it, they took it to a friend for advice. The envelope contained $ 12.300 in cash, and the New York court held in a subsequent claim that the three of them were joint finders. Each child took a third, because the court determined that the lost money was not found in a legal sense until the three children had decided together to claim the money by removing it from the lot.

Under common law, *equitable division* could become reality under the principle of joint ownership. There, two or more people may hold a chattel either as "joint tenants" or "tenants in common".[702]

---

**699** Similarly, John M. Kleeburg, The Law and Practice Regarding Coin Finds, CIM, Compte rendu 53 (2006) 13; M. June Harris, Who Owns the Pot of Gold at the End of the Rainbow? A Review of the Impact of Cultural Property on Finders and Salvage Laws, 14 Ariz. J. Int'l & Comp. L. (1997) 223, at 225–30.

**700** 33 Atl. Rep. (N.J.) (1896) 1055.

**701** Edmonds v Ronella, 73 Misc. 2d 598, 342 N.Y.S. 2d 408 (1973). See also Keron v. Cashman 33 Atl. Rep. 1055 (N.J.) (1896); noted in (1896–1897) 10 Harvard L.R., 63. See also Cummings v. Stone 13 Mich. 80 (1864); Ralph Aigler, Comment, 21 Michigan Law Review (1922–1923) 664, at 681; Robinson v. Western Australian Museum (1977) 51 A.L.J.R. 806, esp. at 822–823 per Stephen and J., at 824 per Mason J.

**702** As to co-ownerhip of chattels see i. e. Judith Hill and Elizabeth Bow–Smith, in: Palmer and Mckendrick (eds.), Interest in Goods (2$^{nd}$ ed. 1998), 251; Dukeminier and Krier, Property (3rd ed. 1993) 325.

Theoretically however, if a finder would obtain title to found antiquities, under the traditional law of finders, the typical finder may accidentally damage the archeological, historical, and other intangible information associated with the newly discovered antiquity.[703] The typical finder is not a learned archaeologist and does not appreciate the importance, and fragility, of the *locus in quo* of the find.[704] The finder's focus is on the tangible antiquity itself, not the intangible archeological, historical, and/or cultural information connected with the find. Accordingly, the most finders will extract the antiquity with little to no care for the intangible components of the find. But often the find will result in at least some of the intangible information being secured. As long as the finder was not trespassing, the finder has an incentive to disclose information concerning the find. This information will help to establish the provenance of the antiquity, and the more information about the provenance, the more valuable the antiquity. Furthermore, giving the finder exclusive and absolute property rights in the newly discovered antiquity will maximize the probability that the antiquity will end up in a foreign country's museum or collector's hands.

Hence, protecting antiquities through the vehicle of finder's law only makes sense when complemented with statutory provision which are especially designed to protect archaeological artefacts. Such provision will have to contain measures to secure the information *in situ*, and to protect the item from damage due to unprofessional excavation. In order for such provisions to be successful, the finder will have to be ensured that the find will be returned to him after the vital information has been secured or provided with compensation for the loss of title.

Such provisions not necessarily would have to be coupled with sanctions or fines. The protection of the archaeological data could already be improved by raising public awareness of the importance of the context in which the item has been discovered.

In fact, the collaboration of finder's law and statutory schemes already proved to be effective. In Germany, several counties voted against state ownership of antiquities owing to the lack of successful reportings in countries which adopted state ownership of heritage items. In Rheinland Pfalz, after six years of "Schatzregal"[705] the reality was that only 2 % of archaeological discoveries could be ascribed to a reported find whereas 98 % were derived from state controlled archaeological excavation. Baden-Württemberg is having a similar de-

703 As to the importance of the historical context see Chapter 1 § III 3.
704 M. L. Dutra, Protecting Cultural Relics in the People's Republic of China, at 65.
705 For the legal institute of the German *Schatzregal* note Part II of this study.

flating experience with only very few finds being acquired by the state through finder's reports. In Bavaria on the other hand, a land which does not provide for state ownership of antiquities, thousands of finds are being reported each year.[706] This may be accounted to the lack of fear that the finds will be taken away from the finders without any compensation. Bavaria also opted against state ownership of antiquities as it contributes to the diversion and corruption of archaeological records as finds are being falsely reported in counties with no state ownership of heritage items.[707]

## II. The Protection of Archaeological Data through the Portable Antiquities Scheme

The English government has recognised the deficiencies of finder's law for antiquities protection. Parallel with the new Treasure Act 1996, it introduced the Portable Antiquities Scheme as an adversarial approach to safe archaeologically valuable information of fortuitously discovered antiquities through members of the public.[708] As opposed to the Treasure Act, the scheme has no effect on the title to finds; however, it provides a mechanism of saving data contained in objects of historical significance.

Before the recent antiquities law reform, the only widespread legal protection in England and Wales granted to antiquities that were not found near protected monuments, was the common law of treasure trove.[709] However, only objects of gold or silver, deliberately hidden with the intention of recovery, qualified as treasure trove and became the property of the Crown.[710] The common law definition was often criticised because it allowed far too many valuable

**706** See Fischer zu Cramburg, Das Schatzregal (2001), at 196.
**707** Niklot Klüssendorf, Der Münzschatz von Niederhohne (1987), at 408.
**708** Generally on the Portable Antiquities Scheme, see e.g. Roger Bland, The Treasure Act and the Portable Antiquities Scheme: A Progress Report, 4 AAL (1999) 191; Roger Bland, Rescuing Our Neglected Heritage: The Evolution of the Government's Policy on Portable Antiquities in England and Wales, 14 Cultural Trends (2005) 257; Roger Bland, A Pragmatic Approach to the Problem of Portable Antiquities: The Experience of England and Wales, 79 Antiquity (2005) 440; Derek Fincham, A Coordinated Legal and Policy Approach to Undiscovered Antiquities: Adapting the Cultural Heritgae Policy of England and Wales to Other Nations of Origin, 15 IJCP (2008) 347–370; N. Palmer Bailment, at 26–069; Portable Antiquities – A Discussion Document, (1996) 1 AAL, Issue 2, 171.
**709** On the English law of treasre trove cp. Part I Chapter 2 § 2 3 a
**710** Attorney-General of the Duchy of Lancaster v. G.E. Overton (Farms) Ltd., 3 All E.R. 503 (1980).

finds to escape regulation because they fell short of the common law definition. These concerns led to enactment of the Treasure Act 1996.[711] If a newly discovered object falls within the scope of the Treasure Act, reporting this find is mandatory, and it becomes property of the Crown. If an object does not meet the treasure threshold, reporting is merely voluntary.

In a government discussion paper published in 1996, the officials stated that only a small percentage of objects found by the public are recorded which "represents a considerable loss to the nation's heritage".[712] In order to complement the Treasure Act, the Department for Culture Media and Sport together with the British Museum and the Heritage Lottery Fund founded the Portable Antiquities Scheme, which encourages voluntary reporting of finds for those objects which fall outside the scope of the Treasure Act.[713] The importance of the Portable Antiquities Scheme lies in its ability to use the public as a tool for archaeologists and researchers – it effectively recruits the public into policing and reporting finds on a totally voluntary basis.[714] Currently, 36 Finds Liaison Officers (FLOs), covering the whole of England and Wales, are employed in the work of the Scheme. They educate the public about the importance of archaeological material and encourage to report finds. The FLOs are based with local 'host' partner organisations, who manage them on a day-to-day basis. The Central Unit is based at the British Museum, though five of the six Finds Advisers are based elsewhere. In 2005/6, 42 part-time Finds Liaison Assistants (FLAs) and 83 volunteers provided an invaluable contribution to the work of the Scheme.[715] During the operation of the Scheme, 360 talks (attended by 13,390 people) have been given about the PAS. At least 468 Finds Days, exhibitions and other events (attended by 14,123 people) have been organised. More than 5,439 children have experienced the educational work of the Scheme. 294 articles about the work of the Scheme have been published or broadcast in the media.

The system has certainly encouraged treasure hunters to report their finds.[716] As a result, a lot more finds are being reported, and an impressive database is

**711** Treasure Act 1996 (c.24).

**712** Cp. Portable Antiquities Discussion Document, at 171. Around 400.000 finds made each year are not covered by the treasure act and thus do not have to be reported.

**713** The Scheme runs an own website to give information to the general public: www.finds.org.uk.

**714** Cp. Roger Bland, A Progress Report, at 191.

**715** Cp. Annual Report 2006/2007.

**716** See Maev Kennedy, 'Unsung Heroes of Heritage' Extolled For Unearthing Hoard of Treasure, Guardian, Jan. 18, 2007, available at http://arts.guardian.co.uk/news/story/0,1992993,00.html.

being created.[717] In 2006/7, the Scheme's Finds Liaison Officers have recorded 57,556 objects; a two-fold increase on 2003/4. Moreover, many important new archaeological sites have been discovered as a result of the finds recorded by the FLOs. These include a new Roman kiln site in Leicestershire, a previously unknown Anglo-Saxon cemetery in Norfolk and a nineteenth-century gunflint production site in Suffolk.[718]

Surprisingly, the voluntary scheme has produced some unexpected benefits. It has not just increased the voluntary reporting of objects which fall below the treasure trove threshold, it has also dramatically increased the reporting of objects which must be reported under the Treasure Act. Before the reporting scheme, few finds were reported. Between 1988 and 1996, there was an average of a little over 23 treasure finds reported annually.[719] In 1998, the first full year of the program, 201 treasure finds were reported. By 2007, 724 treasure finds were reported. This adds to the body of knowledge and precludes a market in unprovenanced objects, as the Scheme produces a better, more responsible attitude among the general public.

Brooches are the most frequently recorded non-coin artefact with 1,780 examples reported. As always, they dominate the category of personal adornment, which also includes pins, finger-rings, bracelets, earrings and beads. Among the items associated with religious activity there have been some remarkable finds, in particular figurines of a three-horned bull from Holbrook, Suffolk and that of a hound from Newchurch.[720]

As a conclusion, the PAS provably succeeded to enhance the protection of heritage items and could serve as a model in order to complement the lack in protection in other jurisdictions. However, it only safes a part of the information adhered to the find. The so important historical context is still being destroyed through the unprofessional removal of the objects from the site. Thus, the Scheme could be complemented through provisions giving incentives to finders to leave archaeological finds *in situ* and informing the relevant Finds Liaison Officers to evaluate the site before the object can be removed.

---

**717** As of 2005, the database had 120,000 objects listed, along with 42,000 publicly available images. See Roger Bland, A Pragmatic Approach to the Problem of Portable Antiquities: The Experience of England and Wales, 79 Antiquity (2005), at 440.

**718** Cp. Annual Report 2006, at http://www.finds.org.uk/documents/report06.pdf

**719** Department of Culture, Media and Sport, Portable Antiquities Scheme Annual Report 2005/6, http://www.finds.org.uk/documents/report06.pdf.

**720** Cp.Annual Report 2006, at http://www.finds.org.uk/documents/report06.pdf

## § 5. Conclusion to Chapter 3

Chapter three comparatively analysed the private law of finds in the common law and civilian jurisdictions as to the general allocation of title to found object. When applying the findings of the analysis to the question how a sovereign can become the owner of treasure under the private law of finds, the analysis of the common law regieme shows that the acqusition of title depends on where the object was found. Objects which became part of the soil cease to be chattels on integration with the land and thereby become the property of the sovereign. However, the intrapolation also revealed that the sole factor that an object has been found on land which belongs to a public authority does not make the sovereign automatically the owner of it. Chattels which were found on the surface of the land can be kept by the person in priority of possession of the item. The owner of the premises will regularly be in priority of possession if he succeeded in manifesting an intention to control chattels which were lost. Objects which were discovered underneath the land but did not become part of the soil are to be treated as an integral part of the realty as against all but the true owner. The law is also not completely clear as to the trespassing finder but leans towards the suggestion that trespass deprives a finder of the title to the found object. As common law does not know any reporting requirements, as is the case in civilian jurisdictions it will be difficult for the soevereign to obtain knowledge of finds which fall foul of the cultural property protection regieme.

Civilian jurisdictions seem more favorable to the finder. The old roman concept of *equitable division* which provides a way to resolve competing claims between the finder of treasure and the landowner that are apt to be about equally strong, is detrimental to the acqusition of title to treasure by a sovereign as it entitles the finder to half of the find. In many jurisdictions however, the state provides for notification and delivery duties. If the antiquity is of interest for the state, it can buy it by compulsory purchase for an amount agreed with the owner and the finder. This for example is the situation in France.

The last section of the chapter elaborated upon the general suitability of private law of finds for antiquities protection. It concludes that while the common law of finders is detrimental to antiquities protection, equitable division as practiced in several civilian jurisdiction constitutes a more favourable system for the protection of movable heritage items through the legal certainty it provides for the finder and landowner.

However, in order to achieve a thorough protection of both the tangible in intangible component of archaeological heritage items, property law provisions which allocate the title to antiquities have to be complemented through special cultural property law provisions which would enable the fortuitously discovered objects to be evaluated *in situ*. Following that, the Portable Antiquities Scheme was presented in the last part of the chapter and although held to be a step in the right direction and a practicable approach to safe archaeological data, it was regarded to be inefficient in protecting the archaeological context of cultural property. In order to improve the scheme's efficiency it could aim to raise public awareness of the importance of archaeological context and the necessity for heritage items to remain *in situ* until the site has been evaluated by professionals.

# Part II: **Turning Rights into Claims**

The aim of Part II of this work is to reflect upon the means of civil recovery of movable cultural property. Although new liberal ideas in respect of dealing with cultural objects such as the idea of the "universal museum", as laid down in the 2002 Declaration on the Importance and Value of Universal Museums,[721] and the notion of the "cultural heritage of all mankind" as laid down in the 1954 Hague Convention[722], have its core of unquestioned validity and indeed constitute important steps to a global understanding of cultural property, it is the author's belief, that cultural objects belong with its original owner, as a matter of law, not as a result of a moral or ethical decision. This is of course subject to the condition that the original owner has a valid claim to the object in terms of title and proof. Moreover, this thesis follows the view that aside from criminal and administrative law, successful cases for the revindication of antiquities will help curbing the illicit trade in cultural objects by discouraging dealers and buyers from acquiring art of uncertain or dubious provenance.

So far, the restitution of art and antiquities gave rise to many unresolved problems and too often, heritage items have not been returned to their original owner. The recovery of stolen or illegally exported heritage items, may it be by a sovereign state or a private individual, creates many unsolved questions. This, on the one hand, stems from the fact that sovereign property interests may not be recognised and enforced in foreign courts. An object being illicitly trafficked is one in respect of which some offence has been committed: such an offence is defined by the laws of the country of origin and may include clandestine excavation, theft, breach of inalienability or rights of pre-emption, failure to comply with trading regulations or violation of export control. Thus, the category of illicit trade constitutes offences based on public laws. Whereas courts of all countries are open to actions for the recovery of stolen property from individuals, they may

---

**721** The 2002 Declaration states that although each case of restitution has to be judged individually, it should acknowledge that museums serve not just the citizens of one nation, but the people of every nation. Museums are agents in the development of culture, whose mission is to foster knowledge by a continuous process of reinterpretation. The Declaration has been signed by 18 major institutions and has been criticised in a number of quarters for its stand on restitution, e.g. Marc O'Neil, Enlightenment museums: universal or merely global? (2004) Museum and Society, 190–202; but see for a different view James Cuno, View from the Universal Museum, in: John H. Merryman (ed), Imperialism, Art and Restitution (2006), at 15–29, arguing that United States courts enforce foreign laws in contradiction of the spirit of the 2002 Declaration and the 1970 UNESCO Convention.

**722** The quoted words are taken from the Preamble of the 1954 Hague Convention. For the notion of common heritage of mankind see further Rudolf Dolzer, Die Deklaration des Kulturgutes zum "common heritage of mankind", in: R. Dolzer/E. Jayme/R. Mussgnug (eds.) Rechstfragen des Internationalen Kulturgüterschutzes (1994), 13.

not enforce a claim instituted by states if it is based on the state's penal or public laws.

On the other hand, inconsistent policies and differences in domestic legislation in many art collecting nations play a part in contributing to the poor recovery rate of art and antiquities. In case an object has been stolen, may it be from an individual or a sovereign, and the case involves a foreign law element, a different result can occur depending on which law will be applied. In such a scenario, international private law will be applied to, to decide the case.

In order to contribute to the depletion of legal obstacles causing a poor restitution rate in illicitly obtained cultural objects, the analysis undertaken in Part II of this thesis takes the following direction: Chapter 4 will discuss the relevant international instruments enacted in order to enhance the protection of cultural property in respect of their quality as a tool to facilitate the restitution of movable cultural heritage. Chapter 5 will deal with the choice of law methodology in respect of the application of foreign law, while Chapter 6 will analyse the national law of several market states in respect of the justiciability of claims that are based on, or, determined by foreign cultural property legislation.

# Chapter 4.
# International Law with Regard to the Recovery of Cultural Objects

## § 1. Introduction

The first international agreements concerning cultural property were born of the necessity to curb the devastation arising from armed conflicts. After having realised the value of cultural property for mankind and the dimension of illicit trafficking in art objects, various international treaties followed to protect cultural property during peacetime. Given the subject of the thesis, this chapter will not focus on the protection of heritage items from devastation and damaging, nor will it differ between treaties protecting such objects in times of war or peace, but it will focus on the relevance of these public international law instruments on the protection of such objects from removal and their subsequent restitution. It will scrutinise the value of the main international agreements concerning the protection of cultural property as to the existence of binding rules on the restitution of illicitly removed heritage objects, and hence, on rules for the application of foreign law by domestic courts. The analysis is structured according to chronology, unless where coherence is better served by discussing an agreement within the context of another treaty. The following chapter will show that the effect of international law so far in force is a limited mechanism for the restitution of antiquities.

## § 2. European Union Initiatives

The European Union embarked on combating illicit trade in cultural property with the dawn of the Single Market and the abolition of border controls within the European Union.[723] Free trade in all goods within the internal market is a guiding principle of the EU, guaranteed under Art. 9 and Art. 28–37 of the Treaty on the Functioning of the European Union [hereinafter: TFEU], formerly also known as EC-Treaty or the Treaty of Rome. Concern was wide that the opening

**723** The Single European Act required the Member States to adopt measures to establish a single integrated internal market by 31 December 1992, cp. Single European Act 1986, O.J. (L.169) 30, entered into force1 July 1987. The Act amended the Treaty Establishing the European Economic Community.

of the market would encourage the illegal removal of national treasures, making it simpler to smuggle them from one Member State to another.[724] The need to reconcile free movement was recognised alongside with that of legitimately protecting Member States' cultural and artistic heritage.[725] Works of art were therefore given special status exempting them from free trade. For intra-EU trade, Art. 36 TFEU provides a derogation from Articles 28–35 TFEU, allowing Member States to adopt or maintain prohibitions, restrictions or measures of equivalent effect on the import, export, or transit within the EU of national treasures having artistic, historic or archaeological value.[726] This exception also applies to third-country exports, that do not conflict with GATT [General Agreement on Tariffs and Trade], which makes similar reference and provisions in its Art. XX.[727] As a result, the Council of the European Union adopted two instruments (1) the Council Directive 93/7/EEC of March 15, 1993 [hereinafter: the Directive][728] on the Return of Cultural Objects Unlawfully Removed From the Territory of a Member State and (2) Council Regulation No. 3911/1992 on the Export of Cultural Goods, which was later replaced by Council Regulation (EC) No 116/2009 of 18 December 2008 on the export of cultural goods [hereinafter: The Regulation].[729] Both measures have the function of a legal rack-wheel, however, the strict requi-

**724** See e.g. N. Palmer, Statutory, Forensic and Ethical Initiatives in the Recovery of Stolen Art and Antiquities, in : Palmer, N., The Recovery of Stolen Art (1998), 1, at 13; A. Müller-Katzenburg, Internationale Standarts, at 112–114; Clare McAndrew/John O'Hogan, Export Restrictions, Tax Incentives and the National Artistic Patrimony, Trinity Economic Paper Series, Paper No 2000/6, available at. http://www.tcd.ie/Economics/research/tep/2000/TEPNo6JOH20.pdf

**725** McAndrew/O'Hogan, Export Restrictions, at 12.

**726** In order to facilitate uniform controls, the Regulation introduces an EU wide system of export licences for the export of cultural goods outside the customs territory of the Community. The system of export licences is further outlined in Commission Regulation (EEC) No 752/93 of 30 March 1993.

**727** McAndrew/O'Hogan, Export Restrictions, at 12.

**728** Council Directive 93/7, 1993 O.J. (L 74) 74–79, amended by Council Directive 2001/38, 2001 O. J. (L 187) 43–44. The statutory instrument which implements the Directive in the UK came into force in 2nd March 1994, The return of Cultural Objects regulations 1994, SI No. 501 (1994). For the German implementation see Richtlinie 93/7/EWG des Rates vom 15. März 1993 über die Rückgabe von unrechtmäßig aus dem Hoheitsgebiet eines Mitgliedstaates verbrachten Kulturgütern, ABl. EG Nr. L 74 (27.03.1993) at 74–79, and Gesetz zum Schutz deutschen Kulturgutes gegen Abwanderung (06.08.1955) as amended on 8. Juli 1999 (BGBl. I 1999, at 1754), and on 18.5.2007 (BGBl. I 2007, at 761–762).

**729** Council Regulation 116/2009 on the export of cultural goods of 18 December 2008 (former Council Regulation (EEC) No 3911/92 of 9 December 1992 on the export of cultural goods, OJ No L 395, 31.12.1992, p. 1, as amended by Council Regulation 2469/96 of 16 December 1996 OJ L 335/9, Council regulation 974/2001 of 14 May 2001 OJ L 137/10 and Council Regulation 806/2—3 fo 14 April 2003 OJ L 122/1.

sition of European Union legislation prevents the gear to have the necessary practical impact on curbing illegal dealings with cultural property.

## I. Council Regulation (EC) No 116/2009

As a respond to the opening of EU borders, Council Regulation (EC) No. 3911/1992 on the Export of Cultural Goods, now Council Regulation (EC) No 116/2009 of 18 December 2008, introduced EU wide uniform export controls. [730] Any object that falls under the scope of application of the Regulation may only be exported to a third country subject to the presentation of a valid Community export licence.[731] The provisions necessary for the implementation of the Basic Regulation are laid down in Commission Regulation (EEC) No 752/93 of 30 March 1993. This Implementing Regulation foresees three types of export licence: the standard licence, the specific open licence and the general open licence.

The Regulation employs a working administrative definition of cultural goods calculated to cover the types of objects which are entitled to protection under Art. 36 TFEU. According to Art. 1 of the Regulation, only such items are covered by the Regulation that fall within the scope categories of cultural goods which are summerised Annex I of the Regulation. As a result, national treasures under the law of any particular Member State of origin that are not covered by the Annex are exempt from the Regulation's export licence requirement. Conversely, cultural goods which are listed in the Annex but not considered a national treasure in the Member States of origin must be accompanied by a licence.

In total, there exist fourteen categories of objects and five ranges of financial values:

Table representing the categories of the Annex with the threshold applicable:

**730** The original basic Regulation was repealed as a result of a codification exercise. Codification brings together in a single new legal act all the provisions of the basic act and its subsequent amendments deleting obsolete provisions and harmonising the terminology thereby rendering legislation more accessible and transparent, cp. Report from the Comossion of the European Parliament on the Implementation of the Council Regulation (EC) No 116/2009 of 18 December 2008 on the Export of Cultural Goods.

**731** Annex 2 shows the way the situation evolved in the period under review as regards the number of issued licences, from EU 15 (2003) to EU 27 (2010). It also shows which share of the total licences issued is accounted for by the different Member States.

| Category of cultural good | Threshold value in Euro |
|---|---|
| Archaeological objects more than 100 years old which are the products of: excavations and finds on land or under water archaeological sites archaeological collections | Regardless of value |
| Elements forming an integral part of artistic, historical or religious monuments which have been dismembered, of an age exceeding 100 years | Regardless of value |
| Pictures and paintings executed entirely by hand, on any medium and in any material (and which are not included in category 3 A or 4) | >150,000 |
| 3 A. Water-colours, gouaches and pastels | >30,000 |
| Mosaics other than those in categories 1 or 2 and drawings executed entirely by hand, on any medium and in any material | >15,000 |
| Original engravings, prints, serigraphs and lithographs with their respective plates and original posters | >15,000 |
| Original sculptures or statuary and copies produced by the same process as the original, other than those in category 1 | >15,000 |
| Photographs, films and negatives thereof | >15,000 |
| Incunabula and manuscripts, including maps and musical scores, singly or in collections | Regardless of the value |
| Books more than 100 years old, singly or in collections | >50,000 |
| Printed maps more than 200 years old | >15,000 |
| Archives, and any elements thereof, of any kind or any medium which are more than 50 years old Regardless of the value | Regardless of value |
| Means of transport more than 75 years old | >50,000 |
| Any other antique items not included in categories A.1 to A.13 between 50 and 100 years old: toys, games, glassware, articles of goldsmiths' or silversmiths' wares, furniture, optical, photographic or cinematographic apparatus, musical instruments, clocks and watches and parts thereof, articles of wood, pottery, tapestries, carpets, wallpaper, arms more than 100 years old | >50,000 |

The export licence is issued by national authorities in accordance with their national law as to the export of cultural objects and in conformity with its regulations.[732] As the Regulation does not intend to protect national cultural objects contrary to the policy of the concerned Member State, Art. 2 (b) third subparagraph provides that the export licence may be refused where the cultural object in question is covered by national legislation protecting national treasures in the

**732** Art. 2 (2).

Member State concerned. The export licence issued by the competent authority is valid throughout the EU.[733]

In 1996, an exception was introduced to the general rule that any object falling under the Regulation's Annex may only be exported subject to a licence. Member States were granted the possibility to waive the need for export licences for archaeological objects of limited archaeological and scientific interest.[734] Art. 2 (b) first subparagraph, provides that no export licences may be required for the following objects: archaeological objects where the objects are more than 100 years old and are the products of excavations and finds on land or under water and of archaeological sites outside of the territory of a Member State. Furthermore, the objects must be of limited archaeological or scientific interest and their presence on the market must be lawful. The reason for introducing this provision was to exclude less important objects from the requirement of an export licence.[735]

In conclusion, the Regulation has a twofold effect: Firstly, it aims to enforce public international law in the form of export rules for the protection of cultural property on an EU wide level. Hence, it prevents the free internal market from being abused for the illegal import of objects protected in their country of origin from being exported into a Member State with less stringent export rules in order to sell them to non-EU-countries. Secondly, the Regulation seeks to co-ordinate the different national policies with respect to the export of national treasures and sets uniform standards for the export laws in force at the borders of the European Union.

Nevertheless, the basic Regulation No. 3911/92 has attracted criticism. Generally, it is being contended that it is difficult to enforce, as its application requires expertise that is generally not present with the customs authorities.[736] This relates generally to all heritage items for which no export licence has been applied for, as well as for archaeological items which fall under the exception of Art. 2 (b) first subparagraph. Items which are not enlisted in the Annex of the Regulation do not require a licence but the value of cultural goods is ascertained according to its material value at the time of the licence application in the country of origin. The customs service however will have to determine the value according to the international market value, which is usually much higher than

**733** Art. 2 (3).

**734** Andreas Peya, Die Ausfuhr von Kulturgütern im nationalen und Geminschaftsrecht (2002) at 147; K. Lubina, Contested Cultural Property, at 232.

**735** Cp. A. Peya, Ausfuhr von Kulturgütern, at 147.

**736** Cp. A. Peya, Ausfuhr von Kulturgütern, 147–148; A. Hipp, Schutz von Kulturgütern in Deutschland, at 270.

its value in the country of origin. Additionally, the attribution of certain items to the categories listed in the Annex creates problems, especially as one of the determining factors is the age of the object in question. Practically, this leads to a situation where art dealers are forced to apply for export licences even for heritage items of minor value, in order not to encounter problems with custom powers at the borders of the EU.[737]

## II. Council Directive 93/7/EEC

EC Directive 93/7/EEC on the Return of Unlawfully Removed Cultural Objects constitutes the counterpart to (amended) Council Regulation (EC) No 116/2009. It introduced domestic obligations in all Member States to return cultural objects "unlawfully removed from another Member State."[738] According to Art. 1 (2) of the Directive, unlawful removal occurs in the case of breach of the Coucil regulation, delineated in the previous of this paragraph, as well as in the breach of national laws, or equally, in the event that an object is not returned after temporary lawful removal.

In order to fall within the scope of the Directive the object must simultaneously fulfill several requirements the multitude of which prevents the Directive from being an effective instrument: (1) It must constitute a "national treasure of artistic, historic, or archaeological value" under national legislation within the meaning of Art. 36 TFEU and at the same time, a cultural object within one of the categories specified in the Annex of the Directive.[739] (2) Requests for return can only be made by a Member State and not by a private individual. Additionally to this second factor (3) requests are subject to a complicated bureaucratic procedure of intra-EU policies under Art 4 of the Directive: Each Member State is obliged to appoint a central authority to carry out the tasks provided in the Directive,[740] and requested Member States are obliged to act as an inter-

737 For an overview of the different points of criticism see e.g. A. Müller-Katzenburg, Internationale Standards, at 122; K. Siehr, International Art Trade, at 226–232.

738 Kurt Siehr, International Art Trade, at 232; Barbara T. Hoffmann, European Union Legislation Pertaining to Cultural Goods, at 191.

739 Art. 1. The Annex is common to both the Export Regulation and the Return Directive

740 Art. 3. Requested Member States are obliged to act as an intermediary between the object's current possessor and the requesting state in order to achieve an amicable settlement; Art. 4 (6). The return mechanism is triggered by an application to the central authority. The application must include all information needed to facilitate this search, with particular reference to the actual or presumed location of the object; to identify the current holder or possessor to notify the requesting Member State that the object has been found and that there are reasonable grounds

mediary between the object's current possessor and the requesting state in order to achieve an amicable settlement. Member States are requested to resolve the proceedings through "non-judicial" methods, such as mediation and arbitration.[741]

According to Art. 7, the return request is subject to two different kinds of limitation periods: the Member State loses its right of action if it either fails to commence proceedings within a year of becoming aware of the whereabouts of the object, or, if it fails to commence proceedings within thirty years of the unlawful removal.

Owing to its restricted scope, the Directive has had very little effect in combating illegal trade with cultural property.[742] Indeed, there is not one reported case ordering the return of an illegally exported object on the ground of the Directive.[743] The reasons are multifaceted: In order to fall under the ambit of the Directive, an item must be both included in the Annex and be classified as a national treasure under the law of the Member State. Thus, an artistic object that is not classified as a national treasure under the law of the requesting Member State is not subject to return, even if it is accompanied by an export licence. This especially excludes objects which have been illegally excavated. The scope of the Directive is additionally limited by the factor that it not only applies solemnly to Member States of the European Union, but it also cannot be invoked by private owners.

The complicated bureaucratic machinery of the Directive may has a major counterproductive effect. Additionally, a successful claimant state will have to compensate the current possessor if he can establish that he "exercised due care and attention in acquiring the object". This means that a state has to buy back its own property even if it can establish enduring title and prove that the item was stolen. This provision contravenes the philosophy of most civil and common law nations where stolen property cannot be acquired in good

for believing that it has been unlawfully removed from that Member State; Furthermore, the central authority has to take any necessary measures, in cooperation with the Member State concerned, for the physical preservation of the cultural object and to prevent, by the necessary interim measures, any action to evade the return procedure, Art. 4 (1) – (5).

**741** Cp. Nicholas J Talbot II, EEC Measures on National Treasures, 16 Loy. L.A. Int"L & Comp. L. J. (1993) 127, at 158.

**742** For the effect of the Directive on the Swiss art market, see for example Marc Weber, Auswirkungen der EU Richtlinie 93 /7/EWG auf den schweizerischen Kunsthandel, 3 Kunst und Recht (2008) 74.

**743** But see however the overview of returns under amicable out-of-court settlements in the Annex of the Fourth Report on the application of Council Directive 93/7/EEC on the return of cultural objects unlawfully removed from the territory of a Member State, 3.05.2013.

faith.[744] However, comparable provisions can be found both under the 1970 UNESCO Convention and the 1955 UNIDROIT Convention.

The Directive does not specify any distinct point in the administrative process at which cooperation the "cooperation" between the Member States is deemed to have failed and court proceedings must be initiated. There should have thus been a time frame starting at the time of the Member State's request, within which the cooperation procedure runs its course. In any event, the requesting Member State must bear the expenses incurred in implementing a court order.

The plethora of hurdles to recover illegally exported or stolen cultural property via the verschlungene wege mechanism of the EC Directive is reflected in a recent return request before the Munich administrative court initiated by the Czech Republic. The decision is also an example of the difficulty to stand in court relying on the Directive.[745] The case concerned a medieval baptismal font, which was stolen from a church in the Czech Republic in 2000. The font constituted a formidable polychromic wood carving with vine and acanthus ornaments dating from the 18$^{th}$ century. It was part of the inventary of the Roman Catholic Church and registered according to Para. 7 of the Czech Cultural Property Statute Law Nr 20/1987. The work of art was illegally exported in contravention with para 18 Law Nr 20/1987 and put up for sale at the art fair in Munich in 2003. The seller was a leading dealer and specialist in sacral antiquities and according to the claimants "well aware of the fact that in the Czech Republic encountered an increase in the theft and illegal export of scaral art". In 2005, the font was forfeited according to the mututal assistance in criminal matters and seized by the Bavarian beauro of invesitgations. In 2006, the Czech Republic sued the Bavarian State in front of the adminstrativ court in Munich for its return on the ground of the German implementtion of the Directive, the "Act on the Return of Cultural Objects 1998".[746] Although the font took the hurdle to qualify as a subject of return proceedings under the German implementaion of the Direc-

**744** But see e.g. Italy, Switzerland and Sweden, where stolen property can be acquired in good faith, cp. Chapter 5 § 2 II.

**745** Decision of the Administrative Court Munich, VG München, 31.07.2008 (Az M 17 K 06.3644), available at openjur 2012, 93323.

**746** Kulturgüterrückgabegesetz (15.10.1998 BGBl I S. 3162 – KultGüRückG1998). After Germany implemented the UNESCO Comnvention 1970, the Act of 1998 was revised. Both, the implementation of the Directive and the 1970 Convention have been consolidated in one Act, the "Act implementing the UNESCO Convention of 14 November 1970 on the means of prohibiting and preventing the illicit import, export and transfer of ownership of cultural property and implementing Council Directive 93/7/EEC of 15 March 1993 on the return of cultural objects unlawfully removed from the territory of a Member State 2007."

tive, the proceedings failed for several reasons: First, the court decided that the font was not "unlawfully removed from the territory of a Member State". Indeed, at the time of its removal, the Czech Republic was not a Member of the European Union. The Act, which declared the font in question to be of "national artistic importance", was only enacted when the Czech Republic entered the European Union. For this reason, the font did not fulfill the requirements of § 6 Abs. 1 Nr. 1 KultGüRückG. The court held that the moment relevant for the fact wheather the claimant was a member of the European Union, was not the moment of the institution of the proceeding but the moment of the removal of the object. In order to substantaite its opinion, the court referred to Art. 28 of the Vienna Convention on the law of the Treaties.[747] There, it is stated that a treaties provisions do not bind a party in relation to any act or fact which took place or any situation which ceased to exist before the date of the entry into force of the treaty with respect to that party.

Similarly complication was the issue concerning the laps of time of the claim: the claim was declared to be time-barred acoording to Art. 7 of the Directive, requiring proceedings may not be brought later than than one year after the requesting Member State became aware of the location of the cultural object and of the identity of its possessor or holder. The line of argument was simple: the Cech cultural ministry was informed about the whereabout of the font in 2003. As the claim was raised in 2006, the one-year period has expired in 2004. The court did not state whether the one year period was triggered by the knowledge of the ministry of culture as the central minisry or any administral body.[748] In an obiter dictum, the court mentioned that the Bavarian Monistry was not the right defendant as it only held the font for the actual owner as a bailee. However, the court pointed out that the claim could be further pursued before the civil courts.

Since it came into effect, the Directive was subject to four evaluation reports.[749] The fourth and most recent report[750] once more points out the ineffec-

---

**747** United Nations Convention on the Law of Treaties Signed at Vienna (23 May 1969), entry into force: 27 January 1980.

**748** But see on this question the Surpreme Court in Vienna, OGH 09.07.2013, Az 4Ob108/13f, holding that the cultural ministry of a member state is accountable for the knowledge of the police or other administrative bodies. The court held that only the knowledge of the cultural ministry itself is decisive for the triggering of the limitation period. The case concerned the illegal removal of an antique statute.

**749** http://ec.europa.eu/enterprise/policies/single-market-goods/internal-market-for-products/cultural-goods/.

**750** Fourth report on the application of Council Directive 93/7/EEC on the return of cultural objects unlawfully removed from the territory of a Member State, 30.05.2013.

tiveness of the Directive and makes a proposal for its amendment, which is due to come into effect in 2015.[751] The Report criticizes limited scope of the Directive, the short limitation period and the overall costly proceedings. For the event of the object being returned, the reported suggest to place the burden of proof on the possessor of the object in question for the purpose of compensation. The possessor will be required to prove that, at the time of its acquisition, he exercised due care and attention when ascertaining the legal origin of the cultural object. In order to encompass and faciliate civil proceedings for the recovery, the proposal also suggests to coordinate the new Directive with Regulation (EU) No 1215/2012 of the European Parliament and of the Council of 12 December 2012[752] on jurisdiction and the recognition and enforcement of judgments in civil and commercial matters.

### III. Iraq Council Regulation (EC) No 1210/2003

Council Regulation (EC) No 1210/2003[753] (hereinafter: the Iraq Regulation) has been enacted following the invasion of Iraq by the United States and the United Kingdom in 2003 (also referred to as Second Gulf War). The Iraq Regulation constitutes the implementary mechanism for UN Security Council Resolution 1483[754] (hereinafter: the Iraq Resolution). The Iraq Resolution was decided upon by the Security Council under Chapter VII of the UN Charter with the consequence that all United Nations Member States are obliged to implement its measures into their domestic law. [755]

---

**751** The proposal can be viewed at http://eur-lex.europa.eu/LexUriServ/LexUriServ.do?uri=COM:2013:0311:FIN:EN:PDF

**752** OJ L 351, 20.12.2012, p.1.

**753** Council Regulation (EC) No 1210/2003 of 7 July 2003 concerning certain specific restrictions on economic and financial relations with Iraq and repealing Regulation (EC) No 2456/96.

**754** Security Council Resolution 1483, P 7, U.N. Doc. S/RES/1483 (May 22, 2003). The United Nations Security Council adopted Resolution S/RES/686 – 1991, at para 2 (d). For an account see Jenschke, Der Völkerrechtliche Rückgabeanspruch, at 176; J. M. Zelig, Recovering Iraq's Cultural property: What Can Be Done to Prevent Illicit Trafficking, Brooklyn Journal of Int. L. (2005) 289, at 311.

**755** For a general account of the Irac Resolution see Kevin Chamberlain, The Iraq (United Nations Sanctions) Order 2003 – Is it Human Rights Compatible? 8 AAL (2003) 357; Mary Ellen O'Connell, Occupation Failures and the Legality of Armed Conflict: The Case of Iraqi Cultural Property, 9 AAL (2004), available at SSRN: http://ssrn.com/abstract=583122. For a detailed analysis of the US legislative response to the Iraq antiquities crisis see Karin E. Borke, Searching for a Solution: An Analysis of the Legislative Response to the Iraqi Antiquities Crisis of 2003, 13 DePaul-LCA J. Art & Ent. L. (2003) 381 (discussing the Iraq Cultural Heritage protection Act, H.R.

Iraq is known as one of the great source countries on the international antiquities market. It lies in the region of ancient Mesopotamia, which marks a beginning in the history of human civilization and claims many firsts, such as the first cities, temples, codified religion, codified law, organized warfare and writing.[756] Iraq's cultural property remained relatively well protected under strict national antiquities laws from post World War I until the First Gulf War in 1991.[757] However, following the wars, both economic strife and lawlessness were present. In the three years following the First Gulf War, ten of Iraq's national museums were attacked and ransacked, resulting in a loss of approximately 3.000 artefacts. 484 manuscripts were stolen.[758] In April 2003, the National Museum in Baghdad (along with several libraries) was plundered.[759] The official U.S. investigation reported that at least 13.515 objects had been stolen from the museum.[760]

The Iraq Resolution and the subsequent Iraq Regulation introduce a prohibition of trade with heritage items covered by the instruments. The items concerned are "historical objects removed from the Iraq National Museum, the National Library, and other locations in Iraq with respect to which reasonable suspicion exists that they have been illegally removed."[761]

Art. 3 (c) of the Iraq Regulation prohibits the "dealing in Iraqi cultural property and other items of archaeological, historical, cultural, rare scientific and religious importance including those items listed in an accompanying Annex". The Iraq Regulation comes in two alternatives: First, the scope of the Regulation includes but is not limited to the dealing in Iraqi cultural objects forming an "integral part of either the public collections listed in the inventories of Iraqi museums, archives or libraries' conservation collection, or the inventories of Iraqi religious institutions".[762] In that way, the Regulation goes further than the UNESCO 1970 Convention which is limited to registered cultural objects only. Second, the Iraq Regulation encompasses objects illegally removed from loca-

---

3497, 108th Cong. (2003) and the Emergency Protection for Iraqi Cultural Antiquities Act 2003, S, 1291. 108th Cong. (2003)).

**756** Cp. Gibson McGuire, Where Civilization began, 56 ARCHAEOLOGY (July/August 2003) 15, at 18.

**757** See the Republic of Iraq Antiquities Law No 59 (1936), as amended in 1974 and 1975.

**758** Cp. Neil Brodie and Colin Renfrew, Looting and the World's Archaeological Heritage: The Inadequate Response, 34 Annu. Rev. Anthropol (2005) 343, at 345.

**759** For an indept account oft he pillage in Iraq cp. M Bogdanos, Thiesves in Bagdad – The Global Traffic in stolen Iraqi Antiquities in: Duncan Chappel/Stefano Manacorda (eds.) Crime in the Art and Antiquities World: Illegal Trafficking in Cultural Property (2011) 143.

**760** N. Brodie/C Renfrew, at 346.

**761** Art. 7 Resolution 2003 and Art. 3 (a) and (b) of the Regulation.

**762** Art. 3 (1) (c) (i).

tions in Iraq if there exists reasonable suspicion that the goods have been removed from Iraq either (i) without the consent of their legitimate owner or (ii) have been removed in breach of Iraq's laws and regulations.[763] The first alternative covers stolen property, whereby the term "owner" may relate to both, private individuals or the Iraqi state as the "owner". The second option suggests that the Regulation generally recognises state ownership in cultural property on the ground of foreign public laws, including penal laws. This view is reinforced by the circumstance that the "breach" of Iraqi law may cover all legislation, including its export laws, ownership declaration and remaining administrative and penal provisions.

As one of very few international law instruments the Resolution is retroactive. It applies not only to objects that were illegally removed from 2003 onwards but instead applies to all objects illegally removed since August 6, 1990.[764] The retroactivity is owed to the first UN Resolution in connection with the Iraq war, which has been enacted right with the beginning of the First Gulf War.[765]

The Iraq Regulation makes a further exception in case the cultural item in question is being returned to Iraqi institutions in accordance with the objective of safe return as set out in Art. 7 of UN Resolution 1483. Here, the Regulation recognises the need to rescue cultural material threatened by armed conflict, illegal excavation, or other insecurity from entering the black market. The Regulation stays unspecific as to who exactly may rely on the exception. While on the one hand it leaves open the possibility for individuals to rely on the exception, at the same time it entails the danger to create a loophole for those who only claim to acquire a restricted object in order to escape from being liable to a fine or incrimination. Equally, the exception does not provide for any definition or procedure for how and when such objects ought to be returned. The exception refers back to the "objective of safe return as set out in paragraph 7 of Resolution 1483 which states that "all Member States shall take appropriate steps to facilitate the safe return to Iraqi institutions" and as such does not offer any assistance in terms of interpretation.

Assistance in matters of interpretation can be found within the "The Guidelines for the Establishment and Conduct of Safe Havens for Cultural Material" (hereinafter: the Guidelines), adopted by the International Law Association in 2008.[766] The Guidelines provide a framework for the establishment and conduct

---

**763** Art. 3 (1) (c) (ii).

**764** Art. 3 (2) (a).

**765** Resolution 661 (1990) of 6 August 1990.

**766** Law Association Guidelines adopted at the he 73rd Conference of the, held in Rio de Janeiro, Brazil, 17–21 August, 2008 are an Annex to the International Law Association Resolution

of safe havens for cultural objects for temporary deposit of cultural material rescued from circumstances of armed conflict and other serious threats. Art. 4 (i) of the Guidelines states that a safe haven must return cultural material items as soon as the "established owner or other established source of the material so requests, provided that the safe haven is satisfied with the conditions for safekeeping and preserving the material by the requesting state or entity".[767] Although the Guidelines are mainly tailored for governmental or nongovernmental institutions, the Guidelines state in the preamble that the initiator of the relocation of an object for safekeeping may be a state, a private owner or museum.[768]

Although it is aimed to facilitate the return of cultural heritage to Iraq, the Iraq Regulation does not provide for an explicit return or restitution mechanism.[769] As the Iraq Regulation is directly applicable, the return process is subject to the national administrative procedure of each Member State. In 2009, the Regulation was subject to proceedings in Germany concerning an Iraqi gold vessel. The case was tried in front of the Financial Court in Munich.[770] After being sold at an auction, the vessel was seized by the custom powers where an expert in archaeology confirmed Iraq to be the source country of the artefact. The auction house initiated proceedings for the return of the vessel from the customs, arguing that the object had been sold by a Swiss dealer who had attested it to be a provincial-roman artefact. After consulting another expert, the court was satisfied that the vessel originated from the royal tombs in the ancient city of Ur, most probably dating back to 2500 B.C., and ordered that the seizure was

---

No 2/2008 Heritage Law. The Guidelines may be found in: 16 Int'l J Cultural Property (2009) 371. The Guidelines contain an annexed Safe Haven Model contract.

**767** Law Association Guidelines, Art. 4 i).

**768** Preamble to the Draft Report 2008 Part I, at 2. Cp also Sophie Engelhardt, Nachrichtenlose Kulturgüter (2013), at 285.

**769** In Paragraph 7, the Resolution obliges all UN Member States "to take appropriate steps to facilitate the safe return". See generally Kevin Chamberlain, The Iraq (United Nations Sanctions) Order 2003 – Is it Human Rights Compatible? 8 AAL (2003) 357; Mary Ellen O'Connell, Occupation Failures and the Legality of Armed Conflict: The Case of Iraqi Cultural Property, 9 AAL (2004) Available at SSRN: http://ssrn.com/abstract=583122. For a detailed analysis of the US legislative response to the Iraq antiquities crisis see Karin E. Borke, Searching for a Solution: An Analysis of the Legislative Response to the Iraqi Antiquities Crisis of 2003, 13 DePaul-LCA J. Art & Ent. L. (2003) 381 (discussing the Iraq Cultural Heritage protection Act, H.R. 3497, 108th Cong. (2003) and the Emergency Protection for Iraqi Cultural Antiquities Act 2003, S, 1291. 108th Cong. (2003)).

**770** Finanzgericht München, AZ 14 K 2754/08 (2009), unreported. On the impact of the resolution on the German trade in Iraqi cultural heritage see Susanne Schoen/Margarete van Ess, Das UN-Handelsverbot von 2003 für irakisches Kulturgut: Folgenlos für Deutschland? 1 Kunstrechtspiegel 2008, 7.

lawful. Basing its judgment on Council Regulation (EC) No. 1210/2003 it ruled the vessel to be returned to the Government of Iraq.

Notwithstanding the direct application of the Regulation, the UK implemented the Resolution and the subsequent EC – Regulation via a criminal law instrument, the Iraq (United Nations) Sanctions Order 2003.[771] Art. 8 of the UK Sanctions Order prohibits the importation or exportation of any item of illegally removed Iraqi cultural property removed from any location in Iraq since August 6, 1990.[772] The implementation introduces two rather controversial offences:

(1) Art. 8 (2) forbids being in possession or control over objects falling under the Order and failing to cause their transfer to a constable.[773]
(2) Art. 8 (3) prohibits dealing in Iraqi items, whereby dealing means "to acquire, to dispose of, to import or export, to agree with another person to do one of the forth mentioned or to make arrangements under which another person does such an act or under which another person agrees with a third person to do such an act."[774]

Art. 8 (2) and 8 (3) reverse the normal burden of proof with regard to the mental element. Unlike most criminal offences, the prosecution is not required to prove guilt intent (*mens rea*). The prosecution has to prove only that the item was an artefact illegally removed from Iraq and that the defendant had the item in his possession and did not cause its transfer to the police, or, under Art. 8 (3), he dealt in the object. Additionally, the offences lack any requirement of dishonesty, causing the defendant to be guilty by merely knowing or believing that the chattel was looted Iraqi cultural property. The burden of proof lies with the defendant that he neither knew nor has had reason to suppose that the item in question was illegally removed from Iraq. This opens up the possibility that a person who acquires looted Iraqi material with the honest intention of returning it to its source may nevertheless commit the offence of dealing, and being in possession but failing to transfer the object to a constable, if he continues to be in possession.[775]

Equally, a person who is not aware of the Iraq Order and comes in possession of a looted artefact will commit the offence if he or she does not transfer the item to a constable. Furthermore, the definition of illegally removed Iraqi cultural property extends to property removed after August 6, 1990, which means that

**771** Statutory Instrument 2003 No. 1519, entered into force on June 14, 2003.
**772** Articles 8 (1) and 8 (4).
**773** Art. 8 (2).
**774** Art. 8 (5).
**775** Cp. N. Palmer, Adrift on a Sea of Troubles: Cross-Border Art Loans and the Specter of Ulterior Title, 38 Vand. J. Transnat'l L. (2005) 947, at 989 (in respect of borrowing museums).

any person who innocently acquired an item after that date, which turns out to be illegally removed from Iraq could be at risk of prosecution, if he failed or fails to hand it over to the police or deals in it.

As a consequence, the British implementation of the Resolution and subsequent Regulation raises serious concerns about its compatibility with the European Convention of Human Rights (ECHR).[776] Specifically, placing the burden of proof on the defendant has been questioned to infringe Art. 6 (2) ECHR, which guarantees to be presumed innocent until proven guilty.[777] Furthermore, the retroactive application of the Iraq Order was criticised, as the definition of illegally removed Iraqi cultural property dates back to property removed since August 6, 1990, possibly being in breach with the requirements of Art. 7 ECHR, which protects from retroactive punishment for crimes.[778]

## IV. Syria Council Regulation (EU) No 1332/2013

Council Regulation (EU) No 1332/2013 introduces a European wide ban on the trade with cultural goods originating from Syria (hereinafter: the Syria Regulation).[779] The Syria Regulation amends EU Regulation No 36/2012 (hereinafter: the basic Regulation),[780] which makes general provisions for sanctioning the trade with Syria, including strategic goods and technologies, chemical weapons, gold metals and diamonds as well as other types of luxury goods.[781]

Historically, Syria included what is now Jordan, Israel and Lebanon as well as the area which we call Syria today. It is often described as the cradle of civilization, since many of the greatest human achievements that later spread to encompass the world had their beginnings right in Ancient Syria. Nowadays, the country is home to exceptional archaeological, urban and architectural sites, six of which have been declared a UNESCO World Heritage Site.[782] Eleven are inscribed on the UNESCO's Tentative List.[783]

**776** For a detailed analysis of the Iraq Order and human rights, see Kevin Chamberlain, The Iraq (United Nations Sanctions) Order 2003 – Is it Human Rights Compatible?, 8 AAL (2003) 357.

**777** Cp. K. Chamberlain, The Iraq Order 2003, at 358.

**778** Cp. K. Chamberlain, ibid, at 359.

**779** Regulation (EU) No 1332/2013 of 13 December 2013 concerning restrictive measures in view of the situation in Syria (O.J. L335, 14.12.13, p.3).

**780** Regulation (EU) No 36/2012 of 18 January 2012 and repealing Regulation (EU) No 442/2011 (O.J. L 16, 19.1.2012, p. 1).

**781** A complete list is available at https://www.gov.uk/sanctions-on-syria

**782** Aleppo (1986); Bosra (1980); Damascus (1979); ancient villages of Northern Syria (2011); Crac des Chevaliers and Qal'at Salah El-Din (2006); Palmyra (1980). For a detailed depiction

All of the sites have been considerably damaged and continue to be damaged during the raging Middle East conflict.[784] There is evidence that the World Heritage properties are being used for military purposes, and subjected to direct shelling and targeted explosions. Extensive illicit excavations are taking place throughout the country and museums are being plundered.[785] Parallel to the ongoing degeneration of the country since 2011, international trade with misappropriated Syrian artefacts exponentially increased. In March 2014, The International Council of Museums published the *Emergency Red List of Syrian Cultural Objects at Risk* (hereinafter: the Red List) with the aim to help art and heritage professionals as well as law enforcement officials identify Syrian objects that are protected by national and international legislation. The Red List illustrates the categories or types of cultural items that are most likely to be illegally bought and sold.[786] However, the Red List is only a help tool, as well as an instrument of self-conduct. Although it has proven useful in the past, for instance with curbing the trade with Iraqi cultural goods, it is not a legally enforceable measure.[787]

The Syria Regulation is the European Union's answer to the continuous loss of Syrian cultural heritage resulting from the escalating crisis in the Middle East. In many points, it resembles the previously discussed Iraq counterpart (both, Iraq Resolution and Regulation). Art. 11 c) of the Regulation prohibits throughout the EU the "import, export, transfer, or provision of brokering services" of Syrian cultural property. The prohibition encompasses "goods of archaeological, histor-

---

of the damage to the UNESCO sites see Mamoun Fansa, Die UNESCO-Weltkulturerbestätten und der Krieg in Syrien, in: Mamoun Fansa (ed.) Syrien – Sechs Weltkulturerbe-Stätten in den Wirren des Bürgerkrieges (2014) 79.

**783** See http://whc.unesco.org/en/statesparties/SY/: Noréas de Hama (1999); Ugrarit (Tell Shamra) (1999); Ebla (Tell Mardikh) (1999); Mari (Tell Hariri) (1999); Dura Europos (1999); Apamée (Afamia) (1999); Un Château du desert; Qasr al-Hayr ach-Charqi (1999); Maaloula (1999); Tartus: la cité-citadelle des Croisés (1999); aqqa-Ràfiqa: la cité abbasside (1999); L'île d'Arwad (1999); Mari & Europos-Dura sites of Euphrates Valley (2011).

**784** For an assessment of the damage cp. http://www.unesco.org/new/en/safeguarding-syrian-cultural-heritage/situation-in-syria/built-heritage/. See also Maamoun Abdulkarim, Archaeological Heritage in Syria during the Crisis in 2011–2013 (2013).

**785** For an assessment of the damage to the Syrian museums cp.http://www.unesco.org/new/en/safeguarding-syrian-cultural-heritage/situation-in-syria/movable-heritage/museums/.

**786** Cp. the ICOM *Emergency Red List of Syrian Cultural Objects at Risk* available at: http://icom.museum/fileadmin/user_upload/images/Redlists/Syria/ERL_SYRIE_EN.pdf.

**787** See the "Emergency Red List of Iraqi Cultural Objects at Risk".The Iraq Red List was drawn up by a group of 12 international experts during a meeting held at the Interpol headquarters in Lyons (France) on 7 May 2003. The List is available at http://icom.museum/fileadmin/user_upload/images/Redlists/Iraq/RedList_Irak_English.pdf.

ical, cultural, rare scientific or religious importance" including but not limited to objects listed in an accompanying Annex.[788]

According to Art. 1 b) of the Regulation, "brokering services" constitutes the "negotiation or arrangement of transactions for the purchase, sale or supply of cultural objects",[789] as well as the "selling or buying" of prohibited goods. In this respect, the Syria Regulation is more specific than its parallel instrument prohibiting the trade with Iraqi cultural heritage, which uses the rather flexible and unspecific term "dealing" with cultural objects from Iraq.[790] By defining the term "brokering services", the Regulation explicitly covers the entire process of illicit art trade: the attempt of trade, the assisting in trading, the actual transaction itself, the handling of objects covered by the prohibition and the assisting in the handling with such objects.

Following the example of the Iraq Regulation, the prohibition is further subject to the condition that the restricted object was taken from Syria either (i) without the consent of the legitimate owner, (ii) in breach of Syrian or in (iii) breach of international law.[791] The first alternative covers stolen property belonging to private individuals or the Syrian state as the "owner".[792] The second option pays tribute to the state ownership in cultural property. The last alternative

---

**788** The accompanying Annex is subdivided in 14 categories of objects: (1) Archaeological objects more than 100 years old which are the products of: excavations and finds on land or under water, – archaeological sites, archaeological collections, (2) Elements forming an integral part of artistic, historical or religious monuments which have been dismembered, of an age exceeding 100 years, (3) pictures and paintings, other than those included in category 4 or 5, executed entirely by hand in any medium and on any material, (4) Water-colors, gouaches and pastels executed entirely by hand on any material, (5) Mosaics in any material executed entirely by hand, other than those falling in category 1 or 2, and drawings in any medium executed entirely by hand on any material, (6) Original engravings, prints, serigraphs and lithographs with their respective plates and original posters, (7) Original sculptures or statuary and copies produced by the same process as the original other than those in category, Photographs, films and negatives thereof, (8) Incunabula and manuscripts, including maps and musical scores, singly or in collections, (9) Books more than 100 years old, singly or in collections, (10) printed maps more than, 200 years old, (12) archives, and any elements thereof, of any kind or any medium which are more than 50 years old, (13) collections of historical, paleontological, ethnographic or numismatic interest, (14) Means of transport more than 75 years old, as well as (15) any other items between 50 and 100 years old.

**789** Art. 1 b (i).

**790** For the Iraq Regulation, cp. this paragraph at III.

**791** Art. 11 (c) 1.

**792** Cp. Art. 3 (c) Council Regulation (EC) No 1210/2003, cp. above.

constitutes a specific referral to the First and Second Protocol of the Hague Convention 1954.[793]

Although the Regulation specifically covers objects removed from Syria if they "form an integral part of either the public collections listed in the inventories of the conservation collections of Syrian museums, archives or libraries, or the inventories of Syrian religious institutions"[794], it is not limited to such heritage.[795] By not closing the provision to only inlclude specifically inventoried or registered items inventoried in a form of administrative procedure, the Syria Regulation consequently pays regard to illegally excavated objects.

The prohibition is further subject to two exceptions: First, it only covers restricted objects exported after the date of 9 May 2011.[796] Compared to its Iraq counterpart instrument, it is not retroactive. Secondly, the Regulation creates an exception for those who can "demonstrate that the restricted goods are being safely returned to their legitimate owners in Syria".[797] Just as its Iraq counter instrument, the Regulation recognises the need to rescue cultural material threatened by armed conflict, illegal excavation, or other insecurity from entering the black market. Again, assistance for interpretation can be seeked within the "The Guidelines for the Establishment and Conduct of Safe Havens for Cultural Material".[798]

The Regulation is a necessary and important measure to protect Syria's cultural heritage, but it repeats the mistake of the Iraq Regulation to miss out on a provision for the explicit return or restitution of objects covered by the Regulation. The return process is subject to the complicated administrative procedures of each Member State. This considerabely slows down the recovery and return process. The recovery may be instituted via a seizure on the ground of criminal provisions, via proceedings in front of the civil courts or ideally both.

Although, as a legal Act of the European Union, the Syria Regulation does not require to be transposed into national law,[799] the UK enacted a technical implementation of the Regulation in order to supplement and detail the enforce-

---

**793** Convention for the Protection of Cultural Property in the Event of Armed Conflict adopted at The Hague (Netherlands) in 1954, see this Chapter, § 3 II 1 and 2.

**794** Art. 11 (c) 1.

**795** But see the UNESCO Convention 1970 which covers only objects which are registered, cp. this Chapter, 3 IV.

**796** Art. 11 (c) 2 (a).

**797** Art. 11 (c) 2 (b).

**798** Law Association Guidelines 2008, cp. above. The Guidelines are available in: 16 Int'l J Cultural Property (2009) 371.

**799** Cp. Article 288 of the Treaty on the Functioning of the European Union (formerly Article 249 TEC).

ment of the restrictive measures against Syria (hereinafter: the Syria Order).[800] The Order amends the earlier Export Control (Syria Sanctions) Order 2013 (S.I. 2013/2012) by consolidating in one single instrument the enforcement of all current trade restrictions against Syria. The Syria Order provides for national offences and penalties, increasing the penalties for offences already existing under the Customs and Excise Management Act 1979.[801] According to Art. 12 A of the Syria Order, a person may commit an offence and may be arrested in the event he or she is concerned in an activity, prohibited by Article 11c of the Syria Regulation. That excludes the offence of being in possession of a restricted object, as provided in the Iraq Order 2003. The offence is subject to the condition that the prohibited activities have been committed "knowingly". The requirement of a *mens rea* element corresponds with the fact that the Order is a criminal law instrument. The Syria Order increase the maximum sentence for importing and exporting property restricted under Regulation up to 10 years of imprisonment.[802]

## § 3. Uniform Law International Instruments

### I. Treaty of Washington 1935

The first multilateral treaty that provided a means for the application of foreign cultural property laws and consequently for the restitution and return of cultural objects was the Treaty on the Protection of Movable Property of Historic Value.[803]

**800** The Export Control (Syria Sanctions) (Amendment) Order 2014 SI 2014 1896 (the Order), in force since 8 August 2014, amending Export Control (Syria Sanctions) Order 2013 (S.I. 2013/2012). The official document available at http://www.legislation.gov.uk/uksi/2014/1896/contents/made.

**801** Cp. sections 50, 68 and 170 of the Customs and Excise Management Act 1979 (1979 c 2).

**802** Cp. Art. 2 (4) of the Order.

**803** Treaty on the Protection of Movable Property of Historic Value, April 15, 1935, OASTS 28. The full text of the treaty is reprinted in: M.O. Hudson, International Legislation – A Collection of the Texts of Multipartite International Instruments of General Interest (1972), at 59 et seq. For a detailed account of the Treaty cp. B. Walter, Rückführung von Kulturgut im internationalen Recht (1988), at 46–48; Sabine v. Schorlemer, Internationaler Kulturgüterschutz: Ansätze zur Prävention im Frieden sowie im bewaffneten Konflikt (1992) at 423–434. The first treaty dedicated to the protection of cultural property was the Roerich Pact on the Protection of Artistic and Scientific Institutions and Historic Monuments (Montevideo, April, 15, 1935, 49 Stat. 3267, TS No. 899, 167 LNTS 279), but its application is geographically limited to the American continent and it does not provide for the restitution of cultural objects, cp. J.H. Merryman, Two Ways of Thinking about Cultural Property, American J. Int'l Law (1986), at 835; K. Odendahl, Kulturgüterschutz,

The Treaty, which is generally known as "Treaty of Washington" (hereinafter: ToW) entered into force on May 1, 1936.[804] In particular, it granted State Parties the possibility to initiate proceedings in the civil courts, which at that time constituted an innovative and workable mechanism of enforcement for the recovery of heritage items. According to Articles 2 and 3 ToW the import of certain narrowly defined objects was subject to the presentation of a valid export licence from their countries of origin. In case an attempt to import an object without this valid export licence was thwarted, the object will be confiscated and returned to the public authorities of the country of origin.[805] For cases in which the illegal import could not be prevented, Art. 6 ToW provided the country of origin with a right to seek the objects return from the state into whose territory the objects had been illegally imported.[806] The holding state has to undertake the necessary steps to return the object to the applicant.[807] This restitution right for the illegally exported and imported objects is complemented by the applicants' state power to initiate court proceedings in the civil courts of the holding state.[808]

Outside the European Community, the Treaty of Washington is unmatched in making the legality of an import of heritage items dependent on the existence of a valid export licence.[809] The relevance of the Treaty of Washington is however limited as it only applies between North America and countries in Middle and South America and it covers a very small group of objects namely, objects dating from pre-Columbian, Colonial times or the "period of emancipation and the republic."[810] One example of heritage items falling within the scope of the Treaty may be the Inca artefacts excavated and exported from Machu Picchu in Peru by

at 1115; for a detailed account of the Roerich Pact see K. Lubina, Contested Cultural Property, at 68 et seq.

**804** It was signed by the member states of the Pan-American Union, the precursor of the Organisation of American States (OAS) on 15 April 1935. It was ratified by Chile (1936), El Salvador (1936), Guatemala (1936), Mexico (1939), and Nicaragua (1935) and went into force on 1 May 1936, cp. K. Lubina, Contested Cultural Property, at 102.

**805** Art. 5.

**806** Art. 6.

**807** Art. 7. See also B. Walter, Rückführung von Kulturgut, at 46–48; S.v. Schorlemer, Internationaler Kulturgüterschutz, at 423–434.

**808** According to Art. 4 ToW "the signatory countries understand that those who have objects declared to be movable monuments, can only enjoy the usufruct, which is transferable only within the same country." What Art. 4 ToW effectively does is to qualify the objects defined under Art. 1 as res extra commercium. Private property is not possible as a consequence of which the state of origin can pursue its claim to the object in the national courts, cp. B. Walter, Rückführung von Kulturgut, at 46–47; K. Lubina, Contested Cultural Property, at 103.

**809** For the European instruments see the above.

**810** Art. 1.

the American explorer Hiram Bingham III at the beginning of the 20th century.[811] In 2010, nearly a century after hundreds of artefacts where brought to Yale, the Yale Peabody Museum decided to return them to the city of Cuzco, the former capital of the Incas. At first, Yale claimed title to the artefacts despite written correspondence in which Bingham acknowledged an obligation to return the objects to Peru after they have been studied.[812] In November 2010, the University of Yale and the Peruvian government signed a memorandum of understanding granting the Peruvian government legal title to all the artifacts and returning all relevant artefacts to Peru.

## II. The Hague Convention 1954

Following the widespread destruction and plunder of World War I and II, the need for a doctrine addressing the protection of national treasures during times of conflict became evident.[813] Guided by the principles concerning the protection of cultural property during armed conflict, as established in the two previous Hague Conventions adopted in 1899 and 1907[814] and in the Treaty of Washington 1935,[815] another international conference in The Hague resulted in the adoption of the Hague Convention 1954 and the First Protocol for the Protection of Cultural Property in the Event of Armed Conflict.[816]

**811** Cp. http://www.yaledailynews.com/news/2011/mar/31/first-artifacts-return-to-peru

**812** Cp. http://www.yaledailynews.com/news/2011/mar/31/first-artifacts-return-to-peru.

**813** On the general problem of looting in times of war or its aftermath, see Neil Brodie, Spoils of War, Archaeology (July/August 2003) 1, at 16.

**814** Convention (II) with Respect to the Laws and Customs of War on Land and its annex: Regulations concerning the Laws and Customs of War on Land. The Hague, 29 July 1899 and Convention (IV) respecting the Laws and Customs of War on Land and its annex: Regulations concerning the Laws and Customs of War on Land. The Hague, 18 October 1907. As the 1899 and 1907 Hague Conventions do not hold provisions for the application of foreign cultural property laws, it was not thought to be necessary to further elaborate upon them here. But see an extensive analysis e.g. K. Lubina, Contested Cultural Property, at 56–61; K. Odendahl, Kulturgüterschutz, at 110–111; D. Schindler, D. / J. Toman, The laws of armed Conflicts: a collection of conventions, resolutions and other documents, 2004, at 55–87.

**815** Cp. this chapter, § 3.

**816** Convention for the Protection of Cultural Property in the Event of Armed Conflict, May 14, 1954, 249 U.N.T.S.215. For a detailed analysis of the convention see e.g. Jennifer Lehman, The Continued Struggle with Stolen Cultural Property: The Hague Convention, The UNESCO Convention and the UNIDROIT Draft Convention, 14, Ariz. J. Int'l & Comp. L. (1997) 527; Joshua E. Kastenberg, The Legal Regime for Protecting Cultural Property During Armed Conflict, 42 A.F.L. Rev.

The convention rests on the premise that cultural property is a valuable possession of humankind deserving universal respect.[817] The 1954 Hague Convention and its two Protocols impose obligations to safeguard and preserve property under military control, to prevent exportation of looted material, and to facilitate its return to countries of origin.[818] In 1954, forty-five countries signed the Convention and forty signed the First Protocol. Today, for the most part, the 1954 Hague Convention has been widely accepted. It is still the fundamental tool for protecting cultural property in wartime and continues to receive new accessions.[819]

It has to be noted that The Hague Convention was the first Treaty to formulate and define the term 'cultural property'.[820] The definition of 'cultural property' in Art. 1 comprises three categories of cultural objects[821]: first movable or immovable property of great importance to the cultural heritage of every people, secondly buildings whose main and effective purpose is to preserve or exhibit movable cultural property (that is of great importance to the cultural heritage of every people) and finally centres containing a large amount of cultural property from the previous two categories.

Although the requirement of Art. 1 that a cultural object must be of "great importance to the cultural heritage of every people" suggests a rather high threshold in order to qualify as cultural property in the sense of the Convention, generally the definition of cultural property of the 1954 Hague Convention allows

(1997) 277; Christoph Jenschke, Der Völkerrechtliche Rückgabeanspruch auf in Kriegszeiten widerrechtlich verbrachte Kulturgüter (Berlin 2005).

**817** Cp. J. E. Kastenberg, The Legal Regime for Protecting Cultural Property, at 278.

**818** Hague Convention, Preamble, 249 U.N.T.S. at 240.

**819** Since the year 2000, 56 new states have accessed the Convention. For a full list of states that ratified or accesses the second protocol see: http://erc.unesco.org/cp/convention.asp?KO=15207&language=E.

**820** See 1954 Hague Convention, at Art. 1.

**821** Art. 1 reads: "For the purposes of the present Convention, the term 'cultural property' shall cover, irrespective of origin or ownership: movable or immovable property of great importance to the cultural heritage of every people, such as monuments of architecture, art or history, whether religious or secular; archaeological sites; groups of buildings which, as a whole, are of historical or artistic interest; works of art; manuscripts, books and other objects of artistic, historical or archaeological interest; as well as scientific collections and important collections of books or archives or of reproductions of the property defined above; buildings whose main and effective purpose is to preserve or exhibit the movable cultural property defined in sub-paragraph (a) such as museums, large libraries and depositories of archives, and refuges intended to shelter, in the event of armed conflict, the movable cultural property defined in subparagraph (a); centers containing a large amount of cultural property as defined in sub-paragraphs (a) and (b), to be known as 'centers containing monuments'.

for a broad, almost unlimited interpretation of the objects that can qualify as cultural property.[822]

The scope of protection granted by the 1954 Hague Convention is outlined in its Articles 2–7. In order to ensure for an efficient protection and in light of the notion of common heritage, the obligations of State Parties already commence prior to the outbreak of a conflict.[823] Once an international or internal conflict has erupted, Art. 4 of the Conventions prohibits:

(1) any use of the cultural property in a manner that will likely expose it to destruction or damage in the event of an armed conflict;
(2) the commission of any acts of hostility or reprisal against cultural property except for reasons of military necessity; and
(3) any form of theft, pillage, or misappropriation of cultural property.

The Hague Convention 1954 does not provide for means to recover cultural objects that have been wrongfully taken during the time of conflict, as provisions for the return of heritage items are covered by the First Protocol.

### 1. First Protocol of the 1954 Hague Convention

The (First) Protocol for the Protection of Cultural Property in the Event of Armed Conflict[824] was adopted together with the 1954 Hague Convention. It entered into force on August 7, 1956. It complements the 1954 Hague Convention in that it imposes additional obligations on State Parties with regard to the protection of cultural property in an occupied territory. As opposed to the Hague Convention itself, it also provides for the restitution of cultural property that has been removed. The obligation to restitute cultural property as provided for in Art. I 3 is far-reaching: it applies also to a State Party that has not been involved in the occupation; it is not subject to prescription, and works also against a *bona fide* purchaser.[825]

In particular, the First Protocol requires an occupying state to:

(1) prevent the export of cultural property from the occupied territory;[826]

**822** C. Jenschke, Der Völkerrechtliche Rückgabeanspruch, at 59.

**823** Articles 3, 6, 7 of the 1954 Hague Convention.

**824** Protocol for the Protection of Cultural Property in the Event of Armed Conflict, signed May 1954, 249 U.N.T.S. 358 [hereinafter Protocol I to the 1954 Hague Convention].

**825** Cp. C. Jeschke, Der Völkerrechtliche Rückgabeanspruch, at 69; K. Lubina, Contested Cultural Property, at 89.

**826** Art. I 1.

(2) seize all cultural property imported into its territory from any occupied territory; [827]
(3) return the seized property to the formerly occupied territory at the close of hostilities;[828] and
(4) pay an indemnity to the holders in good faith of any cultural property which has to be returned.

For the (First) Protocol to apply it is irrelevant whether the occupied country is a State Party. It is sufficient that the occupying country is a State Party.

The rules as provided for in the 1954 Hague Convention and the (First) Protocol have been confirmed in reaction to the conflicts in the Middle East, in particular the First Gulf War (1990 – 91). The United Nations Security Council Resolution from March 1991[829] determined that Iraq, which had ratified the 1954 Hague Convention and its (First) Protocol in 1967, had to return to Kuwait, which had accessed to the 1954 Hague Convention in 1969 and to the (First) Protocol in 1970, all looted (cultural) property.[830] The Hague Protocol lays down no rule as to time limitations on claims.

## 2. Second Protocol of the 1954 Hague Convention

The Second Protocol of the 1954 Hague Convention (Protocol II), which was adopted on March 26, 1999 and entered into force in 2004,[831] addresses the protection of (the substance of) cultural property against damage and destruc-

**827** Art. I 2.

**828** Art. I 3. The obligation to return cultural property at the close of hostilities to the competent authorities of the formerly occupied territory is absolute: it is neither subject to any pre-scription, nor does it recede from any rights that might have been acquired after the export by a bona fide purchaser, cp. C. Jeschke, Der Völkerrechtliche Rückgabeanspruch, at 69.

**829** Resolution S/RES/686 – 1991, para. 2 (d) reads: "(...) that Iraq immediately begin[s] to return all Kuwaiti property seized by Iraq, to be completed in the shortest possible period."

**830** See further on the relevance of the 1954 Hague Convention to the 1990 – 1991 (First) Gulf War: Harvey E. Oyer III, The 1954 Hague Convention for the Protection of Cultural Property in the Event of Armed Conflict – Is it Working? A Case Study: The Persian Golf War Experience (1999) Columbia VLA J. of Law and Arts, 49.

**831** Second Protocol to the Hague Convention of 1954 for the Protection of Cultural Property in the Event of Armed Conflict, signed at The Hague, 26 March 1999. The exact date of entry into force was 9 March 2004, cp. Art. 43 according to which the Second Protocol shall enter into force three months after twenty instruments of ratification, acceptance, approval or accession have been deposited. As of June 2009, 53 countries had become a State Party. See for the actual list: http://www.icrc.org/ihl.nsf/WebSign?ReadForm&id=590&ps=P.

tion.[832] It complements the 1954 Hague Convention, which requires its State Parties to introduce criminal responsibility but does so without explicit reference to the removal of cultural property. It includes a provision to define property under 'enhanced' protection. To qualify for 'enhanced' protection, cultural property must meet three conditions:
(1) it is of the greatest importance to humanity, such as designated World Heritage sites;
(2) it is protected by adequate domestic legal and administrative measures, including existing UNESCO protections, recognizing its exceptional cultural and historic value; and
(3) it is not used for military purposes to shield military sites, and a declaration has been made by the State that has control over the property that it will not be so used.

Furthermore, Protocol II to the 1954 Hague Convention expands upon the provisions in the 1954 Hague Convention for preparatory actions in time of peace to safeguard cultural property against the "foreseeable effects" of an armed conflict. States Parties must therefore:
(1) prepare a national inventory;
(2) plan emergency measures for protection against fire and structural collapse;
(3) remove all movable cultural property from areas that are likely to be damaged during military action or prepare adequate *in situ* protections of such property; and
(4) designate competent authorities responsible for the safeguarding of cultural property.

Protocol II to the 1954 Hague Convention also establishes individual criminal responsibility for violations. A State Party therefore must either prosecute or extradite any person found in its territory who is deemed to have committed serious violations of the Hague/Protocol II rules.[833] In addition, the instrument contains provisions for mutual legal assistance and the establishment of a committee to

**832** See further on the Second Protocol: Thomas Desch, The Second Protocol to the 1954 Hague Convention for the Protection of Cultural property in the Event of Armed Conflict, 2 YIHL ( 1999) 63; J. Hladík, The Control System under the Hague Convention for the Protection of Cultural Property in the Event of Armed Conflict 1954 and its Second Protocol (2004); Andrea Gioia, The Development of International Law relating to the Protection of Cultural Property in the Event of Armed Conflict: The Second Protocol of the 1954 Hague Convention (2003).
**833** See James Nafzinger, The Protection of Cultural Heritage in Time of War and its Aftermath, 6 IFAR Journal No 1/2 (2003).

help implement the protocol and protect the specifically identified cultural property. While the Hague Convention is broad enough to promote respect for cultural property during armed conflict, the specifics do not address the question of restitution or effective enforcement.

## IV. The 1970 UNESCO Convention

### 1. The Principles of the Convention

Whereas the 1954 Hague Convention was drafted to protect cultural property only during military action, the 1970 UNESCO Convention on the Means of Prohibiting and Preventing the Illicit Import, Export and Transfer of Ownership of Cultural Property[834] is the major instrument to protect cultural objects during peacetime.[835] The 1970 UNESCO Convention was designed to curb international trafficking in national treasures by preventing the unlawful export and facilitating the return of cultural property to its nation of origin.[836] It is based on the premise that stolen and illegally exported cultural property shall not be imported. The Convention is comprised of twenty-six articles, those directly relevant to this discussion include Articles 3–10a, which pertain the movement of cultural property between the State Parties of the Convention.

Cultural property is defined in Article 1 to be "property which, on religious or secular grounds, is specifically designated by each State as being of importance for archaeology, prehistory, history, literature, art or science". The six disciplines (archaeology, prehistory, history, literature, art or science) are further explicated in a list of eleven categories.[837]

---

**834** Convention on the Means of Prohibiting and Preventing the Illicit Import, Export and Transfer of Ownership of Cultural Property, Nov. 17, 1970, 823 U.N.T.S. 231 [hereinafter: UNESCO Convention] see also Patrick J. O'Keefe, Commentary on the UNESCO 1970 Convention on Illicit Traffic (2007).

**835** The proposal was based on the preparatory work undertaken in the 1930 s by the predecessor of UNESCO under the League of Nations, K. Odendahl, Kulturgüterschutz, at 134.

**836** See UNESCO Convention Articles 2, 3, 6, 7, 9, 10, 12, 13, 823 U.N.T.S. 231. Previously, it was up to individual states to care for their cultural property, which meant formally constructing unilateral, bilateral or multilateral agreements to protect goods on an international scale.

**837** (a) Rare collections and specimens of fauna, flora, minerals and anatomy, and objects of paleontological interest;
(b) property relating to history, including the history of science and technology and military and social history, to the life of national leaders, thinkers, scientists and artist and to events of national importance;
(c) products of archaeological excavations (including regular and clandestine) or of archaeolog-

The most relevant provisions of the Convention are Articles 3, 6, 7 and 9. Articles 3 and 6 lay down that Parties to the 1970 UNESCO Convention may only import cultural property that has the certified permission to be exported from its source country.

Art. 9 lays down a regulation concerning items of archaeological interest. The provision states that a state whose "cultural patrimony is in jeopardy from pillage or archaeological or ethnological materials" may call on other State Parties "to participate in a concerted international effort to determine and to carry out the necessary concrete measures, including the control of exports and imports and international commerce in the specific materials concerned."

According to Art. 7 of the Convention, "State Parties to the Convention have to:

a. "to take the necessary measures, consistent with national legislation, to prevent museums and similar institutions within their territories from acquiring cultural property originating in another State Party which has been illegally exported after entry into force of this Convention, in the States concerned. Whenever possible, to inform a State of Origin Party to this Convention of an offer of such cultural property illegally removed from that State after the entry into force of this Convention in both States;"
b. (i) to prohibit the import of cultural property stolen from a museum or a religious or secular public monument or similar institution in another State Party to this Convention after the entry into force of this Convention for the States concerned, provided that such property is documented as appertaining to the inventory of that institution;
(ii) at the request of the State Party of Origin, to take appropriate steps to recover and return any such cultural property imported after the entry into force of this Convention in both States concerned, provided, however, that the requesting State shall pay just compensation

---

ical discoveries;
(d) elements of artistic or historical monuments or archaeological sites which have been dismembered;
(e) antiquities more than one hundred years old, such as inscriptions, coins and engraved seals;
(f) objects of ethnological interest;
(g) property of artistic interest, such as:
(h) pictures, paintings and drawings produced entirely by hand on any support and in any material (excluding industrial designs and manufactured articles decorated hand);
(i) original works of statuary art and sculpture in any material;
(ii) original engravings, prints and lithographs;
(iii) original artistic assemblages and montages in any material;
(i) rare manuscripts and incunabula, old books, documents and publications of special interest (historical, artistic, scientific, literary, etc.) singly or in collections;
(j) postage, revenue and similar stamps, singly or in collections;
(k) archives, including sound, photographic and cinematographic archives;
(l) articles of furniture more than one hundred years old and old musical instruments.

> to an innocent purchaser or to a person who has valid title to that property. Requests for recovery and return shall be made through diplomatic offices.

The Convention is thus the first legal instrument to give international effect to property interests on the ground of foreign cultural patrimony laws. It constitutes an acknowledgment of the need for the justiciability of such rights. However, its scope as a tool for the recovery of cultural objects is very limited.

The limitation starts with the requirement that cultural property has to be "designated by each State" as stated in Art. 1 of the Convention. This definition excludes undiscovered or unexcavated items from the range of the Convention's protection.

In terms of the restitution of artefacts, Art. 7 only lays down the obligation to return cultural objects which were stolen from museums or similar institutions and on subject to the condition condition that they had been inventoried. While some authors have argued for a more extensive interpretation of Art. 7 (b) (ii) applying also to illegally exported cultural property as stated in Art. 7 (a),[838] the large majority holds the obligation applicable only to the objects stolen under the circumstances outlined in Art. 7 (b) (i).[839] Consequently, the recognition of foreign export prohibition as proclaimed by the UNESCO Convention is only limited to a general obligation to respect other nations cultural patrimony laws by enacting import prohibitions,[840] but it does not contain a mechanism for the recovery of objects which were taken in violation of foreign nation's export laws. Further, the scope of the Convention is limited to a claim by the "State Party of Origin", which means that private individuals are excluded from the potential claimants.[841] The proceedings have to be initiated via the diplomatic channel. Another limiting factor is the non-retroactivity of the Convention, which can be assumed from customary international law, Art. 28 of the

---

**838** e.g. K. Siehr, International Art Trade, at 207–208. For a detailed account of different methods of interpretation, see K. Lubina, Contested Cultural Property, at 108 and footnote 467.

**839** For example, Christiane Freytag, "Cultural Heritage": Rückgabeansprüche von Ursprungsländern auf 'ihr' Kulturgut? in: F. G. Fechner, Prinzipien des Kulturgüterschutzes. Ansätze im deutschen, europäischen, und internationalen Recht, 175, at 181; Merryman/Elson/Urice (eds.), Law, Ethics, and the Visual Arts, at 187; Simon Mackenzie, Going, Going, Gone (2005), at 90.

**840** But see for example, K. Lubina, stating that the Convention breaks with the principle of public international law that denies the extraterritorial application of national law, at 109. Similarly, Andrea Jaeger, Rechtsfragen des internationalen Kulturgüterschutzes (1993), at 20; A. Hipp, Schutz von Kulturgütern, at 140.

**841** See UNESCO Convention, Art. 7 b (ii).

1969 Vienna Convention on the Law of Treaties, and the *travaux préparatoires* of the 1970 UNESCO Convention itself.[842]

As of today, more than 115 countries have become party to the 1970 UNESCO Convention,[843] however, the Convention is not self-executing and requires the state parties to amend their domestic laws in accordance with its provisions.[844] Only few of the states that ratified the Convention passed the necessary implementing statutes that introduced import control legislation.[845] Where, as in most countries, implementing legislation is missing, the UNESCO Convention does not work properly and there is no obstacle to international art trade.[846]

The lack of clarity in the scope of application has been said to be the main obstacle for a broader acceptance of the Convention.[847] Many states believe that a wide interpretation of Art. 7 of the Convention would interfere with the conduct of the legal trade in cultural property.[848]

Moreover, the 1970 UNESCO Convention raises, without solving, a number of important private law questions such as its impact on the existing rules of national law concerning the protection of the good faith purchaser.[849] The Convention calls for a state party to repatriate cultural property of another State upon request. If the property is returned, the requesting State is required to "pay just compensation to an innocent party or purchaser or to a person who has valid title to that property." This obligation certainly discouraged States from implementing the Convention.

The 1970 UNESCO Convention includes no rule as to the time limitation for claims. This is not necessarily required for requests through the diplomatic chan-

**842** Vienna, 23 May 1969, in force 27 January 1980, 1155 UNTS 331; UNESCO Doc. 78EX/9, Annex, para. 51, 8; and Report of the Special Committee of Governmental Experts to Examine the Draft Convention on the Means of Prohibiting and Preventing the Illicit Import, Export and Transfer of Ownership of Cultural Property: Replies to Draft Convention, UNESCO Doc.16C/17.13 July 1970, Annex 2, paras 18 and 29.

**843** For a full list of state parties to the convention see: http://portal.unesco.org/la/convention.asp?KO=13039&language=E

**844** Cp. Art. 3.

**845** For the different implementations of the Convention see the following paragraph.

**846** For a critical view of the Convention see e.g. Paul Bator, The International Trade in Art, at 27; Jennifer Lehman, The Continued Struggle with Stolen Cultural Property, at 527; Paige Margules, International Art Theft and the Illegal Import and Export of Cultural Property: A Study of Relevant Values, Legislation, and Solutions, 15 Suffolk Transnat'l L.J. (1991–1992) 609; Lyndel V. Prott, Commentary on the UNIDROIT Convention on Stolen and Illegally Exported Cultural Objects 1995 (1997), at 130.

**847** See for example, Kathleen Anderson, International Art Theft, at 10.

**848** Cp. P. Margules, at 621 et seq; Paul Bator, The International Trade in Art, at 94.

**849** See further Chapter 5.

nel, the outcome of which may depend also on political circumstances. However, as each state party implements the Convention in its own way, states may apply their own limitation periods.[850] This uncertainty, however, may have added to the poor acceptance of the Convention. As a consequence, until the 1980s not one art market nation had become state party to the Convention.[851] In 1983, the United States was the first market country to become a party, followed by France in 1997, Japan, and the United Kingdom in 2002, Switzerland in 2003, New Zealand in 2006, Germany in 2007 and also in 2003 on very limited terms Denmark and Sweden. Finally, the Netherlands ratified the Convention on June 9, 2009.

### 2. Implementing the Convention into National Law

The 1970 Convention is not self-executing and provides for a broad or narrow interpretation, depending on the politics of the state concerned, and consequently allows the state parties wide discretion in respect of the manner of implementation. In 1970, the Special Committee of Governmental Experts accepted the view that there would be varying degrees of implementation and decided to make reservations possible.[852] Additionally, many of the Convention's provisions consist of the insertion of phrases such as: "as appropriate for each country",[853] "consistent with national legislation",[854] "to the extent feasible",[855] "consistent with laws of each state"[856] or "as far as it is able".[857] These provisions give state parties great leeway as to how they implement the Convention, provided always that they undertake some means to prevent the illicit trafficking in cultural property.[858] However, it must be recalled that the International Court of Justice, in its

**850** According to O'Keefe, reservations and declarations in this regard are not necessary, P. O'Keefe, Commentary (2007), at 27.
**851** Note that Canada became a State Party as early as in 1977.
**852** The original draft Convention included a provision prohibiting reservations. Such a provision would have ensured acceptance by all parties of all provisions of the instrument but it would have prevented states from becoming a party at all, even if the particular obligations which the state cannot agree with are comparatively minor ones, see UNESCO Dc. SHC/MD/3 Annex 5 Art. 15.
**853** Cp. Art. 5 of the Convention.
**854** Cp. Art. 7 of the Convention.
**855** Cp. Art. 9 of the Convention.
**856** Cp. Art. 13 of the Convention.
**857** Cp. Art. 14 of the Convention.
**858** P. O'Keefe, Commentary, at 98.

opinion concerning the 'Reservations to the Genocide Convention'[859] held that, while states could limit their obligations to an international treaty, there is a certain core content which parties must accept if they wish other states to acknowledge them as parties to a treaty.[860] One fundamental principle on which the implementations are based is *reciprocity*. Generally, it is a principle in international law that international relations and treaties favours, benefits or penalties granted by one state to the citizens or legal entities of another, should be returned in kind.

States have taken widely varying views of their obligations under the 1970 Convention: Many states have not enacted any particular laws for the purpose of implementing the Convention, presumably believing that their existing legal system is capable of fulfilling their obligations under the Convention. The UK thought it unnecessary to implement the Convention as it believed that its existing laws and administrative procedures would enable membership of the Convention without any statutory change.[861] Sweden, for example, ratified the Convention in October 2002, but followed a minimalistic approach.[862] The ratification did not lead to any changes in the Swedish law and it is still legal to import objects smuggled out of other countries.[863] Some States however enacted specific legislation. So far, these are Australia, Canada, Czech Republic, Germany, Japan, Nigeria, the Netherlands, Switzerland, the United Kingdom, the United States of America and New Zealand.[864] The following section outlines their main implementary mechanisms.

#### a. Bilateral Approach

Article 15 of the Convention encourages states to enter bilateral negotiations to resolve claims for cultural objects removed from another state's territory, even prior to its operation. According to this approach, foreign cultural patrimony

---

**859** 1951, I.C.J. 15 (Advisory Opinion of May 28, 1951).

**860** Advisory Opinion at 21–26. See also Lyndel V. Prott, International Control of Illicit Movement of the Cultural Heritage: The UNESCO Convention and Some Possible Alternatives, 10 Syr. J. Int'l L. & Com (1983) 334, at 339.

**861** See Report ITAP 2000.

**862** S. Lunden, The Scholar and the Market: Swedish Scholarly Contributions to the Destruction of the World's Archaeological Heritage, in H. Karlsson (ed.) Swedish Archaeologists on Ethics (2004) 197.

**863** S. Lunden, The Scholar and the Market, at 217.

**864** Note, that New Zealand and Nigeria are the only two states which implemented both, the 1970 UNESCO and the 1995 UNIDROIT Convention, see P. Davies/P. Myburgh, The Protected Objects Act in New Zealand, at 321.

laws will be enforced between two states, if those states have concluded a bilateral agreement in which they specify the type of cultural objects subject to a recovery claim. The agreements restrict imports to the market countries of groups of artefacts noted in a designated list. It is not a blanket ban on all antiquities being imported into the market state with the consequence that legitimate trading is being retained. The bilateral mechanism was chosen, for example, by the United States and Switzerland.

### (1) United States of America

The United States was one of the first market nations to implement the 1970 UNESCO Convention. It adopted a rather restrictive implementation of the Convention's obligations into their domestic law, particularly in respect of foreign export controls. The United States accompanied its acceptance of the Convention by one reservation and six 'understandings' (statements of interpretation).[865]

The implementing legislation known as the Convention on Cultural Property Implementation Act [hereinafter: The CPIA] was enacted in December 1982.[866] As the US interpreted most provisions of the Convention as of a 'ceremonial, rhetorical and ineffective' nature and thus to not having any legal significance,[867] the CPIA explicitly implements only two sections of the Convention – Article 7(b) and Article 9.

Section 308 of the CPIA contains the implementation of Art. 7 (b) (i), stating that "no article of cultural property documented as appertaining to the inventory of a museum or religious or secular public monument or similar institution in any State Party which is stolen from such institution after the effective date of

---

**865** The precise effect of understandings as opposed to reservations is unclear: some consider that they amount to reservations and must be treated in the same way; others that, if a tribunal were to hold the interpretation unwarranted by the text of the treaty, the party making it is still bound by the treaty and cannot maintain its interpretation without breach of its obligations under the treaty, see P. O'Keefe, Commentary, at 26; D.M. Mc Rae, The Legal Effect of Interpretative Declarations, 49 British Yearbook of International Law (1978) 155, at 160.

**866** Convention of Cultural Property Implementation Act, Pub. L. No. 97–446 §§ 301–315, 96 Stat. 2350–63 (1983), codified as amended at 19 U.S.C. § 2601–13. The CPIA is part of the Customs Statute (Title 19 of the U.S. Code) and is trade legislation because it is effectuated through import restrictions. For a discussion of the CPIA see for example P. Gerstenblith, Art, Cultural Heritage and the Law (2008, 2nd ed), at 624; B. Rosecrance, Harmonious Meeting: The McClain Decision and the Cultural Property Implementation Act, 19 Cornell Int'l L.J. (1986) 311; Adam Goldberg, Reaffirming McClain: The National Stolen Property Act and the Abiding Trade in Looted Cultural Objects, 53 UCLA L. Rev. (2005–2006) 1031; P. J. O'Keefe, Commentary, at 107–126.

**867** Cp. P. J. O'Keefe, Commentary, at 28–31.

this title, maybe imported into the US". The term 'cultural property' is defined in reference to the Convention as "including articles described by Article 1 (a) through (k) of the Convention whether or not any such article is specifically designated as such by any State Party for the purpose of such article". This definition is very broad and includes literary every sort of cultural object that might be housed in a museum or other type of institution. The provision gives the Department of Homeland Security (formerly Customs) the authority to seize or forfeit such property at the border or after it has entered the country.[868]

To avoid a general undertaking as set out in Art. 9 of the Convention, the US decided for an interpretation of the provisions that enforces another countries export laws at the national level within narrow limits. Sections 303 and 304 align with Art. of the 1970 UNESCO Convention, splitting it into two parts. Combined, sections 303 and 304 provide prospective prohibitions on import of archaeological and ethnological materials that a foreign state wishes to protect.[869] Section 303 of the CPIA provides a mechanism by which the US can enter into bilateral agreements with other State Parties in order to "apply import restrictions (....) to the archaeological or ethnological material of a State Party the pillage of which is creating jeopardy to the cultural patrimony of the State Party." In consequence, the United States interpretation reduces the Convention to "an agreement to agree."[870] Such an agreement is effective for five years and may be extended for additional periods of five years.[871] Additionally, in order to

---

**868** Cp. P. Gertsenblith, Art, Cultural Heritage and the Law, at 625.

**869** Cp. Katherine D. Vitale, The War on Antiquities: United States Law and Foreign Cultural Property, 84 Notre Dame L. R. (2009) 1835, at 1845.

**870** See also P. J. O'Keefe, Commentary, at 110; Marc B. Feldman, Proceedings of the Panel on the US Enabling Legislation of the UNESCO Convention on the Means of Prohibiting and Preventing the Illicit Import, Export and Transfer of Ownership of Cultural Property, 4 Syr. Int'l L. & Com. (1976) 97, at 114–115.

**871** The U.S. has signed agreements with: Bolivia, regarding antique ceremonial textiles from Coroma; Cambodia, regarding Khamer Stone archaeological material; Canada regarding archaeological artefacts and ethnological material of cultures of Canadian origin; Cyprus, regarding Byzantine ecclesiastical and ritual ethnological material; El Salvador regarding archaeological material representing pre-hispanic cultures of El Salvador; Guatemala regarding archaeological material from sites in the Peten Lowlands of Guatemala and related pre-Columbian material from the highlands and South Coast; Italy, regarding archaeological material representing pre-classical, classical and Roman periods from approximately ninth century B.C. to approximately fourth century A.D; Mali archaeological material from the Niger River Valley Region of Mali and the Bandiagara escarpment forming part of the remains of the sub- Saharan culture and Peru, regarding archeological artefacts and ethnological material.

For a thorough analysis concerning the USA-Italy Bilateral Agreement, see e.g. Gordon Lobay, Border Controls in Market Countries as Disincentives to Antiquities Looting at Source?

enter into a bilateral agreement, the President or his designee must make four determinations: (1) that the cultural patrimony of the foreign state is in jeopardy; (2) that the foreign state has attempted to protect its cultural patrimony; (3) that import controls on the objects requested by the foreign state would substantially benefit the deterrence of their pillage; and (4) that import controls are "consistent with the general interest of the international community in the interchange of cultural property among nations."[872] Without meeting the four criteria, the CPIA does not bar the import of cultural objects unless they are documented as the inventory of a State Party nations museum or other public institution.[873]

Generally, objects are subject to restitution only if they have been included as a listed item in the agreement. Concerning the agreement between the United States and Italy, for example, the import of artefacts is only restricted if they were created between the ninth century B.C. and the fourth century A.D. Cultural property to be included in the agreement is the result of negotiations between the parties.[874]

### (2) Switzerland

In the face of a wide perception that Switzerland was becoming the major market for illicit traffic of art objects, Switzerland became a party to the 1970 UNESCO Convention on January 3, 2004. The Swiss implementing legislation, the Federal Act on the International Transfer of Cultural Property [hereinafter: CPTA], took effect in June 2005.[875] Switzerland implements the Convention in a manner

---

The USA-Italy Bilateral Agreement 2001, in: Simon MacKenzie/Penny Green (eds.), Criminology and Archaeology, 124.

**872** § 304(a), 19 U.S.C. § 2603 (a) CPIA established the Cultural Property Advisory Committee (CPAC) to assist the President in making these four determinations, CPIA § 306, 19 U.S.C. § 2605 (2006).

**873** Merryman/Elson/Urice, (eds.) Law, Ethics and the Visual Arts, at 258.

**874** See the Agreement Concerning the Imposition of Import Restrictions on Categories of Archaeological Material Representing the Pre-Classical, Classical and Imperial Roman Periods of Italy, of January 19, 2001, Federal Register 23/1/2001, 66 (15): 7399. This agreement has been recently prolonged for another 5 years.

**875** Federal Act on the International Transfer of Cultural Property of June 20 2003, in Systematische Rechtssammlung no. 444.1; Bundesblatt (2003): 4475. For a discussion of the CPTA, see G. von Segesser & A. Jolles, Switzerland's New Federal Act on the International Transfer of Cultural Property: An Update and Perspective from the Art Trade 10 AAL (2005) 175; A.F.G. Raschèr, Cultural Property Transfer (Zurich 2005), at 27–67; Marc Weber, New Swiss Law on Cultural Property, 13 IJCP (2006), 99–113; Felix H. Siegfried, Internationaler Kulturgüterschutz in der Schweiz, Das Bundesgesetz über den internationalen Kulturgütertransfer (2007).

that is close to the US model of implementation, through a series of bilateral agreements that impose import restrictions.[876] The new Swiss legislation permits the Swiss Federal Council to enter into agreements with other nations that are party to the UNESCO Convention to protect "cultural foreign affairs interest and to secure cultural heritage", Art 7. Following prerequisites must be fulfilled in order to conclude a bilateral agreement under the CPTA:

(1) the object of the agreement must be cultural property of significant importance for the cultural heritage of the relevant contracting state;
(2) the cultural property must be subject to export provisions in the relevant contracting state for the purpose of protecting cultural heritage; and
(3) the contracting state must grant reciprocal rights (Article 7, para. 2, lit. a–c CPTA).

Cultural property imported contrary to a bilateral agreement is considered an illegal import and their importer is liable to a fine or imprisonment.[877]

The bilateral agreements, which the new legislation authorises the federal states to enter into, may not have been intended to have the Swiss authorities seize property that has been unlawfully imported into Switzerland. However, they may serve as a basis for taking action concerning its seizure. Under Art. 9 of the CPTA, the parties to the agreement may proceed in the Swiss Administrative Court.[878] In order to be able to claim for the return of an artefact, the claiming state will have to prove that the object was unlawfully imported into Switzerland and that it was of significant importance to its own cultural heritage.[879] The Act also provides that all costs associated with the protection, preservation and return of an object have to be paid by the claimant state, which will most probably constitute a powerful deterrent.[880] Claims for repatriation are subject to a statute of limitation of one year after the authorities of the claiming state have become aware of where and with whom the cultural property is located.[881] In addition, if the object concerned has been acquired in good faith by its possessor, the state to which it is to be returned has to pay compensation.[882] Moreover, the

**876** P. Gerstenblith, Art, Cultural Heritage and the Law, at 625.
**877** M. Weber, New Swiss Law on Cultural Property, at 101.
**878** Art. 30 al. 1 Kulturgütertransfergesetz [SR 444.1] in connection with Art. 5, 6 und 44 of the Bundesgesetz über das Verwaltungsverfahren [VwVG; SR 172.021].
**879** Art. 9 para. 1 CPTA.
**880** Art. 9 para. 2 and para. 3 CPTA.
**881** Art. 9 para. 4 CPTA.
**882** Art. 9 paras. 5 and 6 CPTA.

claim of the foreign state expires at the latest 30 years after the cultural property was unlawfully removed.[883]

Unlike the U.S. bilateral agreements, the Swiss agreements are of potentially unlimited duration and do not need to be renewed. Requests for an agreement are not subject to review by a committee of private citizens but are rather negotiated directly by officials of the Swiss Ministry of Culture. So far, Switzerland has entered into agreements only with Italy,[884] Greece,[885] Peru,[886] Egypt[887] and Columbia,[888] however, only the agreement between Switzerland and Italy has been both ratified and enacted.[889]

As opposed to the U.S., Switzerland also decided to implement Art. 10 a), as well as 13 a) of the 1970 UNESCO Convention, which obliges the Member States of the Convention to restrict illicit trade in heritage items by setting certain due diligence standards for antique dealers, especially in connection with the transfer of cultural property.[890] As a consequence, the CPTA imposes duties of care on any person active in the art trade and auction business. Pursuant to Art. 16, para. 1, lit. a–b CPTA cultural property may only be transferred when the person transferring the property may assume, under the circumstances, that the cultural property, was neither stolen, nor lost against the will of the owner, nor illegally excavated and not illicitly imported.

In addition, according to Article 16, para. 2 CPTA, persons active in the art trade and auctioning business are obliged:

**883** Art. 9 para. 4 CPTA.

**884** Agreement between Switzerland and Italy on the Import and Return of Cultural Property, ratified on 20.10.2006, enacted on 27/04/2008.

**885** Agreement between Switzerland and Greece on the Import, Transfer and the Return of Cultural Property, ratified on 15/05/2007.

**886** Agreement between Switzerland and Peru on the Prevention of the Illicit Trade with Cultural Property, ratified on 28/12/2006.

**887** Agreement between Switzerland and Egypt on the Illegal Import, Transfer and Return of Antiquities to its Country of Origin, ratified on 14/04/2010.

**888** Agreement between Switzerland and the Republic of Columbia on the Import and Return of Cultural Property, ratified on 1/02/2010.

**889** All agreements are available on the website of the Swiss Bundesamt für Kulturgut at: http://www.bak.admin.ch/themen/kulturguetertransfer/01985/index.html?lang=de

**890** According to Art. 10 a) of the UNESCO Convention, State Parties of the Convention undertake: to restrict by education, information and vigilance, movement of cultural property illegally removed from any State Party to this Convention and, as appropriate for each country, oblige antique dealers, subject to penal or administrative sanctions, to maintain a register recording the origin of each item of cultural property, names and addresses of the supplier, description and price of each item sold and to inform the purchaser of the cultural property of the export prohibition to which such property may be subject.

(1) to establish the identity of the supplier or seller and require a written declaration from the same of his or her right to dispose of the cultural property;
(2) to inform their customers about existing import and export regulations of the contracting states;
(3) to maintain written records on the acquisition of cultural property by specifically recording the origin of the cultural property, to the extent known, and the name and address of the supplier or seller, a description as well as the sales price of the cultural property;
(4) to provide to the specialized body all necessary information on fulfilling this duty of diligence.

In practice, these due diligence requirements are being implemented through written assurances from the seller that the object in question is of clean provenance.[891]

Switzerland also used the implementation of the Convention as an opportunity to amend their private law.[892] For art objects, the time limit of adverse possession was raised from five years to 30 years,[893] as well as limitation periods concerning defects of quality of an art object.[894]

Although, the Swiss model introduced many novelties into Swiss law which fundamentally improve the protection of art and antiquities in Switzerland, in conclusion, both the American and the Swiss bilateral models are too restrictive to meet the standards of the UNESCO Convention and are not recommendable as a method of implementation. The recovery practice varies from bilateral agreement to bilateral agreemnt and and does not provide for a consistant recovery practice and, in consequence, does not provide for legal certainty in respect of the protection of cultural property for the source states.

### b. Multilateral Approach

As opposed to the U.S. and Switzerland, some countries (Canada, Germany, Netherlands) have not stipulated that property can be recovered only by countries with which a bilateral agreement for such return has been concluded. The only condition for the return of property is that the requirements of the

**891** Cp. Bericht der Bundesregierung zum Kulturgueterschutz in Deutschland (German Report) 2013, at 130.
**892** For a thorough anaysis of the amendments see Heinrich Honsell in: Peter Gauch / Franz Werro / Pascal Pichonnaz (eds.) Das Kulturgütertransfergesetz und das Privatrecht (2008).
**893** Art. 728 (1) and (1ter) of the Swiss Civil Code.
**894** Articles 196a and 210 (1) bis of the Swiss Civil Code.

state's implementary legislation are fulfilled, without the need for the prior conclusion of any agreement. The advantage of this approach is that, where necessary, decisive action can be taken without the necessity of first negotiating an agreement. The implementation by bilateral agreements is constrained by political circumstances and debates between the two contracting states, which essentially contravene the principle of public international law. The implementation via the multilateral approach on the other hand better reflects the purpose of the Convention, but only, of course, if the state parties' implementation has not been interpreted in a rather restrictive manner.

In the European Member States, the implementation follows the lines of Council Directive 93/7/EEC and the legislation transposing it into the Member States law, as many provisions, especially those on good faith acquisition and prescription correspond between the Directive and the Convention. However, the operation of the Directive and its implementing legislation is limited to the Member States of the European Union and the countries of the European Economic Area (EEA). By contrast, the operation of the Convention and the present implementing legislation is global in the sense that it applies to all countries that are party to the Convention, i.e. over 100 countries spread across all continents.

### (1) Germany

Germany enacted implementing legislation for the UNESCO Convention as recently as 2007 via the Act on the Return of Cultural Property of 18/04/2007.[895] The implementation follows the lines of Council Directive 93/7/EEC and the legislation transposing it into German law, the newly amended Cultural Property

895 Gesetz zu dem Übereinkommen vom 14. November 1970 über die Maßnahmen zum Verbot und zur Verhütung der rechtswidrigen Einfuhr, Ausfuhr und Uebereignung von Kulturgut, German Official Journal (BGBl.) 2007 II No. 12 of 25 April 2007, at 626 et seq.; Gesetz zur Ausführung des UNESCO-Uebereinkommens vom 14. November 1970 über Maßnahmen zum Verbot und zur Verhütung der rechtswidrigen Einfuhr, Ausfuhr und übereignung von Kulturgut, BGBl. 2007 I Nr. 21 of 23 May 2007, at 757 et seq. For a first evaluation see Matthias Weller, Zur Umsetzung der UNESCO-Konvention von 1970 aus deutscher Sicht, in Gerte Reichelt (ed.) Rechtsfragen der Restitution von Kulturgütern, Symposium des Ludwig Boltzmann Instituts für Europarecht am 12. Oktober 2007 im Bundesministerium für Unterricht, Kunst und Kultur Wien, (Vienna 2008) 27–38. For an in-depth account from a comparative perspective see also Matthias Weller in: Kulturgüterschutz – Künstlerschutz, Tagungsband II. Des Heidelberger Kunstrechtstags am 5. und 6. September (Baden-Baden 2009) 206.

Restitution Law [Kulturgüterrückgabegesetz, hereinafter: CPRL].[896] Previously, the CPRL implemented only the obligations imposed by Council Directive 93/7/EEC. The amended CPRL[897] now contains the implementation of Council Directive 93/7/EEC, the implementation of the main provisions of the 1970 UNESCO Convention as well as the implementation of the First Protocol of the Hague Convention 1954. Effectively, Germany has only implemented Art. 7 (b) (ii) and Art. 10 (a) of the UNESCO Convention.

Under the German CPRL, the restitution of cultural property is not subject to the conclusion of a bilateral agreement. However, the multilateral implementation of the Convention came with a price. The prerequisites for granting a restitution claim under the Convention are very high:

First of all, according to § 6 (2) sentence 1 of the German CPRL, the requesting state will be entitled to reclaim the object in question only when the heritage item has been classified by the country of origin one year prior to its removal from the countries territory as being of "special importance" and individually recorded in a national inventory of protected property, whose export would constitute an appreciable impoverishment of the national cultural heritage. § 6 (2) sent. 3 CPRL further requires that those inventories are accessible "without any unreasonable obstacles". An unreasonable obstacle would be, for example, an internationally rarely used language.[898] As a consequence, it does not suffice when the cultural property in question is covered by a supranational definition of cultural property as is the case in EC Directive 93/7/EEC of 1993. Heritage items which have not been inventoried prior to its illegal export cannot be subject of a restitution claim in Germany. For example, the Turkish stelae form the Antiquities Museum in Bal, Switzerland, belonging to the Ludwig Collection could not be subject of a return request in Germany as they had not been inventoried in any Turkish cultural property register.[899] In a recent case in front of the admin-

**896** Gesetz zum Schutz deutschen Kulturgutes gegen Abwanderung of 8. July 1999, BGBl. I 1999, at 1754, as amended through Art. 2 of the legislation implementing the 1970 UNESCO Convention, BGBl. I 2007, at 761–762

**897** Gesetz zur Ausführung des UNESCO-Übereinkommens vom 14. November 1970 über Maßnahmen zum Verbot und zur Verhütung der rechtswidrigen Einfuhr, Ausfuhr und Übereignung von Kulturgut und zur Umsetzung der Richtlinie 93/7/EWG des Rates vom 15. März 1993 über die Rückgabe von unrechtmäßig aus dem Hoheitsgebiet eines Mitgliedstaats verbrachten Kulturgütern, BGBl. I 2007, at 757–761.

**898** See explanatory memorandum of the German Parliament to the implementation of the 1970 UNESCO Convention, BT-Drucksache 16/1371, at 18.

**899** See Kurt Siehr, Die Umsetzung des UNESCO- Übereinkommens von 1970 in Deutschland aus der Sicht der Wissenschaft, Tagungsband II des Heidelberger Kunstrechtstages (2009) 79, at 92.

istrative court in Munich, Mexico claimed for the recovery of a convoute fo over 1000 pre-columbian artefacts which were illegally exported from latin America.[900] The artefacts were registered in Mexico's registry of national monuments before they were exported. The registry of those archaeological artefacts which were not registered before they left Mexican territory followed within the German one year-deadline. The Bavarian investigative authorities seized the objects when they were smuggled into Germany lacking an export certificate. The Bavarian court rejected Mexico's claim on the ground that, first, the objects where not of national importance in the sence of § 6 (4) CPRL and second, the national inventory was not "easily accessible" in the terms of the German Implementary Act. According to the court, easily accessible was the right of access via the internet in a common language like Englsh or French, while in this case, the Mexican law only allowed the access to view the Mexican administrative procedure and the registry was only available in Spanish.[901] Mexico argued that in a country where pre-columbian archaeological artefacts are state owned ex lege, it is barely possible to maintain a directory accesibel via the internet, or to deposit a copy of the registry in germany, as the court alternatively suggested. They also argued that Spanish was an in ternationaly common language in order to fulfil the requirement of "easily accessible" in the sence of § 6 (2) CPRL. The judement again proves that countries which protect their heritage via an umbrelle statute have practically no chance to fulfil the srict requirement of Germany's "list principle" rendering the German implementation of the UNESCO Convention for those countries rather useless.

An exception has been introduced for archaeological objects, which were unknown to the government of the Member States prior to their export. According to § 6 (2) sent. 1 No. 1 CPRL, the competent authority must place archaeological objects in the inventory within one year of the time when the country of origin gains knowledge of the excavation. This exceptionally short limitation period practically precludes UNESCO state parties to claim back material which has been subject to illegal excavations, as no state can possible search for its illegally excavated cultural material to this extent.[902] This restrictive interpretation of Art. 7 (b) (ii) has been thought necessary by the German legislator in order to

---

**900** Bavarian Administraive Court, 16 July 2010 [Az 7 CE 10.1097].

**901** For a comment on the case, see Robert Kugler, Die Praxis des Kulturgüterrückgabegesetzes, in: Kulturgütersschutz und politiche Entwicklunge in Mexiko im Jubiläumsjahr 2010, Jahreskongress 2010 der Deutsch Mexikanischen Juristen Vereinigung, Gessaphe (ed.) (2011) 13, at 16.

**902** See also Matthias Weller, Zur Umsetzung der UNESCO-RL, at 35; K. Siehr, Expert Opinions in the Explanatory Memorandum BT Nr 16(22) 049–056, at 6. Available at http://www.bundestag.de/ausschuesse/a22/anhoerungen/unesco/index.html

"preclude an escalating or even abusive amount of restitution claims by state parties which would not be within the meaning of the Convention."[903]

In addition, Germany has implemented the Convention only in respect to illegally exported cultural property, not to stolen property.[904] According to § 6 (2) an object illegally imported into the German Federal Republic is to be returned to the requesting state. § 6 (4) defines illegally imported as "cultural property that has been illegally imported if its export took place in contravention with the state's export laws." Indeed, this restrictive interpretation of the Convention might violate Germany's treaty obligations, and has already been criticised by other State Parties.[905]

The idiosyncrasies in the German implementation start with the fact that claims have to be brought in front of the administrative court and not he civil court. This stems from the fact that the administrative courts succumb to ex officio investigation as opposed to the civil courts, which are ruled by the principle of production of evidence. Indeed, this is the positive side of the medal as the treshhold of ex officio investigation is lower.

Still, for a recovery claim to succeed the requesting state has to prove all conditions of entitlement to the object.[906] In the first place, it will have to prove that it is the owner of the object in question. This entails a practical problem, as in many cases of illegal excavation, it is not easy to exactly attribute an object to a specific area where ther object may have been excavated. Furthermore, claiming an object in Germany includes circumventing a dual time obstacle: The illegal export of the object in question must have taken place after it was registered in the national inventory, and additionally, after the German implementary legislation came into effect.[907] From the perspective of the claiming state this would cause a major problem regarding the burden of proof, as in most cases it will be very difficult or even impossible to pinpoint the exact mo-

**903** Katrin Schenk, Die Umsetzung des UNESCO- Übereinkommens von 1970 aus der Sicht des Gestzgebers in: Tagungsband II des Heidelberger Kunstrechttag (2009) 61, at 66.

**904** See §§ 6 (2) and (4) CPRL.

**905** Report of the Federal Government on the Protection of Cultural Property in Germany (Report on the impact of the Act implementing the UNESCO Convention 1970 on the means of prohibiting and preventing the illicit import, export and transfer of ownership of cultural property and prevention of the expodus of German cultural property (following: German Report 2013), April 2013, at p. 6, available at http://www.bundesregierung.de/Content/DE/_Anlagen/BKM/2013–04–24-bericht-kulturgutschutz.pdf?__blob=publicationFile&v=1.

**906** § 13 (3) CPRL.

**907** The CPRL was enacted on 18.5.2007, see BGBl 2007 I 757, but only came into effect on 26.7.2007, after its publication in the German Federal Law Gazette (Bundesgesetzblatt), see BGBl 2008 II 235.

ment when the object was taken out of its country of origin and illegally imported into Germany. For this reason, the German legislator introduced a legal assumption: in case the exact moment of illegal import into Germany cannot be determined, it is being assumed that the illegal import took place after the effective date of the CPRL, but only if the object in question has been registered in the national inventory before the effective date of the German implementation.[908]

Additionally, the requesting state has to prove the bad faith of the possessor of the object in respect of the circumstances of the objects' illicit acquisition.[909] Especially in connection with interposed acquisitions and sales in third countries, the claimant state will regularly not succeed in producing this evidence. As a result, the claimant state in most cases will have to pay compensation to the possessor of the object according to § 10 CPRL. Equally, the recovery request is subject to a limitation period of only one year, which starts running after the requesting state became aware of the whereabouts of the object in question.[910]

A positive signal of the German implementation is the introduction of import controls placed on cultural property of special importance from the State Parties to the Convention. Before the implementary legislation, import of cultural property was not subject to any system of control. Now, § 14 and § 15 CPRL provide that the import of cultural property into Germany without a valid licence is punished with up to 3 years of imprisonment or a fine. These provisions are supposed to prevent illegally exported items to enter German territory in order to avoid expensive restitution claims by the State Parties to the Convention in the first place.[911] Furthermore, the CPRL introduces duties of care and recording requirements for art and antiquities dealers by fully implementing Art. 10 (a) of the UNESCO Convention. § 18 CPRL requires dealers to maintain written records on the acquired art or antiquity including a description suitable to identify the objects, as well as data on the acquisition of cultural property by specifically recording the origin of the cultural property, to the extent known, and the name and address of the supplier or seller, as well as the sales price of the cultural property. As opposed to the Swiss implenetary legislation, the CPRL, however, did not implement Art. 13a of the UNESCO Convention, which provides that State Parties undertake to prevent by all appropriate means transfers of ownership of cultural property likely to prmote the illicit import or export of such property.

---

**908** Cp. Katrin Schenk, Tagungsband II, at 67; Parliamentary Debate BT-Drucks 16/13750 at 7, available at http://dipbt.bundestag.de/dip21/btd/16/137/1613750.pdf.

**909** § 10 (1) 1 CPRL.

**910** § 11 CPRL.

**911** K. Schenk, Tagungsband II, at 67.

With the adoption of the new Act, the German legislator requested that the Federal Government submited a report on the impact of the Act, in order to investigate whether futhrt adjustments to the law were necessary.[912] The Report, which was subsequently completed in 2013 by the German Ministry of Culture in Cooperation with the competent supreme *Land* authorities and constitutes a complete review of the 2007 Act, proved that although the new legislation was a "politically necessary and correct step",[913] from an overall point of view, the German implementation is too restrictive to be in line with the purposes of the Convention. According to the Report, not one single case since 2008 has led to a return of an object under the act despite numerous requests.[914] During the five years of the evaluation process, the Act's high treshhold for retruns could not be met by any state seeking return, namely the prerequisit that an entitlement for retrun shall exist only for objects which have been entered in a public list of important objects prior to its removal. Numerous illicitly exported cultural objects, especially from the countries of Central America but also from Egypt, Iraq, Iran, Turkey, Russia, China and other states, have been brought to Germany in recent years. In not one single instance could these – in some cases important – cultural objects be returned to their country of origin. In order to meet the policy goals of the UNESCO Convention, return request should be granted if the object in question is covered by the definition of Cultural Property contained in Article 1 of the UNESCO Convention. As such, UNESCO State Parties should generally be treated in the same manner as other EC Member States are treated within the meaning of the EC Directive 1993. Conclusively, the 2013 Report suggests to abandon the list principle, and to introduce import controls at the German borders, which would proclaim illegally exported object automatically to be illegally imported. Moreover, the one year-deadine for instituting proceedings is expected to be extended up to three years. The German legislator plans to consolidate the amendement of the CPRL with the amendment of the EC Regulation EEC 93/7.

---

**912** Resolution of the German Bundestag of 1 February 2007 (Bundestag Printed Paper 16/4145) and Resolution of the Bundesrat of 9 March 2007 (Bundesrat Printed Paper 92/07) [both in German].

**913** Cp. Report fo the Federal Government on the Protection of Cultural Propert in Germany (hereinafter: German Report) 2013.

**914** In many cases however, returns could be achieced according to the mutual assistance in criminal matters, or the UN Iraq Sanctions Order 2003 (Verordnung (EG) Nr. 1210/2003 des Rates vom 7. Juli 2003 zum Verbot der Einfuhr, Ausfuhr und dem Handel mit irakischem Kulturgut).

### (2) Netherlands

The most recent and most generous implementation of the UNESCO Convention was enacted by the Netherlands on June 12, 2009 via the 1970 UNESCO Convention on the Illicit Import, Export and Transfer of Ownership of Cultural Property (Implementation) Act [hereinafter: The Implementation Act].[915] In this connection, the Dutch made amendments *inter alia* to the Code of Civil Procedure, the Civil Code and the Dutch Cultural Heritage Preservation Act. Similar to the German approach, the Dutch implementation follows the lines of Council Directive 93/7/EEC and the legislation transposing it into Dutch law.[916]

The Dutch Government decided to limit the scope of the implementary legislation to "objects of great cultural, historical and scientific importance that belong to the statutorily protected cultural heritage of a country."[917] Accordingly, the definition of cultural property in Section 1 (d) of the Implementation Act corresponds to Art. 1 of the UNESCO Convention and describes cultural property as an object "which has been designated by each state, on religious or secular grounds, as being of importance for archaeology, prehistory, history, literature, art or science" and which belongs to one of the categories of cultural property listed in Article 1. The act of designation does not in itself have to be specific and can instead be couched in general terms.[918] According to the Letter for July 19, 2004 issued by the Dutch House of Representatives, the definition should be viewed partly in connection with the stated purpose of the Convention, namely to protect the cultural heritage of the countries of origin, as expressed in Art. 2 of the Convention.[919] Consequently, "designated" in the sense of the Act may mean any designation of cultural property, even in the form of a declaration of state ownership of certain or even all heritage items. Art. 4 of the Convention defines in more detail what the parties to the Convention should in any event recognise as belonging to the cultural heritage of a state. In any event, unlike

---

**915** Wet tot uitvoering van de op 14 november 1970 te Parijs tot stand gekomen Overeenkomst inzake de middelenom de onrechtmatige invoer, uitvoer of eigendomsoverdracht van culturele goederen te verbieden en te verhin deren (Uitvoeringswet UNESCO-verdrag 1970 inzake onrechtmatige invoer, uitvoer of eigendomsoverdracht van cultuurgoederen. The most recent version ofthe text of the Act can be found, in Dutch, on the website: http://www.wetten.nl, in English in the UNESCO database at www.unesco.org.

**916** Explanatory memorandum to the Dutch Implementation Act, available at UNESCO database, http://www.unesco.org/culture/natlaws/index.php?&lng=en

**917** Parliamentary Papers, House of Representatives 2003/04, 29 314, No. 8 Letter of 19 July 2004.

**918** Expl. Memo, ibid, at 4.

**919** Parliamentary Papers, House of Representatives 2003/04, 29 314, No. 8. Letter of 19 July 2004.

the restrictive German approach, the restitution of cultural property under the Act is not restricted to objects that have been registered in a national inventory prior to their illicit export.

As regards the scope of the Implemenation Act, it should nevertheless be noted that it relates only to cultural property illicitly exported from or unlawfully appropriated in a state party after the entry into force of the Act.

Section 3 of the Implementation Act, which corresponds to Art. 3 of the UNESCO Convention, provides that it is prohibited to import into the Netherlands cultural property which:

a) has been removed from the territory of a State Party in breach of the provisions adopted by that State Party in accordance with the objectives of the Convention in respect of the export of cultural property from that State Party or the transfer of ownership of cultural property; or
b) which has been unlawfully appropriated in a State Party.

"Unlawful appropriation" includes not only theft, but also comparable offences such as embezzlement and obtaining goods under false pretences or unlawful excavation at archaeological sites.[920] Via this provision, the Implementation Act addresses the problem of illegally excavated archaeological objects that are generally unknown to the government prior to their illegal export from their country of origin. In the case of unlawful appropriation it is not necessary to show that a provision concerning the export from the country of origin has also been infringed.[921]

The sanction for infringement of the prohibition in Section 3 is exclusively of private law nature. The prohibition does not confer any extra powers on the Customs or the Criminal Justice Authorities. Infringement of the prohibition constitutes a tort, which can result in an award of damages.[922] Unlike the position in the UK under the Dealing in Cultural Objects (Offences) Act 2003,[923] the Dutch Government decided not to include a provision prohibiting possession of cultural property in respect of which the provisions referred to in Section 3 have been infringed.

---

**920** N.M. van der Horst, UNESCO 1970 en de Bescherming van Culturgoederen, in: Ars Aequi Journal(2009) 666, at 670.

**921** N.M van der Horst (2009), at 670.

**922** Expl. Memo, ibid, at 6.

**923** For a full account of the Act and the UK Implementation of the Convention see this Chapter, further down.

The right to issue proceedings to recover objects in front of Dutch Courts is provided for in Section 4 of the Implementation Act. Cultural property that has been brought into the Netherlands in breach of the import prohibition may be reclaimed by the state party from which the property originated or by the person with valid title to such property. As opposed to Germany, the Netherlands opted to amend its private law in order to implement the Convention, in specific the provisions of the Code of the Civil Procedure and the Dutch Civil Code.[924] The legal proceedings for return of the property are now regulated in Articles 1011a[925] – 1011d of the Code of Civil Procedure. Defences to such proceedings based on acquisition in good faith, acquisitive or extinctive prescription or acquisition of a pledge in good faith are wholly or partly suspended in a series of amendments to the Civil Code.[926] For example, Art. 3:86 Dutch Civil Code "a transfer (...) of a movable object (...) despite the alienator's lack of the right to dispose of the property is valid, provided that the transfer[927] is not by gratuitous title and the acquirer acts in good faith," [928] has been complemented by Art. 3:86 b, which now provides that Article 3:86 may not be invoked against a State Party to the UNESCO Convention or against a person with valid title to such property if, pursuant to Art. 4 of the 1970 UNESCO Convention, they initiate legal proceedings as referred to in Article 1011a of the Code of Civil Procedure for the return of a movable as referred to in that Article." However, as in the German Implementation, the requesting party has to pay fair compensation to the possessor of the objects in question if "it is satisfied that the possessor exercised due diligence in acquiring the movable."[929] For that purpose, Article 3:87a Dutch Civil Code contains the requirements, concerning the diligence to be exercised

**924** According to the Dutch Government, the manner of protecting cultural property of other States Parties is in principle of a private law nature and must to a large extent be regulated in the Civil Code and in the Code of Civil Procedure, see Explanatory Memorandum, at...The relevant provisions on the protection of stolen cultural objects, or rather the protection of the rights and interest of the original owner of a cultural object and a subsequent bona fide purchaser can be found in Book 3 and 5 of the Dutch Civil Code [hereinafter the DCC].

**925** Section 3 (b) is formulated more broadly than is strictly required by 7 (b) (i) of the UNESCO Convention, since it does not include the limitation that the unlawful appropriation must have taken place from a museum or a religious or secular public monument or similar institution.

**926** See Articles 86b, 87a, 88, 99, 238, 310c of the Dutch Civil Code.

**927** The transfer must be in accordance with Articles 3:90, 3:91 or 3:93 DCC.

**928** Cp. Katja Lubina, Protection and Preservation of Cultural Heritage in the Netherlands in the 21$^{st}$ Century, (Vol. 13.2) E. J. Comp. L., (May 2009) 1, at 37, available at http://www.ejcl.org.

**929** Art 3:86 b para. 2 of the Dutch Implementary Act. For a full account of the Provisions contained in the Dutch Civil Code concerning the rules on transferring property and the protection of third parties when acquiring a stolen object, cp. K. Lubina, Protection and Preservation of Cultural Heritage in the Netherlands, 36–38.

by a dealer in cultural property. The provision lists in particular what circumstances must be taken into account in determining whether the possessor of cultural property exercised due diligence when acquiring the property. Paragraph 2 of Article 3:87a Dutch Civil Code provides a private law amplification of Article 10 (a) of the UNESCO Convention by defining in greater detail the requirements of due diligence further specified in Article 3:86b Dutch Civil Code. However, whereas Article 10 (a) merely refers to 'antique dealers', the Dutch provision concerns all dealers under the Bulletin Act and Decree 1992.[930] A separate provision is included in paragraph 3 for auction houses as they do not acquire ownership or possession of cultural property. Similar requirements of due diligence, for example for auction houses, are included in Section 16 of the Swiss Implementation Act.[931] The UNESCO Convention does not compel the adoption of this solution, particularly not as regards the setting aside of the defences listed above. However, the Netherlands is one of the countries that goes to great lengths to protect innocent purchasers and it also has a relatively short period of prescription. As a transit country and market for art and antiques it has been considered necessary to waive such rules in the interests of combating illegal trade with cultural property. As a consequence, the Dutch Implementation goes beyond the requirements of the 1970 UNESCO Convention.

The limited group of cases described in Art. 7 (b) (i) of the Convention concerning cultural property "that has been stolen from a museum or a religious or secular public monument or similar institution in another State Party" are met by Article 1011 b of the Dutch Code of Civil Procedure and did not need extra implementation: Article 1011 b confers on the Minister of Education, Culture and Science the power to take the measures referred to in the existing Article 1010 of the Code of Civil Procedure, which was introduced by the Protection of Cultural Property against Illegal Export (Implementation) Act. The Minister is therefore empowered to take provisional measures at the request of a State Party, for example provisional attachment, taking into custody, appointment of an administrator or application for an interim injunction. The State Party concerned may apply directly to the Minister of Education, Culture and Science for this purpose. The request need not be made through diplomatic offices as stipulated in the Convention.

**930** Article 1 of the Decree of 6 January 1992 (Bulletin of Act and Decree 1992, 36) defines dealers as "wholesale buyers of and dealers in second-hand and unregulated goods, platinum, gold, silver, precious stones, timepieces, art objects, cars, motorcycles, mopeds, bicycles, cameras, film equipment, radios, audio and video equipment and automatic registration equipment."
**931** For the Swiss Implementation of the Convention see above.

According to the amended Art. 310 c of the Dutch Civil Code, proceedings for the return of a movable will be barred five years after the start of the day following that on which the whereabouts of the movable and the identity of the possessor or the holder have become known and in any event thirty years after the start of the day following that on which the movable was removed from the territory of the State Party from which it originates. The latter time limit is seventy-five years in the case of movables that form part of public collections which are listed in the inventories of museums, archives and libraries' conservation collections or in the inventory of an ecclesiastical institution.

The Dutch Act contains no criminal law provisions. Dutch criminal law already includes a series of instruments for tackling the trade in unlawfully appropriated or illicitly exported cultural property.[932]

Altogether, the Dutch Interpretation of the Convention is by far the most generous implementation of the UNESCO Convention and entirely in keeping with Patrick O'Keefe's authoritative book 'Commentary on the UNESCO 1970 Convention on Illicit Traffic',[933] which sets out to give as much meaning as possible to the provisions of the Convention, in accordance with Art. 31 of the Vienna Convention on the Law of Treaties.

#### c. UK Implementation

When the UK acceded the convention on November 1, 2002, it took the view that this could be done on the basis of existing laws and administrative procedures which complied with the treaty obligations.[934] The UK thus decied against a single codified implementation act transporting the UNESCO Convention into UK law. As a consequence, no codified recovery mechnism exists. Kevin Chamberlain notes, that in case an artefact was stolen, illegally excavated or smuggled out of its country of origin, a request for its return in accordance with Art. 7

932 Articles 416 or 417 bis and 437 of the Dutch Criminal Code punish the receiving of stolen property and the deriving of advantages from goods acquired by receiving stolen property, which would also cover the import of illicitly acquired antiquities. The export of cultural property from the Netherlands without the requisite documents constitutes a breach of sections 7, 8, 9 14a and 14b of the Cultural Heritage Preservation Act, which again is an offence according to section 1 (2) of the Economic Offences Act.

933 P. O'Keefe, Commentary on the UNESCO Convention (2007).

934 See e. g. the Report of the Advisory Panel on the Illicit Trade in Cultural Objects, May 2003, at 27 para. 61. However, after Gray J. refused to rule in favour of the Government of Iran in the first instance of the Barakat-case (see Chapter 6 § 3 I 1 b), UK law seemed not to be in line with the UNESCO Convention, at least not until Gray J.'s decision was reversed by the Court of Appeal in Barakat (for an account of the CA decision see Chapter 6 § 3 II 1 a).

(b) (ii) of the UNESCO Convention would first go to the Foreign Commonwealth Office who would then pass it to the Department of Culture, Media and Sport (DCMS).[935] In the case of a criminal offence, the matter would be handed to the police who could seize the object using their powers under the Police and Criminal Evidence Act 1984 to seize and detain any object that is evidence from a crime. Once the object is no longer needed for evidence purpose, the Department's Goods Offices could be employed to persuade the police to apply to the court under sect. 148 of the Powers of Criminal Courts Act 2000 or under the Police (Property) Act 1987 for an order to return the object to the rightful owner.[936] Similarly, the offence of handling stolen goods under sect. 22 of the Theft Act 1968 could apply, as well as the money laundering provisions in the Proceeds of Crime Act 2002. Otherwise, the restitution of the object would have to be pursued through civil proceedings.

Before the UNESCO Convention, UK import control allowed for cultural property to be freely imported. The UK system was introduced by the Import of Goods (Control) Order 1954, an Order made under the Import, Export and Customs Powers (Defence) Act 1939 as amended by the Import, Export and Control Act 1990. The Order requires all goods imported into the United Kingdom to have a licence.[937] In practice, however, the Department of Trade and Industry grants an Open General Import Licence which permits the import of all goods from all sources unless specifically excluded.[938] No items of cultural property are the subject of such an exclusion.

Although the UK believed that it complied with with the 1970 Convention,[939] it passed the Dealing in Cultural Objects (Offences) Act 2003 in order to complement the UK's treaty obligations and reinforce the UNESCO Convention's implementation in the UK.[940] The 2003 Act is a criminal law instrument designed to combat the traffic in unlawfully removed cultural objects by removing the commercial incentive to those involved in the looting by limiting the import of illicitly

---

**935** Kevin Chamberlain, UK Accession to the 1970 UNESCO Convention, 7 AAL (2002), at 247.
**936** Kevin Chamberlain, ibid, at 247.
**937** Sections 1 and 2 of the Order.
**938** Open General Import Licence, dated 4 December 1987, as amended on 1 May 2009, available at http://www.bis.gov.uk/files/file51356.pdf. The goods for which importers need to apply for an individual import licence are listed in the Schedule of the Open General Import, e.g. firearms, ammunition, iron steel and certain textiles, cp. http://www.bis.gov.uk/files/file51478.pdf.
**939** Cp. Report ITAP 2000.
**940** Cp. DSMS guidance on the Dealing in Cultural Objects (Offences) Act 2003, at 2, available at http://www.culture.gov.uk/images/publications/Dealincultural.pdf.

obtained objects into the UK.[941] Under the 2003 Act it is a criminal offence to "dishonestly deal with a cultural object that is tainted, knowing or believing that the object is tainted."[942] According to Sect. 2 (2) an object is tainted, if after the commencement of the act, a person removes the object in a case falling within subsection (4) of the Act or if he excavates the object, and this removal or excavation constitutes an offence. Sect. 2 (2) subsection 4 refers to objects removed from a building or structure of historical, archaeological or architectural interest or from an excavation. For the purpose of the Act, it does not matter whether the excavation or removal took place in the UK or another country or whether the law violated is a domestic or foreign law.

Although the Dealing in Cultural Objects (Offences) Act 2003 in many ways is adequate to meet the requirements of Article 7 of the 1970 Convention, the Act's operation is constricted for various reasons: to begin with, the Act is not retroactive. Under the 2003 Act, a tainted object is only such if it has been stolen after the date the Act came into force.[943] This restricts the application of the Act in respect of objects already in circulation of the market. Non-retroactivity also raises serious problems in relation to the burden of proof. In any successful prosecution it must be proven that the object in question was stolen after the commencement of the 2003 Act, which in the case of antiquities stolen from unregistered sites, and crossing national borders without being recognised or recorded is very difficult.[944] Additionally, the prosecution must prove that the defendant knew or had reason to believe that the object was tainted and his or her dealings in it were dishonest. The DCMS says in its guidelines that: "the burden of proving knowledge or belief that an object is tainted rests with the prosecution and such proof must be beyond all reasonable doubt. This means that a failure by the accused to carry out adequate checks on the provenance of the object will not constitute knowledge or believe."[945] This threshold is so onerous that the UK government estimated the effect of the Act would be fairly limited.[946]

**941** Cp Explanatory Notes to the Act, para 7. For a detailed account of the Act see e. g. S. Mackenzie, Going, Going, Gone: Regulating the Market in Illicit Antiquities (Leicester 2005); S. Mackenzie/P.Green, Criminalising the Market in Illicit Antiquities: An Evaluation of the Dealing in Cultural Objects (Offences) Act 2003, in: S.Mackenzie/P. Green (eds.) Criminology and Archaeology – Studies in the Looting of Antiquities (2009) 178.

**942** Sect. 1 (3) (a) provides for a sentence on conviction on indictment of up to 7 years and/or a fine.

**943** Sect. 2 (2).

**944** Cp. S. Mackenzie/P. Green, Criminalising the Market in Illicit Antiquities, at 189; Ana Filipa Vrdoljak, International Law, Museums and the Return of Cultural Objects (2006), at 245.

**945** DCMS booklet "Guidance on the Dealing in Cultural Objects (Offences) Act 2003, (2004) 8, available at http://www.culture.gov.uk/images/publications/Dealincultural.pdf

Another drawback of the Act is its narrow definition. In practice the Act is concerned with objects of historical, architectural or archaeological interest which had formed part of a building, or are removed from a monument, or excavated contrary to heritage legislation.[947] Objects which have been exported in breach of foreign export prohibitions are not included in the definition of "tainted" objects under sect. 2 (2). By excluding such objects from the scope of the Act the UK did not adequately implement Art. 7 b UNESCO Convention. It made a clear statement that it does not wish to enforce foreign export laws.

As well as declining to engage with the import of illegally exported heritage items from other countries into the UK, the Act raises questions regarding illicit objects already within the UK which are about to be exported. Under the 2003 Act, it is an offence to dishonestly export cultural objects that are tainted, as sect. 3 (1) defines "deals in" to include export. This provision collides with EC Regulation No. 3911/92. In particular, Art. 2 of the Export Regulation creates the obligation to provide an export licence for cultural goods to be exported outside the EU where "the cultural object in question was lawfully and definitively located in the UK on 1 January 1993 or if it is presently located with the UK". That means that objects which have been imported into the UK after 1 January 1993 do not have to be "lawful" in order for them to be entitled to grant an export licence from the UK, unless it has come from an EU Member State. This result creates a situation of conflict between the 3911/92 EC Regulation and sect. 3 (1) of the 2003 Act that seems unlikely to be resolved in the near future.

As a result, the effectiveness of the 2003 Act has been widely criticised and recent interview data suggest that the 2003 Act's impact is only marginal.[948] According to studies conducted by Prof. Simon Mackenzie, the 2003 Act does not appear to have been adopted with energy and enthusiasm by HM Customs as a tool for the prohibition of import of stolen cultural objects.[949] He sees the 2003 Act as "an attempt by Government to signify concern and 'action' which is manifested in a flurry of symbolic legislative activity followed by a sharp decrease in the prominence of the issue on the policy radar."[950]

---

**946** The UK government estimated that there would be one prosecution every two or three years, see Martin Bailey, A New UK Law to Fight Illicit Trade, The Art Newspaper, 11 01.2004, at 8.

**947** Sections 2 (1) and (4).

**948** For the effect of the Act on the UK market see Mackenzie, Going Going, Gone (2005); S. Mackenzie/P. Green (2009) Criminalising the Market in Illicit Antiquities, 178 et seq.; K. Lubina, The Dealing in Cultural Objects (Offences) Act 2003 put through its paces (2007), Issue 199 The Art Loss Review (2007) 25.

**949** S. Mackenzie, Going, Going, Gone, at 103.

**950** S. Mckenzie, ibid, 103.

This statement is not necessarily true as the Act does indeed enhance the already existing criminal law especially by addressing the problem of newly excavated antiquities. The offence of handling stolen goods under sect. 22 of the Theft Act, could also apply in cases involving the handling and the import of stolen antiquities, but it does not cover cases where an item has been illegally excavated or removed in circumstances not amounting to theft. Certainly, however, the most relevant impact of the 2003 Act has been to raise awareness and to appeal to the market players' consciousness. Altogether, it becomes clear that the provisions of English law may help meeting the requirement of Art. 7 of the Convention, but the implementation is footed mainly on Criminal law. The situation where a criminal offence is not involved or cannot be proven, is not addressed by UK legislation. In consequence, many restitution cases will have to go their way through civil proceedings. However, an evaluation of UK case law on the justiciability of foreign claims in Chapter 6 shows that the engagement in civil proceedings does not guarantee a successful recovery, as would be the case when the requested state itself takes action to ensure the recovery. This means that the UK's obligations under Art. 7 of the UNESCO Convention are not automatically met by the existing law, as is considered by the UK government in 2000.

## V. The 1995 UNIDROIT Convention

### 1. Principles of the Convention

After realising the deficiencies of the 1970 Convention, UNESCO asked the International Institute for the Unification of Private Law [hereinafter: The UNIDROIT Convention][951] to create a new mechanism of international law which would help to overcome these shortcomings. As a result, on June 24, 1995, UNIDROIT created the 1995 UNIDROIT Convention on Stolen or Illegally Exported Cultural Objects.[952] The UNESCO Convention does not impose a general duty on state parties

**951** UNIDROIT is the acronym for the International Institute for the Unification of Private Law. It is an intergovernmental organisation based in Rome, founded as long ago as 1926. It has 60 member States from all around the world and its fundamental objective, in the word of the UNIDROIT Statute, is to "examine ways of harmonising and coordinating the private law of States ... and to prepare gradually for the adoption by various States of uniform rules of private law," cp. www.unidroit.org.

**952** UNIDROIT Convention on Stolen or Illegally Exported Cultural Objects, June 24, 1995, 34 I.L.M. (1995) 1330; reprinted in 5 IJCP (1996) 155 [hereinafter: UNIDROIT Convention]. During its 65th session in 1986, the Governing Council of UNIDROIT included international protection of cultural property as a topic of study in the triennial period from 1987 to 1989. The initial draft was presented to UNIDROIT at its 69th session, in April of 1990, cp. K. Siehr, The UNIDROIT Draft Conto procure the return of unlawfully removed cultural objects. The single duty of return which it does impose covers only objects stolen from a limited range of sources.[953] The new UNIDROIT Convention on the other hand specifically focuses on the recovery phase and sets uniform rules and conditions for the restitution of both, stolen cultural objects and the recovery of illicitly exported cultural objects.[954] Unlike UNESCO, the UNIDROIT Convention is self-executing and allows for no reservations.[955]

The Convention addresses two different problems: In respect of stolen cultural property, it aims to reconcile two equally legitimate interests: that of the person (usually the owner) who has been dispossessed of a cultural object by theft and wants to get it back, and that of a purchaser in good faith of such an object who wants to keep it. In respect of illegally exported heritage items it aims to clarify the extent to which importing countries are obliged to recognise and enforce other countries' export-control laws.

The Convention defines cultural objects in Article 2. The categories covered by the 1970 Convention and the 1995 Convention are exactly the same and this has been done on purpose so that the two texts could work together and states could become party to both.[956] However, UNIDROIT does not require that the items be "specifically designated" by the state.[957] The definition thus encompasses objects which have been illegally unearthed.

Stolen cultural objects are addressed by Chapter II of the UNIDROIT Convention. By Art. 3 (1), the "possessor of a cultural object which has been stolen shall

---

vention on International Protection of Cultural Property, 1 IJCP (1992) 321, at 325. For a detailed analysis see Lyndel V. Prott, Commentary on the UNIDROIT Convention on Stolen and Illegally Exported Cultural Objects 1995 (1997); Claudia Fox, The Unidroit Convention on Stolen or Illegally Exported Cultural Objects: An Answer to the World Problem of Illicit Trade in Cultural Property 9 Am. J. Int'l L. & Pol. (1993) 225; P. Margules, International Art Theft and the Illegal Import and Export of Cultural Property: A Study of Relevant Values, Legislation, and Solutions, 15 Suffolk Transnat'l L.J. 609 1991–1992; Norman Palmer, Statutory, Forensic and Ethical Initiatives, In: The Recovery of Stolen Art (1998) 15–17; Bettina Thorn, Internationaler Kulturgüterschutz nach der UNIDROIT-Konvention (2004).

**953** Cp. above.

**954** Lyndel V. Prott, Commentary, at 130.

**955** Art 18 UNIDROIT. A treaty is self-executing when it only requires a signature and ratification in order to gain effect, see e.g. Mirko Ros, Ein Beitrag zur Lehre der self-executing treaties (1984), at 66; Albert Bleckmann, Self-executing Treaty Provisions, in: Encyclopedia of Public International Law, Vol IV (2000) 374, at 374; Andrea Raschèr, Das Schweizer Kulturgütertransfergestezt für einen besseren Schutz des kulturellen Erbes in: Museumskunde Band 67 (2002), at 151.

**956** B. Thorn, UNIDROIT, at 86–88.

**957** 1970 UNESCO Convention, Art. 1.

return it". The Convention emphasizes that, for this purpose, unlawful excavation counts as theft: according to Art. 3 (2) illegally excavated items or those that are excavated legally but are illegally retained, "shall be considered stolen, when consistent with the law of the state where the excavation took place." Thus, as opposed to UNESCO, where archaeological objects are covered only by the interpretation given to Art. 9 by a State Party, the UNIDROIT Convention explicitly protects such objects. The Convention considers an unlawfully excavated cultural object as stolen, when consistent with the law of the state where the excavation took place.[958] This characterisation as theft is a factual recognition of foreign cultural patrimony laws and its ownership declerations and intended to facilitate claims for the return of artefacts if presented in a foreign court. It equally triggers criminal procedures at national level, as well as international co-operation in criminal matters. For example, it gives rise to the application of the National Stolen Property Act in the USA, or similarly, the UK Dealing in Cultural Objects (Offences) Act 2003, which prohibits the dealing in "tainted" cultural objects.[959]

Art. 4 seeks to deal with the technical problems resulting from differences among national rules regarding good faith purchase.[960] According to Art. 4, the possessor of a stolen cultural object required to return it is entitled, at the time of its restitution, to payment of fair and reasonable compensation provided that the he or she neither knew nor ought reasonably to have known that the object was stolen and can prove that he or she exercised due diligence when acquiring the object.[961] In determining whether the possessor exercised due diligence, regard shall be had to all the circumstances of the acquisition, including the character of the parties, the price paid, whether the possessor consulted any reasonably accessible register of stolen cultural objects, and any other relevant information and documentation which it could reasonably have obtained, and whether the possessor consulted accessible agencies or took any other step that a reasonable person would have taken in the circumstances.[962] A major positive change as opposed to the UNESCO Convention is the reversed burden of proof. The possessor has to prove that he/she exercised due diligence

**958** Cp. Marina Schneider, The UNIDROIT Convention on Stolen or Illegally Exported Cultural Objects, Regional Meeting, at 7.
**959** On the Dealing in Cultural Objects (Offences) Act 2003, cp. this Chapter at § 3 IV 2 b.
**960** On the different approaches to the good faith acquisition of movable property, cp. Chapter 5 § 2.
**961** Art. 4 (1).
**962** Art. 4 (4).

when acquiring the object. If he so succeeds, he shall be entitled to payment of a "fair and reasonable compensation" according to Art. 4.

Chapter III of the UNIDROIT Convention deals with the return of illegally exported cultural objects. While the principal problem arising in relation to the theft of cultural objects is that of the position of the *bona fide* purchaser, the main issue to be faced in connection with the illegal export of such objects is the extent to which states may be prepared to recognise rules of foreign public law and, more specifically, the rules of a foreign state of mandatory application.[963] At this point, the UNIDROIT Convention breaks with the principle of territoriality and the non-enforcement of foreign public laws. The Convention states in Art. 5 (3) that "the competent authority of the State addressed shall order the return of an illegally exported cultural object if the requesting State establishes that the removal of the object from its territory significantly impairs one or more [important] interests." Hence, the heritage item has to satisfy three separate tests before it qualifies as an object to be returned under UNIDROIT: First, it must be subject to national export prohibitions in the state of origin at the time of its export and the return request.[964] That requires that the requesting state has enacted specific cultural property legislation. Second, the object must fall within one of the categories listed in the Annex of the Convention.[965] The third test requires the requesting state to establish that the removal of the object from its territory "significantly impairs" one or more of a state's "interests" as listed in Art. 5 (3). Such "interests" for the purpose of the Convention are the physical preservation of the object or of its context, the integrity of a complex object, the preservation of information or the traditional or ritual use of the object by a tribal or indigenous community.[966] Alternatively, the requesting state can submit that the object in question is of "significant cultural importance" for it.[967] This has to be decided by the courts of the requested state where the illegally exported cultural object is located.[968] So far, it is an open question as to what is considered to be of "significant cultural importance" for a nation.[969]

---

**963** Marina Schneider, The UNIDROIT Convention, at 6.
**964** Art. 7 (1) (a).
**965** Art. 2.
**966** Art. 5 (3) (a) – (d).
**967** Art. 5(3).
**968** Art. 8 (1).
**969** Means of determination are proposed by Kurt Siehr, in: The Protection of Cultural Property: The 1995 UNIDROIT Convention and the EEC Instruments of 1992/93 Compared, RDU 1998 – 2/3, 671, at 679.

The possessor who did not know that the object had been illegally exported is entitled to payment of a "fair and reasonable compensation" by the requesting state, provided that the possessor neither knew nor ought reasonably to have known at the time of acquisition that the object had been illegally exported.[970]

As outlined, the obligations laid down in the UNIDROIT Convention concerning both stolen and illegally exported heritage items by far expand the protection of cultural heritage that has been laid down in the UNESCO Convention 1970. The UNIDROIT Convention applies to all stolen cultural goods whereas the UNESCO Convention only applies to objects inventoried by institutions. It also succeeded in dealing with the differences between legal systems of protection of a 'good faith' acquirer.

An additional major improvement instituted by the UNIDROIT Convention is the expansion of eligible claimants to include private parties.[971] The language of Articles 3 and 4 describe participants as "claimants" whereas the 1970 UNESCO Convention only refers to the involvement of "State Parties." As regards illegally exported cultural objects, the recovery is restricted to a State Party.[972]

Moreover, the 1995 UNIDROIT Convention has operational private law provisions, and restitution requests are brought before the court or other competent authority of the State Party where the cultural object is located.[973] The parties may also agree to submit the dispute to another court or to arbitration.[974] The 1970 UNESCO Convention on the other hand favours the international (interstate) cooperation approach, and operates primarily through the diplomatic channel[975] as well as courts, if consistent with the laws of the state party concerned.[976]

Another innovation compared to the previously discussed international instruments is the introduction of a limitation period.[977] The claimant has a time limit of three years in which to bring forth the claim from the time in which the claimant realises "the location of the cultural object and the identity of its

**970** Art. 6 (1). In determining whether the possessor knew or ought reasonably to have known that the cultural object had been illegally exported, regard shall be had to the circumstances of the acquisition, including the absence of an export certificate required under the law of the requesting State, Art. 6 (2).

**971** Articles 3–4.

**972** Articles 5–7.

**973** Art. 8 (1).

**974** Art. 8 (2).

**975** Art. 7 (b) (ii).

**976** Art. 13 (c).

**977** Remember that The Hague Convention 1954 and the UNESCO Convention 1970 do not set an obligatory time limit.

possessor (....)."[978] Furthermore, no claims may be brought after fifty years have passed from the time of the theft.[979] However, there is no time limit imposed for cultural property which is considered "an integral part" of a nation's cultural property; these may include monuments, archaeological sites and items belonging to a public collection.[980] Altogether, the 1995 UNIDROIT Convention can be viewed as complementary mechanism to the 1970 UNESCO Convention.

### 2. Weaknesses Preventing Implementation

At present, there are only twenty-nine states party to the UNIDROIT Convention.[981] The breeding ground for the lack of accessions is Article 18 providing that "no reservations are permitted except those expressly in this Convention." This creates the risk that desirable declarations, for example, as to the meaning of some expressions, will be stigmatised as reservations.[982] For example, the wide definition of cultural property was the reason why many states refused to ratify the Convention on the argument that they could not be expected to enter into such far reaching commitments with regard to such an array of categories of cultural objects, if reservations are not allowed as under UNESCO.[983]

The Netherlands for example signed the UNIDROIT convention but abstained from ratifying it.[984] They proclaimed in the Explanatory Memorandum to the 1970 UNESCO Convention on the Illicit Import, Export and Transfer of

**978** Art. 3 (3).

**979** However, UNIDROIT Convention Article 3 (5) provides that any state may provide in its own law that the time limitation will be set at a period of seventy-five years instead of fifty. The seventy-five year time limit may also be applied to situations in which the cultural object was stolen from a "monument, archaeological site or public collection..."when the claimant state similarly adheres to the seventy five year standard.

**980** Art. 3 (4).

**981** See http://www.unidroit.org/english/implement/i-95.pdf.

**982** Report of the Ministerial Advisory Panel on Illicit Trade 2003, Report 23, bullet point 50.

**983** See for example the proposals for amendments by the German delegation of the preliminary draft of the Convention, Study LXX – Doc. 27, 1.

**984** The UNIDROIT Convention requires a simple signature. This means that when a state signs the treaty, the signature is subject to ratification, acceptance or approval. The State has not expressed its consent to be bound by the treaty until it ratifies, accepts or approves it. In that case, a state that signs a treaty is obliged to refrain, in good faith, from acts that would defeat the object and purpose of the treaty. Signature alone does not impose on the state obligations under the treaty. For states this usually means that the international agreement has to be put before the national parliament for approval, thereby giving the people a direct say in the external activities of the state, see e.g. Mirko Ros, Die unmittelbare Anwendung der Europäischen Menschenrechtskonvention, Ein Beitrag zur Lehre der self-executing treaties (1984), at 66.

Ownership of Cultural Property (Implementation) Act, which implemented the 1970 Convention, that they will not ratify the UNIDROIT Convention as "not only does it have very far reaching consequences, but its definition of cultural objects is also very broad and vague and hence hard to delimit."[985] The lack of possible reservations also inhibited the UNIDROIT Convention from being adopted only in parts, which was another reason for the Dutch government not to implement it.

Britain proclaimed that the length of the limitation period and the limited factors which trigger it constitutes the greatest barrier for adopting the Convention.[986] The normal three-year limitation period in Art. 3 is triggered only by the claimant's actual knowledge of the location of the object and identity of the possessor. A claimant who fails to take obvious and reasonable steps to discover these matters might therefore remain immune from the passing of time for as long as he receives no actual knowledge. Beyond that the only Convention incentive for a dilatory claimant to seek information and progress the claim is the conventional 50-year long period. In certain cases the period is even longer than 50 years and in others there is none: it is indefinite. The Ministerial Advisory Panel on Illicit Trade declared that the principal difficulty lies in the fact that the three-year limitation period cannot be activated by constructive as opposed to actual knowledge of the part of the claimant.[987] The Convention makes no express provisions for situations where the claimant should reasonably have known the location of the objects and the identity of the possessor, but remained ignorant because he failed to take reasonable steps to discover those matters.[988]

A major reason for the unwillingness to implement UNIDROIT may be viewed in Art. 3 (2) UNIDROIT, which lays down the recognition of foreign ownership declarations. Most market nations simply did not wish to implement a document which renders them to generally recognise state ownership of antiquities. According to some opponents, it is an all-encompassing, streamlined return provision.[989] It applies to sites and objects where there is no threat to objects or archaeological context. On top, the convention provides for compensation of the

**985** Cp. The Dutch Explanatory Memorandum to the accession to UNESCO Convention, ibid, at 3.

**986** See Report of the Ministerial Advisory Panel on Illicit Trade 2000, Report 23, bullet point 50; Paul Jenkins, The UNIDROIT Convention on Stolen or Illegally Exported Cultural Objects, 1 AAL (1996) 163.

**987** Report ITAP 2000, at 52.

**988** Report ITAP 2000, at 52.

**989** See e.g. John Henry Merryman, The UNIDROIT Convention: Three Significant Departures from the Urtext, 5 IJCP (1996) 11, at 14.

*bona fide* purchaser after proof of due diligence, but it does not clarify as to how national courts should arrive at a determination of "fair and reasonable compensation."[990] This is indeed an important concern in light of the often exorbitant prices paid by museums, dealers, and collectors for cultural property.

Furthermore, the reversed burden of proof provided by Art. 4 UNIDROIT constitutes a major derogation from the general private law principles of most civil law countries, where the good faith of the acquirer is being presumed until the claimant can proof bad faith.[991] Thus many critics of the UNIDROIT Convention contend that the reversal of the burden of proof in the UNIDROIT Convention contradicts the probably most intrinsic principle of roman law in particular, the principle that the accused is deemed to be innocent, until he has been proved guilty by the courts.[992]

Indeed, the major points of criticism, such as the wide definition of cultural property, the limitation periods, the reversed burden of proof in terms of stolen cultural objects, and the recognition of ownership declarations for archaeological artefacts under Art. 3 (2), constitute a mainstay of the convention and can be regarded as its foremost benefits. Narrowing down the scope of the Convention would undermine its entire effort to combat illicit trade in cultural material.

A solution to the shortcomings of UNIDROIT has just recently been pursued by the Netherlands who based their implementation of the UNESCO 1970 Convention in part on the 'good' elements of the UNIDROIT Convention,[993] for exam-

---

**990** Cp. Brain Bengs, Note, Dead on Arrival? A Comparison of theUNIDROIT Convention on Stolen and Illegally Exported Cultural Objects and U.S. Property Law, 6 Transnat'l L. & Contemp. Probs (1996), 503, at 529; L. V. Prott, Commentary, Art 4, at 41.

**991** Cp. e.g. § 932 of the German Civil Code, see Palandt/Heinrichs, BGB § 932 at 10. This is different in the UK, where in relation to stolen goods section 4 (4) of the Limitation Act 1980 provides for the presumption that "any concersion following the theft is related to the theft". In Switzerland, the amendment of the Swiss Civil Code introduced special due diligence requirements for dealers, Article 16, para. 1, lit. a–b and para. 2 CPTA (above). On the different civil law mechanisms concerning good faith see especially Arthur Salomons, Good Faith Acquisition in English, French and German Law, in: Christian von Bar, Towards a European Civil Code (4th ed. 2011); Jan Winter, The Application of the UNIDROIT Convention on Stolen and Illegally Imported Cultural Objects in Relations between Member states of the European Union, in: Reflections on International Law from the Low Countries in Honour of Paul de Waart (1998), at 362.

**992** See e.g. Ruedie Staechelin, Die Unidroit-Konvention: kulturell verheerend, mit Schweizer Recht unvereinbar, wirtschaftlich ein Eigentor, in: Unidroit: Recht und Ethik im Handel mit Kulturgut (1998) 63–82, at 65; Wolfgang Henze, Unidroit, hehre Ziele verfehlte Mittel, in: UNIDROIT: Recht und Ethik im Handel mit Kulturgut, Tagung der Schweizerischen Akademie der Geistes- und Sozialwissenschaften in Bern (1998) 37.

**993** Dutch Explanatory Memorandum, at 3.

ple by choosing to implement the basic principles of both UNESCO and UNIDROIT Convention by private law mechanisms.[994]

In summary however it must be said that despite its impressive policy solutions to combat illicit trade in cultural objects, the UNIDROIT Convention regrettably has to be considered a failure, owing to the very few accessions and ratifications.

## VI. Commonwealth Scheme for the Protection of the Material Cultural Heritage 1993

Following proposals made by the New Zealand Government after the failure of its action in *Att. Gen. of New Zealand v Ortiz,*[995] the Law Ministers of the Commonwealth agreed on a Scheme which would enable countries of the Commonwealth to mutually recognise their export prohibitions. The Scheme has been adopted in Mauritius in November 1998 [hereinafter: the Scheme].

Generally, Commonwealth Schemes establish a framework within which member countries of the Commonwealth agree to work to deal with a particular problem.[996] They are the preferred way of providing for intra-Commonwealth legal relations.[997] They are not treaties, and therefore no binding obligations are created. Consequently, it is up to the individual Commonwealth countries to pass any legislation necessary in order to bring the principles of the Scheme into operation.[998]

The objective of the Scheme is to surmount the principle of territoriality in respect of misappropriated cultural artefacts and as a consequence to ensure, that such claims are justiciable. As opposed to the UNIDROIT Convention, the Scheme is solely directed against unlawful export and provides for no extra provisions on stolen cultural objects. Items covered by the Scheme are classified items and subject to export control in the requesting state.[999] However, as

**994** Dutch Explanatory Memorandum, at 5.

**995** For accouts of the case see Chapter 1 § 1 II 1 and Chapter 6 § 3 I 1 a.

**996** P. O'Keefe, Commentary on the UNESCO 1970 Convention on Cultural Heritage: The Commonwealth Scheme, 44 ICLQ (1995) 147, at 148.

**997** Three other Schemes are in existence so far. One covers extradition, the second the transfer of convicted offenders and the third concerns mutual legal assistance in criminal matters, see e.g. P.L. Robinson, The Commonwealth Scheme Relating to the Rendition of Fugitive Offenders 33 ICLQ (1984) 614.

**998** Currently, there are 54 Commonwealth Countries, cp. at http://www.thecommonwealth.org/Internal/191086/142227/members.

**999** Paragraph 3 (1) of the Scheme

most stolen artefacts are being exported illegally, the Scheme indirectly enables the return of stolen items.

Complementing the existing provision on export in Commonwealth countries, the Scheme requires each member country of the Commonwealth to do "whatever is necessary to ensure the return of items covered by the Scheme to the country of export when these are exported without a permit".[1000] Earlier drafts of the Scheme had required member countries to prohibit import of such items, with the intention of providing a legal basis for seizure, but most market countries of the Commonwealth refused this proposal.[1001]

The Scheme does not specify the precise legal or administrative means by which return is to be ensured. The steps required would have to conform with the procedures laid down in paragraph 9, but each country can implement these in its own way. Paragraph 9 of the Scheme grants the country of the location of the object two options under which it may proceed when a request has been advanced:

The first option requires the country of location to give notice to the holder of the item that, unless court proceedings are commenced within a stipulated period, the item will be returned to the country of export.[1002] If the holder does not react to the notice, the authorities will seize the item and return it to the requesting state. According to paragraph 10, the central authority in the country of export is required to hold it for 12 months, after having received it from the country of location. During these 12 months, any person who believes to have an interest in this object may come forward and institute proceedings in order to determine questions of title or possessory rights. The second option states that the country of location may institute proceedings or advise the country of export to institute proceedings "with a view to securing an order for the return of the item to the country of export".[1003]

Paragraph 1 (3) of the Scheme clarifies that it is complementary to the existing international agreements and in no way excludes participation in such arrangements. By the time of the enactment of the Scheme, the UNIDROIT Convention was not yet in force, hence the aim of the Scheme at that time was to complement the 1970 UNESCO Convention as well as the EC Directive and the EC-Regulation. Compared to the remaining Conventions in operation, the Commonwealth Scheme presents itself as pretty advanced in relation to the enforcement of property interest footing on foreign export legislation. As opposed to the

**1000** Paragraph 5 (2) of the Scheme.
**1001** Cp. O'Keefe, The Commonwealth Scheme, at 155.
**1002** Paragraph 9 (1) (a) of the Scheme.
**1003** Paragraph 9 (1) (b) of the Scheme.

UNESCO Convention, the Scheme provides for procedures for recovery which the UNESCO instrument lacks. Under the UNESCO Convention, the extent of recovery of unlawfully exported items depends on what interpretation a state gives that Convention, which considerably restricts the scope of the instrument.

In respect of compensation payable to a *bona fide* possessor who has exercised "due care and attention in acquiring the item the Commonwealth Scheme goes further than the EC Directive. The Scheme places the burden of proof on the possessor, while the EC Directive leaves this issue to the legislation of each Member State.

In this respect as in most others, it equals the UNIDROIT Convention which also adopted the reversed burden of proof, but the UNIDROIT Convention, came into force some three years later than the Scheme. Generally speaking, the Scheme may be viewed as the predecessor of the UNIDROIT Convention. Regarding the process of recovery, paragraph 9 of the Scheme even contains more detailed provisions as to how to deal with foreign recovery claims. The UNIDROIT Convention only states in Art. 5 (1) that restitution requests are brought before the court or other competent authority of the requested State Party, whereas the Scheme offers instructions to the country of the location of the object under paragraph 9.

In practical terms, however, the Scheme will be successful only if implemented by the major destination countries for unlawfully exported cultural heritage within the Commonwealth. But so far, only Australia, Canada and New Zealand have effective legislation in this regard. Owing to the parallels between the Scheme and UNIDROIT, the reason for this unwillingness may be similar to the reasons for the reluctance to ratify the UNIDROIT Convention. Without implementation, the Scheme will have no major impact in the Commonwealth arena and so far, no case has been reported which would have taken advantage of the instrument.

## VII. The 2011 UNESCO and UNIDROIT Model Provisions on State Ownership of Undiscovered Cultural Objects

During the session of the UNESCO Intergovernmental Committee for Promoting the Return of Cultural Property to its Countries of Origin or its Restitution in Case of Illicit Appropriation (hereinafter: the Intergovernmental Committee) held in Seoul in November 2008, the Committee Members noticed that many national laws are insufficient in order to secure the protection of cultural objects which have been illegally excavated or otherwise misappropriated from their country of origin.[1004] The Commitee found many laws to be vague or generally lacking important provisions. During this session, the Committee also acknowledged that national laws had often proven to be non-justiciable in foreign courts if presented with a claim for the recovery of misappropriated artefacts. The UNESCO Intergovernmental Committee was set up in 1978 at the 20th Session of the UNESCO General Conference of UNESCO.[1005] It is an intergovernmental body with an advisory role, providing a framework for discussion and negotiation, but its recommendations concerning inter-state disputes are not legally binding. The Committee comprises of 22 Member States, which meet every two years and can also organise extraordinary sessions.[1006]

Following its extraordinary session in Seoul, the Intergovernmental Committee encouraged UNESCO and UNIDROIT to jointly set up a new committee of independent experts who would propose a draft model law aimed at assisting source countries to protect their cultural heritage from illicit trafficking. The model law would be proposed to states as a means that could help to reform their domestic law, whether criminal law or civil law, by integrating the model law in accordance with their legal traditions.[1007]

The aim of the law would be that all states were equipped with sufficiently explicit legal provisions to guarantee their ownership of cultural objects illegally excavated or otherwise misappropriated and equally, to facilitate their return in case of an illegal export. The purpose of the endeavour was also to draft an instrument which would facilitate the application and/or ratification of the 1970 UNESCO Convention and the 1995 UNIDROIT Convention by as many states as possible.

The UNESCO and UNIDROIT Secretariats accordingly set up a committee of independent experts appointed in their personal capacity as representing their relevant geographical area (hereinafter: the Expert Committee). After meeting formally

---

**1004** Cp. Report of the Committee, 16th Session (21–23 September 2010) at 3, all reports of the Committee are available at http://portal.unesco.org/culture/en/ev.phpURL_ID=36205&URL_DO=DO_TOPIC&URL_SECTION=201.html

**1005** The Committee was set up by Resolution 20 C4/7.6/5. The Resolution is available at http://unesdoc.unesco.org/images/0011/001140/114032e.pdf#page=92

**1006** The current Member States are Argentina, Belarus, Burkina Faso, China, Czech Republic, Greece, Guatemala, India, Iraq, Italy, Libyan Arab Jamahiriya, Japan, Mexico, Monglia, Nigeria, Niger, Peru, Republic of Korea, Romania, Senegal, USA, Zimbabwe. The list of current Member States is available at http://unesdoc.unesco.org/images/0018/001857/185754E.pdf

**1007** Cp. Explanatory Memorandum to the model law, November 2011, available at http://www.unesco.org/new/fileadmin/MULTIMEDIA/HQ/CLT/pdf/UNESCO-UNIDROIT_Model_Provisions_en.pdf

on three occasions in Paris, on 20 September 2010, 14 March 2011 and 29 June 2011, the new Expert Committee agreed on a draft model law accompanied by guidelines aimed at better understanding these provisions which was to be called "Model Provisions on State Ownership of Undiscovered Cultural Objects (hereinafter: the model law).[1008]

The model provisions are by no means a binding or normative legal instrument as it is not meant to be submitted to states for formal approval. Its objective is merely to assist source countries in establishing a more sophisticated domestic legislative body for heritage protection. The draft law consists only of six provisions in order to be sufficiently clear and easy to understand by foreign nations. Furthermore, the shortness of the document was intended to avoid having elaborate and costly interpretations of the law of the state bringing an action for the return of an objects that falls within the scope of the model law. Equally, the draftsmen intended to avoid any ambiguity before foreign courts.

Provision 1 of the model law contains a general duty of the state to take all necessary and appropriate measures to protect undiscovered cultural objects, as well as to preserve them. The language of the first provision is already to be found in the Preamble of the UNESCO Convention on the Protection of Underwater Cultural Heritage of 2001, which is not discussed in this research, and in the Preamble of the 1995 UNIDROIT Convention. The first provision is meant to indicate the intent of the law which may be adopted by the relevant state according to its legal traditions, such as being the first clause of a national statute or incorporated in the statutes preamble.[1009]

Provision 2 provides for a definition of the notion "undiscovered cultural objects". It was considered crucial by the Committee to adopt the definition given by the 1970 UNESCO Convention (Art. 1) and the 1995 UNIDROIT Convention (Art. 2) in order to stress that the model law must facilitate the implementation of these two instruments.

Provision 3 is the central rule of the model law. It vests ownership of undiscovered cultural objects in the state, provided there is no prior existing ownership. The provision is aimed to ensure umbrella state ownership in undiscovered antiquities, as adopted by many nations, however, in the most clear and simple terms. The model law uses the term "are owned by" instead of for example "is the property of" in order to exclude any ambiguity in relation to the understanding of the notion of "property".[1010]

**1008** Text and introduction of of the model law see Uniform Law Review 2011, 1024–1034.
**1009** Cp. Explanatory notes to Provision 1 of the model law.
**1010** Cp. Explanatory notes to Provision 3 of the model law.

Provisions 4, 5 and 6 of the model law are intended to facilitate the return of cultural objects which have been illegally excavated and smuggled out of the country, or equally, such objects which have been excavated and exported legally but then illegally retained: Provisions 4 renders all objects excavated contrary to the law of the country or licitly excavated but illicitly retained to be "stolen". The wording of this provisions has been again borrowed from Art. 3 (2) of the 1995 UNIDROIT Convention in order to assist states which are not yet parties to the UNIDROIT Convention to have the legal background in their domestic legislation to benefit from Art. 3 (2) of UNIDROIT. The characterisation of illegal excavation or illegal retention as theft has the advantage that it activates criminal law provisions in the country where the object is illegally situated. This may be for example the National Stolen Property Act in the USA or the Dealing in Cultural Objects (Offences) Act 2003 in the UK. It also triggers international co-operation in criminal matters when international aspects are concerned. From a private international point of view, the characterisation of such objects as stolen may facilitate foreign courts to return such objects to the claimant state.

Provision 4 has to be viewed in correlation with Provision 6 of the model law, which states that "for the purpose of ensuring the return or the restitution of cultural objects excavated contrary to the law or licitly excavated but illicitly retained, such objects shall be deemed to be stolen objects". The provision repeats the wording of Provision 4 but combines it with the phrase "for the purpose of ensuring the return or restitution". The reason for drafting a provision which is so similar in its wording to an already existing provision in the model law may be viewed in the Committees's desire to emphasise the model law's overall purpose to be a mechanism aimed at facilitating restitution. Although the objective of the provision is very nobel, the obstacles which prevent the recognition of foreign ownership declarations, may they be as clear and simple as the model law suggests, are multifaceted, and the phrasing of the provision may be too simplistic in order to ensure the restitution of cultural objects even if they are deemed as "stolen" under Provision 4 of the model law. Provision 6 especially does not address the problem that many countries do not enforce public laws of another country. The effect of this provision probably may be limited to triggering mechanism of international cooperation on criminal matters, which however, in the author's view is already a big achievement in terms of cultural property law.

Following a suggestion of Prof. Patrick O'Keefe, Provision 5 of the model law also suggests that countries render objects which according to Provision 4 are deemed to be "stolen" as res extra commercium. This means that the transfer of ownership of such artefacts is null and void, subject to the exception that the transferor had a valid title to the object at the time of transfer. The latter situation could concern, for example, a private acquirer who validly bought the object before the enactment of the model provisions in the state concerned, or equally, the state itself who according to national law wishes to sell an item from its collection. In its effect, model Provision 5 is the private law counterpart of Provision 4.[1011] The provision is the first international mechanism of its kind to suggest cultural objects illegally excavated to become res extra commercium. The effect of this provision may be viewed with skepticism, as so far, res extra commercium is only subject to very limited acceptance in foreign courts.[1012]

Viewed in the coherent context of this research, the 2011 UNESCO and UNIDROIT Model Provisions are the first international attempt to harmonise domestic cultural property laws for the purpose of facilitating the application of ownership declarations in foreign courts. The model law is clearly a noble an sophisticated attempt by the international community to combat the illicit trafficking with illegally excavated artefacts and constitutes a good leap forward in the right direction. The suggestion that states shall adopt a clear and simple clause that vests ownership in all undiscovered artefacts, as well as the proposition to deem all artefacts which have been excavated contrary to the states law or illegally retained as "stolen" will certainly help such nations recovering their misappropriated cultural heritage in foreign courts. The provisions on inalienability however, as well as Provision 6 of the model law may be too simplistic a mechanism in order to help surmounting the obstacles in civil proceedings which prevent the recovery of cultural heritage. Furthermore, the value of the instrument depends on the amount of nations which will find it useful to incorporate it in their domestic laws. The impact of the model law on a foreign court's decision will have to be awaited.

## § 4. Conclusion

The analysis of international legal instruments aimed at the protection of cultural heritage revealed that the mechanisms so far in force constitute a fairly limited mechanism to promote justiciability of sovereign claims for cultural property in foreign courts. It also depicted, that stolen and illegally exported cultural objects do account for a different level of protection:

EC Directive 93/7/EEC does not concern itself with stolen cultural objects, except if smuggled or illegally removed from one Member State to another. The ob-

**1011** Cp. Explanatory notes to Provision 5.
**1012** Cp. Chapter 2, IV § 3 I.

ligation to return cultural objects exists only where objects have been illegally exported under national law, where the removal breached Regulation 3911/92, or, where an object was not returned after a temporary lawful removal. Furthermore, the Directive encompasses only objects that have been classified as '"national treasures possessing artistic, historic or archaeological value". It must be stressed that it applies only amongst EU Member States and is thus regionally limited. Additionally, it does not provide for private party claims and is subject to complicated bureaucracy. The Directive must be understood as a reaction to the European Single Market. The provisions of the Directive seek first and foremost to prevent the illegal outflow of the Member States' national cultural heritage due to the abolition of customs inspection.

The 1970 UNESCO Convention provides for the return of cultural property stolen from a museum or a religious or secular public monument or similar institution in another State Party after the convention's entry into force. The return is to be achieved by diplomatic channels, and does not include private claims. Regrettably, the obligation to return cultural property as provided for by Art. 7 (b)(ii) does not include unlawfully excavated cultural objects nor does it include illegally exported cultural objects. The Convention is non-selfexecuting and has to be implemented into national legislation in order to be effective. The implementation is subject to a considerable discretion by the State Parties. Against this background, the 1970 UNESCO Convention cannot serve as a satisfactory mechanism for the recognition and enforcement of foreign property interest, despite the significant increase in ratifications.

As opposed to the 1970 UNESCO Convention, the 1995 UNIDROIT Convention is an instrument that does provide for an obligation to return both, stolen and illegally exported cultural objects. It is not limited to the diplomatic channel and grants State Parties access to national courts. Under the 1995 UNIDROIT Convention, stolen cultural property has to be returned, even when acquired in good faith. With regard to the return of illegally exported cultural objects or other illicitly traded objects other than being stolen UNIDROIT is slightly more reserved in granting protection: the obligation to return illegally exported cultural objects is available only to a small portion of cultural objects: only where objects are of significant cultural importance or where their removal impairs one the four listed interests in Art. 5 (3) (physical preservation, integrity, preservation of information, traditional use by indigenous community) will the court in the holding state order for their return. Although the UNIDROIT Convention presents by far the most competent means of applying foreign law in domestic courts, its various drawbacks which prevented states from ratifying the Convention neutralise its legal effect.

The old Treaty of Washington, as well as the Commonwealth Scheme provide for an elaborate system to ensure the return of illegally exported cultural objects. They allow applicant states access to civil courts while at the same time providing for procedural mechanism of recovery for illegally exported cultural objects. However, the Washington Treaty is a regional treaty that is limited in geographical application to the Americas, while the Commonwealth Scheme is limited to Members of the Commonwealth. The Commonwealth Scheme suffers from similar drawbacks than the UNIDROIT Convention, which resulted in the reluctance by Commonwealth Members to implement the Scheme.

As a result, the network of competing international instruments, at least as far as treaty law is concerned, is very reserved in applying foreign property interests in domestic courts.

The recent 2011 UNESCO and UNIDROIT Model Provisions constitute a novel and promising approach. The model law may be feasible of reforming cultural property law 'from the roots' by providing guidance to countries of origin on how to draft workable cultural property domestic legislation. The impact of this endeavour depends on the aptness of source and market countries to revise their existing domestic law. As it is an instrument which is to the sole benefit of countries of origin, and without requiring major effort it could have a significant impact on heritage protection of these countries. One may only hope that many nations will take advantage of the 2011 UNIDROIT and UNESCO initiative. The effect of the draft law on the justiciability of claims in foreign courts will have to be awaited.

# Chapter 5. Choice of Law Methodology in International Cultural Property Cases

## § 1. Introduction

Cases relating to art and cultural property have shown to be ones of multi-state character.[1013] When the journey of the antiquity and the domicile of the claimants link the dispute to more than one state or nation, the multi-jurisdictional factors of the case may substantially complicate the issue of ownership. In order to render a claim for the return of a cultural object justiciable, the first step is to assess which legal regieme is applicable to the case. Indeed, the protection of property interests to cultural objects should start as early as with the choice-of-law methodology that determines which law is applicable to the case in question.

One would assume that the dual nature of art and archaeological artefacts, their tangible and intangible value, submits such objects to special rules within the conflict of laws. In practice however, ordinary rules of private international law still govern legal questions concerning title to cultural property,[1014]and to date, in most countries no special choice of law rules have been introduced in respect of dealings with such property.[1015]

Over the course of time, various connecting factors have been considered by the courts as appropriate to determine the validity of the acquisition and transfer

---

**1013** However, even where such multi-jurisdictional connections exist, the significance of these connections and their relevance to the possible application of another state's or nation's laws must be raised by one of the parties. Thus, the parties may "localise" or "domesticate" a case by either failing to recognise or choosing to minimise multi-jurisdictional links.

**1014** See e.g. Winkworth v Christie's Mason and Woods, [1980] 1 Ch, at 513; City of Gotha v Sotheby's (unreported), reprinted in Norman Palmer, Museum and the Holocaust (1998), Appendix IV, 222; Manuel Fernandez –Montesinos Garcia and others v Manola Saavedra de Aldama [2002] EWHC 2087 (Ch), at 22; Government of the Islamic Republic of Iran v The Barakat Galleries Ltd. [2007] EWCA Civ 1374; Cp. also Reinhardt Mussgnug, Das Kunstwerk im Internationalen Recht, KUR (1985) 15, at 18.

**1015** Sabine Schmeinck, Internationalprivatrechtliche Aspekte des Kulturgüterschutzes (1994), at 73; Pierre Lalive, Une avancée du droit international: La Convention de Rome d'unidroit sur les biens culturels volés ou illicitement exportés, Uniform Law Review (1996) 40, at 43. But compare the Belgium Code de Droit International Prive (16 July 2004) Art. 90.

of rights in movable property: The law of domicile (lex domicilii),[1016] the law of the country where the legal act of purported acquisition or transaction took place (lex loci actus),[1017] the law of the closest connection (lex actus),[1018] the law of the situs of the property in question (lex situs) and the law of the country of origin (lex originis). Which law is applied may determine the outcome in cases concerning cultural property: Different states have chosen to allocate burdens, rights and responsibilities between two relative innocent parties: the original owner and the subsequent purchaser – jurisdictions favour either the first or the latter.

The disharmony in private law can be of particular harm to the interest of nations to protect their cultural heritage. It weakens the position of original owners, good faith purchasers, nations of origin, market nations and the cultural property trade generally.[1019] The French-Italian case *Stato Francese c. De Contestini*[1020] is an illustrative example of this dilemma. In this case, two seventeenth century tapestries, declared in 1901 to be French national treasures, were stolen in 1975, from the Palais de Justice in Riom, France. They were sent to Italy, where they were bought two years later by an antique dealer. The French government raised an action in the Italian courts for the return of the tapestries, alleging that they belonged to the French state. In France, state property or, domaine publique, is inalienable. The action, heard at all levels of the Italian legal system, ultimately failed and the French government had to buy back its own cultural patrimony from the antique dealer. The main argument was that since the sale has taken place in Italy and the tapestries were held in Italian territory, the

**1016** Sill v Worswick (1791) 1 H Bl 690; Sommerville v Sommerville (1801) 5 Ves Jun 750; North Western Bank Ltd v Poynter, Son and Macdonalds (1984) 22 R (HL) 1, per Lord Watson, 12; Dinwoodie's Executrix v Carruthers' Executor ( 1895) 23 R 234, per Lord Traynor, 239; and Provincial Treasurer of Alberta v Kerr [1933] AC 710, per Lord Thankerton.

**1017** See in detail Pierre Lalive, the Transfer of Chattels in the Conflict of Laws (1955) 74–83. See also Alcock v Smith [1892] 1 Ch (CA) 238; North Western Bank Ltd. v Poynter, Son and Macdonalds (1984) 22 R (HL) 1,6; Embiricos v Anglo-Austrian Bank [1905] 1 KB 677, per Vaughn Williams LJ, 683 and Romer LJ, 685; and Carse v Coppen (1951) SC 233, 242.

**1018** See in detail P. Lalive, The Transfer of Chattels, at 74–83.

**1019** Cp. e.g. Patricia Youngblood Reyhan, A Chaotic Pallet: Conflict of Laws in Litigation between Original owners and Good Faith Purchasers of Stolen Art, 50 Duke L. J. (2001) 955, at 962; Jennifer M. Anglim, Crossroad in the Great Race, 45 HARV. Int'l L. J. (2004) 239; Derek Finchham, Adopting the Lex Originis, at 130;

**1020** Tribunale di Roma of 27 June 1987 (Stato Francese c. Ministero per i beni culturali e ambientali e De Contessini), 71 Rivista di Diritto 920 (1988), confirmed by Corte di Cassazione of 24 November 1995, n. 12166, 33 Rivista di Diritto Internazionale e Processuale 427 (1997) – discussed in: A. Biondi, The Merchant, the Thief and the Citizen (1997), at 1174; A. Weidner, Kulturgüter als res extra commercium, at 124.

case was subject to Italian, not French law. In Italy, bona fide purchase of stolen goods is admitted and the dealer was held to have acquired the tapestries in good faith. If French law had governed the case the tapestries would have been held inalienable as domaine public and, consequently, they could not have been transferred by sale. The decision whether to apply the law of the place of the last transaction or the law of the place of origin is thus of severe impact for cultural property law. This chapter intends to contribute to the development of an international consensus about which law should govern the rights and obligations of the disputants once the looted or stolen property surfaces.

## § 2. Acquisition of Title to Stolen Property

In the development of our law, two competing principles exist. The first is for the protection of the original owner: no one can give a better title that he himself possesses. The second protects commercial transactions: the person who acquires in good faith and for value should get a good title. The first principle is enshrined in the Latin maxim "nemo dat quod non principle", the second in the French expression "en fait de meuble, la possession vaut titre".[1021] Certain is that the disharmony in civil law is open to abuse by sophisticated art dealers who wish intentionally to purge objects of known defects in title.[1022] Before we look at the implications that the lack of consistency has on the trade in cultural property, it is thought to be necessary to briefly sketch the different private law approaches that govern the acquisition of title to stolen art.

### I. Jurisdictions favouring the Original Owner

Common law jurisdictions generally tend to favour the original owner.[1023] English law does not allow a person to pass a better title than he had himself with the result that a good title cannot be acquired from a thief.[1024] The title

**1021** Cp. M. Franklin, Security of Acquisition and of Transaction: La Possession Vaut Titre and Bona-Fide Purchase, 6 Tulane Law Review (1932) 589; L. V. Prott, Problems of Private International Law for the Protection of the Cultural Heritage, 5 Recueil des cours (1989) 215, at 275.
**1022** L. V. Prott, Problems of Private International Law, at 264.
**1023** See also Steven Grover, Note, The Need for Civil Law Nations to Adopt Discovery Rules in Art Replevin Actions: A Comparative Study, 70 Tex. L. Rev. (1992) 1431, at 1445–57.
**1024** The general rule is based on the Roman nemo dat quod non habet principle and can be found in section 21 (1) of the Sales of Goods Act 1979, c 54, as well as the 1980 Limitation Act,

that the bona fide purchaser acquires is rendered "void". Furthermore, the purchaser is not entitled to reimbursement if the original owner prevails in the action of conversion.[1025] The original owner has to bring an action in respect of his stolen property within six years from the day of the theft.[1026] The thief, or anyone else who purchases the stolen goods other than in good faith, is not entitled to rely on the six-year limitation period.[1027] Notwithstanding, a good faith acquirer who purchases the goods from a seller who acquired them from their original owner by deception, undue influence, or misrepresentation, receives a good title. This is known as "voidable" title: the title passes if the owner intended to transfer the property to the person with whom he dealt, even if the owner's consent was obtained by gross fraud.[1028]

In the U.S., both under common law and the Uniform Commercial Code, a thief cannot convey good title to a bona fide purchaser.[1029] However, statutes of limitations and the doctrine of adverse possession create exceptions to the nemo dat-rule.[1030] The U.S. also adopted the common law distinction between void and voidable title. Under a void title, a bona fide purchaser has no title to stolen goods,[1031] whereas under a voidable title, a seller who fraudulently obtains possession of goods can pass title to a bona fide purchaser, even thought he seller has no rights to the goods and the seller's fraud turns out to be an offence under criminal law.[1032] The seller must have voluntarily relinquished the

---

Art. 4. The market overt exception which allowed for the good faith acquisition of stolen goods was abolished with the Sale of Goods (Amendment) Act 1994.

**1025** Cp. Richard Crewdson, Some Aspects of the Law as it Affects Dealers in England, in: P. Lalive (ed), International Sales of Works of Art (1988), at 47 and 50.

**1026** Limitations Act 1980, sections 2 and 3.

**1027** Limitations Act, sect. 4 (1). See also Ruth Redmond-Cooper, Time Limits in Actions to Recover Stolen Art, in: N. Palmer (ed.), The Recovery of Stolen Art, 145.

**1028** See Sale of Goods Act (as amended 2003), 1979, ch. 54, § 23. However, note the Limitations Act 1980, sect. 4 (5), which provides that under sec 4 of the Act "theft" includes blackmail (within the meaning of sec 21 of the Theft Act 1968) or fraud (within the meaning of the Fraud Act 2006).

**1029** Cp. the American case Menzel v. List, 267 N.Y.S.2d 804, 819 (N.Y. Sup. Ct. 1966) (holding that "a thief conveys not title as against the true owner"); U.C.C. § 2–403

**1030** Linda F. Pinkerton, Due Diligence in Fine Art Transactions, 22 Case W. Res. J. Int'L L. (1990) 1, at 1–2.

**1031** Cp. Grant Gilmore, The Commercial Doctrine of Good Faith Purchase, 63 Yale L.J. (1954) 1057, at 1059.

**1032** Cp. G. Gilmore, The Commercial Doctrine, at 1059.

good and intended the title to pass.[1033] In the U.S., the time limitation given to the owner to claim the object, 3 years, does not start on the day of theft, but on the day when the owner is able to identify the acquirer.[1034]

## II. Jurisdictions favouring the Good Faith Acquirer

In contrast to the common law jurisdictions, some continental countries favour the good faith acquirer of a chattel.[1035] This is due to the fact that civil law jurisdictions hold the policy of commercial certainty to be one of the most central interests in priavet law.

In *Switzerland*, which for a long time was renowned to be a centre of art smuggling and laundering,[1036] the good faith acquirer of a stolen or lost chattel gets title to the object, even from a thief, if five years have elapsed since the deprivation or loss of lawful possession.[1037] The five-year limitation period begins to run from the date of the theft or loss, irrespective of the original owner's knowledge thereof.[1038] If the original owner reclaims the chattel from the bona fide purchaser before the expiration of the limitations period, the original owner must reimburse the bona fide purchaser for the purchase price. A further important factor for the art trade is the possibility provided by the Swiss Civil Code to acquire in good faith stolen goods at auction. If a bona fide purchaser buys of a chattel at "a public auction in market overt or from a dealer in property of the same kind", he is entitled to refuse the restitution of the chattel until the original owner indemnifies her for the purchase price."

**1033** See the American case Ross v. Leuci, 85 N.Y.S.2d 497, 499 (N.Y. City Ct. 1949) (holding that the seller of an automobile obtained by fraud has a voidable title that passes to a Bona Fide Purchaser unless voided first).

**1034** Generally on the so-called "Discovery Rule", see Patricia Y. Reyhan, Conflict of Laws in Litigation, ibid, at 1023; Tarquin Preziosi, Note, Applying a Strict Discovery Rule to Art Stolen in the Past, 49 Hastings L.J. (1997) 225; Meghan A. Sherlock, Equitble Consistency in International Case of Recovery of Stolen Art and Cultural Property, 8 Tul. J. Int'L & Comp L. (2000) 483.

**1035** Cp. S. Grover, The Need for Civil Law Nations to Adopt Discovery Rules in Art Replevin Action, at 1446.

**1036** Cp. Prott/O'Keefe, Movement, (1989), at 389–408 (stating that Switzerland "has a reputation as a suitable transit State for 'laundering' cultural goods').

**1037** Swiss Civil Code Tit. 20, Art. 714 and Tit. 24, Arts. 933, 934

**1038** Paul-Henri Steinauer, Summary: The Transfer of Ownership of Works of Art in Swiss Law, in: P. Lalive (ed), International Sales of works of Art (1988) 118, at 119.

*Italy* and *Sweden*[1039] are two further countries where the bona fide purchaser acquires good title from a thief unconditionally and the original owner of the good cannot bring an action for its recovery.[1040]

## III. Moderate Jurisdictions

Between those systems, we have for example the French one where the good faith acquirer can receive good title from an apparent owner, however in case of theft, the original owner can reclaim the property within three years.[1041] The Limitation period starts to run on the day of theft. The expiration of this period cancels the original owner's remedy and right of ownership.[1042] In the case of a successful recovery, the original owner must compensate the possessor of the price paid if the object has been acquired in the trade.[1043]

Germany principally follows the common law nemo dat-principle. According to § 935 (1) BGB stolen goods cannot be acquired bona fide.[1044] However, there is an exception: § 935 (2) BGB provides for the good faith purchase of stolen goods at public auctions. The 'doctrine of usucapio' (Ersitzung) permits the purchaser of stolen or lost goods to acquire title, if he purchases and possesses the chattel for ten uninterrupted years after the act of conversion.[1045] The limitation period runs thirty years and starts at the day of the theft.[1046] In case, the original owner

**1039** Swedish Commercial Code, Ch 11:4, 12: 4. See also S. Schmeinck, Internationalrechtliche Aspekte des Kulturgüterschutzes, at 132.

**1040** Italian Civil Code Art. 1153. However, the good faith purchaser cannot acquire good title to archaeological artefacts or to artworks stolen from public museums. Italian law regards such objects as public property and exempt from private commerce, cp. Riccardo Luzzatto, Trade in Art and Conflict of Laws: The Position in Italy, in: P. Lalive (ed.) International Sales of Works of Art (1988) 409, at 418.

**1041** Art. 2279 of the French Civil Code. The same provision can be found in the Bulgarian Ownership Act 1951, sect. 78.

**1042** French Civil Code, Art. 2279. Cp. also S. Grover, The Need for Civil Law Nations to Adopt Discovery Rules, at 1451.

**1043** French Civil Code, Art. 2279.

**1044** Greece, Russia, Latvia and Estonia follow a similar approach in relation to the bona fide acquisition of stolen goods. For a detailed analysis see, Karsten Thorn, Der Mobiliarerwerb vom Nichtberechtigten (1996), at 46; Kurt Siehr, in: Klaus Ebling/Marcel Schulze (eds.) Kunstrecht (2007), at Rn 61.

**1045** Art. 937 (1) and (2) German Civil Code [Bürgerliches Gesetzbuch:BGB]. The 'doctrine of usucapio' is similar to the common law doctrine of adverse possession, cp. S. Grover, The Need for Civil Law Nations to Adopt Discovery Rules, at 1450.

**1046** Arts. 197, 200 BGB.

recovers the stolen chattel from the good faith acquirer before the expiration of the usucaption period, he can sue the seller of the good for damages. Since Germany implemented the 1970 UNESCO Convention, it introduced a discovery rule for the recovery of cultural artefacts that are subject to the German Recovery of Stolen Cultural Property Act 2007.[1047] According to Art. 10 of that Act, a one year limitation period starts to run on the day when the original owner state has knowledge of the whereabouts of the property.[1048]

## § 3. The Application of the Lex Situs and its Consequences

In international property law, which governs the question to the law applicable to in rem relations, the principle of the lex situs is the commonly recognised connecting factor.[1049] According to this principle, the transfer of title to a chattel is determined by the law of the place where the object is present at the time when the transfer is said to have taken effect.[1050] One of the most illustrative examples of the situs rule was the English case *Winkworth v Christie, Manson & Woods Ltd.*[1051] It was a case that concerned cultural objects. Some Japanese works of art were stolen from the claimant Mr Winkworth in England and taken to Italy where they were acquired by the second defendant under a contract governed by Italian law. The second defendant subsequently brought the works of art back to England and delivered them to the first defendant, the London auction house Christie's, in order to be sold. Winkworth brought an action in England seeking a declaration that the works of art had at all material times been his property. The court held that, Winkworth had no legal claim because the sale of the Japanese art works was executed in good faith and Italian law recognised the defendant's superior title.[1052] The validity of the transaction would be deter-

**1047** Kulturgüterrückgabegesetz, § 14 Abs. 3 and § 16 Abs. 2.

**1048** Compare above, Chapter 4.

**1049** Cp. Christopher Staker, Public International Law and the Lex Situs Rule in Property Conflicts and Foreign Expropriations, 58 Brit. Y.B. Int'L L. (1988) 151, at 164; S. Grover, The Need for Civil Law Nations to Adopt Discovery Rules, at 1445–57.

**1050** Cp. Dicey/Morris/Collins, Rule 125, 24–020; Cheshire/ North/Fawcett, Private International Law, at 1209, 1218–1220; Astrid Müller-Katzenburg, Possession and Ownership of Stolen and Otherwise Lost Works of Art, 5 AAL (2000) 105, at 113. For a general account of the lex situs rule, see Janeen Carruthers, Transfer of Property in the Conflict of Laws (2005) Chapter 8.

**1051** Winkworth v Christie, Manson & Woods Ltd [1980] 1 Ch 496. But see also the more recent case Kuwait Airways Corporation v Iraqi Airways Company (No 4 and 5);[2002] UKHL 19; [2002] 2 A.C. 883.

**1052** Winkworth v Christie, at 500–501, per Slade J.

mined according to Italian law, which was the law of the place where the goods were situated at the time of transfer.[1053]

In England, the situs rule has been affirmed in the *Winkworth – case*, but the rule is not one of universal application and subject to five exceptions:[1054] The first exception refers to the acquisition of, or, the transfer of title to goods in transit (*res in transitu*). It is generally assumed that transaction to such goods are governed by the proper law of the transfer.[1055] This exception exists because it would be impossible ex post to determine the situs as at the relevant time. It has been suggested that the proper law of the transfer comprises the law with which the transfer is most closely connected.[1056] The second exception arises where a purchaser claiming title has not acted bona fide. The third exception is the case where the English court declines to recognise the particular law of the relevant situs because it considers it to be contrary to public policy. The fourth exception arises where a statute in force in the country, which is the forum in which the case is heard, obliges the court to apply the law of its own country.[1057] Fifthly, special rules might apply to determine the relevant law governing the effect of general assignments of movables on bankruptcy or succession.[1058]

**1053** Winkworth v Christie, at 514, per Slade J.

**1054** In a more recent decision before the Commercial Court of the Queen's Bench Division, Glencore International AG v Metro Trading Inc [2001] 1 Lloyd's Rep 284, the attempt to expand the categories of exception met with failure.

**1055** See Dicey/Morris/Collins, Rule 125 at 24–020; J. Carruthers, Transfer of Property, at 94. The proper law is the law which governs most aspects of the factual situation giving rise to the dispute, meaning the law with the closest connection governing the case, cp. e.g. FA Mann, The Proper Law Doctrine in the Conflict of Laws, 46 ICLQ (1987) 437. However, jurists have advocated for several laws, such as the law of the owner's domicile, the law of dispatch or the law of ultimate destination, cp. Cheshire/North/Fawcette, Chapter 29, at 1221.

**1056** See especially P. B. Carter, Transnational Sales in Works of Art: The Position in English Private International Law, in P. Lalive (ed.), International Sales of Works of Art (1988) 319. However, there are several potential applicable laws, including the law of the place of dispatch (lex loci expeditionis) and the law of the place of destination (lex loci destinationis), cp. G.C. Venturini, Property, in: International Encyclopedia of International Law (1976) Chapter 21; Martin Wolf, Private International Law (2nd ed. 1950) 520; for a discussion of the different views, see J. Carruthers, Transfer of Property, at 88 et seq.

**1057** In Winkworth v Christie's, at 501, Slade J. suggested that one example of the application of this exception might have been the former sec 24 of the Sale of Goods Act 1893 which stated that "where goods have been stolen and the offender is prosecuted in conviction, the property in the goods so stolen revert to the person who was the owner of the goods, notwithstanding any intermediate dealing with them, whether by sale in market overt or otherwise."

**1058** Winkworth v Christie's, at 501, P. B. Carter, Transnational Sales, at 323.

A number of policy reasons support the application of the lex situs rule. First, it has the advantage of simplicity and legal certainty. If an object has been acquired in good faith, the acquisition will be protected even if the chattel later changes locations. It also facilitates commercial convenience and predictability, as a purchaser needs only ascertain the law of one jurisdiction before concluding a transaction.[1059]

There exists the belief that only the application of the law of the situs will protect creditors or third-party purchasers. Cheshire stated that in questions affecting third parties, "business exigencies require that proprietary rights to movables shall be determined by the lex situs".[1060] Furthermore it is a widely held view that commercial transparency can only be guaranteed if the lex situs is applied. Furthermore, the situs-rule is simple and, in theory, the situs is easily ascertainable.[1061] The popular view is that if a rule of law is framed in simple terms, litigation in respect thereof will decrease.[1062]

Generally, it is argued that simplicity, objectivity, and ease of application of a choice of law connecting factor, in turn, promote certainty, which is regarded as the overarching consideration in the field of property.[1063] So is the uniformity of results.[1064]

It is due to this credos that the lex situs-rule is similarly entrenched in civil law systems: For example, German,[1065] Swiss,[1066] Italian,[1067] Spanish,[1068] and

**1059** Cp. P. Lalive, The Transfer of Chattels in the Conflict of Laws (1955) 101, at 115; S. Schmeinck, Internationalrechtliche Aspekte, at 171 et seq.

**1060** G. C. Cheshire, Private International Law (London 1965) at 411.

**1061** Quentin Byrne-Sutton, Who Is the Rightful Owner of a Stolen Work of Art? A Source of Conflict in International Trade, in: P. Lalive (ed.), International Sales (1988) 545, at 551.

**1062** J. Carruthers, Transfer of Property, at 198; S.M. Nott, Title to movables acquired abroad, 45 Conveyancer and Property Lawyer (1981) 279 et seq.

**1063** See already E. Rabel, The Conflict of Laws: A Comparative Study (1958) at 23. But also Winkworth v Christie [1980] CH 496, at 509.

**1064** Cp. Glencore International AG v Metro Trading Int. Inc, [2001] 1 All ER 103; 1 Lloyd's Rep. 284, per Moore-Bick J., at 294.

**1065** Art. 43 I EGBGB.

**1066** Swiss Civil Code, Tit. 1, Art. 5 (codifying Article 100 of the Swiss Federal Statute on Private International Law).

**1067** P. Benvenuti, Comment to Art. 51 of the New Italian Statute on Private International Law of 1995, 19 Le Nuove Leggi Vivili Commentate 1325, 1334 (1996); R. Luzzatto, Comment to Art. 51 of the new Italian Statute on Private International Law of 1995, 31 Rivista di Diritto Internatzionale Privato e Processuale (1995) at 1157; K. Siehr, International Art Trade, at 77; A. Mueller-Katzenburg, Besitz- und Eigentumssituation bei gestohlenen und sonst abhanden gekommenen Kunstwerken, NJW 1999, 2551, at 2554.

**1068** Art. 10 (I) Introduction of the Spanish Civil Code

Polish[1069] legislators codified this rule in order to advance the nation's public interest in the security of transaction.

In relation to cultural artefacts, however, the lex situs rule indirectly enhances the illicit trade in precious objects.[1070] Antiquities can travel through different jurisdictions and are subject to a constant change of title, without having any connection to the situs of the transaction.[1071] Owing to the differences in the substantive private law of specific jurisdictions, art traffickers are presented with various possibilities to launder the title of the illicitly obtained property by selling it in countries which allow a good faith purchase of stolen goods. As such the rule creates an incentive of forum shopping.[1072]

Furthermore, the rigorous application of the situs-rule in art cases does not allow for security of transaction but rather creates uncertainty for all those who participate in art trade. The result of the transaction will depend upon the substantive content of the law identified by the connecting factor.[1073] The application of, for example, Italian law may prove favourable for the good faith acquirer while the application of US law may prove favourable for the true owner. The latter happened in a case concerning the recovery of two portraits by Albrecht Dürer, which had been stolen from Germany in 1945. In *Kunstsammlungen zu Weimar v Elicofon*,[1074] the Court of Appeal in New York awarded the title to the paintings to the German claimant, the Kunstsammlungen zu Weimar, by making use of the *nemo dat quod non habet – maxim* and the demand and refus-

**1069** Art. 24 para. 1 and para. 2 of the Code on International Private Law 1965, Dz. U. nr 46, poz 290 ze zm.

**1070** For a different view see e.g. Sabine Schmeinck, International privatrechtliche Aspekte des Kulturgüterschutzes (1994) 73.

**1071** Cp. also Olaf Kurpiers, Die lex originis Regel im internationalen Sachenrecht-Grenzüberschreitende Privatrechtliche Ansprüche auf Herausgabe von abhanden gekommenen und unrechtmässig ausgeführten Kulturgütern (2005), at 122.

**1072** Cp. K. Siehr, in Ebling/Schulze (eds.) Kunstrecht, at 61; Sebastian Damm, Kollisionsrechtlicher Erwerbsschutz im Internationalen Kunsthandel, in T. Hoeren/B. Holznagel (eds.) Handbuch Kunst und Recht (2008) 249; Anna Gardella, Nuove perspettive per la protezione dei beni culturali in : 12 Diritto del Commercio Internazionale (1998) 997, at 1006.

**1073** J. Carruthrs, Transfer of Property, at 205.

**1074** 478 F2d 231 (2nd Cir. 1973); cert. denied 415 U.S. 931 (1974); 536 F. Supp. 829 (E.D.N.Y. 1981) affirmed in 678 F. 2d 1150 (2d Cir. 1982). The case concerned the ownership of two paintings by Albrecht Dürer which were stolen in 1945 from Germany during the American occupation and were in the possession of the American art dealer Edward Elicofon. Until 1943, the paintings have been held by the Staatliche Kunstsammlungen zu Weimar. The court awarded title to the German museum.

al rule.[1075] The paradox is that according to German law, the limitation period had already expired and the claimant would not have been able to recover the art if the court had applied German law.

In common law countries, the lex situs-rule may be facing an intermezzo with the Rome II Convention – Since July 2009 it changed the conflict of law regieme in respect of non- contractual obligations within all member States of the EU except Denmark.[1076] Remember that under common law, the recovery of chattels occurs under the law of conversion, which is a claim in tort. The consequence might be that the lex situs rule cannot be applied at all. According to Art. 4 of the Rome II Convention:

> The applicable law to a non-contractual obligation arising out of a tort/delict shall be the law of the country in which the damage occurred irrespective of the country in which the event giving rise to the event occurred and irrespective of the country or countries in which the indirect consequences of that event occurred.

However, as the claimant actually seeks vindication, such a claim should be falling outside the scope of the Rome II Convention altogether. English courts held that the tort of conversion falls under Art. 5 (3) of the Brussles Convention but this provision actually encompasses property matters, whereas property matters per se fall outside the Rome II Convention, as they are not part of the law of obligations. The Court of Justice actually might decide that any interference with property is to be classified as part of the law of property and falls outside the scope of Rome II.[1077] This would mean that Englsih courts would have to apply the lex rei sitae governing in rem relations or the Private International law (Miscellaneous Provisions) Act 1995, which was the Act governing choice of law until the Rome II Convention came into force.

The 1995 Act abolished the former 'double actionability rule' and adopted instead a general choice of law rule under which the applicable rule in tort claims is the law of the country in which the events constituting the tort in ques-

---

**1075** For detailed accounts of the case see e.g. Sylvia Burks, Kunstsammlungen zu Weimar v Elicofon: Theft of Priceless Art Treasures Gives Rise to Protracted International Legal Battle, 19 Tex. Int'l L. J. (1984) 189; Roy S. Kaufmann, Art Law Handbook (2000) 290; Lawrence M. Kaye, The Recovery of Stolen Cultural Property: A Practitioner's View, 5 Vill. Sports & Ent. L. J. (1998) 5.

**1076** Regulation (EC) No 864/2007 of the European Parliament and of the Council of 11 July 2007 on the law applicable to non-contractual obligations (Rome II).

**1077** Cp. also, Andrew Scott, The Rome II Convention on the Law Applicable to Non-Contractual Obligations, John Aherm William Binchy (eds.) 2009.

tion occurred.[1078] The tort of conversion may take place in a number of different ways, which includes the taking possession over the goods with the intention to control the goods but not necessarily with the intention to acquire title. Equally, the unjustified refusal to deliver up a good after a demand is made, constitutes conversion.[1079] Thus the event which constitutes a conversion may not necessarily be congruent with the moment of the last transfer of title to a work of art, which consequently may lead to the application of either the lex situs rule of the tort choice of law rule.

As a consequence, the application of the lex situs-rule is not sufficient per se to ensure uniformity or predictability and has a malign effect on the trade with antiquities. In the following we will thus consider alternative choice of law approaches for claims involving heritage item.

## § 4. Legal Alternatives for Disputes involving Cultural Property

The question whether to apply a special choice-of-law rule for cases involving cultural property only becomes relevant when the law of the country of origin favours the party whom it considers to be the owner of the item, whereas the law of the situs favours the other party, usually the present possessor of the thing.[1080] Additionally, it has to be noted that the party asserting the applicability of a foreign nation's law must plead and prove the content of that law and must establish that the forum law and the foreign law conflict not only on their face but also when applied to the instant case.[1081]

---

**1078** Claims for property which was missapropriated before the enactment of the Private International Law (Miscellaneous Provisions) Act 1995 are still governed by the former common law rule of "double actionabiliy". According to this rule, an action in tort can be adjudicated in a domestic court only if it would be actionable under both the law of the home jurisdiction and the foreign jurisdiction, cp. Dicey/Morris/Collins, Rule 231, at 35–011 et seq; Generally on the double actionability rule see Nicky Richardson, The Double Actionability and the Choice of Law, 32 HKLJ (2002) 497.

**1079** Andrew Tettenborn, Conversion, Trespass and Title to Works of Art, in: N. E. Palmer, The Recovery of Stolen Art (1998) 33, at 35; Norman E Palmer, Conversion, Tort and Restitution, in N E Palmer/ Evan Mckendrick, Interests in Goods (2nd ed. 1998) 825, at 826.

**1080** Cp. S. Symeonides, A Choice of Law Rule for Conflict involving Cultural Property, 38 Vand. J. Transnat'l L. (2005) 1177, at 1188, calling them "direct conflicts" and distinguishing them from "non-conflicts" and "inverse conflicts".

**1081** Cp. P. Y. Rayhan, Conflict of Laws in Litigation, at 1005.

## I. The Law of the Closest Connection

Some jurisdictions give room for a departure of the traditional lex situs rule by adopting the principle of the closest connection. Although they treat the situs-rule as the pre-eminent choice-of-law-rule, there is room for the application of the law which is more closely connected with another jurisdiction.

In Germany, for example, the lex situs rule is codified in Art. 43 EGBGB,[1082] but it is subject to a special evasion clause. Art. 46 EGBGB states:

> "If the law of a state has a significantly closer relationship to the issue than the law which would be decisive according to Art. 43, the law of this state shall be applied."

The application of the exemption clause is restricted to cases where the law that would be decisive according to the lex situs leads to the application of a legal system which is foreign to the case. It has been contended that the exemption rule should only be applied to cases of res in transitu and to cases where the lex situs cannot be identified.[1083] In such a scenario, the court accordingly undertakes a balance of all decisive factors and applies the law with the closest connection to the case.[1084] As the provision is relatively new, so far no case law has emerged to identify its ambit. It is thus worthwhile looking at American private international law, which adopted a similar practice.

In the United States, the Second Restatement of Conflict of Laws provides that property transactions are governed by the law of the state with the "most significant relationship" to the transaction.[1085] However, this principle is the result of the presumption that the lex situs has "the most significant relationship to the parties, the chattel and the conveyance...".[1086] This presumption can be rebutted, if the facts and circumstances of the individual case point to a closer con-

---

**1082** Introductory Act to the Civil Code.

**1083** Mankonwski describes this process as a "grouping and weighing of contacts", in: Christian von Bar/Peter Mankowski, Internationlaes Privatrecht Bd. 1 (2nd ed. 2003), Para 7 at 92.

**1084** Karl Kreuzer, Gutachtliche Stellungnahme zum Referentenentwurf eines Gesetzes zur Ergänzung des Internationalen Privatrechts (1991), at 84.

**1085** Restatement (Second) of Conflict of Laws 6 cmt. C (1971). Cp. also Kunstsammlungen zu Weimar v Elicofon, 678 F. 2d. (2nd Cir. 1982) at 950.

**1086** See, e.g., Green v. Van Buskirk, 72 U.S. (5 Wall.) 307, 311 (1866) (ruling that the choice of law is the law of the location of the property); Lees v. Harding, Whitman & Co., 60 A. 352, 355 (NJ. 1905) (agreeing with the ruling of the federal courts in that "the title of the tangible chattles is determined by the law of the situs"); see also Restatement (second) of Conflict of Laws §§ 244, 246 cmt. a (1971) (stating that in adverse possession and conveyance of interest cases, the nature of the interest transferred is usually determined by the local law of the state where the (personal) property was at the time of the transfer).

necting factor with another jurisdiction. This methodology was applied in the *Goldberg-case*,[1087] a decision concerning the property rights in some valuable Byzantine mosaics, which had been taken from the church Pangia Kanakaria in the northern part in Cyprus, now occupied by Turkey, and then sold on the international art market.[1088] The Cypriot officials filed a civil action for the restitution of the mosaics which were among the few Byzantine works which were not destroyed during the eight century iconoclastic movement. Peg Goldberg, the dealer who tried to sell the artefacts in the United States, based her defence on the lex situs rule, according to which Swiss law was applicable to her purchase. Art. 714 of the Swiss Civil Code provided for a good faith acquisition of stolen goods. The Federal District Court for the Southern District of Indiana, considered not Swiss law, but the law of Indiana to be applicable to the case, as it had the closest connection to the facts of the case: None of the parties' important actors were Swiss; the mosaics had never been in the stream of commerce in Switzerland, and they had only been on Swiss soil for four days.[1089]

Furthermore the Federal Court's decision was reinforced by the fact that Swiss conflict of law rules would have applied the exception with regard to chattels in transit (res in transitu) to which the law of destination applied as opposed to the law place of the transit.[1090] This would have been the law of Indiana, as from the Swiss point of view, the mosaics were in transit, when they were stored in the duty-free area of the Geneva airport.[1091] However, the jurisdiction with the closest connection to the objects was Cyprus, not Indiana.

The decision shows that deciding cases concerning cultural property on a case by case basis can produce arbitrary results, which in the *Goldberg-case* luck-

**1087** Autocephalous Greek-Orthodox Church of Cyprus v Goldberg & Feldman Fine Arts, Inc., 717F. Supp. 1374 (S. D. Ind. 1989); affirmed 917 F.2d 278 (7th Cir. 1990). For details see B. Thorn, Internationaler Kulturgüterschutz, at 260; Stephen L. Foutty, Entrenchment of the Due Dilligence Requirement in Replevin Actions for Stolen Art, 43 Vand. L. Rev. (1990) 1839; Nicholas Augustinos, The Cyprus Experience, in: N.E. Palmer (ed.) The Recovery of Stolen Art (1998) 217; Lawrence M. Kaye, Cultural Property Disputes in Foreign Courts, in: Schneider/Schneider (eds) Cultural Property Protection (2005) 43, at 61; S. Symeonides, On the Side of the Angels: Choice of Law and stolen Cultural Property, in Private Law in the International Arena (The Hague 2000) 748, at 753; Quentin Burne-Sutton The Goldberg Case: A Confirmation of the Difficulty in Acquiring Good Title to Valuable Stolen Cultural Objects, 1 IJCP (1992) 59.

**1088** To the application of the "most significant relationship" principle see also Kunstsammlungen zu Weimar v Elicofon, 678 F. 2d. 1150 (2nd Cir 1982); DeWeerth v Baldinger Wildenstein & Co., Inc., 658 F. Supp. S 688 (US S.D.N.Y. 1987).

**1089** Cypruss v Goldberg 717 F. Supp. 1374 (S. D. Ind. 1989), at 1394.

**1090** See art 101 of the Swiss IPRG (Bundesgesetz über das Internationale Privatrecht).

**1091** Cyprus v. Goldberg 717 F. Supp. 1374, (S. D. Ind. 1989), at 1393–1395.

ily ended with a recovery of the mosaics for Cyprus. If courts are vested with too much discretion in deciding who should be granted possession of cultural property based on a conflict of law analysis which focuses on the most significant relationship, it may manipulate the conflict of laws to arrive at an outcome which the court favours but which is not necessarily the law of the closest connection. Thus in the *Goldberg-case*, the jurisdiction with the closest connection was Cyprus and not Indiana. The defendant's domicile in Indiana could not be deemed more weighty then the claimant's domicile in Cyprus. Unlike the claimants who had every reason to rely on their protective law of their domicile, the defendant could not claim any reliance on the non-protective law of their domicile, especially as non of the acts pertaining the sale took place in Indiana.[1092] Similarly, the situs of the mosaics at the time of the trial should not be deemed any more significant than the situs at the time of the theft, especially because the mosaics were fixed to the church in Cyprus for over 1400 years. Finally, the fact that Indiana was the forum state should not in itself make its relationship any more significant. Indiana's relationship might have been considered significant if, for example, the property had been situated in Indiana for a relatively long time and third parties had dealt with the property in good faith and in justifiable reliance on Indian law. As a consequence, this analysis suggests that the application of the closest connection is not less flawed than the strict application of the situs rule and cannot be viewed as a reliable connecting factor to inhibit the trade with movable antiquities.

## II. Renvoi

Renvoi is a legal doctrine employed in the conflict of laws.[1093] It is a French term which literally means "sending back".[1094] In precise terms, when the choice of law process points a forum court to another jurisdiction's law, the question that arises is: how much of that other jurisdiction's laws should apply? If the reference includes both internal law and conflicts principles, the foreign conflicts

**1092** Cp. S. Symeonides, On the Side of the Angels: Choice of Law and stolen Cultural Property, in: Jürgen Basedow/Siehr Kurt (eds.) Private Law in the International Arena (2000) 748, at 753.
**1093** Cp. Dicey/Morris/Collins, Conflict of Laws, Rule 4 (1); Cheshire/North/Fawcette, Chapter 5 at 57 et seq; G.Kegel/K.Schurig Internationales Privatrecht (9th ed. 2004), § 10 at 386; C.von Bar/P. Mankowski, Internationales Privatrecht Bd I (2003), § 7 IV at 684 et seq.
**1094** Abhishek Bharti, The concept of Renvoi in the Conflict of Laws (2008), available at: http://works.bepress.com/abhishek_bharti/1. Compare also the encyclopedia brittanica at www.britannica.com.

principles may point the inquiring court back to the forum's law or to a third jurisdiction's law.[1095] Despite criticism by scholars and judges, the doctrine continues to appear in international jurisprudence.[1096] The Polish Act on Private International Law 1965 is one of the few jurisdictions that codified the doctrine of renvoi in Art. 4.[1097]

It has even been suggested that the doctrine of renvoi could be applied in cultural property cases as an alternative choice-of-law-rule to the lex situs rule. In the recent case *Iran v Denyse Berend*,[1098] the government of Iran tested this proposition in an English court. The case concerned the recovery of some Persian reliefs belonging to Iran. A French woman in New York purchased the reliefs at an auction. After hanging in her Parisian home for over 30 years, she attempted to sell them at Christies in London. It was common ground that French law should apply as the lex situs. The question was what the application of French law actually meant. Iran argued that the English court should not simply apply French domestic law as the law of the situs, but according to the doctrine of renvoi, it should apply the French conflict of law rules. Ms Berend's lawyers argued that a French court would decline the general lex situs rule in relation to a constituent part of a national treasure such as an ancient palace and would apply the law of the object's state of origin. The basic French rule, that title to movables is determined according to the lex situs, is not established by legislation but by jurisprudence. Hence, it is potentially subject to exceptions which may be developed by judges on a case-by-case basis.[1099] Unfortunately,

---

**1095** See for example, P.R.H. Webb/D.J.L. Brown, A Case Book on Conflict of Laws (London 1960) at 60; Ernst Otto Schreiber, "The Doctrine of the Renvoi in Anglo-American Law", 31 Harvard Law Review (1917) 525.

**1096** See Adrian Briggs, In Praise and Defence of Renvoi, 47 ICLQ (1998) 887; Ernest G. Lorenzen, The Renvoi Theory and the Application of Foreign Law, 10 Colum. L. Rev. (1910) 327; Michael Sonnentag, Der Renvoi im Internationalen Privatrecht (2001); Christian Armbrüster, Privatrechtliche Ansprüche auf Rückführung von Kulturgütern ins Ausland, NJW 2001, 3581; Christian Armbrüster, 10 La revendication de biens culturels du point de vue du droit international privé, rev.crit.dr.int. pr. Vol IV (2004) 723; Larry Kramer, Return of the Renvoi, 66 N.Y.U. L. REV. 979 (1991); Martin Davies, Renvoi and Presumptions about Foreign Law – Case not on Neilson v Overseas Projects Corporation of Victoria Ltd, 30 Melbourne University Law Review (2006), 244.

**1097** For a detailed analysis of the Polish Code, see e.g. Andrzej Maczynski, Polish Private International Law, in Yearbook of Private International Law Vol. VI (2004) 203, at 208.

**1098** Iran v. Berend, [2007] EWHC 132 (QB) 1. For comments on this case see especially Adrian Briggs, The Law which Determines Title to Movable Property, BYIL (2008) 628; Derek Finchham, Rejecting Renvoi for Movable Cultural Property: The Islamic Republic of Iran v. Denyse Berend, 14 IJCP (2007) 111.

**1099** Cp. Iran v Berend, Ibid, at 10.

Iran could not bolster this submission by French authority. Iran further argued that France ratified the 1970 UNESCO Convention and signed the 1995 UNIDROIT Convention. Iran argued that France accordingly would allow recovery of the objects. Although neither Convention has direct bearing on the items in question, Iran maintained that a French judge would not disregard the international instruments and would apply an exception to the lex situs rule. If it had applied the situs rule in this case, the defendant would have obtained title either through a bona fide purchase or through adverse possession, in France.[1100]

So far, there is no direct English authority applying the doctrine of renvoi to movable property in England, and allowing Iran's claim would have meant the first application in this jurisdiction of renvoi to movable property.

After an evaluation of the already existing English case law which was scarce on the question, Eady J. rejected the proposition to apply renvoi to movable property and he saw no reason to extend English law on that point. Consequently, he rejected the application of Iranian law. Although he did acknowledge some potential merits in applying renvoi to cultural property,[1101] he considered such a decision firmly in the province of governments, and not the courts.[1102] Moreover, he considered that it would be "exceeding his function" to determine the application of new legal principles, or a judicial development of French law, such as the application of Conventions in respect of cultural property by a hypothetical French judge. He rather thought it best to determine the relevant law of France "as it stands".[1103] Eady J thus reaffirmed the lex situs rule to be the established policy in relation to movable cultural property.

By that he missed an opportunity not only to make a major step in the development of the conflict of laws, but he missed an opportunity to enhance the protection of cultural property. What the doctrine of renvoi seeks to achieve, is to apply the most appropriate approach to the choice of law issue.[1104] *Renvoi* means that an English court will seek to resolve a legal dispute in the way it would be dealt with by a judge sitting in the place whose law is to be applied. By rejecting this proposition, Eady J. proved that English judges still regard the doctrine of renvoi as an "complication to, and an unjustified subversion of, the English preference for choice of law".[1105] He rather proved that English courts have choice of

**1100** According to either Art. 2229, 2262 and 2279 French Civil Code.
**1101** Iran v Berend, at 30.
**1102** Iran v Berend, at 30.
**1103** Iran v Berend, at 48.
**1104** Cp. Adrian Briggs, The Law which determines Title to Movable Cultural Property, BYIL 2007, 628.
**1105** Cp. Adrian Briggs, In Praise and Deffence of Renvoi, at 889.

law rules which they are satisfied with, and they may not be happy to put them aside in preference for the choice of law rules of a foreign country. However, the application of renvoi may be seen as an integral element of a scheme to control the illicit trade in art and antiquities.

### III. Lex Situs Originis

This chapter argues that in cases of conflicts relating to cultural property the law of the country of origin should prevail. Owing to the incapacity of the lex situs-rule and its consequences for the art trade, there has been a growing movement among scholars for its application as the governing law in relation to title to heritage items.[1106] Academics contend that the importance of cultural heritage for human society justifies bypassing the policies that are considered to be the main pillars of the lex situs-rule, such as the principle of security of transaction and the protection of the good faith purchaser.[1107] Indeed there should be no argument that the country of origin has the closest connection and the most legitimate claim to apply its own law in determining the ownership of objects comprising its cultural heritage.[1108] The prevailing justification for the lex situs rule are inapplicable to art and antiquities disputes because of their value for humankind.[1109] As a result, various international instruments have attempted to harmonise conflict of laws on that matter and adopted the lex originis as the governing law in relation to heritage items. So far, courts have refused to apply the lex ori-

---

**1106** See e.g. Georges A.L. Droz, The International Protection of Cultural Property from the Standpoint of Private International Law, in: International Legal Protection of Cultural Property, Delphi Colloquy (1984) 17 et seq; Derek Finchham, Adopting the Lex Originis Rule, at 111; Erik Jayme, Neue Anknüpfungspunkte für den Kulturgüterschutz in: Dolzer/Jayme/Mussgnug (eds.) Rechtsfragen des internationalen Kulturgüterschutzes (1994) 35, at 52. Guido Carducci, La Restitution International, at 147; P. Lalive, International Sales of Works of Art, 307, 500 and 670; S. Symeonides, A Choice of Law for Conflicts Involving Stolen Cultural Property, 38 Vand J. Trans'l L. (2005) 1177; Patricia Youngblood, A Chaotic Palette: Conflict of Laws in Litigation between Original Owners and Good-Faith Purchasers of Stolen Art, 50 Duke L. J. (2001) 957; Eric Jayme, Internationaler Kulturgüterschutz: Lex originis oder Lex Rei Sitae? IPrax 1990, at 347;
**1107** E. Jayme, Internationaler Kulturgüterschutz: Lex originis oder lex rei sitae -Tagung in Heidelberg, IPrax 1990, 347 at seq.; P. Lalive, Sur le régime des objets d'art volés en droit international privé, Matscher/Karas Valdheim (eds.) Festschrift Fritz Schwind zum 80 Geburtstag (1993) 51, at 59 et seq; D. Fincham, Adopting the Lex Originis (2008) (arguing that adopting the lex originis would allow the market in antiquities to "police itself"), at 149.
**1108** S. Symeonides, A Choice of Law Rule, at 1187.
**1109** D. Fincham, Adopting the Lex Originis, at 148;

ginis,[1110] and the reason for this hesitation may be seen in its "win or loose" attitude and its illusive terminology. Belgium is the sole country who adopted the lex originis to govern cultural property transaction in its recent codification of Private International law.[1111]

This chapter thus proposes the lex originis to be reduced to a rebuttable presumption. The presumption will be rebutted when the country of origin does not provide for bona fide purchaser protection. After an analysis of the international and national legal instruments dealing with the harmonisation of conflict of laws and private law in relation to choice of law methodology and the application of foreign public law, the following paragraph will elaborate a choice of law rule which is based on the lex originis as the starting point of the analysis. It will discuss the critical points of the lex originis which the author believes are the sources for the lack of its appreciation as well as possible answers to the problem.

## 1. The Resolution of the "Institute de Droit International"

The application of the lex originis in relation to cultural heritage has been first introduced by the Institute of International Law.[1112] During its session in Basel from 26 August to 3 September 1991, the Institute adopted the Resolution on the International Sales of Works of Art from the Angle of Cultural Heritage.[1113] It relates to sales of cultural property concluded before or after an illegal export. The Resolution is based on the principle that "every country has the right and the duty to take measure to preserve its cultural heritage, and in some cases such measures entail restrictions on the free movement of works of art which are considered integral elements of the cultural heritage of the country and that such measures should be reconciled as far as possible with the general interest of the international trade of works of art".[1114] Good faith purchasers would have to return stolen or illegally exported cultural heritage against compensation by the owner of the country of origin.

**1110** Cp. Iran v Berend, [2007] EWHC 132 QB; LG Frankfurt a.M., judgment 18.08. 2011–2–13 O 212/10, abailable at BeckRS 2013, 20789.
**1111** Belgian Code on Private International Law of 16 July 2004, cp. further down this Chapter.
**1112** As to this Institute, see Institut de Droit international (ed.) Livre du centenaire 1873–1973 – Evolution et perspectives du droit international (1973).
**1113** Institute of International Law (ed.), Yearbok, 64, Part II (Paris 1992) 402; the text of the Resolution is reprinted in Vol 6 IJCP (1997) 376, and commented upon by Eric Jayme.
**1114** Cp. the Preamble of the Resolution.

According to Art. 2 of the Resolution, the transfer of ownership of works of art belonging to the cultural heritage of the country of origin shall be governed by the law of that country. Art. 1 b of the Resolution defines the country of origin as the most closely linked to the object from the cultural point of view. The Resolution does not resolve how this cultural link is to be determined. In the preliminary expose to the resolution the official rapporteur, Antonio Ferrer-Correia, refers to Art. 4 of the UNESCO Convention. Accordingly, the fundamental question is whether the object is a significant expression ("comme une expression significative") of the national culture of the requesting state.[1115] In order to further specify the assessment of the closest link, the official rapporteur Antonio Ferrer-Correia created a list of six circumstances where a close connection between the object and a specific country may be assumed: 1) Parts of a monument or of monument complexes, 2) religious object of great importance that belong to a living culture of the state concerned, 3) works of art that have been created by outstanding artists who are citizens of the concerned state or who have acquired their artistic knowledge in the concerned state, 4) archaeological objects, 5) works of art from public or private collections, which are of foreign origin but have become an integral part of the specific collection, in that its deaccession from the collection would mutilate its integrity, 6) cultural objects that have been legally acquired in the country or origin and henceforth belong to the cultural heritage of the acquiring state.

The examples created by Ferrer-Correia indeed carry some weight, however, as we will see in the following, the circumstances concerning antiquities pose further questions as to the assessment of the country of origin and have proven to be too unspecific to serve as a determining factor. Moreover, as stated in Art. 1 a, the Resolution is applicable only to cultural items which have been identified as "belonging to the cultural heritage of a country by registration, classification or by any relevant internationally accepted method of publicity". As a consequence, archaeological objects which have been illegally excavated would not be encompassed by the Resolution. The Resolution does not resolve whether Art. 2 only refers to the private laws of the county of origin or whether the provision also encompasses its public laws, including its cultural patrimony laws. The latter is said to contravene the principle of territoriality.[1116] The Resolution as such is non-binding but contributes to the creation of soft-law in this field which might become relevant in cases where courts have to determine the con-

**1115** Antonio Ferrer-Correia, Exposé préliminaire, Annuaire de l'Institute de Droit International, 64-I (1991), at 94.

**1116** Further on this see Chapter 6 on the justiciability of foreign public law.

tent of "good morals" or trade customs by resorting to international standards.[1117] So far, the Resolution has influenced academic debate but no court decisions has referred to it in its judgment.

## 2. Art. 12 of the EC Directive 93/7 EEC

A more than questionable provision concerning the lex originis has furthermore been adopted in the EC Directive 93/7 of 15 March 1993.[1118]
Art. 12 of the Directive states that:

> Ownership of the cultural object after return shall be governed by that law of the requesting Member State.

The wording of the provision has been subject of a lot of academic debate.[1119] Some commentators belief that the provision induces a correction of the traditional situs rule at the time of the acquisition of the object in that the lex originis shall be applicable, if the illegally exported art has been returned.[1120] The lex originis would retrospectively govern all transactions that have taken place after the illicit removal of the chattel and before its return to the original Member State. Other academics argue that the provision is a reference to the property and conflict of law provisions of the requesting Member State, including its special laws governing the protection of cultural property such as res extra commercium rules.[1121]

The commentary to the Commission proposal to the Directive[1122] to Art. 12 states that "the national rules will apply from the moment the cultural item returns to the territory of the requesting Member State, even when the possessor of

**1117** For example, the German provision § 138 BGB dealing with the morality of property and commercial transaction, see the Nigeria-case (German Supreme Court, BGH 22.6.1972); Astrid Müller-Katzenburg, Internationale Standards, at 296; A. Weidner, Kulturgüter als res extra commercium, at 147.

**1118** Cp. Chapter 4 § 2 II.

**1119** For an account of the different opinions see Olaf Kurpiers, Die lex originis im Internationalen Sachenrecht (2005), at 80–102.

**1120** For example E. Jayme, Internationaler Kulturgüterschutz, at 360; the same, Anknüpfungsmaximen für den Kulturgüterschutz im Internationalen Privatrecht, in: C. Dominicé/R. Patry/C. Reymond (eds.) Études des droit international en l'honneur de Pierre Lalive (1993) 717, at 723; Thomas Pfeiffer, Der Stand des internationalen Sachenrechts nach seiner Kodifikation, IPrax (2000) 270, at 278.

**1121** A. Müller-Katzenburg, Internationale Standarts, at 285.

**1122** COM (91) 447 final – SYN 382, in relation to Art. 13 of the Draft Directive. Available at www.prelex.eu.

the object has acquired it according to the provisions of the Member State where the object is situated or according to the law of another Member or non – Member State". That leads to the conclusion that an acquisition of title the law of any other state than the requesting Member State will not be recognised.

A careful reading suggests that it does not change the lex situs-rule by substituting it for the rule of lex originis. Art. 12 is expressly restricted to the period "after the return" of the unlawfully removed cultural good when every Member State is free to apply its own domestic law on such matters, as for example rules on the forfeiture of illegally removed objects or its regular provisions of conflict of laws.[1123] In fact, it creates an exception to the doctrine of vested rights, a principle deriving from the situs rule, according to which the removal of an object across state border shall not undermine per se pre-existing, or vested rights in the object.[1124]

Due to its confusing wording some Member States have refrained from implementing Art. 12 altogether and the provision cannot serve as a prototype for the introduction of the lex originis into international trade in works of art.

### 3. Belgian Code on PIL of 16 July 2004

Belgium is the sole country to adopt a special choice-of-law-rule for movable cultural property in its recent codification of Private International law.[1125] For the purpose of this research it is thus imperative to take the new instrument under closer scrutiny.

The new codification departs from Savigny's traditional approach to select the applicable law without taking into account its contents. Instead, the new Belgian law follows a materialist view which promotes that a foreign law should not be applied if the result appears unacceptable.[1126]

Art. 90 states:

---

**1123** See also K. Siehr, The Protection of Cultural Property: The 1995 UNIDROIT Convention and the EEC Instruments of 1992/93 Compared, Uniform L. Rev (1998) 671; K. Siehr, Die EG-Richtline von 1993 über die Rückgabe von Kulturgütern und der Kunsthandel, in G. Reichelt (ed.) Neues Recht zum Schutz von Kulturgut (1997) 29, at 36.

**1124** Cp. e.g. Janeen Carruthers, Transfer of Property, at 93. And especially Chapter 6 on the justiciability of cultural property claims.

**1125** A translation of the new law is published the in P. Sarcevic / P. Volken / A. Bonami (eds.) Yearbook of Private International Law (2004), at 319–375. The code entered into force on 1st October 2004.

**1126** See Hans van Houtte, Updating Private International Law-The Belgian Experiment, in: Johan Erauw/Vesna Tomljenovic/ Paul Volken, Liber memorialis Petar Šarčević: Universalism, Tradition and the Individual (2006) 66, at 71.

> If an item, which a State considers as being included in its cultural heritage, has left the territory of that state in a way, which is considered to be illegitimate at the time of the exportation by the law of that state, the revindication by the state is governed by the law of that state, as it is applicable at that time, or at the choice of the latter, by the law of the state of the territory of which the item is located at the time of revindication. Nevertheless, if the law of the state that considers the item part of its cultural heritage does not grant any protection to the possessor in good faith, the latter may invoke the protection, that is attributed to him by the law of the state on the territory of which the item is located the time of revindication.

As an answer to concerns expressed in debates in the Belgian Senate, a time-bar was introduced by Art. 127 § 7 of the new code which rules that Art. 90 does not apply retroactively. This was meant to protect the possessions in Belgian museums and art collections from undue reclamations from those few countries who might already have fulfilled the condition of Art. 90 previous to October 2004.[1127]

The new choice of law provision clearly benefits the claimant by providing an option to choose as between the lex originis or the lex situs. The method reminds of the American "better law-approach" which envisioned choosing between or among the law of the involved states the one law that is better.[1128] However, contrary to the American archetype, the most advantageous connection may be chosen by the requesting state, not by the court.

The Belgian legislator weakened this beneficial treatment by emphasising that the possessor in good faith deserves protection under the law of the situs at the time of the recovery request, if the law of the requesting state does not grant protection to third parties. Hence, countries which exclude the bona fide acquisition of cultural property will continue to depend upon bona fide laws of market states. Prof Erauw, who was involved in the drafting process of the new code argued that the reasons for the mitigation of lex originis may be tied to the lobbying of some Belgian museums, who were concerned about losing some or all of their collection with a more generous rule for source nations.[1129]

---

**1127** See J. Erauw, Lex situs and Art Recovery – New Belgian rules, paper presented at the Lex Situs Conference held by the Institute of Art and Law in London, Nov. 2008 (available over the Institute fo Art and Law).

**1128** The better law approach goes back to Prof Robert A. Leflar, Conflict of Laws: More on Choice Influencing Considerations, 54 Calif. L. Rev. (1966) 1584. See also, S. Symeonides, American Choice of Law at the Dawn of the 20th century, 37 Willamette L. Rev. 1, (2001). However, the better law approach was at the discretion of the court, not the claimant.

**1129** See J. Erauw, Lex situs and Art Recovery – New Belgian rules, paper presented at the Lex Situs Conference held by the Institute of Art and Law in London, Nov. 2008 (available over the Institute of Art and Law).

The exportation itself must be illegitimate. No retroactive listing of cultural goods, as provided for example by the German implementation of the 1970 UNESCO Convention,[1130] is permitted.[1131] The rule thus excludes the application of the lex originis to illegally excavated artefacts which have not yet been classified. It is only understood to mean goods stolen and taken out as well as goods legally acquired but exported without permit by the owner. It also comprises the case where an export of a cultural relic was temporary (e. g. on loan or for exhibit) and where subsequently the fact of not returning the good at the foreseen time constitutes an illegal "export". The recovery after a legitimate export is not covered by the rule.

The determination of the nationality of the object which has been the main focus of criticism against the lex originis to be the governing law in cultural property transactions, has been circumvented by the legislator by specifically reducing the application of the provision to the "requesting state". Difficult questions such as the burden of proof in relation to the origin of the antiquity as well as cases, where the antiquity is claimed by more than one country are not being resolved by Art. 90 of the Belgian codification.

Art. 90 is limited to government institutions and excludes all private claimants. Private parties can resort to Art. 92, which is governing ordinary stolen goods. Art. 92 also gives the claimant the choice between lex furti and lex situs under the premise that the law of the country where the object was located upon its disappearance grants protection to possessors in good faith.

Generally, the option to choose between the law which is most protective for the source country is an exceptionally advantageous choice of law rule and so far unprecedented in conflict of laws. Unfortunately, the discretion granted to the claimant contradicts the principle of security of transaction by creating even greater legal uncertainty. To equally protect the acquirer, the applicable

---

**1130** See Gesetz zu dem Übereinkommen vom 14. November 1970 über die Maßnahmen zum Verbot und zur Verhütung der rechtswidrigen Einfuhr, Ausfuhr und Uebereignung von Kulturgut, German Official Journal (BGBl.) 2007 II No. 12 of 25 April 2007, p. 626 et seq.; Gesetz zur Ausführung des UNESCO-Uebereinkommens vom 14. November 1970 über Maßnahmen zum Verbot und zur Verhütung der rechtswidrigen Einfuhr, Ausfuhr und Uebereignung von Kulturgut, BGBl. 2007 I Nr. 21 of 23 May 2007, at 757 et seq. For a first evaluation see Matthias Weller, Zur Umsetzung der UNESCO-Konvention von 1970 aus deutscher Sicht, in: Gerte Reichelt (ed.), Rechtsfragen der Restitution von Kulturgütern, Symposium des Ludwig Boltzmann Instituts für Europarecht am 12. Oktober 2007 im Bundesministerium für Unterricht, Kunst und Kultur Wien, Vienna 2008, 27. For an in-depth account from a comparative perspective see Matthias Weller et al. (eds.), Kulturgüterschutz – Künstlerschutz, Tagungsband des II. Heidelberger Kunstrechtstags am 5. und 6. September 2008 (2009) 206 et seq.

**1131** J. Erauw, Lex situs rule and art recovery, footnote 96.

law should be confined to the lex originis alone. Owing to the raised sensitivity of the subject, nowadays, it can be expected from buyers of antiquities to provide expert knowledge in the field, or to consult an expert when acquiring an object. In fact, antiquities dealers choose their acquisitions according to their art historical or archaeological value and thus should be able to account for an objects provenance. As a result, the application of the lex originis implements a higher level of commercial security than the lex situs or a combination of both.

The relativisation of the provision through implementing an evasion clause in favour of the lex situs takes the wind out of the provision's sails. However, it can also be viewed as an incentive to loosen the rigorous standards of source countries which aim to restrict the trade in antiquities by adopting bona fide acquisition of cultural heritage in a very limited scale. For example, the good faith purchase of antiquities could be allowed under the premise that the due diligence standard was to be set very high and the burden of proof as to whether the acquirer was in good faith could be reversed. Generally speaking, Art. 90 of the Belgian Code on Private International Law is a positive development towards combating the illicit trade in cultural heritage, but the new codification is very restrictive and so far the lex situs-rule is still the predominant governing law in international movable cultural property law.

## IV. The Proposed Choice of Law Rule

### 1. Characterisation of the Object

In order to justify an alternative choice-of-law methodology in a multi-jurisdictional case the court will have to characterise the object in question to be worth different treatment from an ordinary commercial good. The object in question would have to be characterised as 'cultural property'. It has been already discussed that no universally valid definition of cultural property has been agreed upon. It is however, possible to extract common elements from the use of the term 'cultural property' in national, European and international norms.[1132] In order to characterise an object as cultural property for the purpose of conflict of laws, the courts could make use of the definitions in the 1970 UNESCO Convention, the 1995 UNIDROIT Convention and the EC Directive 93/7/EEC. The forth mentioned international instruments combine an abstract definition with the enumeration of objects in a special annex: For an object to qualify as 'cultural object' in the sense of the Directive it must fulfil two require-

**1132** Cp. Kerstin Odendahl, Kulturgüterschutz, at 386.

ments. First it must be classified among the "national treasures possessing artistic, historic or archaeological value" under national legislation or administrative procedures within the meaning of Art. 36 of the Treaty.[1133] Secondly, it must either belong to one of the categories listed in the Annex or must form an integral part of "public collections listed in the inventories of a museum, archive conservation or collection."[1134] The UNIDROIT and UNESCO Conventions additionally include objects important for "prehistory, history, literature, art or science."[1135] They also emphasise the importance of religion and culture. As the Directive, the Unidroit convention lists objects of importance in an Annex.[1136]

Based on the common elements extrapolated from the forth mentioned international, European and national law, Prof. Kerstin Odendahl derived a workable characterisation of cultural property:

> "[o]bjects qualifying as cultural property are corporeal objects, movable or immovable, either unique or consisting of collections / ensembles, which have been either created, changed or formed by human effort or which represent human cultural development, and which are accorded historical, artistic, scientific, architectural, archaeological or any other cultural value of different dimensions."[1137]

By referring to "cultural value of different dimensions", Prof. Odendahl clarifies that it is irrelevant for the qualification whether an object is of value (only) for a certain group of the population, a nation or humanity as a whole.[1138] Neither is it

**1133** Art. 1 (1) Directive.

**1134** Art. 1 (2) Directive.

**1135** Art. 2 Directive.

**1136** Annex: (a) Rare collections and specimens of fauna, flora, minerals and anatomy, and objects of paleontological interest; (b) property relating to history, including the history of science and technology and military and social history, to the life of national leaders, thinkers, scientists and artists and to events of national importance; (c) products of archaeological excavations (including regular and clandestine) or of archaeological discoveries; (d) elements of artistic or historical monuments or archaeological sites which have been dismembered; (e) antiquities more than one hundred years old, such as inscriptions, coins and engraved seals; (f) objects of ethnological interest; (g) property of artistic interest, such as: (i) pictures, paintings and drawings produced entirely by hand on any support and in any material (excluding industrial designs and manufactured articles decorated by hand); (ii) original works of statuary art and sculpture in any material; (iii) original engravings, prints and lithographs; (iv) original artistic assemblages and montages in any material; (h) rare manuscripts and incunabula, old books, documents and publications of special interest (historical, artistic, scientific, literary, etc.) singly or in collections; (i) postage, revenue and similar stamps, singly or in collections; (j) archives, including sound, photographic and cinematographic archives.

**1137** Kerstin Odendahl, Kulturgüterschutz, at 386.

**1138** See also K. Lubina, Contested Cultural Property, at 40.

crucial for the qualification of an object as cultural property that it is of outstanding cultural relevance: cultural property may be of outstanding, special, extraordinary or any other cultural value.[1139] Consequently, territorial and qualitative dimensions are irrelevant to the qualification of an object as cultural property. They become relevant when it comes to the question of whether an object falls under the scope of application of a specific legal norm. As a result, the characterisation suggested by the Belgian Code on PIL 2004[1140] is too narrow and is thus inappropriate to act as a determining factor whether to deflect from the lex situs-rule. Furthermore, a characterisation which relates to the cultural heritage code of the requesting state would contradict the principle of commercial certainty. Parties participating in the art trade can be expected to know the regulations in important international regulations, such as the two Conventions, as well as the Directive, but they should not be expected to inquire into the cultural property statutes of specific source nations in order to ascertain whether an object is to be treated like an ordinary good or like cultural property which is subject to special legal treatment.

### 2. Protection of the Good Faith Purchaser

The application of the lex originis as the governing law for cultural property transaction will find international recognition only if it will provide a mechanism to protect third parties who have acquired the object in good faith.

Both the 1995 UNIDROIT Convention as well as the EC Directive solved the dilemma between original owner and good faith acquirer via a payment of compensation and a raised standard of diligence.[1141] However, payment of compensation to the acquirer in cases of cultural property where objects are of unique significance and collectors value is a cold comfort. Moreover, source countries which are rich in antiquities but poor in recourses will be forced to buying back their own cultural heritage, which considering the prices that are being achieved on the art market would put a strain on the countries already weak economy.

A rebuttable presumption in favour of the lex originis as suggested by the new Belgian Code on Private International Law would ensure that the law of

**1139** K.Lubina, ibid, at 40; A. Müller-Katzenburg, Internationale Standards, at 140

**1140** "If an item, which a state considers as being included in its cultural heritage", Art. 90.

**1141** See Art. 4 1995 UNIDROIT Convention; Art. 9 EC Directive 93/7 stating that where return of the object is ordered, the competent court in the requested states shall award the possessor such compensation as it deems fair according to the circumstances of the case, provided that it is satisfied that the possessor exercised due care and attention in acquiring the object.

the country of origin will apply without leaving out the rights of the bona fide purchaser. The starting point of the choice of law analysis would be the lex originis but the presumption would be rebutted in case the defendant has acquired the object in good faith. In this case the law of the situs of the origin does not provide for good faith purchaser protection, the lex situs will apply. A combination of substantive and conflictual elements in a choice of law rule has already been suggested by Prof. Simeon Symeonides and according to him is "not only permissible but can prove of great benefit in combating the illicit trade in antiquities".[1142] In order limit the application of the less protective lex situs rule, the standard of good faith will have to be raised. The court would be required to take certain value judgments in regard to the state of mind of the acquirer when deciding on the question which law is applicable.

### 3. The Good Faith – Test

Recent quantitative studies highlight the great volume of artefacts with no or forged provenance in the art and antiquities market.[1143] Proof, that many antiquities currently on the market may be illegally excavated. Although it would be incorrect to claim that all objects sold without provenance are stolen or looted, there is no systemic safeguard to ensure that individuals are buying and selling objects legally.[1144] Rather, increased scrutiny of the antiquities trade is needed in which objective evidence of a purchaser's investigation of the legitimate title of the object in question must be the bare minimum for the acquisition of good faith in a given transfer.[1145] There are circumstances in which more research should be conducted when acquiring an antiquity. For example, if a sale takes

---

**1142** Similarly S. Symeonides, has proposed a hybrid model based on both a conflict of laws and a sustantive test, in: A Choice of Law Rule for Conflicts Involving Stolen Cultural Property, 38 Vand J. Trans'l L. (2005) 1177. For the difference between "conflictual" and substantivist" methods and techinques, see S. Symeonides, American Choice of Law at the Dawn of the 21st Century, at 4 et seq.

**1143** C. Chippindale/ D.W. J. Gill, Material consequences of contemporary classical collecting, 104 Am. J. Archaeol. (2000) 463; Ricardo Elia, Analysis of the looting, selling and collecting of Apulian red-figure vases: a quantitative approach, in: N. Brodie/J. Doole /C. Renfrew (eds.) Trade in Illicit Antiquities: The Destruction of the World's Archaeological Heritage (2001) 145.

**1144** Cp. D. Fincham, Adopting the Lex Originis, at 137.

**1145** Cp. Derek Fincham, Towards a Rigorous Standard for the Good Faith Acquisition of Antiquities, 37 Syr. J. of Int'l Law and Com (2009), 1 (arguing for stricter due diligence requirements and the abolition of the presumption of good faith).

place at an unusual location or time as in the *Goldberg-case*.[1146] There are also broad classes of antiquities that, either because of their find-spot or composition, should warrant greater research before a responsible acquisition can take place.[1147] In such circumstances a buyer should be highly alert.

Academic commentators have suggested that rules governing good faith provisions should be adjusted in order to protect the original owner from an abuse of the situs rule by traffickers.[1148] Although various codes of conduct have been developed for the antiquities trade,[1149] setting a standard of diligence for museums and dealers, the new development is not being reflected in the substantive law of most jurisdictions. Instead of harmonising national laws, it would be far easier to adopt a good faith provision into the applicable law-test. If the lex originis does not provide for good faith purchaser protection, the lex situs will only apply if the possessor of the object satisfies a raised standard of due diligence in the acquisition of cultural property. As the term 'good faith' will differ from state to state, the proposed rule will have to either designate the state whose law would provide a definition or provide a self-contained definition of good faith.[1150]

### 4. Reversed Burden of Proof

In order for the rebuttable presumption to work, the good faith purchaser would have to proof that he has complied with the raised standard of diligence as required by the choice-of-law rule. In most jurisdictions however, the good faith of the acquirer of an object is presumed. For example, Art. 2268 of the French

**1146** See e.g., the Goldberg-case (Autocephalous Greek-Orthodox Church of Cyprus v Goldberg & Feldman Fine Arts, Inc., 717F. Supp. 1374, S. D. Ind. 1989), where the sale took place at the airport.

**1147** For example Iraqi cultural objects, which have disappeared after the raid on the Baghdad Museum in 2003, cp. Introduction to this study, Chapter 1.

**1148** See e.g. Heimo Schack, Kunst und Recht (2004), at 509; Anne-Kathrin Arendholz, Gutgläubiger Erwerb gestohlener Kunstgegenstände, in Hoeren/Holznagel/Ernstschneider, Handbuch Kunst und Recht (2008) 217; K. T. Burke, International Transfer of Stolen Cultural Property, 13 Loy. L.A. Int'l & Comp. L.J. (1990–1991) 466; P. Y. Reyhan, Conflict of Laws in Litigation, at 962; A.E. Hayworth, Stolen Artwork: Deciding Ownership is No Pretty Picture, 43 Duke Law Journal (1993) 337, at 357.

**1149** For example, the 1999 CoPAT Codes or the 1986 ICOM Code of Professional Ethics. For an in-depth account of museum codes of ethics see Manlio Frigo, Ethical Rules and Codes of Honor related to Museum Activities: A Complementary Support to the Private International Law Approach Concerning the Circulation of Cultural Property, 16 IJCP (2009) 49; A. Weidner, Kulturgüter als res extra commercium, at 282 et seq.

**1150** Cp. also Symeonides, A Choice of law Rule, at 1190.

Civil Code provides that good faith is always presumed and that the person who alleges bad faith must prove it. A similar principle can be found in Germany and Switzerland.[1151] However, in a field like cultural property, where the objects are of high cultural artistic significance and value academic commentators long since began to question this presumption.[1152] Prof. Marc André Renold even believes that "the sacrosanct principle of the presumption of good faith is loosing its sanctity".[1153] German commentators point to case law in relation to the good faith acquisition of second hand cars, where the acquirer is presumed to be in bad faith where the seller is unable to provide a motor vehicle registration certificate.[1154]

The International Conventions on the subject endorse a reversed burden of proof. Art. 4 (1) of the 1995 Unidroit Convention, specifically with regard to stolen heritage items, takes the position that the presumption of good faith shall be abandoned.[1155] The Convention states that it is the current possessor who must establish that he or she followed the due diligence requirement set out in Art. 4 (4).[1156] In Art. 9, the EC Directive 93/7 provides for a special choice of law rule in favour of the country of origin which rules that the burden of proof shall be governed by the legislation of the requested Member State.

One of the first countries to adopt the reversed burden of proof for objects of cultural value in its national legislation is Japan. In its Act on Controls on the Illicit Export and Import and Other Matters of Cultural Property (ACIEI) of 2002, which implemented the 1970 Convention at national level, it is provided that the bona fide purchaser carries the burden of proof with regard to the question of whether he was acting in good faith at the time of the purchase.[1157] Although not designed to protect cultural objects, England is one of the few countries that provides for a reversed burden of proof for the good faith acquirer.

1151 Argumentum e contrario § 932 BGB (German Civil Code); Art. 3 Swiss Civil Code.

1152 For example P. Lalive, La Convention d'Unidroit sur les biens culturels volés ou illicitement exportés, SZIER / RSDIDE, (1997), at 13, 38, 30; Alejandro M. Garro, The Recovery of Stolen Art from Bona Fide Purchasers, Pierre Lalive (ed), Geneva Workshop on International Sales of Work of Art (1985) 503, at 518; S. Damm, Kollisionsrechtlicher Erwerbsschutz im internationalen Kunsthandel, at 251; O. Kurpiers, Die Lex Originis im Internationalen Sachenrecht, at 124 at seq.

1153 Cp. M.A. Renold, The Ubiquitous Question of Good Faith, in: Resolution of Cultural Property Disputes (Peace Palace Papers 2004) 251, at 263.

1154 For German cases concerning the acquisition of cars see e.g. BHG NJW (2006) 3488; BGH NJW (1996) 2226.

1155 Cp. the Explanatory Report, Uniform L. R. (2001–2003) 476, at 516;

1156 Cp. M-A. Renold, The Ubiquitous Question of Good Faith, at 262.

1157 Toshiyuki Kono, Japanese report, in: T.Kono/S.Wrbka, The Impact of Uniform Laws (2010) 469, at section 3.2.1.

Sect. 4 of the Limitation Act 1980 states that any conversion following the theft of an object is related to the theft unless the contrary is shown.

### 5. A Rule on Discovery

The good faith-test alone is not efficient, if it is not complemented by a "discovery-rule", which would suspend the running of any statute of limitations, until the original owner knows or should have known of the whereabouts of his property. As Symeonides has rightfully pointed out: "without a discovery rule any pretence of protecting owners of stolen property is truly a sham."[1158] Taking Switzerland as an example, the bona fide purchaser of a stolen or lost chattel acquires title, even from a thief, if five years have elapsed since the theft. If we imagine the case wher the bona fide acquirer consigns an object for auction six years after the theft, and after keeping it at home before its resale, the original owner will be unable to recover the artwork if he or she finds out about his property only when the artwork has been put up on sale.

A discovery-rule is based on the reasoning that it is inconsistent with the system of jurisprudence to require a claimant to bring his cause of action in a limited period in which, even with due diligence, he could not be aware a cause of action exists.[1159] Under the discovery rule, an original owner's cause of action does not accrue "until the injured party discovers, or by exercise of reasonable diligence and intelligence should have discovered, facts which form the basis of a cause of action."[1160] When the limitation period expires, the original owner would not be able to bring suit. This would guarantee some degree of security of transaction to a bona fide purchaser of stolen art. Such a flexible approach would not arbitrarily cut off the right to sue of original owners who, despite due diligence, have been unable to identify their defendants.

A prominent example of the application of a discovery-rule to art is the U.S. case concerning three paintings by Georgia O'Keefe that had disappeared from a

**1158** Advocating for the adoption of a discovery rule in art disputes for example S. Symeonides, A Choice of Law Rule for Conflicts Involving Cultural Property, 1177; P. Y. Reyhan, A Chaotic Pallett: Conflict of Laws in Litigation, at 1023; Tarquin Preziosi, Note, Applying a Strict Discovery Rule to Art Stolen in the Past, 49 Hastings L.J. (1997) 225; Meghan A. Sherlock, The Need for Equitable Consistency in International Cases of Recovery of Stolen Art and Cultural Property, 8 Tul. J. Int'l & Comp L. (2000) at 483.

**1159** Autocephalus Greek Orthodox Church of Cyprus v Goldberg & Feldmann Fien Arts Inc 717 F Supp 1374 (1989), per Noland J., at 1387.

**1160** O'Keeffe v Snyder, 416 A. 2d 862 (N.J. 1980). For details on the case see A.Milard, Artful ownership: art law, valuation, and commerce in the United States, Canada, and Mexico (Washington 2000); Derek Finchham, Adopting the Lex Originis Rule, at 125.

New York City gallery in 1946. In *O'Keefe v Snyder,*[1161] the artist only learned of the whereabouts of her paintings nearly 30 years after the theft. In 1975, when the art was put up for sale in a New York auction house, she was then able to obtain information that the paintings were sold by Barry Snyder, the owner of the Princeton Gallery of Fine Art. She demanded the return of the paintings but Snyder arguing that the six-year statute of limitations of the state of New Jersey prevented O'Keefe from bringing the action. The court held that where a court finds that an owner has diligently searched for a stolen painting but "cannot find it or discover the identity of the possessor, the statute of limitations will not begin to run."

The advocators of the theory on discovery particularly point to American cases where courts have found the discovery rule to be "especially appropriate with respect to stolen art, since much art is unavailable to the public and an owner seeking to recover it will almost never learn of its whereabouts."[1162]However, the discovery rule shifts the emphasis from the conduct of the possessor to the conduct of the owner. The focus of the inquiry will no longer be solely whether the possessor has met the test of good faith acquisition but whether the owner has acted with due diligence in pursuing his or her property. The burden of proving due diligence rests on the original owner. The New Jersey Supreme Court proposed that the trial court consider whether O'Keefe exercised due diligence in recovering her paintings, whether there was an effective means of alerting the art world to the theft, and whether registering with an art-theft archive would give a prudent purchaser notice of the theft.

Especially in respect of return proceedings concerning stolen art, New York applies a slightly different form of a discovery rule, the "demand and refusal – rule", under which the limitations period does not begin to run until the owner makes a demand for the return of the property and the possessor refuses.[1163] The so-called New York-rule was set forth in the landmark case of *Guggenheim v. Lubell.*[1164] *Guggenheim,* a decision involving a claim for a painting by Marc Chagall that had been stolen from the Guggenheim Museum. Decades after the theft, the

**1161** 416 A.2d 862 (N.J. 1980).

**1162** De Weerth v Baldinger 836 F 2d 103, 486 US 1056, at 107, per Newman J. DeWeerth involved competing claims to "Champs de Ble á Vetheuil," a painting by Claude Monet, valued at the time of suit at $500,000.

**1163** Generally on the demand and refusal-rule see Laurie Frey, Baklar v Vavra and the Art of Conflicts in New York, 112 Columboa L. Rev. (2012), 1055.

**1164** Solomon R Guggenheim Foundation v Lubell, 77 N.Y. 2d 311 (1991); cp. also the recent case Mirvish v. Mott, Mirvish v. Mott, 18 N.Y.3d 510, 942 N.Y.S.2d 404 (2012), a case concerning the ownership of *The Cry,* an erotically-themed monumental bronze sculpture by Jacques Lipchitz.

museum located its painting at the home of a couple that had purchased it in good faith from a New York gallery. When the the museum sued to recover it, the court pointed out that placing a burden of locating stolen artwork on the true owner and to foreclose the rights of that owner to recover its property in case the burden of proof is not met would encourage illicit trafficking in stolen art. [1165] Te rule has been recently invoked in a case concerning a 3000-year old gold tablet dating to the reign of Assyrian King Tukulti-Ninurta and stolen from the Berlin Vorderasiatisches Museum during World War II.[1166] The tablet resurfaced in 2003, when it was discovered among the possessions of Riven Flumenbaum, a decedent holocaust survivor.

In Germany, the principle of discovery for the maters of the lapsw of time became subject of discussion, after a hoard of master paintings had been discovered in the flat of Cornelius Gurlitt, most of which were allegedly looted during the Holocaust or confiscated as degenrate art in World War II. Hildebrandt Gurlitt, Cornerlius' father, and subsequently Cornelius Gurlitt himself hid the hoard although knowing that many of the paintings must have been confiscated or stolen.

### 6. The Nationality of the Object

One of the major factors speaking against the application of the lex originis are the difficulties in ascertaining the nationality of the object. So far, all suggestions involving the lex originis as a choice of law rule lack a clear definition. The designation of the country of origin by determining the closest connection between the object in question and the requesting country or countries, as suggested by Art. 1 b of the Basel Resolution, is thought to be too vague and does not provide for enough legal predictability.[1167] Belgium elegantly refers to the requesting state as the country of origin. In order to further specify the closest link between the object and the requesting state, additional criteria are necessary. In the judicial practice the attribution to a nation in most cases has been assessed through

---

**1165** Guggenheim v Lubell, 77 NY2d 311 (1991) at 320.

**1166** Matter of Flamenbaum File No. 328146 (N.Y., Surr. Ct. 30.3.2010; Surpreme Court Appelate Decision, File No 2010 – 4400 (N.Y. Sup. Ct. App. Div. 30.5.2012; 2013 NY Slip Op 07510) decided on November 14, 2013 Court of Appeals. For a recent comment see K. Siehr, Bulletin Kunst und Recht 2/2012, 50 – 53.

**1167** See for example A. Weidner, Kulturgüter als res extra commercium, at 194, 204, and 219. But see O. Kurpiers, Lex originis, who wants to determine the closest link through ascription, which is the attribution of an object to a state after consideration of all possible connecting factors, at 194 et seq. Similarly, A. Müller-Katzenburg, Internationale Standards, at 154.

the determination of the "genuine connecting factor" or "cultural importance" of the object for the requesting state. Professor Jayme has suggested several indicators as possible determinants for the nationality of cultural property – the nationality of the artist, the geographical residence of the object in questions, its religious meaning of a certain group, or it's inclusion as part of a particular collection.[1168] The following paragraph refrains from this categorisation as creating diffuse and random results.[1169] It chooses to distinguish between looted and illegally exported artefacts in order to determine the nationality of an antiquity. In the case of looted artefacts, the connecting factor is the place of excavation or the place from which the property has been stolen. In the case of illegally exported artefacts, which has not been illicitly excavated or stolen, the connecting factor has to be determined according to a certain connection or cultural importance of the object for the requesting state. In many cases, the artefact which is being sought to be recovered has been both, illicitly obtained and illegally exported.

### a. The Closest Connecting Factor

The closest connecting factor in relation to objects which have been looted is the place of illegal excavation or theft. In the light of the importance of the archaeological context this would allow to contribute to the understanding of ancient life. The historical evidence of those finds would be lost if looted artefacts were subject to a different attribution. This view is also supported by Art. 4 b of the 1970 UNESCO Convention, which recognises cultural property found within the national territory of a state forms part of its cultural heritage

The attribution of an illegally exported object to a specific nation depends on the extent to which the object in question epitomises the culture of a nation, and to which extent the history of a country is reflected in this specific object. The genuine connecting factor can be determined through an evaluation of facts or balance of interests, which takes into account a conglomerate of possible attribution criteria. One such factor can be the historical importance for a nation as in the case of the Koran manuscripts looted from the National Library in Iraq.[1170] The manuscripts have been a rare example of Arabic calligraphy, which are of grave importance for understanding the history of Mesopotamia. They are said to be an important element of the national identity of today's

---

**1168** E. Jayme, Internationaler Kulturgüterschutz, at 347 et seq.
**1169** See also S. Damm, Kollisionsrecht im Internationalen Kunsthandel, at 202.
**1170** Cp. Haine, Gedächtnisverlust, Der Tagesspiegel, 19.4.2003, at 23.

Iraq. Its theft and the subsequent illegal export are being regarded as "loss of memory" about Iraqi history.[1171]

Another strong indicator for attributing an object to a nation may be its religious or sacral meaning for a certain group. A recent example for the influence of religious traditions on cultural property litigation is the *Bark Etchings-case*,[1172] where a group of aboriginal people in Australian Victoria claimed traditional ownership of three nineteenth-century bark items. One etching shows a series of men dancing in a corroboree or ceremony, together with a watching audience; the other appears to show three men hunting a kangaroo.[1173] The third item is a piece of curved Red Gum bark, shaped with a narrow neck at one end and decorated with red and white ochre.[1174] This piece was used by dancers in an emu dance ceremony. Similar pieces are recorded by nineteenth-century settler-observers as having been discarded at the end of the dance and as having no continuing ceremonial significance.[1175]

In 2004, the ceremonial objects had been loaned by the British Museum to Museum Victoria for an exhibition called "Etched on Bark 1854: Kulin barks from Northern Victoria". The Australian Heritage Department issued a certificate of exemption from export control in respect of the etchings under section 12 of the Commonwealth Movable Cultural Heritage Act 1986. The certificates would allow the etchings to be imported into Australia and subsequently re-exported. During the exhibition however, the Aboriginal Dja Dja Warrung Tribe instituted proceedings for the bark etchings to remain in Australia permanently. The Commonwealth Aboriginal and Torres Strait Islander Heritage Protection Amendment Act in 1984 provided that Victorian Aboriginal people could apply to the Victorian Minister for Aboriginal Affairs for an emergency, temporary, or other declaration if they considered that Aboriginal objects or places were under threat of desecration. Under section 21 E (1) of the Act, the minister was also empowered to compulsorily acquire any Aboriginal cultural property if the minister was satisfied that it was necessary to maintain the relationship between Aboriginals and that object. On the ground of this legislation, the Dja Dja Warrung prevented the

**1171** Cp. Haine, ibid.

**1172** For a comment on the case see L.V. Prott, The Dja Dja Warrung Bark Etchings Case, 13 IJCP (2006) 241.

**1173** Cp. Elisabeth Willis, The Dja Dja Warrung Bark Etchings Case in Australia, 15 IJCP (2008) 49, at 51.

**1174** E. Willis, The Dja Dja Warrung, at 51.

**1175** Carol Cooper, Traditional Visual Culture in South-East Australia, in: Andrew Sayers (ed.) Aboriginal Artists of the Nineteenth Century (1994) 91; Elizabeth Willis, "Exhibiting Aboriginal industry: A story behind a 're-discovered' bark drawing from Victoria, 27 Aboriginal History (2003) 39.

Victoria Museum from returning the etchings to England, although the museum had contractual obligations to return the items to the British Museum as soon as the exhibition had finished. After mediation had failed, legal proceedings were then instituted in the federal court by Museum Victoria and elders of the Dja Dja Warrung people.[1176] The Federal Court however held the emergency declarations to be unlawful.[1177] The Tribes application to the minister for a permanent declaration of preservation also failed. As a consequence, the protective declarations were suspended. The court dissolved the injunction that restrained the museum from permitting the removal of objects in question from Victoria. In the end, the etchings returned back to England.

The case over the bark etchings has generated a major international incident with the British Government, the British Museum and other similar institutions throughout Europe claiming that the proceedings instituted by the tribe would threaten future international loans of indigenous material to Australia. For this reason, the Australian parliament has since adopted an amending bill for the 1984 Act: The Aboriginal and Torres Strait Islander Heritage Protection Amendment Act 2006 was passed in November of that year. It provides that emergence declarations under the 1984 Act as applied for by the Dja Dja Wurrung, in the future will be subject to certificates made under section 12 of the Protection of Movable Cultural Property Act 1986 authorising the export of objects. Although the bark etchings were not repatriated to the Dja Dja Warrung, the case triggered a change in attitude towards the repatriation of aboriginal ceremonial objects to their traditional owners. In October 2005, the National Museum of Ethnography in Stockholm, Sweden, returned the bones of fifteen aboriginals and eleven artefacts from stone age people to their homeland in Australia.[1178] The British Museum returned two bundles of Tasmanian ashes to Tasmania in 2006. Similarly, in May 2007, the Natural History Museum in London returned the remains of 17 Tasmanian Aboriginals.[1179] The Museum's decision followed a report by the British Working Group on Human Remains.[1180]

---

**1176** The litigation is reported in Museum Boards of Victoria v. Carter [2005] FCA 645 May 20, 2005; Carter v. Minister for Aboriginal Affairs [2005] FCA 667 923 May 2005

**1177** Cp. Museum Boards of Victoria v. Carter [2005] FCA 645 May 20, 2005.

**1178** For an account of the case see Janette Greenfield, The Return of Cultural Treasures (3rd ed 2007), at 310.

**1179** Tasmanian Aboriginal Centre v The Trustees of the Natural History Museum, CO/1143/2007 (unreported).

**1180** The Report is available at http://webarchive.nationalarchives.gov.uk/+/http://www.culture.gov.uk/reference_library/publications/4553.aspx

### b. Problematic Constellations

Although the lex originis-rule appears to be the most beneficial choince of law rule in cases concerning cultural property, some unresolved questions remain.

#### (1) Orphaned Objects

Return requests may prove particularly troubling for antiquities by modern states with political boundaries that overlap ancient cultural boundaries. Even if the exact find-spot of the antiquity can be proven.

Invoking the lex originis, may prove particularly troubling with respect to antiquities that have been created by a culture whose boundaries span multiple modern states. If the objects have been illegally excavated their exact find spot will in most cases be unclear. In such cases, one nation may not have a stronger claim to ancient cultural patrimony than any other country that spans the ancient cultural border. For example, it would be difficult for Mexico to make an argument that it has a stronger claim to steward ancient Mayan culture than do the other states that share ancient Mayan territory: Guatemala, Honduras, El Salvador, and Belize.[1181]

This was the exact problem in the famous *Sevso-case*, where Hungary, Croatia and Lebanon claimed ownership of a collection of antique Roman silver.[1182] The Silver is thought to have once belonged to a Roman general Sevso. The lawsuit was commenced by the Republic of Lebanon after Lord Northampton of Great Britain, who held the treasure at the time of the suit, consigned it for sale at an auction in Zurich and arranged to have it exhibited in New York prior to the auction. Subsequently, the former Republic of Yugoslavia and Hungary intervened and asserted claims to the treasure. The trial court instructed the jury that neither Croatia (which succeeded Yugoslavia as a party) nor Hungary could assert an ownership claim to the treasure unless they first proved that the collection originally had been discovered within their respective territory. Notwithstanding expert and factual testimony introduced by Croatia and Hungary during the course of the trial, the jury failed to find that the treasure had

**1181** Cp. Also Marion Forsyth, International Cultural Property Trust, One response to Burden of Proof Challenges in Stolen Antiquities Litigation, 8 Chi. J. Int'l L. (2007) 197, at 202.

**1182** Lebanon v. Sotheby's, 167 A.D.2d 142 (N.Y. App. Div. 1990); Croatia v. Trustees of the Marquess of Northampton 1987 Settlement, 203 A.D.2d 167 (1994), appeal denied, 84 N.Y.2d 805, 642 N.E.2d 325 (1994). But see also Peru v Johnson 720 F Supp 810 (CD Cal. 1989), where the court found that Peru could not succeed in claiming artefacts that could have originated from Equador or Bolivia.

been discovered in and removed from either country's territory.[1183] It is interesting to note that the countries which rumour has associated with the Sevso-Treasure, and which tried to claim possession of the hoard in the New York court case held to establish its ownership have no record of similar material being found in their soil previously. In fact, any one of the Roman Empire's many provinces could have been the home of the treasure.

### (2) State Succession

Questions resembling those in cases of illegally excavated antiquities arise when objects where stolen or illicitly exported from countries which originally shared one territory but today are two or more separate countries, or even totally new countries. This was the constellation in the Swiss *Giant Mogul Gold Coin-case.*[1184] The case concerned the recovery of two giant gold coins minted in 1630 and 1639, which originally belonged to the Nizam of the Indian principality of Hyderabad, India, Mir Osman Ali Khan. In 1988 Mir Osman Ali Khan's grandson, Mukarram Jah, transferred the coins to the Crédit Agricole Indosuez (Suisse) SA as a security for a loan of $25 million granted by the bank to companies controlled by Mukarram Jah. In 1949, India declared particular private antiquity collections to become state property and thus contested the bank's right before the Swiss Courts in 1997. The coins were minted during the seventeenth-century Mogul dynasty and belonged to the personal property of the head of the Hyderabad principality. In 1949, Hyderabad was united to India. As stated in the 1987 auction catalog, the larger coin was minted in Agra, which is today in India, whereas the other was minted in Lahore, which today is in Pakistan. The matter did not come up during the trial but it would have been a difficult issue to decide whether the second gold coin belonged not to the Indian but to the Pakistani cultural heritage.[1185]

**1183** Cp. H. Kurzweil/ L. Gagion /L. de Walden, The Trial of the Sevso-Treasure, in: Kate Fitz Gibbon (ed.), Who owns the Past (2005) 83; Barbara T. Hoffmann, Sevso Follies of 1994, ARCHAEOLOGY, May/June (1994), at 42; Lawrence M. Kaye, The Future of the Past, Recovering Cultural Property, 4 Cardozo J. Int'l & Comp. L. (1996) 23, at 41.

**1184** Union de l'Inde contre Crédit Agricole Indosuez (Suisse) SA, Supreme Court decision, April 8, 2005: ATF 131 III 418; Journal des Tribunaux (2006) I 63 (Summary); Semaine Judiciaire (2006) I 152; Praxis (2006), N 42, 310. For a brief comment on this case, see Art-Law Centre News No. 12 (November 2005); see also Ivo Schwander, Rechtsprechung zum Internationalen Sachen-, Schuld- und Gesellschaftsrecht, Revue Suisse de Droit International et Européen (2006), at 344.

**1185** See Marc-André Renold, Case Note: An Important Swiss Decision Relating to the International Transfer of Cultural Goods: The Swiss Supreme Court's Decision on the Giant Antique Mogul Gold Coins, 13 IJCP (2006) 361.

### (3) Subjective Cultural Importance

Problems arise when ancient treasures which have been part of a major museum collection for a long period of time are requested to be repatriated to the country of origin. It is being argued that the antiquity is bound up with the identity of its holder, with the result that the treasure is viewed as being part of the national heritage of the current holder although it originally has been manufactured for another culture or nation.[1186] In particular, there are artefacts so tied to the identity of the new cultural community that their loss culminates in a loss to their cultural identity.[1187] The growth and shaping of a national identity is open to development and not limited to objects which have been created for another culture, which may long since have been extinct. For example, no one would question Jordan's claim to Roman artefacts in Gerasa (Jerash), although Italy may be viewed as the "successor" of the Roman Empire.[1188]

The debate has gained prominence in the case of the Elgin marbles which are currently housed at the British Museum in London. In 1804, Lord Elgin brought a large part of the Parthenon frieze to London after having stripped down the monuments of the Acropolis. In 1816, the British Government decided to buy the sculptures on the condition that they remain together and be displayed at the British Museum which maintains to this day that the marbles are legally and properly held by it. Greece first called for the return of the marbles in 1829 when it won independence from Turkey and successive Greek governments exert pressure since then.[1189] In the last two decades, the battle for the return of the marbles has constantly increased. The Greek government denies the British claim to the marbles whereas the British argue that the marbles have been in England for more than a century and a half and in that time have become part of the British cultural heritage. Merryman has stated that "the Elgin Marbles and other works in the British Museum have entered British culture,

**1186** See E. Jayme, Die Nationalität des Kunstwerks als Rechtsfrage, in G. Reichelt (ed.) Internationaler Kulturgüterschutz (1992) 7, at 23 and 26.

**1187** Cp. Patty Gerstenblith, Identity and Cultural Property: The Protection of Cultural Property in the United States, 75 B.U. L. REV. (1995) 559, at 570 and 647 (recognising personality theory as conceptual basis to restore control over cultural property to the group that produced it and reasoning that cultural property is "that specific form of property that enhances identity, understanding, and appreciation for the culture that produced it.") See as well J. Moustaka, Group Rights in Cultural Property: Justifying Strict Inalienability, 74 Cornell L. Rev. (1988) 1179; Isabell McBryde, Inntroduction to: I. McBryde (ed.) Who owns the past? Papers from the Annual Symposium of the Australian Academy of the Humanities (1985).

**1188** See S. Damm, Kollisionsrechtlicher Erwerbsschutz im Internationalen Kunsthandel, at 266.

**1189** Information can be found at www.museum-security.org/elginmarbles.

help define the British to themselves, inspire British arts, give Britons identity and community, civilise and enrich British life, and stimulate British scholarship."[1190] Similar can be said of the Obelisk on the Place de la Concorde in France which has been claimed by Egypt or Da Vinci's Mona Lisa, which is a part of both the Italian and the French cultural heritage.

In such cases, the determination of the country of origin might prove impossible as the positions of the claimant and the holder of the antiquity may be considered as roughly equivalent, so that on this point there is a stand-off.

### c. Sharing Agreements as an Alternative Method

All of the forth mentioned constellations seem impossible to resolve, and rather demand a Solomonic judgment.[1191] A possible solution is for the countries in question to collectively pursue a recovery claim. If the states competing for the ownership of a treasure can establish that it was excavated or illegally exported from the territory of either the one or the other country, they could join forces in court and later agree on shared rights of possession.[1192]

An agreement of this kind has already been achieved with *The Three Graces*, which would have been lost to British Heritage, if the Victoria and Albert Museum and the National Gallery in Scotland would not have negotiated to acquire the sculpture jointly in combination with a mutual loan agreement.[1193] The famous sculpture was commissioned by the Duke of Bedford for Woburn Abbey in Bedfordshire in the UK after he saw a previous version commissioned by the Empress Josephine. Finished in 1814, it arrived at Woburn Abbey in 1816 where it stood in a purpose built temple, surrounded by other neoclassical sculptures for nearly two centuries. The museums succeeded in matching the offering price of the J. Paul Getty Museum in California, which attempted to buy the Graces conditionally upon obtaining the necessary export license. The Government refused to grant the export license because they wanted to ensure that items of cultural heritage are retained in this country. Today, the sculpture is ex-

---

**1190** J.H. Merryman, Thinking about the Elgin Marbles, at 1915.

**1191** Fincham admits that such constellations present a difficult problem for any choice-of-law rule, cp. D. Fincham, Adopting the lex originis, at 114.

**1192** Generally to joint ownership of chattels see Judith Hill and Elisabeth Bowes-Smith in: N.E Palmer/E. McKendrick, Interests in Goods (2nd ed. 1998) 251. For joint tenancy in relation to works of art see M. Wantuch, Art Loans as a Diplomatic Solution (LLM Diss 2005), paper available with the author.

**1193** Cp. Sara Bush, Woburn Abbey and The Three Graces, at 269; The Harold Scottland, Three Graces to visit Scottland, 8. July 1995; The Independent, Court ruling likely to end battle for statue: 'Three Graces' set to stay in UK, 14 September 1994.

hibited by each museum in turn, spending approximately three years in each before moving again.

Similarly, in the case of some *Ethiopian tabots* the reason for the decision to lend 11 tabots was the "great religious significance of the tabots to the Ethiopian church".[1194] The tabots are wooden tablets, which are regarded by Ethiopian Christians as representing the original Ark of the Covenant, the wooden chest which once housed the Ten Commandments. They are highly sacrilegious and are not permitted to be touched or even seen by non-believers.[1195] Only a priest of the Ethiopian church is allowed to be near them.[1196] At present, the tabots are being stored in a special room in the basement of the British Museum, where no museum staff, not even curators or conservators are permitted to enter.[1197] On the condition that the tabots will be appropriately stored, the British Museum declared that it is willing to lend the artefacts to the Ethiopian church on a five year renewable loan basis.[1198] The British Museum followed the example of the St John's Episcopal Church in Edinburgh, which sparked huge celebrations in Ethiopia in 2002 when it returned an altar slab that had been given to the church by one of the officers in the campaign.

Marion Forsyth recently suggested the creation of an "International Cultural Property Trust" where countries should come together and establish trusts that would allow for shared responsibility and shared benefit of their cultural heritage.[1199] Such a trust may prove ownership by asserting an ironclad patrimony law that encompasses each country in which cultural objects are found; artefacts, if they are affiliated with that culture, necessarily must have originated in one of the countries party to the trust; the patrimony law will be clear and unambiguous.[1200] Indeed, Forsyth argues that a trust of that kind established by modern states that share ancient cultural boundaries would serve as a deterrent for looting of sites and yield increased scholarship. Furthermore, it would also facilitate international exchange through traveling public exhibitions, interdisci-

---

**1194** Tony Doubleday, legal advisor of the British Museum, in an interview with the author in 2006.

**1195** Martin Bailey, "UK museum face controversial Ethiopian legacy", The Art Newspaper, 18 Oct 2005.

**1196** M. Bailey, ibid.

**1197** Information received from Tony Doubleday legal advisor of the British Museum/London, in a interview with the author.

**1198** However, no contract has been drafted yet to actually make the loan happen, as the Ethiopian church cannot provide the appropriate premises.

**1199** M. Forsyth, International Cultural Property Trust, at 202 (discussing the example of the Japanese Trust for the Preservation of the World Cultural Heritage).

**1200** M. Forsyth, International Cultural Property Trust, at 205.

plinary research among scientists from various countries and fields of expertise, and public education through conferences, seminars, exhibits, and publications.[1201]

## § 5. Conclusion to Chapter 5

The lex situs-rule results in the application of national commercial laws whose solutions are extremely variable. As a consequence, traditional justifications such as commercial certainty, predictability and easy application have turned out to be inapplicable in cases concerning heritage items. Conversely, due to the differences in the substantive laws of certain jurisdictions, the lex situs-rule even creates legal uncertainty. Moreover, it enhances the illicit trade in cultural objects by enabling calculating dealers to buy and sell art in countries whose solution favours their personal transaction. It also encourages forum shopping, which is generally undesirable within the framework of conflict of laws. The divergence between the original owner and the subsequent purchaser is not being resolved by the application of the situs rule. Both parties may prove to be equally innocent. Consequently, the situs-rule governing title to movable cultural property is not an appropriate choice of law methodology in the context of art and antiquities.

This chapter suggests the lex rei sitae originis as an alternative choice of law rule for art disputes. It would allow for the application of heritage laws in foreign courts which would enhance the protection of cultural artefacts. The proposed choice of law rule can be summarised as follows:

> (1) The object in question has to be characterised as cultural property. For this purpose, the court will extrapolate common elements from international and national legislation which could amount to the following definition: "[o]bjects qualifying as cultural property are corporeal objects, movable or immovable, either unique or consisting of collections / ensembles, which have been either created, changed or formed by human effort or which represent human cultural development, and which are accorded historical, artistic, scientific, architectural, archaeological or any other cultural value of different dimensions."
> (2) There is a strong presumption that the lex originis is the governing law. The presumption is being rebutted in cases, where the lex originis does not grant any protection to bona fide purchasers. In such cases the traditional lex situs applies.
> (3) The lex situs-rule will only apply if the defendant can prove, that he has complied with the due diligence test set out by this rule. Otherwise, the lex originis applies.
> (4) Any limitation period invoked by the claimant only starts to run when the claimant has

1201 M. Forsyth, International Cultural Property Trust, at 204.

> or culpably did not discovere the whereabouts of the object.
> (5) The attribution of the object to a specific nation results from the determination of the closest connecting factor between the requesting state and the object. In cases where the nationality of the objects cannot be determined, either due to difficulties in proof, state succession or state division, as well as in cases of subjective cultural importance, the requesting states can act as joint claimants.

Although the proposed choice of law rule will not necessarily ensure the return of cultural property, the application of the lex rei sitae originis by the court, makes a recovery more likely. Of course, there is little question that international conventions and agreements would be a more direct and effective way to combat illicit trade in antiquities than choice of law rules.

# Chapter 6. Cross-Border Enforcement and Justiciability in a Comparative Perspective

## § 1. Introduction

The previous chapter has suggested an alternative choice-of-law-methodology in cases involving art and cultural property. Once it has been determined, according to rules of the conflict of laws, that a foreign law is applicable in a multi-jurisdictional case, the question arises whether that law, or acts based on this law indeed can be enforced.

The principle of justiciability has already been introduced in Chapter 1 of this book. The effect of this this non-enforcement-rule is fatal for sovereign claims for the recovery of cultural objects as – so it seems – courts per se will not apply a property interest stemming from another state's cultural property statute. Especially when a heritage item has been illegally excavated and taken outside the territory of its actual home country, the state will never had obtained possession of the antiquity, unless it has been forfeited during the export attempt. Consequently, it is being argued that a claim for recovery of such an object will amount to the enforcement of the state's prerogative right. In his famous speech in the House of Lords, Lord Denning admitted that "it might be very desirable that every country should enforce every other country's cultural property legislation – by enabling heritage items to be recovered and taken back to their original home. But does the law permit this?", he asked.[1202] It does in some aspects.

To answer this question, Part I of this book has comparatively elaborated legal mechanisms aimed at granting interests in cultural property to sovereigns. The purpose of this chapter is to explore the efficacy of legal mechanisms granting an interest in cultural property to states if presented in a foreign forum. The findings delineated in Chapter 2 in relation to sovereign rights to antiquities will thus be tested here as for their practicability in civil recovery. Many of the mechanisms introduced in Chapter 2 may end up to be non-justiciable if presented in a foreign forum and, as a consequence, can be viewed as rather useless instruments aimed at the protection of cultural property from theft and illegal export at an international level. An important factor in determining whether a claim is justiciable or non-justiciable will be the differentiation beween the recognition of

**1202** Att-Gen New Zealand v Ortiz [1984] AC 1, at 20 per Lord Denning.

a property interest and the enforcement thereof. These notions will be elaborated upon. The following Chapters conduct an analysis of English law in regard of the application of foreign cultural property laws. The results of this extrapolation will be compared to the legal positions upheld in the United States, Germany, and Switzerland.

## § 2. International Resolutions on the Justiciability of Foreign Public Law

Given the principle of territoriality, which is a corollary of each state's independence and equality in international law, courts of one nation do not enforce the public laws of another nation.[1203] According to this principle, the public law of a foreign state shall be exercised only on the territory of the state, which enacted it.[1204] For decades, the principle of territoriality is or was an almost "universal principle."[1205] The question whether foreign public laws may be applied in a national court has been discussed by the international community of several occasions:

### I. The Wiesbaden Resolution 1975

In its session of Wiesbaden in 1975, the Institute de Droit International in The Hague, an association of world-leading private and public international law

**1203** See especially Dicey/Morris/Collins, Conflict of Laws (14th ed. 2008), Rule 3 (1); FA Mann, Prerogative Rights of Foreign States and the Conflict of Laws, 40 Papers by the Grocius Society (1955) 25 (reprinted in F.A. Mann, Studies in International Law (1973) 492)); Christine Freytag, "Cultural Heritage": Rückgabeansprüche von Ursprungsländern auf "ihr" Kulturgut?, in: Fechner F.G., et al. (eds.) Prinzipien des Kulturgüterschutzes (1996) 175; L. Engstler, Die territoriale Bindung von Kulturgütern im Rahmen des Völkerrechts (1964), at 46 et seq; K. Siehr, Öffentliches Recht und internationales Privatrecht beim grenzüberschreitenden Kulturgüterschutz, in: Dolzer/Jayme/ Mußgnug (eds.) Rechtsfragen des internationalen Kulturgüterschutzes (1994) 83; cp. also the English cases: Don Alonso v Cornero, (1613) Hob. 212; Princess Paley Olga v Weisz, [1929] 1 K.B. 718 (CA); Government of India v Taylor [1955] AC 491; Attorney General of New Zealand v. Ortiz [1984] 1 A.C 1, 35 (H.L.).

**1204** Cp. e.g Jan Kroppholler, Internationales Privatrecht (6th ed 2006) at §22 II 2; Ivo Schwander, Einführung in das internationale Privatrecht Bd 1 (3rd ed 2000), at 73.

**1205** Cp. Dicey/Morris/Collins, Rule 3 (1), para 5R-019; Williams and Humbert Ltd v W&H Trademarks (Jersey) Ltd [1986] A.C 368, 428, per Lord Templemen, Derby & Co Ltd v Weldon ( no6) [1990] 1 W.L.R 1139 (CA), at 1154 per Staughton J.

scholars, adopted a resolution on the issue of the application of foreign public law by domestic courts.[1206] According to the "Resolution on the Application of Foreign Public Law", there is no argument for excluding foreign public law a priori from being enforced. The main reasoning of this resolution is that the public law character attributed to a provision of foreign law which is designated by the rule of conflict of laws shall not prevent the application of that provision, subject however to the fundamental reservation of public policy. The same shall apply whenever a provision of foreign law constitutes the condition for applying some other rule of law or whether it appears necessary to take the former provision into consideration.[1207] The Resolution further emphasises, that "the so called principle of the inapplicability of foreign public law", is firstly, "based on no cogent theoretical or practical reason", secondly, "often duplicates with the principle of public policy, and thirdly, it "may entail results that are undesirable and inconsistent with contemporary needs for international co-operation".[1208]

There is only one reservation to these principles: Foreign public law should not be applied if the claim which is based on provisions of public law is of such nature that only States or other public entities could raise it. In conclusion, the Resolution suggests to enforce claims based on provisions of private law which can be raised by any natural or legal person, including states or other public entities acting *iure gestionis*.[1209] This may be the case if the claim is under private law but is grounded on preliminary issues affected or even directly determined by foreign public law. Such a preliminary issue may be for example a question of ownership to a chattel.

## II. Resolution of the "Institute de Droit International"

The 1991 Basel Resolution has already been analysed in connection with the application of the *lex originis* as a choice of law rule to cultural property dis-

**1206** The Institute of International Law was founded on 8 September 1873 in Belgium as an institution independent of any governmental influence in order to be able to contribute to the development of international law and take action for its proper implementation, cp. M. Weller, Kunstrechtspiegel 03/07, 172. More information on the history and ideology of the Institute can be found on: http://www.idi-iil.org.

**1207** For an account on the resolution see M. Weller, Kunstrechtspiegel 03/07, at 173.

**1208** See Report of Pierre Lalive, L'application du droit public etranger, Institute de Droit International, Annuaire Vol. 56, Session de Wiesbaden 1975, at 219 et seq.

**1209** Cp, M. Weller, Kunstrechtspiegel 03/07, 173.

putes.[1210] We remember, the Resolution was designed as a conflict of laws instrument, proposing that the transfer of ownership of works of art belonging to the cultural heritage of the country shall be governed by the *lex originis*.[1211] However, the philosophy of the instrument is equally relevant to the application of foreign public law and the cross- border enforcement of claims to heritage items in general. First of all, the Preamble of the Resolution supports the view that every country has the right and the duty to take measure to preserve its cultural heritage and, in principle, these protective measures shall be recognised by every country. In consequence, the Resolution supports the author's view that property interests arising from a foreign cultural property satute should be recognised in a foreign forum for the purpose of the cross-border enforcement of claims. Secondly, the Resolution expressly addresses the application of foreign export prihibtion relating to cultural objects in Art. 3. There it is provided that "provisions of the law of the country of origin governing the export of works of art shall apply". Art. 1 (2) of the Resolution furthermore affirms that it relates to "sales of works of art concluded *before* or *after* the property has been exported from the territory of the country of origin in breach of the non-retrospective legislation on the latter on the export of cultural property". Here, the Resolution therefore expressly breaks with the traditional principle of territoriality in relation to the application of foreign public law.

However, the application of foreign public law is restricted to to cultural items which have been identified as "belonging to the cultural heritage of a country by registration, classification or by any relevant internationally accepted method of publicity", Art 1 a of the Resolution. The methodology reminds of the implementation of the UNESCO 1970 Convention by Germany which uses the "list principle" in order to narrow down the ambit of the Convention.[1212] As a result, illegally excavated archaeological objects are not encompassed by the Resolution. However, this does not mean that the Resolution excludes the recogition of ownership declarations contained in foreign cultural patrimony laws as such.

The Resolution is non-binding but contributes to the creation of soft-law in this field which might become relevant in cases where courts have to determine the content of "good morals" or trade customs by resorting to international standards[1213]. So far, the Resolution has influenced academic debate regarding

**1210** 64 II Yearbook of the Institute of International Law, at 403–407 (1992).

**1211** Cp. Chapter 5 IV 3.

**1212** Cp. Chapter 4 § 3 IV 2 b (1).

**1213** For example the German provision 138 BGB dealing with the morality commercial transaction, see the Nigeria-case (German Supreme Court BGH 22.6. 1972) – see also Chapter 6 § 5 III.

the application of foreign laws,[1214] but no court decisions has referred to it in its judgment.

### III. Resolution adopted by the International Law Association in 1988

In another conference in 1988, the International Law Association adopted a Resolution in Warsaw concerning the "Transnational Recognition and Enforcement of Foreign Public Laws."[1215] The Resolution adopted by the International Law Association states that "the general presumption in private international law should be that foreign public law ought not per se to be accorded special treatment when considering their entitlement to recognition or enforcement". This latter Resolution goes on to emphasise that a court may "limit its recognition of, or decline to enforce, a foreign law on ground of the forum's public policy, the European ordre public or any related concept; but that exceptional restraint should be exercised in this regard in a transnational context".[1216]

The clear trend of the aforementioned resolutions is consequently in favour of liberalising the traditional approaches in relation to the non-justiciability foreign public laws. The following paragraphs will analyse whether national laws indeed reflect this liberal trend. The analysis will encompass England and Wales, The United States of America, Germany, and, Switzerland.

## § 3. England and Wales

According to the conflict of laws ground work "Dicey, Morris and Collins", Rule 3 (1), English courts have no jurisdiction to entertain an action for the enforcement, either directly or indirectly, of a penal, revenue, or other public law of a foreign State.[1217] This is a principle which according to Dicey is "almost univer-

---

**1214** Cp. e. g. Matthias Weller, Some Observations on the Application of Foreign Public Law by Domestic Courts from a Comparative Perspective, 04 Kunstrechtspiegel (2007), 172.

**1215** The International Law Association is a non-profit organisation founded in Brussels in 1873. Its objectives uder its Constitution are "the study, clarification and development of both private and public interntional law and the furtherance of international understanding and respect for international law.", see www. Ila.org. Conference reports are available via the web-site and www. heinonline.org.

**1216** Proceedings of the Sixty-Third International Law Association Conference 1988 in Warsaw, report available at www.ila-hq.org.

**1217** Cp Dicey/Morris/ Collins, Rule 3 (1), at 5–019.

sal", that according to Lord Denning "no one has ever doubted",[1218] and which Kerr L.J. characterised as being "of general international acceptation".[1219]

The historic justification of reluctance to enforce foreign penal, revenue or other so-called public laws in England was restated by Lord Keith in *Government of India v. Taylor*[1220] when, with specific reference to foreign revenue laws, he said that "enforcement of such laws would constitute an extension of the sovereign power which imposes the taxes", and "an assertion of sovereign authority by one state within the territory of another, as distinct from a patrimonial claim by a foreign state and is contrary to all concepts of independent sovereignties."

However, Dicey Rule 3 (1) does not prevent the recognition of a foreign law. When enforcement does not arise, a foreign law of a type falling into the ambit of Rule 3 (1) will be recognised if it is relevant to the issue,[1221] and provided it is not contrary to public policy.[1222] The question whether a foreign state can sustain a claim for the recovery of cultural property in an English court consequently must depend on whether the claim is characterised to be one of enforcement or recognition. However, the import of the differentiation between recognition and enforcement is unclear. Weller, for instance, holds the view that under English law direct enforcement occurs when a foreign state raises a claim on its rules of public law, whereas recognition could be described as "taking into account or "into consideration" of foreign public laws within the framework of the applicable private law.[1223]

In order to solve the conundrum as to what constitutes recognition and what constitutes enforcement, the author will rely on Lord Keith's distinction as between patrimonial claims, which ought to be recognised in English courts, and prerogative claims, which ought not to be enforced. To substantiate this suggestion the ambit of both types of claims will have to be defined. At the centre of this question stands *Iran v. Barakat Galleries*[1224]. There, the Court of Appeal found that a claim for the return of ancient Iranian artefacts was patrimonial in nature as Iran's claim was one to assert rights of ownership, that could equally adhere to a natural person. The facts of the judgment have already been summar-

**1218** Attorney-General of New Zealand v. Ortiz [1984] A.C. 1, 19.

**1219** In Re State of Norway's Application [1987] Q.B. 433, 478.

**1220** [1955] A.C. 491, 511.

**1221** Re Emry's Investment Trust [1959] Ch. 410; Regazzoni v KC Sethia Ltd [1956]2 Q.B 490, 515 ( CA), affirmed [1958]; Att-Gen of New Zealand v Ortiz [1984] A.C. 1, 20 ( CA), per Lord Denning.

**1222** Re Helbert Wagg & Co Ltd. [1956] Ch 323, 345–349.

**1223** See M. Weller, Iran v Barakat, at 176.

**1224** Government of Iran v Barakat Galleries Ltd. [2007] EWHC 705 (QB); [2007] EWHCA Civ 1374; [2008] 1 All ER 1177; QB 22 [2009].

ised in the introduction to this study but the decision itself will be discussed in different sections of the following paragraph, in order to illustrate the various legal problem areas.[1225]

## I. Enforcement: Prerogative Claims to Cultural Objects

Where a state has not obtained title to a chattel in the same way a private citizen would have obtained the right, it remains unclear whether the state claim is justiciable in English and Welsh courts. Since in the case of newly discovered antiquities the state cannot rely on any previous possession or other root of title, in order to make good his title in the proceedings, it has to rely on the legal statute, which allegedly vests the property right in him. It is being contended that a claim, which is not patrimonial in nature, but grounded on its peculiar powers of prerogative, cannot constitute a case of recognition of a state's property right but will be treated as a claim for enforcement and thus rendered non-justiciable. This approach, which in due course will be called the "public international law approach", relies on the territoriality doctrine and, accordingly, on Dicey Rule 3 (1). It considers claims, which are based on foreign penal, revenue or other public laws to be *acta jure imperii* or in other words, an assertion of a sovereign right.[1226] According to this approach, a state would be unable to recover a looted artefact of which it never obtained possession before it left its territory, as the claim's true purpose was to enforce the state's prerogative right. Consequently, in order to be deemed unenforceable, a cultural property claim will

**1225** Government of Iran v Barakat has also been mentioned in relation to property rights on the ground of an immediate right of possession, note Chapter 2 II.

**1226** For advocates of this view see, FA Mann, Prerogative Rights of Foreign States, in: Studies in International Law (1973) 492, at 497; FA Mann, The International Enforcement of Public Rights, 19 N.Y University J. of Int'l Law and Politics (1987) 603; Ignaz Seidl-Hohenveldern, Internationales Konfikations- und Enteignungsrecht (1952), at 38 et seq.; William H. Kenety, Who Onws the Past? The Need for Legal Reform and Reciprocity in the International Art Trade, 23 Cornell Int'l L.J. (1990) 1, at 35 et seq; J.H. Merryman, Thinking about the Elgin Marbles, 83 Michigan L. Rev. (1985) 890; and also Dicey/Morris/Collins, The Conflicts of Laws, Rule 3(1), at 5–020, although in the most recent issue, Collins admits that a certain degree of flexibility is recommended, cp. also on this recent moderate view Lawrence Collins, Professor Lowenfeld and the Enforcement of Foreign Public Law, 42 Int'l Law and Politics (2009) 125. See also the cases Emperor of Austria v Day (1861) 3 De G& F. J. 217, at 232 and 238; Government of India v Taylor [1955] A.C.491, at 511; A-G of New Zealand v Ortiz, [1984] AC 1; President of the State of Equatorial Guinea v Royal Bank of Scotland, 2006UKPC 7; Mbasago v Logo,[2006]EWCA Civ 1370, [2007] QB 846. See President of the State of Equatorial Guinea v Royal Bank of Scotland [2006] UKPC 7; Mbasago v Logo Ltd. [2007] 2 WLR 1062.

have to be considered *acta jure imperii*, and more specifically, it will have to be based on a foreign penal, revenue, or other public law. In due course, we will discuss the distinction between *acta jure gestionis* and *acta jure imperii*, and further the notions 'penal and 'other public laws' in the sense of 'Dicey Rule 3'. As cultural heritage statutes in most circumstances will not be held to be of a revenue character, it has not been thought necessary to discuss this option.

### 1. Acta Jure Gestionis and Acta Jure Imperii

The public international law approach derives from the works of Dr. FA Mann.[1227] In his essay "Prerogative Rights of Foreign States and the Conflict of Laws"[1228] he concluded that by enforcing prerogative claims, a state would assert its sovereignty within the territory of another state.[1229] Mann bases his doctrine of unenforceability of foreign public laws on international law doctrines of jurisdiction.[1230] The enforcement of a state's public right "involves the infringement of domestic jurisdiction or sovereignty and, accordingly, of public international law insofar as the consent of the forum state is lacking".[1231]

Whether a right is a prerogative right is a question to be answered by public international law, that is to say by reference to what public international law considers as rights exclusively or essentially exercisable within the territorial limits of a state's jurisdiction".[1232] The question to be decided when a state acts by virtue of it sovereign authority, in Mann's view, should not be decided by the forum's conceptions of law. Rather the court should ascertain "the substance of the right sought to be enforced".[1233] This means that it must interpret the claimant state's asserted right in the light of the rule of public international law applicable to interference with the forum's states jurisdiction. Thus, it is not for the forum state to decide whether a state's claim is a public law claim. According to Mann,

1227 FA Mann, Prerogative Rights, at 497.

1228 FA Mann, Prerogative Rights, at 492.

1229 FA Mann, The International Enforcement of Public Rights, 19 N.Y University J. of Int'l Law and Politics (1987) 603, at 624 et seq.

1230 See FA Mann, International Enforcement, at 608.

1231 Mann originally took the view that the attempt of a claimant state to enforce its public law extraterritorially involved a breach of public international law by the claimant state in that it committed an excess of its own jurisdiction, see Mann in Prerogative Rights (1955), at 46; in: International Enforcement, at 609 et seq.

1232 Cp. FA Mann, International Enforcement, at 609.

1233 Cp. FA Mann, International Enforcement, at 613, citing Viscount Simonds in Adams v National Bank of Greece S.A, 1961 A.C. 255, 274 (1960).

the real question is whether international law regards the claim as constituting an infringement of the sovereignty of the forum state.[1234]

In order to distinguish foreign acts, which can be enforced, from acts which cannot, he relies on the classification of *acta jure imperii* and *acta jure gestionis*. The expressions derive from the law of immunity and from the law of state contracts.[1235] The first class – *acta jure imperii* – comprises those acts, which are done by a state's virtue of his sovereign authority, that means activities of a governmental or public nature, the second – *acta jure gestionis* – comprises acts where the state acts otherwise than a sovereign in private or commercial matters.[1236] In Mann's view, it is *acta jure imperii* that shall not be enforced in foreign courts. Although he admits that it does not automatically follow that the courts must refuse the enforcement of *acta jure imperii*, Mann regards the character of the rule as "absolute".[1237]

A claim for the return of illegally excavated artefacts in Mann's view would be regarded an *acta jure imperii*, if the property is situated in a foreign territory and has never been in the possession of the requesting government. To grant such a claim would amount to the enforcement of a prerogative right, which is contrary to public international law. Concerning the protection of cultural heritage, Mann's views have been adopted in the following cases:

### a. Attorney General of New Zealand v Ortiz

The public international law approach was followed by Lord Denning in *Att-Gen of New Zealand v Ortiz*,[1238] where he relied on Mann's distinction as between acta jure imperii and acta jure gestionis.[1239] In this case, which was tried in the early 1980s in the United Kingdom, New Zealand sought the return of Maori panels that had been illegally exported under its cultural property export law in the

**1234** Cp. FA Mann, International Enforcement, at 613.

**1235** See for example Sompong Sucharitkul, State Immunity and Trading Activities in International Law (1959); N.C.H. Dunbar, Controversial Aspects of Sovereign Immunity in Some States, 132 Hague Recueil (1971) 197. Thereby activities acta jure imperii qualify for state immunity under the modern doctrine of "restrictive foreign sovereign immunity", whereas acta jure gestionis do not, cp. William Tetley, Maritime Liens and Claims (2nd ed. 1998), at 1162 and 1184. See also the UK State Immunity Act 1978, c. 33.

**1236** Cp. FA Mann, Prerogative Rights, at 494; William Tetley, Maritime Liens and Claims (2nd ed. 1998), at 1162.

**1237** Cp. FA Mann, International Enforcement, at 611.

**1238** [1984] 2 WLR 809; [1984] A.C. 1. However, Staughton J. expressed a different view in the first instance, cp. [1982] Q.B. 349.

**1239** [1984] A.C.1, at 20.

early 1970s. The claim was rejected because in New Zealand the exporter legally owned the panels so long as the panels were still located within New Zealand and the carvings were not seized before they left New Zealand territory. The key issue of the case was that the seizure of the panels outside New Zealand territory would amount to the enforcement of the government's sovereign right unless the statute provided for automatic forfeiture. If it did, seizure of the panels would not have been necessary and the recovery of the panels from England would not constitute an enforcement of a sovereign right. In case of automatic forfeiture, title to the panels automatically would have passed to the Crown while still on the territory of New Zealand, even though the state never obtained actual possession of them.

According to the New Zealand Historic Articles Act 1962 it is prohibited to export historic articles without an export permit (sec. 5). If any historical article has been illegally exported, sec. 12 (2) provided[1240]:

> "A historic article knowingly exported or attempted to be exported in breach of this Act shall be forfeited to her majesty and, subject to the provisions of this Act, the provisions of the Customs Act 1913 relating to forfeited goods shall apply to any such article in same manner as they apply to goods forfeited under the Customs Act 1913."

The New Zealand Customs Act 1913, replaced by the Customs Act 1966, says in Section 274:

> "When it is provided by this Act or any other of the Customs Acts that any goods are forfeited, and the goods are seized in accordance with this Act or with the Act under which the forfeiture has accrued, the forfeiture shall for all purposes relate back to the date of the act or event from which the forfeiture accrued."

In first instance, Staughton J. concluded that title automatically passed to the Crown upon illegal export of the panels. An English court would recognise the Crown's ownership rights and it was in accordance with public policy to do so. He held that the purpose of the Act, in his view, is to secure the enjoyment of historic articles for the people of New Zealand and that purpose is plainly advanced if articles exported or attempted to be exported become automatically the property of the state and can if necessary be recovered from the Crown.

**1240** See the New Zealand Historic Articles Act 1962, Section 5 and Section 12(2) and the New Zealand Customs Act 1939, Section 274.

Conversely, the Court of Appeal held that New Zealand law did not provide for automatic forfeiture. Seizure was held to be necessary.[1241] Given the absence of automatic forfeiture, the title to the panels had not been vested in the government before they left New Zealand territory. Under public international law, seizure is limited to the territory of the sovereign state.[1242] Because the Maori carvings were not seized in New Zealand, it was not forfeited there. New Zealand had to rely on the Historical Articles Act, as well as on its Customs Act and the export prohibitions it entailed, in order to recover the panels. Consequently, the court had to consider the justiciability of New Zealand's claim.

Lord Denning held in a famous speech that, the New Zealand law was a public law in the sense of Dicey Rule 3 and to enforce New Zealand law abroad would amount to an extra territorial effect of that law, which would violate public international law. He reached the following conclusion:

> "If any court should have legislation prohibiting the export of works of art, and providing for the automatic forfeiture of them to the state should they be exported, then that falls into the category of public laws which will not be enforced by the courts of the country to which it is exported, or any other country because it is an act done in the exercise of sovereign authority which will not be enforced outside its own territory."[1243]

In that manner, Lord Denning has put the inapplicability of foreign public law as a principle generally accepted within the UK conflict of laws.[1244] In the House of Lords, Lord Brightman agreed that the New Zealand law did not have the effect of an automatic forfeiture and that neither ownership nor a right of possession had vested in New Zealand. However, he stated that recovery would be allowed in a case in which title to the historic article had vested in the crown independently of seizure. He thus stated the requirement that the antiquities in question have to be located in the country at the time vesting of title takes place in order to be successfully recovered.

**1241** See already the findings in Chapter 2, at II 2 (1) (a).

**1242** See K. Siehr, International Art Trade, at 186. Compare also Chapter 2 II 2.

**1243** [1984] A.C.1, at 24.

**1244** Conversely, Ackner L.J. held that New Zealand was seeking to enforce a penal law because the statute effected a confiscation of otherwise validly owned historic properties upon illegal export.

#### b. Iran v Barakat: First Instance Decision[1245]

In the first Instance of *Iran v Barakat*, which was later overruled by the Court of Appeal, Justice Gray endorsed the public international law approach as adopted by Lord Denning in the *Ortiz-case*. The two preliminary issues of the case were: (i) could Iran show that it obtained title to the antiquities under Iranian law and (ii) if Iran could show it obtained title, would that title be recognised and enforced in English courts to the extent that it would satisfy a claim in conversion?

The Government of Iran claimed that according to Iranian law it was the owner of the antiquities, even though it does not appear ever to have had actual possession of them, and that this property right is capable of being recognised in an English court. Iran's claim was based on a direct reliance on Iranian cultural property provisions. Justice Gray answered both preliminary questions to the negative: He examined the various laws of Iran that pertain to its archaeological heritage, in particular the National Heritage Protection Act 1930, The Executive Regulations of the National Heritage Protection Act, and the 1979 Legal Bill, which prohibits clandestine digging and illegal excavation to obtain antiquities and historical relics that are more than 100 years old. Justice Gray held that the Iranian provisions could not be construed as conferring title to the antiquities in the Iranian State.

However, the judge upheld the alternative submission that, in the event Iranian law did not confer ownership of the antiquities on Iran, Iranian law did confer an immediate right of possession of the antiquities.[1246] *Obiter dictum*, Justice Gray came to the conclusion that even if he had held Iran to be the owner of the antiquities in question, this title could not be enforced in English courts as it would be an acta jure imperii and thus an exercise of a sovereign right.[1247] By doing so, Justice Gray completely denied the efficacy of national ownership of antiquities. After assuming hypothetically that Iran obtained a valid title to the artefacts it requested to be returned, Justice Gray concluded that property rights which derive from a national ownership statute cannot be enforced in England, because acquisition by means of a national ownership law is a method available only to sovereigns. The judge based his judgment on the following assumptions: First, he recognised the principle that English courts generally will not sustain a claim for the enforcement of foreign penal, revenue or other public laws and called it "well established". He then characterised the act of vesting ownership of antiquities in the government by a public law statute as an act

**1245** [2007] EWHC 705 (QB).
**1246** [2007] EWHC 705 (QB), at 75.
**1247** [2007] EWHC 705 (QB), at 98.

of sovereign authority that is an act jure imperii, which led him to the conclusion that the Iranian provisions were public in nature. As a result, the claim brought by Iran was held to be a claim to enforce a public right for state ownership, as opposed to a patrimonial claim, which would have been justiciable.

In his judgement, Justice Gray even further extended the principles of the public international law approach. By hypothetically assuming that Iran had obtained a valid title and concluding that its enforcement would amount to an exercise of a sovereign authority, he excluded claims for the recovery of artefacts even in the case the state has obtained possession of the antiquities and thus perfected its title before the artefact left its territory.[1248] Hence, his judgment considerably extended the principles laid down in Ortiz by Lord Denning.

**1248** In his judgement, Justice Gray referred to two related cases, which were decided shortly before the Barakat-case commenced and which he found were an authority for the Public International Law approach: President of the State of Equatorial Guinea v Royal Bank of Scotland, 2006 UKPC 7, which was tried before the Privy Council and the parallel proceedings in Mbasogo v Logo [2006] EWCA Civ 1370; [2007] QB 846.

In the Equatorial Guinea-case, the court reaffirmed the public international law approach as proposed by Dr. Mann. The case emerged from the aftermath of an attempted coup in Equatorial Guinea in 2004 that was masterminded by a number of British citizens. Instead, both the state of Equatorial Guinea and its president, Mbasogo, sued the key parties involved for an injunction to prevent a further coup attempt and for damages to compensate the state for losses incurred in repelling the coup. Citing Dicey/Morris/Collins, Rule 3, and referring to what Lord Denning said in *Ortiz*, the Guernsey Court concluded that the claim was not justiciable in English courts as it involved the extraterritorial assertion of sovereign authority, namely, claims to preserve the security of the state and it's ruler, at 24–25, per Lord Bingham of Cornhill and Lord Hoffmann.

In the parallel proceeding in the High Court of England and Wales, Mbasogo v Logo [2006] EWCA Civ. 1370; [2007] QB 846, the case was also dismissed following the argumentation of the Privy Council. The appeal was not pursued by the claimants. The Court of Appeal held that the Government's claim involved "an extension of the sovereign power" (at 63), and could not proceed. The judge expressly emphasised that "it is not in doubt that the courts of one country will not enforce the penal, revenue laws and public laws of another country" (at 29). The Court in Mbasago thought the crucial question to be whether the relevant act were of sovereign character, being acts which may be done by the state alone. The court held that the claims in *Mbasago* arose from the sovereign act of defending the state. However, the claimants in *Mbasogo* were not attempting to apply a foreign law, but were content for the English law of tort to govern the claim. It rightly recognised that the English court had jurisdiction over the claim because it does not involve a foreign public law, but it rules out the possibility of the English court deciding such a case because the issues are not justiciable in an English court. Thus the Mbasago-claim does not fall within the direct scope of Dicey Rule 3. The rationale of the rule was applied analogously as *Mbasago* in the court's view involved the reliance on prerogative rights of the state to found its claim.

Justice Gray clearly misinterpreted the reasoning in the *Ortiz-case*, where Lord Brightman emphasised that New Zealand's claim would have been enforced if it had obtained title before the artefacts left their territory. However, would we hypothetically apply Justice Gray's ratio to the various mechanisms of acquiring and retaining property rights to antiquities, as presented in Chapter 2 of this thesis, none of these legal instruments would be justiciable in English courts.

### 2. 'Penal laws' within the Context of Dicey Rule 3 (1)

If the cultural property legislation the claimant state relies on is characterised as be penal, it is settled that an English court will not lend its aid to its enforcement.[1249] It is being assumed that penal laws *are acta jure imperii.*[1250] The rule against the enforcement of penal laws was said to have its foundation in the principle that crimes are recognisable and punishable only in the country where they were committed, and accordingly no proceeding, even in the shape of a civil suit, which had as its object the enforcement of punishment imposed for breaches, ought to be admitted by the courts of any other country.[1251] Whether a foreign law, or a claim based on foreign law, is to be characterised as penal depends on English law.[1252] It does not depend on the label given to the law by the foreign system.[1253] Generally, English law defines penal to include not only crimes in the strict sense but "all breaches of public law punishable by pecuniary mulct or otherwise at the instance of the state government (…). Thus for this purpose, a penal law is a law which punishes or prevents[1254] an offence.[1255]

Laws may be characterised as penal even if they do not form part of the criminal code of a foreign country.[1256] In *Att-Gen of New Zealand v Ortiz*, Ackner L.J. and O'Connor L.J. held *obiter* that the New Zealand Historical Articles Act 1962 intended to protect the historic heritage by forfeiting cultural heritage ille-

**1249** Cp e.g. Cheshire/North/Fawcett, Ch 8, at 126. See also the cases Ogden v Folliot (1790) 3 Term Rep 726; Wolff v Oxholm (1817) 6 M&S 92; Huntington v Attrill [1893] AC 150; Banco de Vizcaya v Don Alfonso de Burbon y Austria [1935] 1 KB 140; Frankfurter v WL Exner Ltd. [1947] Ch 629; Epmresa Exportadora de Azucar v Industria Azucarera National SA, The Playa Larga [1983] 2 Lloyd's Rep 171; Williams and Humbert Ltd. v W and H Trade Marks (Jersey) Ltd. [1986] AC 368.
**1250** Iran v Barakat [2007] EWCA Civ 1374, at 93.
**1251** Huntington v Attrill [1893] A.C. 150, 156.
**1252** Cheshire/North/Fawcett, Chapter 8, at 126.
**1253** Huntington v Attrill at 155; Iran v Barakat [2008] 1 All E.R. 1177, at 106.
**1254** Schemmer v Property Resources Ltd [1975] Ch. 273, at 288.
**1255** Dicey/Morris/Collins, Rule 3, at 5–027.
**1256** [1984] A.C. 1 (CA), at 33 per Ackner L.J.

gally exported was a penal law in the sense of Dicey Rule 3.[1257] In considering whether sect. 12 of the Act was penal, Ackner L.J. first accepted that forfeiture in certain circumstances may be a penalty. Following that, he noted that the purpose of the New Zealand statute was the preservation of the cultural heritage act of New Zealand and the provisions for forfeiture were but a deterrent by-product of the statute. He also found that the fact that it carries with it unpleasant consequences does not make it penal. However, what made the statute penal in his view was the fact that the vindication of the Maori carvings by New Zealand was not sought by the acquisition of the article in exchange for proper compensation but through confiscation. Ackner L.J. went on to submit that although the general purpose of the Act of 1962 is to preserve the historical articles of New Zealand, a suit to enforce the forfeiture provisions contained in sect. 12 of the Act is still a suit by the state to vindicate the public justice.[1258] He believed it to be unreal to suggest that when a foreign state seeks to enforce forfeiture provisions in another country, it is not seeking to enforce a foreign penal law.[1259] On appeal to the House of Lords, the decision of the Court of Appeal was upheld solely on the narrow point of construction of the New Zealand Statute. The Law Lords, having heard no argument on the point relating to the enforcement of penal law, declined to express any opinion on the correctness of the *obiter dicta* on this matter of the Court of Appeal.[1260]

When categorising a law to be penal and thus unenforceable, the court has to characterise the particular provisions which the claim is based on rather than the statute as a whole. The circumstance that a provision is found within a law, which contains criminal sanctions, such as penalties or forfeiture, does not mean that the provision itself is automatically penal in nature. Equally, the fact that some provisions of a legal statute impose penalties does not render the whole statute penal. This was the important insight of the Court of Appeals decision in Iran v Barakat. While in the first instance of the case, Justice Gray characterised the Iranian provisions to be penal in nature,[1261] the Court of Appeal held the provisions which Iran based his claim on were not penal in nature, notwithstanding the fact that the Iranian 1979 Legal Bill was in large part penal in that it created criminal offences with criminal penalties for unlawfully excavating or dealing with antiquities.[1262] Although the CA did not offer a definition

**1257** Ibid, at 34–35.
**1258** Ibid, at 34.
**1259** Ibid, at 34.
**1260** [1984] A.C. 1 (HL), at 45–49 per Lord Brightman.
**1261** [2007] EWHC 705 (QB), at 90.
**1262** [2007] EWCA Civ. 1374, at 111.

of "penal law", it did offer a methodology of how to ascertain whether a law is penal. It concluded that the changes in title that the provisions of the 1979 bill made in relation to ownership of antiquities were neither confiscatory nor penal. They also did not deprive anyone who already owned antiquities of their title to them. They altered the law as to the ownership of antiquities that had not yet been found, with the effect that these would be owned by the state, subject to the entitlement of the chance finder to a reward.[1263]

As a result of *Ortiz* and *Barakat*, laws which vest ownership in the state *ab initio* will not be considered to be penal in nature whereas, a law which is confiscatory in that it deprives an individual who already became an owner of an antiquity without proper compensation would be rendered penal. Applied to the finding in Chapter 2 of this book, confiscatory laws that vest ownership *ex lege* in the state would not be rendered unenforceable while confiscatory laws based upon an administrative act may end up to be interpreted as "penal" in England. Export laws which work by means of an optional purchase offer may also share this fate, similar to the mechanisms presented in Chapter 2 III 4.[1264]

### 3. 'Other Public Laws' within the Context of Dicey Rule 3 (1)

Given that the cultural heritage provision, which the claimant state relies on, is neither a 'revenue' nor a 'penal law', it will have to be determined whether it may be considered an 'other public law' within the context of Dicey Rule 3 (1). In *Att-Gen of New Zealand v Ortiz* Lord Denning recognised that there was a residual category of foreign public laws, aside from penal and revenue laws, which the English court would not enforce but admitted that the scope of the principle which 'other public laws' cannot be enforced was unclear.[1265] As common law does – as of yet – not recognise any exact distinction between public and private laws, it is difficult to give a precise definition of the concept of 'public laws' which ought not to be enforced in England.

#### a. Unjusiticiable Public Laws – A Conundrum

The part of Dicey Rule 3 (1) referring to 'other public law' has its origin in the 4th edition[1266] when it appeared as 'political law', citing *Emperor of Austria v Day*

**1263** [2007] EWCA Civ. 1374, at 111.
**1264** For export laws on the grounds of an optional purchase offer see Chapter 2 III 4.
**1265** [2007] EWHC 705 (QB), at 20.
**1266** K. Berriedale/A.V. Dicey (ed.s), Conflict of Laws (4th ed. 1927) Rule 54, at 224.

*and Kossuth*,[1267] and distinguishing proprietary rights from claims to enforce political laws. The expression 'political law' was replaced by 'other public law' in the 7th edition.[1268] This was in response to criticism of the expression 'political law' by Dr Mann in his essay 'Prerogative Rights of Foreign States and the Conflict of Laws',[1269] and by Parker L.J. in *Regazzoni v K.C. Sethia*.[1270] The new expression 'public law' was intended to be equivalent to 'prerogative right', the term used by Dr Mann.[1271]

In *Barakat*, the Iranian government made the submission that the Iranian cultural heritage provisions by virtue of which ownership of antiquities vest in the state are not to be classified as 'other public laws'.[1272] Iran argued that the subject matter of such laws is limited to laws whose objectives are determined by the nature and policies of the government of the foreign state for the time being. The category does not extend to laws which are necessary in the long term interest of the state and not exclusively or principally in the political interest of whatever government has enacted them. Iran thus seeked to narrow the ambit of the concept of a 'public law' to what formerly was called a 'political law'.

According to Dicey and Morris, the expression 'public law' refers to all rules (other than penal and revenue laws), which are enforced as an assertion of the authority of a central or local government. It is submitted that the prohibitions of the penal and revenue laws are examples of a wider principle that a state cannot enforce its public law or a prerogative right.[1273] The public laws involved would include, according to Dicey and Morris, such topics as import and export control, trading with the enemy legislation, or price-control regulations.[1274]

In the *Ortiz-case*, Lord Denning suggested that 'public laws' are *eiusdem generis* with 'penal' or 'revenue' laws.[1275] He found a common thread underlying these three categories in the principles applied in international law. Lord Denning, referring to Prof. FA Mann, holds the view that one might have recourse to the distinction between *jure imperii* and *jure gestionis*,[1276] as it derives from

**1267** (1861) 3 De GF & J 217.
**1268** J.H.C. Morris et al (eds.), Dicey, Conflict of Laws (7th ed. 1958) Rule 21, at 159.
**1269** F.A. Mann, Studies in International Law (1973), at 500.
**1270** (1944) Ltd [1956] 2 QB 490, at 524.
**1271** J.H.C. Morris et al (eds), Conflict of Laws (1958) at 162, marginal note 60.
**1272** (2007) EWHC 705 (QB), at 94.
**1273** Dicey/ Morris/Collins, Rule 3, at 5–032.
**1274** Dicey/Morris/Collins, Rule 3, at 5–033.
**1275** [1984] A.C. 1, at 20–21 per Lord Denning.
**1276** [1984] A.C. 1, at 14.

the law of state immunity.[1277] He concluded with regard to the actual circumstances of the case that "if any country should have legislation prohibiting the export of works of art, and providing for automatic forfeiture of the state, then that falls into the category of 'other public laws' which will not be enforced by the country to which it is exported, or any other country, because it is an act done in the exercise of sovereign power."[1278]

P.B. Carter criticises Mann's and Lord Denning's approach as creating anomalous contrasts,[1279] as well as representing "insular attitudes of the bygone age."[1280] In Carter's view, an alternative approach is that penal and revenue laws are separate categories, and that unwillingness to enforce them is based upon differing policy considerations. Moreover, he contends, that either 'other public laws' constitute a third identifiable category, or the phrase 'public laws' simply denotes in this context "a miscellany of foreign laws concerning the enforcement of which a forum will often entertain considerable reservations."[1281]

It is perhaps best, to first assess whether the foreign law under consideration may properly be characterised as a penal or revenue law. It is only if the answer to that question is in the negative that a consideration of the scope of public law in this context should take place. The non-application of a public law in this sense should be limited to the enforcement of claims by the foreign state relating to the exercise of its governmental power.

### b. The Adoption of the 'Governmental Interest' – Test

The question whether a state claim for the vindication of an interest on the ground of a public statute is justiciable was considered by the Hight Court of Australia in the *Spycatcher-case.*[1282] Although the case concerns the protection of intellectual property rights, it was thought imperative to discuss the decision,

---

**1277** For the law of state immunity see for example, Kuwait Airways Corp v Iraqi Airways Co 1 WLR [1995] 1147, at 1156, per Lord Goff of Chieveley. It bears relationship to the distinction, which has been applied by the ECJ to determine whether a claim is a "civil and commercial matter" for the purpose of the Brussels Convention and Brussels I Regulation, where the question is whether or not the state is acting in the exercise of its powers, see Iran v Barakat, [2007] EWCH Civ. 1374 and cases cited in Dicey/Morris/Collins, para 11–025.

**1278** [1984] A.C. 1, at 24 per Lord Denning.

**1279** Cp. P.B. Carter, Transnational Recognition and Enforcement, at 427.

**1280** Carter, ibid, at 428.

**1281** Cp. Carter, ibid, at 427.

**1282** Att-Gen (UK) v Heinemann Publishers Australia Pty Ltd. (1988) 165 CLR 30.

as it produced a test for assertion of an unenforceable public law which was also adopted by English courts.[1283]

In *Spycatcher*, the High Court of Australia rejected any propositions previously made to define public laws and suggested to render actions unjusticiable which enforce the "governmental interest" of a foreign state. The facts of the case are the following: the British Government sought to prevent publication of the book "Spycatcher" on the grounds that Peter Wright, a former member of the British security services and the character on which the book is based, had drawn on confidential information obtained by him while he was an officer. The High Court accepted that there was a principle that the court should not enforce foreign public laws, in the sense that the court would not allow enforcement of claims outside the territory of the foreign sovereign which are based on or related to the exercise of foreign governmental power. The High Court recognised that it was difficult to identify the foreign laws or rights, which fell within the general principle. After having berated Dr. Mann for equating 'public laws' and 'public rights', unfairly, since rights are derived from laws, the court itself equated 'public laws' and 'public interests', the majority of the court suggested that, rather than referring to 'public laws', it would be more apt to refer to 'public interests' or 'governmental interests' to signify that the rule applies to claims enforcing the interests of a foreign sovereign, which arise from the exercise of certain powers peculiar to government.[1284] Their Lordships concluded, that the rule therefore applies to claims to enforce "the interest of a foreign sovereign which arises from the exercise of certain powers peculiar to governments".[1285] Since the British Government was really seeking to protect the efficiency of its Security Service, as part of its prerogative power to maintain national security and thus to advance a governmental interest, its action was not maintainable.[1286]

The theory of analysing the content of the relevant foreign public law in respect of its "governemental interest " is indeed not new. The term "governmental interest" has been first introduced by the late Brainered Currie for the use of deciding choice of law cases in the United States. In his theory, he believed that the anaylsis of the laws involved would reveal the domestic, social or adminstrative policy it contained. In the event these "governmental policies" differed from

---

**1283** Cp. Robb Evans of Robb Evans & Associates v. European Bank Ltd. [2004] NSWCA 82, (2004) 61 NSWLR 75; President of the State of Equatorial Guinea v Royal Bank of Scotland [2006] UKPC 7; Mbasogo v Logo Ltd. [2007] 2 WLR; Iran v Barakat [2007] EWCA Civ 1374, at 118.
**1284** (1988) 165 CLR 30, at 42.
**1285** (1988) 165 CLR 30, at 46–47.
**1286** Cp. J.G. Collier, Conflict of Laws and Enforcement of Foreign Public Laws: Antipodean Attitudes, 48 C.L.J. (1989) 33, at 34.

each other, he determined whether a reasonable basis existed for one or both states to assert a legitimate interest in the application of its policy to the case at hand.[1287] In short, he relied on a case-by-case analysis.

Currie's "governmental interest analysis" has been ever since subject to academic debate. Many commentators criticised it for preventing a uniform system of the conflict of laws and for violating its basic principles.[1288] According to his critics, in private international law the primary goal was to achieve "conflicts justice and not substantive justice".[1289] Similarly, the validity and effectivness of the governmental interest-test, as adopted by the High Court of Australia in *Spycatcher*, was doubted. [1290] Oponents argued that the principle enunciated by the High Court is largely based on "the motivation of the foreign government in bringing the proceedings, rather than upon the intrinsic nature of the foreign law upon which it seeks to rely".[1291] Collins submitted that "governmental policies are not for the courts to decide". [1292]

The drawback of the goverental interest-test is indeed not its prevention of uniformity or ithe fact that it is based on political considerations. However, the

**1287** Brainerd Currie, Selected Essays on the Conflict of Laws (1963) 189; the same, The Constitution and the Choice of Law Governmental Interest and the Judicial Function, 26 Univ. Chicago Law Rev. (1958) 9; the same in: Notes on Methods and Objectives in the Conflict of Laws, Duke L. J. (1959), 171.

**1288** Gerhard Kegel, The Crisis of Conflict of Laws, 112 Recueil des Cours (1964 II) 91, 180; E. Jayme, Zur Krise des "Governmental-Interest-Approach", in: Festschrift für Kegel (1977) 359; Luther McDougal, Comprehensive Interest Analysis versus Reformulated Governmental Interest Analysis, 26 UCLA L. Rev. (1979) 439; Friedrich K. Juenger, Governmental Interest – Real and Spurious – in Multistate Disputes, 21 U.C. Davis L. Rev. (1988) 515; Larry Kramer, The Myth of the "Unprotected-For" case, 75 Va. L. Rev. (1989) 1045; Axel Flessner, Interessenjurispruden im IPR(1990) 249; Lea Brillmayer, Governmental Interest Analysis, 46 Ohio State L. Rev (1985) 459; but see Herma Hill Kay, A Defence of Currie's Governmental Interest Analysis, 215 Receuil des Cours 9 (1989) 78; the same in: Currie's Interest Analysis in the 21[st] Century: Loosing the Battle but Winnin the War, 37 Willamette L.Rev. (2001) 123.

**1289** See Eugene Scoles, Conflict of Laws 1–2 (3d ed. 2000); G. Kegel, The Crisis of Conflict of Laws, Rec des Cours, at 91.

**1290** See, for example, J.G. Collier, Antipodean Attitudes, at 34; P.B. Carter, Transnational Recognition 430–431. In a recent case comment, Whomersley hopes that Dicey and Morris keep avoiding the term "Interest" in future, cp. C.A. Whomersley, Foreign States and British Courts, 125 LQR (2009) 227, at 233; Morris, The Conflict of Law, at 21–020. FA Mann commented: "There appears to be an equally obvious confusion between the governmental "interest" and the exercise of a right peculiar to government; the former is of no significance in law, the latter cannot possibly be said to have been the cause of action in the Spycatcher case", cp. FA Mann, Spycatcher in the Highcourt of Australia, 104 LQR (1988) 497, at 500 .

**1291** Cp. P.B. Carter, Transnational Recognition, at 430.

**1292** Collins in: Dicey/Morris/Collins, Rule 3, at 21–020.

term "interest" is unclear und hardly identifieable. It is simply falls short of pratical realism to suppose that the identification of the purpose behinde a substantive rule of law is so singular that it actually may be discovered in the course of one law suit. This is true for national laws and evene more so for the rules of a foreign law.

Despite some well-deserved scepticism, in *Iran v Barakat* the test was reaffirmed obiter dictum in the context of 'other public laws'.[1293] In the Court of Appeal decision their Lordships stated that the "governmental interest-test" from Spycatcher was not only "consistent" with the English law but was also "a helpful and practical test".[1294] On this basis their Lordships concluded that public laws are "laws that involve the exercise of assertion of a sovereign right, or seek to enforce governmental interest". In respect of cultural property export legislation the CA admitted hat export restrictions on cultural heritage may fall within the category of public laws that are rendered unenforceable under the governmental interest-test, but their Lordships also stressed that this conclusion

---

**1293** Iran v Barakat [2007] EWCA Civ 1374, at 118. The Court of Appeal in Robb Evans & Associates v European Bank Ltd (2004) 61 N.S.W.L.R. 75, appeared to view *Spycatcher* as authority for a wider test, which applies across all three categories of foreign law. It said: "The concept of 'governmental interest', understood in terms of 'powers peculiar to government', encompasses both of the previous well-established categories, i.e revenue laws and penal laws, and also identifies the particular kind of 'other public law' which may also fall within the exclusionary rule, at 38. See also President of the State of Equatorial Guinea v Royal Bank of Scotland, [2006] UKPC 7, where the Privy Council, obiter, seems to have approved the approach of the High Court of Australia in the *Spycatcher*-case in that the application of foreign law depends on whether "the central interest" of the state in bringing the action is governmental in nature, at 25 and 25. But see Mbasogo v Logo [2007] 2 WLR 1062, where English Court of Appeal was careful to express no direct opinion on the governmental intrest test but implicitly rejected it. They have concluded that "this appeal can be resolved by applying the jurisprudence of our courts and without adopting the "governmental interest" approach", at 52. *Evans* appeared to view *Spycatcher* as authority for a wider test, which applies across all three categories of foreign law. It said: "The concept of 'governmental interest', understood in terms of 'powers peculiar to government', encompasses both of the previous well-established categories, i.e revenue laws and penal laws, and also identifies the particular kind of 'other public law' which may also fall within the exclusionary rule, at 38. See also President of the State of Equatorial Guinea v Royal Bank of Scotland, [2006] UKPC 7, where the Privy Council, obiter, seems to have approved the approach of the High Court of Australia in the *Spycatcher*-case in that the application of foreign law depends on whether "the central interest" of the state in bringing the action is governmental in nature, at 25 and 25. But see Mbasogo v Logo [2007] 2 WLR 1062 where English Court of Appeal was careful to express no direct opinion on the governmental intrest test but implicitly rejected it. They have concluded that "this appeal can be resolved by applying the jurisprudence of our courts and without adopting the "governmental interest" approach", at 52.

**1294** Iran v Barakat, [2007] EWCA Civ 1374, at 154.

is "by no means certain."[1295] As an example for legislation that is certainly not justiciable in England, the court named exchange control legislation.[1296] However, although the court approved the governmental interest-test and confirmed its practicality in determining the scope of the public law principle, it did not explicitly apply it to the present case. After submitting that there is no decision which binds English courts to find that there is a rule which prevents the enforcement of all foreign public laws in general, it decided to deal with the case only by reference to whether or not Iran's claim for the recovery of their antique jars was a patrimonial claim in the law of property, subject to a fall-back public policy reservation.[1297]

To sum up the findings on the definition of 'public laws' that ought not to be enforced in English courts, the attempts to introduce clarification to the principle have not succeeded. There is no consent in whether 'public law' is held to be *eiusdem generis* with 'penal' or 'revenue' laws or whether it is considered to be an omnibus clause to penal and revenue. Notions of international law such as *prerogative right*, *acta jure imperii* or *acta jure gestionis* or the "*assertion of a sovereign right*", are of extraordinary width and purport to the state practice and the private international law of inevitably every country in the world. Although the 'governmental- or central interest-test' makes a step towards a workable and more precise definition, it has not yet received sufficient judicial support in order to be called an established rule of law. The appropriateness of the application of traditional, essentially physical, limitations of territoriality to non-physical elements, such as 'governmental interest', might also be questioned in modern times.

## II. Recognition: Patrimonial Claims to Cultural Objects

Under English law, a claim based on rights, which equal those of a private citizen is considered to be a patrimonial claim and will not be treated as a case of enforcement of sovereign rights, but as a case of recognition.[1298] The concept of a

---

**1295** Iran v Barakat, ibid, at 128.

**1296** See e.g. Re Lord Cable, deceased [1977] 1 WLR 7; and Camdex International Ltd. v Bank of Zambia (No. 2) [1997] CLC 714, at 724 (Simon Brown LJ) and 734 (Phillips LJ).

**1297** Ibid, at 125.

**1298** See Princess Paley Olga v Weisz [1929] 1 KB 718; Luther v Sagor [1921] 3 KB 532; Iran v Barakat [2007] EWHC 705 (QB); Union of Soviet Republics v Belaiew (1925) 42 T.L.R. 21. However, note also cases relating to the conflict of laws, such as Williams and Humbert Ltd v W&H Trade Marks (Jersey) Ltd, [1986] 1 AC 368, a case concerning Spanish decrees, by virtue of

patrimonial claim is to be found in a speech of Lord Keith of Avonholme in the old case Government of India v Taylor.[1299] The issue in this case was whether the law sought to be enforced in the claim was a revenue law. Answering this question in the affirmative, Lord Keith said:

> "One explanation of the rule illustrated may be thought to be that enforcement of a claim for taxes is an extension of the Sovereign Power of the state, as distinct from a patrimonial claim by a foreign sovereign."

A patrimonial claim thus must be a claim, which does not involve the extension of the sovereign power of the state. In the case, a state obtained title in the same way a private individual has obtained title to an object, for example through purchase, bequest, gift, or *bona vacantia*, the state will be treated equally. There will be no extension of sovereign power, and consequently, no impediment to recovery. The question is whether this principle equally applies when the title derives from a public statute. If the state owns property in the same way as a private citizen, then the penal law/ public law principle must be inapplicable. In that sense, patrimonial claims are claims under private law, which are based on, or determined by foreign public law. However, for a patrimonial claim to be recognised which is based on public law, the right which the state tries to invoke in a foreign court has to be perfected before it left the state's territory.

### 1. The Recognition of Claims according to the Doctrine of Vested Rights

A state claim for the recovery of cultural property will be patrimonial if the object in question is based on a property right that has been perfected before the chattel has been removed from the state's territory. The justification for this rationale must be seen in the doctrine of vested rights. This principle derives from the lex situs-doctrine, which governs the transfer of title to chattels. Following this general rule, the removal of objects across the border of a state does not undermine

---

which the State of Spain became entitled to control a Spanish company (Rumasa), and indirectly its subsidiary Williams and Humbert Ltd, an English company. The court held that the object of the Spanish decrees "was to acquire direct ownership and control of Rumasa and the two banks and indirect control of Williams and Humbert and that object has been duly achieved by perfection of the state's title in Spain. Accordingly, no enforcement of a foreign penal or other public law took place. Note also the *Banc de Viscaya-case* and the implication that had the securities been deposited at the time of the seizure in a bank in Spain, not in a bank in England, consequential recognition of that seizure would have precluded objection in any subsequent proceedings on the ground that indirect enforcement of an admitted penal law would be involved.

**1299** [1955] AC 481, at 511.

per se pre-existing or vested rights in the object.[1300] As long as the acquisition of the property right has been perfected before it left the territory of the state, it is being recognised in foreign courts, but of course, this rule pertains only so long as there are no further dealings in the object in the new situs.[1301] Subject to certain exceptions, governmental acts affecting proprietary rights will be recognised by an English court as valid if they would be recognised as valid by the law of the country where the property was situated when the law took effect.[1302]

### a. Iran v Barakat – Court of Appeal Decision

In *Barakat*, the Court of Appeal applied the vested rights doctrine in order to distinguish whether Iran's claim was justiciable in England. Instead of applying the governmental interest-test as established in *Spycatcher* the court based its judgment of principles of property law.

The CA first reconsidered the nature of Iran's property interest in the ancient jars and held that it was sufficient to stand to sue in conversion in an English court. First, the CA found that although Iran's law had not clearly declared ownership to fortuitously discovered antiquities, all relevant Iranian provisions viewed in a coherent context were to vest ownership in the state.[1303] Second, the court also considered Iran to have an immediate right of possession in the jars, which alone is enough to institute a recovery claim in England.[1304]

On the ground that Iran indeed obtained a property interest in the antiquities according to Iranian law, the CA held that this interest was to be recognised in an English court. The Court explained that where a foreign state has acquired title under its law of property within its jurisdiction in cases not involving compulsory acquisition of title from private parties, there is no reason why the English court should not recognise its title in accordance with the general principle of vested rights.[1305] The Court found such a claim to be a patrimonial claim as

1300 The underlying theory in German private international law is known as the "imprint theory" (Prägungstheorie), cp. A. Hipp, Schutz von Kulturgüterschutz, at 170; S. von Schorlemer, Kulturgüterschutz, at 538; A. Müller-Katzenburg, at 237.

1301 Cp. e. g. Friedrich K v. Savigny, A Treatise of the Conflict of Laws (1ed 1869, 2nd rev. ed 1980) at 139, 280, 289 and 307. See also J. Carruthers, Transfer of Property, at 93; K. Siehr, International Art Trade, at 77; K. Siehr, The Protection of Cultural Heritage and International Commerce, 6 IJCP (1997) 304; P. Lalive, in: P. Lalive (ed.) International Sales of Works of Art (1988), at 319 and 415.

1302 Kuwait Airways Corporation v Iraq Airways Co [2002] 2 AC 883, at 1077, per Lord Nicholls of Birkenhead.

1303 Cp. Chapter 2 § 2 II.

1304 For the requirements to sue in conversion, cp. later in this paragraph.

1305 Iran v Barakat [2007] EWCA Civ. 1374, at 133.

opposed to a prerogative claim, owing to the fact that Iran owned the antiquities in the same way a private citizen would do. The CA acknowledged that English courts would not enforce penal, revenues or other public laws of another state but found the penal law/public law principle to be inapplicable where the foreign law transfers ownership. In such a case, the CA found it it is not a necessary pre-condition that the foreign state should have reduced the property into its possession.[1306] Comparing the case to *Att. Gen. of New Zealand v Ortiz*, the CA found that *Barakat* was very different from the latter, as the Iranian provisions granted an immediate right of possession. This immediate right of possession would be acquired while the property was within Iran's jurisdiction. The CA believed that a property right of this kind would not be questioned in an English court despite Iran not having acquired possession. Hence, according to the CA, Justice Gray erred in his first instance judgment in that both ownership and an immediate right of possession were property rights, which once acquired within the territory of a state would be non-justiciable in England. He confused the recognition of an already existing property interest and the enforcement of a right based on a public law which would only come to existence if recovery occurred outside the territory of the foreign state. Accordingly the CA held Gray J.'s ruling to be contrary to the doctrine of vested rights and English case law.[1307]

In many ways, the rationale of this judgment is correct. A property interest that was transferred in a party, may it be a private individual or a state, has to be recognised in a foreign court according to the doctrine of vested rights. In that Justice Gray maybe erred. It is also correct that Iran had an immediate right of possession and this is a property right recognisable in foreign courts. However, the vested right-rationale could only prevail as long as the CA did not apply the governmental interest-test to the case. Because if it had, it might have reached the conclusion that Iran's claim indeed gave effect to a governmental interest. One has to consider that Iran's title to the antiquities was the result of a statute that only a state could have enacted. Only a state can vest in itself all fortuitously discovered artefacts on the territory of the state. Although from one point of view Iran's claim was indistinguishable from one that a private citizen may bring, from another point of view, only a state could have brought a claim that was based on a title that the state vested in itself by statutory means. Although the claim was not one to enforce an other public law, it was still a claim giving effect to the governmental interest of Iran.[1308]

**1306** Ibid, at 138.

**1307** Ibid, at 149.

**1308** For a critical analysis of the case see especially Adrian Briggs, The Law which determines Title to Movable Cultural Property, 69 BYIL (2007) 628.

In the end, one has to lend some support for Justice Gray who in the first instance concluded that property rights which derive from a national ownership statute cannot be enforced in England, because acquisition by means of a national ownership law is a method available only to sovereigns.

Although dogmatically the judgment may not stand on secure feet, its outcome still constitutes a great step towards the recognition of title based on foreign cultural patrimony laws and consequently it constitutes a great step in cultural property protection. However, *Iran v Barakat* is not the only case to promote the acquisition of title to antiquities on the grounds of public law.

### b. The Medici-Archives

The vested rights-doctrine was also applied in the older case *King of Italy v Marquis Cosimo de Medici Tornaquinci.*[1309] There, the Italian government sought the recovery of a valuable collection of historical manuscripts covering a period of 700 years. The collection has been in the possession of the Marquis of Medici. Some of the manuscripts were Italian state papers which the Italian government had allowed the Marquis to hold on behalf of the state. Others were family papers, belonging to the Marquis himself. In 1909 the Italian government passed a law ordering that the collection was the property of the state and it was to be kept in Italy. By the same law the government prohibited the export of the family papers belonging to the Marquis without an export licence. The state also proclaimed to have a pre-emption right to buy the family papers. Nevertheless, the Marquis brought the Medici-Archives to England and put it up on sale at Christie's. The Italian government applied for an interlocutory injunction to inhibit the sale. Peterson J. granted the injunction restraining the sale of the state papers, on the ground that they were and always had been the property of the Italian state. No distinction was apparently drawn between enforcement and recognition: Peterson J. found his judgment solemnly on the fact that Italian law had vested title in the Italian state before the papers left Italy. It is not altogether clear whether the judge found that they were or ever had been in the possession of the Italian state. What is clear is that the judge found it was sufficient that the Italian law proclaimed the archive to be the property of the state and the title in them vested in the government before the papers left Italy. The historical documents, on the other hand, had only been exported in breach of Italian law. Peterson J. did not restrain their sale. He thus distinguished between Italy's pos-

1309 King of Italy and Italian Government v Marquis Cosimo de Medici Tornaquinci, Marquis Averado de Medici Tornaquinci, and Christie Manson and Woods (1918) 34 T.L.R. 623.

sessory or proprietary title to the state papers deriving from the Italian legal act and Italy's attempt to recover the historical papers, which were exported in breach of export restrictions and of which it was clearly not the owner. The part of the decision concerning the state papers can be viewed to constitute a patrimonial claim, whereas the claim for the family papers must be regarded to be prerogative in nature and hence rendered unenforceable.

### c. City of Gotha v Sotheby's

Another example for the recognition of a patrimonial claim based on public law is *City of Gotha and the Federal Republic of Germany v Sotheby's and Cobert SA.*[1310] There, the recovery of a painting by Joachim Wtewael "The holy Family with Saint John and Elizabeth", painted in 1603, did not constitute an assertion of a sovereign authority, although the Federal Republic's title derived from a public statute. The Wtewael was taken by the Soviet trophy brigade some time in 1946 from the ducal family of Saxe-Coburg-Gotha at the castle Friedenstein in the City of Gotha, however the exact circumstances of its looting remained unclear. At the time of removal, the painting belonged to the Duke of Saxe-Coburg Foundation for Art and Science [hereinafter: the Foundation]. The picture remained in the Soviet Union until the 1980 s and was then acquired by some Mina Breslov in 1988, consigned to Sotheby's and bought by a Panamanian Corporation, Cobert Finance, in 1989. In the proceedings the Federal Republic of Germany sought to recover the painting on the grounds that it was the successor of the Saxe-Coburg Art Foundation and thus the owner of the painting. The City of Gotha also entered the claim, alleging possessory title to the painting. The question was also, whether Germany's claim is time-barred under the German law of limitation.

Moses J. faced conflicting evidence as to the disappearance of the painting. The questions that arose were whether, as a matter of fact, it can be established that the painting was in Thuringia in 1945 and 1946. Furthermore, whether the title to the painting passed to Thuringia by virtue of the expropriatory Law of 9 October 1945, or on the alternative ground, whether the title to the Wtewael

---

**1310** Unpublished decision, noted by Antony Mair, Misappropriation and Skulduggery in Germany and Russia: Wtewael's "The Holy Family", 3 AAL (1998) 413; Paul Lomas/Simon Orton, Potential Repercussions from the City of Gotha Decision, 4 AAL (1999) 159; Note in IJCP 8 (1999) 584; A. Müller-Katzenburg, Possession and Ownership, 5 AAL (2000) 105, at 120; Ruth Redmond Cooper, 5 AAL (2000) 185, at 190; A. Weidner, Kulturgüter als res extra commercium, at 110. The decision is reprinted in Norman Palmer (ed.), Museum and the Holocaust (1998), Appendix IV, 222.

passed to Thuringia by virtue of the dissolution of the Art Foundation on 14 October 1950. After having examined German law and UK law, the judge came to the conclusion that the painting was the property of Germany, as the dissolution of the Land Thuringia of the Art Foundation in 1950 caused the property in the picture to be transmitted to the Land Thuringia by way of universal succession, the seat of the foundation being at that time in Gotha. Although in 1950, the painting most probably was already in the Soviet Union and the dissolution of the foundation was held to be a governmental act, Moses J. found that it did not amount to an exercise of sovereign authority. The dissolution, in his opinion, was solely concerned with the continuing existence of the Foundation. Thus, bringing an action which seeks to protect proprietary rights, which trace their origin to the dissolution, did not constitute a prerogative claim which would be unenforceable in English courts.

### 2. Recognition based on a Possessory Title

In order to recover a chattel in England, the owner state will claim for vindication under the English law of conversion, relying on its possessory title. The state will be required to plead two things: First, that it had possessory title to the illegally excavated object and second, that the defendant had converted them to its own use. According to the doctrine of vested rights, the argument would follow that neither of these pleadings requires the enforcement of foreign public law: The state's legislation gives the state a possessory title. This was immediately achieved whilst the property was on the claimant state's ground. Therefore, the argument goes, there is no enforcement in such a case, but only recognition of the vested right according to the lex situs rule.[1311]

The English law of conversion asks whether the claimant had an immediate right of possession or whether the claimant had possession in fact.[1312] As the argument goes, an immediate right of possession is a vested right in the sense of the lex situs-rule and accordingly is complete without the claiming state ever being in possession of the goods. Upholding a claim in conversion consequently

**1311** Cp. M. Wolff, Private International Law, at 527; Gerhard Kegel, Internationales Privatrecht (6th ed 1987), at 855.

**1312** See e.g. Andrew Tettenborn, Conversion, Trespass and Title to Works of Art, at 36; Lord Mackay of Clashfern (ed.), Vol 45(2) Halsbury's Laws of England, (4th ed. 2006), at 559: "To sue in conversion a claimant must show that he had either possession or an immediate right of possession, of the chattel at the time of the act in question". See also, W.V.H. Rogers, Winfield and Jolowicz on Tort (18th ed 2010), at 762; Basil Markesinis/ Simon Deakin/Angus Johnston, Markesinis and Deakin's Tort Law (6th ed 2007), at 436.

amounts to recognition and not to enforcement of sovereign rights. However, the rightfulness of this argument is intertwined with questions of English private law and depends on the threshold requirements of the English vindication claim for the recovery of chattels. Whether a mere immediate right of possession qualifies to bring a claim for conversion under English law, was long since an unsettled question. Only if it does, then consequently, this immediate right of possession can be recognised as a patrimonial claim

### a. The Common Law Action in Conversion

In English law, the remedy to recover property is the claim for conversion. As opposed to continental law, where it is a remedy in property law, conversion is classified as a tort. Prof. Palmer describes the law of conversion to have the following functions:[1313] It is a surrogate for the vindication, allowing owners to get back their property or its value from a wrongful possessor,[1314] and it is acting to compensate owners for losses caused by misdealing with their property. An exact definition of how conversion can be committed is probably impossible, but generally it can be agreed upon that the wrong is committed by a dealing with the goods of a person which deprives him or her of the use or possession of them.[1315]

The mere fact that a person owns a chattel does not qualify him to sue in conversion. The reason is that English law does not recognise ownership in the same absolute sense as Roman law did. Roman law recognised a concept of dominium upon which all the civil law systems have modelled their treatment of ownership.[1316] This was to be distinguished from possession. Whoever was entitled to a thing could claim it from anyone else who had control by an action called *vindicatio in rem*. The claimant offered to prove that the thing was his and the proceedings did not even name a defendant.[1317] Possession, on the other hand was a matter of fact.[1318] Nowadays, property protection in civil law

**1313** See generally, Norman Palmer, Conversion, Tort and Restitution, in: NE Palmer/E. McKendrick (eds.), Interest in Goods (2nd ed) 1998, Chapter 32, at 825.

**1314** Palmer calls this the "recovery function", ibid, at 825.

**1315** Cp. Winfield and Jolowicz, at 17–6. See also Howard Perry & Co Ltd. v B.R.B. [1980 1 W.L.R. 1375 at 1380; Hiort v London & North Western Ry Co, (1879) 4 Ex D. 1888, at 194; Kuwait Airways Corp v Iraqi Airways Co (Nos 4 and 5) [2002] UKHL 19, [2002] 2 A.C. 883, at 39 et seq.

**1316** See for example, the Germany Civil Code, Art 985 BGB, according to which the owner of a chattel can recover it from a wrongful possessor. It is not satisfied by the mere showing of a better title to possess. Similarly, the Italian Civil Code, art 948; the Polish Civil Code, Art 222; Art 151 Russian Civil Code.

**1317** Ugo Mattei, Basic Principles of Property Law (2000), at 182.

**1318** Frederick Lawson/Bernard Rudden, The Law of Property ( 3rd ed. 2002), at 114.

jurisdictions is organised in two different actions: the so called 'negatory action', open to the owner against whomever disturbs him or her in the enjoyment of the property, and the *rei vindicatio*, an action that allows the owner to recover possession against the non-owner in possession of the property. These proprietary and possessory actions coexists with personal contractual actions to recover a thing.

Conversely, proprietary actions are unknown in common law, and the concept of ownership in the common law system is less clear-cut than in civil law jurisdiction. Thus in order to deal with the wrongful interference with goods, the common law nowadays only uses possessory action, in the form of the claim for conversion.[1319] In order to sue in conversion, the claimant must show either that he had possession of the goods at the material time, or that he had an immediate right of possession.[1320] If he can show one of these qualifications, he can sue though he is not the owner. It can thus be said that possession in common law counts as title.[1321] Just as possession counts as title, so an immediate right of possession must count as title under English law.[1322]

### b. Immediate Right of Possession as Title under English Law

The contention that possession counts as title has been recently put to the test. It has been demanded that the claimant who pleads an immediate right of possession must show that it arises from a proprietary right meaning a right of possession arising from property.[1323] The demand for a proprietary right as a require-

1319 It has to be noted that under English law, recovery does not occur as of right. Even if wrongful removal is established, the physical return of the object to its claimant owner is only one option available and is generally at the discretion of the court. In some cases courts will prefer to award damages and allow the defendant to keep the work, see N.E. Palmer, Recovery of Unlawfully Removed Works of Art and Antiquity – The Legal Dimension (Paper presented at the Art Crime Conference convened by the Australian Institute of Criminology in Sydney, held in Dec 1999).

1320 Marquis of Bute v Barclays Bank [1955] 1 Q.B. 202. Cp. also Norman Palmer, Conversion, Trespass and Title to Art Works, in: N.E. Palmer, The Recovery of Stolen Art (1998), 37; N.E. Palmer, Possessory Title, in NE Palmer/E.Mckendrick (eds.) Interests in Goods (2nd ed 1998), at 34.

1321 See the case of The Winkfield [1902] p 42 and O'Sullivan v Williams [1992] 3 All E.R. 385, discussed by Norman Palmer in All E.R. Rev (1992), at 22–25.

1322 See Marquess of Bute v Barclays Bank Ltd. [1954] 3 All E.R. 365: "..in order to sue in conversion, it is not necessary fro the plaintiff to establish that he is the true owner of the property alleged to have been converted. It is sufficient if he can prove that at the time of the alleged conversion he was entitled to immediate possession, " per McNair J., at 368.

1323 Cp. Anthony Dugdael/ Michael Jones, Clerk & Lindsell on Tort (19th ed. 2009), at para 17–59. See also Rosenthal v Alderton and Sons Ltd. [1946] KB 374 at 377;

ment to sue in conversion would constitute a convergence to the continental systems of property law, which is mainly based on ownership rights. Common law did not differentiate between possessory title and proprietary title within the tort of conversion. However, interests in a chattel can be shared and it is this fact that has given rise to the distinction between proprietary and possessory. Thus, where an earlier possessor (in common law the bailor) grants possession to a subsequent possessor (the bailee) on terms that reserve to the bailor a reversionary interest in the chattel, the bailor can be said to enjoy a 'proprietary title' and the bailee a 'possessory title' in a chattel.[1324]

Historically, however, wrongful interference with goods used to give rise to two causes of action, which were largely concurrent.[1325] Detinue was used as an action for the interference with the proprietary right of the claimant and conversion, which was used for the interference with the possessory right of the claimant.[1326] Where goods in possession of a bailee were lost or destroyed as a result of breach of his duty to the bailor, the appropriate claim, lay in detinue rather than conversion. Where, however, the claim was brought by the possessor against a third party wrongdoer a claim would lie either in detinue or in conversion. The action of detinue was then abolished by the Torts Interference with Goods Act 1977, which made some simplifications to the old common law in regard of the various forms of actions, but cannot be called a conclusive codification on the interference with goods.

Section 2 of the Act now provides that conversion also covers the case when a claimant was unable to redeliver the goods as a result of their loss or destruction, which was formerly the exclusive province of detinue.[1327] Section 7 makes clear that it is possible to enjoy different interests in goods. It states:

> "Double liability
> (1) In this section 'double liability' means the double liability of the wrongdoer which can arise –
> (a) where one or two or more rights of action for wrongful interference is founded on a possessory title, or
> (b) where the measure of damages in an action for wrongful interference founded on a pro-

1324 Generally on the common law of bailment see Norman Palmer, Bailment, (3rd ed. 2009).

1325 Frederick Pollock/ Frederic W. Maitland, History of English law before the Time of Edward I (2nd ed. 1996), at 179–184; Cecil H.S. Fifoot, History and Sources of the Common Law: Tort and Contract (1970), at 25.

1326 Cp. AWB Simpson, The Introduction of the Action on the Case for Conversion 75 LQR (1954) 364.

1327 W.V.H. Rogers, in: Winfield and Jolowicz on Tort, at 747.

prietary title is or includes the entire value of the goods, although the interest is one of two or more interests in the goods.

(2) In proceedings to which any two or more claimants are parties, the relief shall be such as to avoid double liability of the wrongdoer as between those claimants."

The Act does not define 'possessory title' or 'proprietary title' and the difficulty in this area of the law arises because of an overlap between the two.

An authority for the proposition that conversion demands a proprietary right additionally to the immediate right of possession can be found in the Court of Appeal decision *International Factors Ltd. v Rodriguez,*[1328] a case concerning the conversion of some cheques payable to a company which had entered into a factoring agreement with the claimants, as well as in the Court of Appeal decision *Jarvis v Williams,*[1329] a case in the old law of detinue. In the first case, *International Factors v Rodriguez*, Sir David Cairns held that a mere contractual right was not sufficient in order to bring a claim in conversion, but the right had to be proprietary in nature.[1330] *Jarvis v Williams* on the other hand concerned an owner of goods who sued the defendant to whom the goods have been delivered at the request of a third party, who failed to pay for them. The defendant refused to deliver up the goods. The Court of Appeal held that the claim was not maintainable. The court relied on a passage in the text of Halsbury's Law of England[1331], which stated that "in order to maintain an action of trover or detinue, a person must have the right of possession and the right of property in the goods at the time of the conversion or detention."[1332]

If these contentions were right, claims for the recovery of illegally excavated artefacts of which the state of origin is not the owner but merely has a possessory right to them were to fail in English courts. *Iran v Barakat Galleries*[1333] has now settled this long since unresolved question of English private law. The Court of Appeal accepted that ownership based on a proprietary right is normally the basis for an action in conversion but the mere immediate right of possession without more can also ground the action.[1334] The CA found that Iran had by

**1328** [1979] 1 Q.B. 351, C.A. esp at p 357, per Sir David Cairns.
**1329** [1955] 1 WLR 71 C.A.
**1330** Ibid, at 357, but cp. Buckley L.J. who held that the contractual right of the plaintiffs to demand immediate delivery of the cheques sufficed to found a claim in conversion, whether or not an immediate trust attached to the cheques.
**1331** 2nd ed. Vol. 33 (1932), at 62, para. 98.
**1332** [1955] 1 WLR 71 C.A., at 74.
**1333** [2007] EWCA Civ 1374.
**1334** [2007] EWCA Civ. 1374, at 27–30.

its law the immediate right to the possession of the objects and that such a right was enough to entitle Iran to sue for the recovery of the artefacts. This conclusion was mainly founded on Article 2 (2) of the Iranian Legal Bill 1979 which states:

> "Where the objects named in this Act have been discovered accidentally, the discoverer is duty bound to submit them to the nearest office of Culture and Higher Education as soon as possible."

Even though these objects were deliberately excavated and not the fruits of chance finding, the CA held that the same obligation to submit them must be deemed to apply. The court found that the position of an illegal excavator cannot be better than that of an accidental chance finder.

To sue in conversion the claimant must show either possession of the chattel, or the immediate right to possession, at the time of the conversion. The CA did not opine upon whether Iran had possession of the objects before they were excavated, but it affirmed Iran's right to the possession of them once they were excavated. Furthermore, the CA did not explicitly say whether Iran's immediate right to the possession of the bowls (or indeed any immediate right to the possession of a chattel) was a proprietary interest. However, the CA's judgment neither affirms nor disaffirms that a contractual immediate right to the possession is itself a proprietary interest.

The CA in *Barakat* distinguished *Jarvis v Williams*,[1335] which was relied upon by the defendants, as a case where the plaintiff's right of possession that was contractual and not proprietary, was not immediate. The contract did not purport to confer on him an immediate right of possession. It was held by the court to be only a "conditional contract under which it was agreed that, if the plaintiff recovered possession of the goods, he would receive them in discharge of the third parties obligation to pay for them."[1336] The court also referred to the fact that Jarvis was a case decided under the the old law of detinue and not a claim in conversion,[1337] and it conflicted with more recent authorities.[1338] By rejecting *Jarvis* and *Rodriguez*, the CA returned to the contention that possession counts as title under English law. In doing so, the *Barakat-decision* has achieved that a foreign state who has an immediate right of possession to cultural property under the lex situs, its title will be recognised and enforced in English courts irrespective of whether it has reduced the property into its possession.

**1335** [1955] 1 WLR 71 C.A.
**1336** [2007] EWCA Civ. 1374, at 26.
**1337** [2007] EWCA Civ. 1374, at 26.
**1338** For example, in MCC Proceeds Inc v Lehman Brothers Int ( Europe) [1998] 4 All ER 675.

### 3. Recognition based on Confiscatory Legislation

As already indicated above, a somewhat troublesome question is the extent to which a claim based on confiscatory or expropriatory legislation can constitute a patrimonial claim with the effect that it will be recognised in English courts.

Generally, acts of expropriation are of a prerogative nature, in that they deprive an owner of a property right already vested in him or her.

It would seem that in the UK legislation of this nature may take four forms.[1339]

> First, requisition, which is generally confined to the seizure of property in the public interest for a limited period and in return for compensation.
> Secondly, nationalisation, which is the permanent absorption of property into public ownership in furtherance of some political aim and in return for compensation.
> Thirdly, compulsory acquisition, which is the permanent expropriation of property in fulfilment of some economic or social aim, and in exchange for compensation.
> Fourthly, confiscation, which is the permanent expropriation of private property.[1340] Confiscatory laws are laws, which are penal or financial in nature, and the private owner affected by them is not entitled to compensation.

If an English judge is required to determine the effect of foreign expropriatory legislation, his decision will depend on the situs of the property at the time of the expropriatory act and the question whether the foreign sovereign was in actual possession of the property at the time when the facts giving rise to the litigation occurred.[1341]

#### a. Possession at the Time of the Confiscatory Act

English courts recognise that the ownership of property is conclusively determined by the terms of a foreign expropriatory act if two conditions are cumulatively fulfilled: the property is situated within the jurisdiction of the sovereign at the time of the decree and the sovereign was in possession of the property when the act which gave rise to the litigation took place.

For instance in *Princess Paley Olga v Weisz*,[1342] it was held that works of art, which were confiscated from a princess during the Russian Revolution belonged

---

**1339** The categorisation has been exracted from Williams and Humbert Ltd. v W and H Trademarks (Jersey) Ltd. [1986] AC 368; but see similarly, Cheshire/North/Fawcett, at 132.

**1340** See in relation to discharge of a debt by governmental act, Wight v Eckhard Marine GmbH [2003] UKPC 37, [2004] 1 AC 147.

**1341** Cheshire/North/Fawcett, International Private Law, at 133.

**1342** [1929] 1 KB 718. See also Luther v Sagor [1921] 3 KB 532, at 548; Oppenheimer v Cattermole [1976] AC 249, at 282–283; Buttes Gas and Oil Co v Hammer (No 3) [1982] AC 888, at 931; Williams

to the Russian state, as the Russian state's title had already been complete by virtue of obtaining possession to the items while they were still in Russia.[1343] The works of art have been confiscated by virtue of a decree[1344] which stated that "works of art, antiquities, and articles of historical interest being in museums and depositories, as forming part of the museum funds and being safeguarded by state means, are regarded to be the property of the state." The court decided that the Paley Palace was a museum, which was being safeguarded by state means from funds provided by the Commissariat of Education, and the works of art did form part of it. The second decree on which Russia based its claim was sec. 1 of Decree No. 111 of the Council of People's Commissaries declaring that "the property of all citizens fled outside the confines of the Republic, or hiding themselves to the present time, was to be the property of the Russian government." The facts of the case stated that Princess Paley escaped from Russia without a passport and the court was satisfied that this was considered to be "fleeing from Russia." The princess' claim that the art works still belonged to her thus failed. Whilst not discussed in the case, it is thought that a claim brought by Russia to recover them would have been dismissed, if the cultural objects have had remained in the possession of the princess at all times and, let it be assumed, she would have brought them to England. In this case the true purpose of Russia's claim would have been to enforce a prerogative right.[1345]

Similarly, in *City of Gotha*,[1346] on the alternative ground that the title to the Wtewael did not pass to the Land Thuringia (and hence to the Federal Republic of Germany) through universal succession in 1950, but by the expropriatory law of 9 October 1945,[1347] Moses J concluded that the title based on this expropriatory

and Humbert Ltd. v W and H Trademarks (Jersey) Ltd. [1986] AC 368. But distinguish also Brokaw v Seatrain UK Ltd., [1971] 2 Q.B 476, where it was held that the United states could not claim goods pursuant to a notice of levy by which it claimed title to goods being shipped on a U.S. registered ship by persons alleged to owe tax. In this case Lord Denning said that "if the United States Government had taken these goods into their actual possession, say in a warehouse in Baltimore, (..) that might have been sufficient to enable them to claim the goods, because we would then be enforcing an actual possessory title. But there is nothing of that kind here. The United States Government simply rely on this notice of levy given to the ship owners, and that is not, in my view, sufficient to reduce the goods into their possession", at 482–483.

**1343** See FA Mann, Prerogative Rights, at 503–504; also New Zealand v Ortiz [1984] 1 A.C 1, 35 (H.L.), at 23 per Lord Denning.

**1344** Decree No. 245 (1923) of the All-Russian Central Executive Committee of the Council of People's Commissaries.

**1345** Cp. FA Mann, Prerogative Rights, at 503–504.

**1346** FA Mann, Prerogative Rights, at 503–504

**1347** On 9th October 1945 the Soviet Military Administration in Germany passed a law concerning the securing and expropriation of Nazi property. By Paragraph 19: "The confiscation orders

act was to be given effect to and will be recognised in England. He based his judgment on the fact that, in 1945, the painting was within the territory over which Soviet Military Administration had jurisdiction and was in possession of the trustee. In that, Germany was seeking to protect rights of property, which had vested prior to the action.

The justification for the decisions must be seen in the doctrine of vested rights which states that a title to movables, valid according to the law of the situs at the time of the acquisition, is recognisable in English law.[1348] The law of the situs must prevail in such circumstances unless the rule of the law under which the title has been acquired is so immoral or so alien to the principles of justice as understood by English law that it must be disregarded as being contrary to public policy.[1349] Consequently, expropriatory acts, which have been perfected at the time of the decree and on the territory of the sovereign in that the government has obtained possession of the chattels are regarded to be patrimonial claims and recognisable in English courts. Following that reasoning, the Maori carvings in *Att. Gen. of New Zealand v Ortiz* ought to have been returned to their country of origin if the 1962 statute would have provided for the automatic forfeiture of the carvings prior to their export from New Zealand.

### b. Lack of Possession at the Time of Confiscatory Act

It would follow that expropriatory acts, which have not been perfected at the time of the decree on the territory of the sovereign, are considered to be prerogative claims and effect to such laws will not be given.[1350] If property is not in the possession or control of the foreign state at the time of the proceedings and if it

---

(Verfügung) made pursuant to the police regulations (Verordnung) concerning the confiscation of assets of former memebrs of the national socialist German workers party on 6th July are valid as expropriation orders within the meaning of this Act, even if such orders have not been published."

**1348** See the remarks of Devlin J. in Bank voor Handel en Sheepvart NV v Slatford [1953] 1 QB 248 at 260;

**1349** Cp. Luther v Sagor [1921] 3 KB 532; Williams and Humbert Ltd. v W and H Trade Marks (Jersey) Ltd. [1986] 368 at 431. See generally Cheshire/North/Fawcett, Ch 8. Thus, confiscatory laws which by reason of being discriminatory on grounds of race, religion or that like, constitute so grave an infringement of human rights shall not be given effect to and ought not to be recognised as laws at all, see Williams and Humbert Ltd. v W and H Trade Marks (Jersey) [1986] 1 AC 389, at 392 and 414.

**1350** See on this point Gotha City v Sotheby's (No 2) (1998) Times, 8 October. Other confiscation cases which have not been enforced are Lecouturier v Rey [1910] A.C. 262, 264; Banco de Vizcaya v Don Alfonso de Burbon y Austria [1935] 1 K.B. 140.

was outside of the territorial jurisdiction of that state at the time of the expropriatory act, the rights of the owner are unaffected.[1351] A contrary rule would conflict with the principle of territoriality, but also in the particular case of confiscation with the doctrine that penal laws of another country will not be indirectly enforced in England.[1352]

Conversely, it is being contended, that it makes no difference whether the state has confiscated specific goods by taking them into possession, or whether a general confiscation decree concerns all goods of a certain kind, which provisionally remain in the possession of the former owner.[1353] In so far as the confiscation decree affects property situated within the territory of the confiscating state, its effect is the transfer of the title to the state, and this will be respected everywhere. [1354] Professor Wolf used the example of a British national who resided in Russia during the Revolution and was deprived of his property situated in Russia by confiscation. If the former owner against whom a confiscation order has been issued brings the goods to England, this does not extinguish the ownership of the confiscating state, since the goods were in Russia at the date of confiscation. The Soviet state, as Wolf continues, therefore acquires a proprietary title without ever having possessed the goods.

The position on this issue is now finally settled *Iran v Barakat*,[1355] where the general rule on expropriatory legislation was applied. There, the CA held that the distinction between the two categories of cases, those where the foreign state will be able to claim its property in England even if it has not reduced the property into its possession, and those where it may not claim unless it has reduced the property into its possession, depends on the way in which it has acquired ownership.[1356] If the state has acquired title under public law by confiscation or compulsory process from the former owner then it will not be able to claim the property in England unless it had perfected its title through possession. If however, it has taken the property into its possession then its claim will be treated as a patrimonial claim and thus as a case of recognition. The court did not explain its decision for making a distinction between confiscatory and non-con-

**1351** Tallinna Laevauhisus (A/S) v Estonian State Steamhip Line (1947) 80 Lloyd's Rep 99; Novello & Co Ltd. v Hinrichsen Edition Ltd [1951] Ch 595; Bank voor Handel en Scheepvart NV v Slatford [1953] 1 QB 248. Cp. also Cheshire/North/Fawcett, at 138.

**1352** Fro example, Frankfurther v WL Exner Ltd [1947] CH 629 at 636–637.

**1353** See M. Wolff, Private International Law, at 526–527.

**1354** See also P.B. Carter, who pointed out that "the dominance of the lex situs rule, it would seem, is not easy to be thwarted by inhibitions about the enforcement of the proprietary effects of foreign public or penal law, in: Transnational Recognition, at 421.

**1355** [2007] EWCA Civ. 1374.

**1356** [2007] EWCA Civ. 1374, at 148.

fiscatory cases. Considering the governmental interest-test, the CA most likely regarded acquisitions that are footed on a compulsory process as giving effect to a governmental interest. Maybe, however, the distinction had to be made in order to be in consistence with previous case law, such as the *Princess Paley Olga-case,*[1357] or *Luther v Sagor.*[1358]

The consequence of this distinction is however that claims for the recovery of antiquities which are grounded on a possessory title will be treated as patrimonial in nature only if they are not based on acts which are expropriatory or confiscatory. This reasoning was also the basis for the part of the decision in *King of Italy v Medici,*[1359] in which it was decided that the sale of the historical documents, that had been exported in breach of Italian law would not be restrained.

Practically, this rule excludes all cultural property laws from being applied in English courts which do not provide for state ownership of all artefacts but instead work by means of controlling the illegal export of heritage items. Most export laws must be viewed to be confiscatory or expropriatory laws. India, for example, opted not to introduce state ownership of all newly discovered antiquities. All artefacts are solely protected by Art. 3 (1) of the Antiquities and Art Treasure Act 1972, which provides that "it shall not be lawful for any person, other than the Central Government or any authority or agency authorised by the Central Government on this behalf, to export any antiquity or art treasure." A recovery claim by India would probably not succeed under current English law.[1360]

Consequently, the "lack of possession-rule" applies, even if the act which protects the heritage items from being exported provides for automatic forfeiture. For example, Section 9 of the Australian Protection of Movable Cultural Heritage Act 1986 which, after *Att. Gen. of New Zealand v Ortiz,* was carefully drafted to provide for automatic forfeiture of illegally exported artefacts, says:

- Where a person exports an Australian protected object otherwise than in accordance with a permit or certificate, the object is forfeited.
- Where a person attempts to export an Australian protected object otherwise than in accordance with a permit or certificate, the object is liable to forfeiture.
- A person is guilty of an offence if:

**1357** [1929] 1 KB 718.
**1358** [1921] 3 KB 532.
**1359** King of Italy v Marquis Cosimo de Medici Tornaquinci (1918) 34 T.L.R. 623.
**1360** See also the Giant Mogul Gold Coin-claim recently rejected by Switzerland, this Chapter, § 6, II; cp. also Marc-André Renold, The Giant Antique Mogul Gold Coins, 13 IJCP (2006) 361

- the person exports, or attempts to export, an object; and
- the object is an Australian protected object;
- the person's conduct referred to in paragraph (a) is otherwise than in accordance with a permit or certificate.

Art. 38 (a) of the same Australian Act stresses:

> Where a protected object is forfeited by or under this Act – (a) all title and interests in the object is vested in the Commonwealth without further proceedings

As the law stands now, a recovery of Australian artefacts in England will not be possible as the Australian law is clearly confiscatory in that it deprives someone who already owns antiquities of their title to them without granting any compensation.

The ratio of the confiscatory/non-confiscatory distinction made in *Barakat* has to be put in contrast with the CA's earlier opinion on export legislation where it stated that export laws may be but don't necessarily have to be unenforceable under Dicey Rule 3.[1361] This leaves a potential loophole for laws which are export laws, but do not give effect to a governmental interest in that they are not confiscatory or expropriatory.

### III. Cross-Border Enforcement on the Ground of Public Policy

A more liberal approach in English academic literature and case law suggests to abrogate the rigid non-enforcement of other public laws – doctrine.[1362] Conversely, it is being advocated that courts should adopt a degree of flexibility, correctly pointing to the fact that there is no decision which binds the courts to find that there is a rule, which prevents the enforcement of all foreign public laws.[1363] According to this rationale, the case for withholding or limiting the effect to be given to foreign public laws should generally be assessed on a case-by-cases

**1361** Cp. above.

**1362** M. Wolf, Private International Law, at 504 et seq; P.B. Carter, The Role of Public Policy in in English Private International Law, 42 I.C.L.Q. (1993) 1; Adeline Chong, Transnational Public Policy in Civil and Commercial Matters, Vol. 128 L.Q.R. (2012) 88.

**1363** See e.g. Iran v Barakat [2007] EWCA Civ 1374, at 125; cp. also FA Mann himself in Prerogative Rights, at 513, ad the recent issue of Dicey/Morris/Collins, Rule 3, at 5–040.

basis. More specifically, the test should be one assessed on public policy considerations.[1364]

### 1. The Notion of Public Policy

In order to further dwleve on whether the non-enforcement of other public laws-rule can be abolished in favor of a public policy-test, it is necessary to take a closer look at the theory of public policy in general.

Public policy serves as a correction tool of last resort if the outcome of a legal dispute is incompatible with the general ideas of the law of the forum. The theory of public policy is based on the fundamental economic, legal, moral, political, religious and social standards of a state or legal community.[1365] It is understood to be the credo which does not permit the doing of anything that could harm the basic principles of any society. As the content of what constitutes public policy develops according to the development of the relevant community, public policy has always excaped precise definition. This lack of clarity is one explanation for the hesitant application of the doctrine in common law courts.[1366] As opposed to the practice in civil courts, where public policy consti-

---

**1364** See A. Rushworth, Assertion of Ownership by a Foreign State over Cultural Objects Revoved from its Jurisdiction, L.M.C.L.R. (2008) 123 (following a combined approach of public international law and public policy); P.B. Carter, Transnational Recognition, at 429 (stating that the enforcement of foreign laws should be assessed on individual merits); G. Kegel, Internationales Privatrecht, at 855. Regarding the restitution of cultural property see Quentin Byrne-Sutton, Le traffic international des biens culturels sous 'langle de leur revendication par L'État d'origine: Aspects de droit international privé, 52 Schweizer Studien zum Internationalen Recht (1988), at 175–178; P. Lalive, L'application du droit public étranger, Rapport préliminaire et rapport déf-initif avec projets de-résolutions. – Annuaire de l'Institut de Droit International, session de Wiesbaden, vol. 56, (1975) 157; L.V. Prott, Problems of Private International Law for the Protection of the Cultural Heritage, 5 Recueil des Cours (1989) 215, at 291.

**1365** See Lew/Mistellis/Kroell, at 422; J. Enterria, The Role of Public Policy in International Commercial Arbitration, 21 L & Pol'Y Int'l Business (1989–90) 389.

**1366** Cp. e. g. A.E. Anton and P.R. Beaumont, Private International Law 42 ICLQ (1993) 1, at 3; Cheshire/Fawcette/North, Chapter 18 IV, 741; Neslon Enonchong, Public Policy in the Conflict of Laws: A Chinese Wall Around Little England?, 45 ICLQ, (1996) 631, holding the view that English choice of law rules have an "inbuilt forum-orientated bias which leads to the application of English law in many areas where in other countries, like France and Germany, foreign law will be applicable", at 637; William E. Holder, Public Policy and National Preferences – The Exclusion of Foreign Law in English Private International Law, 17 ICLQ (1968) 926, at 92; Chitty on Contracts, Chapter 16, at 16–003.

tutes a significant factor in the judicial pratice of private international law[1367], judges in England referred to it as "a treacherous ground for legal decision" or "very unstable and unsatisfactory". [1368] Borroughs J. used the famous metaphor of the policy principle being an "unruly horse".[1369] With the constant annaeherung of the two systems of laws, globalisation, as well as the harmonisation of EU law via instruments like the Rome Convention and Regulations, common law courts are becoming friendly with the concept of public policy. Consequently, English courts are creating more room in order to be able to introduce a liberal approach to the application of foreign public law.

It is generally accepted that the instrument of public policy can be devided in two categories:[1370] The first is what can be called "domestic" or "internal" public policy.[1371] Here, public policy is applicable only in a wholly domestic sence and differs considerably in its scope and function from today's principle of public policy in the domain of private international law. The second categroy is called "international public policy" or "ordre public externe".[1372] It is applied by the national courts to disputes that have a foreign element. The "domestic" and "international" – distinction is misleading, as in fact, both situtions refer to principles of national English law. The terminology only adds to the plethora of confusion that surrounds the principle of public policy in the UK.

It has been suggested that the harmonisation of the European Union in the field of private law and private international law may arguably have led to the development of a third category pf public policy in civil and commercial matters, namely EU public policy.[1373] The argument goes that public policy has been codified in the Rome I Convention and Rome II Regulation with no less than six provisions referring to it. The Brussles I Regulation also permits the forum

---

**1367** Batifol and Lagarde have described the freuent and widespread recourse to public policy in France as "abusive, cp. Batifol and Lagarde, Traité de droit international privé. Vol. I (7$^{th}$ ed.), at para 360.

**1368** Janson v Driefontein Consolidated Mines Ltd. [1902] A.C. 484, 500 and 507, per Lord Davey.

**1369** Cp. Richardson v Melish (1824) 2 Bing. 229, 252. Lord Denning M.R. later added: "With a good man in the saddle, the unruly horse can be kept in control. It can jump over obstacles", cp. Enderby Town Football Club Ltd. v Football Association Ltd [1971] 1 Ch. 591, 606 (C.A.).

**1370** See.e.g. W. Holder, Public Policy and National Preferences, at 926. For the history and role of this internal public policy see also W.S.W. Knight, Public Policy in English Law 38 L.Q.R. (1922) 207; Percy Winfield, Public Policy in the English Common Law, 42 Harv. L. Rev. (1929) 76;

**1371** See e. g. Ch. Brocher, Cours de Droit International Prive suivant les principes consacres par les droit postive francais, E. Thorin/Libraries H. Georg (1882), Vol 1, at 106 – 112.

**1372** Dicey/Morris/Collins, at 32 – 236; O. Kahn-Freund, Reflections on Public Policy in the English Conflict of Laws, Grotius Society (1953) 39, at 41.

**1373** Cp. also A. Chong, Transnational Public Policy in Civiland Commercial Matters, at 89.

court to refuse to recognise a foreign judgment if it is manifestly contrary to its public policy. Aside from this, the European Court of Justice has consistently maintained that the concept of public policy is for national courts to decide but at the same time it has reserved for itself the right to set the parameters within which the court may invoke public policy.[1374] The Surpreme Court alrady alluded to "European public policy".[1375]

This work supports the view that there is a fourth type of public policy, which by some proponents is being refered to as "transnational public policy"[1376], "international public policy", "supranational public policy", "world public policy"[1377] or "truly international"[1378] public policy. All of these notions are subject to subtle distinctions, but have in common the idea that public policy considerations can derive from an international source that exists above the state. For the purpose of this study, the term transnational public policy will be adopted as it is a term already familiar in the field of commercial arbitration, where it is used to help decide whether to recognise or enforce an international arbitral awards. Equally, the term "transnational public policy" will draw a contrats to the term "international public policy", which can be found in English private international law, as well as the the French concept of "ordre public international".

## 2. Public Policy and its Function as a Correction Tool

The general idea behind the doctrine of public policy is to creat an "escape route" for the court in order to prevent results which are incompatible forum

**1374** Cp. Krombach v Bamberski (C-7/98) [2000] E.C.R. I – 1935, at 22–23; Apostolides v Orams (C-420/07) [2009] E.C.R. I 3571, at 56; Regie Nationale des Usines Renault SA v Maxica SpA (C-38/98) [2000] EC.R. I-2973, at 27.

**1375** Lucasfilm Ltd. v Ainsworth [2011] UKSC 39; [2011] W.L.R. 487, at 91.

**1376** A. Chong, Transnatonal Public Policy in Civil and Commercial Matters, at 88; Gui Conde de Silva, Transational Public Policy in international Arbitration (2012); D.C. Burger, Transnational Public Policy as a Factor in Choice of Law Analysis 5 N.Y.L.Sch. J Int. & Comp. L. (1983–1984) 367.

**1377** Jan Dolinger, World Public Policy: Real International Public Policy in the Conflict of Laws 17 Texas Int'l L.J. (1982) 167 (and the sources cited therein).

**1378** P. Lalive, Transnational (or Truly International) Public Policy and Interational Arbitration, in: P. Sanders (ed.), Comparative Arbitration Practice and Public Policy in Arbitration (I.C.C.A. Congress Series No.3, 1987); James Fry, Désordre the Ordre Public International under the New York Concention: Wither Truly International Policy, Chinese Journal of International Law 8 No.8 (2009) 81.

law.[1379] The correction may be achieved by refusing to apply a foreign law, which according to the rules of private interational law would normally be applicable. Conflict lawyers call this the "negative function" of public policy.[1380] Equally, the adjustment may be achieved by applying forum law even though the case is indeed governed by a foreign law. This is the "positive function" of public policy.[1381] A third method to create an escape rout for the court is to allow a foreign law to impose itself although, according to the rule of the forum, its application is excluded. The correction takes place on on the ground of what was earlier referred to as "transnational public policy".

### a) Positive Public Policy

The notion "positive public policy" refers to the situation where national forum law may apply although the issue is, in principle, governed by a different foreign law.[1382] The reason for the positive application of a foreign provision is its fundemental importance for the protection of a certain national interest or group, such as rules consumer and employee protection, or equally, national rules on price controles, exchange controle or import or export prohibitions.

The concept derives from the French principle of "lois de police". There, Art. 6 of the French Civil Code states: "on ne droger, par des conventions particulieres, aux lois qui interessent l'ordre public et les bonnes moeors".[1383] In Germany, rules that positivly impose themselves onto forum law are referred to as "Eingriffsnormen", which in a literary sense means "rules that intervene".[1384]

---

**1379** Matthias Kuckein, Eingriffsnormen, Die 'Berücksichtigung' von Eingriffsnormen im deutschen und englischen internationalen Vertragsrecht (2008), at 179.

**1380** Chesire/North/Fawette, at 736; Peter E. Nygh The Reasonable Expectation of the Parties as A Guide to Choice of Law in Contract and Tort, 251 Hague Racueil (1995) 269, at 379–380; Frank Vischer, General Course on Private International Law, I Hague Recueil 9 (1991) 115, at 165; Kegel Schurig, Internationales Privatrecht, at § 16 I, Jan Kroppholler, Internationales Privatrecht, § 36 I, at 244.

**1381** P. Nygh, ibid, at 379–380; F. Vischer, ibid, at 165: Jan Kroppholler, ibid, at 244.

**1382** Cp. Cheshire/North/Fawcette, at 736.

**1383** On the concept of lois de police, see Nelson Enochong, Public Policy in the Conflict of Laws: A Chinese Wall Around Little England?, 45 ICLQ (1996) 631, at 637.

**1384** In Germany, the principle is codified in Art 34 EGBGB, cp. Staudinger Commentary on the German Civil Code (2002) Art. 34 EGBGB. For a detailed analysis of the concept under German law, see e. g. Matthias Kuckein, Eingriffsnormen, Klaus Schurig, Zwingendes Recht, Eingriffsnormen und neues IPR, Rabels Zeitschrift, 217; Andreas Köhler, Eingriffsnormen – der "unfertige" Teil des IPR (2013).

In England, such rules are known as "mandatory rules"[1385], "overriding rules", or "overriding statutes"[1386] and for a long time were not a principle which was widely popular among English jurists.[1387] The UK Law Comission, an independed body created in order to to keep the law under review and to recommend reform, described them as "domestic rules, which are regarded as so important that as a matter of construction or policy they must apply in any action before a court of the forum, even where the the issue is in principle governed by a foreign law selcetd by a choice of law rule".[1388] An example for what is an overriding statute under English law is the Unfair Contract Terms Act 1977 with its provisions of ristricing the parties' freedom to choose the applicable law, the Employment Rights Act 1996, or equally, the the Trade Union and Labour Relations (Consolidation) Act 1992.[1389]

With the adoption of the Rome I Convention[1390] and the subsequent Rome I Regulation 2005[1391], the concept of mandatory rules became obligatory in England. Both, the Convention and Regulation, are meant to establish uniform choice of law rules for contractual obligations throughout the European Community.[1392] In the Rome Convention, mandatory rules are regarded a key concept, with no less than six provisions referring to it.

The definition of the term is found in Art. 3 (3), stating that mandatory rules are "rules which cannot be derogated from by contract", whereas Art. 7 (2) of the Convention states that "nothing in this Convention shall restrict the application of the rules of law of the forum in a situation where they are mandatory irrespective of the law otherwise applicable to the contract". The latter suggests that

**1385** Fawcette [1990] C.L.J. 44.

**1386** Dicey/Morris/Collins, at 1–053

**1387** Cheshire/North/Fawcette, at 728; Matthias Kuckein, Eingriffsnormen, at 2, 155 et seq; Guido Carducci, Mandatory Rules, at 69.

**1388** Law Comission Working Paper No 87 (1984).

**1389** Sect. 289.

**1390** Convention on the Law Applicable to Contractual Obligation 1980 (ratified 1991) or "the Rome Convention", cp. Dicey/ Morris/ Collins, Chapter 32; Peter Kaye, The New Private International Law of the European Community (1993); Hill, International Commercial Disputes, (3rd ed. 2005) Chapter 14; Peter North (ed.), Contract Conflict – the EEC Convention on the Law Applicable to Contractual Obligation: A Comparative Study (1982); Chechire/North/Fawcette, Chapter 18 IV, at 667 et seq.

**1391** Plender/Wilderspin (eds.), The European Private International Law of Obligations (3rd ed, 2009); A.Belohlavek, Rome Convention/Rome I Regulation (2010); Gralf-Peter Callies (eds.) Rome Regulations (2014); Münchener Kommentart zum Bürgerlichen Gesetzbuch Gesetzbuch – IPR, Rom I-VO, Rom II-VO, Rom III-VO (5th ed 2014).

**1392** Rome I Convention, Art 1 (1).

Art. 7 (2) shall be regarded as a general exception to all choice of law rules in the Rome Convention.[1393]

The Rome Convention has been implemented in the UK via the Contracts Applicable Law Act 1990, which states that the Rome Convention shall have the force of law in the United Kingdom.[1394] The Convention is accompanied by the Guiliano and Lagarde Report[1395], which serves as an aid for interpretation of he Convention.[1396] The effect of the implementation was that for contracts made after the convention came into force, the traditional common law rules on contract choice of law are largely replaced by the rules contained in the Convention. It is not possible for the parties to contract out of the Convention as that would defeat its purpose.[1397]

The Rome I Convention 1980 has been replaced by the Rome I Regulation. The Regulation applies to contracts concluded after December 17, 2009 and is a modernised version of the Rome Convention. However, the provision of Rome I still apply to contracts before that date as well as to overseas ountries and territories of the European Union.

### b) Negative Public Policy

Public policy may serve to exclude foreign law.[1398] This negative function of public policy is inherent to most systems of private international law.[1399] Dicey and Morris have placed this rule at the very beginning of their conflict of law handbook, rightly pointing out the importance of the principle for the conflict of law. According to Rule 2,

> "*English courts will not enforce or recognise a right, power, capacity, disability or legal relationship arising under the law of a foreign country, if the enforcement or recognition (..) would be inconsistent with the fundamental public policy of English law*".[1400]

**1393** Cp. Cheshire/Nort/Fawcette, Chapter 18, at 737.
**1394** Sect. 2 (1).
**1395** OJ 1980 C 282.
**1396** Section 3 (3) of the Contracts (Applicable) Law Act 1990 allows for this Report to be considered by the English Courts, cp. Morris, The Conflict of Laws, 11–008.
**1397** Cheshire/North/Fawcette, Chapter 18, at 671.
**1398** N. Neslon Enonchong, Public Policy in the Conflict of Laws, at 47 et seq; Kegel Schurig, IPR (2004), at 516 et seq; Jan Kroppholler, IPR, 244
**1399** Civil law countries have statutory provisions on public policy. E.g. in Germany, this principle has been codified in Art.6 EGBGB (introductory Act of the German Civil Code). Cp. also Poland, Art. 1146 § 1 Nr. 5 Polish Civil Code; Art 31 Italian Civil Code.
**1400** Dicey/Morris/Collins, at 5R-001.

In England, public policy is known to have been applied in a "negative way" in order to give effect to fundamental principles of Human Rights. The courts have held that incapacities imposed on account of slavery[1401], religion[1402], alien nationality[1403] or physical incompetence[1404] and prodigality will be disregarded: In *Oppenheimer v Cattermole,*[1405] it was held obiter that Nazi nationality decrees depriving absent German Jews of their nationality and confiscating their property are regarded to be contrary to English public policy.[1406] Similarly, in *Williams & Humbert Ltd. v W&H Trade Marks (Jersey)*[1407] Ltd it was accepted that in appropriate circumstances the court would disregard a foreign confiscatory decree which offended principles of human rights.[1408]

In *Kuwait Airways Corporation v Iraqi Airways Company (No 4 and 5),*[1409] the court refused to apply an Iraqi Decree on the grounds that it was contrary to public policy. In this case, some aircrafts belonging to Kuwait Airways Corporation had been seized by the Iraqi authorities during the invasion of Kuwait and moved to Iraq. The Iraqi Revolutionary Council passed a Resolution to divest Kuwait Airways of its ownership of the aircrafts and vest ownership in Iraq. Kuwait air sued Iraq for damages, which was accepted as the correct forum. Although generally, confiscatory legislation is recognised when the confiscatory act has taken place on the territory of the confiscating state,[1410] the House of Lords excluded the Iraqi resolution from the bundle of Iraqi laws to be taken into consideration by the court on the grounds that the confiscation of aircrafts in the course of the Iraqi invasion was contrary to the international obligations of the United Kingdom. This was however the case were its courts to adopt an approach which was inconsistent with its duty under the United Nations Charter

**1401** Smith v Brown & Cooper (1701) Holt K.B. 495; Shanley v Harvey (1762) 2 Eden. 126; Sommersett's Case (1771) 20 St. Tr. 1; Chamberline v Harvey (1796) 5 Mod. 182; Forbes v Cochrane (1824) 2 B.& C. 448; Santos v Illidge (1860) 8 C.B. (N.S.) 861.

**1402** Re Metcalfe's Trust (1864) 2 De G.J. & S. 122; Stauart & Prentiss (1861) 20 U.C.R. 513; c.f. von Lorang v Adminstrator of Austrian Property [1927] A.C. 641.

**1403** Wolf v Oxholm (1817) 6 M.& S. 92; Re Krupp AG [1917] 2 Ch. 188; Re Askew [1930] 2 Ch. 259, 275; Re Helbert Wagg & Co Ltd. [1956] 323 at 345.

**1404** Worms v de Valdor (1880) 49 L.J. Ch.261; Re Selot's Trust [1902] 1 Ch. 488; criticised by Cheshire/North/Fawcette, at 129.

**1405** [1976] AC 249.

**1406** [1976] A.C. 249.

**1407** [1986] A.C. 368, 428, per Lord Templeman. See also The Playa Larga [1983] 2 Lloyd's Rep. 171, 190 (CA); Settebello Ltd. Banco Totta and Acores [1985] 1 W.L.R. 1050, at 1056.

**1408** On the recognition of confiscatory acts cp. Part II Chapter 6 § 3 II 3.

**1409** [2002] UKHL 19; [2002] 2. A.C. 883.

**1410** Note Chapter 6 § 3 II 3.

and under the relevant Security Council resolutions: The United Nation declared the invasion illegal, called on all member States not to recognise the invasion and demanded that Iraq rescind its actions purporting to annex Kuwait.

In the light of the previously mentioned case law regading the exclusion of foreign law *City of Gotha v Sotheby's and Cobert Finance SA,*[1411] feels somehow out of the oridinary. The case constitutes a rare example of a decision in relation to section 2 (1) of the Foreign Limitation Periods Act 1984. Sect. 2 (1) of the Act provides that a foreign limitation period shall not be applicable if it conflicts with English public policy.

We recall, that the case concered the recovery of Wtewael painting "The Holy Fmily", where the Federal Republic of Germany sought to recover the painting on the grounds that it was the successor of the Saxe-Coburg Art Foundation and consequently, the owner of the painting. [1412] The City of Gotha also entered the claim, alleging possessory title to the painting. After having examined German law, being the lex situs of the claim, the judge came to the conclusion that Germany's claim to the painting was not time barred as the German statute of limitation was contrary to English public policy. In Moses J.'s view, the German civil code paid no regard to the state of mind of the defendant or to the fact that the painting was stolen and this conflicted with English public policy.[1413] In particular, the City of Gotha could prove that Cobert Finance were not in good faith and had deliberately and unconscionably concealed information relevant to the claim and disregarding these facts for the purpose of English law was contrary to section 2 (1) Foreign Limitation Periods Act 1984.

The judgment caused ripple in the water up until the German parliament. However, althuogh a change in the law has been debated in 1991, the parliament has thwarted to the limitation period in property matters in favor of the principle of commercial certainty. The omission to change the limitation period has not been spoken of until the discovery of some 1200 paintings and drawings at the flat Cornelius Gurlitt in 2013, most of which were allegedly looted during the Holocaust or confiscated as degenrate art in World War II. Hildebrandt Gur-

**1411** The Times, October 1998, unreported; also Federal Republic of Germany v Sotheby's and Cobert Finance SA. For comments on this decision see Norman Palmer, Museum and The Holocaust, Appendix IV; Michael Carl/Herbert Güttler/Kurt Siehr, Kunstdiebstahl vor Gericht (2001); Antony Mair, The case of Wtewawael's The Holy Family 3 Art Antiquity and Law (1998) 413; Paul Lomas/Simon Orton, Potential Repercussions of the City of Gotha Decision 4 AAL (1999) 159.

**1412** The facts of the case have already been introduced in Chapter 6 § 3 II 1 c.

**1413** Moses J. identified a public policy in England that time is not to run either in favour of the thief, nor in favour of any transferee who is not a purchaser in goods faith. According to the judge, the Law favours the true owner of property which has been stolen, however long the period which has elapsed since the original theft.

litt, Cornerlius' father, and subsequently Cornelius Gurlitt himself hid the hoard although knowing that many of the paintings must have been confiscated or stolen. The discovery reheated the public debate regarding the German limitation period to property acquired in bad faith using Moses J.'s arguments to uphold Germany's claim to the Wtawael.

Notwithstanding the forth-mentioned cases, the method to disregard foreign law on the ground of the public policy principle is not frequently practiced by English judges.[1414] In *Kuwait Airways v Iraqi Airways* Lord Nichols emphesised the restricted scope of the public policy principle in England when he stated that "the courts of this country must have a residual power to disregard a provision of the foreign law when to do otherwise would affront basic principles of justice and fairness (..), to be excercised exceptionally and with the greates circumspection."[1415] In *City of Gotha*, Moses J. invoked public policy only with under the advise that "public policy should be invoked only in exceptional circumstances". He opined that "to resort to public policy too readily "would frustrate the English system of private international law which existed to fulfil foreign rights not destroy them."[1416]

### c) Transnational Public Policy

The application of public policy in a positive function can also occur on the ground of what is referred to as transnational public policy, that is public policy derived from supranational sources. It has been already said this concept is not new in the field of arbitration. What is new however, is the advent of the principle in civil and commercial matters, especially in the field of cultural property. For the purpose of this study, it shall be called the "public policy approach."[1417]

Where there can be detect a commonly established principle of international law, or equally a breach thereof, this commonly established principle may become part of the "public policy" of the forum:[1418] In *Oppenheimer v Cattermole*, it was ruled that it is part of English public policy to give effect to "clearly estab-

**1414** Cp. N. Enonchong, 632; P. Roggerson/ J. Collier, The Conflicts of Laws, at 432 et seq.

**1415** Kuwait Airways v Iraqi Airways, at 1077–1078.

**1416** Referring to the Law Commission Report No 114 3.2 (ii), 4.3.5 and Evans J. in Arab Monetary Fund v Hashim [1993] 1 Lloyds Rep. 543, at 592. According to the Law Commission's view, the public policy principle should apply only to "most unusual circumstances", at para. 4.39.

**1417** Martin Wolf called this approach "new" and considered it to be "sound and satisfactory", cp. M. Wolf, International Private Law, at 592.

**1418** Adeline Chong, Transnational Public Policy, 128 L.Q.R. (2012) 88, at 113. But see Jan Kropholler, IPR, § 36 I, at 244.

lished principles of international law".[1419] In *Lorentzen v Lydden*, some Norwegian law has been "positively applied" based on the principle of public policy, although the decree would indeed be unenforceable.[1420] The issue before the English Court was whether a war-time Norwegian decree, requisitioning all Norwegian ships situated outside Norway, affected a Norwegian ship in England. The "policy" at stake in the cases dealing with war-time decrees, was however not the fundamental public policy of the forum_but rather a "political policy".

*Kuwait Airways Kuwait Airways v Iraqi Airways*[1421] was a case in tort that had an underlying property case. In the event, the Iraqi war-time resolution were to be recognised, it would vest ownership in the aircrafts in the Iraqi state. As a consequence, Iraq would not be liable for converting them. The public policy that was applied in order to "escape" this outcome by the court was said to be one which was "truly international in nature". Lord Nichols of Birkenhead regarded it as being "plain beyond argument" that the seizure and assimilation of the aircraft where flagrant violations of rules of international law of fundamental importance".[1422] The actions of the Iraqi authorities breached both customary intrnational law and the UN Charter. Their Lordships emhesisd that the United Kingdom, as a member of the United Nations, had the obligation to accept and carry out decisions of the UN Security Council.[1423]

This study supports the view that transnational public policy may be invoked in order to positively allow the application of foreign sovereign patrimony laws. Staughton J. endorsed the "public policy approach" in *New Zealand v Ortiz*, but his judgment has been reversed by the Court of Appeal and House of Lords. In the trial court, Staughton J. allowed the restitution of the Maori panels, basing his judgment on reasons of what in the author's view can be regarded as transnational public policy. He recognised the fact that there was no specific category of a public law of foreign states that would not be enforced by the English courts and suggested that the enforcement or non-enforcement of such cases should be assessed on its individual merits. The Judge believed that courts had to consider in each case whether "there was a special ground of public policy, which requires the law in question not to be enforced".[1424] He then correctly stated

**1419** [1976] A.C. 249, at 278.

**1420** Cp. Lorentzen v Lydden & Co [1942] 2 K.B. 202. Overruled by Peer International Corp. v Termidor Music Publishers [2003] EWCA Civ 1156. For a different view see, Elsabe Schoemann, Lorentzen v Lydden – Dead and Burried? 10 New Zealand Business L. Rev. (2004) 285.

**1421** [2002] UKHL 19; [2002] 2 A.C. 883.

**1422** Ibid, at 29; at 115, per Lord Steyn; at 114, per Lord Hope.

**1423** Cp. also Apostolides v Orams [2010] EWCA Civ. 9; [2011] Q.B. 519.

**1424** [1982] 1 Q.B. 349, at 371.

that applying the test of public policy, which required the court to respect the national heritage of other countries by recognition and enforcement of their laws, as well as the hope of reciprocity, led him to the conclusion that the court should enforce the provisions of section 12 of the Historic Articles Act 1962. Staughton J. based his judgment on the assumption that "comity requires that we should respect the national heritage of other countries, by according both recognition and enforcement to their laws which affect the title to property while it is within their territory. [1425]

In *Iran v Barakat*, the Court of Appeal declared that there are positive reasons of policy why a state claim for the recovery of antiquities should be enforced. The court overrules the decision of Justice Gray in the trial court and generally agreed with the reasoning of the Wiesbaden Resolution of the Institute of Private International Law[1426] that a certain degree of flexibility should be applied in respect of claims to enforce foreign public laws. The CA stated that there is international recognition that States should assist to prevent the unlawfull removal of cultural objects and there was international acceptance of the desirability of protection of the national heritage. It would be therefore " contrary to public policy for such claims to be shut out.[1427] In consequence, the CA allowed a foreign law to impose itself on the basis of transnational public policy.

Although Lord Denning opined in *Ortiz* that it may be a desirable goal to enforce foreign cultural property laws, the rule of non-enforcement of foreign public laws has been judicially approved.

This may be the reason why, the CA's ruling is in some respects progressive as concerns public policy, but stays traditional regarding its findings on export laws. Indeed, the Court shut out most claims footed on export legislation by restricting the scope of laws recognisable in English courts via the confiscatory/non-confiscatory distinction.[1428] If the CA was consistent in its approach to apply public policy as a positive factor in claims for the recovery of cultural property, then claims grounding on export legislation may have to be recognised even if the the foreign act is considered to be confiscatory or expropriatory.

In fact, the courts ruling seems inconsistent in it earlier finding that "it might be contrary to public policy not to enforce certain types of laws, such as legal acts for the protection of the environment or national heritage items". This

**1425** [1982] 1 Q.B. 349, at 372.

**1426** Cp. Chapter 6 § 2

**1427** [2007] EWHC Civ. 1374, at 154.

**1428** In Lorentzen v Lydden, the Norwegian decree was held to be non-confiscatory, note above.

also includes foreign export laws whose aim is to protect cultural property from being illegally acquired and smuggled out of their country of origin.

### 3. Cultural Property as a Policy Consideration

Commentators criticised that ultimately public policy alone is too unspecific a concept to rely upon in formulating a legal rule to define the fine margin between recognition and enforcement,[1429] the concept of public policy being not nearly as sophisticated in England as that of its continental European counterparts.[1430] Indeed, the non-enforcement-rule as stated in *Dicey* can be abrogated in favor of a test based on policy consideration only if a transnational public policy to enforce the law in question is evident. In *Peer International Corp v Termidor Music Publishers Ltd. (No. 1)*,[1431] a dispute about the ownership of the English copyright in certain musical works, composed by Cuban nationals.

Termidor Music Publishers Ltd. claimed to be the exclusive licensees of the English copyright that belonged to a Cuban company, EMC. EMC based their claim on ownership on the operation of Cuban Law 860 which came into effect in August 1960 after the Cuban Revolution.[1432] The Cuban Decree purported to have the effect of divesting UK companies of ownership of UK copyright. Aldous L.J. and Mance L.J. rejected EMC's submission that the Cuban legislation should be given effect on the grounds of public policy and comity as they could not detect any internationally accepted public policy as to the assignment of copyright. Hence they rejected the positive application of the Cuban law.

As opposed to the fats of the cace in *Termidor*, there exist a vast amount of legislation that has been enacted in order to ensure the protection of cultural heritage, to prevent their illegal appropriation or to or to facilitate its return to their countries of origin. Hence, there is strong crendece to the view that a transnational public policy of protection of cultural heritage in general has emerged.[1433]

Since the decision in *Ortiz*, most EU countries have implemented Council Directive 1993 and ratified both, the UNESCO and UNIDROIT Conventions. Interna-

---

**1429** C.A Whomersley, Case Commen: Foreign States and British Courts, LQR (2009) 277, at 231 et seq.

**1430** See N. Enonchong, Public Policy in the Conflict of Laws, at 637.

**1431** [2004] 2 WLR 849.

**1432** For a detailed comment on the case see Elsabe Shoeman, Lorentzen v Lydden – Dean and Burried?, 10 New Zealand Buisness Law Quarterly (2004) 285.

**1433** Cp. L.V. Prott, Problems of Private International Law for the Protection of Cultural Heritage, 217 Hague Receuil de Cours (1989) 218; Adeline Chong, Transnational Public Policy, at 105.

tional awareness as to cultural property protection has largely increased. Conversly, in Ortiz, no such awareness existed. Although the UNESCO Convention entered into force in 1970, the Convention was not mentioned in the decision. Lord Denning actually emphasised the need for "an international convention on the matter where individual countries can agree and pass the necessary legislation."[1434]

In *City of Gotha v Sotheby's*, Moses J. considered the statutory codified public policy in relation to art objects when deciding about the application of the German limitation period, but decided against it, although admitting that it would be "attractive" to apply some special considerations to a work of art when there exists a possibility of it being displayed to the public.[1435] He feared, however, to be numbered among the "idiosyncratic interferences of a few judicial minds," if doing so.[1436]

Some three dacades later, however, the CA in *Barakat* was satisfied that the variety of instruments enacted by the international community to protect cultural heritage indicated a certain common public policy. In its judgment, the CA referred to Articles 2, 3 and 13 of the UNESCO Convention,[1437]to EC Directive 93/7,[1438] and to Articles 3 (2) Arts. 4, 5 (1) and 6 (1) of the 1995 UNIDROIT Convention.[1439] It also mentioned the Commonwealth Scheme for the Protection of the Material Cultural Heritage, adopted in Mauritius in November 1993, following proposals made by the New Zealand Government after the failure of its action in the *Ortiz-case*.[1440] The court admitted that none of these instruments directly affected the outcome of the appeal, but it stressed that such instruments do illustrate an international acceptance of the importance to protect cultural herit-

**1434** Lord Denning stated that "there should be an international convention on the matter where individual countries can agree and pass the necessary legislation", [1982] 3 WLR 571, at 585. See further, J.F. Nafziger, The New International Legal Framework for the Return, Restitution or Forfeiture of Cultural Property, NYU Journal of Int'l L. and Pol. (1983) 799.

**1435** He referred to EC Directive 93/7/EEC 1993 and the Council Regulation on the Return of Cultural Objects 1994, but noted that the acts did not apply in this case. He could further not identify any public policy deriving from these acts, which extended to objects stolen after the war.

**1436** Citing P.B. Carter, The Foreign Limitation Periods Act 1984, 101 LQR (1985) 68, at 71.

**1437** [2007] EWCA Civ. 1374, at 156.

**1438** [2007] EWCA Civ. 1374, at 160. The Directive was incorporated into English law with effect from March 2, 1994 by the Return of Cultural Objects Regulations 1994, SI 1994/501, as amended by SI 1997/1719 and SI 2001/3972, cp. Chapter 4.

**1439** The Convention was signed by the UK in June 1995, and came into force in 1998 when the necessary five ratifications had been effected, cp. Chapter 4.

**1440** The Commonwealth Scheme is based on mutual recognition of export prohibitions, but it has not resulted in concrete action.

age.[1441] Against the background of *Ortiz* and *Barakat*, it can be concluded that the recent case law exhibits a strong public policy in respect of the protection of a foreign nation's cultural heritage.

Irrespective of positive public policy concerning the protection of cultural heritage, it remains open to a defendant to plead that there might be competing positive reasons of public policy not to enforce the claim in question, such as the principle of security of transaction or the fact that the property in question was expropriated without compensation, when the expropriation was at the same time discriminatory or contrary to established principles of public international law.[1442]

## IV. Reflections on England and Wales

The previous chapter depicts that the rule of "non-enforcement of other foreign public laws" has been judicially approved by the English Courts in cases where the foreign law had been considered to be confiscatory, as well as in cases on the revolution against foreign governments.[1443] In cultural property cases however, the rule leads to anomalous results: Wheather a claim is held to be justiciable in Enland depends on whether it will be held a prerogative claim or a patrimonial claim. This again hinges on the distinction between recognition and enforcement. That once more relies on the factor whether the foreign state was able to perfect its title to the cultural object while it is still within its jurisdiction. It is obvious that this legal technique can only produce unsatisfactory result.

In *New Zealand v Ortiz*,[1444] the Court of Appeal considered the New Zealand heritage law to be a prerogative claim and thus unenforceable because to allow the claim for the recovery of the maori panels would entail an excersice of a sovereign authority outside its own jurisdiction which contravees the principle of territoriality. If however, New Zealand would have perfected its title through gaining possession of the panels, a claim to assert this title would have been

**1441** [2007] EWCA Civ. 1374, at 163.

**1442** In Kuwait Airways Corp. v Iraqi Airways Co. (Nos. 4 and 5) [2002] UKHL 19, [2002] 2 A.C 883, the House of Lords declined to recognise Iraqi legislation transferring Kuwaiti aircrafts to Iraq Airways following the Iraqi invasion of Kuwait because the invasion and occupation was in breach of international law including Iraq's obligation under resolutions of the United Nations Security Council.

**1443** President of the State of Equatorial Guinea v Royal Bank of Scotland International [2006] UKPC 7; Mbasogo v Logo (No.1) [2006] EWCA Civ 1370; [2007] Q.B. 846.

**1444** Ibid.

held to be justiciable. Via *Barakat*, English courts made an important step to circumvent this anomaly. First, by relying on the vested rights-doctrine and drawing a line between the recognition and enforcement of soverein claims: Iran's claim was held to be patrimonial as Iran was able to establish an immediate right of possession that would be recognised in England. Secondly, by invoking transnational public policy. Thirdly, the *Barakat-decision* has put the UK in alignment with the 1970 UNESCO Convention which requires that illegally obtained artefacts ought to be returned. The court's findings also complement the recent Dealing in Cultural Objects and Offences Act 2003, which is not retroactive and applies only to objects taken after 2003. *Barakat* on the other hand applies to antiquities stolen anytime after the requesting state has enacted its cultural heritage statute.

But *Barakat* does not resolve the anomaly completely: While the acquisition of a possessory or proprietary title based on a foreign cultural property law will be recognised if the title was perfected within the territory of the requesting state, the recognition of rights based on export legislation is unclear. The CA does not exclude per se claims based on export legislation, as it does not expressly deem such laws to be giving effect to a "governmental interest". It also admits that claims based on an immediate right of possession are to be recognised. But it sticks to the "confiscatory – non confiscatory" – distinction and excludes expropriatory laws as unjusticiable. This distinction is inconsistent with the court's findings on transnational public policy. How, for example, an English court would decide if a claim was brought on the grounds of export legislation which is confiscatory but grants the state an immediate right of possession?

Although *Barakat* suffers drawbacks, the public policy-test as adopted by the Court of Appeal in order to justify the application of foreign public law is a much welcome and modern development. To rely on a test based on policy considerations in order to enforce or not to enforce foreign public law could rid the law of anomalies as produced in *Ortiz* and save the courts from having to bend established doctrines in order to make space from previous antiquated case law. The test may even lead to the application of foreign export laws protecting cultural heritage.

The conclude, the public policy-approach recognises the fundamental problem with illegally excavated antiquities that are looted directly from the ground and unrecorded before their theft. It normalises the role of national ownership statutes, putting them on a par with other forms of ownership by both nations and individuals.

# § 4. The U.S. Approach

Although the U.S. conflicts-of-law rules exclude claims based on foreign penal law or foreign revenue laws,[1445] U.S. courts recognise foreign cultural property laws within the application of the National Stolen Property Act [hereinafter: NSPA|,[1446] which imposes criminal liability on anyone who transports stolen property in interstate or foreign commerce, knowing it is stolen.[1447] In particular, goods, which were illicitly exported from its country of origin, have been deemed "stolen" in the sense of the NSPA. Consequently, the U.S. courts recognise and indirectly enforce certain types of foreign public law through interpreting criminal law provisions.

## I. The McClain-Doctrine

The so-called McClain-doctrine gives an answer to the question whether taking cultural objects in contravention of a foreign cultural property law creates a recognisable claim under the NSPA, especially in relation to antiquities that have never been possessed physically by the state asserting ownership.[1448] The NSPA is a federal criminal statute whose purpose is to help with the recovery of tangible, movable property where the possessor is aware of its illicit status.[1449] Sections 2314 and 2315 of the Act seek to prevent the interstate transport of such goods by prosecuting "whoever transports, transmits, or transfers in interstate or foreign commerce any goods, wares, merchandises, securities or money, knowing the same to have been stolen, converted or taken by fraud."[1450] If convicted, a defendant may be both fined and imprisoned. As the NSPA stands today, there is no express reference to the protection of cultural property, however, American courts have been using the Act to prosecute dealers of stolen antiquities. Under

**1445** See for example. J. Moore, A Digest of International Law (1906), at 236. Equally the cases The Antelope, 24 U.S. (10 Wheat.) (1825) 66; The SS Lotus, [1927] P.C.I.J., ser A, No 10; Banco Nacional de Cuba v Sabatino, 376 U.S. 398, 414 (1964).

**1446** National Stolen Property Act, ch. 33, Paragraph 3, 48 Stat. 749 (1934) (current version at 18 U.S.C. (1982).

**1447** See 18 U.S.C. sections 2314, 2315. The NSPA criminalises the transport and possession of stolen property but it does not define what "stolen" means.

**1448** Cp. J.H. Merryman/J. Nafzinger, The Private International Law of Cultural Property in the United States, 42 Am.J.Comp.L. Supp (1994) 221, at 225.

**1449** Kelly E. Yasaitis, National Ownership Laws as Cultural Property Protection Policy: The Emerging Trend in United States v Schultz, 12 IJCP (2005) 95, at 96 et seq.

**1450** See Sect. 2314.

the NSPA, the United States government, in effect, prosecutes the offender on behalf of the foreign government by applying that foreign country's national ownership law as the basis for finding the object stolen. This raises the question of whether something should be considered 'stolen' in a United States criminal proceeding when the object was unknown to its true owner prior to its theft.

The relationship between national ownership of antiquities and the NSPA was first litigated in *United States v Hollinshead.*[1451] In this case, an American court considered the application of foreign public law by interpreting the term 'stolen' of the NSPA.[1452] The case involved the taking of a rare Mayan stele in the Guatemalan jungle, sawed into pieces and imported the pieces into the Unites States. Guatemalan law purported to establish State ownership of all pre-Columbian artefacts located in the country.[1453] The court in the second instance convicted the dealer Hollinshead of transporting and conspiring to transport 'stolen property' under the NSPA. Hollinshead was thus prosecuted in the U.S. for a theft which is a crime only under Guatemalan law.[1454] In upholding his conviction, the Ninth Circuit reiterated that all the NSPA required was that Hollinshead knew that the stele was stolen. It was not necessary to show, that he was aware of applicable Guatemalan law.[1455] However, in *Hollinshead*, the Guatemalan government had knowledge about the stele and already took possession of it after it was excavated, and inventoried as Machaquila-Stele No. 2. Hollinshead discovered the piece and literary stole it from the excavation site. As such, the case does not raise problems of direct enforcement of public law, as the object was possessed physically before it was illegally exported to the U.S.[1456]

---

**1451** 495 F.2d.1154 (9th Cir. 1974).

**1452** J.H. Merryman, Protection of Artistic National Patrimony Against Pillaging and Theft, in: Leonard Duboff (ed.) Art Law: Domestic and International (1971) 236, at 245; Cynthia Ericson, United States of America v Frederick Schultz: The National Stolen Property Act Revives the Curse of the Pharaos, 12 Tul. J. Int'l & Comp.L. (2004) 509, at 515. For a detailed account of the case see William Hughes, United States v Hollinshead, 1 Hastings Int'l & Comp.L.Rev (1977) 149; Judith Church, Evolving U.S. Case Law on Cultural Property Disputes, 2 IJCP (1993) 47.

**1453** The laws of Guatemala under which the country claimed title included Articles 107 and 129 of its 1965 Constitution, Congress Decree No. 425 of 19 September 1947 as amended by Decree-Law No. 437 of 24 March 1966.

**1454** Cp. A. Müller-Katzenburg, at 190; Jonathan S. Moore, Enforcing Foreign Ownership Claims in the Antiquities Market, 97 Yale L.J. (1988) 470.

**1455** Cp. William J. Hughes, United States v. Hollinshead, at 153.

**1456** See also A. Müller-Katzenburg, at 69; Prott & O'Keefe, Movement (1989), at 722.

Using *Hollinshead* as its main precedent, the *United States v McClain-cases*[1457] established certain principles for analysing the nature of foreign national ownership laws, which later became known as the McClain doctrine.[1458] The two related decisions, colloquially known as *McClain I* and *McClain II*, concerned some pre-Columbian cultural artefacts from Mexico which were illegally imported by some art smugglers.[1459] Mexico claimed ownership of the objects by virtue of its cultural property statute.

In both decisions, the Fifth Circuit Court of Appeals affirmed that taking possession of cultural objects in violation of foreign treasure trove statutes can give raise to criminal liability under the NSPA. More specifically, the court constituted that an object may be considered 'stolen' within the meaning of the NSPA, if a foreign nation has assumed ownership of the object through its artistic and cultural patrimony laws.[1460]

In *McClain I*, the court undertook an analysis of the NSPA's use of the term 'stolen'. The court recognised national ownership declarations as an attribute of sovereignty, finding no legal distinction between property claimed by foreign cultural property legislation and property possessed in the more conventional sense. The court held that: "The state comes to own property only when it acquires such property in the general manner by which persons come to own property, or when it declares itself the owner, the declaration is an attribute of sov-

**1457** United States v McClain, 545 F.2d 988 (5th Cir. 1977), rehearing denied, 551 F.2d 52 (5th Cir. 1977) [McClain I]; United States v McClain, 593 F2d 658 (5th Cir. 1979), cert. denied, 444 U. S. 918 (1979) [McClain II]. The cases have already been introduced in Chapter 2 § 2 I 6 in reation to the "quality of the properitary title".

**1458** Cp. Adam Goldberg, Reaffirming McClain: The National Stolen Property Act and the Abiding Trade in Looted Cultural Objects, 53 UCLA Law Rev. (2006) 1031, at 1040. The McClain-doctrine became subject to severe criticism by US commentators, for example Judith Church, Evaluating the Effectiveness of Foreign laws on National Ownership, 30 Colum.J. Transnat'l L. (1992) 179; JH Merryman, Case Note: Limits on State Recovery of Stolen Artifacts: Peru v Johnson, 1 IJCP (1992) 169, at 171 et seq.; P. Bator, An Essay, at 351 ("What will be the impact of McClain in controlling the import of looted antiquities?"); William G. Pearlstein, Claims for the Repatriation of Cultural Property: Prospects for a Managed Antiquities Market, 28 Law & Pol'y Int'l BuS (1996) 123, at 135–36 (noting that "other than in McClain and Hollinshead, in no case to date" had any defendant come close to receiving an NSPA conviction under McClain doctrine). W.J. Hughes, United States v. Hollinshead, 149; R.S. Kaufmann (ed.), The Art Law Handbook, at 411–12 (stating that the McClain doctrine principles put the United States in a position of enforcing foreign laws that are poorly understood or not properly applied by the government involved).

**1459** Cp. A. Golberg, Reaffirming McClain, at 1031 et seq; K. Yasaitis, National Ownership Laws as Cultural Property Protection Policy: The Emerging Trend in United States v Schultz, 12 IJCP (2005) 95.

**1460** Cp. A. Goldberg, Reaffirming McClain, at 1041.

ereignty."[1461] Further the court stated: "Possession is but a frequent incident, not the sine qua non of ownership, in the common law or the civil law."[1462] The court correctly cited U.S. law under which a state or national government may be an owner even though it never had possession of the goods it owns.[1463] The court added however that "the mere violation of export restrictions does not make possession of the illegally exported property a violation of the NSPA."[1464] In other words, foreign umbrella statutes are unenforceable in the United States unless they establish national ownership.[1465] Consequently, the court allowed a criminal conviction under the NSPA arguing that Mexico's law declared itself the owner of all antiquities "with sufficient clarity to survive translation into terms understandable by American citizens" and the antiquities count as 'stolen' under sections 2314 and 2315 of the NSPA. The smugglers were convicted of both violating the NSPA and conspiring to violate the NSPA. The defendants appealed on two grounds. First, they argued that 'stolen' as used in the NSPA means only the wrongful deprivation of physical possession. Mexico had never alleged such deprivation, and the defendants insisted they had engaged only in unauthorised export, a conduct which is not penalised under U.S. law. Additionally, the defendants contested the lower court's determination that Mexican law had established state ownership of all pre-Columbian artefacts at the time the relevant objects were removed from Mexico and additionally, they argued that Mexican laws were too vague and inconsistent to give the defendant proper notice of the status of the objects in question.[1466]

In *McClain II*, the court stated that "(...) we agree with the earlier panel that it is proper to punish through the NSPA encroachments upon legitimate and clear Mexican ownership, even though the goods may never have been physically possessed by agents of the nation".[1467] However, the court held that property claim-

**1461** U.S. v McClain I 545 F. 2d 988 (1977), at 1002.

**1462** U.S. v McClain II, 593 F. 2d 658 (1979), at 671.

**1463** See for example, United States v Plott, 345 F. Supp. 1229, 1232 (S.D.N.Y.1972), United States v Klapisch, No. 77–620, slip op (E.D.N.Y. July 28, 1978), concerning state ownership of alligators; Geer v Connecticut, 161 U.S. 519, 529 (1896), concerning state ownership of wild life.

**1464** McClain I, at 1002.

**1465** McClain I, at 1002. See also A. Goldberg, Reaffirming McClain, at 1042. The distinction is significant, the general rule in the U.S. is that one does not violate U.S. law by importing an object in violation of another countries export laws, see for example Leonard Duboff, Art Law (1975), 295–300; J.H. Merryman, The Retention of Cultural Property, 21 U.S. Davis L.Rev. (1988) 477.

**1466** McClain II, at 690.

**1467** McClain II, at 671. See also Barbara Rosecrance, The McClain Decision, 19 Cornell Int'l L.J. (1986) 311.

ed by virtue of a foreign ownership vesting law cannot be considered 'stolen' under the NSPA unless the relevant ownership declaration is clear enough for U.S. citizens to understand. It only upheld the conspiracy conviction of the smugglers.[1468]

Taken together, *McClain I* and *McClain II* established the core of the McClain doctrine.[1469] The main principle of the doctrine is that taking possession of cultural objects in violation of foreign cultural property legislation can give rise to criminal liability under the NSPA. However, this principle is subject to certain limitations: The NSPA does require a high evidentiary burden of proof, because as a criminal statute, the elements of the crime must be proven beyond all reasonable doubt and there is an intent requirement that the prosecution must prove on the part of the defendant. First, the ownership declaration must be sufficiently clear so as to give adequate notice of what conduct is prohibited, particularly in a criminal prosecution.[1470] Second, the claimant must prove that the antiquity was found within the modern territory of the nation, and the act giving raise to the prosecution must have taken place after the effective date of the vesting legislation.[1471] These requirements are necessary in order to avoid giving the national legislation extraterritorial or retroactive effect. [1472]

The McClain doctrine was largely criticised by supporters of the 'free-market-approach'.[1473] Paul Bator, for instance, argued that applying the NSPA to property which had never been known or possessed by the states blurred the lines between the enforcement of export control and the recognition of ownership declaration.[1474]

Another argument put forward against the McClain doctrine was the overlap between the application of the NSPA for the purpose of cultural property protection and the U.S. Cultural Property Implementation Act [CPIA], which implemented the 1970 UNESCO Convention in the United States.[1475] The United States signed UNESCO before *McClain* was decided, but it was not until 1983 that the CPIA

**1468** Cp. J. Church, Evaluating the Effectivness, at 185.

**1469** Cp. A. Goldberg, Reaffirming McClain, at 1042; Andrea Cunning, U.S. Policy on the Enforcement of Foreign Export Restrictions on Cultural Property & Destructive Aspects of Retention Schemes, 26 Hous. J. INT'L L. (2004) 449, at 486 – 487; P. Gerstenblith, The Public Interest in the Restitution of Cultural Objects, 16 Conn. J. Int'l. L. (2001) 198, at 216.

**1470** McClain II, at 670 – 671.

**1471** McClain I, at 1000 – 1001.

**1472** Cp. P. Gerstenblith, Schultz and Barakat, at 25.

**1473** For the 'free-market-approach' see Chapter 1, Introduction.

**1474** P. Bator, An Essay on the International Trade in Art, at 348 – 349 (quoting McClain I).

**1475** For the Implementation of the UNESCO Convention via the CPIA see Chapter 4 § 3 IV 2 a. (1).

was enacted to implement the Convention.[1476] Critics of *McClain* argued that the CPIA precluded the application of the NSPA. The CPIA was specifically designed to protect cultural property while the NSPA was not. According to some scholars the CPIA was intended to be the sole Congressional statement on international cultural heritage policy.[1477] The CPIA imposes import restrictions only under limited circumstances,[1478] and the NSPA allegedly could not criminalise a broader range of cultural-objects-related activities.[1479]

Proponents of the McClain doctrine contended that the language of the statute in no way indicates preemption of the NSPA.[1480] To the contrary, the CPIA's legislative history indicates expressly that Congress never intended the Act to preempt or modify any existing federal law.[1481] Additionally, senators who believed that the CPIA should replace the McClain doctrine as the sole expression of American cultural objects policy tried twice after the CPIA's passage, without success, to introduce new legislation mandating preemption.[1482]

Despite the implementation of the CPIA, courts continue to apply the reasoning of the McClain doctrine to find national ownership laws as grounds for declaring cultural property as 'stolen'.[1483] Pursuant to the *McClain* decisions, the state department moved to conclude a bilateral treaty with Mexico and executive agreements with Peru and Guatemala, that have been necessary in order to implement the UNESCO Convention in the United States.

---

**1476** See in detail Chapter 4.

**1477** See e.g. Merryman/Elsen/Urice (eds.), Law, Ethics and the Visual Arts, at 262. Senator Daniel Patrick Moynihan argued in 1985 to amend the NSPA and expressly limit its reach in situation where the CPIA should apply, cp. Brief of Amici Curiae in Support of the Appeal of Defendant-Appelant Frederick Schultz, 333 F. 3d 393 ($2^{nd}$ Cir. N.Y. 2003).

**1478** See Chapter 4, at IV 1.

**1479** Cp. Merryman/Elsen/Urice (eds.), Law, Ethics and the Visual Arts, at 262.

**1480** See e.g. A. Goldberg, Reaffirming McClain, at 1059; P. Gertsenblith, The Public Interest in the Restitution of Cultural Objects, at 220; James F. Fitzpatrick, A Wayward Course: The Lawless Customs Policy Toward Cultural Properties, 15 N.Y.U. J. Int'l L. Pol. (1983) 857, at 862–864.

**1481** The Senate Report on the CPIA states that the it "neither pre-empts state law in any way, nor modifies any Federal or State remedies that may pertain to articles to which [CPIA] provisions apply." Schultz, 333 F.3d at 408 (quoting S. REP. NO. 97–564, at 22 (1982), reprinted in 1982 U.S.C.C.A.N. 4078, 4099). Significantly, the Senate Report also states that the CPIA "affects neither existing remedies available in state or federal courts nor laws prohibiting the theft and the knowing receipt and transportation of stolen property in interstate and foreign commerce .... " (emphasis added). The NSPA is just such a law.

**1482** James F. Fitzpatrick, A Wayward Course, at 864; A. Goldberg, Reaffirming McClain, at 1059.

**1483** K. Yasaitis, U.S. v Schultz, at 100.

## II. McClain Revisited – United States v Schultz

In 2003, the McClain-doctrine was reaffirmed in the case *United States v Schultz*,[1484] where the defendant Frederick Schultz, one of the most prominent art dealers in the U.S. and president of the National Association of Dealers in Ancient, Oriental and Primitive Art was convicted under the NSPA of transporting and conspiring to receive stolen Egyptian antiquities in violation of Egypt's national ownership law No. 117.[1485] With his conspirator Jonathan Tokeley-Parry, a British conservator, Schultz purchased various looted antiquities, dipped them in plastic, and painted them to represent cheap souvenirs to smuggle them out of Egypt. [1486] In addition, Schultz and Tokeley-Parry copied 19th century pharmaceutical labels onto paper that had been baked and tea stained, claiming the artefacts belonged to the Thomas Alcock – Collection, whereby they turned newly excavated antiquities into 'legitimately owned' English pieces.[1487] If objects were legitimately owned before the 20th century, it would be harder to prove they were taken under violation of the ownership law which was in force in Egypt by that time. When British authorities investigated Tokeley-Parry's illegal trade, they discovered Schultz's illicit activities, as Tokeley-Parry implicated Schultz both in his personal documents and in his trial testimony.[1488]

The *Schultz-trial* began in 2002. Schultz argued that Egyptian Law No. 117 was an export law and consequently no real ownership rights could vest in Egypt. He claimed that because Egypt never actually possessed the objects in question, the state's ownership was triggered only by their export and that it was against U.S. Policy to enforce another countries export control law. Without considering whether this assessment of U.S. policy was correct, the court in

---

**1484** United States v. Schultz 333 F. 3d 393 (2nd Cir. June 25 2003). See also Martha Lufkin, The Schultz-Case, 8 AAL (2003) 321. Furthermore, United States v Pre-Columbian Artefacts 845 F. Supp. 544 (N.D. 111.1993), where a federal district court in Illinois held that a Guatemalan treasure law could provide the basis for an NSPA claim, even though the law did not vest national ownership until objects were exported illegally.

**1485** United States v. Schultz, 333 F.3d 393 (2d Cit. 2003). See e. g. Cynthia Ericson, Note, United States of America v. Frederick Schultz: The National Stolen Property Act Revives the Curse of the Pharaohs, 12 TUL. J. INT'L & COMP. L. (2004) 509, at 521 (noting that before his indictment, Schultz had been the president of the National Association of Dealers in Ancient, Oriental, and Primitive Art, and also had served as the president of the International Association of Dealers in Ancient Art).

**1486** Peter Watson, The Investigation of Frederick Schultz, 10 Culture Without Context (2002) 21.

**1487** Cp. J.H. Marryman, Symposium III, Ownership and protection of Heritage: Cultural Property Rights of the 21st Centruy: Panel Discussion, 314.

**1488** K. Yasaitis, U.S. v Schultz, at 103.

Schultz dismissed the argument on the ground that Law No. 117 indeed is an ownership vesting law and not an export law.[1489] Both Egyptian witnesses for the United States "confirmed the purpose of Law 117 [as] . . . to bring all newly discovered antiquities within the direct possession and control of the Egyptian government in order to ensure that they are properly preserved and documented."[1490] Interestingly, although not taken up in the written opinion to the case, at oral argument one of the judges implied that sec. 2315 of title 18 NSPA, which states that "whoever receives, possesses, conceals, stores barters, sells, or disposes of any goods, (..) which have crossed a state or Unites States boundary after being stolen, unlawfully converted or taken," might also encompass the illegal export of artefacts.[1491] The court in Schultz further emphasised that other United States courts had previously prosecuted foreign thefts through the NSPA to deter United States citizens specifically from dealing with internationally stolen goods.[1492] While the trial court underlined the significant property interest a state has in protecting its symbolic heritage, seemingly whether or not that heritage is in its actual possession, the appellate court stated that, "the fact that the rightful owner of the stolen property is foreign has no impact on a prosecution under the NSPA."[1493]

The *Schultz*-judgment effectively established the McClain doctrine in the State of New York, which is the centre of the art trade in the United States. It also finally cleared out the argument brought up by critics of the McClain doctrine that the enactment of the CPIA which implemented the UNESCO Convention in the States,[1494] precluded the application of the NSPA and that the CPIA is intended to be the sole Congressional statement on international cultural heritage policy.[1495] The argument was rejected by the court, which concluded that the potential overlap of the two legal instruments is no reason to limit the reach of the NSPA. First, the court pointed out righly that the CPIA is am import law while the NSPA is a criminal law. Second, the court stated that through the plain language of the CPIA's legislative history, the CPIA was intended to exist concurrently with other criminal laws. Although the CPIA and the NSPA may overlap in certain areas, it was expressly stated in the CPIA's accompanying Senate report that "the implementation of Article 7 (b) of the [Cultural Property Im-

**1489** United States v Schultz, 333 F. 3d 393, at 407–408.
**1490** United States v Schultz, at 405.
**1491** See P. Gerstenblith, Schulz and Barakat, at 30.
**1492** United States v Schultz, at 448.
**1493** United States, v Schultz, at 402; 178 F. Supp. 2d 445, 446 n5.
**1494** For the Implementation of the UNESCO Convention via the CPIA see Chapter 4 I a) (1).
**1495** Cp. Merryman/Elson/Urice (eds.), Law, Ethics and the Visual Arts, at 262.

plementation] Convention affects neither existing remedies available in State or Federal courts, nor laws prohibiting the theft and the knowing receipt and transportation of stolen property in interstate and foreign commerce."[1496]

As a result of *Schultz*, the McClain doctrine provides more than moral censure, and the NSPA criminal sanctions allegedly have cooled the demand on the U.S. market for illicitly obtained objects.[1497] The decisions affirmed the trend whereby foreign cultural property ownership laws can be the basis for the prosecution of violators under the NSPA.[1498] However, the doctrine does not restrict the trade in cultural objects severely. Rather, it sets a low moral bar below which collectors should not be allowed to trade. Source countries have to comply with the strict limitations of *McClain* in order to succeed in a recovery claim. However, as a result of *McClain* and *Schultz*, the Metropolitan Museum of Art, the Boston Museum of Art, the Princeton Art Museum, the J. P. Getty Trust and the Cleveland Art Museum have returned approximately 100 works of ancient art to Italy. Although none of these returns were the result of litigation, it can be assumed that the threat of litigation contributed to these voluntary restitutions.

### III. Civil Recovery on the Grounds of McClain – An Antique Platter of Gold

The McClain doctrine was further utilised in the civil forfeiture and recovery of antiquities on the basis that they are stolen property. In United States v An Antique Platter of Gold,[1499] the U.S. government intervened on behalf of the Italian government to seek the forfeiture and return of an ancient gold platter to Italy purchased by a New York art collector.[1500] The platter was originally found on Italian soil and was eventually sold to an art dealer in Switzerland. It came to the attention of a New York art dealer, who agreed on behalf of one of his clients to purchase the object and import it into the United States. Some three years

**1496** S. Rep. No. 97–564, Title II.

**1497** A. Goldberg, Reaffirming McClain, at 1060.

**1498** Kelly Yasaitis, U.S. v Schultz, at 107.

**1499** United States v An Antique Platter of Gold, 991 F. Supp. 222, 230 (S.D.N.Y. 1997); Harlan Levy/Constance Lowenthal, Stolen and Smuggled Art, N.Y. L. J, (1997) 1; Jordana Hughes, Liberal Enforcement, at 139; Martha Lufkin, Criminal Liability for receiving State Claimed Antiquities, AAL (2003) 1, at 3; K. Yasaitis, National Ownership Laws, at 102.

**1500** The case is often called the *Steinhart-case*, after the collector who tried to regain his confiscated object. Another U.S.-case ordering the forfeiture of a moon rock belonging to Honduras and referring to McClain and the Antique Platter decision, is United States v One Lucite Ball containing Lunar Material, 252 F. Supp 2d 1367 (S. D. Fla. 2003).

after the purchase, the Italian government discovered the transaction and requested the assistance of the U.S. to recover the item. *Customs Directive No. 5230–15*, on which the court relied, requires customs officials to look into the place of origin of an object and whether that place has a national ownership law which could potentially support a claim for ownership. Specifically, the Customs Directive specifies that the "leading case construing the National Stolen Property Act as it relates to claims of ownership of cultural property by foreign countries is United States v. McClain."[1501]

U.S. customs officials succeeding in seizing the platter from the collector and a civil forfeiture trial against the collector ensued. The court held that the platter has been imported in violation of firstly, some prohibitions on the illegal importation of goods based on material false statements, and secondly, the NSPA.[1502] Despite the fact that the platter had been purchased in good faith, and for a substantial amount of money, the court held that by virtue of the old 1939 Italian Cultural Property Law, the object rightfully belonged to the government of Italy and had in effect been stolen. According to the Italian law, all archaeological finds and antiquities found on Italian territory automatically belong to the state unless a part can establish title predating the year 1902. As opposed to *Hollinshead*, in *Antique Platter*, there was no suggestion of the defendant's knowledge that the platter was stolen from Italy.[1503] To the contrary, the object originally was sold to someone other than the defendant. The only basis for concluding that the platter was stolen under the NSPA was the fact that the original sale and export of the object was in violation of Italy's cultural property statute.[1504] On that ground, the forfeiture of the platter was considered rightful, and the antiquity could return to Italy.[1505]

1501 Customs Directive 5230–15, Detention and Seizure of Cultural Property (Apr. 18, 1991) 8.
1502 See H. Levy/C. Lowenthal, Stolen and Smuggled Art, at 6; Jordana Hughes, Liberal Enforcement, at 140.
1503 United States v An Antique Platter of Gold, 991 F. Supp. 222, 230 (S.D.N.Y. 1997), at 225.
1504 991 F. Supp. 222, 230 (S.D.N.Y. 1997), at 231–232.
1505 But note Government of Peru v Johnson, 720 F. Supp. 810, 933 F.2d 1013 (9th Cir. 1991), where the court found that the requirements of the McClain-doctrine were not satisfied. The district court found that Peru's national umbrella statute was not sufficiently clear and it was not possible to prove that the Pre-Columbian antiquities where excavated within the modern borders of Peru. Compare also Republic of Croatia v The Trustee of the Marquess of Northhampton 1987 Settlement, 610 N.Y.S. 2d 263 (1st Dept. 1994).

### IV. Reflections on U.S. Law

Following this analysis, the American approach mirrors in several aspects the principles of the vested rights-doctrine and the public policy-approach, as well as the rules established in the 1975 Wiesbaden Resolution and the Resolution invoked by the International Law Association. Foreign public law is being applied by concretising the term 'stolen' under the National Stolen Property Act. By using this technique, American courts support the contention that foreign public law is not being excluded a priori from its application in a foreign forum. The recognition of foreign vesting statutes and even foreign export restrictions as exemplified by the *McClain* and *Hollinshead* decision not only complement the United States ratification of the UNESCO Convention but reflect its underlying spirit. Because the American implementing legislation does not accommodate the Conventions broad policy goals,[1506] enforcement of foreign public laws under the NSPA is a necessary concomitant to the Cultural Property Implementation Act.

## § 5. The German Approach

### I. General Rules

German law includes a claim for the recovery of chattels in § 985 BGB (German Civil Code).[1507] The claim is based on the Roman principle of *vinidicatio in rem* and requires the claimant to establish and prove ownership, meaning title based on a proprietary right. Furthermore, the German Civil Code allows for the recovery of chattels according to § 861 and § 1007 BGB, which are claims based on a possessory title, without the requirement of ownership. To the detriment of cultural heritage protection, German law provides for a reversal of the burden of proof in favor of the defendant. According to § 1006 BGB, the current possessor of the object in question, namely the defendant, is per se assumed to be the rightful owner of the object in question, unless the caimant proves that he has a better proprietary right.[1508] The rule is universal and has never been questioned but is subject to an exception. In case the object was stolen or otherwise illegally appropriated, § 1006 I 2 BGB reverses the burden of proof back in favor of the claimant.

---

**1506** Compare Chapter 4 § 3 IV 1 a (1).
**1507** Bürgerliches Gesetzbuch (German Civil Code).
**1508** Cp. e.g. Christian Baldus, in: Münchener Kommentar, § 1006 ($5^{th}$ ed. 2009).

For claimants of misappropriated artefacts this requirement often constitutes a significant hurdle. In a recent case in front of the Munich Court of Appeal[1509], a claim concerning a large collection of archaeological artefacts allegedly illegally exacavated in Nothern Cyprus was rejected and referred back to the regional court as Cyprus was unable to submit enough proof for the facts that the objects in question were excavated after the enactement of the Cypriotic Cultural Heritage Act 1930. The Act provides for state ownership of the government and is still valid law on the territory of Nothern Cyprus, which was invaded by Turkey in the 1970s.[1510] Cyprus was equally unable to submit proof that the objects were of Cypriotic origin. The court expressly denied the possibility of a reversal of the burden of proof in favor of the claimant and stressed that it would apply the principle of evidence as laid down in the German Code of Civil Procedure. On the other hand, Cyprus's claim for the collection of some ecclesiastical icons, which was pursued in the same proceeding, was successful as Cyprus accomplished to prove ownership to the objets via the testimony of an expert in Cypriotic art.[1511] The icons were all stolen from various chruches, abbeys and museums during the Turkish invasion in Nothern Cyprus. After their repatration, the icons can be now viewed at the Byzantine Museum in Nicosia. As opposed to that, the case in respect of the archaeological artefacts has to be continued in front of the regional court which will hear the testimony of further witnesses.

## II. Rules on Cross-Border Enforcement and Justiciability

### 1. The Imprint Theory

German courts lack jurisdiction to hear claims based on foreign public law, such as claims based on revenue laws or penal laws. However, the application of foreign public law is not excluded per se, if the legal act is relevant to preliminary issues of a claim is footed on private law.[1512] A claim based on private law is equivalent to what English courts consider a patrimonial claim. A patrimonial

**1509** OLG München, judgment of 18.03.2013 [AZ 19 U 4878/10].

**1510** The court held that Cyprus and not Turkey was indeed allowe to pursue the claim, as apart from Turkey, the Republic of Nothern Cyprus is not accepted by the community of states as an independent state according to international law. As a consequence, Cyprus did not loose the capacity of right of action as a result of the establishment of the Turkish Republic of Nothern Cyprus.

**1511** OLG München, ibid.

**1512** See e.g. G. Kegel/K. Schurig, Internationales Privatrecht, at 1092, with further references. Further more on German law concerning the application of foreign public law see, Matthias Weller, Iran v Barakat, at 174 et seq.

claim under German law would be, for example, a claim for the recovery of an ancient artefact, where foreign law has to be applied in order to determine the ownership of the chattel as a result of a preliminary issue. The fact that the claimant is a state or a private individual, or whether the title to the chattel originates from foreign public law or foreign private law does not make any difference under German law. What is relevant, however, is that the title stemming from the foreign act has to be perfected while the chattel was still on the territory of the claimant state. The reasoning behind this principle is based on the so-called 'imprint theory', which may be considered an equivalent to the vested rights doctrine common in English and American law.[1513] This principle is also not being undermined in the event an object had been obtained through an expropriatory measure. If assets are the target of acts of expropriation or confiscation, the effects of these measures, such as a subsequent change of title, will be recognised by German courts subject to the condition that the assets were present on the territory when the expropriatory legislation entered into force and subject to a public policy test.[1514]

### 2. Cross-Border Enforcement on the Ground of Public Policy

Public policy control is an established principle in Germany and per se affects any application or recognition of foreign law by German courts.[1515] German law clearly draws a distinction between "negative public policy" codified in Art. 6 EGBGB[1516] and "positive public policy". The term "international public policy" has been used less frequent in Germany, but occasionally appears in German lierature and case law and referes to what is here regarded as transnational public policy.[1517]

---

**1513** Cp. J. Kropholler, Internationales Privatrecht § 21 I (commenting on the vested rights-theory from the German perspective); M. Weller, Iran v. Barakat, at 175, see also A. Müller-Katzenburg, NJW (1999) 2554; A. Hipp, Schutz von Kulturgütern, at 170; S. von Schorlemer, Kulturgüterschutz, at 538.

**1514** See Federal Court of Justice (BGH), judgment of 28 April 1988 – IX ZR 127/87, NJW 1988, at 2173; Federl Court of Justice (BGH) judgement of 22 March 2006 – IV ZR 6/04, at no. 21, NJW-RR 2006, at 1091. Cp. also M. Weller, Iran v Barakat, at 175.

**1515** See e.g., Federal court of Justice (BGH) NJW (2002), 2389; Federal Court of Justice (BGH) NJW (1991), 1597 et seq.; Thomas Rauscher, Internationales Privatrecht (3rd ed. 2009), at 126 et seq.; J. Kroppholler, Internationales Privatrecht, § 21 I 2 c.

**1516** Introductory Act to the German Civil Code (EGBGB).

**1517** Albert Bleckmann, Sittenwidrigkeit wegen Vertosses gegen den ordre public international; BGZ 59, 83 (22.06.1972), concerning some Nigerian masks and figunrines, cp. further down this

According to Art. 6 EGBGB, foreign law is excluded where its application would lead to a result manifestly incompatible with the fundamental principles of German law. On the other hand, forum law positively imposes itself in cases where national "mandatory rules" provide so.[1518] These are the forum law's rules of a public character that pursue certain economic-political or social goals.[1519] The ratio of the positive function of public policy was enshrine in Art 34 EGBGB before the rule was abolished in 2009, with the enactment of the Regulation (EC) No 593/2008 of the European Parliament and of the Council of 17 June 2008 on the law applicable to contractual obligations (Rome I).[1520] The idea of the theory of "mandatory rules" was subject to a lot of criticism in Germany for creating legal uncertainty and inhibiting the harmonisation of judicial decisions in Europe and it remains so under the new European regulation.[1521]

### 3. Cross-Border Enforcement Jurisprudence

In respect of the application of foreign public laws, the following German cases are relevant to this study:

---

Chapter; BGH Z 98, 70 (at 73), a German case concerning the cross-border enforcement of an English arbitral judgment.

**1518** In Germany the term is known as "Eingriffsnormen", cp. F.A Mann, Sonderrecht und Eingriffsnormen im Internationalen Privatrecht, FS Beitzke, (1979), 607; Klaus Schurig, Zwingendes Recht, Eingriffsnormen und neues IPR, RabelsZ 1990, 217; Matthias Kuckein, Die Berücksichtigung von Einriffsnormen im deutschen und englischen internationalen Vertragsrecht (2008).

**1519** For example, the provision in respect of misleading promises of financial benefits enshrined in § 661a BGB was considered to be a mandatory rule, cp. BGH Z. 165, 172, at 180 et seq (1.12.2005) with a commen by Stephan Lorenz, IPrax 2006, 602.

**1520** See Johnathan Harris, Mandatory Rules and Public Policy under the Rome I Regulation, in: Franco Ferrari/Stefan Leible (eds), Rome I Regulation – The Law Applicable to Contractual Obligation in Europe (2009). On the former provisiosn of Art. 34 EGBGB, which was based on Art. 7 of the European Convention on the law applicable to contractual obligations 1980.

**1521** Cp. Andreas Köhler, Eingriffsnormen – Der 'unfertige Teil' des europäischen IPR (2013), referring to it as the "mandatory rules problem". The ‚raison d'être' of mandatory rules was recently confirmed by the German Federal Court of Justice (BGH) in a case concerning an agency contract provideding for the exclusive jurisdiction of the Courts of Virginia and for the application of U.S. laws. The court held this jurisdiction clause was in-applicable as it was in violation of Germany's mandatory rules, cp. BGH, Beschluss vom 5.9.2012 – VII ZR 25/12, for a comment see Jeniffer Antomo, IHR 2013, 35.

### a) The Egyptian Sarcophagus-Case[1522]

In the *sarcophagus-case*, the Higher Regional Court in Berlin (Kammergericht) ruled that German courts recognise the proprietary effects of umbrella statutes, as long as the acquisition or change of title has been completed before the object left the jurisdiction of the claimant state, subject to the condition that the effect of the transaction does not contravene German public policy.[1523] The case concerned a claim raised by Egypt against a German art dealer, the Millenium Art Holdings Limited. Egypt had applied for interim measure to prevent the export of some precious grave goods belonging to the Egyptian princess Meretites amongst others her famous sarcophagus, which for several years were stored in a German warehouse. The artefacts were to be shipped from to a buyer in the United States.

Egypt relied on Art. 6 of the Egyptian Law No. 117/1983 on the Protection of Archaeological Objects which vests ownership of all archaeological objects in the state. However, as in the Barakat-case, Egypt never had obtain possession to the artefacts before thy left Egyptian soil. The German Kammergericht held that as a consequence of the imprint theory it will generally apply foreign vesting laws, subject to a public policy-test as to the conformity of the Egyptian Act's proprietary effects with the German constitutional guarantees. The case was still dismissed on grounds of evidence, as Egypt was unable to prove when and where the artefacts have been excavated. Before the enactment of the 1983 Law, export of Eyptian artefacts in private ownership was legal according to Law No. 66/1963. The defendants submitted that the arefacts were sold by a private collector in 1969 and exported legally. The case thus failed on factual and not on legal grounds. Theoretically, had the artefacts been located in Egypt at the time of the enactment of the 1983 law, and Egypt was able to proof this fact, the court would have accepted Egypt as the owner of the artefacts by virtue of the Egyptian Cultural Property Act (No. 117). The application of the law would have been subject to a test of public policy according to Art. 6 EGBGB.

The Kammergericht rejected Egypt's claim on the grounds that the export of archaeological heritage items to be a criminal offence according to Law No. 66/1963. After having interpreted Law No. 66/1963, the Kammergericht held that the Egyptian law could not be construed as conferring title to the objects in question. Especially, it did not contain provisions on automatic forfeiture of illegally exported goods. The court nevertheless, did not express any doubts as to the ap-

**1522** Kammergericht Berlin, Judgement of 16.10.2006 – 10 U 286/05. NJW 2007, 705; for a short comment on the case cp. M. Weller, Iran v Barakat, at 174.

**1523** See also Christian Armbrüster, Privatrechtliche Anspruee auf Rueckfuehrung von Kulturgütern ins Ausland, NJW (2001) 3581, at 3583.

plicability of law Law No. 66/1963, in case it did provide for a vesting of title in the Egyptian state. Thus it can be implied from the court's reasoning that the law would have been applicable irrespective of the fact that it contained penal provisions.[1524] Owing to the fact that the artefacts were held to be exported from Egypt legally, the Kammergericht did not consider the justiciability of the export law No 66/1963. The case shows to be consistent with the recommendations made by the Institute de Droit International and Law Association Resolutions. The Kammergericht expressly held that Egypt's claim for the return of the antiquities would be justiciable on the gorunds of the 1983 Law, if Egypt were able to prove that the Artefacts were misappropriated after 1983, despite not having obtained possession of the artefacts. The German court thus recognised the problem of illegally excavated and missapropriated antiquities.

### b) The Greek Coins-Case[1525]

In the *Greek coin-case*, the High Court in the federal state of Schleswig held that ownership vesting statutes were generally consistent with German public policy. The judgment further affirmed the application of the vested rights-doctrine to cultural property matters. The case concerned a claim by the Greek government for the seizure and recovery of certain antique coins, which were illegally excavated and exported to Germany by a Greek citizen. Greece grounded its request on the base of the European Convention on Mutual Assistance in Criminal Matters.[1526] The court ruled in favour of Greece and ordered the seizure of the coins. Greece footed its claim on Art. 15 of the Greek Law No. 5351/1932, which vests all archaeological artefacts in the state, and which at the time of the trial, was the applicable statute.[1527] Greece contended that the defendant committed a crime under Art. 375 I b-a Greek Criminal Code and Art. 1 sec. 1 Greek Law No. 1608/50, as amended by Art. 7 of Law No. 1271/82.[1528] The defendant argued that he

**1524** Cp. M. Weller, Iran v. Barakat, at 175.

**1525** Hight Court (Oberlandesgericht) Schleswig, judgment 10–02–1989–1 Ausl. 2/89, NJW (1989) 3105. See also A. Weidner, Kultugüter als res extra commercium, at 112; Michael Anton, Illegaler Kulturgüterverkehr (2010), at 221.

**1526** http://conventions.coe.int/Treaty/EN/Treaties/Html/030.htm (21.05.09).

**1527** Greece enacted a new law in June 2002. For Greek cultural property law see Chapter 2 § 2 I 2 as wll as e.g. Spyridon Vrellis, The new Act no 3028/2002 on the Protection of Antiquities and Cultural Heritage in Greece, in: E. Schneider/R. Schneider (eds.) Cultural Property Protection (2005), 97; Daphne Voudouri, Law and the Politics of the Past: Legal Protection of Cultural Heritage in Greece, 17 IJCP (2010) 547.

**1528** Under this provision a person who illicitly acquires archaeological artefacts commits a criminal offence.

had inherited the coins as he discovered them on his land. The Schleswig court ruled that the defendant never acquired ownership to the coins as the Greek state was the owner of the antiquities at all times, according to Art. 15 of Law No. 5351/1932. The court expressly underlined that "German law recognises this proprietary right." Moreover it concluded that the Greek claim would only be held non-justiciable in case it grossly contravened the principles of Germany property law. As German law knows the concept of state ownership of antiquities and codified it in Art. 73 of the EGBGB, the court held that the recognition of the state's title was not contrary to German public policy.[1529] Consequently, the German court holds claims for the return of cultural property to be justiciable on the grounds of the doctrine of vested rights und subject to the public policy doctrine.

### 4. Recognition within the Scope of the Immorality of Conduct

Another mechanism for determining the justiciability of foreign law in Germany is the application of foreign law within the scope of provisions concerning the immorality of conduct.[1530] This does not amount to the immediate application of the law but it may influence the result of the proceedings. Similarly to the application of foreign public law by American courts, openly framed conditions may be affected by foreign public law, in particular, terms such as 'good faith', 'legitimate interest', 'immorality', or 'public policy'.[1531]

#### a) The Nigeria-Decision

This mechanism has been applied in the famous *Nigeria-decision* of the German Federal Court of Justice. The case concerned the transport of several antique masks and figurines from Nigeria to Hamburg, without previously obtaining a valid export certificate.[1532] The freight was insured with a German insurance

---

**1529** See on this point, judgment of the German Surpreme Court, BVerfG, NJW (1988) 2593 (a case concerning treasure trove statutes in Germany).

**1530** See also Kurt Siehr, International Art Trade and the Law, at 190; M. Weller, Iran v Barakat, at 176.

**1531** See M. Weller, Iran v Barakat, at 176.

**1532** BGHZ 59, 82 [1972]; NJW (1971) 1575. See also A. Bleckmann, Sittenwidrigkeit wegen Verstosses gegen den ordre public international, Anmerkung zum Nigeria Urteil, in: 34 ZaöRV (1974) 112; Kurt Siehr, Nationaler und Internationaler Kulturgüterschutz. Eingriffsnormen und der internationale Kunsthandel, in: B. Pfister/M.R. Will (eds.) FS fur Werner Lorenz (1991) 526; Albert Bleckmann, Sittenwidrigkeit wegen Verstosses gegen den ordre public international, in: ZaöRV 34 (1974) 112; Hans W Baade, "The Legal Effects of Codes of Conduct for Multinational Enterprises", Germ. YB Int'l L. (1979) 40; cp. also FA Mann, case note on the Nigeria case,

company. During the transport, six valuable bronze figures were lost. After the insurance company denied to pay compensation, the Nigerian company filed a law suit in Germany, but the claim failed in all instances. Being the court of last instance, the Federal Surpreme Court (BGH) relied on a provision in the standard terms and conditions of the insurance contract according to which the conract was valid only if it related to a "legitimate" interest to be insured.[1533] The BGH held that the insurance contract was null and void as it was to be considered immoral under § 138 (1) BGB. In the end, no compensation had to be paid to the policyholder.

First, the BGH had to interpret § 138 BGB which constitutes that "a legal transaction which is immoral and contrary to public policy is null and void".[1534] Usually, "public policy" and "morality" in the sence of § 138 BGB are violated when the conduct in question contradicts common business practices, integrity requirements, rationality and principles of fairness in Germany. In the *Nigeria-case*, the court found that the term "public policy" likewise includes "international public policy" which is based on internationally accepted common values and rules of fairness and, equally, may inlcude interests of foreign states. The court reasoned that foreign public law should be applied if the policy of the law has been recognised by the international community, as for example in an international convention. Having come to this conclusion, the judges referred to the 1970 UNESCO Convention. The BGH found that "in the interest of safeguarding the morality of the international trade in cultural goods, the export of heritage items in violation of export prohibitions of the state of its origin does not deserve the protection through private law including the insurance contract." The court inferred from the 1970 Convention a consensus of the international community on the necessity to protect cultural property and thereby indirectly applied Nigerian export law within the term of "immorality of conduct.[1535]

The court's reasoning relates to American and English legal practice where "the non-appliocation of foreign law may constitute a breach of the duty of comity owed by one state to another".[1536] However, the decision is remarkable in that the court based its reasoning on the 1970 UNESCO Convention, which, at that

---

NJW (1972) 2179, who approves the decision; G. Reichelt, International Protection of Cultural Property, 1 Uniform Law Rev. (1985), 43.

**1533** M. Weller at 176; K. Siehr, Nationaler und Internationaler Kulturgüterschutz, at 527.

**1534** For a comprehensive comment on the provisions see e.g. C. Armbrüster, in: Münchener Kommentar, (2006) § 138.

**1535** G. Reichelt, International Protection of Cultural Property, at 46; M.Weller, Iran v Barakat, at 176.

**1536** Cp. D. Lloyd, Public Policy – A Comparative Study in English and French Law (1953).

time, was in force only since two years, and Germany was not even a party. It applied the UNESCO Convention within the principle of what is here being referred to as "transnational public policy" which again has been held to be part of German public policy. This ratio mirrors the reasoning in the *Barakat-decision* rather precisly. The difference to *Barakat* is that Iran pursued its claim based on its ownership right. In the *Nigeria-case*, the claim footed on Nigeria's export prohibition, which the court did not apply directly but within the interpretation of § 138 BGB.[1537] A direct application on the ground of § 134 BGBwhich constitutes that "legal transactions that violate a statutory prohibition are void" has been rejected by the BGH, as according to the court, the Nigerian export law was a foreign act and § 134 BGB only referred to domestic law. Notwithsanding its generous application of the prinicple of public policy on the ground of the international consensus in respect of the protection of cultural heritage, the court stated that – as a general rule – foreign laws as such were only to be enforced if so provided by an applicable treaty.[1538] The UNIDROIT Convention constitutes a treaty in this sence, but has not been retified by Germany so far.

#### b) Three Phrygian Offering Cups and Two Byzantine Incense Burners

In a recent case, which was dismissed both by the Frankfurt administrative court[1539] and the Frankfurt regional court (Landgericht),[1540] Turkey made an attempt the recover three Prygian offering cups and two Byzantine incense burners, allegedly illegally excavated at the Phrygian burial mounds of Gordion, located west of Ankara.[1541] The five artefacts were discovered at an antique market in Istanbul by a German couple, both employed in Turkey as teachers since many years. During the purchase of a carpet, they noticed the antique vessels which later became subject of the claim. The artfacts were then allegedly wrapped in carpets purchased by the couple of teachers and, in 1980, sent to Germany as "additional surprise presents" for the buyers of the carpets. In October 2007, the claimant, a German art dealer, bought the antiquities without inquiring

1537 See also BGHZ 94, 268 (judgement 8.05.1985), a decision of the German Federal Supreme Court concerning an estate agent contract accomplished through bribery.
1538 K. Siehr, Nationaler und internationaler Kulturgüterschutz, at 527.
1539 VG Frankfurt a.M., judgment 2.06.2010 – 5 K 1082/10.F, available at BeckRS 2011, 51903.
1540 LG Frankfurt a.M., judgment 18.08. 2011 – 2 – 13 O 212/10, abailable at BeckRS 2013, 20789.
1541 For a comment of the case, see Suzan Topal-Gökceli, Rechtlicher Schutz archäologischen Kulturgutes in der Türkei, in: Gerte Reichelt (ed.) Denkmalschutz in Europa (Schriftenreihe Forschungsgesellschaft Kunst und Recht, Band 3, 2012) 45; K. Siehr, Rückführung gestohlener Kulturgüter durch internationale Rechtshilfe, Bulletin Kunst und Recht 2/2011, 12.

about the provenance of the objects. In 2008, the artefacts where seized by the German police in relation to the suspicion against the art dealer of dealing with stolen goods. He chelleneged the seizure in front of the adminstrative court and succeeded.

First, the administrative court completely ruled out the possibility that the German couple may have been acting in bad faith. According to the court, the main fact was the low price for which the art dealer purchased the items from the German couple.[1542] In any event, the court continued, they acquired the artefacts by means of advers possession on the ground of § 937 BGB. As a consequence, the Frankfurt administrative court found no indication that the art dealer was not the rightful owner of the objects in question. The artefacts were returned to him in 2010. The return request which Turkey filed in parallel proceedings on the grounds of the Kulturgüterrückgabegesetz, the German implementory Act to the 1970 UNESCO Convention, was rejected owing to the fact that Turkey was unable to satisfy the strict formalities laid down in the Act.[1543]

A few weeks later, Turkey filed a civil law suit against the art dealer for the recovery of the artefacts in front of the civil court in Frankfurt (Landgericht), claiming that the artefacts were illegally excavated and later exported from Turkey in breach of the Turkich Cultural Porperty Statute. Using this line or argument, Turkey argued that it was the owner of the objects. Turkey alleged that the artefacts showed rather fresh streaks of clay and this was irrefutabile proof for the fact that they stem from a recent illegal excavation. Furthermore, they asserted that being a a professional art dealer, the defendant must have been aware of Turkey's strict cultural property legislation, especially its export laws. Turkey additionally argued that the objects could not be acquired in good faith as they "count as stolen in the sence of § 935 German Civil Code". § 935 I BGB prohibits the good faith acquisition of stolen goods. Here, Turkey's reasoning is footing on the 1995 UNIDROIT Convention, as well as the UNESCO and UNIDROIT Model Law 2011 which both state that "illegally excavated goods count as stolen".[1544]

Referring to the *Nigeria-decision,* Turkey continued that, under German law, transactions which violate foreign export prohibitions are to be considered void according to § 138 German Civil Code.[1545] All of Turkey's arguments were rejected by the Frankfurt court. First, the Landgericht confirmed that the *lex situs* was the

---

**1542** For all five vessels the dealer paid 200 Euros.

**1543** For a critical examination of the German Implementation of the UNESCO 1970 Convention see Part II, Chapter § 3 IV 2 b 1).

**1544** Art. 3 (2) UNIDROIT Convention 1995.

**1545** Cp. above.

applicable law to the case. It pointed out that the principle of the *lex situs* is governing not only transaction in respect of oridinary chattels but also transactions in respect of cultural heritage items. An application of the *lex originis* has not been considered. Furthermore, the Landgericht ruled that Turkey was unable to prove ownership to the objects in question in the terms of a "better proprietary right." Remember that, under German law, § 1006 BGB provides for a rebuttable presumption of ownership in favor of the current possessor unless the objects in question has been stolen, § 1006 I 2 BGB. The Frankfurt court held that the term "stolen" in § 1006 II 2 BGB was to be interpreted in the same manner as in § 935 I BGB. In consequence, the court continued, an item counts as stolen, when "the owner lost the immediate possession to the objects in question against his will." Owing to the fact that the antquities were illegally excavated, the court held that Turkey could not "loose possession" of the antique vessels as it never obtained possession in the first place. As a result, the exception to § 1006 I 2 BGB did not apply with the consequence that Turkey carried the burden of proof fro the ownership to the artefacts which it was unable to substantiate. The court found that the residue clay on the surface of the objects as well as the fact that similar items were recently excavated at the burial mounds of Gordion does not constitute enough proof that the artefacts were actually excavated on the territory of Turkey. The court followed the argument of the art dealer who submitted that the artefacts in question could equally stem from Syria or Armenia.

Athough Turkey lost the case owing to a lack of substantiate proof of ownership, the key factor for this failure was the courts ruling in respect of the rebuttable presumption arisng out of § 1006 I 2 BGB. The court's reasoning follows the arguments of Judge Gray in the first insance of the *Barakat-decision*, which was later overruled by the Court of Appeal and the House of Lords. [1546] Both, the Court of Appeal and the House of Lords agreed that Gray J.'s ruling was not in line with the UNESCO and UNIDROIT Convention and was thus not in line with English public policy. In the event that the Frankfurt court had followed Turkey's argument that the items "count as stolen", both § 1006 II 2 BGB and § 935 BGB would have applied. As a result, the objects could not have been aquired in good faith and Turkey would have come to enjoy the simplification of the German rules concerning the taking of evidence.

---

**1546** Note that in 2009, the Constitutional Act 2005 came into force, which established an independent Judicial Appointments Commission and, from October 2009, sts up a supreme court, independent from the House of Lords, with its own appointments system, staff, budget and building, cp. House of Lord Report Library Note 2010 available at http://www.parliament.uk/documents/lords-information-office/House%20of%20Lords%20Reform%201997–2010 %20-%2028 %20 %20June%202010.pdf

The Frankfurt Landgericht also rejected Turkey's second line of argument which followed the rationale of the *Nigeria-decision.*[1547] The court contended that transactions within the Republic of Germany were not to be considered void according to § 138 BGB "just because they were in breach of a foreign countrie's export prohibition". After comparing the case to the *Nigeria-decision,* the judge came to the conclusion that § 138 BGB was not applicable as the transaction took place within the territory of Germany and after the objects have been exported. Opposed to that, in the *Nigeria-case*, it was the actual contract governing the transport of the Nigerian artefacts which violated the Nigerian export laws.[1548] Additionally, the judge pointed out that § 138 BGB requires "knowledge" in the sence that the defendant being aware of the illegality or immorality of his conduct, which the court answered to the negative. In his reasoning, the judge applied the principle of territoriality, similar to the ration in the *Ortiz-case* and the first instance of the *Barakat-decision.*

The judgment is indeed a disappointing retrograde step for the protection of cultural property in Germany as it practically denies the recognition and cross-border enforcement of a source countrie's ownership statute, although it is a well-known fact that Turkey is a major source country. In 2011, the Turkish authorities seized over 25.000 illegally excavated objects and over 500 were registered as of special cultural importance.[1549] The Frankfurt Landgericht's reasoning that illegally excavated antiquities do not count as stolen under German law contradicts the recent positive developlment in cultural property law as heralded in *Barakat.* There, the C.A. referred to both the 1970 UNESCO and 1995 UNIDROIT Convention although England did not implement the UNESCO Convention and did not ratify UNIDROIT. Equally, the Landgericht's assumption that Turkey cannot be the owner of the artafects as it never had obtained possession of the objects contradict previous German decisions. The Landgericht acted blind and deaf to the growing awareness of the transnational public policy to return misappropriated antiquities which was recognised in the German *Nigeria–case* as early as in 1972 and later confirmed and solidified in *Barakat.* Likewise, the decision contradicts the U.S. approach where illegally excavated goods count as

**1547** Cp. above.

**1548** For the opposite view see Arndt Koch, Antiken, Recht und (kein) Markt? Zivil und strafrechtliche Probleme des Handels mit archäologischem Kulturgut, KUR (2009) 49, at 52; C. Armbrüster, NJW 2001, 3581, 3584.

**1549** Cp. Turkish Report on Anti-Smuggling and Organised Crime 2011 undetaken by the Cultural Ministry of the Interior, available online at http://www.kom-gov.tr/TR/Dosyalar/2011_Ingilizce.pdf (8.6.2012)., at 14. In 2010, 32.612 archeological artefacts were seized.

"stolen" under the National Stolen Property Act.[1550] The court's rationale as to the application of the Turkish export prohibition within the immorality of conduct as provided by 138 BGB contractицts the reasoning of the Surpreme court in *Nigeria*. There, the BGH clearly stated that the public policy principle as defined in § 138 BGB referres to "transactions" as such. That consequently must also include transactions performed within the territory of Germany.

## III. Reflections on German Law

The analysis of German judicial practice shows a contradictory attitude: On the one hand, German case law stands out in that Germany recognised the necessity for protecting cultural objects by applying foreign public law rather early. The *Nigeria-decision* footed its reasoning by referring to the 1970 UNESCO Convention shortly after the instrument came into force. Germany does not per se render foreign public law non-justiciable. According to the *lex situs-rule*, a sovereign claim for the recovery of antiquities remains a patrimonial claim even if preliminary issues such as title to an object are affected by foreign public law. The mere fact that the state seeks to rely on its title does not alter the characterisation of the claim as being one raised under private law, and the state's action does not amount to an attempt to enforce acts of state in a foreign forum as such. The state is held to act in its capacity as a private owner like any other owner of a chattel.

This reasoning mirrors the principles as laid down in *Government of Iran v Barakat*. German *opinio juris* goes even further than *Barakat*, in that it recognises changes of title footed on expropriatory or confiscatory legislation. Further, the legal technique of "taking account" of foreign public law within the framework of the applicable contract law in order to concretise openly framed conditions resembles the U.S. approach as laid down in the McClain doctrine.

On the other hand, the judgement in the Phrygian vessels-case ignores the principles as well as the international consensus laid down in the 1970 UNESCO Convention, the 1995 Unidroit Convention and the Model Provisions 2011. None of the Conventions have been mentioned by the court although at the time of the judgemnt they were in effect. The judges did not consider enforcing Turkey's export law on the ground of transnational public policy following into the *Nigeria-decision's* footsteps.

**1550** Cp. Chapter 6, § 4.

As a last point, claimants – both states and individuls – seeking to recover cultural objects need to be aware, that the Achilles heel of the German system certainly is its strict approach on the taking of evidence and the burden of proof. The presumption that the current possessor is assumed to be the owner of the subject of the claim inhibits many states from recovering their property especially in the case of illegally excavated antiquities. If German courts would accept the proposition that illegally excavated goods count as stolen, as is laid down in the Unidroit Convention 1995 and the UNESCO and UNIDROIT Model Provisions 2011, the presumption could be reversed.

## § 6. The Swiss Approach

### I. Swiss Federal Act on Private International Law 1987

In Switzerland the principle that the application of foreign public law is not excluded per se is codified in Art. 13 (1) of the Federal Act of Private International Law 1987 (IPRG). The provision prescribes that the selection of a foreign law by the choice of law rules of the IPRG comprises all provisions of that foreign law that are applicable to the situation in question. Section (1) makes clear that "the applicability of a provision of the foreign law is not excluded in by the mere fact that it is characterised as public law".[1551]

The Swiss government's report that was issued when the private international law act was adopted states that the goal of this provision was to overcome the Supreme Court's reservation regarding the applicability of foreign public law.[1552] This choice of law rule thus provides for the application of foreign public law and a Swiss judge, although he is not obliged to, may theoretically enforce foreign law even in the form of export prohibitions.[1553] Unfortunately, this liberal rationale was not adopted by the Swiss courts.

**1551** Cp. Marc Weber, Unveräusserliches Kulturgut im nationalen und internationalen Rechstverkehr (2002), at 410.

**1552** Cp. Message relating to the Swiss PIL-Act, November 10, 1982; Feuille fédérale 1983 I 255, 299–300.

**1553** Marc Weber, Unveräusserliches Kulturgut, at 410.

## II. India v Crédit Agricole Indosuez

The case that has already been mentioned under the name *Mogul Gold Coin-case* concerned the recovery of two gold coins minted in 1630 and 1639, which originally belonged to the Nizam of the Indian principality of Hyderabad, India, Mir Osman Ali Khan.[1554] In 1988 Mir Osman Ali Khan's grandson, Mukarram Jah, transferred the coins to the Crédit Agricole Indosuez (Suisse) SA as a security for a loan of $ 25 million granted by the bank to companies controlled by Mukarram Jah. In 1949, India declared this particular private antiquity collection t to become state property and thus contested the banks' right before the Swiss Courts in 1997. The coins that were minted during the seventeenth-century Mogul dynasty belonged to the personal property of the head of the Hyderabad principality until the transfer of sovereignty to the newly independent State of India in 1949. In 1992, India filed a request for judicial assistance in criminal matters, asking that the coins be seized on the grounds that they had become national treasures of India when the principality of Hyderabad was united to India in 1949. In May 1997, India filed a possessory and proprietary claim for the recovery of the coins against the bank based on Arts. 933 f., as well as Art. 641 para. 2 of the Swiss Civil Code (SCC). As Indian law does not provide for state ownership of newly discovered antiquities, the Indian government based its action on the ground that the coins were a national treasure that had been illegally exported from India.

In 1972 India enacted the Antiquities and Art Treasures Act, and according to this statute, antiquities such as the gold coins in question could not have been exported without the authorisation of the Indian government.

The Supreme Court of Switzerland rejected India's claim. Quoting the *New Zealand v Ortiz,* it stated that Switzerland would not apply Indian public law.[1555] Additionally, it argued that at the time when the gold coins were handed over as s security to the bank, no international conventions were in force.

Another question to decide by the court was the validity of the 1988 security agreement between the bank and Ali Khan's grandson. Under Swiss law, the creation of a security must be based on a valid title, and this title can only be the

**1554** Union de l'Inde contre Crédit Agricole Indosuez (Suisse) SA, Supreme Court decision, April 8, 2005: ATF 131 III 418; Journal des Tribunaux (2006) I 63 (Summary); Semaine Judiciaire (2006) I 152; Praxis (2006), N 42, 310. For comments on the case, see e.g. Marc-André Renold, The Giant Antique Mogul Gold Coins, 13 IJCP (2006) 361; Ivo Schwander, Rechtsprchung zum internationalen Sachen-, Schuld- und Gesellschaftsrecht, Revue suisse de droit international et européen (2006) 344.
**1555** ATF 131 III 418, at 424.

contract by which the security is created.[1556] Based on Art. 19 of the Swiss Private International Law Act (PIL-Act), as well as on the principle of universal public order, a contract that violates foreign rules prohibiting the export of national treasures could be considered null and void independently of its validity on the basis of the Swiss substantive law applicable to the contract. Art. 19 PIL-Act provides the application of foreign mandatory rules to the condition that it be required by "legitimate and manifestly overwhelming interests with regard to the Swiss legal order."[1557] The court rejected the application of Art. 19 on the grounds that, firstly, the international conventions and national statutes that could serve as the basis for a universal public policy are not applicable in the present case: Switzerland has not ratified the 1995 Unidroit Convention and the Convention has no retroactive effect. The CPTA[1558] which has implemented the 1970 UNESCO Convention, is only effective as of June 1, 2005 and is not retroactive. Secondly, Art. 7 CPTA provides that international bilateral agreements should be entered into in order to enable foreign states to claim the restitution of illegally exported cultural objects (Art. 9 CPTA). No such agreement has been entered into at the present stage. Thus the clear interest of the Supreme Court lies in its support for the non-retroactivity of the applicable rules, be it the 1970 UNESCO Convention, the 1995 Unidroit Convention, or the recent CPTA.

As a result, the decision clearly contradicts the reasoning of the Swiss legislator who expressly ruled against the non-applicability of foreign public law in Art. 13 of the Swiss PIL-Act. The use of comparative analysis by the court should also be viewed with criticism. Although it is perfectly legitimate to refer to a case like *New Zealand v Ortiz* in this circumstances, the court should also have discussed the German Nigeria decision, which held that the insurance contract relating to cultural goods was void because it was in breach with Nigerian export regulations.[1559]

The Supreme Court also disregarded that Switzerland has once allowed the return of artefacts on the grounds of public policy. In an older Swiss case,[1560] a painting stolen in France was located in Switzerland and the French owner

**1556** M-A. Renold, The Giant Antique Mogul Gold Coins, at 365.
**1557** M-A. Renold, The Giant Antique Mogul Gold Coins, at 365.
**1558** Cp. this chapter above.
**1559** For the Nigeria-case, cp. this Chapter, sect. on German law.
**1560** Tribunal Federal Suisse 1 April 1997 (l. c. Chambre d'Accusation du Canton de Geneve), 123 II Arrets du Tribunal Federal Suisse 134, at 143–144. See also P. Lalive, Réflexions sur un ordre public culturel, in: E. Wyler/A. Papaux (eds.), L'Extranéité ou le dépassement de l'ordre juridique étatique: actes du colloque des 27 et 28 novembre 1997 organisé par l'Institut d'études de droit international de la Faculté de droit de l'Université de Lausanne (1999) 155.

asked the Swiss authorities to return the painting as the proceeds of crime according to the 1959 European Convention on Mutual Assistance in Crime Matters. At the very end of the decision the Swiss federal court added:

> "If, as in the present case, the claim is for restitution of cultural property, the judge of international legal assistance should pay regard to the international public interest which, in Switzerland as well as in France, is bound to protect these objects. These provisions [under the UNESCO and UNIDROIT Conventions], based on a common inspiration, express such an international public policy already in force or in the making. These provisions demand an effective international fight against the illegal trade of cultural objects".[1561]

### III. Reflections on Swiss Law

Although Switzerland recently implemented the 1970 UNESCO Convention and Swiss law has opted for the liberal approach towards the application of foreign public law, this development is not reflected in in the *Giant Mogul-case.* Whereas this statement might go too far and another court might reverse this rigid opinion concerning the application of a state's title to cultural property, the decision at least reflects the general legal mood that foreign export laws will not be enforced in Swiss courts.

The judgement aims at restricting the application of foreign cultural patrimony laws to the system of bilateral treaties set forth in Art. 7 of the Swiss CPTA, and it concludes that without such agreements there is no need to consider foreign rules prohibiting the export of cultural goods. This justification reminds of the argument put forward by the American critics of the McClain-doctrine which argue that the U.S. Cultural Property Implementation Act is the only means by which treasure trove statutes shall be enforced in America. However, this reasoning is incompatible with the general goals of the 1970 UNESCO Convention. The CPTA also states that Switzerland seeks to make a contribution to the protection of the cultural heritage of mankind and prevent theft, looting, and both, the illicit export and import of cultural property (Art. 1 para. 2). Consequently, the CPTA should not be the exclusive means by which Switzerland wishes to fight against the illicit traffic of cultural property.

---

**1561** Tribunal Federal Suisse 1 April 1997 (l. c. Chambre d'Accusation du Canton de Geneve), 123 II Arrets du Tribunal Federal Suisse 134, at 143–144, but cp. also Kurt Siehr, The Beautiful One has Come to Return, in: J.H. Merryman (ed.), Imperialism, Art and Restitution (2006) 114, at 122.

## IV. Conclusion to Chapter 6

Chapter 6 has comparatively elaborated the judicial practice as to the justiciability of foreign cultural property laws in the main market states England, United States, Germany, Switzerland. The purpose of this elaboration was to undermine the rigid opinion that courts generally do not enforce public laws of another country. Conversely, the Chapter aimed at proving that a static non-enforcement of foreign public laws – rule is an antiquated attitude and contrary to the development of international law. Especially in the case of movable antiquities, successful recovery cases of such objects in foreign courts may create a notion of deterrence in the market states and influence the motivation of collectors to acquire illegally excavated antiquities. In order to contribute to the fight against the illicit trafficking of cultural property, it would be an imperative for such claims to be enforced in foreign courts.

A comparative analysis of international *opinio juris* indeed shows a shift towards the "public policy-approach". The analysis has revealed that national courts have the liberty to recognise or to enforce the law of another state based on the doctrine of vested rights and subject to the principles of public policy. Any classification of foreign laws for the purpose of limitation upon their recognition or enforcement should consider and reflect specific policies. This certainly concerns policy considerations that are "transnational" or "truly international". This study purports the view that cultural property protection is such a "truly interational" policy.

Chapter 6 further argues that the distinction between recognition and enforcement is an imprecise one why only limited effect should be accorded to it in order to assess the justiciability of claims for misappropriated cultural material. This is being reflected in the differences in national attitudes, when it comes to drawing this distinction between the enforcement of public law and its recognition. German and American courts apply foreign public law in order to determine preliminary questions of the claim, such as the 'ownership' of a missapproraited cultural object or the term 'stolen'. This process may be called "taking into account" of foreign public law. On this ground, German and American courts will recognise a sovereign's title if the title to the chattel in question has been acquired according to the doctrine of vested rights, and secondly, if the claim does not grossly contravene the public policy of the forum state. English courts on the other hand will reject a claim for the recovery of misappropriated cultural arefacts if the state obtained its title by an act that can only adhere to the sovereign power a state, such as an expropriation, confiscation, or any other kind of compulsory acquisition. Such a claim will be held to be a prerogative claim, as opposed to a patrimonial claim, which would be enforced. In the event that the act which vests title to the object in the state was prerogative in nature, the court will deny the sovereign's claim, even if the movable in question was present within the state's territory at the time of the expropriatory act and even if public policy reasons would require the court to allow the claim. The same is true for claims which are based on laws that seek to enforce a "governmental interest". If however, the state obtained title to the antiquity in the same manner an individual would have obtained title to it, then the claim will be treated as patrimonial and the state's claim will be recognised in England, subject to the public policy exception, and provided that the vested rights doctrine is not infringed.

An unforseen development, however, is about to manifest itself in the Swiss judicial practice. Although Switzerland is the only market state which has codified the principle of justiciability of foreign public laws in its choice-of-law rules, the rationale is not being followed by the Swiss courts. Even though Switzerland is now a party to the 1970 UNESCO Convention and has implemented the instrument into national law, the principles of the Convention have not been taken into consideration in recent case law concerning the recovery of some artefacts from India.

So far, the *Barakat-decision* brings England not only into alignment with Germany and the United States, but can be considered a leader in the protection of cultural objects. A laudable goal however, would be international uniformity as to the application of foreign cultural property laws.

# Summary

The overall aim of this study was to promote the view that misappropriated movable cultural objects should be returned. This credo had to be reinforced by legal argument. As in most cases, chattels are being restituted by means of civil recovery, this research contended to investigate the various types of rights that sovereigns can obtain in cultural objects, and to elaborate upon the corss-border enforcement and justiciability of claims based on these rights.

Consequently, the direction of the research was twofold: In a first step, a selection of national laws aimed at the protection of cultural objects were scrutinised in respect of mechanisms that vest ownership of movable cultural objects in their sovereign, in case of illicit, licit excavation, or export. Alternatively, these laws were analysed with regard to mechanisms that create any other proprietary interest in the state. These rights and interests have been tested as to their quality as property. Furthermore, in order to provide for an integrated approach, national civil law systems have been compared in view of allocation of title to fortuitously discovered antiquities under the private law of finds. In a second step, this study took stock of the existing international and national laws regarding the application of these previously discovered rights and interests in cross-border litigation. Additionally, the thesis made an attempt to recommend an alternative route to the traditional choice-of-law methodology in multi-jurisdictional cases where cultural objects are concerned.

The analysis of national legal systems revealed that various mechanisms exist by means of which states extract control over cultural objects. These mechanisms were divided in two broad categories, namely legal mechanisms that aimed at acquiring property rights to antiquities which were not yet in the ownership or possession of the state, and legal mechanisms that were meant to retain cultural items already held by the state within the public domain. The analysis of the first category revealed that while all national legal frameworks grant their sovereign certain rights to heritage items upon their discovery or export, there exist a great variety of forms and techniques employed to empower the state with property rights to cultural heritage. Such include property interests based on declarations of ownership, interests based solely on rights of immediate possession, and property interests arising out of export declarations and rights of pre-emption. Some of these mechanisms, such as carefully designed umbrella laws, may create a strong title to the benefit of the state while others do not grant any property rights to their sovereign upon their violation. Such laws, for example, are export laws where the illegal export of heritage items entails solely criminal or pecuniary sanctions. In relation to misappropriated antiquities, the thesis revealed that claims for the return of cultural objects may be in danger of failing if the wording of the statute is imprecise and does not account for state ownership of all fortuitously and illegally discovered artefacts. It is therefore strongly recommended to states whose laws do not contain ownership declarations to implement the recently drafted 2011 UNIDROIT and UNESCO Model Provisions on the State Ownership of Undiscovered Cultural Objects into their existing domestic law.

As far as pre-emption rights are concerned, the extrapolation allows to conclude that a state achieves title to a heritage item only if it has a statutory pre-emption right which it exercised. In the event it did not, this thesis adopted the view that pre-emption rights do not confer title upon their violation as their nature brings with it that they are entirely dependent on an uncertain future contingency. However, if the pre-emption right provides for a specific degree of certainty, it may be treated as a contingent interest in property for the purpose of enforcement under the patrimonial interest. The same is true if the pre-emption right gives rise for an automatic forfeiture in favour of the state.

The analysis of legal mechanisms aimed at retaining cultural property in the public domain revealed that such rules provide the state with an interest, in the sense that they prevent an involuntary loss of the state's title, but they do not create property rights upon their violation and are thus not capable of being enforced in a foreign court in that event. This may be different with the German "*öffentliche Dienstbarkeit*" where the art object can be divested only under the premise that the chattel is charged with a real right for the object to be used only within the limits of a specific public purpose. The same is true for the Ecuadorian "*dominio eminente*", a real right ipso jure, similar to the "*öffentliche Dienstbarkeit*" which precludes the good faith acquisition of the object free of this right. In such case, the state has always an immediate right of possession to recover the chattel in order to display it on its territory.

As the acquisition of title under the law of finds is concerned, the sovereign acquires title to cultural objects unde two condictions. Either the object in question has been found on land which belongs to the public authority. In this case, the sovereign will become owner of the object if the private law of finds allocates title to the object to the land owner. The analysis of the common law of finds however revealed that the acquisition of title to found objects is unpredictable and beares many unsolved questions. The factor that an object has been found on land which belongs to a public authority does not make the sovereign automatically the owner of it. Chattels which were found on the surface of the land can be kept by the person in priority of possession of the item. Moreover, unnecessary distinctions are being drawn between finds on the ground and finds that are attached or merely loose in the ground. In case, the object was not found on private land, the sovereign will only acquire title to the object, if the title holder to the find, may it be the finder or the landowner, transfers the object to the sovereign, for example in return for a reward, or because criminal law or public law provisions oblige the finder to do so.

It can be concluded that the common law of finders is detrimental to antiquities protection, while equitable division as practiced in several civilian jurisdiction constitutes a more favourable system for the protection of movable heritage items through the legal certainty it provides for the finder and landowner. Thus, in order to achieve a thorough protection of both the tangible and intangible component of archaeological heritage items, property law provisions which are aimed at allocating title to fortuitously discovered antiquities have to be complemented through special cultural property law provisions in order to enable antiquities to be evaluated *in situ*.

In its second part, which was devoted to the practical implementation of sovereign rights in a foreign forum, the study was able to detect an emerging trend towards a general willingness to apply foreign cultural property laws in foreign courts. Judging from the fact that the relevant international legal instruments so far in force show some serious drawbacks, and so far have proven to be a fairly limited mechanisms for the recovery of misappropriated cultural objects, this emerging trend proves to be a necessary and welcome step in order to guarantee a thorough and holistic protection of cultural property. A comparative analysis of *opinio juris* in England, Germany and the United States shows to mirror this development and suggests that courts start to endorse the view that claims for the return of cultural property based on sovereign rights should not be excluded per se but rather held to be justiciable. As a consequence property rights on the ground of cultural patrimony laws are being recognised in foreign courts, if the claim to recover a chattel can be viewed to be 'patrimonial' in nature. The basic position that courts do not entertain an action for the enforcement of foreign public law is developing into a modern rule that courts should enforce such claims subject to the public policy reservation.

In fact, it was as early as 1975, that principles for a liberal application of foreign public laws have been formulated. The Wiesbaden Resolution, as adopted by the Institute de Droit International, promotes the view that the public law character attributed to a provision of foreign law shall not prevent the application of that provision, subject to the fundamental reservation of negative public policy.

Today, this newly emerging liberalism even suggests to determine the justiciability of foreign public law on the grounds of a positive public policy – test. In other words, if reasons of public policy mandate the application of a foreign provision, then it would be contrary to international law for a claim based on this provision to be shut out. Such reasons of transnational public policy may be extrapolated from international legal instruments aimed at the protection of cultural heritage. For this reason, the recent decision *Government of Iran v Barakat Galleries Ltd.*, which for the first time explicitly spoke about a positive obligation to apply foreign cultural property laws, hovers at the forefront of the development in this legal field. However, *Barakat* once again proves that courts entertain a general hesitation towards the enforcement of property interests on grounds of export legislation or equally, of legislation which beares a prerogative character. The recent Swiss decision concerning the giant Mogul gold coins confirms this basic tenor, although Switzerland belongs to the few countries that have codified in their choice of law rules that foreign laws should not be disapplied per se.

Based on the reasoning of the Institute de Droit International and in view of the general respect for the doctrine of vested rights, this limitation should be reconsidered with regard to export legislation that grants the claimant state an immediate right of possession. As an immediate right of possession equally forms a property right that is feasible of being recognised in foreign courts, interests based on such possessory rights should be taken into account no matter if they are footing on expropriatory or confiscatory legislation. This argument is in line with the view that cultural heritage has evolved to be a policy consideration which is "transnational" or "truly international".

In order to further provide for an exhaustive protection movable cultural property, the application of foreign cultural patrimony laws has to begin as early as with the question, which law should be applied to a multi-jurisdictional art case. Indeed, the choice of law methodology in respect of dealings with art and movable antiquities calls for a new, if not even a novel approach. This book promotes the idea that as far as cases involving cultural property are concerned, the *lex originis* is the more suitable choice-of-law-rule as compared to the traditional *lex situs*-rule, which so far dominated commercial transactions. The *lex situs*-rule results in the application of national commercial laws whose solutions are extremely variable. As a consequence, traditional justifications such as commercial certainty, predictability and easy application have turned out to be inapplicable in cases concerning misappropriated heritage items. Conversely, due to the differences in the substantive laws of certain jurisdictions, the *lex situs*-rule even creates legal uncertainty. The *lex originis* however, allows for the application of the heritage laws of source countries in foreign courts, which would enhance the protection of cultural artefacts.

To resume, this study was able to reinforce the view that claims for the return of cultural property should be held justiciable in foreign courts. What was called by Lord Denning to be a "desirable goal" is proving to become legal reality. For the future, national courts should work towards a uniform application of foreign public laws, at least when cultural property is cincerned. A recommendation would be the application of foreign provisions on the grounds of a ‘positive public policy’ – test. In the end, as Moses J. once contended in *City of Gotha*, “the system of private international law exists to fulfil foreign rights not to destroy them”.

# Bibliography


Abhishek, B., The Concept of Renvoi in the Conflict of Laws (2008)

Abdulkarim, M. Archaeological Heritage in Syria during the Crisis in 2011–2013 (2013)

Adlercreutz, T. Property Rights and Protection of Cultural Heritage in Sweden, 7 IJCP (1998) 410

Alder, C., The Illicit Traffic in Asian Antiquities, Paper presented at the Australian Registrars Committee Conference in Melbourne (9 October 2001)

Aigler, R., Comment, 21 Michigan Law Review (1922–1923) 664

Alibrandi T./Fierri P., I beni culturali e ambientali (1985)

Anderson, K., International Art Theft, 8 New Eng. Int'l & Comp. L. Ann (2002) 411

Anglim, J. M., Crossroad in the Great Race, 45 Harv. Int'l L. J. (2004)

Anton, M., Zivilrecht – Guter Glaube in Internationalen Kunsthandel (2010)

Arendholz, A.K., Gutgläubiger Erwerb gestohlener Kunstgegenstände, in: Hoeren T./Holznagel B./Ernstschneider T., Handbuch Kunst und Recht (2008) 217

Armbrüster, C., Privatrechtliche Ansprüche auf Rückfuehrung von Kulturgütern ins Ausland, NJW (2001) 3581

Armbrüster, C., 10 La revendication de biens culturels du point de vue du droit international privé, rev.crit.dr.int. pr. Vol IV (2004) 723

Augustinos, N., The Cyprus Experience, in: N.E. Palmer (ed.) The Recovery of Stolen Art (1998) 217

Aust, A., Handbook of International Law (2010)

Axer, P., Widmung als Schlüsselbegriff des Rechts der öffentichen Sachen: Zur Identität des Rechst der öffentlichen Sachen als Rechtsgebiet (1994)

Axer, P., Das Hamburger Stadtsiegel – ein Problem des Rechts der öffentlichen Sachen, NWVBl. 1992, 354

Baade, H. W, The Legal Effects of Codes of Conduct for Multinational Enterprises, Germ. YB Int'l L. (1979) 40

Bamforth, N., Protecting the National Heritage? Judicial Review and the Three Graces, 1 Art, Antiquity & Law (1996) 147

Batiffol H./ Lagarde P., Traité de droit international privé (7th ed 1993)

Belohlavek, A., Rome Convention/Rome I Regulation (2010)

Bharti, A., The concept of Renvoi in the Conflict of Laws (2008), available at: http://works.bepress.com/abhishek_bharti/1

Basedow, J./Siehr K., Private Law in the International Arena (Privatrecht in der Internationalen Arena, Liber Amicorum Kurt Siehr (2000)

Bengs, B., Note, Dead on Arrival? A Comparison of the UNIDROIT Convention on Stolen and Illegally Exported Cultural Objects and U.S. Property Law, 6 Transnat'l L. Contemp. Probs. (1996) 503

Bernsdorff N./ Kleine-Tebbe A., Kulturgüterschutz in Deutschland (1996)

Biondi, A., The Merchant, the Thief and the Citizen: Circulation of Works of Art within the European Union, 34 Common Market L. Rev. (1997) 1173

Blake, J., Export Embargoes and the International Antiquities Market – The Turkish Experience, 2 ART, ANTIQUITY & LAW (1997), 233

Blake, J., On Defining the Cultural Heritage, 49 ICLQ (2000) 61

Blake, J., Illicit Antiquities and International Litigation- The Turkish Experience, Antiquity (1998) 824

Bland, R., The Treasure Act and the Portable Antiquities Scheme: A Progress Report, 4 ART, ANTIQUITY & LAW (1998) 191

Bland, R., Rescuing Our Neglected Heritage: The Evolution of the Government's Policy on Portable Antiquities in England and Wales, 14 Cultural Trends (2005) 257

Bland, R., A Pragmatic Approach to the Problem of Portable Antiquities: The Experience of England and Wales, 79 Antiquity (2005) 440

Bleckmann, A., Self-executing Treaty Provisions, in: Encyclopedia of Public International Law, Vol IV (2000)

Bordkey, A.K., The failure of the Nationalisation of Cultural Patrimonies, in: M Briat/J.A. Friedberg (eds), Legal Aspects of International Trade in Art (1996)

Borodkin, L., The Economics of Antiquities Looting and a Proposed Legal Alternative, 95 Colum. L. Rev. (1995) 378

Borke, K. E., Searching for a Solution: An Analysis of the Legislative Response to the Iraqi Antiquities Crisis of 2003, 13 DePaul-LCA J. Art & Ent. L. (2003) 381

Bow-Smith, E./ Hill, J., in: Palmer N.E./ McKendrick E. (eds), Interest in Goods ($2^{nd}$ ed. 1998) 251

Bowstead, W./Reynolds, F.M.B./ Watts, P., Bowstead and Reynolds on Agency (2010)

Briggs, A., The law which determines title to movable property, 79 BYIL (2008) 628

Briggs, A., In Praise and Defence of Renvoi, 47 ICLQ (1998) 887

See e.g. Brocher, Cours de Droit International Prive suivant les principes consacres par les droit postive francais, E.Thorin/Libraries H. Georg, Vol 1 (1882)

Brodie, N.J. /Doole, J./ Renfrew, C., Trade in Illicit Antiquities: The Destruction of the World's Archaeological Heritage (2001)

Brodie, N., Spoils of War, Archaeology (July/August 2003) 1

Brodie N./Renfrew C., Looting and the World's Archaeological Heritage: The Inadequate Response, 34 Annu. Rev. Anthropol. (2005) 343

Browman D.L./ Givens D.R., Stratigraphic Excavation: The First New Archaeology, 98 Anthropologist (1996) 80.

Burke, K. T., International Transfer of Stolen Cultural Property, 13 Loy. L.A. Int'l & Comp. L.J. (1990–1991) 466

Burks, S., Kunstsammlungen zu Weimar v Elicofon: Theft of Priceless Art Treasures Gives Rise to Protracted International Legal Battle, 19 Tex. Int'l L. J. (1984) 189

Bush, S.E., The Protection of British Heritage: Woburn Abbey and The Three Graces, 5 IJCP (1996) 269

Byrne-Sutton, Q., Who Is the Rightful Owner of a Stolen Work of Art? A Source of Conflict in International Trade in: P. Lalive, International Sales of Works of Art (1988) 545

Byrne-Sutton, Q., The Goldberg Case: A Confirmation of the Difficulty in Acquiring Good Title to Valuable Stolen Cultural Objects, 1 IJCP (1992) 59

Byrne-Sutton, Q., Le traffic international des biens culturels sous l'angle de leur revendication par L'État d'origine: Aspects de droit international privé, 52 Schweizer Studien zum Internationalen Recht (1988) 175

Cadena, L.R., Derecho Civil, Bd I (Quito 1974)

Calhoun, A., De-accessioning: Why not? (1985)

Cameron, S., Non-Justiciability in Australian Private International Law: A Lack of "Judicial Restraint"? 10 Melb. J. of Int'l L. (2009) 102

Carducci, G., La Restitution Internationale des Biens Culturels et des Objets d'Art (1997)
Carl M./Güttler H./ Siehr K., Kunstdiebstahl vor Gericht (2001)
Carleton, J., Protecting the National Heritage: Implications of the British Treasure Act 1996, 6 IJCP (1997) 343.
Carman, J., Valuing Ancient Things – Archaeology and Law (1996)
Carter, P.B., Transnational Sales in Works of Art: The Position in English Private International Law, in: P. Lalive (ed), International Sales of Works of Art (1988) 319
Carter, P.B., Transnational Recognition and Enforcement of Foreign Public Laws, 48 Cambridge L.J. (1989) 417
Carter, P.B., The Foreign Limitation Periods Act 1984, 101 LQR (1985) 68
Carruthers, J., Transfer of Property in the Conflict of Laws – Choice of Law Rules in *Inter Vivos* Transfers of Property (2005)
Callies, G.-P., (eds.) Rome Regulations – Commentary on the European Rules of the Conflict of Laws (2014)
Chamberlain, K., The Iraq (United Nations) Sanctions Order 2003 – Is it Human Rights Compatible?, 4 ART, ANTIQUITY & LAW (2003) 357.
Chamberlain, K., UK Accession to the 1970 UNESCO Convention, 7 ART, ANTIQUITY & LAW (2002) 231
Carducci, G., Conflict of Laws, Uniform Law, Mandatory Rule, in: Barbara T. Hoffmann, Art and Cultural Heritage, Law, Policy and Practice, 68.
Chatelain, J./Chatelain, F., Oeuvres d'art et objets de collection en droit français (1990)
Chatelain, F., Rapport national sur le sujet 1. Liberté des musées de procéder à des transactions d'objets d'art, in: Briat, M./Freedberg, J., A. (eds.), International Sales of Works of Art: International Art Trade and Law (1991) 109
Cheesman, C., Religious Offerings and the Intention to Recover in the Law of Treasure Trove, 1 ART, ANTIQUITY & LAW (1996) 27
Cheng, J.M., The Problem of National Treasure in International Law, 12 Oregon Rev. Int'L L . (2010) 141
Cheshire J./North P./Fawcett J., Private International Law (14th ed. 2008)
Chippindale, C./Gill, D., Material Consequences of Contemporary Classical Collecting, 104 Am. J. Archaeol. (2000) 463
Church, J., Evaluating the Effectiveness of Foreign Laws on National Ownership, 30 Colum.J. Transnat'l L. (1992) 179
Church, J., Evolving U.S. Case Law on Cultural Property Disputes, 2 IJCP (1993) 47
Church, J., Foreign National Ownership Statutes in U.S. Courts, 30 Colum.J.Transnat'l L. (1993) 179
Coggins, C., United States Cultural Property Legislation IJCP 7 (2005) 94
Cohan, J. A., An Examination of Archaeological Ethics and the Repatriation Movement Respecting Cultural Property (Part One), 27 Environs Envtl. L. Pol'y J. (2004) 1
Collier, J. G., Conflict of Laws and Enforcement of Foreign Public Laws: Antipodean Attitudes, 48 C.L.J. (1989) 33
Collins, L., Professor Lowenfeld and the Enforcement of Foreign Public Law, 42 Int'L L and Politics (2009) 125
Cookson, N., Archaeological Heritage Law (2000)
Cooper, C., Traditional Visual Culture in South-East Australia, in: Sayers A. (ed) Aboriginal Artists of the Nineteenth Century (1994) 91

Cordero, J. S., The Protection of Cultural Heritage – A Mexican Perspective, in 8 Uniform Law Review (2003), No 1–2, 565
Cornu, M., French Report, in: T. Kono/S.Wrbka, The Impact of Uniform Laws on the Protection of Cultural Heritage and the Preservation of Cultural Heritage in the 21st Century (2010) 337
Cornu, M., Le droit culturel des biens – L'intérêt culturel juridiquement protégé (1996) 476
Crewdson, R., Some Aspects of the Law as it Affects Dealers in England, in: P. Lalive (ed.) International Sales of Works of Art (1988) 47
Cunning, A., U.S. Policy on the Enforcement of Foreign Export Restrictions on Cultural Property & Destructive Aspects of Retention Schemes, 26 Hous. J. Int'l L. (2004) 449
Cuno, J., View from the Universal Museum, in: John H. Merryman (ed.), Imperialism, Art and Restitution (2006)
Damm, S., Kollisionsrechtlicher Erwerbsschutz im Internationalen Kunsthandel, in: Hoeren T./Holznagel B./Ernstschneider T. (eds.) Handbuch Kunst und Recht (2008) 249
Davies P./Myburgh P., The Protected Objects Act in New Zealand: Too Little, Too Late, 15 IJCP (2008) 321
Debbasch, C., Droit administrative des biens (1994)
Dörner, H., Zivilrechtliche Probleme der Bodendenkmalpflege (1992)
Del Piano, A. J., The Fine Art of Forgery, Theft and Fraud: Corruption in the World of Art and Antiquities, 8 Criminal Justice (1993) 16–20, 56–57
Dicey, Morris & Collins on the Conflict of Laws, 14th ed. Mainwork and 4th Supplement (2006)
Dolinger, J., World Public Policy: Real International Public Policy in the Conflict of Laws 17 Texas Int'l L.J. (1982) 167
Doyal S., Implementing the UNIDROIT Convention into Domestic Law: The Case of Italy, 39 Colum. J. Transnat'l L. (2001) 657
Drela, M., Własność zabytków (in Polish: The Ownership of Relics, 2006)
Droz, G.A.L., The International Protection of Cultural Property from the Standpoint of Private International Law, in International Legal Protection of Cultural Property, Proceedings of the 13th Colloquy on European Law, Delphi 20–22 Sept 1983 (1984) 17
Duboff, L., Art Law (1975)
Duboff, L., Art Law in a Nutshell (2nd ed, 1993)
Dugdael A./ Jones M., Clerk & Lindsell on Tort (19th ed. 2009)
Dukeminier J./ Krier J., Property (3rd 1993)
Dunbar, N.C.H. Controversial Aspects of Sovereign Immunity in Some States, 132 Hague Recueil (1971) 197.
Dutra M., Sir, How much is the Ming Vase in the Window? Protecting Cultural Relics in the People's Republic of China, Protecting Cultural Relics in the Peoples' Republic of China, 5 Asian-Pacific L. & Pol'y J. (2004) 62
Ebling K. /Schulze S. Kunstrecht – Zivilrecht, Steuerrecht (2007)
El-Bitar, J., Der deutsche und der französische Kulturgüterschutz nach der Umsetzung der Kulturrückgaberichtlinie (2006)
El-Bitar, J., Der Schutz von Kulturgut als res extra commercium in Frankreich: Ein Vorbild für Deutschland? In: Im Labyrinth des Rechst? Wege zum Kulturgütershcutz, Koordinierungsstelle für Kulturgutverluste (ed.) (2007) 173
Elia, R., Analysis of the looting, selling and collecting of Apulian red-figure vases: a quantitative approach, in: N. Brodie/J. Doole /C. Renfrew (eds.) Trade in Illicit

Antiquities: The Destruction of the World's Archaeological Heritage (McDonald Inst 2001) 145
Engstler, L., Die territoriale Bindung von Kulturgütern im Rahmen des Völkerrechts (1964)
Engelhart, S., Nachrichtenlose Kulturgüter (2013)
Enonchong, N., Public Policy in the Conflict of Laws: A Chinese Wall Around Little England?, 45 ICLQ (1996) 631
Enrichsen H.-U.,/D. Ehlers, Allgemeines Verwaltungsrecht – Recht der öffentlichen Sachen (13th ed. 2005)
Enterria, J.,The Role of Public Policy in International Commercial Arbitration, 21 L & Pol'Y Int'l Business (1989–90) 389
Erauw, J., Lex Situs and Art Recovery – New Belgian Rules, paper presented at the Lex Situs Conference held by the Institute of Art and Law in London, Nov. 2008
Erichsen H-U./ Ehlers D., Allgemeines Verwaltungsrecht – Recht der öffentlichen Sachen (13th ed. 2005)
Ericson, C., Note, United States of America v. Frederick Schultz: The National Stolen Property Act Revives the Curse of the Pharaohs, 12 Tul. J. Int'l & Comp. L. (2004) 509
Fallon, R.H., Justiciability and Remedies – And their Connection to Substantive Rights, 92 Virginia L. Rev. (2006) 633
Fansa; M. (ed.) Syrien – Sechs Weltkulturerbe-Stätten in den Wirren des Bürgerkrieges (2014)
Feldman, M.B., Proceedings of the Panel on the US Enabling Legislation of the UNESCO Convention on the Means of Prohibiting and Preventing the Illicit Import, Export and Transfer of Ownership of Cultural Property, 4 Syr. Int'l L. & Com. (1976) 97
Feroozi, A.W. and Tarzi, Z., The Impact of War upon Afghanistan's Cultural Heritage (2004)
Ferrer-Correia, A., Exposé prelimiaire, Annuaire de l'Institute de Droit International, (1991) 64-I
Fifoot, C. H.S., History and Sources of the Common Law: Tort and Contract (1970)
Fincham, D., A Coordinated Legal and Policy Approach to Undiscovered Antiquities: Adapting the Cultural Heritgae Policy of England and Wales to Other Nations of Origin, 15 IJCP (2008) 347
Fincham, D., How Adopting the Lex Originis Rule Can Impede the Flow of Illicit Cultural Property, 32 Colum. J. L. & Arts (2008) 111
Fincham, D., Rejecting Renvoi for Movable Cultural Property: The Islamic Republic of Iran v. Denyse Berend, IJCP, (2007) 111
Fincham, D., The Fundamental Importance of Archaeological Context, in Noah Charney (ed.) Art and Crime (2009)
Fincham, D., Towards a Rigorous Standard for the Good Faith Acquisition of Antiquities, 37 Syr. J. of Int'l Law and Com (2009) 145
Fincham, D., Why U.S. Federal Criminal Penalties for Dealing in Illicit Cultural Property are Ineffective, and a Pragmatic Alternative, 25 Cardozo Arts & Entertainment L. J. (2007) 597
Fischer zu Cramburg, R., Das Schatzregal (2001)
Fitz Gibbons, K., Who Owns the Past – Cultural Policy, Cultural Property and the Law (2005)
Fitzpatrick, J. F., A Wayward Course: The Lawless Customs Policy Toward Cultural Properties, 15 N.Y.U. J. Int'l L & Pol. (1983) 857
Fox, C., The Unidroit Convention on Stolen or Illegally Exported Cultural Objects: An Answer to the World Problem of Illicit Trade in Cultural Property, 9 Am. J. Int'l L. & Pol. (1993) 225

Franklin, M., Security of Acquisition and of Transaction: La Possession Vaut Titre and Bona-Fide Purchase, 6 Tulane L. Rev. (1932) 589
Freytag, C., "Cultural Heritage": Rückgabeansprüche von Ursprungsländern auf 'ihr' Kulturgut? in: F. G. Fechner, Prinzipien des Kulturgüterschutzes-Ansätze im deutschen, europäischen, und internationalen Recht (1996) 175
Frigo, M., Ethical Rules and Codes of Honor Related to Museum Activities: A Complementary Support to the Private International Law Approach Concerning the Circulation of Cultural Property, 16 IJCP (2009) 49
Frigo, M., Cultural Property v. Cultural Heritage: A "Battle of Concepts" in International Law?, 86 International Committee of the Red Cross (June 2004), 367
Frigo, M., La Protezione dei Beni Culturali nel dritto internazionale (1986)
Foutty, S.L., Entrenchment of the Due Dilligence Requirement in Replevin Actions for Stolen Art, 43 Vand. L. Rev. (1990) 1839
Forsyth, M., International Cultural Property Trust, One response to Burden of Proof Challenges in Stolen Antiquities Litigation, 8 Chi. J. Int'l L. (2007) 197
Galindo, N.G., Fundamentos de derecho administrativo (Quito 1984)
Gardella, A., Nuove perspetti per la protezione dei beni culturali : La convenzione dell'UNIDROIT del 24 guigno 1995, in : 12 Diritto del Commercio Internazionale (1998) 997
Garner, B. A., Black's Law Dictionary (8th ed 2004)
Garro, A. M., The Recovery of Stolen Art from Bona Fide Purchasers, in: Lalive P. (ed), Geneva Workshop on International Sales of Work of Art (1985) 503
Geldart W./ Yardley D., Introduction to English Law (11th ed 1995)
Gerstenblith, P., Art, Cultural Heritage and the Law – Cases and Materials (2nd ed 2008)
Gerstenblith, P., Controlling the International Market in Antiquities: Reducing the Harm, Preserving the Past, 8 Chi. J. Int'l L. (2007) 169
Gerstenblith, P., Schultz and Barakat: Universal Recognition of National Ownership of 14 ART, ANTIQUITY & LAW (2009) 21
Gerstenblith, P., The Public Interest in the Restitution of Cultural Objects, 16 Conn J. Int'l L. (2000–2001) 197
Gerstenblith, P., Identity and Cultural Property: The Protection of Cultural Property in the United States, 75 Boston U. L. REV. (1995) 559
Gibbons, K. F. (ed.), Who Owns the Past – Cultural Policy, Cultural Property and the Law (2005)
Gilgan, E., Looting and the market for Maya objects: a Belizean perspective, in: Brodie N./Doole J./Renfrew C., Trade in Illicit Antiquities: the Destruction of the World's Archaeological Heritage (2001) 73
Gilmore, G., The Commercial Doctrine of Good Faith Purchase, 63 YALE L.J. (1954) 1057
Gioia, A., The Development of International Law Relating to the Protection of Cultural Property in the Event of Armed Conflict: The Second Protocol of the 1954 Hague Convention (2003)
Goldberg, A., Reaffirming McClain: The National Stolen Property Act and the Abiding Trade in Looted Cultural Objects, 53 UCLA L. Rev. (2005–2006) 1031
Gray, K. / Gray, S.F., Elements of Land Law (4th ed. 2005)
Greenfield, J., The Return of Cultural Treasures (3rd ed 2007)
Grover, S., Note, The Need for Civil Law Nations to Adopt Discovery Rules in Art Replevin Actions: A Comparative Study, 70 Tex. L. Rev. (1991–1992) 1431

Harbison, J.S., Private Enforcement of Public Values in US Courts: Justiciability Barriers in Environmental Law, 4 Environt'l L. Rev. (2001) 264.
Harris, J., Who Owns the Pot of Gold at the End of the Rainbow? A Review of the Impact of Cultural Property on Finders and Salvage Laws, 14 Ariz. J. Int'l & Comp. L. (1997) 223
Harvey, B.W./ Meisel F., Auctions Law and Practice (1995)
Hayton D./ Mitchell C., Hayton and Mitchesll's Commentary and Cases on the Law of Trusts and Equitable Remedies (13th ed. 2010)
Hayworth, A.E., Stolen Artwork: Deciding Ownership is No Pretty Picture, 43 Duke Law Journal (1993) 337
Helmholz, R.H., Equitable Division and the Law of Finders, 52 Fordham L. Rev. (1983–1984) 313
Henze, W., Unidroit, hehre Ziele verfehlte Mittel, in: UNIDROIT: Recht und Ethik im Handel mit Kulturgut, Tagung der Schweizerischen Akademie der Geistes- und Sozialwissenschaften in Bern (1998)
Hickey, R., Curbin the Enthusiasm of Finders, in: Elizabeth Cook (ed), Modern Studies in Property Law (2007) 97
Hill, C., in Norman Palmer (ed), The Recovery of Stolen Art (1998) Chapter 10, 181
Hill, G., Treasure Trove in Law and Practice (1936)
Hill, J./Bowes-Smith, E. in Palmer N.E/McKendrick E. (eds.), Interests in Goods (2nd ed 1998) 251
Hipp, A., Schutz von Kulturgütern in Deutschland (2000)
Hladík, J., The Control System under the Hague Convention for the Protection of Cultural Property in the Event of Armed Conflict 1954 and its Second protocol (2004)
Hoath, D. C., Some conveyancing implications of "finding" disputes, Conveyancer and Property Lawyer (1990) 348
Hoffman, B.T., European Union Legislation Pertaining to Cultural Goods, in: B. T. Hoffmann (ed) Art and Cultural Heritage (2006) 191
Hoffman, B., Sevso Follies of 1994, Archaeology (1994) 41
William E. Holder, Public Policy and National Preferences – The Exclusion of Foreign Law in English Private International Law, 17 ICLQ (1968) 926
Honsell, H. in: Peter Gauch / Franz Werro / Pascal Pichonnaz (eds.) Das Kulturgütertransfergesetz und das Privatrecht (2008)
Hosford, I,. Options or Rights of First Refusal?, 17th Annual Advanced real Estate Drafting Course Paper (2006) available at http://www.texasbarcle.com/Materials/Events/5853/44891_01.pdf
Hönes, E-R., Das Schatzregal, DöV (1992) 425
Hudson, A.H., Is Divesting Abandonment Possible in Common Law? 100 LQR (1984) 110
Hudson, M.O., International Legislation – A Collection of the Texts of Multipartite International Instruments of General Interest (1972)
Hughes, J., The Trend Toward Liberal Enforcement of Repatriation Claims in Cultural Prop erty Disputes, 33 GW J. INT'L & ECON. (2000) 131
Hughes, W., United States v Hollinshead: A New Leap in Extraterritorial Application of Criminal Laws, 1 Hastings Int'l & Comp. L. Rev. (1977), 149
Irsheid, C., The Protection of Cultural Property in the Arab World, 6 IJCP (1997) 11
Jaeger, A., Rechtsfragen des internationalen Kulturgüterschutzes, (1993)
Jahn, I., Loan versus Gifts, Determining the Donor's Intention, Lord Beaverbrook v. The Beaverbrook Art Gallery, 12 ART, ANTIQUITY & LAW (2007) 81

Jayme, E., Anknüpfungsmaximen für den Kulturgüterschutz im Internationalen Privatrecht, in: C. Dominicé C. /Patry R./ Reymond R. (eds), Études des droit international en l'honneur de Pierre Lalive : Recueil/Faculté de Droit de l' Université de Genève, Institute Universitaire de Hautes Etudes Internationales Christian Dominicé (1993) 717
Jayme, E., Die Nationalität des Kunstwerks als Rechtsfrage, in G. Reichelt (ed) Internationaler Kulturgüterschutz (1990) 7
Jayme, E., Internationaler Kulturgüterschutz: Lex originis oder lex rei sitae-Tagung in Heidleberg, IPrax (1990) 347.
Jayme, E., Neue Anknüpfungspunkte für den Kulturgüterschutz, in : Dolzer/Jayme/Mussgnus (eds) Rechtsfragen des internationalen Kulturgüterschutzes (1994) 35
Jayme, E., Protection of Cultural Property and Conflict of Laws, 6 IJCP (1997) 376
Jenschke, C., Der Völkerrechtliche Rückgabeanspruch auf in Kriegszeiten widerrechtlich verbrachte Kulturgüter (2005)
Jenkins, P., The UNIDROIT Convention on Stolen or Illegally Exported Cultural Objects, 1 ART, ANTIQUITY & LAW (1996) 163
O. Kahn-Freund, Reflections on Public Policy in the English Conflict of Laws, Grotius Society (1953) 39
Kastenberg, J. E., The Legal Regime for Protecting Cultural Property During Armed Conflict, 42 A.F.L. Rev. (1997) 277
Kaufmann, R.S., The Art Law Handbook (2000)
Kay, H.H., A Defence of Currie's Governmental Interest Analysis, 215 Receuil des Cours 9 (1989) 78;
Kay, H.H. Currie's Interest Analysis in the 21st Century: Loosing the Battle but Winnin the War, 37 Willamette L.Rev. (2001) 123
Kaye, L. M., Cultural Property Disputes in Foreign Courts, in: Schneider E./ Schneider R. (eds.), Cultural Property Protection, Deutsch Türkische Rechtsstudien (Istambul Conference) Band 4 (2005) 43
Kaye, L. /Main, C. T., The saga of the Lydian hoard antiquities: from Uşak to New York and back and some related observations on the law of cultural repatriation, in: Tubb K.W. (ed.), Antiquities, Trade or Betrayed. Legal, Ethical and Conservation Issues (2002) 150
Kaye, L. M., The Recovery of Stolen Cultural Property: A Practitioner's View, 5 Vill. Sports & Ent. L. J. (1998) 5
Kaye, M., The Future of the Past, Recovering Cultural Property, 4 Cardozo J. Int'l & Comp. L. (1996) 23
Kegel, G., Internationales Privatrecht (6th ed. 1987)
Kegel, G. / Schurig, K., Internationales Privatrecht (9th ed. 2004)
Kenety, W.H., Who Onws the Past? The Need for Legal Reform and Reciprocity in the International Art Trade, 23 Cornell Int'l L.J. (1990) 1
Kenny, P/H., What is a Right of Pre-Emption? Conveyancer and Property Lawyer (2001), 295
King, J.A., Institutional Approaches to Judicial Resraint, OJLS (2008) 409
King, J.A., The Pervasiveness of Polycentricity, Public Law (2008) 101
Kleeburg, J. M., The Law and Practice Regarding Coin Finds, CIM, Compte rendu 53 (2006) 13
Klüssendorf, N., Der Münzschatz von Niederhohne (1987)
Knapp, B., La protection des biens culturels, in Rapports suisses présentés au XIII Congrès international de droit comparé (1990) 227
Knight, C.J.S., Of Coups and Compensation Claims: Mbasago Reassessed, K.L.J. (2008) 176

Koch, A., Antiken, Recht und (kein) Markt? Zivil und strafrechtliche Probleme des Handels mit archäologischem Kulturgut, KUR (2009) 49

Kobyliński, Z., The Protection of Archaeolgical Artefacts in Europe (Ochrona dziedzictwa archaeologicznego w Europie, Warsaw 1998)

Kohls, F., Kulturgüterschutz – Die Wirkung von Verstössen gegen Ausfuhrverbote und Möglichkeiten der Rückführung illegal verbrachter Kulturgüter – eine vergleichende Untersuchung mit den Rechten Dänemarks, Norwegens und Schwedens (2001)

Kono T./Wrbka S., General Report in: Kono T./Wrbka S., The Impact of Uniform Laws on the Protection of Cultural Heritage and the Preservation of Cultural Heritage in the 21st Century (2010) 1

Kramer, L., Return of the Renvoi, 66 N.Y.U. L. REV. (1991) 979

Kreuzer, K., Gutachtliche Stellungnahme zum Referentenentwurf eines Gesetzes zur Ergänzung des Internationalen Privatrechts (1991)

Kroppholler, J., Internationales Privatrecht (6th ed. 2006)

Kuckein, M., Eingriffsnormen, Die 'Berücksichtigung' von Eingriffsnormen im deutschen und englischen internationalen Vertragsrecht (2008)

Kugler, R., Die Praxis des Kulturgüterrückgabegesetzes, in: Kulturgütersschutz und politiche Entwicklunge in Mexiko im Jubiläumsjahr 2010, Jahreskongress 2010 der Deutsch Mexikanischen Juristen Vereinigung, ed Karl August Prinz von Sachsen Gessaphe (2011) 13

Kurpiers, O., Die lex originis im Internationalen Sachenrecht (2005)

Kurzweil H./ Gagion L./ de Walden L., The Trial of the Sevso-Treasure, in: Fitz-Gibbon K. (ed.), Who owns the Past (2005) 83

Lalive, Réflexions sur un ordre public culturel, in: E. Wyler/A. Papaux (eds.), L'Extranéité ou le dépassement de l'ordre juridique étatique: actes du colloque des 27 et 28 novembre 1997 organisé par l'Institut d'études de droit international de la Faculté de droit de l'Université de Lausanne (1999) 155

Lalive, P., La convention d'UNIDROIT sur les biens culturels volés ou illicitement exportés (du 24 juin 1995), Vol 7 Revue suisse de droit international et de droit européen, (1997) 13

Lalive, P., Une avancée du droit international: La Convention de Rome d'UNIDROIT sur les biens culturels volés ou illicitement exportés, Uniform Law Review (1996) 40

Lalive, P., Sur le régime des objets d'art volés en droit international privé,, in: Matscher/Karas-Valdheim (eds.) Europa im Aufbruch: Festschrift Fritz Schwind zum 80 Geburtstag (1993) 51

Lalive, P. (ed.), International Sales of works of Art (La vente international d'oevres d'art, 1988)

Lalive, P., Report, L'application du droit public étranger, Institute de Droit International, Annuaire Vol. 56, Session de Wiesbaden 1975, 219

Lalive, P., The Transfer of Chattels in the Conflict of Laws (1955)

Lalive, P., Transnational (or Truly International) Public Policy and Interational Arbitration, in: P. Sanders (ed.), Comparative Arbitration Practice and Public Policy in Arbitration (I.C.C.A. Congress Series No.3, 1987)

Lawson F./ Rudden B., The Law of Property (3rd ed. 2002)

Lee, R.W., Elements of Roman Law (1956)

Lehman, J., The Continued Struggle with Stolen Cultural Property: The Hague Convention, The UNESCO Convention and the UNIDROIT Draft Convention, 14 Ariz J. Int'l & Comp. L. (1997) 527

Lemme, F., Il "Korous" ritrovato: reflessioni e meditazioni, in: Tra Arte e diritto, (2nd ed. 1996) 62
Lepsius, O., Besitz und Sachherrschaft im öffentlichen Recht (2002)
Levy, H./Lowenthal, C., Stolen and Smuggled Art, N.Y. L.J, (1997) 1
Lew, J.D.M./Mistelis, L.A./Kroell, S. Comparative Interational Commercial Arbitration (2003)
Lindsay, E.W., The Recovery of Cultural Artefacts: The Legacy of our Archaeological Heritage, 22 Case W. Res. J. Int'l (1990) 165
Lloyd, D., Public Policy – A Comparative Study in English and French Law (1953)
Lobay, G., Border Controls in Market Countries as Disincentives to Antiquities Looting at Source? The USA-Italy Bilateral Agreement 2001, in: MacKenzie S./Green P. (eds.), Criminology and Archaeology – Studies in Looted Antiquities (2009) 124
Loewenthal, D., Why Sanctions Seldom Work: Reflections on Cultural Property Internationalism, 12 IJCP (2005) 293
Lomas P./Orton S., Potential Repercussions from the City of Gotha Decision, 5 ART, ANTIQUITY & LAW (1999) 159
Lorenzen, E. G., The Renvoi Theory and the Application of Foreign Law, 10 Colum. L. Rev. (1910) 327
Lubina, K., Protection and Preservation of Cultural Heritage in the Netherlands in the 21st Century, 13 Elec. J. Comp. L. (2009) 1
Lubina, K., The Dealing in Cultural Objects (Offences) Act 2003 put through its Paces Issue 199 The Art Loss Review (2007) 25, http://www.tracemagazine.co.uk/legal/legalarchive.php?id=9
Lubina, K., Dutch Report, in: T. Kono/S.Wrbka, The Impact of Uniform Laws (2010) 563
Lufkin, M., Criminal Liability for Receiving State-Claimed Antiquities in the United States: The 'Schultz'- Case, 8 ART, ANTIQUITY & LAW (2003) 321
Lunden, S., The Scholar and the Market: Swedish Scholarly Contributions to the Destruction of the World's Archaeological Heritage, in: H. Karlsson (ed.) Swedish Archaeologists on Ethics (2004) 197
Luzzatto, R., Trade in Art and Conflict of Laws: The Position in Italy, in: P. Lalive (ed.) International Sales of Works of Art (1988) 409
Lyman R.L./O'Brien M., Americanist Stratigraphic Excavation and the Measurement of Cultuaral Change, 6 J. Archaeol. Method and Theory (1999) 55
Maczynski, A., Polish Private International Law, Yearbook of Private International Law Vol. VI (2004) 203
Mackenzie S./Green P., Criminalising the Market in Illicit Antiquities: An Evaluation of the Dealing in Cultural Objects (Offences) Act 2003, in: Criminology and Archaeology – Studies in the Looting of Antiquities (2009), 178
Mackenzie, S./Green, P., Criminology and Archaeology – Studies in Looted Antiquities (2009)
Mackenzie S., Dealing in Cultural Objects – A New Criminal Law for the UK, 71 Amicus Curiae (2007) 8
Mackenzie, S., Going, Going, Gone: Regulating the Illicit Market in Antiquities (2005)
Margules, P., International Art Theft and the Illegal Import and Export of Cultural Property: A Study of Relevant Values, Legislation and Solutions, 15 Suffolk Transnat'l L.J. (1991–1992) 609
McAndrew C./O'Hogan, J., Export Restrictions, Tax Incentives and the National Artistic Patrimony, Trinity Economic Paper Series, Paper No 2000/6, available at http://www.tcd.ie/Economics/research/tep/2000/TEPNo6JOH20.pdf

McBryde, I., (ed.) Who owns the past? Papers from the Annual Symposium of the Australian Academy of the Humanities (1985)
McElroy, J., War against the Illegal Antiquities Trade: Rules of Engagement for Source Nations, 27 Hastings Comm. & Ent. L.J. (2004 – 2005) 549
McGoldrick, D., The Boundries of Justiciability, 58 ICLQ (2010) 981
McIntosh, S. K., The Good Collector: Fabulous Beast or Endangered Species? Debates between Susan Kean McIntosh and Colin Renfrew 1 Public Archaeology (2000) 73
Mc Rae, D.M., The Legal Effect of Interpretative Declarations, 49 British Yearbook of International Law (1978) 155
Mair, A., Misappropriation and Skulduggery in Germany and Russia: Wtewael's "The Holy Family", 3 ART, ANTIQUITY & LAW (1998) 413
Malaro, M.C., A Legal Primer on Managing Museum Collections (2nd ed. 1998)
Manisty, E. & Smith, J., The Deaccessioning of Objects from Public Institutions: Legal and Related Considerations, 15 ART, ANTIQUITY & LAW (2010) 1
Mann, F. A., Spycatcher in the Highcourt of Australia, 104 LQR (1988) 497
Mann, F. A., The International Enforcement of Public Rights, 19 N.Y U. J. of Int'l L. & Pol. (1987) 603
Mann, F.A., The Proper Law Doctrine in the Conflict of Laws, 46 ICLQ (1987) 437
Mann, F.A., Case note on the Nigeria case, NJW 1972, 2179
Mann, F. A., Prerogative Rights of Foreign States, 40 Papers by the Gropius Society (1955) 25, reprinted in: Studies in International Law (1973) 492
Mann, F. A., The Effect of Changes of Sovereignty Upon Nationality, 5 Modern Law Rev. (1942) 218
Manssen, G., Der Hamburger Stadtsiegelfall, JuS (1992) 745
Markesinis B. /Johnston A./Deakin S., Markesinis and Deakin's Tort Law (6th ed 2007)
Marks P, The Ethics of Dealing (1998)
Mattei Ugo, Basis Principle of Property Law (2000)
Maurice, C. and Turnor, R., The Export Licencing Rule in the United Kingdom and the Waverley Criteria (1992)
Merryman, J.H., Imperialism, Art and Restitution (2006)
Merryman, J. H./ A. Elsen/ Urice, S. (eds.), Law, Ethics and the Visual Arts (2007)
Merryman, J. H., Cultural Property, International Trade, and Human Rights, Occasional Papers in Intellectual Property from B. N. Cordozo Law School University No 9 (2001)
Merryman, J. H., The UNIDROIT Convention: Three Significant Departures from the Urtext, 5 IJCP (1996) 11
Merryman, J. H., A Licit Trade in Cultural Objects, 4 IJCP (1995) 11
Merryman J.H./Nafzinger J., The Private International Law of Cultural Property in the United States, 42 Am.J.Comp.L. Supp (1994) 221
Merryman, J. H., Limits on State Recovery of Stolen Artifacts: Peru v Johnson, 1 IJCP (1992) 169
Merryman, J. H., The Retention of Cultural Property, 21 U.S. Davis L. Rev. (1988) 477
Merryman, J. H., Two Ways of Thinking about Cultural Property', 80 Amer. J. of Int'l. L. (1986) 831
Merryman, J. H., Thinking about the Elgin Marbles, 83 Michigan L R (1985) 1881
Merryman, J. H., American Law and the International Trade in Art, in: Pierre Lalive (ed.) International Sales of Works of Art (1985)

Merryman, J. H., Protection of Artistic National Patrimony Against Pillaging and Theft, in: L. DuBoff (ed.) Art Law: Domestic and International (1975) 236

Mayer, K., The Plundered Past (1973)

Mayer, O., Der gegenwärtige Stand der Frage des öffentlichen Eigentums, AöR 21 (1907) 499

Miller, M. A., Looting and the Antiquities Market, 4 Athena Rev., No 2, editorial notes.

Moore, J. S., Enforcing Foreign Ownership Claims in the Antiquities Market, 97 Yale L.J. (1988) 466

Moore, J., A Digest of International Law (1906)

Morris, J.H.C., The Conflict of Laws ($6^{th}$ ed. 2005)

Morris J.H.C., et al (eds), Conflict of Laws, ($7^{th}$ ed. 1958)

Moustaka, J., Group Rights in Cultural Property: Justifying Strict Inalienability, 74 Cornell L. Rev. (1988) 1179

Müller-Katzenburg, A., Possession and Ownership of Stolen and Otherwise Lost Works of Art, 5 ART, ANTIQUITY & LAW (2000) 185

Müller-Katzenburg, A., Besitz- und Eigentumssituation bei gestohlenen und sonst abhanden gekommenen Kunstwerken, NJW (1999) 2551

Müller-Katzenburg, A., Internationale Standards im Kulturgüterverkehr (1996)

Münchener Kommentart zum Bürgerlichen Gesetzbuch, Allgemeiner Teil (2006)

Münchener Kommentart zum Bürgerlichen Gesetzbuch, Sachenrecht (2009)

Murphy, J.D., Plunder and Preservation: Cultural Property Law and Practice in the People's Republic of China (1995)

Mussgnug, R., Museums- und Archivgut als res extra commercium? in: Dolzer R./Jayme E./Mussgnug R. (eds.) Rechtsfragen des internationalen Kulturgüterschutzes, Symposium 22/23 Juni 1990 im internationalen Wirtschaftsforum Heidelberg 1994, (1999)

Mussgnug R., Das Kunstwerk im Internationalen Recht, KUR (1985) 15

Muszalski, E., Kodeksy cywilne obowiązujące na ziemiach centralnych Polski (Civil Codes Binding in Central Poland, 1936)

Nafziger, J.F. The New International Legal Framework for the Return, Restitution or Forfeiture of Cultural Property, NYU Journal of International Law and Politics (1983) 799

North, P. (ed.), Contract Conflict – the EEC Convention on the Law Applicable to Contractual Obligation: A Comparative Study (1982)

Nott, S.M., Title to movables acquired abroad, 45 Conveyancer and Property Lawyer (1981) 279

Nygh, P., The Reasonable Expectation of the Parties as A Guide to Choice of Law in Contract and Tort 251 Hague Racueil (1995) 269

O'Connel, M.E, Occupation Failures and the Legality of Armed Conflict: The Case of Iraqi Cultural Property, 9 ART, ANTIQUITY & LAW (2004)

Odendahl, K., Kulturgüterschutz (2005)

Ong, E.-L., Non-Justiciability in Private International Law: Principle or Discretion? 31 Comp. L. World Rev. (2002) 35

Özel, S., The Basel Decisions: Recognition of the Blanket Legislation Vesting State Ownership over the Cultural Property Found within the Country of Origin, 9 IJCP (2000) 325

Özel, S., The Protection of Cultural properties in Turkey, in: E. Schneider/S.Schneider (eds.) Cultural Property Protection (2005) 23

Olsburgh, C., Authenticity in the Art Market: A Comparative Study of Swiss, French and English Contract Law (2005)

O'Connor, T., Intelligence-Led Policing and Transnational Justice, J. Just. Int'l Stud. (2006), 2333
O'Keefe, P.J., Commentary on the UNESCO Convention (2007)
O'Keefe, P.J., Trade in Antiquities – Reducing Destruction and Theft (1997)
O'Keefe, P.J., Provenance and Trade in Cultural Heritage, 95 Brit. Colum. L Rev, (1995) 259
O'Keefe, P.J., Commentary on the UNESCO 1970 Convention on Cultural Heritage: The Commonwealth Scheme, 44 ICLQ (1995) 147
O'Keefe, P.J./Prott L.V., Law and the Cultural Heritage, Vol 3, Movement (1989)
O'Keefe, P.J./Prott L.V., Law and the Cultural Heritage, Vol 1, Discovery and Excavation (1984)
O'Keefe, P.J., Export and Import Controls on Movement of the Cultural Heritage: Problems on the National Level, 10 Syracuse J. Int'l L. & Com. (1983) 352
Ortiz, G., The Collectors and the Regulation of the Art Market, in: La Libre Circulation des Collections d'objects d'art (1993) 147
Ortiz, G., The Cross-Border Movement of Art, 3 ART, ANTIQUITY & LAW (1998) 53
Osman, D. N., Occupiers' Title to Cultural Property: Nineteenth-Century Removal of Egyptian Artifacts, 37 Colum. J. Transnat'l L. (1999) 969
Oyer III, H.E., The 1954 Hague Convention for the Protection of Cultural Property in the Event of Armed Conflict – Is it Working? A Case Study: The Persian Golf War Experience (1999) Columbia VLA J. of Law and Arts, 49
Palmer, N. Acquiring Property in Treasure and the Duty to Notify: The Coroners and Justice Act 2009 and the New Criminal Offence, 15, Issue 2 ART, ANTIQUITY & LAW (2010), 125
Palmer, N., Responding to Conscience – The Holocaust Return of Cultural Objects Act 2009, 15 ART, ANTIQUITY & LAW (2010) 87
Palmer, N., Bailment (3rd ed. 2009)
Palmer, N., Adrift on a Sea of Troubles: Cross-Border Art Loans and the Specter of Ulterior Title, 38 Vand. J. Transnat'l L. (2005) 947
Palmer, N., Repatriation and Deaccessioning of Cultural Property: Reflections on the Resolution of Art Disputes, in: Current Legal Problems (2001) 475
Palmer, N., Bad Apples and Blighted Windfalls: Finding, Bailment and the Fruits of Crime, in: Meisel F./Cook P.J. (eds.) Property and Protection: Essays in Honour of Brian Harvey (2000) 1
Palmer, N., Recovery of Unlawfully Removed Works of Art and Antiquity – The Legal Dimension (Paper presented at the Art Crime Conference convened by the Australian Institute of Criminology in Sydney, held in Dec 1999)
Palmer, N.E., Conversion, Tort and Restitution, in Palmer N.E/Mckendrick E. (eds.), Interests in Goods (2nd ed. 1998) 825
Palmer N. (ed.), The Recovery of Stolen Art – A Collection of Essays (1998)
Palmer, N., Statutory, Forensic and Ethical Initiatives in the Recovery of Stolen Art and Antiquities, in: Palmer, N., The Recovery of Stolen Art – A Collection of Essays (1998) 1
Palmer, N., Quality and Duration of the Finder's Title: Free-Standing of Free-For-All? 3 ART, ANTIQUITY & LAW (1998) 223
Palmer, N., Title to Antiquarian Finds: Perpetuating the Impenetrable, (1996) ART, ANTIQUITY & LAW, 15
Palmer, N., Treasure Trove and Title to Discovered Antiquities, in: Palmer and McKendrick (eds), Interests in Goods (1993) 305, reprinted in: 2 IJCP (1993) 275
Papapetropoulos, A., The Decision of the Council of State, 7 Environment and the Law (2003) 693

Pawlowski, M., Rights of Pre-emption, (2004) L. & T. Review 39
Pearlstein, W.G., Claims for the Repatriation of Cultural Property: Prospects for a Managed Antiquities Market, 28 Law & Pol'y Int'l BuS (1996) 123
Penner, J.E., The Law of Trust (5th ed. 2006)
Peters, C., Die Ersitzbarkeit von Gegenständen öffentlich–rechtlichen Eigentums in besonderer Beziehung auf Stücke aus Archiven des Staates oder anderer öffentlich-rechtlicher Körperschaften in Preussen, VerwArch 24 (1916) 167
Peya, A., Die Ausfuhr von Kulturgütern im nationalen und Gemeinschaftsrecht (2002)
Pfeiffer, T., Der Stand des internationalen Sachenrechts nach seiner Kodifikation, IPrax (2000) 270
Piatkowski, J. S., The system of private law (Polish: System Prawa Cywilnego t. II, 1977)
Pinkerton, L.F., Due Diligence in Fine Art Transactions, 22 CASE W. RES. J. INT'L L. (1990) 1
Plutschow, M., Staatliche Vorkaufsrechte im internationalen Kulturgüterschutz (engl: Pre-Emption Rights in International Cultural Property Law) Studien zum Kunstrecht 14 (2002)
Poli, J.F., La Protection de biens culturelles meubles (1996)
Poli, J.F., Le classement d'un tableau de Van Gogh comme monument historique : Mote sous Conseil d'Etat, 31 juillet 1992 : M. Jaques Walter, in: 10 Revue Française de Droit Administratif (1994) 259
Pollock F./ Wright S., Essays on Possession in the Common Law (1888)
Pollock F./Maitland F.W, History of English law before the Time of Edward I (2nd ed. 1996)
Polonsky M./ J-F. Canat, The British and French System of Control of the Export of Works of Art, 45 ICLQ (1996) 557
Preziosi, T., Note, Applying a Strict Discovery Rule to Art Stolen in the Past, 49 Hastings L.J. (1997) 225
Prott, L.V., The Dja Dja Warrung Bark Etchings Case, 13 IJCP (2006) 241
Prott, L. V., The International Movement of Cultural Objects, 12 IJCP (2005) 225
Prott, L. V., Commentary on the UNIDROIT Convention (1997)
Prott, L. V., Problems of Private International Law for the Protection of the Cultural Heritage, 5 Recueil des Cours (1989) 215
Rabel, E., The Conflict of Laws: A Comparative Study (1958)
Radwanski, R., System Prawa Cywilnego, Vol I, at 522; System Prawa Prywatnego, Vol. II, Prawo Cywilne – Czesc Ogolna (2002)
Ramier, T.P., Agent Judiciaire du Tresor v Walter: fait du Prince and a King's Ransom, 6 IJCP (1997) 337
Raschèr, A., Cultural Property Transfer (2005)
Raschèr, A., Das Schweizer Kulturgütertransfergesetzt für einen besseren Schutz des kulturellen Erbes in: Museumskunde Band 67 (2002) 28
Rauscher Thomas, Internationales Privatrecht (3rd ed. 2009)
Reichelt, G., International Protection of Cultural Property, 1 Uniform Law Rev (1985) 43
Renfrew, C., Collectors are the Real Looters, 46 Archaeology (1993) 16
Renold, M-A, Case Note: An Important Swiss Decision Relating to the International Transfer of Cultural Goods: The Swiss Supreme Court's Decision on the Giant Antique Mogul Gold Coins, 13 IJCP (2006) 361
Renold, M-A, The Ubiquitous Question of Good Faith, in: Resolution of Cultural Property Disputes (Peace Palace Papers 2004) 251

Renold, M-A, A Landmark Decision in Art Law by the European Court of Human Rights: Beyeler v Italy, 5 ART, ANTIQUITY & LAW (2000) 73
Reyhan, P.Y., A Chaotic Palette: Conflict of Laws in Litigation Between Original Owners and Good-Faith Purchasers of Stolen Art, 50 Duke Law Journal (2001) 955
Richardson, N., The Double Actionability and the Choice of Law, 32 HKLJ (2002) 497
Rigaux, F., Libre circulation des biens culturels et protection des tresors nationaux, 2 European Review of Private Law (1994) 95
Robinson, P.L.,The Commonwealth Scheme Relating to the Rendition of Fugitive Offenders 33 ICLQ (1984) 614
Rogers, W.V.H., Winfield and Jolowicz on Tort (18th ed. 2010)
Ros, M., Die unmittelbare Anwendung der Europäischen Menschenrechtskonvention, Ein Beitrag zur Lehre der self-executing treaties, (Zurich 1984)
Rosecrance, B., Harmonious Meeting: The McClain Decision and the Cultural Property Implementation Act, 19 Cornell Int'l L.J. (1986) 311
Rudolph, B., Beyeler v Italy, 94 Am. J. Int. L., No. 4 (Oct., 2000) 736
Rushworth, A., Assertion of Ownership by a Foreign State over Cultural Objects Removed from its Jurisdiction, L.M.C.L.Q. (2008) 123
Rutter P.S./Montgomery D.M., Options, Rights of First Refusal, Rights of First Negotiation and Rights of First Offer- A Guide Through the Maze, California Real Estate Journal (1999) 1
Ryngaert, C., Jurisdiction in International Law (2008)
Salomons, A., Good Faith Acquisition in English, French and German Law, in: Christian von Bar, Towards a European Civil Code (4th ed. 2011)
Samuels, A., Comment, 116 National L. J. (1966) 1009
Sarcevic P./ Volken P/ Bonami A. (eds) Yearbook of Private International Law (2004)
Savigny, F. K v., A Treatise of the Conflict of Laws (1ed 1869, 2nd rev. ed. 1980)
Schack, H., Kunst und Recht (2004)
Schenk, K., Die Umsetzung des UNESCO- Übereinkommens von 1970 aus der Sicht des Gestzgebers, in: Weller, M., Kulturgüterschutz – Künstlerschutz Tagungsband des Zweiten Heidelberger Kunstrechtstags am 5. und 6. September 2008 in Heidelberg (2009) 61
Schmeinck, S., Internationalprivatrechtliche Aspekte des Kulturgüterschutzes (1994)
Schurig, K., Zwingendes Recht, "Eingriffsnormen " und neues IPR, 54 Rabels Zeitschrift fuer neues und auslaendisches Privatrecht, 217.
Scott, A., The Rome II Convention on the LawApplicable to Non-Contractual Obligations, in: John Aherm/ William Binchy (eds.) 2009
Seidl-Hohenveldern, I., Internationales Konfikations- und Enteignungsrecht (1952)
Sherlock, M., Equitble Consistency in International Case of Recovery of Stolen Art and Cultural Property, 8 Tul. J. Int'l & Comp L. (2000) 483
Smyte, Q., Pre-Empting the Problem, Property Law Journal (2003) 109
Sexton R./ Bogusz B., Complete land law: texts, cases and materials (2009)
Schindler, D./Toman D.J., The laws of armed conflicts: a collection of conventions, resolutions and other documents (2004)
Schneider E./Schneider R.M (eds.)., Cultural Property Protection, Deutsch-Türkische Rechtsstudien, Band 4 (2005)
Schoen S/van Ess, M., Das UN-Handelsverbot von 2003 für irakisches Kulturgut: Folgenlos für Deutschland? 1 Kunstrechtspiegel (2008) 7

Schoemann, E., Lorentzen v Lydden – Dead and Burried? 10 New Zealand Business Law Rev. (2004) 285
Schreiber, E. O., The Doctrine of the Renvoi in Anglo-American Law, 31 Harv. Law Review (1917) 525
Schultz, F., Classical Roman Law (1951)
Scott, A., The Non-Justiciability of Sovereign Foreign Claims, LMCLQ (2007) 296
Schwander I., Rechtsprechung zum Internationalen Sachen-, Schuld- und Gesellschaftsrecht, Revue Suisse de Droit International et Européen (2006) 344
Schwander, I., Einführung in das internationale Privatrecht Bd 1 (3rd ed. 2000)
Scott, A., The Rome II Convention on the LawApplicable to Non-Contractual Obligations, John Aherm William Binchy (eds.) 2009
Staudinger, v. J, Kommentar zum Bürgerlichen Gesetzbuch mit Einführungsgesetzt und Nebengesetzten (2005)
Staudinger, v.J, Einfuehrungsgesetz zum Buergerlichen Gesetzbuch (2002)
Shyllon, F., The Right to a Cultural Past: African Viewpoints, in: UNESCO/Institute of Art and Law (eds) Cultural Rights and Wrongs: A Collection of Essays in Commemoration of the 50th Anniversary of the Universal Declaration of Human Rights (1998) 103
Siehr, K., Der Nigeria Fall des BGH, in: Festschrift für Werner Lorenz (1991) 526
Siehr, K., Die EG-Richtline von 1993 über die Rückgabe von Kulturgütern und der Kunsthandel, in G. Reichelt (ed.) Neues Recht zum Schutz von Kulturgut (1997)
Siehr, K., Die Umsetzung des UNESCO-übereinkommens von 1970 in Deutschland aus der Sicht der Wissenschaft, in: Weller, M., Kulturgüterschutz – Künstlerschutz Tagungsband des Zweiten Heidelberger Kunstrechtstags am 5. und 6. September 2008 in Heidelberg (2009) 79
Siehr, K., Kulturgüterschutz, in: Klaus Ebling/Marcel Schulze (eds.) Kunstrecht (2007) 104
Siehr, K., The Beautiful One has Come to Return in: J.H. Merryman (ed.), Imperialism, Art and Restitution (2006) 114
Siehr, K., Reforms and Developments in the Member States of the European Union, in: Schneider E./Schneider R (eds.) Cultural Property Protection, Deutsch-Türkische Rechtsstudien Band 4, (2005) 77
Siehr K., Das Sachenrecht der Kulturgüter: Kulturgütertransfergesetz und das schweizerische Sachenrecht (2003)
Siehr, K., European and Swiss Law of the Protection of Cultural Property, Aktuelle Juristische Praxis (1999) 962
Siehr, in: The Protection of Cultural Property: The 1995 UNIDROIT Convention and the EEC Instruments of 1992/93 Compared, RDU (1998) 671
Siehr, K., The Protection of Cultural Property: The 1995 UNIDROIT Convention and the EEC Instruments of 1992/93 Compared, Uniform L. Rev (1998)
Siehr, K., The Protection of Cultural Heritage and International Commerce, 6 IJCP (1997) 304
Siehr, Die EG-Richtline von 1993 über die Rückgabe von Kulturgütern und der Kunsthandel, in G. Reichelt (ed.) Neues Recht zum Schutz von Kulturgut (Wien 1997) 29
Siehr, Öffentliches Recht und internationales Privatrecht beim grenzüberschreitenden Kulturgüterschutz, in: Dolzer/Jayme/Mussgnug (eds.) Rechtsfragen des internationalen Kulturgüterschutzes (1994) 83
Siehr, K., International Art Trade and the Law (1993)

Siehr, K., Nationaler und Internationaler Kulturgueterschutz. Eingriffsnormen und der internationale Kunsthandel, in: B. Pfister/M.R. Will (eds) Festschrift fur Werner Lorenz (1991) 526

Siehr, Expert Opinions in the Explanatory Memorandum BT Nr 16 (22) 049–056, available at http://www.bundestag.de/ausschuesse/a22/anhoerungen/unesco/index.html

Siehr, K., The UNIDROIT Draft Convention on International Protection of Cultural Property, 1 IJCP (1992) 321

Siegfried, H., Internationaler Kulturgüterschutz in der Schweiz, Das Bundesgesetz über den internationalen Kulturgütertransfer (2007)

Sikuta, J./Hubalkova, E., European Court of Human Rights, Case Law of the Grand Chamber 1998–2006 (2007)

Simpson, AWB, The Introduction of the Action on the Case for Conversion 75 LQR (1954) 364

Smyte, Q., Pre-empting the Problem, 109 Property Law Journal (2003) 10

Sonnentag, M., Der Renvoi im Internationalen Privatrecht (2001)

Soudijin M./Tijhuis E.,Some perspectives on the illicit antiquities trade in China, 8 ART, ANTIQUITY & LAW (2003) 149

Spiegler, H. N./Kaye, L. M., American Litigation to Recover Cultural Property – Obstacles, Options and Proposals, in: Brodie N./ Doole J./ Renfrew C. (eds.) Trade in Illicit Antiquities (2001) 121

Staker, C., Public International Law and the Lex Situs Rule in Property Conflicts and Foreign Expropriations, 58 Brit. Y.B. Int'L L. (1988) 151

Staechelin, R., Die Unidroit-Konvention: kulturell verheerend, mit Schweizer Recht unvereinbar, wirtschaftlich ein Eigentor, in: Unidroit: Recht und Ethik im Handel mit Kulturgut; Tagung der Schweizerischen Akademie der Geisteswissenschaften Bern 1998 (1998) 63

Staudinger, J v., Kommentar zum Bürgerichen Gesetzbuch (2005)

Steinauer, P.-H., Summary: The Transfer of Ownership of Works of Art in Swiss Law, in: P. Lalive (ed.), International Sales of works of Art (1988) 118

Stevens, J., Land Law, (4th ed. 2008)

Sucharitkul, S., State Immunity and Trading Activities in International Law (1959)

Sultan, J., Comment, Combating the Illicit Art Trade in the European Union: Europol's Role in Recovering Stolen Artwork, 18 J. INTL. L. BUS. (1998) 759

Symeonides, S., A Choice of Law Rule for Conflict involving Cultural Property, 38 Vand. J. Transnat'l L. (2005) 1177

Symeonides, S., On the Side of the Angels: Choice of Law and stolen Cultural Property, in: Basedow, J./Siehr K., Private Law in the International Arena (Privatrecht in der Internationalen Arena, Liber Amicoru Kurt Siehr (2000) 748

Symeonides, S., American Choice of Law at the Dawn of the 21st Century, 37 Willamette L. Rev. (2001) 1

Talbot II, N.J., EEC Measures on National Treasures, 16 Loy. L.A. Int'l & Comp. L.J. (1993) 127

Tamm D./Ostrup A., Danish Report, in: T.Kono/S.Wrbka, The Impact of Uniform Laws (2010) 297

Techera E.J., Safeguarding Cultural Heritage: Law and Policy in Fiji, 12 J. Cultural Heritage (2011) 329

Tetley W., Maritime Liens and Claims (2nd ed. 1998)

Tettenborn, A., Conversion, Trespass and Title to Works of Art, in: Palmer N.E/McKendrick E. (eds.) Interests in Goods (2nd ed. 1998) 33

Thorn, B., Internationaler Kulturgüterschutz nach der UNIDROIT-Konvention (2004)
Thorn, K., Der Mobiliarerwerb vom Nichtberechtigten (1996)
Tooher, J., Jubilant Jamie and the Elephant Egg: Acquisition of Title by Finding, 6 Australian Property L.J. (1998) 117
Topal-Gökceli, S., Rechtlicher Schutz archäologischen Kulturgutes in der Türkei, in: Gerte Reichelt (ed.) Denkmalschutz in Europa (Schriftenreihe Forschungsgesellschaft Kunst und Recht, Band 3, 2012) 45
Tubb, K. W., The Antiquities Trade: An Archaeological Conservator's Perspective, in: Tubb K.W. (ed.), Antiquities, Trade or Betrayed. Legal, Ethical and Conservation Issues (2002) 256
van Hecke, G. A., Confiscation, Expropriation and the Conflict of Laws, 4 Int'l L. Q. (1951) 345
van Heesch, J., Belgian Laws Regarding Coin Finds, 43 CIN, Compte Rendu (1996) 82
van Houtte, H., Updating Private International Law? The Belgian Experiment, in: Erauw J./Tomljenovic V./ Volken P. (eds.) Liber memorialis Petar Šarčević: Universalism, Tradition and the Individual (2006) 66
Venturini, G.C., Property, in: International Encyclopedia of International Law (1976), Chapter 21
Vincent S., The Good Collector, Debates between Susan Kean McIntosh and Colin Renfrew, 1 Public Archaeology (2000) 73.
Van Heesch, J., Belgian Laws Regarding Coin Finds, 43 CIN, Compte Rendu (1996) 82
Van Houtte H., Updating Private International Law-The Belgian Experiment, in Johan Erauw/Vesna Tomljenovic/ Paul Volken, Liber memorialis Petar Šarčević: Universalism, Tradition and the Individual (2006) 66
Vitale, K. D., The War on Antiquities: United States Law and Foreign Cultural Property, 84 Notre Dame L. R. (2009) 1835
Vischer, F., General Cource on Private International Law, I Hague Recueil 9 (1991) 115
von Bar, C., Towards a European Civil Code ($4^{th}$ ed. 2011)
von Bar, C./ Mankowski, P., Internationlaes Privatrecht Bd. 1 ($2^{nd}$ ed. 2003)
von Schorlemer, S., Internationaler Kulturgüterschutz: Ansätze zur Prävention im Frieden sowie im bewaffneten Konflikt (1992)
Von Segesser, G./Jolles, A., Switzerland's New Federal Act on the International Transfer of Cultural Property: An Update and Perspective from the Art Trade ART, ANTIQUITY & LAW (2005) 175
Voudouri, D., Law and the Politics of the Past: Legal Protection of Cultural Heritage in Greece, 17 IJCP (2010) 547
Voudouri, D., Circulation et protection des biens culturels dans l'Europe sans frontieres, in: Rev. de Droit Public Rev. de Droit Public (1994) 479
Vrellis, S., Protection of Antiquities and Cultural Heritage in Greece, in: Schneider E./Schneider R. (eds.), Cultural Property Protection (2005) 97
Vrdoljak, A. F., International Law, Museums and the Return of Cultural Objects (2006)
Walker Tubb, K., Antiquities Trade or Betrayed-Legal Ethical and Conservational Issues (1995)
Walter, B., Rückführung von Kulturgut im internationalen Recht (1988)
Watson, P., The Investigation of Frederick Schultz, 10 Culture without Context (2002) 21
Warren, E. H., Trover and Conversion: An Essay (1936)
Warring, J., Underground Debates: The Fundamental Differences of Opinion that Thwart UNESCO's Progress in Fighting the Illicit Trade in Cultural Property, 19 Emory Int'l L. Rev. (2005) 227

Weber, M., Unveräußerliches Kulturgut im nationalen und internationalen Rechtsverkehr (2002)
Webb P.R.H./Brown, D.J.L, A Case Book on Conflict of Laws (1960)
Weber, M., Auswirkungen der EU Richtlinie 93 /7/EWG auf den schweizerischen Kunsthandel, 3 KUR (2008), 74
Weidner, A., Kultugueter als Res Extra Commercium im Internationalen Sachenrecht (2001)
Weller, M., (ed.) Kulturgüterschutz – Künstlerschutz, Tagungsband II. Des Heidelberger Kunstrechtstags am 5. und 6. September (2009) 206
Weller, M., Zur Umsetzung der UNESCO Konvention von 1970 aus deutscher Sicht, in: Gerte Reichelt (ed.) Rechtsfragen der Restitution von Kulturgütern, Symposium des Ludwig Boltzmann Instituts für Europarecht am 12. Oktober 2007 im Bundesministerium für Unterricht, Kunst und Kultur Wien (2008) 27
Weller, M., Iran v Barakat: Some Observations on the Application of Foreign Public Law by Domestic Courts from a Comparative Perspective, 04 Kunstrechtspiegel (2007) 172
Wendel, P., Protecting Newly Discovered Antiquities- Thinking Outside the Fee Simple Box, 76 Fordham L. Rev. (2007) 1016.
Whomersley, C.A., Foreign Sates and British Courts, 125 LQR (2009) 227
Wieling, H. J., Property Law, Vol I: Chattels, Possession and the Rights to Movables (1990)
Wilderspin, M./Plender R., (eds.), The European Private International Law of Obligations (3rd ed. 2009)
Willis, E., History, Strong Stories and New Traditions: The Case of "Etched on Bark 1854", 4 History Australia (2007) 13
Willis, E. Law, Politics and "Historical Wounds": The Dja Dja Warrung Bark Etchings Case in Australia, 15 IJCP (2008) 49
Willis, E., Exhibiting Aboriginal industry: A Story Behind a "re-discovered" bark drawing from Victoria, 27 Aboriginal History (2003) 39
Winter, J., The Application of the UNIDROIT Convention on Stolen and Illegally Imported Cultural Objects in Relations between Member states of the European Union, in: Reflections on International Law from the Low Countries in Honour of Paul de Waart (1998)
Wolf, M., Private International Law (2nd ed. 1950)
Yasaitis, K. E., National Ownership Laws as Cultural Property Protection Policy: The Emerging Trend in United States v Schultz, 12 IJCP (2005) 95
Youngblood, P., A Chaotic Palette: Conflict of Laws in Litigation between Original Owners and Good-Faith Purchasers of Stolen Art, 50 Duke L. J. (2001) 957
Zelig, J. M., Recovering Iraq's cultural property: what can be done to prevent Illicit trafficking, Brooklyn J. of Int. L. (2005) 289
Zsunay, E., Protection of Cultural Heritage in Turkish Private Law, 6 IJCP (1997) 278

# Annex

United Nations
Educational, Scientific and
Cultural Organization

Organisation
des Nations Unies
pour l'éducation,
la science et la culture

Organización
de las Naciones Unidas
para la Educación,
la Ciencia y la Cultura

Организация
Объединенных Наций по
вопросам образования,
науки и культуры

منظمة الأمم المتحدة
للتربية والعلم والثقافة

联合国教育、
科学及文化组织

## 1970 UNESCO CONVENTION ON THE MEANS OF PROHIBITING AND PREVENTING THE ILLICIT IMPORT, EXPORT AND TRANSFER OF OWNERSHIP OF CULTURAL PROPERTY

(Paris, 14 Nov 1970, Entry into force 24 April 197)

The General Conference of the United Nations Educational, Scientific and Cultural Organization, meeting in Paris from 12 October to 14 November 1970, at its sixteenth session,

**Recalling** the importance of the provisions contained in the Declaration of the Principles of International Cultural Co-operation, adopted by the General Conference at its fourteenth session,

**Considering** that the interchange of cultural property among nations for scientific, cultural and educational purposes increases the knowledge of the civilization of Man, enriches the cultural life of all peoples and inspires mutual respect and appreciation among nations,

**Considering** that cultural property constitutes one of the basic elements of civilization and national culture, and that its true value can be appreciated only in relation to the fullest possible information regarding is origin, history and traditional setting,

**Considering** that it is incumbent upon every State to protect the cultural property existing within its territory against the dangers of theft, clandestine excavation, and illicit export,

**Considering** that, to avert these dangers, it is essential for every State to become increasingly alive to the moral obligations to respect its own cultural heritage and that of all nations,

**Considering** that, as cultural institutions, museums, libraries and archives should ensure that their collections are built up in accordance with universally recognized moral principles,

**Considering** that the illicit import, export and transfer of ownership of cultural property is an obstacle to that understanding between nations which it is part of UNESCO's mission to promote by recommending to interested States, international conventions to this end,

**Considering** that the protection of cultural heritage can be effective only if organized both nationally and internationally among States working in close co-operation,

**Considering** that the UNESCO General Conference adopted a Recommendation to this effect in 1964,

**Having before It** further proposals on the means of prohibiting and preventing the illicit import, export and transfer of ownership of cultural property, a question which is on the agenda for the session as item 19,

**Having decided**, at its fifteenth session, that this question should be made the subject of an international convention,

**Adopts** this Convention on the fourteenth day of November 1970.

**Article 1**

For the purposes of this Convention, the term `cultural property' means property which, on religious or secular grounds, is specifically designated by each State as being of importance for archaeology, prehistory, history, literature, art or science and which belongs to the following categories:

(a) Rare collections and specimens of fauna, flora, minerals and anatomy, and objects of palaeontological interest;

(b) property relating to history, including the history of science and technology and military and social history, to the life of national leaders, thinkers, scientists and artist and to events of national importance;

(c) products of archaeological excavations (including regular and clandestine) or of archaeological discoveries ;

(d) elements of artistic or historical monuments or archaeological sites which have been dismembered;

(e) antiquities more than one hundred years old, such as inscriptions, coins and engraved seals;

(f) objects of ethnological interest;

(g) property of artistic interest, such as:

(i) pictures, paintings and drawings produced entirely by hand on any support and in any material (excluding industrial designs and manu-factured articles decorated by hand);

(ii) original works of statuary art and sculpture in any material;

(iii) original engravings, prints and lithographs ;

(iv) original artistic assemblages and montages in any material;

(h) rare manuscripts and incunabula, old books, documents and publications of special interest (historical, artistic, scientific, literary, etc.) singly or in collections ;

(i) postage, revenue and similar stamps, singly or in collections;

(j) archives, including sound, photographic and cinematographic archives;

(k) articles of furniture more than one hundred years old and old musical instruments.

**Article 2**

1. The States Parties to this Convention recognize that the illicit import, export and transfer of ownership of cultural property is one of the main causes of the impoverishment of the cultural heritage of the countries of origin of such property and that international co-operation constitutes one of the most efficient means of protecting each country's cultural property against all the dangers resulting there from.

2. To this end, the States Parties undertake to oppose such practices with the means at their disposal, and particularly by removing their causes, putting a stop to current practices, and by helping to make the necessary reparations.

**Article 3**

The import, export or transfer of ownership of cultural property effected contrary to the provisions adopted under this Convention by the States Parties thereto, shall be illicit.

**Article 4**

The States Parties to this Convention recognize that for the purpose of the Convention property which belongs to the following categories forms part of the cultural heritage of each State:

(a) Cultural property created by the individual or collective genius of nationals of the State concerned, and cultural property of importance to the State concerned created within the territory of that State by foreign nationals or stateless persons resident within such territory;

(b) cultural property found within the national territory;

(c) cultural property acquired by archaeological, ethnological or natural science missions, with the consent of the competent authorities of the country of origin of such property;

(d) cultural property which has been the subject of a freely agreed exchange;

(e) cultural property received as a gift or purchased legally with the consent of the competent authorities of the country of origin of such property.

**Article 5**

To ensure the protection of their cultural property against illicit import; export and transfer of ownership, the States Parties to this Convention undertake, as appropriate for each country, to set up within their territories one or more national services, where such services do not already exist, for the protection of the cultural heritage, with a qualified staff sufficient in number for the effective carrying out of the following functions:

(a) contributing to the formation of draft laws and regulations designed to secure the protection of the cultural heritage and particularly prevention of the illicit import, export and transfer of ownership of important cultural property;

(b) establishing and keeping up to date, on the basis of a national inventory of protected'property, a list of important public and private cultural property whose export would constitute an appreciable impoverishment of the national cultural heritage;

(c) promoting the development or the establishment of scientific and technical institutions (museums, libraries, archives, laboratories, workshops . . . ) required to ensure the preservation and presentation of cultural property;

(d) organizing the supervision of archaeological excavations, ensuring the preservation `in situation' of certain cultural property, and protecting certain areas reserved for future archaeological research;

(e) establishing, for the benefit of those concerned (curators, collectors, antique dealers, etc.) rules in conformity with the ethical principles set forth in this Convention; and taking steps to ensure the observance of those rules;

(f) taking educational measures to stimulate and develop respect for the cultural heritage of all States, and spreading knowledge of the provisions of this Convention;

(g) seeing that appropriate publicity is given to the disappearance of any items of cultural property.

**Article 6**

The States Parties to this Convention undertake:

(a) To introduce an appropriate certificate in which the exporting State would specify that the export of the cultural property in question is authorized. The certificate should accompany all items of cultural property exported in accordance with the regulations ;

(b) to prohibit the exportation of cultural property from their territory unless accompanied by the above-mentioned export certificate;

(c) to publicize this prohibition by appropriate means, particularly among persons likely to export or import cultural property.

**Article 7**

The States Parties to this Convention undertake:

(a) To take the necessary measures, consistent with national legislation, to prevent museums and similar institutions within their territories from acquiring cultural property originating in another State Party which has been illegally exported after entry into force of this Convention, in the States concerned. Whenever possible, to inform a State of origin Party to this Convention of an offer of such cultural property illegally removed from that State after the entry into force of this Convention in both States;

(b) (i) to prohibit the import of cultural property stolen from a museum or a religious or secular public monument or similar institution in another State Party to this Convention after the entry into force of this Convention for the States concerned, provided that such property is documented as appertaining to the inventory of that institution;

(ii) at the request of the State Party of origin, to take appropriate steps to recover and return any such cultural property imported after the entry into force of this Convention in both States concerned, provided, however, that the requesting State shall pay just compensation to an innocent purchaser or to a person who has valid title to that property. Requests for recovery and return shall be made through diplomatic offices. The requesting Party shall furnish, at its expense, the documentation and other evidence necessary to establish its claim for recovery and return. The Parties shall impose no customs duties or other charges upon cultural property returned pursuant to this Article. All expenses incident to the return and delivery of the cultural property shall be borne by the requesting Party.

**Article 8**

The States Parties to this Convention undertake to impose penalties or admin-istrative sanctions on any person responsible for infringing the prohibitions referred to under Articles 6(b) and 7(b) above.

**Article 9**

Any State Party to this Convention whose cultural patrimony is in jeopardy from pillage of archaeological or ethnological materials may call upon other States Parties who are affected. The States Parties to this Convention undertake, in these circumstances, to participate in a concerted international effort to determine and to carry out the necessary concrete measures, including the control of exports and imports and international commerce in the specific materials concerned. Pending agreement each State concerned shall take provisional measures to the extent feasible to prevent irremediable injury to the cultural heritage of the requesting State.

**Article 10**

The States Parties to this Convention undertake:

(a) To restrict by education, information and vigilance, movement of cultural property illegally removed from any State Party to this Convention and, as appropriate for each country, oblige antique dealers, subject to penal or administrative sanctions, to maintain a register recording the origin of each item of cultural property, names and addresses of the supplier, description and price of each item sold and to inform the purchaser of the cultural property of the export prohibition to which such property may be subject;

(b) to endeavour by educational means to create and develop in the public mind a realization of the value of cultural property and the threat to the cultural heritage created by theft, clandestine excavations and illicit exports.

**Article 11**

The export and transfer of ownership of cultural property under compulsion arising directly or indirectly from the occupation of a country by a foreign power shall be regarded as illicit.

**Article 12**

The States Parties to this Convention shall respect the cultural heritage within the territories for the international relations of which they are responsible, and shall take all appropriate measures to prohibit and prevent the illicit import, export and transfer of ownership of cultural property in such territories.

**Article 13**

The States Parties to this Convention also undertake, consistent with the laws of each State:

(a) To prevent by all appropriate means transfers of ownership of cultural property likely to promote the illicit import or export of such property;

(b) to ensure that their competent services co-operate in facilitating the earliest possible restitution of illicitly exported cultural property to its rightful owner;

(c) to admit actions for recovery of lost or stolen items of cultural property brought by or on behalf of the rightful owners ;

(d) to recognize the indefeasible right of each State Party to this Convention to classify and declare certain cultural property as inalienable which should therefore ipso facto not be exported, and to facilitate recovery of such property by the State concerned in cases where it has been exported.

**Article 14**

In order to prevent illicit export and to meet the obligations arising from the implementation of this Convention, each State Party to the Convention should, as far as it is able, provide the national services responsible for the protection of its cultural heritage with an adequate budget and, if necessary, should set up a fund for this purpose.

**Article 15**

Nothing in this Convention shall prevent States Parties thereto from concluding special agreements among themselves or from continuing to implement agreements already concluded regarding the restitution of cultural property removed, whatever the reason, from its territory of origin, before the entry into force of this Convention for the States concerned.

**Article 16**

The States Parties to this Convention shall in their periodic reports submitted to the General Conference of the United Nations Educational, Scientific and Cultural Organization on dates and in a manner to be determined by it, give information on the legislative and administrative provisions which they have adopted and other action which they have taken for the application of this Convention, together with details of the experience acquired in this field.

**Article 17**

1. The States Parties to this Convention may call on the technical assistance of the United Nations Educational, Scientific and Cultural Organization, particularly as regards:

(a) Information and education;

(b) consultation and expert advice;

(c) co-ordination and good offices.

2. The United Nations Educational, Scientific and Cultural Organization may, on its own initiative conduct research and publish studies on matters relevant to the illicit movement of cultural

property.

3. To this end, the United Nations Educational, Scientific and Cultural Orga-nization may also call on the co-operation of any competent non-governmental organization.

4. The United Nations Educational, Scientific and Cultural Organization may, on its own initiative, make proposals to States Parties to this Convention for its implementation.

5. At the request of at least two States Parties to this Convention which are engaged in a dispute over its implementation, UNESCO may extend its good offices to reach a settlement between them.

**Article 18**

This Convention is drawn up in English, French, Russian and Spanish, the four texts being equally authoritative.

**Article 19**

1. This Convention shall be subject to ratification or acceptance by States members of the United Nations Educational, Scientific and Cultural Organization in accordance with their respective constitutional procedures.

2. The instruments of ratification or acceptance shall be deposited with the Director-General of the United Nations Educational, Scientific and Cultural Organization.

**Article 20**

1. This Convention shall be open to accession by all States not members of the United Nations Educational, Scientific and Cultural Organization which are invited to accede to it by the Executive Board of the Organization.

2. Accession shall be effected by the deposit of an instrument of accession with the Director-General of the United Nations Educational, Scientific and Cultural Organization.

**Article 21**

This Convention shall enter into force three months after the date of the deposit of the third instrument of ratification, acceptance or accession, but only with respect to those States which have deposited their respective instruments on or before that date. It shall enter into force with respect to any other State three months after the deposit of its instrument of ratification, acceptance or accession.

**Article 22**

The States Parties to this Convention recognize that the Convention is appli-cable not only to their metropolitan territories but also to all territories for the international relations of which they are responsible; they undertake to consult, if necessary, the governments or other competent authorities of these territories on or before ratification, acceptance or accession with a view to securing the application of the Convention to those territories, and to notify the Director-General of the United Nations Educational, Scientific and cultural Organization of the territories to which it is applied, the notification to take effect three months after the date of its receipt.

**Article 23**

1. Each State Party to this Convention may denounce the Convention on its own behalf or on behalf of any territory for whose international relations it is responsible.

2. The denunciation shall be notified by an instrument in writing, deposited with the Director-General of the United Nations Educational, Scientific and Cultural Organization.

3. The denunciation shall take effect twelve months after the receipt of the instrument of denunciation.

**Article 24**

The Director-General of the United Nations Educational, Scientific and Cultural Organization shall inform the States members of the Organization, the States not members of the Organization which are referred to in Article 20, as well as the United Nations, of the deposit of all the instruments of ratification, acceptance and accession provided for in Articles 19 and 20, and of the notifications and denunciations provided for in Articles 22 and 23 respectively.

**Article 25**

1. This Convention may be revised by the General Conference of the United Nations Educational, Scientific and Cultural Organization. Any such revision shall, however, bind only the States which shall become Parties to the revising convention.

2. If the General Conference should adopt a new convention revising this Convention in whole or in part, then, unless the new convention otherwise provides, this Convention shall cease to be open to ratification, acceptance or accession, as from the date on which the new revising convention enters into force.

**Article 26**

In conformity with Article 102 of the Charter of the United Nations, this 'Convention shall be registered with the Secretariat of the United Nations at the request of the Director-General of the United Nations Educational, Scientific and Cultural Organization.

ANNEX 1

**UNIDROIT CONVENTION ON STOLEN OR ILLEGALLY EXPORTED CULTURAL OBJECTS**

(Rome, 24 June 1995)

THE STATES PARTIES TO THIS CONVENTION,

ASSEMBLED in Rome at the invitation of the Government of the Italian Republic from 7 to 24 June 1995 for a Diplomatic Conference for the adoption of the draft UNIDROIT Convention on the nternational Return of Stolen or Illegally Exported Cultural Objects,

CONVINCED of the fundamental importance of the protection of cultural heritage and of cultural exchanges for promoting understanding between peoples, and the dissemination of culture for the well-being of humanity and the progress of civilisation,

DEEPLY CONCERNED by the illicit trade in cultural objects and the irreparable damage frequently caused by it, both to these objects themselves and to the cultural heritage of national, tribal, indigenous or other communities, and also to the heritage of all peoples, and in particular by the pillage of archaeological sites and the resulting loss of irreplaceable archaeological, historical and scientific information,

DETERMINED to contribute effectively to the fight against illicit trade in cultural objects by taking the important step of establishing common, minimal legal rules for the restitution and return of cultural objects between Contracting States, with the objective of improving the preservation and protection of the cultural heritage in the interest of all,

EMPHASISING that this Convention is intended to facilitate the restitution and return of cultural objects, and that the provision of any remedies, such as compensation, needed to effect restitution and return in some States, does not imply that such remedies should be adopted in other States,

AFFIRMING that the adoption of the provisions of this Convention for the future in no way confers any approval or legitimacy upon illegal transactions of whatever kind which may have taken place before the entry into force of the Convention,

CONSCIOUS that this Convention will not by itself provide a solution to the problems raised by illicit trade, but that it initiates a process that will enhance international cultural co-operation and maintain a proper role for legal trading and inter-State agreements for cultural exchanges,

ACKNOWLEDGING that implementation of this Convention should be accompanied by other effective measures for protecting cultural objects, such as the development and use of registers, the physical protection of archaeological sites and technical co-operation,

RECOGNISING the work of various bodies to protect cultural property, particularly the 1970 UNESCO Convention on illicit traffic and the development of codes of conduct in the private sector,

HAVE AGREED as follows:

ANNEX 2

## CHAPTER I - SCOPE OF APPLICATION AND DEFINITION

### Article 1

This Convention applies to claims of an international character for:

(a) the restitution of stolen cultural objects;
(b) the return of cultural objects removed from the territory of a Contracting State contrary to its law regulating the export of cultural objects for the purpose of protecting its cultural heritage (hereinafter "illegally exported cultural objects").

### Article 2

For the purposes of this Convention, cultural objects are those which, on religious or secular grounds, are of importance for archaeology, prehistory, history, literature, art or science and belong to one of the categories listed in the Annex to this Convention.

## CHAPTER II - RESTITUTION OF STOLEN CULTURAL OBJECTS

### Article 3

(1) The possessor of a cultural object which has been stolen shall return it.

(2) For the purposes of this Convention, a cultural object which has been unlawfully excavated or lawfully excavated but unlawfully retained shall be considered stolen, when consistent with the law of the State where the excavation took place.

(3) Any claim for restitution shall be brought within a period of three years from the time when the claimant knew the location of the cultural object and the identity of its possessor, and in any case within a period of fifty years from the time of the theft.

(4) However, a claim for restitution of a cultural object forming an integral part of an identified monument or archaeological site, or belonging to a public collection, shall not be subject to time limitations other than a period of three years from the time when the claimant knew the location of the cultural object and the identity of its possessor.

(5) Notwithstanding the provisions of the preceding paragraph, any Contracting State may declare that a claim is subject to a time limitation of 75 years or such longer period as is provided in its law. A claim made in another Contracting State for restitution of a cultural object displaced from a monument, archaeological site or public collection in a Contracting State making such a declaration shall also be subject to that time limitation.

(6) A declaration referred to in the preceding paragraph shall be made at the time of signature, ratification, acceptance, approval or accession.

(7) For the purposes of this Convention, a "public collection" consists of a group of inventoried or otherwise identified cultural objects owned by:

(a) a Contracting State
(b) a regional or local authority of a Contracting State;
(c) a religious institution in a Contracting State; or
(d) an institution that is established for an essentially cultural, educational or scientific purpose in a Contracting State and is recognised in that State as serving the public interest.

(8) In addition, a claim for restitution of a sacred or communally important cultural object belonging to and used by a tribal or indigenous community in a Contracting State as part of that community's traditional or ritual use, shall be subject to the time limitation applicable to public collections.

**Article 4**

(1) The possessor of a stolen cultural object required to return it shall be entitled, at the time of its restitution, to payment of fair and reasonable compensation provided that the possessor neither knew nor ought reasonably to have known that the object was stolen and can prove that it exercised due diligence when acquiring the object.

(2) Without prejudice to the right of the possessor to compensation referred to in the preceding paragraph, reasonable efforts shall be made to have the person who transferred the cultural object to the possessor, or any prior transferor, pay the compensation where to do so would be consistent with the law of the State in which the claim is brought.

(3) Payment of compensation to the possessor by the claimant, when this is required, shall be without prejudice to the right of the claimant to recover it from any other person.

(4) In determining whether the possessor exercised due diligence, regard shall be had to all the circumstances of the acquisition, including the character of the parties, the price paid, whether the possessor consulted any reasonably accessible register of stolen cultural objects, and any other relevant information and documentation which it could reasonably have obtained, and whether the possessor consulted accessible agencies or took any other step that a reasonable person would have taken in the circumstances.

(5) The possessor shall not be in a more favourable position than the person from whom it acquired the cultural object by inheritance or otherwise gratuitously.

**CHAPTER III - RETURN OF ILLEGALLY EXPORTED CULTURAL OBJECTS**

**Article 5**

(1) A Contracting State may request the court or other competent authority of another Contracting State to order the return of a cultural object illegally exported from the territory of the requesting State.

(2) A cultural object which has been temporarily exported from the territory of the requesting State, for purposes such as exhibition, research or restoration, under a permit issued according to its law regulating its export for the purpose of protecting its cultural heritage and not returned in accordance with the terms of that permit shall be deemed to have been illegally exported.

(3) The court or other competent authority of the State addressed shall order the return of an illegally exported cultural object if the requesting State establishes that the removal of the object from its territory significantly impairs one or more of the following interests:

(a) the physical preservation of the object or of its context;
(b) the integrity of a complex object;
(c) the preservation of information of, for example, a scientific or historical character;
(d) the traditional or ritual use of the object by a tribal or indigenous community,

or establishes that the object is of significant cultural importance for the requesting State.

(4) Any request made under paragraph 1 of this article shall contain or be accompanied by such information of a factual or legal nature as may assist the court or other competent authority of the

State addressed in determining whether the requirements of paragraphs 1 to 3 have been met.

(5) Any request for return shall be brought within a period of three years from the time when the requesting State knew the location of the cultural object and the identity of its possessor, and in any case within a period of fifty years from the date of the export or from the date on which the object should have been returned under a permit referred to in paragraph 2 of this article.

**Article 6**

(1) The possessor of a cultural object who acquired the object after it was illegally exported shall be entitled, at the time of its return, to payment by the requesting State of fair and reasonable compensation, provided that the possessor neither knew nor ought reasonably to have known at the time of acquisition that the object had been illegally exported.

(2) In determining whether the possessor knew or ought reasonably to have known that the cultural object had been illegally exported, regard shall be had to the circumstances of the acquisition, including the absence of an export certificate required under the law of the requesting State.

(3) Instead of compensation, and in agreement with the requesting State, the possessor required to return the cultural object to that State, may decide:

(a) to retain ownership of the object; or
(b) to transfer ownership against payment or gratuitously to a person of its choice residing in the requesting State who provides the necessary guarantees.

(4) The cost of returning the cultural object in accordance with this article shall be borne by the requesting State, without prejudice to the right of that State to recover costs from any other person.

(5) The possessor shall not be in a more favourable position than the person from whom it acquired the cultural object by inheritance or otherwise gratuitously.

**Article 7**

(1) The provisions of this Chapter shall not apply where:

(a) the export of a cultural object is no longer illegal at the time at which the return is requested; or
(b) the object was exported during the lifetime of the person who created it or within a period of fifty years following the death of that person.

(2) Notwithstanding the provisions of sub-paragraph (b) of the preceding paragraph, the provisions of this Chapter shall apply where a cultural object was made by a member or members of a tribal or indigenous community for traditional or ritual use by that community and the object will be returned to that community.

**CHAPTER IV - GENERAL PROVISIONS**

**Article 8**

(1) A claim under Chapter II and a request under Chapter III may be brought before the courts or other competent authorities of the Contracting State where the cultural object is located, in addition to the courts or other competent authorities otherwise having jurisdiction under the rules in force in Contracting States.

ANNEX 2

(2) The parties may agree to submit the dispute to any court or other competent authority or to arbitration.

(3) Resort may be had to the provisional, including protective, measures available under the law of the Contracting State where the object is located even when the claim for restitution or request for return of the object is brought before the courts or other competent authorities of another Contracting State.

**Article 9**

(1) Nothing in this Convention shall prevent a Contracting State from applying any rules more favourable to the restitution or the return of stolen or illegally exported cultural objects than provided for by this Convention.

(2) This article shall not be interpreted as creating an obligation to recognise or enforce a decision of a court or other competent authority of another Contracting State that departs from the provisions of this Convention.

**Article 10**

(1) The provisions of Chapter II shall apply only in respect of a cultural object that is stolen after this Convention enters into force in respect of the State where the claim is brought, provided that:

(a) the object was stolen from the territory of a Contracting State after the entry into force of this Convention for that State; or
(b) the object is located in a Contracting State after the entry into force of the Convention for that State.

(2) The provisions of Chapter III shall apply only in respect of a cultural object that is illegally exported after this Convention enters into force for the requesting State as well as the State where the request is brought.

(3) This Convention does not in any way legitimise any illegal transaction of whatever nature which has taken place before the entry into force of this Convention or which is excluded under paragraphs (1) or (2) of this article, nor limit any right of a State or other person to make a claim under remedies available outside the framework of this Convention for the restitution or return of a cultural object stolen or illegally exported before the entry into force of this Convention.

**CHAPTER V - FINAL PROVISIONS**

**Article 11**

(1) This Convention is open for signature at the concluding meeting of the Diplomatic Conference for the adoption of the draft UNIDROIT Convention on the International Return of Stolen or Illegally Exported Cultural Objects and will remain open for signature by all States at Rome until 30 June 1996.

(2) This Convention is subject to ratification, acceptance or approval by States which have signed it.

(3) This Convention is open for accession by all States which are not signatory States as from the date it is open for signature.

(4) Ratification, acceptance, approval or accession is subject to the deposit of a formal instrument to that effect with the depositary.

## ANNEX 2

**Article 12**

(1) This Convention shall enter into force on the first day of the sixth month following the date of deposit of the fifth instrument of ratification, acceptance, approval or accession.

(2) For each State that ratifies, accepts, approves or accedes to this Convention after the deposit of the fifth instrument of ratification, acceptance, approval or accession, this Convention shall enter into force in respect of that State on the first day of the sixth month following the date of deposit of its instrument of ratification, acceptance, approval or accession.

**Article 13**

(1) This Convention does not affect any international instrument by which any Contracting State is legally bound and which contains provisions on matters governed by this Convention, unless a contrary declaration is made by the States bound by such instrument.

(2) Any Contracting State may enter into agreements with one or more Contracting States, with a view to improving the application of this Convention in their mutual relations. The States which have concluded such an agreement shall transmit a copy to the depositary.

(3) In their relations with each other, Contracting States which are Members of organisations of economic integration or regional bodies may declare that they will apply the internal rules of these organisations or bodies and will not therefore apply as between these States the provisions of this Convention the scope of application of which coincides with that of those rules.

**Article 14**

(1) If a Contracting State has two or more territorial units, whether or not possessing different systems of law applicable in relation to the matters dealt with in this Convention, it may, at the time of signature or of the deposit of its instrument of ratification, acceptance, approval or accession, declare that this Convention is to extend to all its territorial units or only to one or more of them, and may substitute for its declaration another declaration at any time.

(2) These declarations are to be notified to the depositary and are to state expressly the territorial units to which the Convention extends.

(3) If, by virtue of a declaration under this article, this Convention extends to one or more but not all of the territorial units of a Contracting State, the reference to:

(a) the territory of a Contracting State in Article 1 shall be construed as referring to the territory of a territorial unit of that State;
(b) a court or other competent authority of the Contracting State or of the State addressed shall be construed as referring to the court or other competent authority of a territorial unit of that State;
(c) the Contracting State where the cultural object is located in Article 8 (1) shall be construed as referring to the territorial unit of that State where the object is located;
(d) the law of the Contracting State where the object is located in Article 8 (3) shall be construed as referring to the law of the territorial unit of that State where the object is located; and
(e) a Contracting State in Article 9 shall be construed as referring to a territorial unit of that State.

(4) If a Contracting State makes no declaration under paragraph 1 of this article, this Convention is to extend to all territorial units of that State.

**Article 15**

(1) Declarations made under this Convention at the time of signature are subject to confirmation upon ratification, acceptance or approval.

ANNEX 2

(2) Declarations and confirmations of declarations are to be in writing and to be formally notified to the depositary.

(3) A declaration shall take effect simultaneously with the entry into force of this Convention in respect of the State concerned. However, a declaration of which the depositary receives formal notification after such entry into force shall take effect on the first day of the sixth month following the date of its deposit with the depositary.

(4) Any State which makes a declaration under this Convention may withdraw it at any time by a formal notification in writing addressed to the depositary. Such withdrawal shall take effect on the first day of the sixth month following the date of the deposit of the notification.

**Article 16**

(1) Each Contracting State shall at the time of signature, ratification, acceptance, approval or accession, declare that claims for the restitution, or requests for the return, of cultural objects brought by a State under Article 8 may be submitted to it under one or more of the following procedures:

(a) directly to the courts or other competent authorities of the declaring State;
(b) through an authority or authorities designated by that State to receive such claims or requests and to forward them to the courts or other competent authorities of that State;
(c) through diplomatic or consular channels.

(2) Each Contracting State may also designate the courts or other authorities competent to order the restitution or return of cultural objects under the provisions of Chapters II and III.

(3) Declarations made under paragraphs 1 and 2 of this article may be modified at any time by a new declaration.

(4) The provisions of paragraphs 1 to 3 of this article do not affect bilateral or multilateral agreements on judicial assistance in respect of civil and commercial matters that may exist between Contracting States.

**Article 17**

Each Contracting State shall, no later than six months following the date of deposit of its instrument of ratification, acceptance, approval or accession, provide the depositary with written information in one of the official languages of the Convention concerning the legislation regulating the export of its cultural objects. This information shall be updated from time to time as appropriate.

**Article 18**

No reservations are permitted except those expressly authorised in this Convention.

**Article 19**

(1) This Convention may be denounced by any State Party, at any time after the date on which it enters into force for that State, by the deposit of an instrument to that effect with the depositary.

(2) A denunciation shall take effect on the first day of the sixth month following the deposit of the instrument of denunciation with the depositary. Where a longer period for the denunciation to take effect is specified in the instrument of denunciation it shall take effect upon the expiration of such longer period after its deposit with the depositary.

## ANNEX 2

**Article 20**

The President of the International Institute for the Unification of Private Law (UNIDROIT) may at regular intervals, or at any time at the request of five Contracting States, convene a special committee in order to review the practical operation of this Convention.

**Article 21**

(1) This Convention shall be deposited with the Government of the Italian Republic.

(2) The Government of the Italian Republic shall:

(a) inform all States which have signed or acceded to this Convention and the President of the International Institute for the Unification of Private Law (UNIDROIT) of:

(i) each new signature or deposit of an instrument of ratification, acceptance, approval or accession, together with the date thereof;

(ii) each declaration made in accordance with this Convention;

**Article 20**

The President of the International Institute for the Unification of Private Law (UNIDROIT) may at regular intervals, or at any time at the request of five Contracting States, convene a special committee in order to review the practical operation of this Convention.

**Article 21**

(1) This Convention shall be deposited with the Government of the Italian Republic.

(2) The Government of the Italian Republic shall:

(a) inform all States which have signed or acceded to this Convention and the President of the International Institute for the Unification of Private Law (UNIDROIT) of:

(i) each new signature or deposit of an instrument of ratification, acceptance, approval or accession, together with the date thereof;

(ii) each declaration made in accordance with this Convention;

ANNEX 2

United Nations
Educational, Scientific and
Cultural Organization

Organisation
des Nations Unies
pour l'éducation,
la science et la culture

Organización
de las Naciones Unidas
para la Educación,
la Ciencia y la Cultura

Организация
Объединенных Наций по
вопросам образования,
науки и культуры

منظمة الأمم المتحدة
للتربيـة والعلم والثقافة

联合国教育、
科学及文化组织

UNIDROIT

Expert Committee
on States' Ownership of Cultural Heritage

**Draft model provisions on State Ownership of Undiscovered Cultural Objects**

# Explanatory Report with draft model provisions and explanatory guidelines

The Expert Committee established by the UNESCO and UNIDROIT Secretariats met formally on three occasions in Paris, on September 20, 2010, March 14, 2011 and June 29, 2011. Several exchanges among the members of the Committee also took place via e-mail.

The members of the Committee were the following: As Co-chairs, Dr. Jorge Sánchez Cordero (Mexico) and Prof. Marc-André Renold (Switzerland) and, as members, Thomas Adlercreutz (Sweden), James Ding (China), Manlio Frigo (Italy), Vincent Négri (France), Patrick O'Keefe (Australia), Norman Palmer (United Kingdom) and Folarin Shyllon (Nigeria). Both the UNIDROIT and UNESCO Secretariats were represented by Marina Schneider and Edouard Planche.

## 1. Mandate of the Expert Committee

At its first meeting the Expert Committee discussed its mandate which is the "working on model provisions with explanatory guidelines (in French: '*dispositions modèles accompagnées de lignes directrices'*) on State Ownership of Undiscovered Cultural Objects" (Minutes of the September 20, 2010 meeting, page 2).

The Expert Committee's understanding of its mandate was confirmed by the Intergovernmental Committee for Promoting the Return of Cultural Property to its Countries of Origin or its Restitution in Case of Illicit Appropriation in its September 23, 2010 Recommendation: "[A]cknowledging the

ANNEX 3

obstacles faced by many countries in applying for restitution of cultural property, especially when it comes to materials from cultural sites where there is no inventory or provenance documentation, in particular objects coming from illicit excavations" the Intergovernmental Committee recommends "the preparation of model provisions with explanatory guidelines to be made available to States to consider in the drafting or strengthening of national laws" (Recommendation N° 3, 16th session of the Intergovernmental Committee, Paris 2010, CLT-2010/CONF.203/COM.16/5).

### 2. Preliminary Draft Model Provisions

At the first meeting of the Expert Committee (September 20, 2010), a preliminary draft was discussed. This preliminary draft contained several proposals that were deemed by the Committee as being too broad and based more on the language of an international convention than that of model provisions of national law. Hence they were redrafted and presented orally to the Intergovernmental Committee for Promoting the Return of Cultural Property to its Countries of Origin or its Restitution in Case of Illicit Appropriation at its 16th session. The discussions that followed indicated that a certain number of amendments would be necessary. These were incorporated in the draft model provisions discussed at the second formal meeting of the Expert Committee on March 14, 2011.

### 3. Draft Model Provisions

The second meeting of the Expert Committee (March 14, 2011) discussed further these draft model provisions. All experts present agreed that much progress had been made with this draft. A certain number of comments and additional proposals were made and discussed and the result of these was incorporated in a document which was circulated to all members of the Committee.
The text as it stood after the March meeting was submitted, with short comments, to the 90th session of the UNIDROIT Governing Council in May 2011. The Council took note of the state of advancement of the work on drafting model legislative provisions and reiterated its support and involvement for the project. The Council will examine and endorse the Provisions on State Ownership of Undiscovered Cultural Objects with explanatory guidelines when they are finalized.

Based on additional comments a third version was prepared by the chair and discussed at the final meeting of the experts on June 29, 2011. Coined by certain as being "by far the best so far" this document was approved by all members of the Committee, even if certain minor points were still discussed and solved at the final meeting.

The text that follows below is the result of that third and final meeting of the Expert Committee. It is meant to be presented at the 17th session of the Intergovernmental Committee for Promoting the Return of Cultural Property to its Countries of Origin or its Restitution in Case of Illicit Appropriation on June 30, 2011 by the Chair of the Expert Committee.

It is important at this stage to note that the Expert Committee made great efforts to come to a short text, with only six provisions, which aims, in line both with the 1970 UNESCO and the 1995 Unidroit Conventions, both to encourage the protection of archeological objects and to favor their restitution to the State where illicit excavations took place.

The Co-chairs would like to take this opportunity to thank all members of the Committee for their time and effort and hope that the result of their involvement, presented herewith, will enable

States who wish to do so to claim the return or the restitution of unlawfully removed cultural objects.

**Draft Model Provisions on State Ownership of Undiscovered Cultural Objects**

**Provision 1 (General Duty)**

**The State shall take all necessary and appropriate measures to protect Undiscovered Cultural Objects and to preserve them for present and future generations.**

*Guidelines:*

It is felt that the model provisions should start with a general clause stating the general duty of the State regarding cultural objects that have not yet been discovered.

The duty relates both to the *protection* and *preservation* of such objects.

The State's duty applies both in the present times (i.e. on the date the model provisions are adopted by a State) and for the future (i.e. after they have been adopted). The model provisions will not affect past situations as they are not intended to be retroactive.

This provision may, according to the legislative tradition of the enacting State, either be the first clause of a national statute, or be incorporated in the statute's preamble.

**Provision 2 (Definition)**

**Undiscovered cultural objects include objects which, consistently with national law, are of importance for archaeology, prehistory, history, literature, art or science and are located in the soil or underwater.**

*Guidelines:*

The model provisions definition is based on the general definition given by the 1970 UNESCO Convention (art.1) and the 1995 Unidroit Convention (art. 2). As it is a model of a national legislation a reference to the national law is appropriate.

The definition incorporates both types of Undiscovered Cultural Objects, i.e. those found in the *soil* and those found *underwater.*

It should be stressed that the list of categories is not exhaustive (for example, are also covered anthropological objects, human remains, etc.). Similarly, the location of the object should be understood broadly (for example, an undiscovered object could be located in a building or in ice).

ANNEX 3

**Provision 3 (State Ownership)**

**Undiscovered Cultural Objects are owned by the State, provided there is no prior existing ownership.**

*Guidelines:*

This provision is the central rule of the model provisions. The principle adopted - State ownership - follows that of many existing national legislations, but in the most clear and simple terms.

A restriction should be made in case prior ownership by a third party can be established (e.g. a person buries a cultural object belonging to him/her in order to protect it during a conflict, intending to retrieve it later so that he/she has not abandoned ownership). Some existing statutes go in the same direction when they require for State ownership that the discovered object "belong to no one".

Seeing the general and abstract nature of a model law, it does not appear necessary that it provide in detail what are the precise circumstances in which "prior existing ownership" is to be considered as established. The national legislator might wish to provide an (illustrative or exhaustive) list of such circumstances, based on local understandings or traditions.

The enacting State may wish to consider the effect of national and international human rights laws on the validity of an extended ownership of the State.

**Provision 4 (Illicit excavation or retention)**

**Cultural objects excavated contrary to the law or licitly excavated but illicitly retained are deemed to be stolen objects.**

*Guidelines:*

Among the several possible definitions of what the "illicit excavation or retention" of a cultural object can be, the definition given by art. 3 paragraph 2 of the 1995 UNIDROIT Convention should be followed, since one of the purposes of the model provisions is to facilitate the enforcement by national courts of the UNIDROIT Convention. Model provision 4 (and 6 as well) follow that purpose, although they also have an autonomous existence.

It should be reminded here that art. 3 paragraph 2 of the 1995 UNIDROIT Convention provides that "[f]or the purpose of this Convention a cultural object which has been unlawfully excavated or lawfully excavated but unlawfully retained shall be considered stolen when consistent with the law of the State where the excavation took place".

In case an object is lawfully excavated and lawfully exported on a temporary basis, but not returned after expiry of the term, it should be deemed stolen.

ANNEX 3

**Provision 5 (Inalienability)**

**The transfer of ownership of a cultural object deemed to be stolen under Provision 4 is null and void, unless it can be established that the transferor had a valid title to the object at the time of the transfer.**

*Guidelines:*

Model provision 5 is the private law complement of provision 4. An undiscovered cultural object is a *res extra commercium* and remains such once it has been discovered. It can therefore not be validly acquired by a further acquirer (by purchase, donation, succession, etc.).

A reservation should, however, be made in case the transferor has a valid title (e.g. a State archeological museum that decides, validly according to its national law, to sell an item in its collection or a private person who validly acquired the object prior to the entering into force of the model provision in the State concerned). If this is the case, the museum or the private person are the actual owners of the object and they may as such dispose of it.

The enacting State should be conscious of the limited scope of the provision: if the object is transferred abroad, the nullity of the transfer of ownership will be effective only if the foreign State has adopted Provision 5 or a similar rule.

**Provision 6 (International enforcement)**

**For the purposes of ensuring the return or the restitution to the enacting State of cultural objects excavated contrary to the law or licitly excavated but illicitly retained, such objects shall be deemed stolen objects.**

*Guidelines:*

Model provision 6 aims to facilitate the return or the restitution of a cultural object that has been exported after having been discovered and unlawfully removed. If the object is considered stolen, international judicial cooperation in criminal matters will generally enable its return to the country where it was discovered.

Also, from a private international law point of view, a foreign court, seeing that the country where the object was discovered considers it as stolen on the basis this provision, will have little difficulty in returning it on the basis of that state's law. This will even more so be the case if the States involved have ratified the 1995 UNIDROIT Convention (see its art. 3 paragraph 1).

It should also be noted that the model provisions cannot intend to answer all the questions linked to the legal status of excavations and discoveries of cultural objects. For example, the model provisions do not deal with the issue of "treasure trove" (i.e. to what extent should the discoverer be rewarded for his or her discovery), nor do they purport to solve the vexed issue of the protection of the good faith acquirer and his or her duty of diligence. Such issues, if the national legislator deems them to be relevant, will have to be dealt with separately according to the legal perception of the national legislator.

Paris, June 29, 2011

For the Expert Committee,
its Co-chairs:

Prof. Marc-André Renold, Geneva

and

Dr. Jorge Sánchez Cordero, Mexico

ANNEX 3

New Zealand: Five Māori wooden panels excavated in Motunui (Tanaraki) in 1972 and illegally exported from New Zealand. The panels were thought to have lined the back walls of a pātaka, a storehouse on stilts or a pole that was used to keep preserved food.

Iran: chlorite jar and cup dating from 3000 BC and excavated from the Jiroft region of South East Iran. The artefacts were illegally exported from Iran and exhibited for sale by Barakat Galleries in London.

FSC
www.fsc.org
MIX
Papier | Fördert
gute Waldnutzung
FSC® C083411

Kolibri 360 GmbH
Ferdinand-Jühlke-Straße 7
99095 Erfurt, Deutschland
produktsicherheit@kolibri360.de